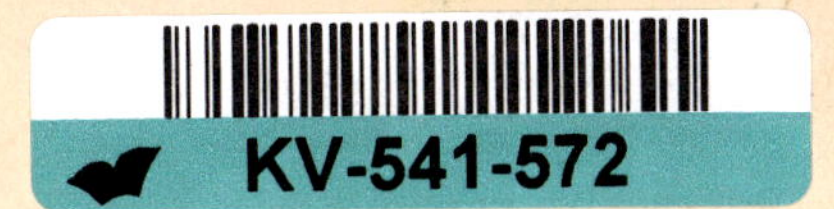
KV-541-572

A HISTORY OF JEWISH LITERATURE

FROM THE CLOSE OF THE BIBLE TO OUR OWN DAYS

By

MEYER WAXMAN, Ph. D

VOL. II

From the Twelfth Century to the Middle of the Eighteenth Century

NEW YORK

BLOCH PUBLISHING CO.

"The Jewish Book Concern"

1933

PRINTED IN THE UNITED STATES OF AMERICA
THE MEYERSON PRESS, CHICAGO, ILL.

PREFACE

In coming again before the reading public after an interval of three years and prefacing the second volume of A History of Jewish Literature, the author finds that but little can be added to what was said in the preface to the first volume regarding his undertaking of the work and its aim and purpose. The conditions described there which in the opinion of the author made the connected presentation of the content of the entire post-Biblical Jewish literature a necessity still exist. The knowledge of Jewish literature, of its teachings and ideals in intellectual circles, both Jewish and non-Jewish, has not been augmented to an appreciable degree, and a book supplying reliable information on these subjects still fills an urgent need.

Nor is it necessary to explain again the character, method and plan of the volume, inasmuch as it is a continuation of its predecessor. Moreover, the judgment pronounced by a majority of the reviewers of Volume I, both in this country and abroad, largely substantiated the judiciousness of the author in the selection of the particular method and plan followed in these volumes, and in addition demonstrated to him that his labors were not in vain.

However, the author found it necessary to alter his original plan to condense the history of the extensive literature of the Jews into two volumes and expand it to three volumes. The wide ramification of the mass of literature produced during the second half of the Mediæval Ages made such change not only desirable but absolutely necessary. Again, the versatility of expression of the Jewish genius during the modern period, the vicissitudes of Jewish life and the kaleidoscopic change of ideas, ideals and views during that span of time require that a separate volume be devoted to a survey of its extensive literature. It is hoped that the third volume will appear in a shorter interval of time than the one separating the first and second volumes.

The author wishes to record his recognition of the services rendered him in the course of preparation of the book by a number of persons. Such is due to Dr. A. S. Oko, librarian emeritus of the

Hebrew Union College Library who has continuously supplied him with the necessary books; to Prof. Alexander Marx of the Jewish Theological Seminary for his furnishing the photostats for the illustrations and especially for his revision of and important additions to the bibliographies of both volumes; to Prof. Charles S. Braden of Northwestern University for his reading a large part of the manuscript and making valuable suggestions for improvement in style; to Mr. Shemaryahu Swirsky and Mr. David Shapiro, his students at the Hebrew Theological College, to the first for industrious labor in assisting in the compilation of the index, and to the second for his rendering into rhyme a large number of the poetical selections; to Mr. Benjamin Meyer for his drawing the maps for this volume as well as for the first; and finally to his wife who read both the manuscript and proofs with painstaking care and attention.

He is also thankful to his friends who procured a part of the funds necessary for the publication of the work. These are: the Central Conference of American rabbis, Drs. Solomon Goldman, Felix Levy, Joseph Stoltz, Tobias Schoenfarber of Chicago and Dr. Charles Shulman of Glencoe, Illinois.

Chicago, September 1933.

TABLE OF CONTENTS

CHAPTER IV

RABBINIC LITERATURE

CHAPTER V

PHILOSOPHY, THEOLOGY AND ETHICS

MAP OF JEWISH LITERARY CENTERS DURING THE AGES.

This map will convey to the reader the importance of the role certain countries and cities played in the development of Jewish literature during the period.

Spain and Italy as leading centers of literary activity during the greater part of the period are placed at the top, and beneath them the countries included in their sphere of influence.

Literary activity in northern Africa was stimulated by the influx of immigrants from Spain, and the revival of intellectual productivity in Palestine and Egypt was wholly due to the settlement of the Spanish exiles who often came by way of North Africa. Likewise, France and Germany, directly influenced the establishment of the Polish-Lithuanian center of learning. Provence, in this period as in the preceding one, was influenced by the countries surrounding it, and this fact explains its central position.

Dates of maps:

Spain—1492
France and Provence—1350.
North Africa—1600.
Italy, Germany, Poland, Palestine and Egypt—1700.

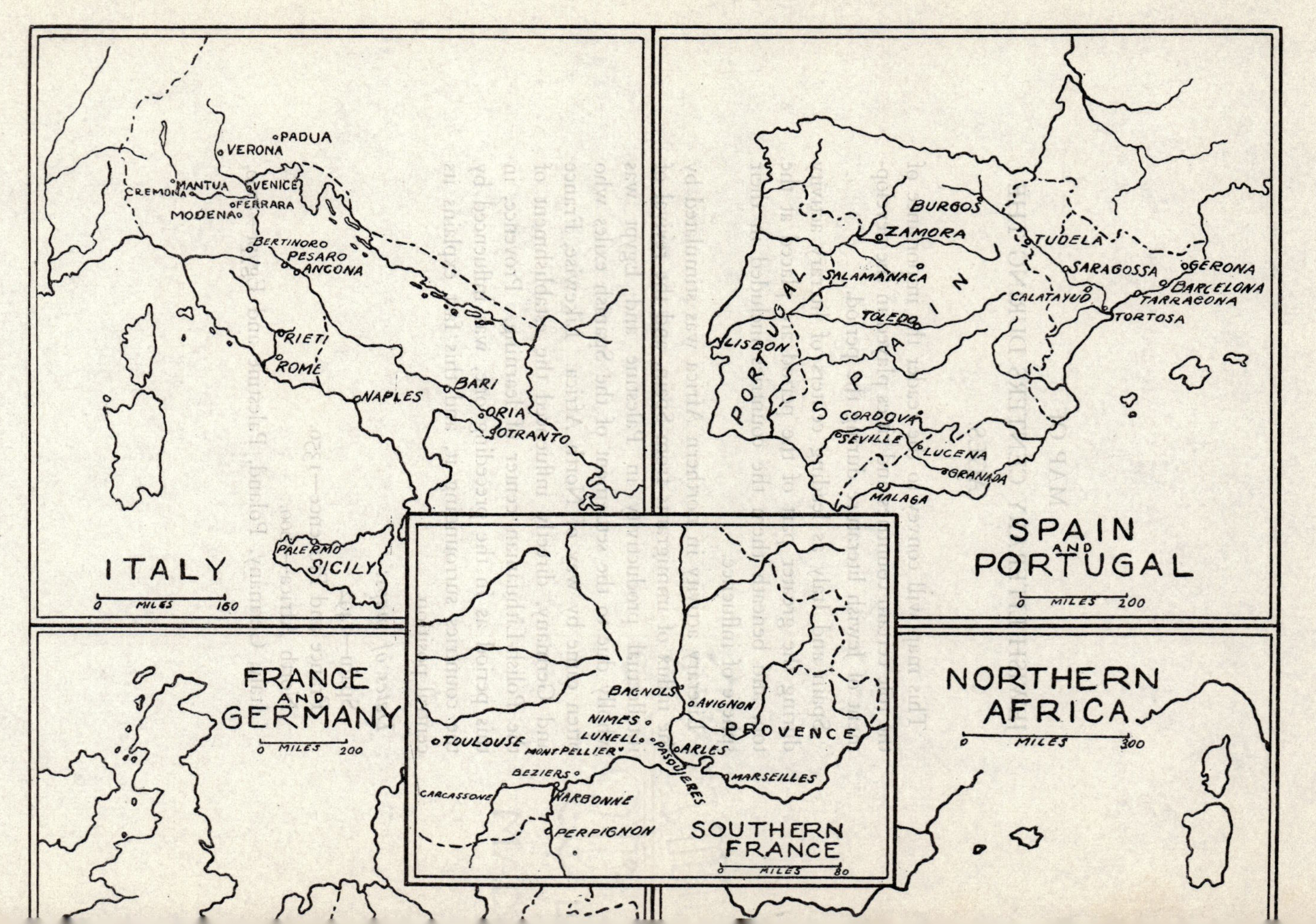
ITALY
0 MILES 160
PADUA
VERONA
MANTUA
CREMONA
VENICE
FERRARA
MODENA
BERTINORO
PESARO
ANCONA
RIETI
ROME
NAPLES
BARI
ORIA
OTRANTO
PALERMO
SICILY
SPAIN AND PORTUGAL
0 MILES 200
BURGOS
ZAMORA
TUDELA
SARAGOSSA
GERONA
BARCELONA
TARRAGONA
TORTOSA
CALATAYUD
SALAMANACA
TOLEDO
LISBON
PORTUGAL
SPAIN
CORDOVA
SEVILLE
LUCENA
GRANADA
MALAGA
FRANCE AND GERMANY
0 MILES 200
NORTHERN AFRICA
0 MILES 300
SOUTHERN FRANCE
0 MILES 80
BAGNOLS
AVIGNON
NIMES
LUNELL
PROVENCE
TOULOUSE
MONTPELLIER
ARLES
PASQUIERES
MARSEILLES
BEZIERS
CARCASSONE
NARBONNE
PERPIGNON

COUCY
SOISSONS
PARIS
METZ
CORBELL
TROYES
RAMERUPT
ORLEANS
SENS
CHINON
WORMS
MAINZ
FURTH
FRANKFORT
SPIRES
NUREMBURG
PRAGUE
REGENSBURG
AUGSBURG
VIENNA
DAMPIER
EMPIRE
FRANCE
FEZ
MOROCCO
ALGIERS
ALGERIA
KAIRWAN
TUNIS
POLAND
AND
LITHUANIA
0 MILES 50
VILNA
GRODNO
POSEN
KALISZ
LUBLIN
LUTZK
CRACOW
LEMBERG
POLAND
LITHUANIA
TURKEY
AND
PALESTINE
0 400
ADRIANOPLE
CONSTANTINOPLE
SALONIKI
GREECE
OTTOMAN
EMPIRE
TIBERIAS
SEPPHORIS
SAFED
LOD
JABNEH
JERUSA
GAZA
ALEXANDRIA
FUSTAT
CAIRO
EGYPT
0 MILES 200

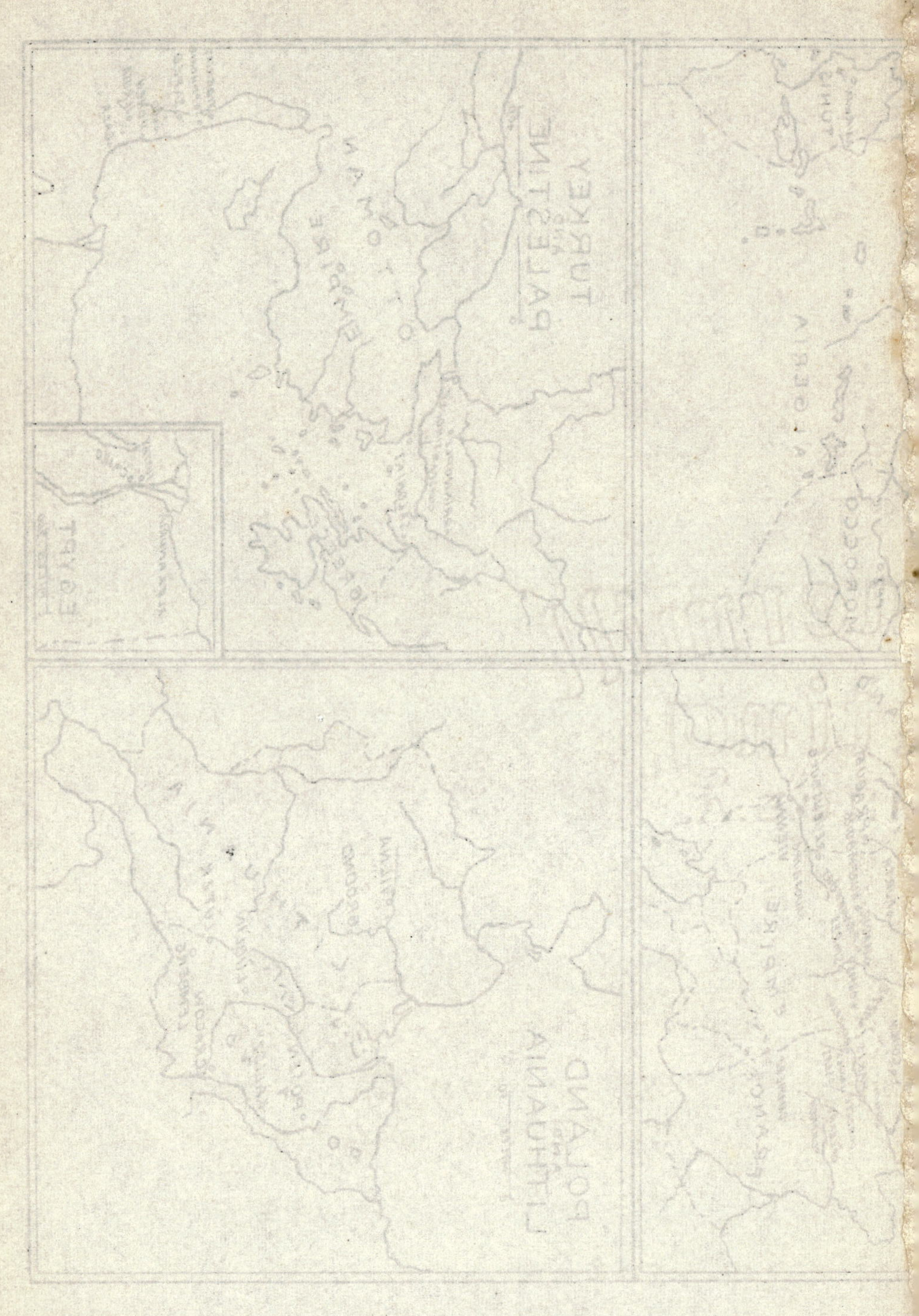

Book III

MEDIAEVAL PERIOD

DIVISION II

From 1200 C. E. to 1750

MEDIAEVAL PERIOD

Division II

INTRODUCTION

1. NATURE AND CHARACTER OF THE LITERATURE OF THE PERIOD

The ramified mass of literature of the second period of the Mediaeval Ages, with which the following pages deal, differs from the literature of the first period not quantitatively but qualitatively. As will be seen, all currents of literary expression reviewed in the preceding volume continued to flow through the centuries, each one in its own peculiar way, swelling the mighty stream of Jewish culture. The line of demarcation between these two periods is then primarily that of quality. If the period closing with the twelfth century has been named by almost unanimous consent the Golden Age, the successive layers of the second period, continuing the metallic nomenclature, will have to be denominated the silver and brass ones respectively.

The causes that brought about this change both in the quality and tone of Jewish literature are: first, the general lassitude which usually follows a long period of literary activity and great display of mental energy; second, the change in the centers of literary activity; third, the absence of great personalities; and finally, a general tendency to follow the beaten track trodden by those who have gone before. That these factors interlap each other and often serve both as causes and effects is needless to say. As for the first cause, it is hardly necessary to dwell upon it, for it is a frequent phenomenon in all cultural efforts both in that of the individual and that of the group. An intellectual strain on the part of any organism is followed by a reaction resulting in a lessening of mental activity for a stated period. The history of human culture furnishes us with ample examples where a period of splendid literary activity by any nation is followed by one of mediocrity and barrenness. Jewish literature is, therefore, no exception to the rule. Here and there, an individual may appear in one field or another who excels in depth of thought or elegance of expression even the great masters of the Classic age, but the quality of the entire literature remains, on the whole, on a lower level.

Of greater importance was the change of centers. The line that formerly divided the world Jewries into those under Islamic and those under Christian rule, though not obliterated, lost its importance almost completely. By the beginning of the thirteenth century, the power of the Crescent began to wane; Mohammedan rule in Spain gradually receded before the militant cross; and before long, almost the entire Pyrenean Peninsula, with the exception of a small strip of territory on the coast, reverted to its former Christian rulers. In the East, the Mohammedans still held sway, but their dissensions and the frequent sweeping of hordes of Mongols, Seljuks and Turks through Western Asia, broke up the once powerful Caliphate into small shattered fragments, laid waste the once fertile provinces, and considerably reduced the population of the great cities. The result of these conditions was the decline of the Arabic culture, whose bloom had faded long before, and degeneration set in.

And that which transpired in the gentile world was reflected more intensely in the Jewish world. Eastern Jewries began to dwindle, and correspondingly, their literary activity ceased almost completely. For nearly three centuries, from the beginning of the thirteenth to the end of the fifteenth, the East hardly produced any author of note or any work of literary value. Verily, during that period, glory had departed from the East. It was only after the fall of Constantinople and the establishment of the Turkish Empire, that Turkey and especially Palestine rose as centers of literary activity.

Under these circumstances, Jewish cultural activity for the greater part of the period was concentrated almost entirely in the West, in Christian Europe. This change of center caused a corresponding change in the tone and character of the literature. On the one hand, it brought about a uniformity of spirit, inasmuch as Jewish life throughout Europe assumed a unified character, and on the other hand, it caused a narrowing of tendency and an intensified concentration on a limited number of subjects, such as the field of Rabbinic law, mysticism and pietistic literature. The broad-mindedness, the closeness to general life, the variety of interest in all aspects of life which characterized the literary productions of the Classical period in Spain were gone, for no more was Jewish life in that country unimpeded in its development as it was in the preceding centuries.

Jewish life in Spain, as well as in all other countries in Europe, assumed a very gloomy aspect during the second half of the Middle Ages. In fact, the really dark spirit of these Ages, as far as the Jews were concerned, was displayed primarily during that epoch. From the thirteenth century on, the Church concentrated all its efforts, if not to destroy the Jews, at least to humiliate, harass, and distress them. The history of the Jews in the centuries that follow is one long tale of woe and suffering caused by persecutions, attacks, massacres, exiles and innumerable discriminations. In the first three centuries alone, we note two great massacres, one caused by the plague of the Black Death in 1348, which swept through France and Germany, and the other in 1391 in Spain, each of which far exceeded the outrages of the Crusades, besides numerous daily attacks in various cities of Germany and France. Each of these centuries witnessed a general exile of Jews from England, France and Spain respectively, the three important countries of Europe.

Is it to be wondered at, then, that under such conditions, when whole Jewries were tossed like a ball over the plains of Western Europe, when even the struggle for mere existence was of the severest kind, Jewish literature lost the ease and grace of former days, or that mysticism which afforded some comfort to the aching heart should have taken the place of philosophy? On the contrary, the wonder is how any literature developed at all under such unbearable conditions.

Yet, not only did the Jew cling to his sacred possessions, the Bible and the Talmud, not only did he seek in them shelter from the storms of the time, but he did not neglect other branches of literature as well. Having once tasted the joys of poetry, the charms of philosophy, the satisfaction arising from search in the field of science, and the broadness of mind resulting from the study of history and geography, the Jew continued to cultivate them with avidity and assiduity. For three centuries, from the thirteenth to the sixteenth, we see such a tremendous production of literature in all these branches, that we might even say that what was lost in quality was probably made up in quantity. Wherever the Jew managed to obtain a breathing spell from continuous persecution, there literature flourished. When Spain ceased to be the center, Provence took its place for a century and a half, and when exile and persecution crushed the spirit of the Jew there, Italy became conspicuous on the literary map of Israel. Thus, the hunted and driven genius of the people wandered from place to place, and wherever it alighted, it struck root, and beautiful blossoms sprouted forth.

It was only with the end of the sixteenth century that the Jewish spirit throughout Western Europe, especially in Germany, began to show signs of extreme weariness and the production of Jewish literature began to abate. The one hundred and fifty years from the end of the sixteenth to the middle of the eighteenth century have been called by writers on the history of literature, a period of stagnation. And while this judgment can not be fully sustained, for it was then that Talmudic learning reached its zenith in Poland, and some literary contributions were made by Palestine and Turkey, yet we may concede that it is partially true. On the whole, this period marks the lowest point in the ebb of Jewish literature, and the deepening of shadows before the rise of a new and brighter period, that of modern times.

As the literary productivity of the period under consideration exceeds in quantity that of the preceding one and is as varied as the former, it is very difficult to outline its nature in detail, and we will, therefore, point out only a few of its conspicuous characteristics. First, there is a change in the language. While the literature of the Classical period was, to a great extent, written in Arabic, the literature of this period is written almost entirely in Hebrew with only a small fraction in other languages, of which the Judaeo-German was the one most commonly used.

The reason for this change is simple. With the gradual conquest of Spain by the Christians, the Arabic language ceased to be the spoken tongue of the Jews of that country, while Latin, the literary language of Europe, was never adopted by the Jews as a medium of expression. As for the other European languages, they were hardly used for literary purposes by the very peoples who spoke them, and the Jews, who were hemmed in in the ghettoes and forcibly separated from the general currents of life, certainly could not employ them as a vehicle of literary expression. Only in such countries as Spain and Italy, where Jewish life was comparatively more in tune with the environment, do we meet with books written in Spanish or Italian.

The second characteristic is the popular nature of the books. In fact, the popular tone and character of the books was primarily a result of the extensive use of Hebrew as the medium of expression. This increased the study and the reading of books, and created a thirst for knowledge among the large masses. And since a book which was destined for the initiated few could be circulated only in a limited number of copies every author strove, therefore, to adapt his work rather to the level of the large educated classes than merely to appeal to the few deep and penetrating minds.

Another factor in the production of the popular level of the literature of the period is the tendency evinced by the writers who succeeded the Classical epoch, to follow in the footsteps of the great who had gone before. This tendency, which increased as time went on, brought about the creation of certain schools of method and thought, the fixation of standards, and the stabilization of literary canons. Very few individuals dared to break new paths, but followed in the old track, only widening it to a certain degree. It is for this reason that we note in all fields, be it grammar, lexicography, or exegesis, or even Rabbinic learning, so many digests, compendia and compilations. Only here and there, did an individual dare to soar above the level and make a real contribution to literature.

The popular level to which the literature adapted itself had also its advantages. Not only did it influence the development of Hebrew prose in making its style more elastic and precise, but it also introduced a wider ramification in Jewish literature. In no period, the Classical not excepted, did Hebrew prose reveal such a wide variety of subjects and multiplicity of branches as in the period under discussion. It can justly be denominated the great epoch for Hebrew prose. The fact that the literature produced was the only means of obtaining knowledge as well as spiritual pleasure generated in the public a desire for different types of literature. Not only did the Jew want to be instructed in law and ethics, but he desired also to be introduced to science in all its branches, as well as to the lighter and aesthetic side of life. The gloomy life of the ghetto needed some rays of cheerfulness. Hence, we have the great mass of translations produced during the thirteenth and fourteenth centuries in the Provence, the large number of books of tales and fables, and the considerable quantity of humorous and satirical works written in the Provence and in Italy.

We must also not overlook the fact that exclusive as Jewish life was during the latter part of the Mediaeval Ages, some contact existed between it and the general life of which it formed a part in most countries of Europe. Movements and stirrings which took place in the larger sphere were always echoed and reflected in the Jewish world, and first, of course, in its literature. It is thus that the great Renaissance movement with its humanistic spirit, its idealism as well as its attitude of levity towards life left its traces upon Jewish literature. Not only do we have numerous parodies of the works of the great writers of the Renaissance, but we meet with much of that levity towards life even in original works. Nor did the critical spirit of the late Renaissance and the early Modern Period pass by unnoticed in Hebrew literature. It left its imprint upon it, and thus we can hear the pulse of general life beating in a great part of the Jewish literature of the period. Only in the East-European centers of Jewry, such as Poland and the neighboring countries, was its influence weaker and hardly noticeable. There, through a concatenation of circumstances, Jewish life was more exclusive, and consequently, its spirit was concentrated primarily on such aspects of literary productivity which were of a purely Jewish nature, as Rabbinic law, ethics, and pietistic works.

CHAPTER I

GRAMMAR AND LEXICOGRAPHY

2. *GENERAL FEATURES*

The Classical period in the field of Hebrew grammar and lexicography closed, as we know, with David Kimhi. He was the last of the great builders of the science of the Hebrew language, the foundations of which were laid three hundred years before by Saadia. But the building was far from complete as there was still much to be done and perfected, and this work was undertaken by his successors. In fact, it was the works of Kimhi and some of his predecessors, such as Ibn Ezra and a few others, which gave the impetus to an extensive activity in the field of the science of language, even in such countries as France and Germany where previously it had been only scantily cultivated. Hitherto, it was Spain which produced most of the workers in this field. Henceforth, during the succeeding centuries, with two or three exceptions, Spain will come in but little in our survey of this branch of literature, as other lands take its place. The great services performed by the Tibbonides (Vol. I, Chs. VII, XI), the family of translators in Provence, in translating the works of Hayyuj, Ibn Jannah and others from the Arabic into Hebrew, together with the works mentioned above originally written in Hebrew, threw open the doors of philological knowledge to the Jews of Western Europe who were not acquainted with Arabic. This created a desire in the hearts of Jewish scholars in those countries not only to study the science of language, but also to produce works of their own.

As the books produced were of a popular and practical nature, i. e. compendia and text books, their number is quite considerable and they hail from all countries of Western Europe, France, Germany and Italy. It is, therefore, best to survey the literature in the chronological order of the centuries rather than take up each country separately, the method followed hitherto.

3. *THE THIRTEENTH CENTURY*

The thirteenth century was quite productive in the field of grammar and lexicography. Of the most important works, first in time and probably in value, is the Lexicon written by Moses ben Isaac of England, surnamed *Ben ha-Nesiah* (The Son of the Princess). The exact time when the author lived is not definitely determined. Some scholars were inclined to place him at the end of the twelfth century, and some, on the other hand, relegated him to the fourteenth, but it is now commonly assumed that he lived in the first half of the thirteenth century. The name of the book is the *Sepher ha-Shoham* (Book of the Onyx), so called because it contains the letters of the author's name *Moshe,* i. e. *Mem, Shin, He.* As the author informs us in the introduction, he wrote in his youth a short grammar of the Hebrew language entitled *Leshon Limmudim* (Language of Instruction), but it has not come down to us.

The *Sepher ha-Shoham* is preceded by a grammatical introduction which is devoted primarily to two things, the use of the functional or servile letters, namely those which do not belong to the root but serve a certain purpose, as the Waw conjunctive or conversive, or denote the person and time in the verb inflexion etc., and the changes of letters in many words in the Bible. On this point, Moses makes many elucidating remarks which help to clear up a number of dark passages in the Bible. Towards the end of the introduction, he discusses the forms of the inflexion of the verb, but leaves the subject incomplete. The author shows a fair acquaintance with the grammatical literature. He knows of the works of Hayyuj and Ibn Jannah's polemics against him, but not of the works of Jannah himself. Ibn Tibbon's translation of Jannah's *Book of Roots* and the *Rikmah* evidently did not reach him, and although he knew some Arabic, he probably could not read them in the original. He knows of the works of Joseph and David Kimhi, of Parhon, against whose theories he makes a number of strictures, as well as of those of Rabbi Berakhya ha-Nakdan (punctator) and others. He even communicated with distant scholars, as he quotes a rather far-fetched explanation of the Hebrew root, *Yabem* (to contract a Levirate marriage) by analogy with a Russian verb imparted to him by Isaac of Chernigow, Russia.

The Lexicon proper is divided into three parts which are based on the division of all words in Hebrew into verbs, nouns and words of relation, such as adverbs, numerals etc. The book is not arranged alphabetically, but according to grammatical construction. Thus, the first part which explains the verbs is subdivided into seven portals corresponding to seven classes of verbs, such as the sound or complete verbs (shlemim), *Yod* and *Nun* quiescent or missing, etc. The second part includes all nouns, divided according to Kimhi's classification into one hundred and sixty-two forms. The third embraces the numerals, adverbs and Aramaic words found in the Bible, and also a few chapters on rules of vocalization and accents.

Another important grammatical work belonging to this century is an anonymous book called *Petah Debarai,* literally the *Opening of My Speech.* The name is borrowed from Ps. CXIX, 130, where it is said, "The opening of thy words giveth light; it giveth understanding to the simple." Our author likewise meant to say that his words or teachings will give light and understanding to those who are ignorant of the subject. The book is supposed to have been composed by a Spanish grammarian in the middle of the century, and has even been ascribed to Moses Kimhi. This supposition, however, may be rejected on many grounds. The purpose of the author was to give a popular statement of the principles and rules of Hebrew grammar, and in his introduction, he endeavors to show how a knowledge of grammar is necessary for the understanding of the Bible. It is divided into two parts, the first of which is devoted to the verbs, where an exhaustive study of their classification and inflexions is presented, together with paradigms of the conjugations. The other part deals with the nouns, particles, verbal suffixes giving the paradigms of such, and at the end, a few chapters are devoted to the rules of phonetics, vowels and accents. Among the earlier grammarians cited in the book are Hayyuj, Ibn Jannah and Ibn Ezra. Although David Kimhi is not mentioned there, it was he who influenced our author most as he followed him in his method.

The Orient contributed its share to the science of language. Isaac ben Eliezer ha-Levi wrote two grammatical works to which he gave titles already used by other authors, one *Sephath Yether* (The Excellence of Language) used by Ibn Ezra, and the other *ha-Riḳmah* employed by Ibn Jannah (Vol. 1, Sect. 101). The first is a Hebrew digest of Hayyuj's two chief works together with Jannah's supplements to these works; the second deals with various subjects, such as homonyms, synonyms, two-stemmed verbs and other matters.

Work of a more original character was done at the beginning of the century by a Palestinian scholar, Tanhum Yerushalmi. He wrote a commentary in Arabic on a number of books of the Bible, to which he prefixed a lengthy introduction dealing with grammatical problems. In these chapters, he enunciates the principle, already advanced by Ibn Koreish, of the great value of comparative study of the Semitic languages, especially the Aramaic and the Arabic. In accordance with his principles, he elucidates many problems in Hebrew grammar in the light of his philological studies in the other languages. Tanhum also wrote in Arabic a lexicon to Maimonides' Code, the *Mishnah Torah,* where he explains the skillful use made by Maimonides of the Hebrew language, the elasticity he introduced in the meaning of words, and the new nuances and shades he imparted to an exceedingly large number of Biblical and Mishnaic expressions.

Even Germany produced a lexicographical work of some importance during the first half of the century. This lexicon was written by a certain Shimshon. We find that he was acquainted with Parhon's work but his main authority is still Menahem ben Saruk, as he follows him in assuming bilitteral and even monolitteral roots. He introduces a novel feature in his lexicon, inasmuch as he translates many words into German. This marks the beginning of a series of later works of a similar nature.

4. ABRAHAM BEDERSI

In the second half of this century, a work was produced in the field of lexicography which far surpassed the others composed in the period. This is the Dictionary of Synonyms named *Hotham Tokhnith* (The Sealed or Closed Pattern) by Abraham ben Isaac Bedersi, i. e. of Beziers, a city in the Provence, the father of the more famous son, poet and moralist, Yedayah ha-Penini. Though Abraham himself was also famous, especially as one of the leading poets of the day, yet we know few details of his life. It is surmised that he was born about 1240 at Beziers as his surname indicates, but that he left that city when very young and settled at Perpignan, where he was instructed by the poet Joseph Ezobi. For some time, he wandered around in various cities of the Provence, as we find him in Narbonne and several other cities in 1285. He returned to Perpignan a second time, for we find that some of his letters written in 1290 were dated at that city. Towards the end of his life, he must have settled again at Beziers, as we find references to that fact. The date of his death can likewise be determined only approximately, for it seems that in the year 1304, when the war on the study of science and philosophy was renewed by the zealous and pious rabbis of Spain and France, Abraham was no longer among the living. He, therefore, must have died around 1300.

The *Hotham Tokhnith* was not only the first of its kind in the treatment of the subject of Hebrew synonyms, but even to the present day remains unique in its character, inasmuch as it is the only work which treats the subject exhaustively. It consists of twenty-two parts, the number of the letters of the alphabet, subdivided into three hundred and sixty portals, each of which treats a group of synonyms. The work is executed with great skill, and while it deals mostly with nouns, it also includes a number of verbs and adverbs. The author is exhaustive in his treatment of the subject and explains the shades of each synonym according to its derivation from the root and the meaning of that root. He corroborates his opinion by citing analogies from passages of the Bible, or from the Aramaic translations, (Targumim), or from the Talmud, or from the analogies of usage in Arabic and even from popular usage. He exhibits great discernment in distinguishing between delicate shades of words. His method is the conceptual one, namely, he deals with each group of synonyms which denote one general concept. Thus, there are in Hebrew five words expressing speech, seven expressing power, etc. The meaning of each word of these conceptual groups is then determined, elucidated and distinguished. The Lexicon has great value not only for the science of the Hebrew language but for Biblical exegesis as well, for by determining the exact meaning of similar words, many different passages in the Bible become clear. Bedersi was widely read not only in the literature of his subject but in other fields as well. Among the authorities he cited are found, besides all leading grammarians, with the exception of David Kimhi, also Sherira Gaon, Rashi, Maimonides and Jacob Tam.

5. *THE PUNCTATORS*

In Germany and northern France, where the scientific study of grammar was not well developed, there were always certain people who devoted themselves, as was already pointed out above, (Vol. I, Sect. 110) to a certain branch of grammar necessary in daily practice, namely that of punctuation or vocalization. These people were called, on account of their specialty, *Nakdanim,* i. e. punctators, (sing. Nakdan). It was they who carried on the grammatical tradition, for they vocalized the Biblical books, compiled Masoretic notes and supplied the accents. As the knowledge of grammar increased with the production of Hebrew books on the subject, these punctators studied them assiduously and became authors themselves. During the thirteenth century, there were numerous punctators whose works were left to later generations, either in notes on the margin of Biblical books or in special treatises on the subject.

The most important among them was Shimshon the Nakdan (fl. about the middle of the century), who wrote a book on the rules of vocalization and accents under the title *Hibbur ha-Kanim,* called also *Shimshoni* after his name. He is well acquainted with the words of Hayyuj, Ibn Ezra, Jacob Nakdan and others. Other *Nakdanim,* such as Joseph ha-Hazan (The Cantor) of Troyes and Moses ben Zeli wrote similar books. In the second half of the century, we have Yekuthiel Ben Judah of Prague who wrote a fine treatise on the rules of vocalization entitled *En ha-Korē* (The Eye of the Reader), a work which won the praise of later grammarians. Even a great Talmudic scholar, Mordecai ben Hillel (d. 1928), found it necessary to try his hand at a grammatical work, writing two poems in which he recites all the rules affecting the changes of four vowels, namely, the *Kametz, Patah, Tzere and Segol.*

6. FOURTEENTH CENTURY

Work in the field of the science of language was continued during the fourteenth century, Italy and the Provence taking the lead. Benjamin ben Judah of Rome wrote two works on grammar, a shorter tractate and a larger compendium entitled *Mebo ha-Dikduk* (Introduction to Grammar). The first one was primarily meant to serve as a supplement to the current text books on the subject. In his introduction, the author complains that most of the text books are devoted to the verb and its forms, but that other parts of grammar are neglected. His book is devoted to the supplying of these deficiencies. In his larger manual, the first two chapters cover the subjects treated in the short tractate, while the other eight deal primarily with the verbs and nouns, their inflexions and conjugations. A chapter on prosody and rules of Hebrew meter is also included.

Some grammatical contributions were made by another famous Italian writer, the poet Immanuel ben Solomon (Ch. III, Sect. 30) in his book *Eben Bohan* (The Touchstone), although it was intended mainly as a handbook for Biblical interpretation. It consists of four parts, the first three of which are devoted to the explanations of omissions of words or of additions and exchanges of letters found in the Bible. These parts contain numerous grammatical, lexicographical, and rhetorical notes and remarks which enrich these subjects.

Noteworthy additions to this branch of literature are the works of the exegete and moralist, Joseph Ibn Kaspi (Ch. II, Sect. 17). They are named, in accordance with the custom of this author to combine the names of all his works with the word *Keseph* (silver), his own surname, *Sharsheroth Keseph, Zeror ha-Keseph* and *Rithukoth Keseph,* (Chains of Silver, A Package of Silver, and Silver Fastenings, respectively). The first of these three is an abridged dictionary, where an attempt is made to open a new path in lexicography and grammar, that is to introduce the element of logic in the explanation and derivation of words, as well as in laying down the rules of grammar. In it, the endeavor is made to deduce from the fundamental meaning of each root all secondary and borrowed meanings of the root itself, as well as of kindred nouns. The second is mainly an outline of the logical principles underlying language in general, and Hebrew in particular. It may thus be denominated a philosophy of grammar. The third contains chapters on the rules of the holy language, practically a grammar. Ibn Kaspi was a great adherent of the trilitteral theory, and even endeavored to supply trilitteral roots to bilitteral nouns.

Of the other grammatical works, the first is the *Menorath ha-Maor* (The Lamp of Light) by Joseph ben David ha-Yevani, i. e. the Greek. It consists of a dictionary and a grammatical introduction. It was, however, preserved only up to the eighth letter. The second is a complete grammar called by the oft-employed name *Leshon Limmudim* by Solomon ben Abba Mari Jarhi, i. e. of Lunel. It was he, who finally fixed the number of the conjugations of the Hebrew verb at seven, which number was adopted by all subsequent grammarians. The older grammarians counted six, David and Moses Kimhi added two more, but Jarhi's number seems to be the more correct and scientific one.

Several works in Talmudic and Aramaic lexicography were produced in Germany during the century. There is very little originality in them as they are merely digests of the *Aruk,* the Talmudic Lexicon of Nathan of Rome (Vol. I, Sect. 148), but they evince a practical tendency, inasmuch as they translate the words into German. The first is a digest of the *Aruk* entitled *Aruk Goren* (literally *Goren* means a heap of grain, by which is probably meant that he compiled his words from many sources) by Menahem ben Eliakim of Bengen, Germany. The author omitted the Talmudic citations of the sources, and merely gives the meaning of the words. Another one is the *Aruk ha-Katzer* (Shorter Aruk) written by an anonymous German author. In this work, almost every word is translated into German and a number of new words added, and while the citation of sources is omitted, references are given for the added words. Of this work, several slightly different versions were current which were printed in Constantinople, Krakow and other places. Each version contains some additions. Thus, the Constantinople edition added explanatory words in Italian and Spanish beside the German.

7. *THE FIFTEENTH CENTURY*

The fifteenth century was, in general, a very productive one for Jewish literature, the field of grammar and lexicography proving no exception. Of the works produced, the first both in time and importance, is the *Maasē Ephod* (The Work of the Ephod, a fine woven garment of the high priest) by Isaac ben Moses Profiat Duran. It is euphemistically called so on account of its delicate composition.[1] The author who distinguished himself otherwise as a controversialist and philosopher (Chs. V, X, Sects. 75, 149) brought his philosophic spirit to play upon his grammatical work. He carried Ibn Kaspi's attempt to found grammar upon the principles of logic and philosophy much farther and treated the entire subject philosophically. The work consists of a lengthy and interesting introduction and thirty-three chapters. In the introduction, Ephodi, as he is usually called, examines the various opinions of the scholars of his day regarding the study of the Torah. Some of the Talmudists considered the legal method of study the proper one; the philosophers, on the other hand, tried to explain the Torah by allegories; while the Kabbalists emphasized mysticism. He disapproves of all three methods and claims that the right way to study Torah is the study of the plain meaning of the Bible. But since it is impossible to understand the Bible properly unless we are well acquainted with the grammar and the laws of the language in which it is written, he was moved to compose this work. He is aware that the great masters, such as Judah Hayyuj, Ibn Jannah,

[1] Also because the author used the name אפודי as a surname. It stands for the initials of the sentence, "Amar (said) Profiat Duran."

Ibn Ezra and others have covered the subject, but he claims that the later scholars, referring mainly to the Kimhis, made some mistakes and these he endeavors to correct. He concludes his introduction by outlining fifteen points for the proper study of the Torah.

The first eight chapters of the book deal with introductory and general matters; thus the first with a definition of language in general, the second and third with the final and the efficient causes of language, and the fourth with the parts of speech. Here, the author, true to the philosophy of his time, tries to show that the three parts of speech, the nouns, the verbs, adverbs and particles, reflect the tripartite division of the universe; thus the nouns correspond to the world of the separate intelligences which exist without mutation; the verb which changes and moves in time to the world of the spheres which move constantly; while the adverbs and particles correspond to the lower world, since like it, their existence is dependent upon the words to which they are joined. Of the other four chapters, the first two are devoted to a definition of the letters, their sounds and vowels, and to a discussion of the organs of speech. He deviates from his predecessors in limiting the number of vowels to five which represent exactly the sounds of human speech. The other two vowels, namely the *Kametz, O* and the *Segol, E,* he considers only as nuances of the *Patah, A* and the *Tzere, Ai,* following the Sephardic pronunciation. The succeeding two chapters are devoted to the state of the Hebrew language and the development of its grammar. Ephodi considered Hebrew the most perfect language on account of its brevity of expression and other qualities.

With chapter nine, the grammar proper begins. That chapter where the classes of nouns are given is followed by three others (X-XII) on the principles of the verb, a chapter on the functional or servile letters, and another on the mutation of letters and vowels. (Ch. XIV.) He devotes Chapters XV-XXIII to the forms and conjugations of the verb, making many original suggestions, among them that the *Niphal* form is not the passive of the *Kal,* but denotes rather reflexive action. Chapters XXIV-XXVI describe the roots of nouns, adverbs, and verbal suffixes, and are followed by Chapters XXVII-XXIX which deal with rules for the interpretation of the Bible and by three others on particles and pronunciation. The book closes with a short chapter discussing the question of why Hebrew is called the sacred tongue. As can be seen, Ephodi did not deal with all parts of grammar, as he omitted many subjects, but the novelty of his method and depth of insight into the nature of language and his brilliant suggestions make his work an important contribuion to Hebrew lexicography.

Of the other works is to be noted the *Leshon Limmudim* (Language of Instruction) by David ben Solomon Ibn Yahya of Lisbon (1440-1504), a concise grammar of the text book type, systematically arranged. It is divided into four parts dealing with vowels and punctuation, verbs, nouns and particles respectively. He was influenced to a certain degree by Ephodi. Another grammarian who likewise hailed from Lisbon but who later settled in southern Italy was Moses ben Shem Tob Ibn Habib. He wrote a few books on the subject, a larger grammar called *Perah Shoshan* (Flower of the Lily) which was lost and of which only citations are preserved, and two smaller works, one a very brief outline of the principles of grammar in the form of questions and answers by the name of *Marpē Lashon* (The Cure of the Tongue), and one on poetics entitled *Darḵē Noam* (The Ways of Sweetness), where the rules of prosody are given.

Italy produced a number of grammatical and lexicographical works. Joseph ben Judah Tarco wrote in 1429 a book entitled *Rab Poalim* (Master of Deeds), a play on the word *Poalim* which also means verbs, dealing with the verb only, and followed it up by a lexicon named *Baal ha-Lashon* (Master of Language). Judah ben Jehiel Messer Leon, physician and philosopher, composed the *Libnath ha-Sapir* (Whiteness of the Sapphire), a grammar consisting of two parts, the first dealing with the theories of pronunciation, vocalization and prosody, the second with the verbal and nominal forms. The same Messer Leon wrote a very important and exhaustive rhetoric, the first of its kind and almost the only one in Hebrew, under the title *Nopheth Zuphim* (The Sweetness of Honey), where he propounds the theories of Cicero and Quintilian on rhetoric and oratory. His contemporary Solomon Urbino wrote in 1480 the *Ohel Moed* (The Tabernacle of the Congregation), a dictionary of synonyms, so named because all words are brought together there. It differs greatly in arrangement from the dictionary of Bedersi, but on the whole, is of an inferior quality. There is no attempt made to explain the various nuances of the synonyms, but in each article, a list of synonyms is given, and only on rare occasions, a more extensive explanation is offered. Urbino, of course, supplies Biblical references for the words.

The *Meir Natib* (The Light of the Path), the first Hebrew concordance, was written in Provence about the year 1447 by Isaac ben Kalonymos of the family Nathan. The author wrote his book for the purpose of facilitating the quoting of verses from the Hebrew Bible by Jewish scholars in cases of controversy with gentiles. He took as his model the Latin Concordance of the Franciscan Monk Arlottus (1290). It is needless to say that this work served more than the purpose intended by the author, inasmuch as it furthered the progress of Biblical study and exegesis, and in turn served as a model for later improved concordances. Isaac ben Kalonymos was the first to introduce in the Hebrew Bible the division into chapters, which is an addition to the older Masoretic division into weekly portions (Parshioth). This division was followed in the Greek and Latin Bibles and was taken by our author from the Latin. The printers of the first Hebrew Bible followed Isaac in this matter and introduced the double division, both that of the weekly portions and that of the chapters.

There are two more lexicographical works produced in this century, both intended for popular use, as the authors added a translation of the words in one or two other languages. The first is the anonymous *Makerē Dardekē* (Instructor of Children), a Hebrew, Italian and Arabic Biblical dictionary. The author must have lived in southern Italy, where Arabic was still known, at the beginning of the century, as he bewails the expulsion of the Jews from France in 1305. This proves that the memory of that expulsion was fresh in his mind. He had a double purpose in writing this book, one to help people to understand the Bible, especially since they neglected the Scriptures in their eagerness for Talmudic studies, and secondly, like Nathan, to help scholars in cases of controversy. The author follows Kimhi's arrangement in his *Book of Roots* and also follows him as well as Rashi in the explanation of the words. He very often quotes their French and Provencal translation of words. The second dictionary is that of Saadia Ibn Danon, Rabbi of Granada. To this dictionary, he prefixed a lengthy introduction dealing with the principles of grammar and prosody. This introduction was originally written in Arabic, but the author himself translated it into Hebrew.

8. *THE SIXTEENTH CENTURY*

During the sixteenth century, there were few works produced in the field of the science of language, but the lack of quantity was made up in quality. The works produced were of a very high order. The two outstanding authors are the famous Elijah Levita (1467-1549) and Abraham de Balmes (d. 1524), both of Italy. The first performed an exceptional service to the cause of the science of the Hebrew language, not only by his books but by his acting for many years as teacher of Hebrew and Bible to Christian scholars, both Catholic and Protestant. Of him it can be veritably said that he was a teacher of the gentiles (*Nabi La-Goyim,* Jeremiah I, 5), and much of the contributions by Christian scholars to Hebrew philology and lexicography from the sixteenth century on is due to his inspiration.

Elijah was born in Neustadt, Germany, and devoted a great part of his life to a thorough study of Hebrew grammar, the Bible, the Masora and the Targumim. In 1504, he settled in Padua, where he occupied himself for five years in instructing both Jews and gentiles in these subjects. In 1509, he went to Rome where he made the acquaintance of the Humanist, Cardinal Egidio de Viterbo, a Semitic scholar, by whom he was supported for thirteen years in order that he might devote himself to his studies. In 1527, he went to Venice at the invitation of Daniel Bomberg, the famous printer of Hebrew books, to serve as a corrector in his printing house. In later life, he returned to Germany at the invitation of the Hebraist and printer Paul Fagius, one of his famous pupils, to help him in the printing of Hebrew books. There he made many friends among the gentile scholars of Hebrew of his day and acquired many followers, the most famous among whom was Sebastian Münster. This scholar translated most of Levita's works into Latin, and Elijah thus became known to the learned world. He was even invited by the king of France, Francis the First, to become teacher of Hebrew at the Sorbonne, but for some unknown reasons, he declined this offer.

The works of Levita cover the entire field of the science of the Hebrew language and lexicography as well as that of the Masorah and Biblical Aramaic. They are divided into the following classes: (a) grammar proper; (b) Masorah; (c) Hebrew and Aramaic lexicography. To the first class belongs first the grammatical work entitled *ha-Bahur* (The Chosen One), so named because it contains the selected rules of grammar, and also because the term *Bahur* was Elijah's cognomen, probably on account of the fact that he married late in life—as *Bahur* in late Hebrew signifies an unmarried man. The book was written at the request of his patron, the Cardinal Egidius de Viterbo and is dedicated to him. It treats only of the verbs and nouns, its excellence consisting not in the originality of the content, but in its logical and systematic arrangement and lucidity of its style. It consists of four sections, two devoted to the verb and its inflexions and two to the noun and its derivations and declensions. Each section is divided into thirteen articles (Ikkarim), the number of the Maimonidean Articles of Faith.

This book was supplemented by another called *Pirkē Eliyahu* (The Chapters of Elijah) which consist of grammatical essays dealing with phonetics, particles, gender of nouns, and prosody. In addition, Levita also wrote a book on accents under the name *Tob Taam* (literally Good Judgment, but *Taamim* in Hebrew is also the name for accents) and finally, the *Sepher ha-Harkabah* (The Book of Combinations), an alphabetical list of compound words in the Bible, explaining their composition and derivation. Elijah's grammatical books, on account of their clearness and preciseness, gained great favor among the Christian Hebrew scholars of the sixteenth century, and several of them, including his *Bahur,* were immediately translated into Latin.

To the second class, namely, the work on the Masorah, belongs first of all his little book *Masoreth ha-Masoreth,* that is the *Masorah of the Masorah* of the Bible (Sect. 93). In spite of its brevity, it is an epoch-making work. The Masorah which is of exceptional importance for the study of the text of the Bible, Hebrew orthography and grammar was a closed book to Jewish and gentile scholars on account of its obscure terminology, cryptic signs, and extreme brevity of language. Elijah opened its gates by explaining its terminology, its sign language and laid down a large number of rules by means of which one can find his way in its devious paths.

The book is divided into three sections, curiously named, *The First Tables* (Luhoth Rishonoth), *The Second Tables* (Luhoth Shnioth), and *The Broken Tables* (Shivrē Luhoth). In these three sections, the first two of which are subdivided into ten commandments each, in analogy with the Tables of the Law, every phase of the *Masorah* is discussed and explained. The book is introduced by three prefaces of which the third is the most important. It is in itself a short treatise on the origin of the changes in the text of the Bible known as *Keri* and *Ketib* (Vol. I, Sect. 91) and that of the vowel points and accents. There Elijah first declared the later accepted opinion, that both the vowel points and the accents were neither given from Sinai, as heretofore asserted, nor were they known throughout the Talmudic period, but were invented by the Masorites after the close of the Talmud. This view called forth much criticism on the part of the Orthodox, but as stated, was later accepted by all. His third introduction was immediately translated into Latin by Sebastian Münster. Later the entire book was translated into that language, and went through several editions. Levita wrote a larger book on the Masorah entitled *Sepher Zikhronoth* (The Book of Remembrance). It is a masoretic concordance, dealing with all its subjects in alphabetical order, and is a valuable contribution to the grammatical and lexicographical knowledge of the Bible. It was, however, never printed though it was sent to Paris for that purpose and was left in manuscript form.

To the last class of Elijah's works belong a number of important books, the first of which is the *Tishbi.* The *Tishbi* contains the definitions of seven hundred and twelve words (the numerical sum of the letters of Tishbi, a cognomen of Elijah), partly Biblical and mostly Talmudic and post-Talmudic, which possess special importance. It was originally intended to include only such words as were omitted both by Kimhi and Nathan, author of the *Aruk,* but later even words recorded by them were included. It is a fine specimen of a partial encyclopaedic dictionary, for not only are the derivations of the words given, the Greek, Latin and Arabic origins quoted, but the different uses of the words in the Bible, the Targum, the Talmud, or the post-Talmudic literature are also stated. Again, if it is a verb, the various meanings in each form and all nuances arising from changes in the forms are then listed. The book was published with a Latin translation by his friend and pupil, Paulus Fagius.

Of greater importance is his larger work, the *Meturgeman* (The Interpreter). This is a complete dictionary of all the *Targumim,* i. e. the Aramaic translation of the Bible, as well as of the Aramaic words found in the Bible proper. It was the first dictionary of its kind and in it, Levita wanted to accomplish for the *Targumim* what David Kimhi accomplished by his Book of Roots for the Hebrew Bible. It is very skilfully done, each word is derived from its root, and references to the *Targum* given. All derivatives, such as nouns and adjectives derived from the verb are grouped under the root articles. Of special importance is the fact that the author notes the different Aramaic expressions used by the *Targumim* to translate a Hebrew word or phrase, explaining the reason for such deviations.

A noteworthy contribution to Hebrew grammar was made by the above-mentioned Abraham de-Balmes in his bulky book *Miknē Abraham* (The Acquisition of Abraham). Of the life of the author we know little, except that he was a famous physician and scientist as well as a Talmudic scholar. In his old age, he lived at Venice where at the request of the printer, Daniel Bomberg, he composed his book which was printed in the year 1523. Shortly after that, he died. The book is of a much heavier calibre than Levita's works, inasmuch as it is a systematic treatment of the entire field of Hebrew grammar, including syntax. It is divided into eight portals or sections, the first three of which are devoted to phonetics, mutation of letters and vowels and punctuation (Nikud). The fourth and the fifth portals deal with the noun and the verb respectively. Especially exhaustive is the treatment of the noun, for the author enters into a detailed classification of the nouns dividing them into three hundred and eleven classes. The sixth portal is devoted to adverbs and particles, while the seventh deals extensively with the syntax and the eighth with the accents. The last chapter was left incomplete, for the author died before it went through the press, but was completed by Kalonymos ben David. The method of the book is the philosophic one, each section being prefaced by a number of philosophical and logical definitions which elucidate the grammatical principles scientifically. De Balmes quotes many authorities, among them also his teacher, Messer Leon. He devotes much space to criticism of the theories of his predecessors, especially the Kimhis. Although the book was immediately published with a Latin translation, yet it did not gain much popular favor on account of its rather lengthy treatment of the subject as well as the heaviness of style and terminology, but it was greatly appreciated by scholars.

9. *THE SEVENTEENTH AND EIGHTEENTH CENTURIES*

The one hundred and fifty years from the beginning of the seventeenth century to the end of the Mediaeval period were quite productive for the science of language. A considerable number of text books on grammar, dictionaries, and glossaries were composed by various authors in various countries. However, most of them are mere compilations or digests of the books of their predecessors, and only a few rise above the average.

Of these in the field of grammar, the first is the *Arugath Habosem* (A Bed of Spices) by Samuel Arkevolti of Padua, printed in 1602. This grammar, besides being well organized, is especially distinguished for its chapter on the forms of the Hebrew meter as employed by the Mediaeval poets. Samuel's study of the subject is exhaustive, and he enumerates twenty-two different meters. The book contains also several chapters on rhetoric, where a number of rules for fine writing is given, and a few curiosities, such as chapters on how to write code letters or how to employ the vanishing script, etc.

A second book of a high quality is the Grammar of the Hebrew Language written around 1660 by the famous philosopher, Baruch Spinoza, at the request of some of his friends. The author planned to write his book in two parts, an etymology and a syntax, but he completed only the first. The work is characterized by the scientific terseness and philosophic depth of its author. It is divided into twenty-four chapters, the first four of which are devoted to the letters, vowels and accents, the next five to the nouns, three to adverbs, particles and suffixes, and the rest to the verb. It is interesting to point out the philosopher's conception of the relation between nouns and verbs. According to him, all Hebrew words with the exception of the particles have the quality of a name, thus the infinitive is only a *nomen agentis,* that is, a name of an action, and the finite modes or moods, such as the past and future are only adjectives of the noun of action. In this theory, we see a reflection of his philosophy that there is one substance, and all other things are only attributes and modes. His remark about the Hebrew tenses is worth noting. Hebrew, says he, has only two tenses, the past and future, for the present was considered by the Jews as a point at which the past ends and the future begins. Hence, what we would otherwise call the present is only a participle in Hebrew.

The third grammatical work of importance which appeared in 1733 is the *Zohar Hatebah* (literally the Window of the Ark, but figuratively there is a play on the word *Tebah* which means both word and ark). It was written by Solomon Hanau (d. 1746), a German grammarian. The book covers the entire field of grammar with a chapter on accents and another chapter on rhetoric and syntax. Hanau was considered a great authority on grammar in his time, and he wrote a series of books on this subject, of which the above-mentioned is the most complete. He exerted great influence in his day, and on account of the fact that he was himself a German Jewish scholar, his book which was adapted to the German way of pronouncing Hebrew, became the favored grammatical text book among the German and Polish Jews, who henceforth were the leaders in literary productions.

In the field of the *Masorah,* we have a few noteworthy contributions. These are Menahem Lonsano's *Or Torah* (The Light of the Torah) and Solomon Norzi's *Minhat Shai* (The Gift of the Offering). Lonsano was a Palestinian who came to Italy in his old age, in the year 1618 and there produced his work *Shete Yodoth* (Two portions), a book dealing with various subjects, of which the *Or Torah* forms a part. The work deals with the closed and open passages of the Pentateuch,[2] and the number of words to be written *plena* or defective. It serves as a guide to writers of the Scrolls of the Law.

Norzi's book consists of notes, grammatical and Masoretic, to the entire Pentateuch which are of great value to specialists in vocalization and scroll writing. Norzi hailed from the city of Norzia but later settled in Padua, where he finished his work in the year 1626.

Very little was produced by Jewish scholars during these centuries in the field of lexicography besides a few glossaries in Yiddish translation. Only several additions to the *Aruk*, the great Talmudic Lexicon by Nathan of Rome were made. Benjamin Mussafia of Hamburg (1605-1675), physician and philosopher, also poet and philologist wrote notes to the *Aruk*, entitled *Musaph ha-Aruk* (Addition to the Aruk). The notes are very valuable, inasmuch as Benjamin was a thorough Greek and Latin scholar and he supplied the derivations of hundreds of Talmudic words from these languages with their proper meanings. Besides, he added many words omitted or overlooked by Nathan. The above mentioned Lonsano also wrote notes to the *Aruk* by the name of *ha-M'aarik* (The Adjuster), in which he added a considerable number of words, and like Benjamin, utilized his knowledge of Greek and Latin, though he was not as proficient in these languages as the former.

[2] Certain passages in the Torah are separated from the following portion of the text by a larger interval of space and others by a smaller one. The first are called *Petuhoth*, i. e. open, the other *Setumoth*, closed.

CHAPTER II

BIBLE EXEGESIS

10. GENERAL REMARKS

Bible exegesis which reached its highest point during the twelfth century in the commentaries of Rashi, Samuel ben Meir (Rashbam), Ibn Ezra and the Kimhis was characterized, as we have seen, by its tendency towards the *Peshat,* namely the interpretation of the verse in accordance with the grammatical and linguistic connotation of the words. It might, therefore, have been expected that the exegesis which was produced during the centuries subsequent to the Classical period should follow the trodden path of the Classic exegetes. Yet the case was not so. The great mass of exegetical writings brought forth in the post-Classical age by numerous writers deviate to a large extent from the *Peshat* method of interpretation. That there are a number of notable examples is self-evident.

The factors that brought about this swerving from the accepted method are the two intellectual currents, philosophy and mysticism, which became very conspicuous in Jewish life with the beginning of the thirteenth century.

Philosophic exegesis was, of course, not a new thing in the history of Bible interpretation. Saadia laid its foundation by declaring that there is nothing in the Bible which contradicts the principles of reason, and by endeavoring to reconcile many apparent contradictions. We have already seen (Vol. I, Ch. XI, Sect. 179) that some of his followers made this principle their main motive of Biblical interpretation. But this tendency became more prevalent from the twelfth century on. A great impetus towards its development was given by Maimonides, who though himself not a commentator on the Bible, yet dealt extensively in his *Guide* with many portions of the Bible and with hundreds of difficult verses, endeavoring to rationalize not only the story of creation, prophetic visions and miracles, but most of the laws and precepts. Those that succeeded him not only adopted his method, but went much further. A great number of these philosophic exegetes revived the Philonic method of allegory, and not only used but abused it to a great extent. The protagonists of this method saw in many Biblical stories and narratives, as well as in many precepts, not actual events or commandments but philosophic allegories, where the struggle of man to attain intellectual perfection and his striving to unite with the Active Reason are depicted, or moral lessons enjoined. That this tendency was a dangerous one, inasmuch as it stripped the Bible of its plain human teaching and sublimated it into a string of abstract philosophic dicta and ethical teachings, is quite evident. It called forth severe strictures in its own time, and as a result, declined. Fortunately, not all philosophic exegetes carried things to such an extreme. Many of them kept within bounds and followed the way of Maimonides. These made important contributions to a rational understanding of the Bible and its problems. The most typical and important of such philosophic exegetes was Levi ben Gerson or Gersonides.

The second current, that of mysticism began, with the advent of the thirteenth century, to take hold of the minds of the leading scholars and became a powerful factor in the spiritual life of the Jews. Under its new name, Kabbala (Ch. VII), it colored all manifestations of that life, and of course, that of Bible interpretation. This method was likewise based on an old principle, which in its essence is akin to the one of the extreme philosophers, namely that the words of the Bible have besides their apparent also a hidden meaning and that it contains all truths that the human mind can conceive regarding God, the world, man and creation. That this principle was frequently abused by the mystic interpreters is needless to say. Mysticism, which as we have seen (Vol. I, Ch. XII), considered every letter of the Bible of special significance and even invested the vowel points and the numerical value of the letters with hidden meanings, found in exegesis ample room for the exercise of its methods. This type of exegesis arose first in Germany where, at the end of the twelfth century, its early mystics began to comment on the Bible in that spirit and to utilize combinations of letters and initials of words, as well as the numerical value of letters in order to derive certain teachings from the text. Later, with the development of the Kabbala in Spain and other countries, it spread also thither. There, this exegesis assumed a more dignified aspect; verses and passages were made to yield secrets and to corroborate the main teachings of the Kabbala. Such commentaries multiplied but differed little from each other. Of course, even among the mystics there were some exceptions to whom the mystic interpretation was a secondary matter and the *Peshat* method the primary motive. These, likewise, made noteworthy contributions to Biblical exegesis, the typical one being Moses ben Nahman or Nahmanides, as he is usually called. That there were also exegetes who followed neither current but continued to explain the Bible in the *Peshat* way of interpretation goes without saying. However, with the exception of Isaac Abrabanel, these commentators contributed very little to exegesis, repeating mostly in one form or another what had been said by the great commentators of the Classical age.

There is yet another species of exegesis, the homiletic, where the Bible is interpreted in a sermonic way and the verses are made to yield a moral lesson, or a practical rule, or even a religious exhortation. In reality, this is a revival of the old Midrashic way, but it differs from it both in quality and in quantity.

As the quantity of exegetic literature during the post-Classical period is very extensive, while the high quality of such works is limited only to a few commentaries, the review will deal primarily with the representative commentators who typify the different currents of interpretation and will note only briefly the less important exegetes.

11. BIBLE EXEGESIS IN THE EAST

With the death of Maimonides, Jewish learning in the East began to decline. Yet, for a century or so thereafter, literary activity was still kept alive by a few individuals who were influenced by the spirit of the great master. Maimonides himself, as noted above, wrote no commentary on the Bible, but the interest aroused in the Bible by his writing bore fruit. His favorite pupil, Joseph Ibn Aknin (Vol. I, Ch. XI, Sect. 173), wrote a commentary on Canticles in Arabic, where in accordance with the current philosophic spirit, he explains this book allegorically and makes it yield philosophic thoughts.

Abraham, the son of Maimonides, wrote a commentary on the first two books of the Pentateuch which deals with the important problems presented by these books in a philosophic manner. Moses ben Shesheth, who originally hailed from Spain but later settled in Babylon, wrote at the beginning of the thirteenth century commentaries on Isaiah and Ezekiel reproducing to a great extent the interpretations of others.

A commentator of note was the above-mentioned grammarian and philologist Tanhum of Jerusalem. As he was both a scientific student of Hebrew and a philosopher, being an ardent devotee of Maimonides, his commentaries are distinguished by a close adherence to the *Peshat* method and by a free philosophic spirit. He wrote them in a scientific manner, prefacing each book with an introduction in which the general principles underlying the interpretation are enunciated. He displays a keen critical sense when discussing historical events in the Bible, especially in the Book of Judges. His commentaries were written in Arabic and covered a great part of the prophetic books. Several of them, namely those on the Books of Judges and Habakuk were published by various scholars.

Little was produced during the following centuries. We hear only of two commentators of the fourteenth century; one Eliezer ben Nathan Ashkenazi who probably lived in Egypt, wrote in the year 1364 a Hebrew commentary on the Pentateuch permeated by a rationalistic spirit. The other, a certain Nathaniel ben Isaiah wrote an Arabic commentary on the Pentateuch earlier in the century (1339) which is also pervaded by the philosophic spirit of the age.

12. MOSES BEN NAHMAN

Spain, for centuries the home of Bible exegesis, also showed signs of decline, during the post-Classical period, in this branch as well as in other branches of Jewish literature with the exception of Rabbinics. Philosophy, on the one hand, and mysticism on the other hand, engaged the attention of the scholars outside of the Talmud. Still it succeeded in producing during the thirteenth century two great commentators, each one representing a type of exegesis. The first is Moses ben Nahman referred to above (1195-1270).

Nahmanides was born in Gerona, a city in Aragon. He was endowed with great intellectual capabilities and an aptitude for learning. While yet a mere youth, he acquired a great name as a Talmudic scholar, and at twenty, he had already written a number of commentaries on various tractates of the Talmud. It seems that he was by profession a physician, as many other Jewish scholars of his day, but in spite of that, medicine was only his avocation, his vocation being Jewish scholarship. He acted as official rabbi in the city of his birth and on account of his profound erudition and great piety was accepted by almost the entire Spanish Jewry as its spiritual leader. When the conflict about the teachings of Maimonides broke out in the middle of the century, Nahmanides who was somewhat averse to philosophy but a great admirer of Moses ben Maimon, tried at first to mediate between the parties, namely the Maimonists and the rigorists, but when Maimonides himself was censured, he defended him warmly. In the year 1263, Namhanides was invited by King James I of Aragon to participate in a religious controversy with the convert Pablo Christiani, in which he distinguished himself as a skillful disputant. But when he later published in book form the arguments advanced at the dispute, he was brought up on charges by the Dominicans for insulting the Christian religion, and though the king was kindly disposed towards Nahmanides, a sentence of two years' exile was passed upon him. He then left Spain altogether and settled in Palestine where he spent the remainder of his life.

The spiritual and intellectual makeup of Nahmanides was of a composite character. He was deeply religious, and while still a youth, was attracted by the revived and invigorated mystic teachings of the Kabbala. In fact, later mystics referred to him as one of the founders of the secret knowledge. His relation to philosophy as a rationalistic interpretation of Judaism was, therefore, a negative one. He believed that by the proper study of the Bible itself, a deeper knowledge of Judaism can be gained than any philosophy might offer. Yet, he was not averse to speculation in general nor to science. Being a Spaniard and a physician, he could not disparage secular knowledge. He even encouraged religious speculation and considered the proving of religious principles rationally a duty, but objected to dogmatic Greek scholasticism. Hence, his rather peculiar relation to Maimonides. He admired him greatly, both on account of his Halakic writings and also on account of his *Guide,* yet he objected strenuously to the leading principles laid down there. Even his strong mystic leanings did not lead him, like other Kabbalists, to view Judaism under that aspect. He believed in the sanctity of the Kabbala and in the truth of its teachings, but thought that its knowledge should be limited to the few and that the great masses should be taught a Judaism based on faith as well as on reason as much as possible, and be permeated with a broad spirit of common sense and piety.

As a medium for the broadcasting of such teachings of Judaism, he chose the writing of a commentary on the Pentateuch, the basis of the Jewish religion. The commentary was written and completed during his last years in Jerusalem, but was begun earlier and planned for decades. It may be said to have been practically his life work. In his introduction, he defines rather modestly the purpose of the commentary which is, "To satisfy the need of students who, weary of the yoke of exile and suffering, read the Bible on the Sabbaths and holidays for a better understanding of it; and to rejoice their hearts with explanations both pleasant and palatable." But there is really more to it than the mere enjoyment of pleasant interpretation. To Nahmanides, the Torah was Divine, containing all wisdom and the solution of all problems, as he says in his introduction, "The Torah contains all fifty portals of understanding, but we must know how to open them." Yet, in spite of this mystic view of the Torah, he made, as stated, the mystic teachings secondary, his main purpose being to give a comprehensive view of the Torah in its entirety, in all its parts, legal as well as narrative, in the most natural way.

Nahmanides did not aim to make his commentary a mere series of explanations of the meaning of words and phrases as previous commentators had done, nor to derive any ethical teachings, but really to bring out the essence of the Pentateuch in all its aspects. Hence, his disagreement both with Rashi and Ibn Ezra, his two predecessors whom he quotes so frequently. With the first, he is dissatisfied on account of his Midrashic tendency, and with the second, on account of his rather free spirit.

His main principle was that the Torah is to be understood not by forcing it to yield philosophic truths but in its own way and in the way understood by tradition. His problem was to show the reason for every law and precept and to prove how it is really enfolded in the meaning of the words. Still, Nahmanides with all his legal piety had an extremely healthy sense for *Peshat* and believed that there are several meanings to the words of the Torah, that of Halakah, Agada, and that of *Peshat*. He, therefore, often gives two interpretations to verses, the traditional Halakic and the one independent of it. It is interesting to note that in such places, Nahmanides had a penetrating insight into the Bible and some of his *Peshat* interpretations resemble very closely those of the best modern commentators. On the whole, it may be said that he endeavors to reconcile the Rabbinic interpretation with the *Peshat* only in such cases where a different interpretation would directly overthrow Rabbinic law, but in passages where such is not the case, he discards the Talmudic explanation if he finds it does not agree with the natural sense of the verse.

His love for naturalness was so great that not only did he try to find satisfactory reasons for precepts which are, as a rule, known as *Hukim,* i. e. Commandments by the pure will of God, but he notices every deviation from a natural state of human life apparently implied by the wording of a law and tries to correct it. Thus he is not afraid to say that the precept, "And thou shalt love thy neighbor as thyself" (Lev. XIX, 18), is an exaggeration, for it can not be taken literally, as it is contrary to human nature. What it really means, says he, is that man is enjoined to love his friend in all ways just as he loves himself, and not limit the love to any particular aspect of his character, but the degree of love of the other man can never equal that of the love of self.

In his endeavor to present as comprehensive a view as possible of the Torah, Nahmanides had to grapple with grave problems, such as those of the sacrifices, miracles, prophecy and similar ones. In all such cases, he takes issue with Maimonides' rationalism. Thus, in the case of the sacrifices, he rejects the view of the former, that they were instituted by God in order to detract the attention of the Jews from sacrificing to idols, as not compatible with the spirit of the Torah. He offers, therefore, his own view which is that the act of sacrifice is symbolic representing the complete inner change in the soul of the sinner. The slaughtering and the burning of the sacrifices visualize to the sinner the punishment due him but which was averted by the grace of God. There is a certain psychologic insight in this explanation but little historical truth. The problem of miracles presented a very difficult aspect. Nahmanides believes in miracles, for it is to him the very proof for God's creation of the world and His constant conduct of it. Otherwise, he argues quite logically, all the promises of the Bible of reward to the righteous and punishment to the sinner have no meaning. In the natural order of events, the sinner should not suffer more than the righteous, nor should the latter prosper. Hence, the belief in miracles is inherently connected with the fundamental principles of faith. Furthermore, he sees many hidden miracles embodied in the very process of nature. Yet he claims that God limits himself in the performance of miracles, and whenever possible, lets nature take its course. At times, he even endeavors to reconcile miraculous events with nature. Thus, he does not consider the rainbow, spoken of in Genesis IX, 9, 13, 14 as a sign of the covenant that no flood will ever come upon the earth, as a new creation, for it is a natural phenomenon which can be produced by any one. He says that it was always there from the very beginning of the world, but that after the flood it was considered as a sign of the covenant between God and the human species. The symbolic meaning is new, but not the rainbow itself.

Thus, and in many other ways, does Nahmanides endeavor to present the entirety of the Torah in the light of deep piety as well as in the light of understanding and human reason. On the whole, it can be said that he succeeded in presenting the teachings of Judaism in a comprehensible way. His commentary is a noteworthy contribution to the exegesis both of the spirit of the Torah as well as of the words and verses. Whenever Nahmanides turns to *Peshat,* he displays remarkable insight and skill. His work was greatly valued by generations of scholars who speak of the commentary in the highest terms of praise, and many a modern student can still peruse it with great profit.

13. BAHYA BEN ASHER

A decade or two after the completion of the commentary of Nahmanides, there arose in Spain a commentator who utilized the teachings of the Kabbala as an important element in Biblical exegesis. This was Bahya ben Asher of Toledo or Saragossa (d. 1291). He was greatly influenced by Nahmanides, but unlike him, failed to see the real purpose of exegesis, which is to make the Bible more comprehensible to the average man so that its teachings may become clarified rather than mystified. However, even he, being a Spanish Jew, felt that the mystic interpretation of the Torah would not be sufficient, and he, therefore, relegated mysticism to the place of a fourth element in his commentary. In his introduction, he tells us, imitating Ibn Ezra, that there are four methods of Bible exegesis. The first is the *Peshat* whose representatives are Rashi and Rabbi Hanannel, the second is the Midrashic, the third the philosophic, and the fourth the one "where light dwelleth, the path of the soul when it is illuminated by the light of life." This is, of course, the way of mysticism. He claims that the originator of this method of interpretation was Nahmanides, but says that while the latter only alluded to it, he will explain the matter more fully.

Bahya thought that in order to produce a perfect commentary, it was best to follow all four ways. He accordingly explains such verses as he deems fit in four ways, Midrashically, philosophically, mystically and by *Peshat.* This attempt to satisfy everybody did not, however, enhance the value of the commentary. He displays, on the whole, little originality except probably in the mystical aspect. In all other ways, he is an eclectic. Most of his *Peshat* explanations are borrowed from the commentaries of Rashi, Hanannel and Nahmanides. Although he promises faithfully in his introduction to quote everyone by name, he fails to credit Nahmanides for numerous explanations he excerpted from his commentary, and only occasionally refers to him by name. In his philosophic aspect, he seems to have excerpted a number of remarks from various philosophic exegetes on different verses and incorporated them in his commentary. His main purpose in incorporating these remarks in the commentary was, as he states in the introduction, to show that the Torah contains all sciences, only "that the latter are attained by investigation and speculation, while the Torah is revealed."

More valuable is his Midrashic interpretation, for Bahya was careful to select from the vast Agadic and Midrashic literature a large number of passages, rich in thought and feeling, and arrange them according to the verses. He was well versed in this literature and we often meet in his book passages from lost Midrashim. The Kabbalistic way of interpretation is, as said, the most original, for although he claims to be only an expounder of Nahmanides' mystic versions, he really added much of his own.

The commentary of Bahya, in spite of its eclectic character, and maybe because of it, was considered a very popular book and exerted great influence on future generations. His remarks are quoted by numerous later authors. Especially popular were his Midrashic comments which contain deep feeling and pathos, and a large number of them were incorporated in religious books intended for the masses and written in the German-Jewish vernacular (Yiddish), such as the embellished translation of the Pentateuch known as the *Teitsch Chumesch* and others.

14. JACOB BEN ASHER

The mystic current in exegesis having once been set in motion continued to flow, as is evident in a number of commentaries written during the fourteenth and fifteenth centuries in Spain, some endeavoring to find in the Bible the hidden teachings of Kabbala, and some only using its method of playing wtih letters and their numerical value in order to derive ethical teachings. The typical commentary of the latter type is the one written by Jacob ben Asher (1280-1340), known as *Baal ha-Turim,* literally the author of the Turim, his Magnum Opus, the Great Code (Ch. IV, Sect. 57).

Rabbi Jacob was known as one of the greatest Talmudists of his time. Like his father Asher, he devoted himself mainly to the study of Rabbinics and knew but little of the secular sciences. Being very pious, he was attracted by the Kabbala, yet, not being thoroughly permeated by its spirit, he did not lose the sense for the plain meaning of the Bible. His commentary, therefore, contains a good deal of *Peshat,* in which he follows Nahmanides, giving him full credit in his introduction for material borrowed from his commentary. However, the more interesting part of it is his original contribution, and that is his interpretation of passages by means of *Notaricon* and numerical value of words.

His method is as follows: He notes that a certain expression or word is found in the Bible a number of times, and by a dialectic method, he finds a common thought running through these different verses, no matter in what context they may be found. The ingenuity of this device can be seen from the following example. On Genesis I, 14, which contains God's commands to the two luminaries, Rabbi Jacob remarks as follows: "The word *l'Ototh"* (For Signs) is found only in this verse and in Isaiah VIII, 18 where the prophet says, "Behold I and the children whom the Lord hath given me are *l'Ototh* and for wonders in Israel." Hence, he says, we must understand that the term children refers to scholars, for as the word *l'Ototh* in Genesis refers to luminaries, so does it similarly refer in Isaiah, for the scholars are the luminaries of the community. This is a frequent method of comment with him. Quite frequent also is the *Notaricon,* that is constructing words or passages either from the initials of words in a verse or from the final letters. Similarly common is the *Gematria,* that is calculating the numerical value of one word to equal that of another, and consequently including the meaning of the latter in the former. Another device of his is to attach special significance to the number of times a certain word appears in a passage and derive from this fact a certain teaching.

To illustrate these devices, we will quote a few examples. On Genesis I, 4, Rabbi Jacob comments: The final letters of the first three words, "And God saw the light and it is good" (Vyar Elohim Eth, etc.) form together *Emeth* (truth), that is the *Aleph* of the first, *Mem* of the second and *Tau* of the third, to show that truth is the foundation of creation. In the same chapter (v, 27) which ends with the words,

"Male and female he created them," our commentator notes: *Zakar* (Male) equals *Berakah* (Blessing) while *Nekebah* (Female) equals *bi-Klalah* (with a curse). This means that the numerical value of *Zakar* equals that of *Berakah* (Betn equals 2, Resh equals 200, Kaf equals 20, Hē equals 5—227; again Zein equals 7, Kaf equals 20, Resh equals 200—227). Similarly, the letters of *Nekebah*[1] equal 167, the same as that of bi-Klalah. The implication is clear, that man brings blessing, while woman brought the curse of death upon humanity. On Genesis, IX, 21, he says: "Wine equals wailing" (Yayyin equals 75, Yelalah equals 75) which means that excessive drinking leads to misery and wailing. On Genesis I, 5, the rabbi remarks, "The word light is mentioned in the story of the first day of creation five times, which number implies the Five Books of Moses, the source of light." He, at times, offers a fanciful explanation of words in order to unfold a Rabbinic thought. Thus, to Genesis, V, 20, "And he called her name Eve, for she was the mother of all living," he offers a different explanation for the name of Eve, *Hava* in Hebrew. It is derived from *Havē,* to speak, so named because of her fluency in speech, as the rabbis said: "Of the ten measures of speech in the world, woman took nine."[2] Such are the curious comments of Jacob ben Asher. They are, as a rule, brief and very often brilliant and scintillating. It is interesting to note that this part of the commentary wherein these peculiar devices are employed became very popular, so that the *Peshat* part was ultimately separated from it altogether. In the printed Bibles, only an abbreviated version of Rabbi Jacob's commentary was included. That is the part containing all the comments of the nature described above. It seems that such juggling with words and letters and the employment of these interpretations suited the mood of the large masses of students in Germany and Poland, who admired the skill and keenness evinced in the notes and comments of Jacob ben Asher.

15. MINOR EXEGETES IN SPAIN

The work of exegesis continued in Spain up to the time of the expulsion. To the more important of the works, belong first the notes to the Pentateuch of Asher ben Jehiel the great Talmudist, the father of the above named Jacob, then the commentary on Job, Daniel

[1] In order to make the equation correct, the author writes the word Nekebah thus נקיבה with an extra Yod as it was often the custom in Germany to insert an extra Waw or Yod in words when unpunctuated.

[2] Kidushin 49a.

and Chronicles composed by Samuel ben Nissim. His commentaries are denoted by the author himself and others as Midrash, as they contain a large number of Midrashic excerpts, but he also quotes profusely Saadia, Ibn Jannah, Rashi and Ibn Ezra.

Commentaries were also written during the fifteenth century by the great Rabbinic authorities, Simon ben Zemah Duran, originally of the island of Majorca but later of Algiers, Joseph Hasan of Portugal (1450-1480) and Joel Ibn Shaib of Tudela (1485). The first wrote a commentary on the Book of Job in the spirit of *Peshat,* the second on a number of books including Canticles, and the last on Psalms and Lamentations. The last great exegetical work written by a Spanish scholar is the *'Akedat Yitzhak* (The Sacrifice of Isaac) by Isaac 'Arama (1450-1490), but as it is in the form of philosophic sermons, it belongs to homiletic literature and will be discussed in its proper place.

16. EXEGESIS IN PROVENCE

The southern part of France or the Provence was, as we know, a great center of learning and literature during the thirteenth and fourteenth centuries, and exegetical activity flourished there in a considerable measure. Special impetus in that direction was given by the great exegetes of the previous century, the Kimhis. As Provence was the heir to the Spanish type of Jewish learning, namely the cultivating of philosophy, science, and the study of the languages in equal measure as that of Rabbinics, it follows that the *Peshat* and the philosophic currents were well represented in the exegetical productions. As a matter of fact, the latter was more prevalent. It was there where the allegoric method of interpretation was carried to the extreme.

Of the exegetes in the Provence, the first to be mentioned are two of the Ibn Tibbon family, the famous translators, Samuel Ibn Tibbon and his son Moses. The first wrote a lengthy commentary on the first chapter of Genesis, where the question of creation is discussed in a philosophical manner, and also a commentary on Ecclesiastes in a similar vein. The second composed a commentary on Canticles with a lengthy introduction, where the poetic form and the allegoric character of the book are discussed.

Towards the end of the thirteenth century, we have commentaries written by the famous Talmudist, Menahem ben Solomon Meiri (of the family Meiri, 1249-1306) on a large number of the books of the Bible. Only the commentaries on the Books of Proverbs and Psalms are left to us, the others are known only by quotations. The commentary on Proverbs is written in two ways. At first, the writer explains the verses in plain *Peshat,* called by him the revealed way (Nigleh), and then in a hidden (Nistor) allegoric-philosophic one. As an illustration of this method which was, as we know, prevalent in the Provence during this period, we will quote one example. The verse 31, chapter XXI in Proverbs, "The horse is prepared against the day of battle, but safety is of the Lord," is explained by Meiri thus: The horse that is the active intellect of man is preparing or struggling to conceive the final purpose of life and the world; but, says the sage, "God is all, and real salvation lies in knowing His essence."

The fourteenth century opens up with the commentaries of Nissim ben Moses of Marseilles on the Pentateuch, called *Maasē Nissim* (literally the Work of Nissim; but there is a play on the words, as *Maasē Nissim* may also mean miraculous deeds). It is of the philosophic type and is prefixed by a lengthy inroduction dealing primarily with prophecy. However, he and others were soon to be overshadowed by two great commentators whose works occupy an important place in the history of exegesis. These are Joseph Ibn Kaspi and Levi ben Gerson.

17. JOSEPH IBN KASPI

Joseph ben Abba Mari of Argentier (1280-1340), hence Kaspi* was one of the most prolific authors of his time. He contributed to almost every branch of Jewish literature except Rabbinics. His grammatical works were noted above, but he is primarily a philosopher and exegete, and it is in these two branches that he excels. The number of his works reaches twenty and most of them are compounded with the name *Keseph.* Only a few facts of his life are known. He was born, as said, in Argentiers but lived a great part of his life in Tarascon. However, he seemed to have wandered about for quite a number of years and visited many cities in the Provence and Spain. He even made a journey to Egypt in the hope of gaining more philosophic knowledge in the city where Maimonides lived and wrote. He was, though, disappointed in his quest, for he found the descendants of Maimonides good Talmudists but poor philosophers. He seems to have possessed wealth and was thus able to devote himself unperturbed to his beloved studies.

* Argent and Keseph both meaning silver.

Kaspi wrote commentaries on the entire Bible. Like all philosophers of his time, he expected to find all philosophic teachings in the Bible, yet his commentaries can not be classed as typical philosophic exegesis, for he had a strong sense for *Peshat*. In his introduction to Proverbs, he openly reprobates the allegorists who see in it and in several other books of the Hagiographa discussion about matter and form, and boldly states that we should understand the words of the Torah and the prophets in their plain meaning as we do the books of Aristotle on logic and physics. By this, though, he does not mean to say that he places the Bible on the same level as the books of Aristotle, for Kaspi was a deeply religious man and considered the Scriptures holy and the revealed word of God. Yet, he did not always adhere to his own declaration, and occasionally uses a bit of allegory himself, especially in some of the Hagiographic books. Besides, he wrote special books where he discusses the question of miracles in the Bible and other important theological subjects from a philosophic point of view. The commentaries were intended for the average intellectual student and much of the discussion of the difficult subjects was left out.

His commentaries, on the whole, reflect the duality of his own character. Kaspi was, as said, a deeply religious man yet he was equally permeated by the spirit of philosophy, so that he often rebelled against tradition in quite a striking manner, and contrary to Ibn Ezra who veiled his heterodox remarks in cryptic language, he frequently expressed himself rather bluntly. Hence, we find in his commentaries that while he praises the Masorites, he often disregards them and dares to make a number of irreverent remarks about some of the patriarchs, not sparing even Moses whom he considers a perfect man. It sems that Kaspi had a jocular vein in him, which he could not restrain even when writing on the most exalted subjects.

Kaspi aimed to be original, and he says, therefore, that he will endeavor to explain only those verses where he can offer something new. He quotes Ibn Ezra by name frequently when he differs with his view, and more rarely when he agrees with him. This tendency gives a disjointed character to his commentary and makes it appear more like a series of notes and glosses. In general, we can discern three different strains in his commentaries, corresponding to the three parts of the Bible, namely, the Pentateuch, the Prophets and the Hagiographa, as each of these commentaries bears a different character. The one on the Torah is more in the nature of lengthy notes to selected verses rather than a running commentary. There he devotes himself primarily to the explanation of difficulties connected with certain verses, on account of either theological or historical reasons. Only on rare occasions, does he explain merely the plain meaning of the verses. In these notes, he often carries on a polemic against Ibn Ezra's and Maimonides' interpretations, and also expresses his philosophic views on prophecy and miracles, though he devoted a special book to these matters. His commentary on the Prophets deals more with the *Peshat* of the verses, while that of the Hagiographa, with the exception of the Proverbs and Lamentations, is more in the nature of a discussion of the contents of the books and contains little exegesis.

Kaspi was well versed in the grammatical literature, and made much use of its principal works, especially of Jannah's *Book of Roots*. He, however, brought into the commentary his great knowledge of logic which, as we have seen above, he combined with grammar. He, therefore, lays down quite frequently many logical definitions before he explains a passage, and often uses to great advantage the niceties of logical distinctions in discerning nuances of Biblical expressions. He was versed in the Latin translation of the Bible, and made it a point to contravert Christological references or interpretations. In general, he warns his readers not to rely on translations, and takes special pleasure in pointing out errors in the Latin version, showing that the author misunderstood the text of the Bible. In spite of his being a philosopher and of a critical turn of mind, he is quite conservative in his commentary, and like Ibn Ezra, he champions the integrity of the text and opposes every emendation. At times, he even offers very strange explanations rather than admit the necessity for changing a letter or the vocalization in a word.

In his commentary on the Hagiographa, he evinces sound understanding of the sense of the books. In his introduction to Proverbs, he remarks that though he believes Solomon to be the author of the book, yet he does not believe that he wrote the book himself, but that he uttered proverbs on various occasions which were written down by his scribes and later edited by him. Kaspi, however, thinks that only Part I (Ch. I-X) was edited by Solomon himself, while Part II, (Chs. X-XXV) was edited by the scribes, hence the repetitions. He warns the readers not to look for allegories in Proverbs, nor for unity in the chapters. The individual proverbs teach practical wisdom and ethics, and each carries its own thought. He also makes pointed remarks about their form, balance and antithesis. Yet, he at times, hints at the hidden meaning of some of the sayings.

His commentary on Job is primarily a discussion of its contents, and he strongly disagrees with Maimonides who identifies the opinions of Job and his friends with those of Aristotle and the various philosophic views of the Arabs of his time, namely the Mutazilia and Asheria. Strange to say, Kaspi who, on the whole, kept aloof from allegoric interpretation excepts the Book of Canticles and believes it to be an allegory. The book, in his opinion, tells the story of the struggle of the human intellect to unite with the Active Reason of the universe and describes in terms of love the passionate desire of that intellect to attain the coveted union.

The commentaries of Kaspi, as a whole, contain many fine remarks, interpretations and logical exegesis, and certainly are important contributions to Jewish exegesis. But because of their disjointedness and the frequent forced interpretations of verses, as well as on account of some irreverances and crude witticisms, they did not exert the proper influence upon exegetic literature, and the larger part of them remained unpublished until recently.

18. LEVI BEN GERSON

Levi ben Gerson, known either as *Ralbag* (Rabbi Levi ben Gerson) or Gersonides was one of the outstanding scholars of his time. He was born at Bagnols in 1288, and lived successively at Perpignan and Avignon. He mastered almost all the sciences of the time, distinguishing himself especially in mathematics, astronomy and philosophy. (Ch. VI, Sect. 78.) His works in the field of astronomy were translated into Latin, and he was known to the gentile scholarly world as Maestro Leon de Bagnols or as Leo Hebraus. Like all Jewish scholars, he practiced medicine as a profession, distinguishing himself in that science. He died in 1340.

To the Jewish world, however, Gersonides is known primarily as commentator and philosopher. He wrote commentaries on the Pentateuch, on all of the Hagiographa except the Psalms, on the Five Scrolls and on the First Prophets, namely the prophetical historical books. Of these, the commentaries on the Pentateuch, Job and Proverbs are the most representative both in quantity and quality.

Being permeated with the spirit of philosophy, it is, of course, understood that Gersonides followed the philosophic method of interpretation, but did not carry it to extremes and wrote valuable commentaries from an exegetic point of view. In his general view of the Bible, he follows the one of Maimonides, which holds that the Bible is a revelation of God just as nature is. He, however, improved upon that view by undertaking to show in detail, in his lengthy commentary on the Pentateuch, that the Torah teaches the ethical rules and maxims of conduct. For this reason, he added at the end of his exegesis of each chapter of the Pentateuch a summary of the principles of ethics derived from it.

His point of view is, as he explains in the introduction to the commentary on the Pentateuch, that the Scriptures are the highest expression of Divine Providence in relation to the human species, inasmuch as it aims to guide man towards spiritual perfection which is the final aim of human life. And in order to carry out this aim, the Bible contains three elements which are conducive to this purpose in various ways. These are, (1) the precepts both positive and negative (Asē and lo-Tasē) which intend to regulate both religious practice and beliefs; (2) theories of ethical conduct of the individual and of society contained in the historical narratives of the lives of our ancestors; (3) beliefs and principles of knowledge which might have been ascertained by philosophic speculation accessible only to the select few, but were revealed to all by the prophets in their utterances.

After laying down these principles, he tells us that the purposes of his commentary are first, to derive speculative truths from the Torah, though not always in the way the Talmud does; second, to elucidate the precepts and commandments of the Law; third, to find the fundamental principles from which the particulars of each precept as enumerated by oral law result, and to derive these principles from the verses. In this derivation, Gersonides does not always follow the Talmudic mode of deduction, inasmuch as he considers the method not binding, but believes that he can reach the same conclusions by means of plain exegesis. He also endeavors to ascertain as far as possible the reasons for such precepts (Taamē ha-Mitzvoth). In this way, the commentary of Gersonides resembles in its scope and character that of Nahmanides, namely, that it aims to bring out the entire teaching of the Bible in all its aspects. That a more liberal spirit and broader view prevails in the latter than in the former is needless to say.

The method of Gersonides in his commentaries is a peculiar one though it has some resemblance to the one employed by Ibn Ezra in some of his commentaries. It consists of a triple explanation. At first, he explains the meaning of the words in the chapter in accordance with the grammatical and lexicographical sense, then he gives the connected thought and interpretation of the entire chapter, and finally, either a summary of the speculative ideas and ethical maxims arranged in numbered statements, or an abstract of the philosophic view of the passage. Ibn Ezra and Maimonides are the two authorities whom Gersonides usually follows in his commentary, as he rarely quotes any one else with the exception of Saadia. Of the two, the former is his guide in pure exegetic matters, and the latter in philosophic and general interpretation of the teachings of the Torah. Yet he deviates from both many times. He often interprets the words differently from Ibn Ezra, but not, however, on the basis of differences in grammar but from philosophic purposes, as Gersonides derives philosophic ideas even from the etymological meaning of the words. In the explanation of the most important theological questions, he usually follows Maimonides, although he differs from him in a number of subjects, such as the creation of the world and other matters where Gersonides developed his own view (Ch. V, Sect. 76). But even where he follows Maimonides, he is, as a rule, more explicit and endeavors to show that his view is derived from the verses themselves.

Thus, while he agrees with Maimonides in his view that the sacrifices were a means to detract the Jews from idol worship, he also attaches to them a deeper meaning, and dwells at length on the symbolism involved in each kind of sacrifice. Likewise, in regard to miracles, he accepts the Maimonidean view that each miracle is a special temporal act and was not predetermined by God at creation, but differs from him greatly in ascribing miracles to the Active Reason and not to God Himself. He also tries to minimize as much as possible the supernaturalness of the miracles. He lays down a rule that the miracles conform somewhat to the rules of nature, inasmuch as they are not essentially contrary to nature. For instance, the turning of the rod of Aaron into a snake is only miraculous, insofar as the *causes* that brought about the existence of *this* snake are not natural, but not as regards the existence of the snake itself. Were there no snakes in existence, that miracle could not have taken place, just as a square can not become a circle by any miracle.

The characteristic feature of the commentary of Gersonides is that it intends to explain every detail of the Pentateuch and make it more rational or more in accordance with the philosophic conception of his time. This tendency caused him to use a good deal of symbolism and allegory in the manner of the day. One example will suffice. In explaining the two cherubim placed on the cover of the arc, he remarks that they symbolize the human reason and the universal Active Reason or Intellect, and therefore it is written, "And their faces are turned one towards the other" (Ex. XXV, 20), as human reason always turns to the Active Reason, its source.

Notwithstanding all such deviations and flights into allegory, his Pentateuch commentary has great exegetic value in the broad conception of the term. It throws light on many subjects and offers to the intelligent student a wide and more comprehensive view of the Torah. Especially elucidating are the portions dealing with legal matters, where he endeavors to explain each law in relation to its ramifications and particulars in a logical and rational manner. Of great value are also his summaries where the ethical teachings of the Pentateuch are enhanced. These summaries were held in great esteem by the scholars of succeeding generations, and they were later reprinted separately with notes and comments.

Of the other commentaries of Gersonides, the one on Job is the most important. In it, he follows his triple method and explains the single words in each chapter first, his main purpose being to clarify the content of the book. In rather lengthy discussions he endeavors to give a complete view of the problem of Divine Providence which he accomplishes in a perfect philosophic manner, treating each side of the question. The opinions of Job and his friends represent, according to him, the different views that can be expressed on this subject. He finds in it, of course, his own view which agrees with that of Elihu (for his view on the subject see Ch. V, Sect. 76).

In Koheleth and Proverbs, Gersonides finds the main Aristotelian theories of practical ethics, the former dealing with the principles and the general statements of conduct and the latter with their application and the particular means for obtaining the aims involved in those principles.

The contradictions in Koheleth, he explains by the fact that the author includes views with which he does not agree in order to afford people a choice of action. Canticles he explains entirely as an allegory depicting the soul, its faculties and the reigning spirit. His commentary on this book is of little exegetic value and is only of interest, inasmuch as it affords a glimpse into the curiosities of the human mind.

With all his philosophic temper, Gersonides like Ibn Ezra, was addicted to the science of astrology and believed in the influence of the constellations upon human destiny. This, of course, produced in him a mystic vein which is noticeable in his commentaries. It is not to be wondered at, therefore, that at the end of his commentary on the Book of Daniel he calculated the date of the coming of the Messiah and even fixed the year to be that of 1358.

The commentaries of Gersonides were greatly cherished by the intellectuals of the subsequent generations and were well preserved. In some editions of the Bible, they received a very prominent place, next to Rashi and Ibn Ezra. In the Basel edition of the Biblia Magna (1550), the commentary of Gersonides on Job even displaced that of Rashi which is given on the margin.

19. FRANCO-GERMAN AND ITALIAN EXEGESIS

With Rashi and his disciples, Samuel ben Meir and Joseph Karo, the great period of Biblical exegesis in northern France and the adjacent German provinces closed. What followed during the succeeding centuries were merely sporadic attempts to interpret parts of the Bible in one way or another, mostly in a mystic way. That this activity went on, and at times, in a prolific manner is needless to say, for the Bible was always of great interest to Jewish scholars, but little original matter was produced.

To the most important commentaries of the period composed in northern France belong the following: First, a commentary on the Pentateuch, known as the *Gan* (The Garden), so named from the fact that the numerical value of the two letters *Gimmel* and *Nun* amount to fifty-three, the number of the weekly portions in the Pentateuch,[3] written by Aaron ben Joseph in 1250; second, *Tosofoth* compiled by an anonymous author at the end of the thirteenth century under the name of *Daath Zekenim* (The Knowledge of the Elders). The latter, as its name indicates, is really a collection of glosses and remarks by various scholars, in the manner of the Tosofoth to the Talmud. (Vol. I, Ch. X, Sect. 146). More than fifty commentators are quoted there by name besides many whose remarks are quoted anonymously. This commentary from its very nature, bears a heterogenous character. Various kinds of comments are found there, some of a

[3] It is true that in the printed Pentateuchs, the number of the portions is fifty-four, but in the Colophon at the end of Deuteronomy,, where the number of the weekly portions is stated, two versions are cited, fifty-four and fifty three. It seems that the Jews of France where the author of the commentary, the *Gan,* lived, counted only fifty-three.

mystic nature, some more in the nature of *Peshat* and some distinguished by brilliancy and wit. The third is the *Heskuni* a commentary on the Pentateuch written by Hiskia ben Menoah about the year 1240. He followed Rashi to a great exent with only a few additions of his own. Finally, two more commentaries were written at the end of the thirteenth and the beginning of the fourteenth centuries. These are: *Paaneah Rosa* (Uncovering of the Secrets) by Isaac ben Jehudah ha-Levi and *Minhath Yehudah* by Jehudah ben Eleazar. On the other books of the Bible, we have only one commentary, that on Ezekiel, Isaiah and the Minor Prophets by Eliezer of Beaugence.

In Germany, but little was produced during four centuries. Of those most noted, we may mention first, the commentaries of the famous Kabbalist and codifier, Eleazar ben Jehudah of Worms, known after his code as the *Rokeah* (Vol. I, Ch. X, Sect. 156). They are, of course, of the German mystic type. The second is the one on the Pentateuch by the name of *Zioni,* written by Menahem ben Meir Zioni in the fifteenth century. It is primarily a collection of Kabbalistic comments culled from mystic works chiefly from the Zohar, the standard work of the Kabbala. Partial commentaries were also written by Avigdor Kara of Prague (d. 1349), Israel Krems (Isserlin) of Marburg and Lippman of Mülhausen, author of the famous polemic book ha-Nitzahon (Ch. X, Sect. 149).

Of the Italian commentators, there are to be noted Isaiah di Trani the younger, who lived in the second half of the thirteenth century and wrote commentaries on a number of books of the Bible following the *Peshat* method, and the grammarian, Benjamin ben Jehudah (Sect. 6). Zerahia ben Isaac ben Shealtiel, the philosopher, composed, at the end of the century, a philosophical commentary on the Books of Proverbs and Job where he displays considerable originality.

The outstanding Italian exegete in the fourteenth century was the poet Immanuel of Rome (Ch. III, Sect. 30). He wrote commentaries on the entire Bible mostly in a rational *Peshat* way, but some, especially those on Proverbs and Canticles are written in a philosophic and allegorical manner. Almost at the same time, Shemaria Ikriti (The Cretan) of Negroponti undertook, at the order of Robert, the king of Naples, to write a commentary on the Scriptures which aimed to defend every word of the Bible against philosophical criticism and at the same time to take into account the demands of logic, grammar and rhetoric, but it was not completed. A mystical commentary on the Pentateuch by Menahem of Reccanti, known under the name of *Reccanti* also belongs to the first half of the fourteenth century. The century and a half that followed was, on the whole, barren, and only the commentary on Proverbs by Jehudah Messer Leon (Ch. I, Sect. 7), grammarian and rhetorician, is worth mentioning. However, after a long period of comparative sterility in the field of exegesis, there arose once more a great commentator who hailed from Spain but who wrote most of his commentaries in Italy, Don Isaac Abrabanel.

20. *DON ISAAC ABRABANEL*

Isaac ben Jehudah Abrabanel, statesman, Bible commentator and philosopher, was born in the year 1437 at Lisbon, Portugal, whither his father had escaped after the persecution in Spain in the year 1391. He received a thorough Jewish and secular education, knowing besides Spanish, Portuguese and Hebrew also Latin and was well read in philosophical and theological literature. A distinguished financier and diplomat, he was in great favor with Alfonso, king of Portugal, and managed his financial affairs. In Lisbon he also began his literary activity by undertaking to write his commentary on the Pentateuch beginning with Deuteronomy. But when king Joao succeeded to the throne of his father, Abrabanel, together with other friends of Alfonso, fell into disfavor, and was forced to flee for his life. He escaped into Spain and settled in 1483 in Toledo, where he was received with honor by the Jewish community. For a short time, Abrabanel lived as a private citizen, devoting himself to literary activity, and in less than a year completed his commentary on the Books of Joshua, Judges, Samuel, and Kings, the early prophetical books. However, he was soon called by Ferdinand and Isabella, king and queen of Spain, to state service, in which he was engaged until the expulsion of the Jews in 1492.

After the expulsion of the Jews from Spain, Don Isaac settled for a while in Naples where he was again pressed into state service. But again through the vicissitudes of fortune, he was forced to flee together with the king of Naples to Sicily. At Messina, whither he accompanied his king, he began his commentary on Isaiah but interrupted his work when he discovered at Corfu the lost manuscript of his commentary on Deuteronomy which he had begun in his youth. Moving to Monopoli, a small town near Naples, he spent eight years there from 1496 to 1503 in literary activity, and completed his commentaries on Isaiah, Daniel, and Deuteronomy, besides writing other works. Abrabanel spent the last five years of his life in Venice, where he wrote commentaries on the other four books of the Pentateuch, and those of Jeremiah, Ezekiel and the Minor Prophets. He died in 1509. His life was a very active one, both as a man of the world and author, for his literary productivity was exceedingly great. Yet, while Abrabanel contributed to several branches of Jewish literature, it is upon his work as a commentator on the Bible that his fame rests.

As a commentator, Abrabanel belongs to the class of Nahmanides and Gersonides, who endeavored to explain the general content of the Bible, its principles, views and moral teachings more than the actual meaning of the words and passages. But while Nahmanides in a larger degree and Gersonides in a lesser degree paid great attention to the *Peshat* of the text, Abrabanel neglected this phase almost entirely. He says quite frequently that as far as the grammatical construction of words and phrases and their derivation are concerned, he relies upon his predecessors. His commentary is, therefore, primarily a philosophical, theological, ethical and to some degree an historical exposition of the Bible. Its main characteristic is that it undertakes to explain all possible difficulties that may arise in the interpretation of the Bible whether from a philosophical, theological, historical or other point of view. But inasmuch as exegesis, in its wider meaning deals with the general content of the book as well as with that of the words and phrases, Abrabanel's exposition is a great contribution to exegetic literature in affording a better understanding of the Bible, ist teachings and moral value.

He was properly prepared for his great task of bringing out the best that there is in the Bible. He was well versed in the entire Jewish literature, especially in the philosophic and exegetic phases, and though he knew no Arabic, yet mastered thoroughly the Arabic-Greek philosophy from Hebrew and Latin translations. He was equally versed in the writings of the Christian commentators on the Bible. He was the first Jewish exegete who quotes considerably from Christian commentaries, and at times adopts their views. In one instance, he places the opinion of Nicholas da Lyra, the famous scholastic commentator, on a par with that of Ibn Ezra, Nahmanides and others. He was also a voracious reader of history, knew Josephus in the Latin translation and other histories, and made good use of his historical knowledge in the commentary.

Abrabanel introduced a modern note in exegesis, as with the exception of the Book of Numbers, to which he wrote only a short preface, he prefixed lengthy introductions to each book, carefully analyzing and discussing its purposes and contents. In the introductions to the historical books, the question of authorship, time of composition and chronology are discussed. In those to the prophetic books, the character of each prophet and his style are taken up. As a matter of fact, the introductions themselves throw light upon many knotty questions of the Bible.

His method is an entirely novel one in Jewish exegesis. It is best characterized by calling it the problematic method and it certainly suited his purpose. Since his aim was to straighten out all difficulties in the Bible, it could best be accomplished by raising such difficulties and then removing them. He, therefore, prefaces each section of each book with a number of questions or doubts, as he sometimes calls them, and then interprets that section in such a manner as to gradually solve all the problems. The problems, as stated are of various natures, philosophical, theological, historical, that of the order and sequence of the sections or any that bear upon the elucidation of a given passage. This method of placing the questions or problems before each section is followed throughout the Bible, in the prophetic and historical books as well as in the Pentateuch, and they vary from five or six to as many as thirty to the section.

Abrabanel possessed a keen, clear and analytical mind, and though he is generally conservative, yet he discerns many difficulties which are brought forward today only by Bible critics, and likewise in his interpretation, he makes suggestions which have found their full development only in modern Biblical exegesis. On the whole, Abrabanel's relation to the Bible is that of a rational conservative. He is, of course, severely opposed to Gersonides, Kaspi and others who attempted to rationalize all evident supernatural events in the Bible, and often rebukes even Maimonides though he revered him exceedingly and generally followed him in his opinions. Abrabanel can thus be spoken of as one who seeks compromises and tries to follow the middle way. Thus, he adopts Maimonides' view of the sacrifices as being only a means to wean the Jews away from idol worship. Yet, he is not wholly satisfied with the view and attaches to it an additional symbolic importance. He is more conservative than Gersonides and even than Maimonides on the question of certain miracles, taking them either as actual events or as experiences of certain persons in a wakeful state through visions of angels and not as a matter of dreams. Yet, whenever possible, he explains a miracle fairly rationally. The turning of the wife of Lot into a pillar of salt is a fair example of this. He says that Lot's wife did not become a pillar of salt because she turned around, but explains the words, "And his wife looked back from behind him and she became a pillar of salt" (Gen. XIX, 26) to mean that she remained behind in Sodom to look after her property and thus was consumed with the rest, and her body together with the bodies of the others were covered with a deposit of salt. The sin of the builders of the Tower of Babel and the consequent descent of God and his punishing them by confusing their language, is rationally explained. These people, says Abrabanel, were just turning from the simple pastoral life to a city life with high buildings, industries and inventions. This life is more artificial and requires diversity of occupation and consequently of terms. This diversity ultimately brought about a difference in language as well as quarrels which caused the scattering of people upon the face of the earth. The descent of God is merely a figure representing His foresight as to what will happen to them as a result of the new mode of life. Such an explanation, while it may not stand the test of science, yet represents a fair attempt to rationalize a very difficult story of the Bible.

He displays great skill in dividing the books of the Bible according to their contents and subject matter, disregarding the arbitrary traditional division into sections and portions based on the weekly readings in the synagogue. The endeavor to find a logical connection in the sections of the Bible, made him offer a number of ingenious explanations for their sequence in which he often preceded modern Biblical exegesis. Thus, he points out that chapters XXI-XXIV in Exodus, which are now called by Bible critics the Books of the Covenant, and which contain a summary of the most important Mosaic laws, are an extended explanation of the Ten Commandments which precede them, namely a statement of particulars included in the general commandments, a suggestion which has been repeated again and again in modern exegesis. Similar explanations showing ingenuity abound in his commentary.

While on the whole, Abrabanel endeavored to explain the contents of the Bible in a modified rationalistic way and can by no means be said to be inclined to mysticism, yet he retained enough of the spirit of his age which was permeated with mysticism and Kabbala. We find him, therefore, frequently wandering off into symbolism, allegory and mystic interpretation, at times even borrowing an allegorical explanation from Christian commentators. This brought him, on occasion, to devote lengthy discussions to some Kabbalistic teachings. Thus, in his interpretation of the precept enjoining levirate marriage if the brother dies without issue (Deut. XXV, 8-11), he discusses at length the question of metempsychosis or the theory of transmigration of souls.

Abrabanel utilizes the interpretations of the previous exegetes to a great extent and quotes them repeatedly. Ibn Ezra, Maimonides, Nahmanides and Gersonides are his favorites but there are many others. He ransacked the entire exegetic literature and wherever he discovered some remark deserving of mention, excerpted it. As a matter of fact, he usually quotes before the interpretation of a section the opinions of the principal commentators on certain points discussed there. He analyzes them carefully, after which he either selects with or without modification one opinion with which he agrees, or rejects them all and offers his own view. He entertained great respect for his predecessors, but when he finds their views unacceptable, he minces no words but expresses himself very sternly. He spares no one, not even the great Maimonides himself on whose *Guide* he wrote a commentary.

With the purpose Abrabanel had in mind and with the method he employed, it would be futile to expect him to explain the verses singly, as other exegetes have done. His is, as stated, a commentary on the contents and accordingly he disregards the verses, but explains the section as a whole. However, in the exposition or paraphrase of the content, the interpretation of single verses are also often included.

In his commentaries on the First Prophets, i. e. the historical books and on the Last Prophets (Isaiah-Malachi), he follows the methods employed in the Pentateuch. He divided each book in his own way, according to the individual logical subjects treated, without paying attention to the traditional division. Thus, in the Book of Joshua, he discerns only sixteen divisions instead of twenty-four, in the Book of Judges twelve instead of twenty-one and in both Books of Samuel which he treats as one, twenty-five instead of fifty-five of the traditional divisions. In the prophetic books proper, he first divides each book according to the number of prophecies it contains, and then subdivides these prophecies into sections. As a rule, his division is always smaller than the traditional division into chapters. Thus, he finds the number of prophecies in both parts of Isaiah to be only thirty-five instead of sixty-six chapters, in Jeremiah only seventeen instead of fifty-two chapters. His divisions are very valuable as they are based on logical insight into the content of the books and contribute greatly to a comprehensive exegesis, as the modern type intends to be. Here, as in the Pentateuch, he prefaces each section or prophecy with a series of problems or questions which his exegesis intends to solve.

However, his greatest contribution to the exegesis of the historical and prophetical books are his introductions. In his general introduction to the "First Prophets" (Nebiim Rishonim), he discusses first the classification of the books of the Canon. After giving the traditional classification into Torah, Prophets and Hagiographa (Tanakh i. e. Torah, Nebiim and Ketubim) and the literary one adopted by gentile scholars into legal, historical, prophetical books and books of wisdom, he offers his own historical classification. He divides the books of the Canon into those which were written before the Jews settled in Palestine, i. e. the Pentateuch; those which were written during the period of the First Commonwealth which include the early historical books and most of the prophetic ones; and the post-exilic ones. The question of the time of composition of the Books of Joshua, Judges, and the Books of Samuel is taken up next. Here Abrabanel evinces considerable critical acumen. He differs with the Talmudic opinion that Joshua wrote his own book on the ground that it contains expressions and records of events which clearly show a later date. He concludes, therefore, that Samuel was the author of the book. He, likewise, offers a novel view regarding the Books of Samuel, namely, he accepts partly the Talmudic opinion that Samuel had written the records of the events up to his death, and that these were supplemented by the later prophets, such as Gad and Nathan, contemporaries of David, but claims that it was edited by Jeremiah who also wrote the Book of Kings. This view he corroborates by critical observation.

Abrabanel was practically the first Jewish commentator to devote considerable attention to the question of Biblical chronology, primarily that of the period of the Judges and the following period up to the division of the kingdom. Both in the introduction and in the text of the commentary, he discusses the question widely and really elaborates a system of chronology for that period, which while not exactly solving that most difficult problem, contributed greatly to the attempted solution by subsequent commentators both Jewish and Christian. He, of course, also discusses the moral purpose of the historical books and elucidates their ethical value.

In his introductions to the prophetic books proper, he analyzes in each one the nature, character of the content of the prophecies and quality of style. He does it in good Aristotelian manner and discusses first the questions of time and character of the prophet himself, then the form, style, and quality of the prophecies, and finally the subject matter. However, as a result of his trend of mind, looking upon the prophets as the exponents of a completed Judaism and as those who deal with the distant future, he often reads more into their prophecies than they contain. Thus, he evolves out of the Book of Isaiah a complete and detailed eschatology. Yet, on the whole, Abrabanel's commentaries and introductions are a distinct contribution to Biblical exegesis from the historical point of view, as they blazed the path for a better understanding of the Bible in all its phases for many a modern commentator.

With Don Isaac the long period of activity of Mediaeval Jewish exegesis practically closes. The commentaries that follow during the two and a half centuries either have little literary value, inasmuch as they are mere compilations or belong primarily to homiletic literature.

CHAPTER III

POETRY

21. GENERAL CHARACTERISTICS

The poetic productions of the post-Classical period partake of the nature of the Jewish literature of that period in general, namely, they are rich in quantity but not in quality. In the five centuries, extending from the thirteenth to the eighteenth, we hardly find an outstanding poet who could compare favorably with the poets of the former periods either in loftiness of poetic spirit or elasticity of style. In the entire mass of literary productions which go under the name of poetry, there is seldom a new note struck or flight of the spirit noted. All poets, with probably the exception of Immanuel of Rome, follow the wide track trodden out for them by their predecessors. But the track is not followed by these successors in its entire breadth and length, for out of the wide way of the poets of the Golden Age, they mapped out for themselves only a narrow path from which they did not turn nor swerve. The secular poetry of the first few centuries of this period does not present the variety of content and form of the earlier poetry. The cheerful spirit of the poet of the former age which broke out in song at the sight of the gleaming wine or of beauty in nature and man is almost entirely absent in the poetic literature of this period. We rarely meet with a nature or wine poem in the centuries that follow the Classic epoch. Only later, in the fourteenth century in Italy, do we again hear Immanuel breaking into song in praise of the brimming cup. Love songs, of course, were still produced in abundance. They were, however, composed more from a sense of duty than from inspiration invoked by the sight of beauty.

On the other hand, there is a superabundance of eulogistic poems on friendship. This species of poetry which was quite in evidence even in the former period grew considerably in the later centuries, and at times seemed to be the chief staple of poetic production. From praise to blame is but one step, and once poetry became a means for elegant expression rather than a fount of inspiration, it was pressed into all kinds of service. And as the times were turbulent and division was rampant in Israel, and hatred ran high, poetry became the chief vehicle of polemics and conflict of opinion. Hence, polemic poetry grew luxuriantly in those days.

The change in the content of poetry was, of course, due to the change in Jewish life. The second half of the Middle Ages was, as far as the Jews were concerned, the more turbulent one. The happy days of Moslem Spain were gone forever. As the Pyrenean Peninsula gradually became Christianized, the Jews were more and more subjected to oppression and restrictions. Upon them as well as upon their brethren in other countries always hung the Damoclean sword of persecution, and as in the other Jewish centers, such as France and Germany, Jewish life assumed a darker hue.

As a result, the poetic spirit was hampered and its flight checked. It limited itself, as Judaism in general, to the confines of the spirit. And just as other forms of literature were gradually limited to constant admonition to the Jews to cling to the Torah and to the inculcation of the teachings of religion and morality, so did poetry become to a large extent didactic and theologic. Moral poems were produced in abundance, both long poems where the ethical teachings of the philosophers are stated in detail and short pointed ones where a flash of thought is clothed in happy expressions or a parable is told.

As humor and satire are useful allies both in polemic and didactic teachings, a tendency for the use of the epigram ensued. Epigrams and epigrammatic poems form, therefore, a considerable portion of the poetic productivity. As a rule, however, the shorter didactic pieces of poetry in its various forms were not collected in separate works but were inserted in books of parables, popular ethical treatises and moral tales. There they were used to epitomize the teaching of the chapter or the moral of the tale or parable.

As if to compensate for the poverty of the spirit, a conscious attempt is made by the poets of this period at artfulness of style. All kinds of devices are used to make the style more artistic, various acrostics, peculiar rhymes and special use of certain words with a meaning different from ordinary connotation. Of all these devices, the most popular were the lengthy monorhymes, the use of words beginning with the same letter a hundred or even a thousand times, and dexterous use of Biblical verses, phrases or words. Thus, we have poems ending in a monorhyme *Ri,* two hundred and ten times, other poems consisting of a thousand words beginning with *Aleph* (Eleph-Alphin), or *Mem* and other letters. But in all these devices, the impress of conscious artificiality and laboriousness is evident, and as a result, the more the style was cultivated the more ornamental it was, the heavier and less beautiful it became. Poets vied with each other in twisting the sense of the words, in changing their meaning, in fanciful rhyming, in making allusions to Biblical or Talmudic interpretations of words, and thus artificiality took the place of poetic fancy, and versification replaced poetry.

All that was said about the secular poetry of the period can with equal justice be applied to the sacred poetry produced during the time. This branch of poetry which was predominant in the Classical period and which served as a source of religious inspiration to the generation had likewise fallen from its former state. In the first two centuries of the period, we still find poems of the admonition type (Tokheha) where the poet's call to the soul to reflect upon its state and upon its destiny is made with more or less vigor. But except for this form of *Piut,* all others are mere reiterations of old themes reworked with less skill. This type of sacred poetry where a flicker of the old spirit is still seen was produced mostly in Spain and the Provence. In the West-European countries and in Italy, the lands where *Piut* flourished luxuriantly during the eleventh and twelfth centuries, the sacred poetic activity was limited mostly to the *Selihah and Kinah* (elegy) types. The constant persecutions afforded the pious souls sufficient cause for outpourings of heart at the miseries their people endured. But in all this mass of *Kinoth* and *Selihoth,* we hear only a sick soul wailing at its suffering rather than the vigorous protest and the bold demand upon God for redemption which reverberate in the *Piutim* of the former generations. As time speeds on, even the moan is silenced and Paitanic productivity ceases altogether, until its revival in the sixteenth and seventeenth centuries in Palestine and other Oriental countries, and to a certain extent also in Europe.

22. *EPOCHS AND GEOGRAPHIC EXTENT OF POETIC ACTIVITY*

This rather long period of poetic activity embracing five and a half centuries is not of a homogeneous character but is divided into several epochs, the heterogeneity of which is made more complicated by the wide geographic extent of the activity. Unlike the Classical period, when literary activity in general and poetic productivity in particular was primarily centered in the Pyrenean Peninsula, the poetic literature of the period under discussion has the world for its stage. The Jewries of almost all countries contributed their quota to the sum total of poetic literature. Yet, as in all spiritual phenomena, there are always some centers where the activities are manifested with greater vigor than in other places.

Combining, therefore, time and space, we can conveniently divide the period into two epochs, separated by half a century of low poetic productivity during which hardly anything worth while was produced. Each of these epochs had one or two countries as centers. The first epoch embraces the two and a half centuries from the twelfth to the middle of the fifteenth, during which time the Spanish-Provence schools, on the one hand, and the Italian school, on the other hand, predominated. The second represents the period of time from the sixteenth century to the middle of the eighteenth. This epoch had Palestine and the other Oriental countries together with Italy as its centers.

From a literary point of view, the first epoch may be called the post-Classical, for as stated, the poets of the time merely followed in the footsteps of the great masters of the past hardly adding a new note. The second epoch, however, should rather be called the epoch of the revival of poetry, as during that time, a stronger and more vigorous spirit is evident. Here and there, poets arise, who in their depth of feeling and beauty of language remind us of the former singers of Israel. The epoch is also distinguished by attempts to introduce new poetic forms hitherto unknown in Jewish literature. This came as a result of the influence of European literature upon the writers of poetry. The leaven of this new spirit was Italy. In that country, which took the place formerly held by Spain, the Jews were always closer to the general life than they were in other countries, and the spirit of the Renaissance penetrated to a certain degree even the thick walls of the ghetto. Hence, it was there where Jewish poetry began to swerve from the old Arabic and Oriental models and adopt some of the newer European forms. As a result, the sonnet and the drama make their appearance in Jewish poetry, forms entirely unkown to earlier ages.

In conclusion, we may remark that while, on the whole, the poetry of this long period is by comparison considerably poorer in quality than the preceding one, yet it is not without its special value. The poets of distinction who arose during that period have in their way enriched Jewish poetry, and in its many colored web, their strands shine with a particular hue adding lustre to the entire artistic work. What is more important, however, is the fact that at no time was the Jewish muse entirely silenced, except possibly for a few decades. During all these centuries of misery and agony, the chosen spirits of Israel had not forgotten the ancient lyre and poured forth the noble sentiments of their hearts in measured and rhymed song. Furthermore, these children of a tortured and hunted people did not forget to laugh, and quite often cheer and laughter are heard in the poetic compositions of this period, which as far as the Jew was concerned, is the darkest one of the Mediaeval Ages. Great indeed was the spirit of optimism in Israel.

A. First Epoch (1200-1450)

23. *THE SPANISH SCHOOL*

Poetic productivity in Spain during the thirteenth century reflects in its tone and manner the lassitude of spirit which, as a rule, follows a period of great mental effort. Many were the writers who tried their hand at poetry, but few were there who achieved distinction. As indicated above, poetry writing became a very popular mode of expression and its services were sought by all, so that poetry, instead of being a mistress became the hand-maiden of all movements of the time, especially that of polemics and morality.

During that century, there raged the great war between the followers of philosophy or Maimunists and the opponents of philosophy or anti-Maimunists. Poetic missiles and darts in the form of lampoons, epigrams and short or long poems in praise or abuse of philosophy were therefore employed by the champions of both sides. Thus, a new species of poetry was created—the polemic one. To this kind of poetry, almost all the writers of the time contributed. Shem Tob ben Joseph ben Shem Tob, Shem Tob Ibn Falaquera, Abraham Ibn Hasdai and many others championed the Maimunist side. Meir Zarfati, Judah Ibn Al-Fakhar and Meshullam da Piera were the protagonists of the other side and attacked the teachings of philosophy with poetic weapons. The center of attack was the *More Nebuḳim,* and a great deal of wit and humor was expended by the opponents in shooting their darts at the book and its teachings or in warding off blows. As a rule, the polemic poems bear a dignified tone, and the opponents of

Maimonides spare his great name, but at times, in the heat of battle, the limits of dignity are transgressed and some aspersions are cast even upon Maimonides himself. The poetic champions of Maimonides, on the other hand, devote themselves mostly to eulogies on the greatness of the master. In the defensive and offensive poems, puns on the name of Moses and *More* (teacher) are used profusely, yet, with all the good intentions of the lovers of philosophy, their poetry is mediocre and their epigrammatic wit dull and insipid.

The anti-philosophic side, however, succeeded in putting forth as one of its champions a man with considerable poetic spirit, the above mentioned Meshullam ben Solomon da Piera.* He was a great master of Hebrew and his several poems against those who interpreted the Bible allegorically and spoke of miracles as visions in dreams, are written with great skill and mastery of style. There is pathos in them for we hear the cry of one who defends his cherished beliefs against those who want to rob him of them.

Da Piera wrote also other poems, especially poems on friendship and epigrams which are distinguished by their style. Most of the poems, however, were not published and are found only in manuscript.

Another poet of note of the thirteenth century was Todros ben Judah ha-Levi Abulafia (b. 1247). His poems in praise of the members of the Shoshan family in Navarre, recently published, display poetic talent and great skill in the mastery of the language. Though he uses mostly the monorhyme, his poems are light and pleasant, as he employs many devices to adorn the rather hackneyed theme, i. e. praise of a notable. In one of such poems dedicated to the Shoshan family, the poet stages a dispute between the various flowers, each flower singing its own praise and describing its beauty. Finally, the lily (Shoshan) advances its claim to fame not on the ground of its exceptional beauty but because of the fact that the Shoshan family was named after it. Then the poet launches upon a panegyric to that family. The prelude, however, possesses a charm of its own, for in it, Abulafia evinces a keen sense of appreciation of the beauty of nature.

* He had lived for some time in the Provence but seemed to have spent the greater part of his life in Spain.

24. *DIDACTIC POETRY*

Many were the poets in this age who used poetry as a vehicle for moral teachings, but not much has remained of their writings. The work of two of such poets was preserved, inasmuch as they interwove the poems in their ethical works. The first is Abraham ben Samuel ha-Levi Ibn Hasdai (first half of the thirteenth century). He was also famous as a translator of works from the Arabic, the best known of which is the translation of *Ben ha-Melek we-ha-Nazir* (The Prince and the Dervish). In this book, he included many poems which epitomize the moral teachings of the various sections.

In these poems which are, as a rule, short and of an epigrammatic nature, Ibn Hasdai displays not only skill in the mastery of the language and in the handling of rhyme and meter, but brilliancy of thought and deep worldly wisdom. The following are some of his best known ethical epigrams. Observing the sad lot of noble people, he bitingly remarks:

At treacherous Time that seizes the noblest of men[1]
And hurls them into a foul narrow pen
I look on with rage.
It likens them unto the sweet singing bird,
Which, when its melodious voice is but heard,
Is thrown in a cage.[2]

Discussing the right method of training children, he pithily summarizes his view on the subject in a short epigram:

Go out, provide your son of five with food
If labor you must even like an ox;
And when he's ten instruct him steadily;
Then he will heed your words and wisdom gain.
Hold him in full esteem when he's fifteen,
So that when twenty, he will honor you.[3]

Observing the vicissitudes of human life, he sings:

The world is a pen;
The shepherds are the days;

[1] "Time" in Mediaeval Jewish poetry is synonymous with life, destiny and the course of events in the world.

[2] Ben ha-Melek we-ha-Nazir, p. 25.

[3] Ibid, p. 38.

The sheep are the men.
Death is the plain wide,
Where old and young abide.
The grave is the gate,
Through which all pass;
But what is beyond
That secret none doth possess.[4]

Such and many more didactic poems, brief and pointed, are scattered through the book.

The second didactic poet is the philosopher, Shem Tob ben Joseph Ibn Falaquera (1225-1290). In addition to his philosophical works, he wrote a popular treatise, *The Searcher* (ha-Mebakesh), on the various ways of life and the occupations a man may choose. In that book which opens with a poem on the search of wisdom as the purpose of human life, many epigrams and short poems are scattered. Falaquera possesses besides poetic skill also a pleasant sense of humor, and his epigrams are tinged with a delicate irony which drives the moral teaching deeper into the soul. Mocking at inconstancy in the conduct of some men who plead exigency of circumstances, he says:

Conduct yourself according to your time and place,
For then you will abound with joy and peace.
Be wise when in the midst of sages and the wise;
But when you see a fool—let all your wisdom cease.
And when you see a lion—don't forget to roar,
And when you meet an ass—bray and say no more.[5]

Disparaging excessive credulity on the part of the people, he remarks:

The credulous is like a rock
For both lack understanding;
He's like an ox that chews his cud—
Nothing else comprehending.[6]

Regarding courage, he sings:

If misery is like a rock—then I am like a hammer;
I am like the water—if trouble's like a spark.

[4] Ibid, p. 83.
[5] ha-Mebakesh, p. 10.
[6] Ibid, p. 13.

Adversity imbues my heart with strength, just as the glamour
Of the moon increases nightly with the dark.[7]

Ridiculing the ways of the physician of his time, Falaquera says:

"Be a physician," said Time to the fool,
"Far better than th' Angel of Death you will be;
You will take money and rob them of life,
While he kills his men but forgets the fee."[8]

Falaquera wrote many poems of all kinds, but it is in his satiric and didactic epigrams that he excels.

25. *POETS OF NORTHERN SPAIN*

The first half of the fourteenth century in Spain was, on the whole, a period of silence as far as poetry was concerned. Only towards the end of the century, the voice of song rises again, and poetic activity continues for some time. The religious debates between Jews and Christians which were popular at the beginning of the fifteenth century, culminating in the debate at Tortosa in the years 1413-1414, gave a new impetus to polemic poetry. But the polemics were at this time addressed not against the opinions of the Jews, but against Christianity and Jewish apostates. We have, therefore, a number of epigrams directed against the teachings of the Church and against apostates who presumed to teach their former co-religionists. This period is also distinguished by the influence exerted by Spanish culture upon Jewish poetry both in form and in content. Yet, the influence is light, the poets following mostly the old models. Only occasionally, do we hear of a poet who parodied the Spanish songs in his Hebrew productions. Of the many poets of this period, two are outstanding. These are Solomon ben Meshullam da Piera (1340-1417) and Solomon ben Reuben Bonfed. Da Piera left a whole Diwan of poems and hymns which are extant largely in manuscript. He wrote both secular and sacred poetry but excelled in the latter. A number of his hymns which bear evidence of his mastery of style and of his feeling heart were published. Like all poets of his time, he wrote didactic pieces in the old form of poems of admonition (Tokhahoth). In one where he admonishes men to

[7] Ibid, p. 34.
[8] Ibid, p. 49.

forsake the pursuit of pleasure in their youth and devote themselves to wisdom, we find the following strong passage:

And then when the passions of youth pass away,
No more willing to stay—
Their splendor and glamour so empty then seem,
So illusive their gleam—
The days of old age come when wisdom is sought.
But can it be bought?
Then Age reprimands them: "Why came ye so late?
Now closed is the gate.
Shall iron when washed become white, or can sand
Retain impress of hand?"[9]

Da Piera wrote also a number of friendship poems and epigrams, among them also a few wine poems.

Solomon ben Reuben Bonfed (1380-1450) was a prolific poet, but primarily a secular one. His Diwan is still in manuscript and only a part of it was published by Dr. Kaminka. He wrote a large number of poems on friendship and still more on love. But in all his love poems, he is only an able imitator of ancient models, as there is little originality in them. One of his poems has special value for the history of Hebrew literature in the fourteenth and fifteenth centuries. In it, he bewails the decline of poetry and reviews its entire history, enumerating the great poets who have gone before. From it, we learn the great esteem in which some poets were held in their time, though only their names have come down to us. Bonfed distinguished himself also in polemic poems and a number of his satirical epigrams against apostates and some doctrines of Christianity display a biting humor.

Of the minor poets of the time are Solomon Ibn Labi, Benveniste Ibn Labi (d. 1412), Vidal Joseph Ibn Labi and Joseph ben Astruc. Solomon and Benveniste Ibn Labi are highly praised by Bonfed, as he calls them the father and mother of poetry, but we must allow for the usual exaggeration of the Mediaeval style. Vidal Ibn Labi seemed to have been greatly influenced by Spanish poetry, for he himself wrote Hebrew parodies of Spanish models.

26. THE PROVENCE SCHOOL

As indicated on previous occasions, Provence or the South of France became, in the post-Classical period, the heir to the literary

[9] Mibhar ha-Shirah, ed. Brody, p. 324.

glory of Spain. For a period of two centuries, the thirteenth and the fourteenth, it took the leadership in intellectual activity. Grammarians, Bible commentators, philosophers and translators vied with each other in literary productivity so that the Provence became the center of Jewish literature. And along with the other branches of literature, there flourished also Jewish poetry, both secular and sacred. As in other places, likewise in the Provence, the ability on the part of one to express himself in poetic form was considered a mark of intellectual attainment, and consequently, we have a large number of poets there during the thirteenth century. But though many called themselves poets, only a few really deserved that name. These were Joseph Ezobi, Abraham Bedersi and his son, Yedayah, surnamed ha-Penini (The Pearly-mouthed) because of his exquisite style.

27. *JOSEPH EZOBI*

Joseph Ezobi (fl. 1230) was a native of Perpignan and was considered in his day an accomplished scholar and great poet. He had many disciples of whom Abraham Bedersi was one. His fame as poet rests primarily on the long poem entitled *Kaarath Keseph* (The Silver Bowl) which he dedicated to his son Samuel, on his wedding day. It is a didactic poem intended to teach the moral ways of life. It bristles with brilliant thoughts and pointed epigrams, one of which enjoins generosity of spirit.

> Bestow thy generosity on the poor;
> But if thou art short of means,
> And thy hand perforce must close;
> Let thy mouth be wide open
> And let words of kindness thence flow.[10]

28. *ABRAHAM BEDERSI*

Abraham Bedersi who, as we have seen above (sect. 4), was a distinguished linguist, was considered also a leading poet in his time. He composed both sacred and secular poems. The secular are mostly friendship and didactic poems. They were collected in a Diwan by his son but are still largely unpublished, with the exception of a few of the more important ones which were published by various scholars. To these belongs first a long poem by the rather euphemistic name of The Turning Sword (Hereb ha-Mithapekheth) which is bor-

[10] Kaarath Keseph, p. 10.

rowed from Genesis IV, 24.[11] It contains two hundred and ten verses, all ending in a monorhyme of *Ri,* which is a reference to the number of verses (Resh 200, Yod 10 equals 210). Its content is variable. In the first half, Bedersi describes the vicissitudes of life, and calls upon the soul to remember its purpose in the world and its ultimate destination in the manner of the admonition poems. In the second half, he bewails the lack of interest in poetry and recalls sorrowfully the bygone days when great poets flourished and poetry was the favorite pursuit of men of intellect. In speaking of the glory of former days, he mentions a long list of poets whose muse he admires. It thus has special value for the history of literature, as we learn from Bedersi the names of many poets who are otherwise unknown.

Another rather curious poem, or to be more exact a semi-poetic composition which is ascribed to Abraham Bedersi is a prayer of one thousand words, each beginning with an *Aleph,* known as *A Thousand Alephs* (Eleph Alphim). The poem is divided into four parts, the first dealing with the attributes of God, His kindness to the creatures and the poet's longing for Him; the second and third containing a description of the sufferings of Israel at the hands of the mocking enemies and a plea to alleviate the suffering. The fourth part is a confession of sin which concludes with an expression of unbounded trust in the mercy of God. As an exhibition of dexterity in the mastery of Hebrew and skill in choice of words, it is almost incomparable.

29. *YEDAYAH HA-PENINI*

Yedayah, the son of Abraham Bedersi (1280-1340) made a name for himself in several branches of literature. His fame, though, rests principally on the work known as *Behinath Olam* (The Examination of the World). It is primarily an ethical book and its contents will be discussed in the proper place. Here and there, we find passages which rise to poetic heights though written without rhyme or meter. Discussing the vicissitudes of the world and that of human life, Yedayah draws the following picture:

> The world is a stormy sea, deep and wide—
> Life is but a frail bridge thrown over it.

[11] The meaning of the name seems to be as follows: The letters of Hereb equal in numerical value 210, Heth 8, Resh 200, Beth 2, the number of verses in the poem, while the adjective ha-Mithapekheth is given to it because it is intended to revert against those who forsake the life of religion.

One end of the bridge is supported by pillars
Which for destruction are destined.
The other leads to happiness eternal,
To the sight of the king who rules in light.
The bridge is but an ell wide,
Nor are there rails to its side.
Man, perforce dost thou live
And the bridge must cross.
O, man, what wilt thou do,
When the sea into roars doth break
And thy habitation doth tremble and quake?[12]

In addition to the *Behinath Olam,* Yedayah wrote a didactic piece known as *Bakashath ha-Memim,* where each word begins with a *Mem.* The work is written in masterful style and is a display of dexterity in the manipulation of the language. It is quite a remarkable feat to express a series of connected thoughts in words limited to one form.

The poem is divided into nine chapters, each dealing with a certain subject. Chapter I describes the creation of the world out of nothing. The second chapter tells of God's greatness as manifested in the order of the universe and especially in the creation of man, while the third praises the dealings of God with man in giving him the Torah, rewarding the righteous and punishing the wicked. Chapters IV and V contain a description of the vicissitudes of human life and a complaint to God for placing man in such a precarious position where he is beset by dangers on all sides. Chapter VI gives a vivid description of the ways of the sinful man and the remorse following upon sin. Chapter VII is a confession of sin and a plea for forgiveness, while the last two chapters contain a plea to God for the redemption of Israel.

It was his dexterity in the use of language and the fineness of expression and especially the happy turn of words and phrases which earned for Yedayah the name of *Penini.* Yet with all these, he is more *Melitz* (euphuistic writer) than poet, and that title can be conferred upon him only in the same sense as it was bestowed upon many of his contemporaries, who, like him, excelled in the skilful use of the language and only rarely attained poetic heights.

[12] *Behinath Olam* Ch. VIII.

30. POETRY IN ITALY; IMMANUEL BEN SOLOMON HA-ROMI (The Roman)

In the poetic literature of the post-Classical period, Italy occupies a most prominent place. In that land, the Classic tradition never died out even during the darker period of the Middle Ages, and love of poetry was almost a national trait with the Italians. With the middle of the thirteenth century, the first signs of the Renaissance became evident. The love for poetry was intensified, the poet became the hero of the day, and his art the most favored and admired. The ability to compose poetry was prized above all, even by the nobility and the clergy. Statesmen and political leaders vied with each other in the writing of songs.

This trend in the general life of the country found imitators among the Jews. The Jews in Italy were always in closer touch with the general life than the Jews in other Christian countries. Persecutions were never severe there, and consequently the influence of the general culture penetrated through the walls of the ghetto. Life in Italy in the thirteenth century was stormy politically and gay socially. Politically, the country was divided into many republics and municipalities which warred with each other, and the din of battle was heard there constantly. Socially, it was a gay affair; frivolity, looseness of morals and merry making were the order of the day, and not even the severe Catholic Church could stem or slacken the mad rush of gay life. No wonder then that the ghetto could not withstand its lure and followed suit. Hence, the poetry of Italy reflects a different type of life than that of other countries, and it is Immanuel ha-Romi who typifies that life in all its vicissitudes.

Immanuel (1265-1330) was descended from one of the leading Roman Jewish families and received a many-sided education. He was deeply versed in the Talmud and Jewish philosophy and mastered the Hebrew language with exceptional skill. Besides, he also knew Latin and Italian. By profession, he was a physician and seemed to have occupied an important position in the Roman Jewish community, and was also respected by the gentiles, especially by the literati of the age. He was a friend of Dante and wrote a fine elegy in Italian after his death.

His literary career was as checkered as his life. He wrote commentaries on all the books of the Bible (Sect. 19), a grammar of the Hebrew language and many other books. But his fame rests primarily on the collection of his poems in the *Maqama* form* which he called *Mahbaroth* (A Collection of Maqamas). And like his literary career so was his personality a mixture of many elements, for at one and the same time, he was a God-fearing man, a scholar with a wide knowledge in many branches of science, a moral preacher and a writer of frivolous songs which very often passed the bounds of decency.

All these conflicting traits are reflected in his poetry. Yet, on the whole, Immanuel represents the extreme secular side of Jewish poetry in which he excels. He wrote love songs, wine ditties, friendship poems, epigrams on all matters serious and trivial and even didactic pieces. As a poet, Immanuel ranks high because of his exquisite style, the beauty of the rhyme and verses, and the flashes of thought and inspiration permeating them.

The outstanding characteristics of Immanuel are, (1) his exceptional linguistic ability and dexterous workmanship; (2) his keen humor and biting satire; and finally, (3) his love of life and cheerful optimistic spirit. Immanuel's mastery of the Hebrew language in all its devious ways and forms of expression almost equalled that of the great masters of the Classic period. Like them, he ransacked the treasures of the language and utilized his wide knowledge of the Bible and the entire Jewish literature to great advantage. With great skill, he juggles with whole or fragments of verses, twists them into different meanings and combinations, and as a result, dazzles us with the wealth of the language and its many colors. Not less was his power of poetic technique. He was, of course, a follower of the great Classic poets and used the heavy Arabic meter of *Yated* and *Tenuah* (Vol. I, Ch. IX, Sect. 116) with great agility. His rhymes are light and the meter short, so that consequently his verses are mobile and spirited. Immanuel, influenced by the rising Italian poetry, introduced into Hebrew a new poetic form, the sonnet, which consists of fourteen lines divided into four strophes, the first two strophes of four lines each called quatrains, and the last two of three lines each called tercets. There are thirty-four such sonnets by Immanuel, and though bound by all the rules of Hebrew meter, they possess certain peculiar beauty.

* The name Maqama which literally means assembly, was applied by the Arabs to a species of literature wherein the exploits of a wandering scholar or poet and his victories over rivals are humorously described. See also Vol. I, p. 466.

As great as his mastery of style, so intense was his love of life and cheerfulness of spirit. The Classic poets of Spain also sang of love and wine, but even there the serious vein can be detected. In Immanuel, life is bubbling, gay and buoyant. His love poems are, on the whole, more passionate than noble, coming from a heart stormy with passion, but they also breathe a genuine sense of admiration for beauty. Hence, they contain passages of real poetic value. In the usual exaggerated style of his day, Immanuel utters in praise of his beloved the following words:

Of what avail indeed will be the sun's rebellion?
And e'en if all of heaven's host refuse to shine?
The light of my gazelle the sun's at perihelion
By far exceeds. Why needst thou fear, O heart of mine?
My love reveals her beauty—lo! behold then,
The sun shine out in glory and in full array.
But when she hides, conceals her splendor golden,
I know—'tis parting day.[13]

In another place he sings:

My lovely gazelle, I ask you
Are thy eyes that shine so bright
Taken captive from the sky by day
And returned there night by night?
Or do they merely resemble
The stars, and the spheres—thy face?
For no beauty is like thy beauty
And there's nothing like thy grace.[14]

The love poems of Immanuel are not only passionate but also grossly erotic. Eroticism was the fashion of the time and Immanuel desiring to show that the Hebrew language is sufficient for all kinds of expressions sprinkled a great many erotic and pornographic phrases in his poems.

He had a genuine admiration for beauty and an equal abhorrence of ugliness, hence he admired in women only their beauty. Otherwise, they meant little to him and when they happened to be ugly, they represented to him the personification of evil. We, therefore,

[13] Mahbaroth, Maqama, 1.
[14] Mahbaroth, Maqama, 16.

find among Immanuel's poems some where women, especially ugly ones, are spoken of derogatively and are the butt of his jests. One such poem distinguished for its satirical levity deserves to be quoted. Says Immanuel:

My soul, I suspect is desirous
Of renouncing its portion in Heaven;
'Twould rather prefer as its haven
—Much abused Hell.

For there one can find milk and honey,
And charming young ladies galore—
And temptresses—can one wish more?—
And many a sweet-voiced gazelle—

Of what good can Paradise be
When the company there is so boring
—Old, homely hags always snoring—
I'd rather my Paradise sell.[15]

The satire of Immanuel is a bubbling well of humor and hilarity. It knows no bounds; at times, it is a mere good-natured jest, and at times, it is biting and stinging, expressed in insults hurled at his antagonists. He jested at everything and every subject was worthy of a poem. As he was a great parodist, he imitated some of his predecessors, such as Ibn Ezra and Harisi who wrote poems on the months of the year (Maqama 9). He was asked to write a poem on the constellations which he did, interspersing it with many humorous remarks such as, "I think the stars of heaven are old men or eunuchs as they have a virgin (Virgo) among them and do not care to clothe her," or "the bull (Taurus) is placed in heaven only to guard the ram (Aries) and the goat (Capricornius) against the lion (Leo)."

That Immanuel's satire found expression in epigrams goes without saying. Many are the epigrams scattered in his *Mahbaroth,* but we will quote only two. On poems:

They asked me, "Which of songs do you deem best?"
I answered, "One that's of a tender age."[16]
"And which the worst?" I said to them, "The one
That 'fore its master in the grave is flung."[17]

[15] Ibid.
[16] The meaning is that the poem is new and not merely an elaboration of an old theme.
[17] Maqama, 19.

On physicians:

In seasons of sickness I shudder;
  I tremble in times of travail;
They asked me, "Why need your heart flutter?"
  I answered, "My sins I bewail."

"What do you desire?" they queried.
  My reply was, "Forgiveness of sin."
"A physician?" To answer I hurried,
  "The malady was sent by Him."[18]

Hilarity and jesting do not last forever. There comes a time when the poet, awakened from his mad rush for pleasure, sees the world in a different light and the seriousness of human life is impressed upon him. Then his lyre strikes a new chord, one of pain and sorrow. And in this role, Immanuel is as distinguished as in the former. Especially moving are his songs of old age. This life-loving poet, observing the fleeting days and slowly approaching old age is seized with terror, and pours forth his complaints in beautiful poems. Thus, he says:

My time I see fleeting and flying;
My glorious sun—it doth set;
I see my pains hastening, hieing;
My day dies—I rue and regret.
The pegs of my tent the storms shatter;
I see the cruel world seize me;
And tear my best cloak and then scatter
The tatters all over the sea.[19]

In another place, he wails:

Oh, my heart to heaven did rise but yesterday,
And its joys topped the skies;
But sorrow-laden is my soul to-day
And my heart is bitter, no more happy and gay.[20]

[18] Ibid.
[19] Maqama, 1.
[20] Ibid.

In such strain did Immanuel sing of old age and approaching death. He is especially sorrowful when he remembers the joys of former days, his love making and the "gazelles" whose beauty he admired in his youth. Looking upon them in their faded glory, he is filled with pity both for their former bloom which had passed so quickly and for himself. One of such poems devoted to his former paramours is remarkably striking for its pathetic beauty as well as for its note of sorrow which reminds us of Ecclesiastes' mournful cry "Vanitas Vanitatum." But even here his humor does not forsake him, and from time to time, we meet lines which sparkle with its spirit. Thus in one of his poems, he makes the following pithy remark:

"Oh, who ever thought that the day would come,
When instead of their beauty (the gazelles')
I will admire only their clothing."

With all his hilarity and love of joy in life, Immanuel possessed deep religious and ethical feeling, and when that spirit moved him he sang religious poems which possess depth and emotion. The following is a gem of Mediaeval sacred poetry. Turning to God, he says:

Oh Lord! if Thou wilt slay me, yet will I trust in Thee.
I'll flee from Thy stern presence—to Thee to seek my aid.
In sorrow I'll seek refuge in Thy cloak's fold, and there
Will from Thy scorching anger find shelter cool and shade.

In days tenebrous—darkness by Thy wrath sent holds sway,
I hope to bask in brilliance, to gaze on Thy sweet light.
My heart with Thine own people's unites in prayer and praise
The people who for Thy sake die wilfully and fight.[21]

Observing human life and its vanity, he sings:

The days of man are three in number;
The day gone by—its step 'twill ne'er retrace;
To-day it fleeteth, fleeteth onward;
The morrow—hidden, recondite of face.[22]

[21] Maqama, 19.
[22] Ibid.

In such moments, he is conscious of his own nobility of soul and its mastery of the passions and emotions. When pressed to explain his superiority over other men, he composed a short poem of which the following is a part:

> My friends inquired:
> "How did your intellect attain such heights?"
> I answered, "By subjecting things to me
> And not myself to them."[23]

Such is the many-phased and many-sided poetic spirit of Immanuel, a full appreciation of which can only be acquired by reading his poems, songs, epigrams and sonnets in the original.

The poems and songs are set in the *Maqama* form. It seems that Immanuel took the *Tahkemoni* of Harisi as a model. But while Harisi chose in true Arabic fashion a certain witty poet as the hero of the *Maqamas,* and he himself acts as his companion under the assumed name of Heman ha-Ezrahi (Vol. I, Ch. XVI, Sect. 204), Immanuel is the hero himself, and for a companion he chooses, in the manner of his day, a certain prince (Sar) who acts as his patron. Whether such a patron actually existed or not is of little count. The poet makes the patron his good angel who rewards him materially for his poetic efforts, inspires him and constantly urges him on to sing on one occasion or another.

The prince and Immanuel roam around together as boon companions and meet with various adventures, and when these end either successfully or otherwise, the prince commands the poet to strike his lyre. At times, the prince who is a man of culture and himself aspires to poetic laurels participates in poem making. We have then a number of poems where certain parts are supposed to have been contributed by the prince. Sometimes, they are really duets, the prince contributing the opening half of the line (Deleth) and the author the closing half (Sooger, Maqama 5), or the poems consist of a series of questions and answers, the patron propounding the questions and the poet giving the answers. (Maqamas 5 and 6.)

The narrative parts of the *Maqamas* are written in rhymed prose, but in Immanuel's *Mahbaroth,* unlike the *Tahkemoni* of Harisi, the prose forms the minor part while the poetic part is twice as large or even more. The subjects of the *Maqamas* are of great variety as they

[23] Maqama, 1.

were written largely at the request of the patron in accordance with his changing moods. If he happened to be hilarious, he bade the poet write love or wine poems; if in a religious mood, Immanuel had to bow to his will and sing of God or extol ethical virtues. There are even two poetic novels in the book where a complete short story is told. One called *Megillath ha-Heshek* (The Scroll of Passion) deals with love, and the other with ethics.

The *Mahbaroth,* as Immanuel himself tells us in the preface, were written in his old age in order to collect all the poems composed by him during his life. The *Maqama* form was considered by him to be the most suitable for a collection of poems of such varied nature. He then either adopted the device of a prince or patron companion in order to give the proper setting to the book, or it is also possible that a prince actually existed who was both jovial and cultured and a patron of letters who acted as his good "genius." If so, though unnamed, he deserves the thanks of lovers of Hebrew poetry.

In conclusion, we must make mention of Immanuel's parody of Dante's Divina Commedia which forms the last *Maqama* of his book, the twenty-eighth, and is called Hell and Paradise (Topheth we-Eden). It was written, as he informs us in the introduction, after he passed the age of sixty, that is between the years 1320-1330. As the last part of Dante's work was published in 1320, the year of his death, it most likely served Immanuel as a model.

In the introduction to this *Maqama,* he tells us how he came to visit hell and paradise. It happened at the time that a dear friend of his, a man of great deeds and of a noble family, died. His death made a deep impression upon the poet and caused him to take account of his own life, of his sins and transgressions. And while thus sunk in sorrow and contemplation, a vision appeared to him in the form of an old man by the name of Daniel who offered to act as his guide in the other world. Immanuel consented to follow him and the visit was made. Immanuel's description of hell falls much below that of Dante. It is brief and incomplete and only the general features are given, while Dante gives a full description of the architecture of hell, divides it into the Inferno and Purgatory, and each division into circles and compartments, and also assigns a place for each class of sinners. Of all this there is no trace in the work of Immanuel. He does mention several names, such as the Valley of the Carcasses (Emek ha-Pgorim) and *Neshia* which seem to indicate different departments for different classes of sinners, but on the whole, he does not distinguish between them. Thus, he places Aristotle, Plato and Galen in the company of Nebuchadnezzar, Titus and Belshazzar, though their sins are slight as compared with those of the latter, as they consist only in the belief in the eternity of the world, in the existence of ideas, and an utterance against Moses, respectively. In the description of the inhabitants of hell, Immanuel finds ample room to revenge himself upon some of his contemporaries. Accordingly, we find a number of allusions to some well known persons in his time whom Immanuel meets in hell and is greatly surprised, as they had passed as righteous men on earth. The description also gives a picture of Jewish life in his day for we can see there the vices which were frequent in Jewish communities. We learn of quarrels in the synagogue for distribution of honors, of the loose morals of cantors, of their ignorance and of their bad conduct otherwise.

Seeing all the tortures the inhabitants of hell are undergoing, trembling seizes Immanuel lest he also suffer for his sins. But his guide reassures him that his place is in *Eden,* his great merit being his commentary on the Bible, and that all the prophets whose books he commented are his friends and advocates. They then direct their steps to paradise. In the description of paradise, Immanuel is even more sparing than in that of hell. He simply mentions certain degrees and gradations, and thrones and canopies of various grades. In paradise are placed, of course, all those who are designated in the Bible as righteous, a large number of Tannaim, very few Amoraim and a number of his contemporaries, including his mother, mother-in-law and father-in-law. Among the contemporaries, he names a certain Daniel who was then still alive but for whom a magnificent throne is reserved in paradise. It seems that the last part especially was written in a hurry for of the great men of Mediaeval days scarcely half a dozen are mentioned. Such names as Saadia, Gabirol, the saintly Bahya, Rashi and his grandsons, the great Tosafists and a host of other pious men are absent from Immanuel's roll of honor. On the other hand, he does not forget to place the pious gentiles in paradise, though with the exception of Cyrus, he does not refer to any one by name. He also devotes considerable space to a description of the reception given to him by the prophets and by kings David and Solomon, on whose books he commented. He is quite lavish in the praises bestowed upon him and makes David acclaim him the best commentator on the Psalms, even superior to David Kimhi, the only other commentator whom Immanuel mentions.

There was a good deal of speculation among scholars as to the identity of the Daniels spoken of in the poem, the guide and the one for whom a throne was waiting in paradise. Some asserted that the guide Daniel was none other than Dante. Another opinion was advanced that he was the prophet Daniel, while still another averred that he was merely a friend. The second opinion seems to be the more plausible one, for as Dante had selected the famous Virgil as his guide, Immanuel, in imitation, chose a prophet as his mentor. Likewise, we may dismiss the notion that the Daniel for whom a throne was waiting was Dante, as advanced by some scholars, for besides the fact that a Christian could not have been given so much honor in paradise, he was already dead when Immanuel wrote his poem, while the Daniel of the book was still alive.

Immanuel exerted great influence upon the later poets who tried to imitate him, but the pious Jewish world bore him a grudge for his levity and immodesty of expression. A special interdiction against reading his poems was inserted by Joseph Karo in his *Shulhan Aruḳ* (Code). Yet it was not strong enough to make the Jews forget him. His works were preserved in entirety and thus constitute one of the finest contributions to Mediaeval poetic literature.

31. BENJAMIN BEN ABRAHAM ANAVI (Di Mansi)

Benjamin ben Abraham of the family of Anav or Anavim (the pious or humble), was most likely an older contemporary of Immanuel and to him, some assert, belongs the honor of introducing secular poetry in Italy. His secular poetry was primarily didactic tempered with satire and humor. He wrote a long satirical poem without meter under the name of The Burden of the Valley of Vision (Massa Ge-Hisoyon), a title borrowed from Isaiah, Ch. XXII.

In the prologue, he bewails the conditions of his time which he paints in rather dark colors. Love of money prevails, pleasure is sought after and wisdom is despised. He is especially severe at the tendency toward finery in clothes and dressing. Reflecting on this state of affairs, he falls asleep and sees a vision. In a wide valley, there stood a man in the likeness of the image seen by Nebuchadnezzar in his dream as related in the Book of Daniel (Ch. II, 31-36). The head of the man was of gold, the arms and breast of silver, the sides of copper, the legs of iron, and the feet part clay and part iron. A stone then rolled down and crushed the man and the fragments of his body were scattered by the winds. The interpretation of the vision is given by an angel. The image of the man symbolizes the human world, the golden head represents the very rich, the silver hands the less rich, the copper sides the middle class, the iron legs the nobles and the soldiery, the feet of iron and clay are the poor, the first symbolizing the wise, the second the ignorant poor. Finally, the stone that smote the image is the symbol of death, the great leveller of all.

After viewing the whole of human life in this imaginary form, the author goes on to teach the way of life. There are, he says, three cardinal vices and three cardinal virtues. The former are, lust, jealousy and pursuit of honor, the latter are, temperance, good will and humility. He then proceeds to tell us of the ramification of virtues and vices by way of a parable.

Reason and ignorance were searching for life partners; the first chose humbleness as his consort, while the second chose pride. Of these two unions, prudence, morality, patience, kindness, trust, truth and deliberation were born to the first couple, and impudence, flattery, haste, stinginess, anger and mockery, to the second. These are the progenitors of all vices and virtues. The author in relating these hypothetical marriages praises each virtue and disparages each vice in forceful epigrams and pithy sayings, and thus completes his vision.

Benjamin wrote also another poem of an ethical nature entitled The Portals of the Tree of Life (Shaare Etz Hayyim). It consists of sixty-three stanzas, alphabetically arranged. The letters of the alphabet are repeated three times, each letter beginning three stanzas. He, however, omitted the letters Waw and Yod and instead substituted the acrostic of his name. There is no meter, but he uses a monorhyme of the word *Hayyim,* life. Each stanza contains a practical ethical precept and is intertwined with Biblical verses.

Benjamin's poetic spirit did not rise very high. He was more of a *Melitz,* i. e. euphuistic writer, than poet, but his dexterous use of the poetic form for ethical teaching and the introduction of the parable influenced some of his successors to imitate him, and produce highly poetic moral dramas, such as those of Moses Hayyim Luzzatto.

32. MOSES RIETI

The remainder of the fourteenth century was, on the whole, a period of barrenness for Jewish poetry in Italy. The mantle of Immanuel seemed not to have found a suitable person to fall upon and for a time he had no imitators. Only at the beginning of the fifteenth century do we meet with a poet of considerable power, though he falls far below Immanuel. That poet was Moses ben Isaac Rieti (1393-1460). Rieti was a physician by profession and a philosopher and poet by inclination. His poetic work is called *Mikdash Meat* (Little Shrine) and was intended to give a general review both of the sciences and the entire Jewish literature. It is divided into two parts, the *Ulam* (the Ante-room) and the *Hekal* (The Palace).

The *Ulam* consists of five cantos. In the first canto, after offering a short prayer, Rieti tells us that he modeled his book after a certain work written by a Christian, explains the name and the purpose of the poem, and maps out its divisions. The second canto is devoted to philosophy and the conception of God. The principal works of the Jewish philosophers are described, especially those of Maimonides and Gersonides. The third canto deals with the classification of the sciences, their uses and purposes. He even gives a brief description of their contents. Cantos four and five deal in a detailed manner with logic, especially with Aristotle's book on the Categories and Porphyry's Isagoge.

The second part, the *Hekal* consists of eight cantos and is devoted to Jewish literature. It is written in the manner of Dante's *Paradiso,* and describes a visit to the heavenly place where the heroes of Israel dwell. The first canto is primarily a description of the place proper; the second, a fine prayer; the third tells of the city of God and its dwellers. In the fourth and fifth cantos, the poet gives in allegorical fashion an account of the Mishnah, its order and its contents. The remaining cantos are devoted to an enumeration of all the Tannaim, Amoraim, and Gaonim, and other scholars who dwell in the city of God, the recitation of the miracles that were performed by pious men at various times, as well as the wonders of Palestine.

The poem is written in rhyme and consists of fourteen hundred and two tercets, that is three line stanzas. Rieti exhibits a mastery of the language and skill in rhyming, but little poetic spirit. On the whole, it is not much more than a rhymed literary chronicle. Rieti, however, displays a remarkable knowledge of the entire field of Jewish literature, as his list of names and books is almost a complete one. Though a philosopher and poet himself, he yet excludes Immanuel from his Paradise because he sang of love, as well as the philosophers Gersonides, Isaac Albalag and Moses Narboni for their heretical views. It is, however, doubtful whether they were much the worse for it, as his Paradise is rather a prosaic one.

Rieti, however, was very popular among his contemporaries, for the second canto of the *Hekal* which is a prayer, was accepted into the ritual of the Italian Jews, and was divided into seven parts each to be recited on a different day of the week. Rieti's contribution to Hebrew poetry consists mainly in his popularizing the tercet, thus introducing more variety in its form.

33. *SACRED POETRY*

The sacred poetry produced during the period is large in quantity, but displays little originality. There is hardly a new note struck or a deep religious feeling expressed. The Paitanim tread in the footsteps of their predecessors, and the subjects are the same which were dealt with by the earlier poets. The didactic tendency which we noticed in secular poetry is also quite evident in the sacred. And to compensate for lack of poetic feeling, there is a conscious endeavor at artificiality of construction. Devices, like those mentioned above, namely beginning every word of the poem with the same letter (Taus or Alephs or Memim), or fanciful rhyming and peculiar acrostics are constantly employed.

The prevailing poetic types are the *Selihah* and the *Kinah* in all their phases, the admonition to the soul (The Tokheha), the plea to God, the martyr story, all are represented. The number of Paitanim is considerable and they hail from all European countries, especially from Italy and the Provence. These two countries became, during the thirteenth and the fourteenth centuries the centers of Paitanic activity. Yet Germany contributed its quota of *Selihah* and *Kinah* writers, excelling especially in the latter. The constant suffering which the Jews of Germany underwent turned their poetry into one monotonous complaint to God, in which they poured forth their hearts and pleaded for alleviation of that suffering. Even Greece brought forth a number of prolific Paitanim who showed skill and dexterity in their *Selihoth*.

It is impossible to enumerate all the Paitanim of the period who tried their hand at composing sacred poetry. We will, therefore, only mention the most outstanding during the centuries. At the beginning of the thirteenth century, we have a great Paitan in Catalonia, northern Spain, Isaac ben Jehudah, known as the Seniri (fl. c. 1220). He is said to have written more than thirty *Piutim* and *Selihoth* to all festivals. His style is clear and lucid and the themes of his poems deal mainly with the suffering of the nation. In one of his poems, an introduction to the *Kadish,* he turns to God and says:

> Thy dove is struggling on from place to place;
> Her nightly lodging is a frightful space;
> And there the ravens lie in ambuscade;
> Thy dove cries out: Redeem me by Thy grace.
>
> O dove! Because thou still dost trust in Me,
> I see thy sorry plight and misery.
> Thou wilt yet don thy garments beautiful.
> My daughter! Happy days will come to thee.[24]

He also wrote a long Admonition poem (Tokheha), where the contrast between the vanity and fleetness of human life on the one hand, and the lasting misery and agony of death on the other hand, is drawn in a graphic manner. He concludes with an exhortation to the soul to devote its life to the service of God.

To that century and that country belong also three other Paitanim, Abraham ben Isaac, Solomon Moses and Moses ben Nahman, the great Talmudic scholar and exegete known as Nahmanides. The last named wrote a very fine poem of one hundred lines using monorhyme. The poem bewails the flight of time, the swift passing of youth and its pleasures, and calls upon man to utilize old age for contemplation and meditation upon lofty subjects, such as the Godhead and the higher world. The opening lines emit a very pathetic note:

> My comrades cry out and inquire:
> The days that exulted with pride
> Where are they? Dost know where to seek them?
> They're borrowed from you—and denied.
> O tell us: those days will they ever
> Return, and restore all they robbed?
> The happiness, joy, and the beauty,
> The glory for which our hearts throbbed,
> The sweetness and soulful desire—
> That vanished as th' tune of a lyre?[25]

[24] Anthology of Hebrew poetry, ed. Brody, p. 259.
[25] Ibid, p. 281.

Another poet of this century, who probably lived in southern Spain was Nahum who wrote a number of Redemption *Piutim* (Geuloth) in light meter and style, in which comfort and hope are held out to a martyred people by picturing the coming of the redeemer. The poems containing allusions to verses in Canticles, where the beloved invites the lover to come to her bower, are replete with love similes and short descriptions of awakening spring.

From Provence, there hail many Paitanim during the thirteenth and fourteenth centuries, among them Joseph Ezobi, Abraham Bedersi, and his son Yedayah who wrote a poem on the soul where its vicissitudes from the time it comes to dwell in man until its departure is described. Other Provence Paitanim are Abraham ben Hayiim, Phineas ha-Levi, Abba Meir ben Moses and Israel Crescas.

Italy brought forth a host of writers of sacred poetry the most important of whom are Benjamin ben Abraham, the physician, most probably the one discussed above (Sect. 31), his brother Moses, Moses ben Joseph, Jehiel ben Jekutiel, Abraham ben Joab, the gay Immanuel and others. Many of these, especially Benjamin specialized in *Selihah* writing. A very prolific *Selihah* writer was also Mordecai ben Sabbatai, surnamed the Long One (ha-Aruk) whose place or time is not definitely known. It is surmised that he hailed either from southern Italy or Greece and lived in the middle of the thirteenth century. From Greece, there hailed also a number of other Paitanim.

From Germany and France, we have mostly *Kinah* (elegy) writers. To France belong Nathaniel ben Joseph from Chinon who died the death of a martyr in 1306, perishing in flames, Solomon ben Simha, Eliezer ben Judah ha-Cohen, Abraham ben Menahem and others. Among the German *Kinah* writers, the important ones are Yehiel of Eisenach (fl. 1235) who wrote a long *Kinah* for the ninth of Ab, Meir ben Yehiel of Halle, Saxony, and Meir ben Baruch of Rothenburg. (Ch. IV Sect, 43.) The first wrote an elegy on the ten martyrs (Arzē ha-Lebanan) which is included in the standard collection of *Kinoth* recited on the ninth of Ab. The poem is primarily an epic relating in detail the death of these martyrs during the Hadrianic persecutions in the year 135-138 C. E. Meir's *Kinah* written on the occasion of the burning of the Scrolls of the Law in 1254 is likewise included in the *Kinoth* selection and is recited on the ninth of Ab. It is a powerful cry of an agonized soul at seeing the

Torah, the dearest possession burned and is addressed to the Torah itself. Its opening lines run as follows:

O burnt on the pyre!
Inquire after the peace of thy mourners
Who long for thy courtyards, but wallow
Instead on the ground, while the scorners
Pour out their contempt for thy scrolls
And for us, who in pain unexpressed
Are astonished to see
That a fire had power o'er the light of our souls.

O burnt on the pyre!
Inquire after the peace of thy lovers,
Who walk in the dark
Of a night that seems endless, yet hopefully wait
For the coming of day, for the song of the lark.

O burnt on the pyre!
Inquire after the peace of a heart-broken man
Who is constantly crying—
A man who with jackal and ostrich is vying
In bewailing, bemoaning thy fate.[26]

To the pertinent question, the poet found no answer.

The second half of the fourteenth century and the first four decades of the fifteenth brought forth a number of Paitanim, especially in the southern countries, such as Italy and Greece, but Provence and Spain can also boast of some Paitanic activity. At that time, a new center of literary activity also rises in Algiers, northern Africa whither the Spanish Jews fled after the persecutions in 1391. Of the names of the Paitanim in that center, only a few deserve to be mentioned, and even these, more for the name they acquired in other fields of literature than for their poetic productions. These are the two great Rabbinic scholars, Rabbi Isaac ben Shesheth Barfath (1330-1408) and Rabbi Simon ben Zemah Duran (1361-1444). The former came from Spain, the latter from the island of Majorca both settling in Algiers. Barfath left us a number of *Kinoth,* several of them composed on the occasion of the massacres of 1391. Duran wrote a long poem on Palestine under the name of *Eretz Hemdah* (The Desired Land), which seems to be an imitation of Judah ha-Levi's Ode to

[26] Ibid, p. 295.

Zion, but of a much inferior quality. Of those who hail from other countries, probably the most prolific of the Italian Paitanim was Moses ben Abraham ha-Hazan, who left a large number of *Selihoth,* and the Bohemian Abigdor Kara (fl. 1380-1400) of Prague, whose *Selihoth* for certain fast days were included in the standard selections. He lived through the persecutions, and that painful experience is reflected in the stirring poem entitled the God of Revenge (El-Nekomoth).

B. Second Epoch (1500-1750)

34. SECULAR POETRY IN ITALY

The conditions during the opening decades of the second epoch were not favorable for poetic productivity. The end of the fifteenth century was marked by the expulsion of the Jews from Spain, and the gradual decline of the Jewish communities in the Provence. By this time, the number of Jews there was an insignificant one. Under these circumstances, we must turn for poetic inspiration to Italy, the country where literary activity was not interrupted since its revival in the thirteenth century. In the two and one half centuries which still remained of the Mediaeval period, Jewish secular poetry found its only home there.

During the sixteenth century, there arose a number of fine verse writers in Italy, but hardly a single poet deserving of that name. The first was Israel of Cortina who in 1530 wrote a long poem on women under the name of *Toḳhahath Nashim* (A Reproach of Women). It consists of eighty-four tercets with two quatrains as a conclusion. As the name indicates, the poem speaks of women in a derogatory tone, though the author admits of the existence of some noble women. This subject of women served as a theme also for later poets. In the second half of the century, Judah Sommo da Porta Leone of Bologna, a friend of Azarya de Rossi, the famous historian, wrote another long poem by the name of *Magen Nashim* (The Defender of Women), where woman is defended and eulogized. Jacob de Fano, as if desiring to strike a middle way on the question, composed a poem on the same subject named *Shiltē ha-Giborim* (The Shields of the Mighty), where he admits of the good qualities in women, but claims the supremacy of men.

Three famous scholars of that century who distinguished themselves in other fields also wrote some good poetry. These are the historian Azarya de Rossi, Judah Moscato (d. 1594), the commentator on the Kuzari and Menahem Lonzano (d. 1610), the Masorite and lexicographer. The first included six poems in his historical work, *Meor Enayim* (Sect. 143). They deal mostly with the description of the nature of the book, praise of wisdom and derision of the enemies of light and truth. While he does not rise to great poetic heights, the style is elegant and forceful. The second wrote a number of elegies on the death of famous scholars, including one on Joseph Karo and even three elegies on the death of Margarita, Duchess of Savoy. The third was a more prolific poet. In his lexicographical work, *Shnē Yodoth* (Two Hands), he devoted several sections to poetry, a large part of which is primarily sacred, and only two are devoted to secular poetry. The fourth of these sections denominated *Dereḳ ha-Hayyim* (The Way of Life) is a didactic poem of two hundred and ninety-eight verses containing moral sayings and ethical teachings in fine and forceful style. The fifth section called *Toḳhahoth Musar* (The Reproof of Instruction), divided into fifteen cantos, is a fine satire on the manners and ways of life of his contemporaries.

Samuel Arkevolti (Sect. 9) the grammarian, can also be classed as a poet. In his grammar, *Arugath ha-Bosem,* he devotes a chapter to prosody where he discussed the various meters and the technique of versification, illustrating the rules with specimens of his own poetry. While he can not lay claim to true poetic spirit, yet he does not fall behind many of his contemporaries. His style is pure and the diction Biblical, and here and there, we sense a lyrical touch and note a humorous vein.

The seventeenth century marks the rise of a new trend in Hebrew poetry in Italy. The trend is an upward one, for during the time, there appeared a few poets who truly deserved that name. There is also a marked improvement in the style and meter. The language becomes purer, approaching that of the Bible, the rhyme becomes varied and Italian forms are introduced. The eight line, the six line stanza and the tercet are frequently employed. Likewise, the horizon of poetry is widened, and dramatic poetry which was almost unknown in the previous centuries makes its appearance in Italy.

Judah Leon de Modena (1571-1648) is the first poet of the seventeenth century. De Modena, a man of great talent but of a rather dubious character who distinguished himself in many fields of knowledge did not pass by poetry. As of everything else, he made of poetry a profession, a means for earning money. He wrote on almost every theme, elegies, eulogies, poems on friendship, and especially wedding songs and epitaphs. Yet in spite of all that, some of his poems possess great beauty and even pathos, and strange to say it is the epitaphs which he made to order that display these traits. He was a master of parody and employed it with great skill, parodying expressions of Biblical verses and allusions to names in a befitting manner. Most of these epitaphs can not be translated as they lose their forcefulness, but we will attempt to reproduce one which was written on the grave of a woman named Simha (Joy). It reads:

In the midst of the thorns she is lying,
  A queen among women, a rose.
As the grass that grows up and then withers
  Was the woman that here doth repose.
This world is a lodging for travellers
  Joy comes and is followed by woes.[27]

Very beautiful is a line from an epitaph written on an infant.

Woe for the dawn which passed out before the break of day.[28]

35. *JACOB AND EMANUEL FRANCES*

The two brothers, Jacob (1615-1677) and Emanuel (1618-1703) Frances are the two most distinguished poets of the century. They were great Rabbinic scholars, especially Emanuel whose Responsa and decisions are quoted with great deference by contemporary Rabbinic authorities. They also possessed much secular learning, mastered the Italian language and the philosophy and the science of the day, and held an esteemed social position. Possessing a sane and clear view of Jewish life, they entered upon a war with mysticism and the Kabbala, which at the time penetrated all phases of Judaism. They were especially vigorous against the pseudo-Messianic movement of Sabbatai Zevi which was rampant in Italian Jewry. In a Jewish world which went mad with the false hopes kindled by Sabbatai, these two brothers were almost the only clear-sighted men who foresaw the evil consequences of the movement, and with daring courage threw down the gauntlet to the deluded ones and fought

[27] Luhoth Abanim, collection of epitaphs. Pub. by Berliner, 1881, No. 63.
[28] Ibid, No. 158.

bitterly and with great passion the spread of Sabbatainism. They employed, of course, polemic poetry as their weapon. The *Zevi Mudah* (The Hunted Stag), an allusion to Sabbatai Zevi, is a collection of poems written by both brothers against the false Messiah and his followers. The book was edited by Emanuel who appended to it an introductory poem. It consists of two parts, the first containing the poems of Jacob and the second that of Emanuel. The poems are distinguished by a sharp satiric vein. All invectives are hurled against Sabbatai, his prophet Nathan and other leaders, and a warning issued to the Jews not to be misled by the sect. The style is light and the darts pointed and penetrating, breathing hatred, as Jacob says:

"My quill is charged with fire,
My pen point is a dart;
My tongue a poisoned arrow,
To strike him in the heart."[29]

These poems, of course, made many bitter enemies for the brothers among the Sabbataians who used all possible means to vilify their names. To these attacks, they replied with more poems and Jacob attacked even the Kabbala itself in a poem where he mockingly remarks that ignorant youngsters who do not know the rudiments of physical science scan "the circles of the heavens" and those who do not know the most elementary rules of the Talmud delve into the mysteries of the spheres and the Sephiroth or try to interpret the visions of Ezekiel. He calls upon them to devote themselves to the study of the Torah and to acquire some knowledge before venturing upon the mysteries. The poem which was well written was a shock to many rabbis to whom the Kabbala was the acme of knowledge and the persecutions against Jacob doubled. He was finally compelled to leave his native city Florence and wander about. These wanderings and persecutions shortened his life, for he died in the year 1667, at the age of fifty-two.

Of the other poems written by Jacob against his traducers, some are included in a dialogue written in rhymed prose by Emanuel called *Vikkuah Libni we-Shimmi*. In them, he is not only bitter against his enemies, but bewails his own suffering and complains against his

[29] Kovetzal-Yad, p. 103. Translation taken from Rhine's Secular Poetry in Italy, J. Q. R. N. S. VII, p. 379.

miserable lot. To these, Emanuel added in that dialogue several of his own poems where he defends his brother and hurls defiance at his enemies. Emanuel calls to them:

Oh haste, ye dogs, that bark aloud,
That shout: "Bow-wow, your song is trite";
They can but thunder, I can shoot;
They can but bark, while I can bite.[30]

When his mood of sorrow and bitter satire departed, Jacob wrote fine elegies on the death of scholars, also some wedding poems and epigrams full of humor. Thus reads one of his epigrams against a woman who leaves her house too often:

For every woman great or small
To go out there are three times in all.
The first is when from mother's womb
She doth come forth;
The second is when from home she departs
For the house of her husband;
The third is when, alas, for the tomb she leaves,
Yet perhaps, this may be the best of all.[31]

More prolific than his brother and more versatile and even deeper in poetic feeling was Emanuel. He wrote both secular and sacred poetry. His secular poetry is varied. Besides his polemic poems mentioned above, he wrote a large number of elegies, friendship poems and wedding songs. In his younger days, he wrote elegant love sonnets, some of them with an erotic tinge, for which he later apologized in a long poem. But the few poems of this type that are left us are beautiful in their tone without being indelicate. One sonnet written to his fiancee, Honore Grazia, is especially Biblical in tone.

Thy stature is that of a palm;
Thy eyes—the eyes of a dove.
As sweet as the odor of balm,
Is that of thy nostrils, love.

Like sparks of the sun—thy curls,
How beautiful is thy speech!

[30] Translation taken from Rhine's Sacred Poetry in Italy, Ibid, p. 382.
[31] Kol Ugob, ed. A. B. Paper, No. 15.

Lovely thou art—and perfect
Thou'rt beyond compare and reach.[32]

Emanuel distinguished himself in his numerous epigrams. He wrote a large number of them, and even a dialogue by the name of *Vikkuah Itiel we-Ukol* where woman is the subject of the contest. There are many epigrams of a very clever nature. Thus, Ukol wrote an epitaph on his wife's grave.

This is not a tombstone,
It's a weight
Set upon the grave of my beloved wife;
Lest God forbid
She raise the lid
Of the coffin, and return home to ruin my life.[33]

Another epitaph on the grave of a fool:

A fool is buried in this grave.
I warn you, reader, shun this view.
For even when he's dead and safe,
The presence of a fool eschew.[34]

Or on the grave of a quarrelsome fellow:

In this grave lies man despicable,
Slanderer and teller of tales.
Oh, were he only able,
His trade even among dead he would ply.[35]

Again, speaking of begging, he says:

The poor who begs with bated breath,
And asks for alms with tearful eyes
Is surely not afraid of death:
Who begs a thousand times he dies.[36]

[32] Metek Sphatayim, p. 49.
[33] Ibid, p. 17.
[34] Ibid, p. 25.
[35] Ibid.
[36] Kol Ugob, No. 47. Translation taken from Rhine's Secular Poetry in Italy. Ibid, p. 388.

Complaining of fools, he wittingly sings:

That speech alone distinguishes
The brute from man is wrong:
Else why did God upon the fool
Bestow a speaking tongue?[37]

But Emanuel was not always humorous or polemical. His life was full of misery and misfortune, persecuted as he was by enemies and the vicissitudes of time. His first wife died young and his two children followed her. He remarried, but his second wife also passed away soon, and to cap the misery, his only son from the second marriage died in infancy. He was thus left alone in the world, and as the feeling of loneliness oppressed him, its echo is heard in his elegies and poems. In one sonnet of particular sadness, after complaining of his sufferings, he comforts himself with the following lines:

Do not be disquieted nor cast down, Oh my soul,
Even in pain, years do pass,
Nor does suffering last forever.[38]

Very pathetic are the lines of one of his Admonition poems (Tokhahoth), where he sings mournfully of the passing of life:

Passed are days of youth happy and gay;
Quickly they sped and flower-like withered away.
Days of spring like smoke dispersed,
Fall is upon me and winter
Winds destroy fruit and flower
And sweep ice and sleet in my life's bower.[39]

Our author also wrote a book on poetry in the form of a dialogue under the name of *Meteḳ Sphatayim* (Sweetness of Lips), where he gives all rules of poetic composition, and discusses the various meters and verse constructions, such as the eight-line stanza, the sestet, the tercet and the sonnet. He gives ample illustrations from his own poetry, as well as from that of his brother of all the poetic forms. He

[37] Kol Ugob, No. 48. Translation taken from Rhine. Ibid.
[38] Metek Sphatayim, p. 86.
[39] Kol Ugob, No. 51.

exhibited great skill in his mastery of the language and in this he was incomparable in his generation. We can discern his dexterity in his use of language from the fact that among his numerous poems there is one of ten lines, four words to the line composed entirely of proper names, and it is not a mere jingle of rhymes but expresses a fine prayer for the redemption of Israel.

Emanuel wrote a large number of sacred poems for almost all festivals and also for the day of Purim and for many other occasions. These are distinguished by beauty of style and depth of religious feeling.

36. MOSES ZACUTO

A poet of great power and ability in this century was Moses Zacuto (1625-1697). To him belongs the honor of introducing the drama into Hebrew poetic literature. Until the time of Zacuto, we scarcely have any attempt at dramatic production. The nearest approach to it was a short dramatic poem by Emanuel Frances where we have a trilogue between the evil *Yetzer,* the good *Yetzer* (the good and bad thoughts personified) and a child, each endeavoring to persuade the child to follow his ways. There are also two groups of people introduced there, one residing in hell, and the other in paradise. But this poem lacks elaboration, as it is very brief, and there is hardly any action. The Hebrew drama begins with Zacuto.

Moses Zacuto was born and educated in Amsterdam, having attended the Jewish school *Etz Hayyim,* simultaneously with Baruch Spinoza. He showed in his early youth a great proclivity to mysticism, and he devoted the rest of his life to the pursuit of the Kabbala. In his eagerness for its study, he went to Poland to be initiated into its mysteries by the famous Kabbalist, Rabbi Sheftal of Posen. He later left that country in order to go to the Holy Land, but on passing through Italy, he was offered the Rabbinate at Venice which he accepted. Later, he was called to Mantua where he resided until his death.

Together with his study of the Kabbala, Zacuto also occupied himself with poetry, composing many religious poems. But his fame rests on his two dramas *Yesod Olam* (The Foundation of the World) and the *Tofteh Aruk* (Hell prepared), especially the latter.

The *Yesod Olam,* published in 1673 is a popular Biblical play suitable for Purim, the day when the Jews allowed themselves to make merry and seek amusement. The hero of the play is our father, Abraham, and the plot is as follows:

Abraham having destroyed the idols in his father's house, is brought to trial by Nimrod, the king of Mesopotamia, on the complaint of his own father. At the trial, he declares his belief in one God and is sentenced to death by fire. His brother Haran is undecided as to whether to follow Abraham or not. But when news is brought of Abraham's miraculous delivery, he also declares himself a believer in one God. He is then sentenced to be burned and is consumed. Abraham's family, namely Terah, Lot, Sarah and Milka, the wife of his brother Nahor, are converted to the worship of one God, while Nahor himself still persists in worshipping idols.

The plot is really an elaboration of a Midrashic story, but it is a worthy attempt at dramatization. The work is, of course, still crude, has little action, and consists mostly of dialogue, but the character of Abraham is well drawn. He appears as a philosopher and zealous champion of high ideals and is also endowed with the power of swaying the masses.

Equally well drawn is the character of Nimrod who typifies Oriental despotism, and is represented as a calm self-possessed tyrant. The conflict between these two forms the central point of interest in the play. There is, however, a lack of technique in the drama, as it is not divided into acts and scenes. The style of the poem is pure and lofty and the rhyme is mostly of the quatrain form, though here and there, a number of sonnets are scattered throughout the drama.

Of much higher value is the second work of Zacuto, the *Tofteh Aruk*. However, its value consists mainly in the poetic and artistic spirit permeating it, and not in the technique or dramatic construction which is even more primitive than that of the *Yesod Olam*. It is a typical mystery play, one of those plays which were current in Mediaeval European literature, but is thoroughly impregnated with the Jewish spirit. Its subject is, like the one in most mystery plays—death and life beyond the grave—the great mystery which formed the center of interest in Mediaeval life.

The hero of the drama is a dead person, and the other of the active dramatis personae is one of the demons of hell. Non-participating personae are the family of the dead man, people engaged in the burial of the dead, groups of sinners, and groups of demons. The scenes are laid first in the cemetery and then in hell. It is divided into two acts. In the first act, the dead man awakes immediately after the burial and is amazed at his new state. In a long soliloquy, he passes judgment upon the physicians who were unable to save him, ridicules their ignorance and their greed for money, and then compares his present state with his former during life, bewailing his position. Suddenly a noise is heard which terrifies him and he attempts to rise but in vain. Then the dead man together with his grave slide down to the very bottom of the earth, and hell with all its terrors appears before him.

Here the second act begins. A marvelous description of hell, its occupants, their suffering, and the demons who inflict that suffering is given by Zacuto in the opening scene. It is not detailed, as that is reserved for a later scene, but a general aritstic picture is drawn. The dead man is terrified at all this and trembles. A demon then approaches, and a remarkable dialogue takes place between the two. The dead man offering ransom pleads and bewails his state in five line stanzas while the demon replies with only one word which seems to fit in exceptionally well with the thought expressed in the stanza and also rhymes with it.

After the dead man has exhausted all his arguments and pleadings, the demon, in a lengthy monologue, draws a gloomy picture before his interlocutor delineating the points of difference between the life in the world above and the present state. Then in order to convince the dead man of the grim reality of hell, he leads him through its seven circles. The description of each circle then follows giving in detail the type of suffering in each and the kind of sinners. The scene is interrupted with a confession uttered by the sinners who justify the judgment visited upon them. This is repeated several times. The demon then points to paradise and gives a brief description of it. A song of the just is heard at a distance. Finally, pointing at the contrast between the lot of the righteous and the sinners, the demon concludes his monologue with a few stanzas, justifying the judgment of God. The dead man repeats the stanzas of the demon and likewise proclaims God's justice.

The drama of Zacuto was probably, like the previous attempts of Immanuel and Rieti, influenced by Dante's Inferno. Zacuto's work excels though by its dramatic elaboration, by the psychological analysis of the character of the hero and especially by the wonderful description of the moments of the drama. The awakening of the dead man, his reflections, his meeting with the demon, the dialogue and the description of hell and its terrors are all artistically portrayed.

The style is pure and graceful, the meter light, the rhyme is that of the five line stanza, namely the last two lines rhyme with the first, while the middle two, rhyme with each other. But of still greater value is the moral of the play, for the poems bring out vividly the vanity of human life and the futility of sin, which would make even a non-believer in hell reflect upon his conduct.

Besides his dramatic poems, Zacuto wrote also a semi-dramatic elegy on the death of his teacher, Saul Mortara of Amsterdam. In the elegy, the virtues of the master are personified and dramatically described. He also wrote a large number of *Piutim* collected under the name of *Hinē Kol Hadash* (Here is a New Voice), a parody of Ecclesiastes I, 9, where it is said, "En Kol Hadash Tahat ha-Shemesh" (There is nothing new under the sun). These poems do not rise much above the *Piutim* of his contemporaries, only occasionally bertaying the poetic power which Zacuto really possessed.

37. *MINOR ITALIAN POETS*

The seventeenth century was, in a measure, a flourishing period for Jewish poetry in Italy. Besides the important ones heretofore discussed, there was a host of poets who wrote a large number of poems of the current types and forms. The most important of them are the following: The first is Eliezer ben Gerson Hephetz, who composed a number of philosophical poems, among which is one on the manifestation of God in the world of life and nature, and a sonnet to the soul, where he calls upon it to remember its permanent habitation in heaven, and utilize its stay on earth merely for the adding of glory on its return thither. The second is Abraham ben Sabbatai Cohen (1670-1729), a native of Crete who settled in Italy. He wrote the *Kehunath Abraham* (Priesthood of Abraham), a poetic paraphrase of the Psalms. This work is written in fine style and good meter, and at the end of each psalm the content is given. Others are Israel, Benjamin Bassan, Isaiah Bassan, the teacher of Moses Hayyim Luzzatto, Abraham Isaac Castelo, his son Joseph, and Emanuel Kalbo who composed long wedding songs, elegies and sonnets on various occasions. Their merit consists in the fact that they helped popularize the Italian forms of poetry, the sonnet, the quatrain and the sestet, which added grace and variety to Hebrew poetry.

38. SACRED POETRY

The sacred poetry of this epoch is quite extensive and the number of *Piut* and *Selihah* writers considerable, but the quality of the *Piutim* and other sacred poems is much lower than that of those produced in the former epoch. Yet, we have even in this epoch a few poets who possessed great depth of feeling and intensive religious fervor. The larger number of Paitanim hail from Sephardic communities which were situated in countries under Mohammedan rule. The Spanish exiles who settled in North Africa, Turkey and Palestine produced numerous Paitanim. Samuel David Luzzatto copied from only one edition of a Tetuan (Morocco) *Mahzor* the names of fifty poets who are otherwise unknown, all hailing either from North Africa or from Turkey and Palestine. As it would take too long to enumerate all of them, we will mention only several names. These are Solomon Al-Khabetz whose fine hymn to the Sabbath, "Come my beloved towards the bride," known as *Leḳo-Dodi* was accepted in the Friday night service; the famous Kabbalist, Isaac Luria, whose Hebrew and Aramaic Sabbath poems form an important part of the after-meal songs (Zemiroth); and the greatest of them Israel Najara of whom anon.

Of the European countries, Italy leads in Paitanic activity. All those secular poets, such as Modena, the brothers Frances, Menahem Lonsano, Gershon Hefez, Samuel Arkevolti, Azarya de Rossi wrote *Piutim, Azharoth* (Vol. I, Sect. 115) and *Selihoth.* Besides these, there were numerous other Paitanim. The Italian poets introduced into sacred poetry the same forms they employed in the secular ones, namely the sonnet, the eight line stanza, and the tercet, thus introducing a new note in this type of poetry.

Germany contributed its quota of Paitanim, *Selihah* and elegy writers. Persecutions were frequent and special tragic occurrences in the form of exiles from provinces or cities were almost daily phenomena. These gave impetus to the *Selihoth* and *Kinoth.* Many were there who tried their hand at this work, and even Poland produced a number of Paitanim in this age. The massacres in the Ukraine in 1648 brought forth a host of *Kinah* writers. Among those of German Polish Paitanim are Akiba ben Jacob of Frankfort (d. 1597) a *Selihah* writer of talent, Solomon Luria, the famous Talmudic scholar and Samuel Edels known under the pseudonym of MaHarsha (Morenu Samuel Edels) another great Talmudic scholar. *Selihoth* and elegies on the massacres of 1648 were also written by

Yom Tob Lippman Heller, commentator on the Mishnah, Sabbatai Cohen, the commentator of the Code of Karo (Sect. 65) and by many others. Thus, the production of sacred poetry which began to bloom in Palestine continued to express the deep religious feeling of the singers of Israel, their yearning for redemption and their cry for alleviation of suffering for twelve centuries in all lands of the diaspora, under all kinds of vicissitudes and changes. And no matter how varied the form and different the style and ability of the singers might have been, the purpose was one. It all grew out of the deep pathos and tragedy of Jewish life, the life of a people in exile.

39. ISRAEL NAJARA

We can not close our review of sacred poetry during the post-Classical period without devoting some space to the poetry of Israel Najara, who is undoubtedly the oustanding sacred poet of the entire period. He restored to the *Piut* its pristine glory and gave once more articulate expression to the sufferings of his people and its intense longing for redemption.

Israel Najara was born in Damascus about 1560, and most likely received his education from his father Moses, who was himself a great scholar and wrote many books including some notes to the *More Nebukim* of Maimonides. Little is known of Israel's life otherwise, except that he was a devotee of the Kabbala which flourished at that time at Safed, Palestine, and that he served as Rabbi of Gaza where he died. The year of his death is unknown.

Najara was endowed with all the qualities for poetic activity. He possessed a feeling heart, a fine sense of language, great skill in rhyming and above all real poetic spirit. The writing of sacred poetry was his main vocation in life, his deep pious spirit clamoured for constant expression, and consequently his poetic output was very large. There are several hundred of his poems extant, and many of them were received in the ritual of the Oriental and some also in that of the German Jewries. Najara himself boasted that he never wrote any love poems and that he devoted his pen entirely to the glory of God and Israel. Yet there is an erotic tinge even in his sacred poems, as many of them are written in the form of love dialogues between God and Israel. Najara, on the whole, in spite of his extreme piety, gave to his poetry a secular aspect. He imitates the forms and meters of all languages known to him, Turkish, Arabic, Spanish, Italian and Greek, and uses the quatrain and the tercet forms very frequently. In addition, he intended his poems to be sung and always designated at the beginning of each the melody to which it was to be sung.

There are three motives in Najara's poetry, God, Israel and redemption. His love for God is great, but still greater is his love for Israel, and still more intense is his yearning for redemption. He lived in a time of Messianic hope, in the age when the Kabbala and mysticism flourished, when hearts fluttered with expectation of the arrival of the son of David, and Najara being of the inner circle of the Safed Kabbalists was the spokesman of these hopes. He, therefore, differs from the earlier poets in his songs. They are not cries and pleas for redemption as much as the expression of hope that it is coming and near at hand. They thus instilled comfort in the hearts of his suffering brethren who were weary of exile and persecution. Thus, he sings:

My dove! why dost thou wander,
  Fluttering from nest to nest
And like a mother in birth-pangs
  Can'st thou find no rest?
Thou'lt yet be sweet and lovely
  In gorgeous apparel dressed.
My beloved, my sweet, my sister
  In glorious jewels thou'lt shine.
For soon I'll gather thy exiles
  Come sister, come bride of mine.[40]

In such and other endearing epithets, he expresses his love for Israel which is unbounded and infinitely tender. Israel is Najara's beloved, his gazelle to whom he devotes one love poem after another with untiring energy. He sings of his people as of a beautiful maiden and describes her beauty and charms in exquisite fashion. At times, he himself seems to be the lover, and at other times, he makes God address Israel in love terms. Thus he says:

My beauty! O why do thy eyes shoot darts
  On all who set their eyes on thee?

[40] Zemiroth Israel, Pt. I, No. 16.

All who behold thee tremble like fish,
  When caught in a net that's thrown at sea.
They yearn to approach thee and draw in thy light;
  But they dare not come near, and thy presence must flee.
For thy light is more blinding than ever the sun's
  Or the moon's and the heavenly orbs could be.[41]

or

The light of thy cheeks causes many a heart
  To tremble and heavily palpitate.
Their hearts are enkindled, they can find no rest
  Whom thy heavenly beauty did captivate.
Have pity on those who are caught in the meshes
  Of passion, and longingly thy love await.
Give them thy remedy, hasten thy cure,
  Save them before it shall be too late.[42]

But at times, Najara speaks to God on behalf of his people, his beloved who is waiting for the return of her lover who has forsaken her and calls to him in pleading and tender tones, thus:

To my tent, O pray return
And there in joy ascend,
For the fire of thy forsaking doth in me burn.
Thy gazelle from might do save
Living Redeemer, redemption bring near;
See Thy dove the pursuing hawk doth fear.[43]

In his religious poems, Najara expresses his deep love for God, his own littleness as compared to the infinite Divine greatness. In one of such poems, he says:

To Thee, who dwelleth on high
My hand do I spread,
And lowly do I bow my head.
As a poor man humble do I pray,
Thou bring salvation to my soul nigh.[44]

[41] Ibid, No. 100.
[42] Ibid, No. 107.
[43] Zemiroth Israel, No. 6.
[44] Ibid, No. 56.

As all religious poets, Najara wrote a considerable number of Admonition poems where the vanity of human life is bewailed and a call is made to the soul to prepare for its permanent habitation. In one of these poems, Najara sings:

The pleasures of life, its desires
  Pass swiftly like phantoms away;
And yet man strives on and aspires
  To gain them, though long they'll not stay.

'Twould rather be proper and fitting
  For man to prepare for his way.
Who knows what will happen to-morrow?
  Who knows what may happen to-day?[45]

In another song, he mournfully chants:

The creatures of Time are the vine,
The vintager—Death.
God sends his decree
And they're plucked in a breath.
The vintager picks luscious grapes
And unripe fruit,
Old and young, poor and rich;
He hastens to carry off his loot
And who can dare with him to dispute?
Therefore men of reason
Will prepare provision,
Turn from the splendour of time
And passion subdue,
In order perfection of soul to pursue,
For God lacks not strength nor desire
To pay every man what him is due.[46]

Najara wrote a large number of Piutim for every Sabbath of the year as well as for the festivals. Most of the Piutim, while they deal with the same themes, are brought in some connection with the story of the week as told in the portion of the Bible. His festival poems are long and possess an epic element. Thus, his poems for the festivals of Passover, Purim and Hanukah are really epic narratives, inas-

[45] Ibid, Pt. III, No. 33.
[46] Ibid, No. 52.

much as the entire story of the Maccabean struggle, that of Esther and the Exodus are told in great detail. Our poet wrote also a small number of secular poems consisting of eulogies to friends and great men, wedding songs, polemics and elegies on the death of great men. In the manner of the day, Najara also displayed his skill in the writing of poems in Aramaic. One of these poems called God the Master of the World (Yo Ribon) which is both an ode and a plea for redemption became so popular that it was accepted by all Jewries of the world in the *Zemiroth* (Sabbath meal songs), set to tunes and is still sung by the Jews the world over.

The style of Najara is a very artistic one, employing as stated all forms of poetry and poetic devices. He uses alliteration, *Taganis* and the refrain. He collected his own poems and the largest part of them was published during his life time, the first collection having appeared at Safed in 1587. A second edition, containing some additional poems appeared in Venice in 1599. We possess the two collections of his sacred poems. The first called *Zemiroth Israel* (The Songs of Israel, allusion to his name) is divided into three parts, *Olath Tamid* (The Permanent Offering) containing poems of a general nature; (2) *Olath Shabbath* (The Sabbath Offering) *Piutim* for the Sabbaths of the Year; and (3) *Olath ha-Hodesh* (The Offering of the Month) containing poems for the first of the month and the festivals. The second named *Pismonim* contains all of his refrain poems (Pismon being the name for refrain poem). Najara himself published a collection of his secular poems under the name *Mi-Mē Israel* (From the Waters of Israel) which he divided into several sections, giving each a euphuistic name in accordance with the subject with which it deals.

Chapter IV

RABBINIC LITERATURE

40. *INTRODUCTORY REMARKS*

The second half of the Mediaeval Ages extending as it did for five and one-half centuries was one of extreme productivity in the field of Rabbinic literature. As persecutions increased, and as oppression became more burdensome and suffering more acute, the isolation of Jewish life became more pronounced. More and more did the Jews withdraw into their own shell and out of its confines created their spiritual home. In the center of that home was the study of the Talmud. In the solving of the intricate problems, the oppressed Jewish soul found the much desired consolation, and in the unravelling of the difficult knotty passages, the keen Jewish mind, clamoring for expression, found the joy and comfort sought for.

It was not, however, all a matter of interest in mental dialectics, but to a great extent one of intense practical interest. The spirit of piety which prevailed in all Jewries of Europe was greatly intensified by persecution and suffering, and the Jews of Mediaeval Germany and France, and for that matter, even those of Spain, were constantly worried over the problem of their daily religious conduct. It was of great concern to them whether they really fulfilled all the prescribed duties or inadvertently missed one of them. To these pious Jews, intoxicated with religion, the many precepts and the constantly growing mass of ceremonies and customs were no burden. They experienced no hardship in their performance, but joy and exultation. To know the right way of conduct and the exact manner of performance of the precepts was of prime importance. The rabbis and scholars, therefore, delved into the Talmud and the earlier codes, interpreting their meanings in various ways,, straightening out contradictions, smoothing out difficulties in order to ascertain the exact decision and arrive at a definite conclusion. Hence, the feverish activity of code making which went on for several centuries, when almost every great scholar found it necessary to compile his own code though often adding little that was new except some special interpretations of the sources affecting certain laws. On account of the strict piety of the codifiers, these decisions are permeated with a spirit of severity. That exceptions abound is, of course, needless to say.

It is no wonder then, that when the study of the Talmud and the codes became almost the chief mental occupation of the entire European Jewry, that the literary activity in the field of Rabbinics constantly ramified and increased, and that the number of books reached enormous proportions. This activity went on throughout western and southern Europe, Spain not excepted. In fact, during the three centuries, from the thirteenth to the end of the fifteenth, namely the time of the expulsion of the Jews, Spain occupied the most prominent place in the productivity of Rabbinic literature. Its Talmudic commentators and codifiers far outshone those of Germany or France. In those countries, on account of the frequent perseutions and periodic exiles, literary activity was stunted and its growth checked. In Spain, however, though persecutions were not unknown, the Jews enjoyed up to the end of the fourteenth century, a comparative measue of security and extensive privileges, conditions which enabled them to develop great literary productions.

For the very same reason, we note that Spain and Germany changed places in regard to the type of literature produced in each country. In the Classical period, the Talmudic scholars of Spain devoted their attention to the compilation of codes in order to facilitate the arrival at decisions and to spare the people the trouble of delving into the mysteries of the Talmud themselves. The German scholars, on the other hand, immersed themselves in the depths of the Talmud proper to unfold its meaning, and thus produced the best commentaries and keen dialectical glosses and analytical discussions, known as the *Tosofoth*. (Vol. I, Ch. X, Sect. 145-146.) The role is now reversed. The commentaries and analytical discussions come from Spain, while the code-making and compiling of decisions constitute the principal contribution of Franco-German Jewish scholarship. The Jews of the latter countries lacked the leisure and mental repose necessary for the work of the first kind, while those of Spain did possess the required conditions for an extensive and deep study of the Talmud.

It is also to be noted that Spain not only took the place of Germany in producing the type of Rabbinic literature formerly cultivated in the latter country, but that it also borrowed the peculiar spirit of intensive and analytical study of Rabbinics which characterized the Franco-German Tosafists. The Spanish commentaries of the post-Classical period, with some exceptions, lack to a great extent, the logical systematization on the part of the author found in like works of the former period, as well as the endeavor to explain the Talmud clearly and lucidly. They are more a display of keen analysis and mental acumen which testify to the dialectic and scholastic ability of their authors.

At the end of the fifteenth century, the two great centers of Rabbinic learning, Spain and Germany, ceased their literary productivity, the former because of the expulsion of the Jews, and the latter on account of the constant suffering the Jews had undergone there. But in both cases, it was only a change of locale and not an actual cessation of literary activity on the part of these groups of Jews, the Sephardic and Ashkenazic. In the place of the old centers, these Jews who migrated to other countries built up two new ones which left their mark upon the history of Rabbinic literature. These were Turkey, Egypt and Palestine in the East, and the Slavonic countries, chiefly Poland, in the West. The first was established by the Spanish immigrants who settled there early in the sixteenth century, and for two centuries, the center in the East produced great literary monuments. It seems that the freedom and extensive privileges which the immigrants enjoyed gave a fresh impetus to the genius of Spanish Jewry, and it blossomed forth in intensive intellectual productivity. It was in this period that the final code of Jewish civil and religious law, the *Shulhan Aruḳ* was produced by a Spanish Jew, Joseph Karo. For some reason or other, this fresh activity of the Spanish Jewry in the field of Rabbinics as well as in other fields, was of short duration, for by the beginning of the eighteenth century it began to decline.

Of more endurance and greater persistency was the Slavonic center. As early as the thirteenth century, the Jews from Germany began to migrate into the neighboring Slavonic countries, at first into Bohemia and then into Poland and Lithuania. These new centers gradually grew and by the end of the fifteenth century, they became the great store-house of Talmudic learning and held that position for over three centuries, extending into the modern period. There, especially in Poland, the Talmud reigned supreme. It was the Alpha and Omega of Jewish education and its knowledge bestowed upon its possessor honor and distinction. It was quite natural then that in this center there should develop an extensive and intensive literary activity. There, the *pilpul* system of Jewish study (derived from the Aramaic word *pilpal,* i. e. pepper, sharp-mindedness) flourished and developed to its highest degree. There, where the chief intellectual output was Rabbinic literature, all its forms and phases flourished simultaneously. Talmudic commentaries, code compiling, responsa writing, all were produced in considerable numbers. However, in view of the fact that at the time of the rise of the Polish center of learning, the great standard works in the field of Rabbinic literature were already written and even printed, the scholastic ingenuity of these scholars found expression mostly in supercommentaries and in annotations both on the Talmud and codes, and only occasionally in compiling new codes. Still, that did not in any way check the luxurious growth of that literature, for there was no end to interpretations, additions and refutations of the decisions of the predecessors or ingenious reconciliation of contradictory statements of authorities. In short, it became an endless chain of mental exercises where minds bent upon one aspect of study, i. e. the legal one, vied with each other in a display of keenness and penetration into the meaning of texts.

It is understood, of course, that in a survey of half a millenium of literary activity in one field where the number of books reach into the thousands, where commentaries upon commentaries, annotations upon annotations, and glosses upon glosses are constantly added, where many books resemble each other in tone and character, justice can not be done to even a fair part of this literature. At the best we can note only its outstanding landmarks, its lines of development and contours together with a number of the most prominent works. The rest will have to be left to the imagination of the readers.

For the very same reason, namely on account of the quantity of the works produced, as well as the fact that the differences between the schools of scholars from various countries were obliterated and a certain homogeneity in all these productions exists, it is thought best to adopt in this chapter as in chapter XVII the chronological method, rather than to treat each country separately as was done when dealing with the literature of the Classical period.

A. Commentaries

41. *THE THIRTEENTH CENTURY*

With the close of the schools of Rashi and that of the Tosafists (Vol. I, Sect. 145), the Talmud became, on the whole, an open book; its ways were explored, its difficulties solved and contradictions straightened out. Yet, in spite of all this, the work of commentation did not cease. On the contrary, the very method of the Tosafists inspired the students who followed them to probe still deeper into the ways of the Talmud and find some dark corners still unexplored by the great pathfinders of the former period, often stumbling upon new contradictions in the very commentaries of the earlier scholars which needed reconciliation. Again, here and there, weak spots were found in the explanations of the former teachers, for in many places they were either too brief or not clear in their interpretations, and even the great Rashi with all his lucidity and endeavor to explain was no exception. All this induced many later scholars to attempt to write new commentaries, or in most cases, additions to commentaries, and novel and ingenious remarks which threw new light upon passages in the Talmud. These exegetic remarks, however, are as a rule, only interspersed in long discussions full of twists and turns, of objections to the statements of the earlier scholars, together with keen answers to these objections.

There was one part of the Talmud, however, which really needed commentation and that was the Mishnah. Rashi, whose aim was to explain the Talmud as a whole, commented on the Mishnah very briefly, relying upon his explanation of the Gemarah which is itself a commentary upon the Mishnah. In addition, he wrote no commentaries at all on the Mishnaic orders *Zeraim* and *Taharoth* to which there is no Gemarah. The only commentary on the entire Mishnah was that of Maimonides. But, it being too general in nature, could not satisfy the Franco-German scholars who looked for detail in a commentary, and besides was not available to them as it was not as yet translated into Hebrew. It was, therefore, natural that when the Mishnah became a special subject of study separate from the Gemarah, a tendency to explain it independent of the Gemarah should develop, and accordingly, we find during the post-Classical period a number of excellent commentaries on the Mishnah.

The first commentary produced during the thirteenth century was one on the two orders of the Mishnah, *Zeraim* and *Taharoth* by the Tosafist Samson ben Abraham of Sens (Vol. I, Ch. X, Sect. 146). Rabbi Samson who headed the migration of rabbis from France and Germany to the Holy Land in 1210, settled in Acco which was at the time in Christian hands, and lived there for twenty years until 1235. It seems that the commentary was written there, for he makes extensive use of the Palestinian Talmud. It is detailed, explaining both the words and expressions of the Mishnah as well as its content by quoting frequently the interpretation of Mishnaic passages found in the Gemarah in other tractates of the Talmud, as these Sedarim have no Gemarah in the Babylonian Talmud. In the case of the order of *Zeraim* to which the Palestinian Talmud has a Gemarah, the commentator continually quotes passages also from that Gemarah to each Mishnah to elucidate its meaning. He also explains the passages from the Palestinian Talmud quoted, and as they are very numerous, Rabbi Samson indirectly comments upon a considerable part of the Palestinian Talmud to *Zeraim*.

In the commentary on the last order of the Mishnah, *Taharoth,* to which there is no Gemarah either in the Babylonian or Palestinian Talmud, Rabbi Samson utilizes for purposes of elucidation statements from the Tosephta (Vol. I, Sect. 58) to these tractates. In the entire commentary, the gist of Talmudic discussions of the Mishnaic passages, explained anywhere in the Talmud, are quoted. Rabbi Samson is primarily a commentator, but being also a Tosafist of note, he can not refrain from interspersing here and there a discussion in the Tosafist manner, that is raising difficulties and removing them. In such passages, the great Tosafists, Rabbi Jacob Tam and Rabbi Samson's teacher, Rabbi Isaac ben Samuel of Dampierre (Vol. I, Ch. X, Sect. 146) are often quoted and their opinions elucidated. The commentator, is on the whole, scrupulous to explain the meaning of each expression in the Mishnah and each word in a grammatical way as far as such knowledge was available to him. In such cases, he draws upon the great source of information, the *Aruk* of Rabbi Nathan of Rome (Vol. I, Ch. X, Sect. 148). Rabbi Samson's commentary on the Mishnah was held in great esteem by the scholars of the generations, and is usually quoted by the abbreviation *Rash,* i. e. Rabbi Samson.

42. *MOSES BEN NAHMAN AND SOLOMON BEN ADRET*

Moses ben Nahman or Nahmanides was one of the greatest Rabbinic scholars of his day (for his life see Sect. 12). He, being a disciple of Rabbi Jona of Gerona, who followed the French method of the study of the Talmud, namely the intensive and pilpulistic, gave great impetus to the spread of that method in Spain. He practically transplanted it to that country where it took root and in time bore fruit. Nahmanides is the father of the commentaries or quasi-commentaries known as *Novellae* (Hidushim) which consist primarily of remarks and discussions upon selected passages. The main purpose is to analyze more deeply the meaning of these passages, to criticize the explanations offered by previous commentators by rasiing objections to their comments and offering new ingenious explanations. Very often, an extensive discussion is devoted entirely to the defense of a certain decision on a point of law against the contrary opinion. The decision defended may be either that of Al-Fasi, or of Maimonides, or of Rashi or of any other codifier. This type of defense involves great skill, for it implies the refutation of the previous interpretations of the passage or passages in question, smoothing out contradictions, and consequently, a reinterpretation of the Talmudic passages. Hence the value of these *Novellae* as commentaries.

The Novellae of Nahmanides are extant almost to three full orders of the Talmud, which deal with laws practiced even after the destruction of the Temple, namely *Moed, Nashim, Nesiḳin.* In the last order, the two tractates *Baba Kama* and *Sanhedrin* are left out. In addition, he commented also on the tractates *Beraḳot, Hulin* and *Niddah* of the orders *Zeraim, Kodashim* and *Taharoth* respectively. These three tractates deal with laws practiced at the present day. His *Novellae* are distinguished by a brilliancy of discussion, penetrating legal thought and keenness of analysis. Still, all these discussions had a practical aim in view, for there was still room for additions and deviations as Jewish law was not as yet stabilized. Nahmanides has, therefore, an eye for the ultimate decisions of the law in his Novellae and after long discussions, he points out the decisions according to his opinion, often deviating from those of his predecessors.

His *Novellae* and commentaries were greatly revered by the scholars of the succeeding generations, and some of the decisions arrived at by Nahmanides through his discussions in the commentaries were later incorporated in the adopted codes.

Besides his *Novellae,* Nahmanides also wrote an Halakic book called *Milhamot Adonai* (The Wars of the Lord), in which he defends Isaac Al-Fasi against the objections and refutations of Zerahia ha-Levi in his book *Ha-Maor* (Vol. I, Ch. X, Sect. 149). He is very zealous for the honor of Al-Fasi, as it was his general tendency to consider the words of the earlier scholars as authoritative and any deviation from their opinion as an irreverence. This tendency biased his method of defense in two ways. First, it is evident in the treatment of his opponent Zerahia towards whom he displays a spirit of intolerance in making caustic remarks which do not agree with his otherwise meek and humble character. Second, it is reflected in his endeavor to defend Al-Fasi at all events. In fact, he declares in the preface to the second part of the *Milhamoth* which covers the order *Moed* of Al-Fasi's Compendium, "We will defend the words of our master at all times even in places where his words may be doubted, for it is our duty to do so in regard to the writings of our predecessors. Besides they are not here to defend themselves." This method, of course, gave a peculiar ring to the book. Nahmanides used all his keenness of mind to accomplish his purpose. His discussions bear, therefore, an extreme pilpulistic character. Still, in view of the fact that as the result of such discussions, there emerged a new interpretation of passages in Al-Fasi's Compendium, high value is attached to his remarks, and the *Milhamoth* may be considered a commentary on the Al-Fasi.

Nahmanides who firmly established the Franco-German method of Talmud study in Spain left many disciples, the greatest of whom was Solomon ben Adret (Rashba) (1245-1310), a native of Barcelona and rabbi of that city for half a century. Ben Adret was a man of great piety and an ardent student of the Talmud. In fact, he specialized in this field, and though he knew other sciences as he himself testifies,[1] yet he wrote little on other subjects save Rabbinics. He also studied under Rabbi Jona of Gerona, the master of Moses ben Nahman himself and Isaac ben Nahman of Gerona.

Ben Adret was a prolific writer in all fields of Rabbinic literature, that of commentaries, codes and Responsa. Of the last two, we will speak later. His commentaries or *Novellae* (Hidushim) extend to

[1] Minhat Kanaoth, epistle 43.

sixteen tractates, covering most of the three important orders of the Talmud, *Moed, Nashim, Nezikin*, also the three tractates of *Berakot, Hulin* and *Niddah* of the other three orders. His method is, in a way, a further development of that of Nahmanides, that of isolated discussions on selected passages where the opinions of previous scholars are analyzed, elucidated, confirmed or rejected. In his keenness of analysis and ability to reconcile contradictions, he surpasses Nahmanides, while on the other hand, he is more of a commentator than the former. The passages he discusses and comments upon are more numerous and are frequently consecutive. There is hardly a page in the Talmud from which he does not select a few passages for explanation. He also devotes considerable attention to the elucidation of their meaning pointing out the insufficiencies of the previous commentators. For this purpose, he is very painstaking in ascertaining the right readings (Girsoth) and offers many excellent emendations. He quotes the Palestinian Talmud, as well as many earlier commentators especially Rashi and the Tosafists, frequently for the purpose of clarifyng cretain passages.

Like Nahmanides and other Spanish commentators, he does not forget the practical aim of the *Novellae,* and whenever necessary indicates the ultimate decision of the Law. In general, the commentaries of the *Rashba* resemble the *Tosofoth* in spirit and manner. His *Novellae* were studied assiduously by subsequent scholars and were held superior even to those of his master.

43. *ASHER BEN YEHIEL AND OTHER COMMENTATORS*

One of the great Rabbinic scholars of the century was Asher ben Yehiel (Rosh) (1250-1327). He was born in Germany and studied under the great Rabbi Meir of Rothenburg, one of the last Tosafists, and it was in that country that he spent a great part of his life. When his master was seized by the Emperor Rudolph and confined as prisoner in the fortress of Ensisheim in 1286, Asher because of the fact that the Emperor sought to hold him for the ransom of Rabbi Meir, left Germany. The exact year of his departure is not known. He wandered around in many lands, stayed for some time in Montpelier and other cities of the Provence until in 1304, he was invited to become the Rabbi of Toledo, the leading community in Spain. There he spent twenty-three years, and was acknowledged as the spiritual leader of the entire Spanish Jewry. His influence, however, went beyond the borders of Spain, and homage was paid him by Jewish scholars of all lands. The academy which he established at Toledo was crowded with students from all Jewries, hailing even from distant Slavonic countries, such as Bohemia and far Russia.

The attitude of the *Rosh* towards other studies outside of the Talmud was typical of one who spent the greater part of his life in Germany. It was one of contempt, as he considered all other sciences inferior to the knowledge of the Torah and not worth spending time on. Yet he was not a blind fanatic, though he took an active part in the issuing of the ban against the study of philosophy (Ch. X, Sect. 153), for his statements in that regard were actuated by a belief that the knowledge of the Torah was all sufficient and intrinsically higher than all other studies. He even acknowledged the great value of philosophy *per se* and praised the philosophers, calling them wise men, but he was suspicious of its study fearing that it would ultimately lead men away from tradition. Rabbi Asher was distinguished not only by his great learning, but also by his noble character. He was a man of truth and justice, and his court was so famed for that quality that even the government referred many cases to him for decision. In spite of his exalted position, he was meek and humble in his relations with people and never forced his opinion upon others, but presented it in such wise as to make it acceptable to all. It was both on account of his learning and his high ethical qualities that he was considered the leader of Jewry in his day.

It is to be expected that a man of great ability devoting himself to one branch of study should be prolific in his literary output, and the *Rosh* was no exception to the rule. Like Solomon ben Adret, he contributed to every branch of Rabbinic study. His Magnum Opus is the Code or the Compendium (Sect. B), but he also wrote commentaries and many Responsa. The commentaries of the *Rosh* are of two kinds, commentaries proper and *Tosofoth* which are printed under the name of *Tosofoth ha-Rosh* (The Additions or Glosses of Rabbi Asher). These *Tosofoth* extend to seventeen tractates. They are like other *Tosofoth,* glosses and remarks. On the whole, Rabbi Asher's remarks are distinguished by their simplicity and logical explanation and not by keenness of analysis and the ability to unravel intricate scholastic knots which are displayed in the *Novellae* of Nahmanides and ben Adret. Most of his *Tosofoth* are still in manuscript, only those to eight tractates having been printed. His commentaries proper are only on three tractates, that of *Nedarim,* dealing with vows and their annulment in the order of *Nashim,* and *Tamid* and *Midoth* in the order of *Kodashim*. The two tractates deal with the order of the sacrifices in the Temple and the description of the Temple respectively. These commentaries are devoted primarily to the explanation of the text in regular order. They are brief, concise and elucidating, and resemble the work of Rashi though he seldom quotes him. Instead he mentions frequently the comments of some Tosafists, especially Rabbi Eliezer of Metz who most likely had written commentaries on some tractates.

Rabbi Asher also wrote commentaries on the Mishnah of the orders *Zeraim* and *Taharoth*. But these are almost supercommentaries on those of Rabbi Samson, as they contain only notes and additions to his explanations. However, in the commentary on *Taharoth,* he is more original and not so dependent on Rabbi Samson. Yet, with all this prolific work, Rabbi Asher's fame does not rest on his commentaries and *Tosofoth* but on his great Compendium.

Of the other commentators of this century, the first in time and in importance was Rabbi Meir ben Todros ha-Levi Abulafia, Rabbi of Toledo (1180-1235). He was a man of rigorous piety and great religious zeal. It was he who first dared to attack Maimonides for his too liberal views on resurrection, immortality and kindred matters, and thus gave impetus to the anti-Maimunist movement (Ch. X). Rabbi Meir, though born and reared in Spain, preferred the Franco-German method of Talmud study, devoting himself entirely to Rabbinics. He wrote commentaries on a number of tractates, of which those on *Sanhedrin* and *Baba Bathra* are extant. These bear the name *Yad Ramah* (The Exalted Hand, *Ramah* being the initials of Rabbi Meir ha-Levi). His commentaries really deserve the title, as they are quite consecutive and hardly any passage is omitted. In spite of his great admiration for the Franco-German method of Talmud study, he follows in his commentary the Spanish method and gives the gist of the discussion in each passage in his own words with explanations and remarks. He is very careful to explain each difficult expression tracing it to its source, the Bible or the Talmud. His style is clear and lucid but too verbose. On the whole, it is a fair specimen of the Spanish type of commentaries.

Two other prominent scholars, contemporaries of Rabbi Meir, also wrote commentaries on various tractates of the Talmud. The first was Rabbi Jonathan of Lunel (d. c. 1215 in Palestine), a friend and admirer of Maimonides who championed his cause against Rabbi Meir ha-Levi. His commentaries are extant in manuscript on the tractates of *Shebuoth* and *Sanhedrin*. In addition, he was the first to write a complete commentary on one of the tractates of Al-Fasi's Compendium, that of *Erubin*. The second was Rabbi Jonah Gerundi, the teacher of Nahmanides and ben Adret. He was one of the leaders in the camp of the anti-Maimunists, not out of disrespect to the great teacher but rather out of a feeling of pure piety, fearing that the too liberal ideas of Maimonides might injure the simple faith. However, he was the first to retract his statements against Maimonides publicly when this strife in Jewry led to disastrous results. The commentaries of Rabbi Jonah extend to the tractates of *Sanhedrin* and *Baba Bathra* and are more in the nature of *Novellae* than the standard type of commentaries. A commentary on the tractate *Berakot* of Al-Fasi's Compendium was also ascribed to him and was even printed under his name. But critical investigation has shown that it is not from the hand of Rabbi Jonah himself, but was written by one of his pupils from notes taken of the lectures of the master. This commentary is complete as it explains the passages consecutively, gives the gist of Talmudic discussions omitted by Al-Fasi, and also utilizes other devices, such as comparison of passages in the Babylonian and Palestinian Talmuds in order to clarify the meaning of the discussion.

Of the commentators of the time of ben Adret we may note Rabbi Aaron ha-Levi (1235-1300), a great Rabbinic scholar of the generation who distinguished himself in the other fields of Rabbinic literature. His commentaries are extant on two tractates, *Ketuboth* and *Kedushin* of the order of *Nashim* and are still in manuscript form.

The Franco-German center of learning contributed during this century, besides many *Tosofoth* collections to various tractates of the Talmud, only one commentary on the Mishnaic order of *Taharoth* by Rabbi Meir of Rothenburg (1230-1293), the master of the *Rosh*. This together with his editing of the printed *Tosofoth* on the tractate *Yoma* are his only contributions to the explanation of the Talmud. His main work lay in the field of Responsa which will be discussed later.

A commentator of note was Menahem ben Solomon Meiri (1249-1306) or as he was called Don Vidal of Perpignan, Provence. Menahem, like most of the Provence scholars of his day, was a man of versatile knowledge. He was a friend of the sciences and in the great controversy about the works of Maimonides defended him vigorously. He also possessed a keen historical sense and wrote a history of Jewish tradition which served as an introduction to his commentary on Aboth.

Meiri wrote commentaries on all the tractates of the Talmud, thirty-six in number, but only eight of them were printed, while the rest are still in manuscript. The method of his commentaries differs greatly from those of his contemporaries, resembling that of Maimonides whom he most likely took as his model. It is a logical one and proceeds as follows: At the beginning of each tractate a brief introduction is given explaining the reason for the proper place of this tractate in the order of the Talmud, its theme, the subjects discussed, and the division of such discussion. Each chapter is again introduced by an analysis of the subjects treated in the group of the Mishnoth contained therein. The commentary proper centers around the Mishnoth. Each Mishnah is extensively explained with reference to the discussion in the Gemarah and with a view to the ultimate decision. The Gemarah is explained in a much briefer way and the old Gaonic method is followed in giving the gist of the discussion in the passage with additional explanations. The comments on the Gemarah are not intended for young students but for those who already possess a knowledge of the Talmud. On the other hand, the explanations offered of the content of the Mishnah are those of a real commentary, detailed and clear. Rabbi Menahem had also the practical phase in mind, and quotes at the end of each discussion of a subject the proper decision.

The author drew upon quite a number of sources for his commentary. He quotes frequently the Palestinian Talmud and also the previous commentators, even a few of those whose works are no longer in existence. These predecessors are usually quoted by special titles of respect and not by their names. Thus, the title, "The great Rabbis" (Gedolē ha-Rabbanim) refers to Rashi, "The great writers of books" (Gedolē ha-Mehabrim) to Maimonides, "The great commentators" to Abraham ben David (Raabad) and so on. On the whole, the commentary of the Meiri is an excellent specimen of the Spanish-Provence type of commentaries.

44. THE FOURTEENTH AND FIFTEENTH CENTURIES

The earliest commentator of the fourteenth century is Rabbi Yom Tob ben Abraham (otherwise known as *Ritba*) Ibn Ashbilla (d. 1360). He was a disciple of both ben Adret and Rabbi Aaron ha-Levi. Like his masters, he devoted himself primarily to the study of the Talmud, though he seemed to take some interest in philosophic studies and even wrote a book defending Maimonides against the objections raised by Nahmanides in his Bible commentary. Rabbi Yom Tob wrote only comemntaries, for no other Halakic book is ascribed to him. They cover almost every tractate of the important orders, *Moed, Nashim, Nesikin* with a few exceptions and also tractates *Berakot* and *Niddah*. His method was like that of his master's *Novellae,* consisting of keen remarks and analytic discussions where refutations of the opinions of previous commentators and glossators are frequent. On account of his great love for inventing new differentations in the meaning of legal concepts and scholastic suppositions, his commentaries were very lengthy. Recognizing their impracticability for students in this form, he himself revised them, making a shorter edition where only the best of his *Novellae* are retained. The first edition, however, was not entirely destroyed and is extant to some tractates. The printed commentaries, though, are all of the second edition. Yet in spite of his love for ingenious pilpulistic discussion, we find in Rabbi Yom Tob's *Novellae* many remarks which explain the meaning of the passages, and since he was also careful to ascertain the correct readings their value is considerable.

A commentator of considerable importance was Rabbi Nissim ben Reuben Gerundi (d. c. 1375) who like ben Adret occupied the post of Rabbi at Barcelona, and exerted great influence over the entire Spanish Jewry. He was primarily distinguished as a commentator on the Compendium of Al-Fasi. We possess his commentary on fourteen tractates of the Compendium, and he is considered one of the two standard commentators of that work. In his Al-Fasi commentary, he inclines towards the analytic-discussion method of Nahmanides and ben Adret, and displays great skill in making ingenious interpretations. He relies mostly on his own mental powers and pays little respect to authority if he is in disagreement with its pronouncement. He, therefore, does not hesitate to refute Rashi's inerpretations or those of his predecessors. When necessary, he explains the meaning of certain words or expressions very briefly, but his explanations of entire passages are lengthy. There, he quotes the views of previous commentators, sometimes for purposes of refutation, and sometimes for confirmation of his own views. Rabbi Nissim also wrote commentaries on eleven tractates of the Talmud proper, but while most of them are of the *Novellae* type, the one on the tractate *Nedarim* is an excellent specimen of real commentation. This tractate which deals with vows and the modes of their annulment was not studied by the Gaonim in their academies, and was to some degree neglected by other commentators. Even the great Rashi did not do justice to its intricate subjects. Rabbi Nissim is the only commentator who explained it adequately. But even here, he combined together with plain commentation the Tosafist method of raising difficulties and removing them, so that nothing might be left unintelligible. Very frequently, Nissim gives the Halakic decision derived from the passage. The Palestinian Talmud is quoted often by our author for purposes of elucidation, and likewise Nahmanides and ben Adret are quoted quite frequently in connection with the Halakic decision. (Pesak.)

Joseph Habiba, the disciple of Rabbi Nissim who lived during the second half of the fourteenth century, was the second commentator to devote himself primarily to the Compendium of Al-Fasi. We know very little about his life, not even the name of his father. We can only infer from the fact that he calls both Rabbi Nissim and Rabbi Hasdai Crescas his teachers that he was younger than either, and since Crescas died in 1410, Habiba most likely lived some years after that. It seems that he undertook to complete his teacher's commentary on the Compendium of Al-Fasi. We find, accordingly, in print Habiba's commentary on seven tractates, those which were not commented upon by Rabbi Nissim. His commentary, the *Nimuḳē Yoseph* (The Penetrations or Deep Reasons of Joseph) is a clear and simple one. He evidently did not belong to the keen-minded pilpulists, but concentrated his efforts upon clarifying the meaning of the passages as well as at arriving at Halakic decisions. For this purpose, he quoted copiously the remarks of both his predecessors and contemporaries. These quotations occupy the greatest part of his commentary. On account of his efforts to ascertain the correct decision of the Halakah, Habiba was highly esteemed by later codifiers and his commentary is frequently quoted by them. He also wrote *Novellae* on several tractates of the Talmud.

With Habiba the list of commentars of the fourteenth century closes. The following century the fifteenth, produced scarcely any important commentator whose work is worth recording. On the whole, it was a century of decline for Rabbinic literature both in Spain and in Germany. This decline was, of course, partly due to the exceptional suffering the Jews of both centers experienced, especially in Spain. There, the fifteenth century was ushered in by the terrible persecutions of the year 1391, and closed with the expulsion in 1492. These were merely the outstanding tribulations sustained by that Jewry besides many smaller ones that occurred between these termini. Under such circumstances, literary contributions in a field which demands great mental acumen could hardly be expected. The situation in Germany was little better, and the results were similar.

45. *THE SIXTEENTH CENTURY*

The sixteenth century was a period of great productivity in Rabbinic literature. During that time, as pointed out above, two new centers of learning made their appearance, that of the East and that of the North, the Slavonic. These took the place of the two older ones, Spain and Germany respectively, and on the whole, their literary productions retain the characteristics of the type of literature produced in the centers they superseded.

The Eastern center brought forth a few noted commentators. The first one was Rabbi Obadiah di Bertinoro (1470-1520) i. e. from the city of Bertinoro, in Italy. At the end of the fifteenth century, he emigrated to Palestine and settled in Jerusalem, where he wrote his commentary on the Mishnah. It comprises the entire Mishnah covering every tractate, and is as complete as possible. It is written with a view of explaining the Mishnah to those who make a special study of it apart from the Gemarah. His method is exceptionally well adapted for this purpose. He explains every word and expression which needs explanation, but his primary interest lies in clarifying the meaning of whole passages. His treatment is both detailed and inclusive, inasmuch as he interprets the Mishnah in accordance with the results arrived at in the discussions of the Gemarah. Bertinoro also supplies all necessary details regarding the subjects treated in the various Mishnoth, even if these are not given in the Gemarah immediately adjoining these particular Mishnoth. He does not deviate from his main purpose, that of commenting upon the text, and therefore, his work contains no pilpulistic or scholastic discussions. Hence its great value. As a rule, he gives one interpretation to a passage, only on rare occasions offering two, quoting the second in the name of its author. Very few sources are given by our commentator except that of Maimonides' commentary on the Mishnah which is mentioned quite frequently. His stay in Palestine was of great assistance to Obadiah in his work, for the conditions of life there in his time resembled the life reflected in the Mishnah, and his acquaintance with it as well as with the Arabic language enabled him to explain many words and customs mentioned in the text. He made special use of this knowledge in his commentary on the orders *Zeraim* and *Taharoth* which treat of the daily life of the Jew in the home, field and workshop. It was to the ascertaining of the names of implements, fruits and utensile and their descriptions that he applied the knowledge gained from experience. To all other qualities, we must also add that of style which is clear and concise and very seldom verbose. All these qualities made the work of Obadiah the standard commentary on the Mishnah which is printed in all editions. For the sake of brevity, it is called *R'aab,* i. e. Rabbi Obadiah Bertinoro.

From Egypt hails another commentator or, to be more exact, a collector of commentaries, Rabbi Bezallel Ashkenazi (d. 1530) of Alexandria, a disciple of David Aba Zimri (Sect. 69). He compiled a collection of excerpts from commentaries under the name of *Shitta Meḳubezet* or *Asephat Zeḳenim.* The first title means a Composite Way or Method of Interpretation, the meaning of the second is An Assembly of Elders, that is a collection of the remarks of early commentators. The greater part of his collection which covers twenty-one tractates is printed, while a part is still in manuscript. The excerpts are arranged in the order of the pages of the tractates from the beginning to the end. On each page of the Talmud, passages are selected and their interpretations by the various commentators are given. Among the commentators whose works are frequently excerpted are: Hanannel Gaon, Joseph Ibn Migash, Abraham ben David, Nahmanides, ben Adret, Nissim Gerundi and many others. He also excerpted the various editions of the *Tosofoth,* many of those which are not printed with the Talmud, and translated many excerpts from commentaries written in Arabic. Ashkenazi thus performed a great service to Rabbinic literature, inasmuch as he preserved many parts of excellent commentaries from oblivion. He himself also wrote glosses to a number of tractates.

46. THE POLISH CENTER OF LEARNING

During this century, Poland rises into prominence as a great center of learning. Literary activity which hitherto was non-existent, or at least not noticeable, suddenly bursts forth and the number of books in Rabbinics in all its branches becomes exceedingly large. This sudden outburst of literary productivity was the result of accumulated and stored up energy. For although, we have exceedingly few books by Polish authors prior to the sixteenth century, we have, on the other hand, numerous references by German and Spanish authors of the previous centuries to Russian and Polish scholars who visited academies in Western lands. These scholars, on returning to their country had undoubtedly established small academies of their own where pupils congregated and sat at the feet of their masters. Thus, Torah was not unknown in Poland. Nevertheless, this blossoming forth of scholarship needed an impetus from without. That impetus was found in the migration of prominent scholars from Germany into Poland who, with their coming, stimulated the study of the Talmud, and made that country the seminary of great scholars for many generations to come.

Of these savants, the most important one was Rabbi Jacob Polack (d. 1541), who is often called the father of Torah in Poland. Little is known of Rabbi Jacob's early life, as not even the date of his birth can be accurately determined. We know, though, that he was the disciple of Rabbi Jacob Margolis of Nurenburg, Germany, and that in the year 1490, he shared the Rabbinical post in Prague with Rabbi Isaac, the son of the former. At the beginning of the sixteenth century, around the year 1507, Rabbi Jacob Polack left for Poland and became rabbi and head of a Talmudic academy at Krakow, where he carried on his activity for over three decades.[2]

Rabbi Jacob is considered the inventor of a new method in the study of the Talmud. This is the extreme pilpulistic method known as the Hiluk, i. e. division and analysis. It consisted primarily in taking an apparently unified Talmudic subject and with fine analytic ability dissecting it into its component parts, drawing nice distinctions in their meanings, and then building up a new subject out of these newly defined parts. This method afforded ample room for mental ingenuity and hair splitting definitions which enchanted the young students. It was for this reason that Rabbi Jacob's academy was crowded with students who later became scholars themselves. His leading disciple was Rabbi Shakhnah, Rabbi of Lublin, the teacher and father-in-law of Rabbi Moses Isserlis, the greatest codifier of Poland. Yet, in spite of his great learning and sharp mind Rabbi Jacob left no books. Only a few Responsa and decisions in

[2] It is almost the consensus of historians that Rabbi Jacob was first rabbi in Prague and then came to Krakow. There is, however, a dissenting opinion which asserts that Rabbi Jacob was born in Poland and was first rabbi at Krakow and thence went to Prague. It bases itself on the fact that his name Polack would indicate his Polish origin. See Rabbi Hayyim Nathan Dembitzer in his introduction to his Kelilath Yofi, pp. 2-4.

certain religious matters are quoted in his name in the books of later authors. He must also have written some glosses and addenda to the code of Moses of Coucy, known as the *Semag* (Sect. B), as such are referred to by Solomon Luria, but they were lost. Likewise, little is left of the writings of his disciple, Rabbi Shakhnah. It was left for a younger contemporary to begin the period of literary activity in Poland.

That scholar was Solomon Luria (1510-1574), known briefly as *Rashal* (Rabbi Solomon Luria). Rabbi Solomon was born in Posen, the son of Rabbi Yehiel of Worms who traced his descent to Rashi. In his youth, he studied in Worms under his maternal grandfather, Rabbi Isaac Korbin, and later returned to Poland where for some time, he studied privately in the city of Ostroh where his father-in-law, Rabbi Kalman held the post of rabbi. At the age of forty, he succeeded his father-in-law to that office. Later, he was invited to Lublin to take the place of Rabbi Shakhnah and resided there until the day of his death. Solomon Luria, though considered one of the greatest Rabbinic authorities of his day, did not enjoy a peaceful life, as he had many opponents who often attacked him severely despite the fact that he was himself of peaceful disposition and of a high moral nature. The cause of the antagonism was Luria's love of truth, and his fearless criticism of the opinions of others if these did not stand the test of reason. It is this characteristic, the indefatigable search for truth which stamps his numerous writings.

Luria wrote commentaries, codes and Responsa. His most important book was the *Yam Shel Shlomoh* (The Sea of Solomon, with reference to his name and to Kings, Ch. VII, 23), which is both a code and a commentary on seven tractates of the Talmud, viz. *Betza, Gittin, Kidushin, Yebamoth, Ketuboth, Baba Kama* and *Hulin*. While it is primarily a code, it contains many comments on a large number of passages in the Talmud.

His method is not the pilpulistic one, but of a very plain and lucid nature. He usually quotes the explanations of others, and where these are not, in his opinion, suitable, offers his own. His real value as a commentator is, however, not based upon the *Yam Shel Shlomoh* but upon his other book, *Hokmath Shlomoh* (The Wisdom of Solomon) which covers the entire Talmud. This contains glosses and comments on passages both in the Gemarah proper and in the commentaries of Rashi and the *Tosofoth*. It can, therefore, be considered both as a commentary and supercommentary. The great value of the book consists not so much in the comments, as in the correction of readings. Luria spared no effort in ascertaining the correct readings in the Talmud, searching diligently all ancient manuscripts of the Talmud, comparing the readings in the quotations of passages by early authors and employing his own reasoning powers to determine the proper word, when such seemed to him doubtful. As a result, he substituted in his *Hokmath Shlomoh* hundreds of correct readings in place of the faulty ones. These corrections extend both to the Gemarah, to Rashi and to Tosofoth. Their value is exceedingly great, for a correct reading removes many a difficulty in the interpretation of a passage. His comments are brief and clear and contribute greatly to the understanding of the Talmud. The glosses and comments of Luria were considered of such importance that they were reprinted in subsequent editions of the Talmud at the back of each tractate. The later editions of the Talmud have also incorporated in the text proper many of his readings, thus improving the text of the Gemarah greatly.

47. *RABBI MEIR LUBLIN AND RABBI SAMUEL EDEL'S*

The most prominent supercommentators or *Novellae* writers of the century were Rabbi Meir Lublin, known as *Maharam* (Morenu ha-Rab Meir) and Rabbi Samuel Eliezer ha-Levi Edel's, known as *Maharshah* (Morenu ha-Rab Samuel Eliezer). He was also known as Samuel Edel's after his famous mother-in-law. The first (1558-1616) born in Lublin, studied in Krakow under Rabbi Isaac Shapiro who later became his father-in-law. At the age of twenty-four, he became the head of the academy at Lublin, and five years later, was invited to succeed his father-in-law in the Rabbinical post at Krakow. From there, he went to Lemberg and ultimately back to Lublin, where he died. Rabbi Meir was one of the leading scholars of his day and was greatly respected for his learning, but his irascible temper caused a number of differences between him and the other scholars of his generation, which differences were at times the reason for his leaving one rabbinical post and accepting another.

Rabbi Meir wrote Responsa as well as glosses and *Novellae* to most of the tractates of the Talmud, but is known chiefly for the latter. The *Novellae* contain primarily explanations of passages in Rashi and the *Tosofoth,* and only here and there, comments are offered on passages in the Gemarah proper. He is brief in his comments and really clarifies many a difficult passage in Rashi or *Tosofoth.* His method is that of the commentator, endeavoring to straighten out contradictions in the statement of the Tosafists and make their remarks more comprehensible. He possessed a critical and fearless spirit and very often criticized the opinions of other commentators in harsh words. Rabbi Meir was primarily interested in Halakah and passed over any Agadic parts of the Gemarah without any comment.

The second, Rabbi Samuel Eliezer Edel's (1565-1632) was born in Krakow and studied under his father, Rabbi Judah ha-Levi. After marrying the daughter of Rabbi Moses Ashkenazi of Posen, he settled in that city and conducted there an academy for twenty years. His mother-in-law Edel, a rich woman, maintained that academy at her own expense, and after her death, Rabbi Eliezer was forced to disband the school because of lack of support. He then held rabbinical posts successively in Chelm, Lublin and Ostroh.

Samuel Edel's was primarily a teacher of Talmud and greatly rejoiced in imparting instruction to the hundreds of students who flocked to his academy. To this work, he devoted his entire energy and the keenness of his intellect. The results of his teaching and expounding of the Talmud during a life time are embodied in his *Novellae* to almost the entire Talmud. Like those of Rabbi Meir Lublin, his glosses and commentaries are primarily intended to elucidate the passages in Rashi and the *Tosofoth,* but they differ greatly from the *Novellae* of the former in their character. They are distinguished by a spirit of keen logical analysis and sharp-mindedness. In fact, Rabbi Samuel applied to his *Novellae* the same method employed by the Tosafists themselves, that of testing the veracity of the statements made by Rashi and *Tosofoth* by raising objections to them and refuting these objections by a deeper interpretation of the meaning of the statements. At times, however, he turns plain commentator and interprets the difficult passages of the Gemarah, Rashi and Tosofoth. Rabbi Samuel, unlike Rabbi Meir Lublin, was greatly interested in the Agadic part of the Talmud and wrote extensive *Novellae* to such portions of the Gemarah (Hidushē Agadoth). His comments on the Agada are permeated with a spirit of rationalism, which testifies to a deep study on his part of the works of the Jewish philosophers.

48. THE SEVENTEENTH AND EIGHTEENTH CENTURIES

The last two centuries of the Mediaeval period were, on the whole, a period of decline in the field of Rabbinic literature. In most of the Jewries of the world, there was a marked lassitude in intellectual productivity. The mass of literature which was constantly accumulating, especially in the field of Rabbinics, weighed heavily upon the later scholars. Very little that was new could be added to all that had already been said by the scholars of the previous generations, and hence the lessening of productivity. There were, of course, other causes which brought about this state of affairs, chief among which was the weariness experienced by West-European Jewries, particularly that of Germany as a result of the continued suffering which in turn caused mental exhaustion. Poland formed an exception to the rule. There, in spite of the fact that the Jews experienced in the middle of the seventeenth century one of the most terrible persecutions, that of the Cossack massacres,[3] the study of the Talmud was never interrupted. As soon as the country quieted down, the academies were reopened and teachers and students resumed their work. Poland continued its intellectual supremacy during the entire period. In fact, it became the very center of Talmudic learning, exercising great influence upon the Jewries of other countries. Almost all the great rabbis and scholars of Germany, during these centuries, were either born in Poland and only later in life settled in German countries or were studenets of Polish scholars.

In Poland, therefore, literary activity in Rabbinics continued unabated. Many were the scholars who contributed to one or another branch of Rabbinic literature, and consequently a considerable number of them still wrote commentaries on the Talmud.

One of the most important of these commentators was Rabbi Yom Tob Lippman Heller Wallerstein (1579-1654). He was born in western Germany but studied at Prague under the famous Rabbi Judah Liwa ben Bezallel, the reputed creator of the legendary *Golem.* At the age of eighteen, he was appointed judge (dayan) in the same city, and a short while later was elected rabbi of Vienna. From there, he again went to Prague as chief rabbi where he was involved in a quarrel with some of the leaders of the community who brought false charges against him to the government and he was put into prison. He then left for Poland serving as rabbi at Nemerow in the

[3] These massacres took place in the years 1648-1649, and are known as the massacres of *Tah* and *Tat,* i. e. the 5408 and 5409 according to the era of creation, their cause was the uprising in the Ukraine of the Cossacks under the leadership of Bogdon Chmelnicki, against the Poles. During these two years, the Cossack hordes swept through the Ukraine and Galicia, perpetrating the most atrocious massacres in many cities upon the Poles and Jews. It is estimated that a quarter of a million Jews perished as a result of these butcheries.

Ukraine, Ludmir, and finally at Krakow. During his stay in Ludmir, Rabbi Yom Tob met with an incident similar to the one experienced at Prague. On account of his endeavors to combat simony among the rabbis in Poland, his enemies informed against him to the government, whereupon he was ordered to leave the city, but later at the trial was acquitted and exonerated from all charges.

Rabbi Yom Tob differed greatly from the other rabbis of Poland. Though like them he devoted himself to the study of the Talmud and codes yet he did not neglect other studies as he was well versed in mathematics and knew Latin and German. His other studies, especially that of Jewish philosophy, made him more liberal in his views and opinions, which liberality is reflected in his writings. Rabbi Yom Tob was a prolific writer and composed numerous works covering all phases of Rabbinics. But his fame rests chiefly on his commentary on the entire Mishnah, known as *Tosofoth Yom Tob* (The Additions or Glosses of Yom Tob). In his introduction to the commentary, Rabbi Yom Tob states the reason which impelled him to compose it. His teacher, Rabbi Judah Liwa instituted the custom that groups of people should make the study of the Mishnah a daily affair, and as this custom spread to other cities, the study of the Mishnah became a regular part of instruction in Jewry. There arose, therefore, a need for an adequate and all sufficient commentary on the Mishnah. Upon examining the previous commentaries, Rabbi Yom Tob found them all wanting. Even that of Bertinoro, the most extensive and explicit, did not, in his opinion, fill all requirements. Still, because of its excellent qualities, he took it as a basis and called his own *Tosofoth,* namely additions to that of Bertinoro. His purpose is, he says, to straighten out contradictions between Mishnaic statements not noticed by the former, and at times to explain the comments of Bertinoro himself. It was his intention that the Mishnah should become an open book to all, and that no passages should remain obscure.

Rabbi Yom Tob carried out his purpose almost to perfection. His *Tosofoth* really do clarify many a Mishnah, and his comments, on the whole, add much to its understanding. He quotes extensively from the commentaries of his predecessors, always mentioning the name of the commentator. Very often, he criticizes these explanations and shows their inadequacy, and then offers his own. He is especially ingenious in his interpretation of the Agadic part of the Mishnah. Yom Tob's commentary on the tractate *Aboth* reflects his great learning and wide study of Jewish philosophy and ethics, as well as the liberality of his views. On account of all these qualities to which we may add also that of his fine Hebrew style, the *Tosofoth Yom Tob* gained wide popularity among the students of the Mishnah, and took its place of honor beside that of the commentary of Obadiah Bertinoro.

Another commentator of note was Rabbi Meir Schiff (1608-1644) known as *Maharam Schiff* (Morēnu Rabbi Meir Schiff). He was born in Frankfurt on the Main, was rabbi first in Fulda and later in Prague where he conducted a large academy and was respected greatly by the scholars of his generation. His activity at that famous seat of learning, however, did not last long, as death overtook him at the early age of thirty-six.

He wrote a number of books including homilies and a commentary on the Bible, but his fame rests on his *Novellae* to the Talmud. They are the gist of his discussions in the academy and covered originally the entire Talmud, but a large part was burned at the time of the great conflagration in Frankfurt in 1711. The part that remains covers ten tractates. Rabbi Meir did not like the pilpulistic system of his generation but endeavored rather to elicit the plain meaning of the Talmudic passages upon which he commented. He, therefore, does not propound in his *Novellae* any questions in order to find for them an ingenious answer, but merely elucidates the content of the passages as he sees fit. Very often, he rebukes his predecessors, such as the *Maharshah* or *Maharam* for their pilpulistic explanation of a passage and remarks that it can be explained very simply. He also disliked verbosity and was very economical in his style. This last feature ultimately undid his entire effort which was to explain the Talmud as briefly as possible. On account of the excessive brevity of his comments, a large number of them are difficult to understand and need a supercommentary. In fact, such a commentary was written by Rabbi Mordecai Mordush and is appended to Rabbi Meir's own commentary.

49. OTHER COMMENTATORS

Of the many writers of *Novellae* and glosses to the Talmud from the second half of the seventeenth to the end of the eighteenth century, the following are of special importance and deserve to be mentioned. The first is Rabbi Jacob Joshua Falk (1680-1754). He was rabbi in Lemberg, Berlin, Metz and Frankfurt on the Main, and gained a great reputation as one of the leading scholars of his day. While at the last named city, he participated in the strife between the Rabbis Jacob Emden and Jonathan Eibeshütz, taking the side of the former and accusing the latter of Sabbatainism, i. e. being a follower of the false Messiah, Sabbatai Zevi. His great work was the collection of *Novellae* in five parts to most tractates of the Talmud, under the title of *Penē Yoshua* (The Face of Joshua). The work is distinguished by mental brilliancy and keenness of analysis in the manner of the day. It gained great popularity in his day, as well as during the succeeding generations. The *Penē Yoshua* is still a favorite handbook with many a Talmudic student who wants to delve into the intricate Halakic discussions.

The second figure of importance was Ezekiel Landau (1713-1793), rabbi in several leading Jewish communities and ultimately in Prague. Rabbi Ezekiel was one of the giants of Talmudic learning at the beginning of the modern period and was considered, in his day, the greatest authority on Rabbinic questions. He took an active part in the Emden-Eibeshütz strife and endeavored to pacify the opposing sides. He was also one of the rabbis who witnessed the dawn of the modern period and opposed bitterly Mendelsohn's German Pentateuch translation, in which he saw the herald of a new spirit that was destined to change the entire life of the Jews.

Rabbi Ezekiel is especially known for his collection of Responsa, but he also wrote a book of *Novellae* to a number of tractates of the Talmud by the name of *Zelah,* the abbreviation of the words *Ziun l'Nefesh Hayya* (A Monument to a Living Soul). The book is an example of the extreme pilpulistic method of the day as well as of the great learning of the author.

The third was Rabbi Pinchas ha-Levi Hurwitz (1740-1805). He hailed from Lithuania, but was famous for his great learning throughout Jewry, and he was later called to the leading rabbinical post of Frankfurt on the Main. Like the other rabbis of the day, he fought bitterly the rise of the Enlightenment Movement (Haskalah), but towards the end of his days, he saw the futility of his struggle. He was the last of the line of Frankfurt rabbis who contributed to Rabbinic literature. He wrote *Novellae* to two tractates of the Talmud, *Ketuboth* and *Kidushin*. The former is called the *Book of Ketubah* (Marriage Contract) or the *Sepher Haflaah* (The Book of Distinction), the second the *Sepher ha-Makne*. Both contain *Novellae* of the pilpulistic type with many comments on various passages. These books gained favor with the Talmudic students and are still used in Talmudic academies.

B. Codes

50. CENTERS AND METHODS OF CODIFICATION

Just as the commentary of Rashi and the glosses and additions of the Tosafists did not stop the process of commentation, but even gave it fresh impetus in a measure, so did the Code of Maimonides, complete as it was, not stop the process of codification of the laws in Jewry. As noted above, it went on without interruption. There were a number of reasons for the continuation. First, the division of opinion as well as the difference in customs between the two Jewries, the Spanish and the Franco-German. Second, the Code of Maimonides, though it enjoyed great authority, was found wanting by the scholars who succeeded him, mainly for the reason that he did not quote the sources whence he derived his decisions, nor did he mention the authorities whom he followed. The lack of sources and authorities gave to the Code of Maimonides the aspect of a one man's work, a thing which was always distasteful to the mind of Talmudic scholars who delighted in discussions and arguments pro and con. The third and most important is that the intensive study of the Talmud going on in all Jewries and the resultant meticulous care in observing the laws must have necessarily called forth a desire on the part of scholars to introduce certain modifications in the decisions. As long as there was no generally adopted code, there was always room for the individual scholar to compile his own code, which compilation afforded him the opportunity for self expression, for each code though on the whole differing little from the others, yet bore the mark of the author. There was in each one some change either in method, decisions or interpretations of sources. Thus the activity went on for centuries.

As remarked above, greater interest in code making was displayed in Germany. Still, Spain did not lag behind, and many were the codes produced there. In fact, while the number of codes of Franco-German origin was probably larger than the Spanish, the latter excelled in quality and in bulk. The former were mostly, with few exceptions, manuals for local use by rabbis of certain districts, only a few enjoying sufficient authority to have their decisions quoted and accepted by the final codifiers. The Spanish codes, on the other hand, were written with a view of making them authoritative and are, on the whole, more inclusive and complete.

The codifying activity went on for four centuries from the end of the twelfth to the beginning of the seventeenth century, and on the whole, during this period, it was limited to two Jewries, the Spanish and the Franco-German. The contribution of other countries to the process of codification of the laws is slight, as we have but a few codes emanating from the hands of Italian scholars. With the completion of the *Shulhan Aruk* by Joseph Karo, the process of code making practically came to an end. Yet, the activity did not cease for even this code was not considered complete, but needed explanation and complementing. This work was almost entirely carried on in the new center of learning, Poland. For a time, attempts were made even there by various scholars to compile codes of their own, but their attempts were soon given up, and the work of the later scholars was limited to commentation and the writing of glosses and additions to the adopted code.

The methods of codification followed by the numerous codifiers were various, and all of them, with the exception of one, had already been used by the codifiers of the first period. They were as follows: (a) that of Compendium, where the gist of the discussion of the tractates of the Talmud is given and decisions indicated; (b) of arrangement according to the precepts of the Torah, treating each precept separately; (c) an arrangement of the laws according to the order in which they are stated in the Pentateuch; (d) compilation of groups of laws according to their general kindred nature or according to some special peculiar arrangement.

Most of the codes of the period follow the source method and give extensive excerpts of the Talmud and of the works of earlier codifiers to indicate the reason for their decisions. Some, however, and these are the most authoritative, follow the pure code method, where the decision is given with as little reference to the sources as possible.

51. THE FRANCO-GERMAN CODES

The earliest code produced in the thirteenth century by a French scholar was the *Semag,* abbreviation for the full title *Sepher Mitzvoth Gadol* (The Large Book of Precepts) by Rabbi Moses of Coucy (1200-1260). Rabbi Moses was one of the later Tosafists and is quoted frequently in the *Tosofoth* printed with the Talmud. He was a very pious man and spent a number of years in traveling through France and Spain, visiting the Jewish communities for the purpose of strengthening their faith in God and urging the scrupulous observance of the laws. On account of his great scholarship, deep piety and religious zeal, he was considered an authority on all matters pertaining to Jewish law.

He was moved to compose his code, though he was a great admirer of the Code of Maimonides and always spoke of it with great reverence, by the following considerations: Maimonides, says Rabbi Moses, evidently performed a great service by compiling the Mishnah Torah, but he gave no sources for his decisions. As a result, any rabbi who would teach the people according to his code would be unable to prove the reasons for such teachings. Second, some of his decisions differ from those of the great Franco-German scholars, such as Rashi, Rabbi Jacob Tam and other Tosafists. Third, there is also a division of opinion regarding the proper counting of the precepts which lies at the basis of the Code of Maimonides (Vol. I, Sect. 173). Rabbi Moses felt, therefore, that there was need for a new code which should remedy the enumerated defects, and he proceeded to compile one. He even claims that he was urged in a dream from heaven to carry out this work. He began to compile his work about the year 1241 and it must have consumed a number of years. It thus represents the fruit of the author's mature scholarship.

The order of arrangement employed by Rabbi Moses is a novel one, as it is arranged according to the six hundred and thirteen precepts contained in the Pentateuch. It is true that the author of the *Halakoth Gedoloth* (Vol. I, Ch. X. Sect. 152) prefaced his code with a list of the six hundred and thirteen precepts, and Maimonides took the statement of these precepts as the basis of his code, but both of these codifiers followed a different method of arrangement of the material in their works. Rabbi Moses, however, bases his entire arrangement on these precepts and takes up each precept separately, grouping the ancillary laws under it. As there are two kinds of precepts, affirmative and prohibitive (Asē and Lo-Tassē) the former numbering two hundred and forty-eight and the latter three hundred and sixty-five, the author accordingly divided his book into two parts. In the first part, he treats all affirmative precepts, and in the second the prohibitive. As these include all laws, those practiced even after the destruction of the Temple and those which ceased to be practiced after that time, the *Semag* is, therefore, a complete digest of the entire oral law and resembles in this respect the Code of Maimonides which influenced it also otherwise.

In the grouping of the precepts, he was only partly influenced by the order adopted in the Code of Maimonides, but on the whole, he had a system of his own. It seems to be as follows: He divided the entire sum of the laws, written and oral, into six large divisions; (1) those concerning the individual in relation to God and fellow-man, whether in matters of belief or practice; (2) those relating to family life; (3) those regarding prohibited and permitted foods; (4) those relating to society, namely all civil and criminal laws, including the laws connected with the conduct of the state; (5) laws, the operation of which depends on the possession of Palestine; and (6) those connected with the Temple service. The same division is followed in both parts, and on the whole, the scheme is carried out in a logical manner, that is the laws grouped under the divisions have a close relation to each other, in accordance with the plan. There are, of course, some exceptions and the relation of certain laws to the particular division in which they are placed may be at times a loose one, but in a work of this kind, such loose spots are bound to occur. At the end of the second book, the author treats in an appendix the five Rabbinical precepts, including the institutions of Hanukah and Purim and all such laws connected with them.

As one of the main purposes of Rabbi Moses in compiling his code was the statement of the sources together with the decisions, he is very careful to give the source of each rule and decision in the Talmud or other Halakic books. He displays great skill in this work, as the sources are quoted very briefly and yet not one is omitted. In addition, wherever necessary, the interpretations of the various commentators of Talmudic statements which affect the decisions are given together with the statements themselves. The earlier authorities, such as the Gaonim, Al-Fasi, Maimonides, Rashi and others are quoted frequently and their decisions are incorporated. As the code includes all precepts relating to beliefs and ethics, excerpts from the writings of the Jewish philosophers, especially Saadia and Maimonides, are given in the proper places.

Great skill is also displayed in the intertwining of the sources among the statements of decisions. These are not two different things but are dexterously united into one harmonious whole. For this purpose, Rabbi Moses very frequently gives the source not in the original language but in his own words. Finally, it is to be noted that the style of the *Semag* is not the least of its fine qualities. It is easy, simple and precise, resembling much the style of Maimonides in his code. Undoubtedly, Rabbi Moses who was a great admirer of the former was influenced by the charm of the language of the Mishnah Torah and unconsciously imitated it. All these characteristics made the *Semag* a great work, and one of the important codes compiled during the post-Classical period. It was held in great esteem by the scholars of the succeeding generations and was frequently cited in the later codes.

The second important code of that century is the *Or Zorua* (Light is Sown, after Psalms XCVII, 11) by Rabbi Isaac ben Moses of Vienna. The author was one of the great Talmudists of the day. He was the pupil of Rabbi Eliezer ben Joel ha-Levi (Vol. I, Sect. 156) and of Rabbi Judah of Paris, a leading Tosafist. In turn, he was the teacher of the famous scholar, Meir of Rothenburg.

The code is limited to the religious laws practiced in exile, as it does not deal with civil or criminal laws. It seems that Rabbi Moses had a practical aim in view, and as the religious laws in all their phases relating to the individual, family and the synagogue were the principal concern of the Jewish masses in Franco-German Jewry, the author deals primarily with them.

No particular method is followed in the arrangement of the laws. The work is merely divided into two parts, the first covering the greater part of the religious laws, such as those of prayer, benedictions, family purity, prohibited foods, marriage and divorce and others. The second is devoted entirely to the Sabbath and the festivals.

The method of the presentation of the subject matter is the source method, and eminently so, as the sources are quoted copiously and extensively and in the original language without the slightest change. The author also adduces numerous interpretations of the passages and the decision is only given at the end. In fact, the book of Rabbi Isaac stands midway between a Compendium and a Code. It is not arranged according to the tractates of the Talmud as the former, but the large number of excerpts together with a partial grouping of laws according to the order of the chapters in certain tractates give the *Or Zorua* the aspect of a compendium. The value of the *Or Zorua* consists in the extensive use of post-Talmudic sources, as Rabbi Isaac was exceptionally well versed in the entire Rabbinic literature. The Gaonic Responsa, their codes and commentaries, as well as those of the Franco-German school were all open to him and hardly anything in the great mass of Halakic literature escaped him. Besides, he carried on an extensive correspondence with all the famous scholars of his time and placed before them cases on various matters for decision, which decisions he included in his code. At times, however, he differs from the opinions propounded by his teachers and colleagues and takes great pains to explain his reasons for such difference of view.

All these characteristics make the *Or Zorua* a valuable Halakic work but not a code in the strict sense of the word. In fact, it was not written for the large masses of pious Jews, but for the scholars who utilized it to a great extent in their own works.

A third code emanating from the hands of a French scholar in the second half of the thirteenth century was the *Semaḳ,* initials of *Sepher Mitavoth Katan* (The Small Book of Precepts) by Isaac ben Joseph of Corbeil, one of the Younger Tosafists. This is, in a way, based on the larger book of Rabbi Moses of Coucy, but with many great changes. First, it was intended not for scholars but for scholarly laymen, and was aimed to be primarily a popular code. For this reason, the sources are reduced to a minimum, and the decision is given clearly and precisely. Second, the author adopted a different division of the precepts. He divided them into seven groups: (1) those related to the heart, namely to thought and feeling; (2) precepts depending upon individual action and those for the performance of which a definite time is set, such as festivals and others; (3) laws connected with the organ of the tongue, namely precepts regarding the pronouncement of vows, prayers, and various benedictions; (4) precepts connected with manual labor, including parts of the festival laws, laws of marriage and divorce, and kindred family laws; (5) laws of food dealing with all kinds of prohibited foods; (6) laws involving either a money transaction or expenditure of the same, covering most of the civil laws; (7) the laws of the Sabbath. This division, it must be admitted, is not a very logical one and is quite forced. The main purpose of the author was to find a seven fold division, as the book is divided into seven parts corresponding to the seven days of the week, and he intended that the readers or the students should cover one part on each day of the week. This intention indirectly influenced the grouping of the laws, for he often joins a group of laws to a section for no other reason but that it has some connection with the day on which it is to be studied. Thus the family laws are joined to the fourth division merely because this division is to be studied on the fourth day and in Talmudic times, marriages usually took place on Wednesday. For the same reason, the laws of the Sabbath are treated in a separate section and reserved for the seventh day. These divisions are also connected with seven of the Ten Commandments, but this connection is rather loose and forced.

The method of presentation of the subject matter is, as can be inferred from the name of the book, one dealing separately with each precept and the group of laws evolved from it. The author, however, does not follow Rabbi Moses of Coucy in treating the affirmative and prohibitive precepts in two different parts, but in each division, he treats first the affirmative and then the prohibitive ones. The Rabbinical precepts are likewise treated at the end of each section. In addition to references to Talmudic sources, interpretations and decisions of the post-Talmudic authorities are also given very briefly, especially those of Maimonides and the Franco-German scholars. Very often, the adopted usage or custom of the country is given in support of a certain decision. As the book was intended to be a popular one, it is interspersed with many Agadic statements, moral maxims and ethical teachings which enhance its value, serving as introductions to the discussions of many precepts.

The last thirteenth century code produced by a German scholar was the *Mordecai* by Mordecai ben Hillel of Nuremberg. He was a disciple of Rabbi Meir of Rothenburg and died a martyr's death in the year 1298. The *Mordecai* is a veritable encyclopaedia of Rabbinic literature containing comments, decisions and Responsa placed together in a quite unsystematic way. It is supposed to have been arranged according to the tractates of Al-Fasi's Compendium, and is usually printed in this way in the editions of that work. In reality, however, it has little to do with that Compendium, for the passages selected follow the original order of the Talmud more than that of Al-Fasi's Compendium. The method of the *Mordecai* is as follows: Certain passages are selected to serve as the key to a discussion in regard to the decision on a particular subject. An exceedingly large number of interpretations of the passage in question bearing upon the ultimate decision is then given, and finally the author's own view is stated. Many Responsa, especially by the teacher of the author, Rabbi Meir of Rothenburg, are usually incorporated in the discussions. These Responsa are, of course, part of the code, as they give definite decisions on certain cases.

On the whole, the *Mordecai* is little systematized and looks like a Rabbinic note-book wherein the author collected material for a code. Yet, here and there, attempts have been made by him to collect and arrange certain subjects in proper order, such as quoting passages of the Talmud from various places, bearing on a certain subject and covering all its phases. At other times, laws relating to one subject are grouped together. Thus, in the *Mordecai* on the tractate *Shebuoth,* dealing with oaths, all laws regarding oaths are arranged in excellent order, and we find similar groups in other places. It is possible that the author was interrupted in the middle of his work by his untimely death, and had he lived longer, would have produced an excellent code. Yet, with all these defects, the *Mordecai* was held in exceptional esteem by all later codifiers, for it served them as a source book for decisions upon all subjects. The scholars made great use of it, and it is very frequently quoted by them.

52. *THE ITALIAN CODES*

Italy, which was, during the thirteenth century, a great center for Rabbinic studies also produced some codes of importance. The most noted of these was the *Shibolē ha-Leḳet* (The Gathered Sheaves) by Zedekiah ben Abraham Anavi, the physician. Little is known about the author's life except that he lived about the end of the thirteenth century, was descended from a very distinguished family which produced many scholars, and that his brother was the physician and poet, Benjamin Anavi, whose work was described above. (Ch. III, Sect. 31.)

The code is not a complete one, as it deals only with the laws of the ritual and the festivals. Its name indicates its character. The contents are gathered from many sources, such as other codes, Responsa and commentaries. The author explains in the introduction that it was his purpose to sift out from the mass of opinions and decisions contained in the many books the right ones, and select such material as might be relied upon in teaching the proper way of religious conduct. He modestly apologizes for his presumption in acting as arbitrator between the opinions of greater scholars than himself, and in rejecting some of them. In justifying his presumption, he quotes the remark of a philosopher, that as the dwarf standing on the shoulders of a giant sees farther than the giant, so the later scholars, though of inferior ability, may view the subject in a clearer manner than their more gifted predecessors.

The book is divided into twelve sections which he calls *Arugoth* (Beds of Flowers) as the subject is compard to a field, each section dealing with a different legal subject. Thus, the first section deals with the laws of prayer, the second with those of the Sabbath, the third with benedictions and so forth. The sections are subdivided into paragraphs discussing individual laws in detail.

The book follows the code method, very few quotations of the sources being given, though many opinions are mentioned. The rules for practice are given in detail, and wherever necessary, reasons for their performance as well as for certain prayers are supplied. The opinions quoted are always stated in the name of the authors. Zedekiah must have done a prodigious amount of work, as the authorities cited are very numerous, extending from the Gaonim to his own contemporaries. Of the Italian scholars, he quotes several of his teachers, Rabbi Meir ben Moses, Rabbi Nathan ben Menahem and Rabbi Isaiah di Trani the younger, and very frequently his brother, the poet Benjamin, who was also a great Rabbinic scholar .

Rabbi Zedekiah exercised great skill in his decisions, but on the other hand, shows little logical judgment in his offering of reasons for the performances of certain customs or recitations of peculiar prayers, as many of them are based on superstitious beliefs. In this, though an Italian who cultivated the science of medicine, he did not rise above the simple pious codifiers of the Franco-German school. His style, on the other hand, possesses many excellent qualities. It is almost pure Hebrew and very clear.

The *Shibolē ha-Leḳet* was highly esteemed by the author's contemporaries in Italy, and even by later generations. A short time after its appearance, an Italian scholar by the name of Yehiel thought it necessary to make a digest of it under the name of *Tanya Rabatha*. For a long time it was thought that the *Tanya* was a new code, and since the author did not place his name on the title page only inserting it casually in the book with the words, "I Yehiel," it was erroneously ascribed by the printers to Rabbi Yehiel, son of Rabbi Asher of Toledo. But a comparison of the two codes, the *Tanya* and the *Shibolē ha-Leḳet* easily shows that the former is only a digest of the latter. True, there are some additions by the author, but the greater part of the work is taken from the code of Rabbi Zedekiah. The

Tanya covers the same subjects, quotes the same authorities and very frequently the decisions are given in the words of the *Shibolē ha-Leḳet.*

Rabbi Yehiel's aim was to compile a brief and popular code. He, therefore omitted many laws that are not practiced regularly, abbreviated the proofs offered by Rabbi Zedekiah for his decisions, the reasons for rejecting one opinion and selecting another, as well as many other statements which he deemed unnecessary. He also changed the order of arrangement of the statements of rules included in the general divisions, and thus greatly improved the connection between them. Hardly anything is known of the author of the *Tanya* except his name, Yehiel. It is surmised by Weiss that this Yehiel was Rabbi Yehiel ben Jekutiel, a grandson of Rabbi Benjamin Anavi, the brother of Rabbi Zedekiah.

53. *LATER GERMAN CODES*

Of the many codes and compilations that were produced in Germany during the fourteenth and fifteenth centuries, only a small number which were considered authoritative and were quoted by the final codifiers are worthy of note. The first of these is the *Shaarē Dura* (The Portals of Dura, the Hebrew pronunciation of the German word Düren, the residence of the author) by Isaac ben Reuben of Düren (c. 1320). The book is a partial code, as it treats only of food laws and kindred subjects. This group of laws was a great favorite with German codifiers, and many codes on the treatment of this subject were compiled. The reason for the frequent codifying of these laws is clear. Since they affected the daily life of the Jew and especially the conduct at home, they became an object of scrupulous observation, and hence an object of special study, and great care was exercised in decisions concerning them. The treatment of these laws received even a special name, *Isur we-Heter* (Prohibition and Permission) which indicates the significance attached to decisions on the subject. Hence, the *Shaarē Dura* bears also a second title, *Isur we-Heter.*

The book is divided, as the name indicates, into portals or chapters which take up the various groups of laws in fine order. The sources and the reasons for the decisions are stated and authorities are quoted. The authorities are almost all Franco-German scholars. Of the Spanish codifiers, Al-Fasi is quoted once and Maimonides three times. Of the German authorities, Rabbi Asher is the last one quoted. The author was most likely one of his disciples.

The code enjoyed exceptional authority in this branch of laws, and was frequently commented upon by later scholars. Rabbi Solomon Luria (Sect. 46) and Moses Isserlis (Sect. 60), the great Rabbinic scholars of the sixteenth century are among those who wrote commentaries and glosses to the book, besides many others.

The next code is the *Agudah* (The Bond) by Alexander Süslein of Frankfurt. We know little concerning the author except his name and place. It is deduced, however, that he lived during the first half of the fourteenth century, and that consequently the book was written about 1340-1345. Rabbi Jacob Mölin, a fifteenth century scholar says that the author lived before the persecutions. This refers to the massacres that occurred during the Black Plague in 1348-49, hence, the book was written during the years stated.

The book is a brief compendium of laws deducible from important passages of the Talmud together with the additional decisions of the later authorities. It is arranged, like the Al-Fasi and the *Mordecai,* according to the tractates of the Talmud, covering it entirely, even the orders *Zeraim* and *Taharoth* which deal with laws not practiced today. His order of tractates is very peculiar. He begins with the fourth order *Nesiḳin,* followed by *Nashim, Zeraim,* and then by *Kodashim* and *Taharoth.* The reason for such arrangement must have been the importance he placed on the laws contained in the first two orders which deal with civil and family matters.

The Talmudic sources are given very briefly, but the comments and deductions are given at greater length. The author excerpted many passages from the *Mordecai* without even mentioning him. He does, however, name many authorities quoting extensively from the writings of both Franco-German and Spanish scholars, and of the latter especially Al-Fasi and Maimonides. Of the commentators, he is particularly fond of the great Tosafist, Isaac ben Samuel. The author not only decides between the opinions of earlier codifiers and authorities but deduces many decisions himself directly from the Talmud. On the whole, Rabbi Alexander omits all lengthy discussions and states the results briefly. When treating of the orders *Zeraim* and *Taharoth* to which there is no Gemarah, he is exceptionally brief and merely quotes the opening sentence of the Mishnah pointing out the law derived from the statement and indicating where it is discussed in the Gemarah to other parts of the Talmud.

The *Agudah* was not a popular book, as it was intended primarily for scholars and was accordingly esteemed and quoted by them. It was not printed until the year 1591.

A code which is quite often quoted by the final codifiers is the anonymous work, *Isur we-Heter* first printed at Ferrara in 1555. On the title page of the first as well as those of subsequent editions, it is ascribed to Rabbi Jonah Gerundi. But even a hasty perusal of the book will convince any one acquainted with this literature that it could not have emanated from his pen. The authorities quoted there, such as the *Mordecai,* the *Rosh* and others lived more than a generatoin after the death of Rabbi Jonah. It must, therefore, be assumed that the book was written at the end of the fourteenth century, or even at the beginning of the fifteenth century by a German scholar.

From its title, we can infer its contents, for as stated, all books that bear the title *Isur we-Heter* deal with food laws. Likewise, our book deals primarily with these subjects, though it contains several chapters on some of the laws of the Sabbath and other subjects. The book is divided into sixty portals (Shearim) which are subdivided into sections. Each portal deals with a single law and the section with its particulars. It is arranged primarily in the form of a code where the decision is given without discussion yet the sources are likewise stated and the authorities quoted. The title of this code as well as the arrangement of the subject matter resemble closely the *Shaarē Dura.* Its novelty consists merely in the changing of a number of decisions and the introduction of different practices current in certain localities.

A most important phase of religious life is the synagogue ritual. In this particular matter, however, there was always great variety of practice. In a number of things, the customs of one locality differed from another, and since the ritual consists of a large number of details, the variety was correspondingly great. To remedy this situation and to standardize the practice of the ritual, three scholars have written codes dealing primarily with this subject, where all the customs of Germanic communities were collected and given legal authority. These were Rabbi Abraham Klausner of Vienna (d. 1408), his disciples, Rabbi Jacob ha-Levi Mölin (1365-1427) known as *Maharil* and Rabbi Isaac of Tyrna. These three scholars collected the customs of Jewish communities regarding the ritual and other subjects affecting religious life in works which they called *Minhagim* (Customs).

Of these three works, the most important is the Book of *Minhagim* by Rabbi Jacob Mölin. It is the most comprehensive as it contains the largest number of popular practices concerning the ritual and other phases of religious life. It is also the most authoritative, for Rabbi Jacob Mölin was considered the greatest scholar of his day, and his name gave to the work the weight of authority. It was, therefore, accepted by all subsequent scholars as a source of citation.

The latest code written by a German scholar before the final code the *Shulhan Aruk* was compiled, was the *Agur* by Rabbi Jacob Baruch ben Judah Landau. Rabbi Jacob was born and educated in Germany but emigrated about 1470 to Italy. There he studied under Judah Messer Leon and other scholars, but in spite of all this, his work is based primarily on the results of German learning and scholarship in the field of codification.

The *Agur* contains fourteen hundred and thirty-nine sections which are arranged in the code method, following the order of the Code of the *Tur* (sect. 57). It deals to a large extent with ritual and Sabbath and festival laws. Its main purpose was to add the decisions of the later German scholars upon laws which either were omitted by Rabbi Jacob, the author of the *Tur* or were added after the compilation of that code. Among the authorities that he quotes most are Rabbi Jacob Mölin and Israel Isserlin.

54. *THE SPANISH CODES*

As was pointed out above, there was from the twelfth century on, little difference in the method of Talmud study between the Spanish and Franco-German scholars. The dialectic form of study which, during the Classic period was primarily the share of the French and German scholars, penetrated into the Spanish schools and the scholars of that country were henceforth as greatly distinguished by their analytic and pilpulistic legal discussions as their Franco-German brethren. This trend is, of course, also reflected in the codes of the Spanish school. Yet, we note that the old method of arranging the subject matter in a systematic way and in logical sequence was not abandoned entirely and that there is in the works of this school a manifest effort on the part of the authors to preserve these characteristics in a substantial measure. Another differentiating characteristic of the Spanish codifiers is that while they do not omit to include every important decision of law and every opinion of practice, they are not so rigorous and severe in their decisions. The excessive severity which is usually expressed in Franco-German codes by the phrase, "It is customary to follow the severe opinion" (ve-Nehagin l'ha-Hamir) is on the whole, absent from these codes. The weight of the *Minhag,* i. e. the custom of excessive piety did not hang so heavily upon these codifiers.

The first codes produced during the thirteenth century were those of Rabbi Moses ben Nahman (Nahmanides). He wrote two small collections of the laws of vows and laws of the first born (Nedarim and Bekhoroth) arranged in the form of Al-Fasi's Compendium. These were intended as supplements to the latter's Compendium and follow his method, namely selecting the Talmudic passages which contain the decisions and omitting the unnecessary part of the discussion. His other partial codes are the *Torath ha-Adam* (The Laws of Man) embracing the laws of purity (Nidda) and mourning, and the *Hilkoth Bedikah* (The Laws of the Examination) dealing with the examination of the lungs in a slaughtered animal. In these codes, Nahmanides sometimes follows the pilpulistic source method, where the derivation of each law is extensively discussed, and sometimes the pure code method, giving each decision briefly in the manner of the Code of Maimonides.

A very important code written at this time was the *Torath ha-Baith* (The Law of the House) by Rabbi Solomon ben Adret (Rashba). Its name indicates its scope, as it is devoted primarily to the laws practiced in the Jewish home. It is divided into seven sections or "Houses" as he calls them and each section into portals. The sections embrace laws of slaughtering, *terepha,* salting of meat, other dietary laws, and laws of purity of women. In this code, the source method of Jewish codification reached its highest point. Ben Adret not only gives the original sources of the Talmud for the derivation of each decision, but also a lengthy exposition of the interpretation of these passages by previous commentators and codifiers. This exposition is often followed by a discussion aiming either to refute the opinions quoted or to confirm them. His own decision is given at the end.

However, he himself understood that such a method of arriving at decisions would make his code extremely unpractical. He, therefore, appended to each portal a resume of the discussions where the decisions are given briefly and decisively. This resume he called *Torath ha-Baith ha-Kotzar* (The Brief Teaching of the House). In the printed editions, this resume is placed on the margin. To this code of ben Adret, Rabbi Aaron ha-Levi, a colleague of the author, added glosses and notes under the name of *Bedek ha-Baith* (The Repair of the House), where he discloses some weak spots in the argumentation of the author. And again, ben Adret added some notes under the name of *Mishmereth ha-Baith* (The Guard of the House), refuting the difficulties raised by Rabbi Aaron. The work, on account of the authority of ben Adret was greatly esteemed by later codifiers and is repeatedly quoted by them.

Worthy of mention is also the book *ha-Hinuk* (The Training) by Aaron ha-Levi, which though not properly a code, can serve as a good introduction to one. The purpose of the book was, as the name indicates, a pedagogic one, that those who read the Pentateuch in weekly portions should become acquainted with the precepts derived from each portion. The author, therefore, adopted the table of precepts elaborated by Maimonides and rearranged it according to the chapters of the Bible where these precepts are found. The author, however, is not satisfied with a mere indication as to where this or that precept is found, but explains the manner of its derivation, the ethical reasons for its performance, and above all, he defines the application of the precept to life. The last is the most important phase of the work, for there he displays his great knowledge of Rabbinical literature. In defining the application of a precept, whether an affirmative (Asē) or a prohibitive one (Lo-Taasē), he utilizes all the interpretations placed upon this precept in the Talmud and the subsequent legal books, its specifications and its various connotations.

True, Aaron does not give the particulars as to how the precept is to be observed, or in case of a prohibitive one, what particular things are not to be done, but the broad statement of the precept, its definition and description helped codifiers greatly in arriving at a decision in each case. He usually indicates the chapters of the tractates of the Talmud where these particulars are discussed. Rabbi Aaron also tells at the end of each section to which class of Mitzvoth the precept belongs, whether it possesses eternal validity independent of time and place, or is dependent for its observance on the existence of the Temple and the possession of Palestine; again, whether it is obligatory on one without distinction of sex or class, or vice versa. All these qualities together with that of the style, which is pure Hebrew, give the *ha-Hinuk* an important place in the codification literature.

55. *THE COMPENDIUM OF RABBI ASHER (Rosh)*

The most important code emanating from Spain during the thirteenth century was the Compendium of the Talmud made by Rabbi

Asher ben Yehiel (Sect. 43) which like the one of Al-Fasi bears no other name than that of the author's, *Rosh* (initials of Rabbi Asher). It resembles to a great extent the code of Al-Fasi, but it also differs considerably from it. That of Al-Fasi represents primarily the opinions and decisions of the author himself and to a lesser degree, the views of the Gaonim. Likewise, the Code of Maimonides embodies only his decisions, and in addition, gives no sources. The study of the Talmud, however, had been going on for centuries in France and Germany, and eminent scholars had, as we have seen, written commentaries, Responsa, and codes. Their views had not, however, found any expression in the two great codes which were gradually becoming authoritative.

To remedy this situation, to give expression to the views of the Franco-German scholars in matters of decision of laws, and also to supply the sources, Rabbi Asher wrote his Compendium. It aimed, like that of Al-Fasi's to show scholars how to derive the decision of the law directly from the Talmud by abridging the Talmudic discussions and excerpting such passages as bear on the point of law in question. Rabbi Asher, of course, included the views of the *Halakoth* (Legal Statements) of Al-Fasi, but did not always accept them, differing from them whenever he saw fit. The importance of his work, however, consists not in his deviations from Al-Fasi, but in the new matter which he added. He incorporated the interpretations of the Talmudic passages and the decisions of the Franco-German scholars, especially the work of the Tosafists. His Compendium, therefore, contains not only sources and decisions, but also discussions and comments, both of which clarify the subject and supply the reason for the ultimate decisions. Rabbi Asher also introduces new cases which are not included in the Talmudic sources and decides upon them by analogy. Many authorities are quoted, most of them French and German, and great weight is given to the opinions of his teacher Rabbi Meir of Rothenburg.

The work of Rabbi Asher, though written in Spain, represents to a great extent German Rabbinic scholarship. Since, however, we note in it the influence of the Spanish school, it thus represents the amalgamation of the scholarship of both schools. Like Al-Fasi's, the Compendium of the *Rosh* covers only such tractates of the Talmud or such parts of tractates as treat of laws observed today, omitting the others. The Compendium of the *Rosh* was accepted by the succeeding generations as of great authority. Its decisions are continually referred to and were made the basis for the great code of his son, Rabbi Jacob, the Tur.

56. THE PROVENCE CODES

The codifying activity which was carried on in France and Germany also spread into the Provence. This country which became a great literary center during the thirteenth and fourteenth centuries did not lag behind the other two centers in Rabbinic scholarship. Many were the scholars who arose there and left their mark upon the development of Rabbinics. In the field of codification, we have two codes produced by Provence scholars which were accorded certain authority.

The first is *ha-Manhig* (The Guide) by Rabbi Abraham ben Nathan of Lunel. The book deals primarily with the synagogue ritual and other matters of daily conduct. It was written early in the thirteenth century (1205) and is frequently quoted by later codifiers on matters of ritual.

The other code is one with a peculiar name, *Toldoth Adam we-Hava* (The Generations of Adam and Eve) by Rabbi Yeruham (fl. in 1300-1340), a disciple of Rabbi Asher. The purpose of Rabbi Yeruham was to give a more popular code than the Compendium of the *Rosh*. The book covers practically all parts of Jewish law except those dealing with civil law. The name is given to it because of its peculiar arrangement. The author divided his book into two parts, the first dealing with all the laws obligatory upon a Jew when in single state hence its name *Adam,* and the second deals with laws that apply only to married life, hence the name *Hava*. As the laws applying to Jewish life independent of the state of marriage form the largest part of Jewish religious law, the first part, therefore, occupies three-quarters of the work. Of the twenty-eight sections or paths (Nethiboth) into which it is divided, twenty-one are devoted to the first part and seven to the second.

As the life of man is taken as the basis of arrangement for the subject matter, the author endeavors to carry out this scheme even in the grouping of the laws. Accordingly, the first section deals with the laws affecting the life of the child, namely those attending its birth, circumcision, the duties of the father to the child and the duties of the child to the father and mother. The second describes the process of education and the study of the Torah, including all laws regarding the writing of scrolls and phylacteries. The third deals with prayers, embracing all the laws of the synagogue ritual. Then follow a number of sections on the Sabbath and festivals, on dietary laws, and so on. The second part deals with the laws of marriage, divorce and other matters of family practice. There are, of course, many flaws in this arrangement as groups of laws are often joined without any close relation to each other. But on the whole, there is a general endeavor to carry out the scheme.

The book is primarily a pure code and the decisions are given without discussions and without quotations of sources. These are only indicated, authorities are mentioned briefly, and only occasionally, are several opinions quoted regarding a decision. There are many defects in the makeup of the book, its style is not clear and inaccuracies in the quotations and decisions occur frequently. It can not be definitely determined whether these errors emanated from the hands of the author or from those of the copyists. The book, however, in spite of its defects, is quoted and relied upon by later codifiers.

57. *THE CODE OF RABBI JACOB (The Tur)*

As indicated above, the Compendium of the *Rosh* still left a place for the compilation of a code which should really deserve the name. where the law should be stated clearly and concisely. We also noted that an attempt was made by Rabbi Asher's disciple, Rabbi Yeruham to perform this task. But he did not possess the ability to arrange the work in the form necessary for the code to gain authority and be accepted by a large part of Jewry, nor did he possess that scholarly prestige which would impart to his work that authority. This task was more ably performed by Rabbi Jacob, the son of Asher. (1280-1340.)

As preparatory work for his code, he compiled the tables of decisions derived from the Compendium of his father under the name of *Piske ha-Rosh* and appended them to each tractate of the Talmud. On the basis of these decisions, he wrote his code which he named *Sepher ha-Turim* (The Book of the Rows). The name is an allusion to the four rows of stones which were set in the breast plate of the High Priest (Ex. XXVIII, 15-16) called in Hebrew *Turim,* used according to tradition as an oracle for decisions of judgment.

Rabbi Jacob, like his father, was interested only in the laws practiced at all times, and did not include those which ceased to operate with the destruction of the Temple. These laws he divided into four classes: (a) those which affect the daily life of the Jew and which every Jew can decide for himself with the help of a proper book;

תרעז אין מבדילין בה במוצאי שבת

תרעח הזכרת חנוכה בתפילה וברכת המזון ואם אומ' בשם שעשית ניסים וכו'

תרעט לגמור ההלל בח' ימי חנוכה

תרפ סדר היו' בחול ובשבת ובשחל ר"ח טבת בחול ובשבת

תרפא סדר הפרשיות של חנוכה

תרפב טעם לתענית של י"ג באדר וכו' פורים ביום ראשון מתענין ב' ביום ה' שלפניו

תרפג איזה דבר מתבטל מפני מקרא מגילה

תרפד זמן קריאתה לעיירות ולכרכי' המוקפי' ומה נקרא מוקף ומי שרוצה לילך בשיירא ובן עיר שהלך לכרך או איפכא ודין קריאתה באדר ונתעברה השנה

תרפה מי חייבין בקריאתה ואם נשים מוציאות לאנשים

תרפו הכשר קריאתה מיושב וסירוג' וסירוגין וסירוסין ומתנמנם ובאה קורין ואם אינה כתובה כולה או השמיט בה הסופר אותיות ואם קרא על פה ובאיזה לשון נקראת ואם נקראת ביחד וכל דיני קריאתה

תרפז הכשר תיקון עיבודה וכתיבת ואם כתובה בין הכתובים ות התפירתה וכל דיני תיקונה ו ואם אין לו כשירה ואם יוצא' בגזולה

תרפח ברכותיה אם לא בירך לפניה ולא לאחריה ואם שח בה ומי שקורא מגילה לחולה

תרפט דין סדר הלילה והיום וכל די' דיניו

תרצ מתנות אביונים ומעות שגבו לצורך עניים

תרצא זמן סעודת פורים ושלוח מנות

תרצב היתר מלאכה ואיסור הספד ותענית ומי שמת לו מת בו ביום או קודם לכן וכיצד יתנ' יתנהג האבל

תרצג דין ארבעה עשר וחמשה עשר שבאדר הראשון

נשלמו הרמזים בעזרת השם
נתיבה במים עזים

חזק חזק חזק

סדר עשיית הקשר של תפילין למעתיק יכניס הרצועה במעברתא מפני הרצועה לפני הבתים ויחפר הכל בידו והרצועה שהיא עתה לצד שמאלו יהפכנה ב' פעמים לצד ימינו ויכפלנה במקום הקשר דרך המסה לצד הבתים ויקח הרצועה שהיא עת עתה לצד ימינו ונשיבה על אותו כפל וכפלה דרך מסח ומכניסה ב' פעמים בתוך אותו כפל ובפעם שנייה מניחה רפויה והרצועה הראשונה שבכפל לצד הבתים מב מביאה בין ב' הרצועות המסבבות הראש ומכניסה באותו כפל הרפוי ומהדקו ופני השניים של הקשר הוא נעשה ממילא וכל זה ע"פ סליק עשיית הקשר

חזק ונתחזק הסופר לא יוזק
עד שיעלה חמור בסולם

A page from the Tur Orah Hayyim, ed. princeps, Pieve de Sacco, 1475. (Copy in possession of the Jewish Theological Seminary, New York)

(b) those relating to prohibited and permitted things (Isur we-Heter) which are of a more difficult nature and need the decision of a scholar, such as the dietary laws, laws of purity of women and kindred matters; (c) laws which deal with family relations; (d) laws that bear on civil life and the dispensation of justice in all its phases. Accordingly, the code is divided into four divisions or rows. The first is named *Tur Orah Hayyim* (The Path of Life) embracing (a) all laws of religious conduct of a Jew from the time he rises in the morning until he retires in the evening, namely all laws of prayer, benedictions, synagogue ritual, law of phylacteries and similar subjects; (b) laws of the Sabbath; (c) laws of all festivals. The second row is named *Tur Yore Deah* (The Teacher of Knowledge) and deals with the laws of the second class. The third is called *Tur Eben ha-Ezer* (The Stone of Help). The name is taken from I Samuel, III, 13 and is an allusion to both the stone of judgment of the High Priest's breastplate, and to the fact that the woman is called in Gen. II, 20 *Ezer,* a helpmate, as this part deals with the law of the family. The fourth is called *Hoshen ha-Mishpat* (The Breast-Plate of Judgment) borrowed from Exodus XXVIII, 15, as the division deals with civil law. The divisions are further subdivided into sections, containing groups of laws and these into chapters.

The method of Rabbi Jacob is to state the law in a brief and concise manner without quotation of sources, only at times referring briefly to a Talmudic statement. However, this manner of statement is only followed when there is total agreement by the authorities, but when there is a difference of opinion, he quotes the various authorities, for while the code is based on the decisions of his father, the opinions of others are also mentioned giving the view of the *Rosh* at the end. Rabbi Jacob was a very modest man, and does not undertake to decide between the opinions leaving that to the student. Often, though, he indicates his predilection for an opinion by saying, "I am inclined to accept this view." Of the authorities quoted, we note that those whose views are mentioned in the *Orah Hayyim* are largely Franco-German scholars, while in the *Hoshen ha-Mishpat,* the views of Spanish scholars predominate. The book is interspersed with many ethical sayings and moral maxims and dicta culled from Talmudic literature, aiming to inculcate the fear of the Lord and love for the observance of the Law. The style is light, clear and simple, which adds greatly to the value of the book.

The *Tur,* on account of all these qualities, was accepted during several centuries as the authoritative code by a large part of Jewry, and ultimately served as the basis for the final code, the *Shulhan Aruk.*

The *Tur* with all its excellent qualities, which made it a useful and practical code, did not bring to a close the codifying activity. Scholars still found it necessary to compile codes of their own, either complete or partial. There were, of course, some new features in their works, for they either amplified the subject matter and made it more popular or added some new matter. Of such codes, we have several, produced in Spain and the Provence.

The first is the *Abudraham,* so named after its author, David ben Joseph Abudraham of Seville (fl. 1300-1345), who is said to have been a disciple of Rabbi Jacob. The book deals only with the synagogue ritual, namely prayers and benedictions. As this was intended to be a popular book, its scope is more inclusive than a mere code. The author says in the introduction that he was moved to write his work because he saw that many people do not understand the meaning of prayers, nor do they know the exact way of conduct as customs differ. The book accordingly gives not only the rules, laws and customs in detail, but devotes much space to giving reasons for many *Minhagim* (Customs), and especially to comments on prayers and on some of the most important *Piutim.*

This last phase of the book is very valuable, and it served during the ages as an encyclopaedia on matters of ritual and custom. Later codifiers refer to the *Abudraham* frequently.

The second one is the *Zedah l'Derek* (Provision for the Road) by Menahem ben Zorah of Navarre, a disciple of Judah, the son of Asher (1308-1385). It is a kind of encyclopaedia of Jewish knowledge, inasmuch as it embraces not only legal decisions but matters of ethics, bits of science and other subjects. He was impelled to write his book on account of the conditions of the times. These were days of persecution when the study of the law had ceased and ignorance was rampant. In addition, there were many people who, while delving in philosophy, scoffed at the law altogether and made light of the observance of the precepts. It was, therefore, the intention of the author to give to the people a book which would unite both the decisions of the law and a rational presentation of the beliefs, ethics and principles of Judaism.

The work is divided into five sections dealing with (a) prayers and benedictions; (b) dietary laws; (Isur we-Heter); (c) family laws; (d) festivals; (e) fasts, mourning, Messiah and resurrection. The decisions of the laws are given very briefly with no difference of opinion and no authorities quoted. The author attempts to rationalize many customs and rules of conduct, and also gives explanations for the observance of many precepts. It seems that Menahem being a man of great erudition and versed in many branches of knowledge was anxious to display that knowledge in his book. He, therefore, included many irrelevant matters in his work, which only confused the reader, and were a great factor in preventing the code from becoming popular.

The third code produced at this time was the *Orhoth Hayyim* (The Ways of Life) by Rabbi Aaron ben Jacob ha-Kohen of Lunel (c. 1330-1360). It is divided into two parts, the first one dealing with laws and customs of the ritual for the entire year, the second with the laws of the Sabbath and festivals, dietary laws and miscellaneous matters. The purpose of the code was a very practical one. Rabbi Aaron lived at the time of the expulsion from France (1308) and was himself one of the exiles. Seeing that his brethren were scattered to different lands and that during the exile books were lost, authority was weakened and established customs forgotten, he composed his code in order to teach the wanderers the way of Jewish life. It is, therefore, written in the form of brief decisions without any sources or discussions. The book was composed earlier than the *Tur,* and evidently the author had no knowledge of its appearance. The *Orhoth Hayyim* is based primarily on the *Semag* (Sect. 51), the additions to that book by Rabbi Peretz and on an anonymous early code by the name of *Melamed* (The Teacher). The author endeavors also to supply reasons for the precepts and customs and to explain their meaning. The reasons are sometimes given in a philosophic manner, borrowed from the works of Jewish philosophers, and sometimes in a Kabbalistic manner, namely by using *Gematrias* (numerical value of words) and *Notaricons* (initials of words) to explain the origin of a certain custom.

To this Rabbi Aaron, there is ascribed by a number of scholars another code which passed for a long time as an anonymous one, the *Kol-Bo* (Miscellany). It deals, as its name indicates, with a number of things. These are the laws of ritual, some Sabbath and festival laws, selected dietary laws, a part of the family laws and a number of miscellaneous subjects. The book contains also excerpts from a number of earlier codes, such as the *Teruma* (Vol. I, Ch. X, Sect. 156), the codes of Rabbis Eliezer ben Nathan, Peretz, Isaac ben Samuel the Tosafist and others. It contains also the texts of a number of legal and public documents, among them the long text of the *Herem* (Formula of Excommunication) used on rare occasions, as ordinarily the shorter form was used. On the whole, the work bears the character of a note book which the author compiled for his own use as material for a later work. It is, therefore, thought by scholars that it represents the first draft of the *Orhoth Hayyim,* as the resemblance between the two is very great.

58. THE SHULHAN ARUK OF JOSEPH KARO

The period, a century and a half, which elapsed from the composition of the *Tur* to the expulsion of the Jews from Spain (1492) was not a very fruitful one for the production of Rabbinic literature in Spain. Times were turbulent, the great persecutions in 1391 resulting in fearful massacres of the Jews throughout the country, devastated many Jewish communities and reduced the entire Spanish Jewry to a state of weakness and poverty, both economic and spiritual, from which it could not recover during the entire fifteenth century. It is not to be wondered at then that literary activity in all fields was reduced to a minimum, and accordingly, we have few books of importance in any branch produced during the period, Rabbinic literature not excepted. It was only after the expulsion, when the Spanish exiles founded new centers in the lands of the East that the genius of Spanish Jewry blossomed forth once more and made its contributions to Jewish literature. And not the least of these contributions was the code produced by Rabbi Joseph Karo, one of the exiles who settled in Palestine.

Rabbi Joseph ben Ephraim Karo (1488-1575) was born in Spain or in Portugal. After the expulsion, his father settled in the city of Nicopoli, Bulgaria, and there young Joseph was educated by him and other immigrant Spanish rabbis. The family later removed to Adrianopole, where Joseph acted for a long time as head of an academy. There he began to compose his great work called the *Beth Yoseph* (The House of Joseph), which is usually considered a commentary on the Tur, but in reality, as will be seen, is an independent code. He spent twenty-five years on this work, and before he finished it, he settled in Safed, Palestine. Twelve years more he spent in revision of the work, and it finally appeared in 1554. Later, he compiled a digest of this larger work which he called the *Shulhan Aruk* (The Set Table) indicating by that name that he set forth the spiritual food for the people in a manner ready to be consumed. It was this digest which became the adopted code.

Joseph Karo was also, like most of the scholars of Safed, a Kabbalist and practiced an ascetic manner of life, and even believed that a voice from heaven was speaking to him at certain times, instructing him both in matters of Jewish law and mystic lore. He named this voice, the *Magid* (The Preacher) and thought that it was the spirit of the Mishnah. He even wrote a book by the name of *Magid Mesharim* (The Preacher of Righteousness) which is supposed to contain the content of the conversations held by him with that spirit. Among other things, the spirit told him that he was the greatest man in his generation, that his name would become known throughout Jewry and that he was destined to accomplish great things. It is not impossible to imagine that secretly Karo entertained Messianic aspirations, as the age was surcharged with mysticism and Messianism. Yet, his Kabbalistic inclinations did not influence his treatment of the law.

As stated the *Shulhan Aruk* was only the digest of the larger work, the *Beth Yoseph*. It was the latter which Rabbi Joseph considered his Magnum Opus. The motive for its composition was as follows: A number of scholars including Karo were not satisfied with the *Tur* on account of its brevity and insufficiency of sources. Karo, therefore, planned to write a larger work which should give the derivation of the decisions from the sources and should also include other opinions not mentioned by Rabbi Jacob. At first, he intended to append his work to the Code of Maimonides but later changed his mind because Maimonides stated only his individual view and there would be no connection between the two; he therefore attached it to the *Tur*. But though the *Beth Yoseph* is joined to the *Tur,* there is only a slight connection between them. It is not a commentary but an independent work following the order and arrangement of the *Tur*. In this work, Karo follows up the derivation of all the laws through all the sources up to the Talmud, quotes a number of opinions and interpretations, analyzes the reasons for the views, and finally gives his own decision.

It seems quite clear that Karo intended the *Beth Yoseph* to be his code. But later, he composed the digest, as he says, to serve as a manual of study for the younger students before they entered upon his larger work. The time for just such a digest was an opportune one. The greater part of the exiles were not definitely settled in their new lands of habitation, academies were not opened as yet and the rabbis of the newly settled communities not having much leisure for intensive study rejoiced at the appearance of the *Shulhan Aruk* which gave them the ready decisions without any shadow of doubt. On the other hand, Kabbalist rabbis who wanted to devote their time to the study of the mysteries also welcomed the *Shulhan Aruk* as a time saver in pronouncing decisions. Thus it was not long before the digest which Karo himself considered as a student's manual became the most popular code, and later when the additions of Isserlis were joined to it, (Sect. 60) the code of entire Jewry.

Yet it was not entirely due to the exigencies of the time that the book was accepted by the larger part of Jewry, but to a great extent to the merits of the work itself. The *Shulhan Aruk* is divided into four parts, the same as the *Tur,* and the arrangement and the grouping of laws is exactly the same. But while the *Tur* quotes a number of opinions and seldom decides, only indicating at times an inclination towards a decision, the *Shulhan Aruk* gives the decision without any difference of opinion. Only rarely is a second opinion mentioned with the formula, "And some say" (We-Yesh Omrim). No sources are quoted but a plain statement of the rule is given.

Karo also introduced the division of chapters into paragraphs called *Seif* (Branch), the number of paragraphs varying according to the contents of each chapter. Each paragraph deals with a specified point of law. Such a division made the book more serviceable and more practical. The style of the book is, of course, that of Rabbinic Hebrew but of a very pure kind, light and lucid, offering no difficulties to the reader in his endeavor to understand the content. Style thus became a factor in the acceptance of the book. However, the greatest factor in the spread of the work was the reputation of the author for possessing vast erudition and deep learning. Karo was considered by the scholars of the day as one of the great men in the generation, and the ability he displayed in his works, notably in the commentary on the Code of Maimonides and in the *Beth Yoseph* was considered sufficient guaranty for the authority of his decisions in the *Shulhan Aruk.*

The *Shulhan Aruk* of Karo can be considered a pure Sephardic code, for he ignored most of the German authorities and based his decisions upon those of Al-Fasi, Maimonides and Rabbi Asher. His concessions to the German views consist only in that he took Rabbi Asher as one of his authorities, and as we have seen (Sect. 55), the latter had relied mostly on the views of the Franco-German scholars. Karo, however, does not accept the views of the *Rosh* when they are opposed to those of the other two authorities. His principle was to rely on any two against the third one.

This particular characteristic made the *Shulhan Aruk* at first unacceptable to the entire Germanic Jewry which in a broad sense included also all Jewish communities in the Slavonic countries. During the first twenty years, the Code of Karo was only authoritative for the Spanish communities. In order to become that which it ultimately did become, namely the final code of all Jewry, it had to be completed and receive many additional decisions which represented the results reached by the many codifiers in France and Germany. Only after this was done, and only after a struggle lasting for almost a century, it gradually received the sanction of the entire Jewry. This work of completing the *Shulhan Aruk* was done by a Polish scholar, Rabbi Moses Isserlis.

59. *THE POLISH SCHOOL OF CODIFIERS*

As was already noted, the Polish scholars continued in their manner and method of study the traditions of the Franco-German schools. It follows from this that they clung to these traditions also in their legal decisions and code compilations, preferring the German views and opinions to those of the Sephardic or Spanish codifiers. It was, therefore, natural that the *Shulhan Aruk* of Karo should have been met on its appearance with great opposition on the part of the Polish scholars. Some of them disregarded it entirely and set out to compile their own codes in their own way.

The first of these was Rabbi Solomon Luria (Sect. 46). He was greatly dissatisfied with Karo for his following only the three above mentioned authorities and disregarding all the German authorities. He speaks very harshly of his work and warns people not to follow the decisions of the *Shulhan Aruk*. His own work, the *Yam Shel Shlomoh* (The Sea of Solomon), though containing a good deal of commentary, is primarily intended as a code. It is a source code and is arranged on seven tractates of the Talmud, covering some of the festival laws. Luria's method of decision was to select certain passages from the Talmud which serve as the original source for the derivation of the law, and then through a discussion of the various interpretations placed upon them by subsequent authorities arrive at the ultimate decision. He was very extensive in his discussion and quoted the opinions of most of the authorities, especially those of the Franco-German school. He also laid great stress upon custom (Minhag) and German tradition.

In addition to his chief work, Rabbi Luria wrote also glosses and notes to the old German code *Shaarē Dura* and a commentary on the *Semag*.

60. *RABBI MOSES ISSERLIS (Ra-Maa)*

However, as great a scholar as Luria was and as careful as he was in his decisions, he did not succeed in making his views prevail, and the work of standardizing the German-Polish opinion on matters of Jewish law and stamping it with the impress of authority was left to one of his colleagues, Rabbi Moses Isserlis (1520-1572), known as the Ra-Maa (initials of Rabbi Moses Isserlis).

Rabbi Moses was born in Krakow, and after studying for some time under the famous scholar, Rabbi Shakhnah at Lublin whose son-in-law he later became, he returned to the city of his birth and remained there for the rest of his life. He established an academy there, and also acted as the rabbi of that famous city. Rabbi Moses Isserlis was considered one of the greatest scholars of his day and mastered practically all branches of Jewish learning. Unlike his colleague, Rabbi Luria who devoted himself to Halakah only, Isserlis took great interest also in Jewish philosophy and history, and wrote glosses to the *Guide* of Maimonides and to Zacuto's book on history, the *Yuhasin* (Sect. 128). He also studied the Kabbala and wrote several works of a Kabbalistic nature.

His forte, however, was the Halakah and in this field he was a very prolific author. He wrote commentaries on a number of tractates of the Talmud, two commentaries, a long and a short one, on the *Tur,* glosses to the *Mordecai,* a digest of the early code, *Shaarē Dura,* under the name of *Torath Hatath* (The Law concerning Sin), referring to the laws of Isur we-Heter, included in that digest. Besides all these, he also wrote a book of Responsa. But all these works were really preparatory to his Magnum Opus, the addition to the *Shulhan Aruk* which completed this work and made it the code of Israel. Isserlis, like the other Polish scholars, was dissatisfied with Karo's code for its one-sided decisions, but unlike them, he did not disregard its excellent qualities and decided to remedy its defects. He then wrote his additions to it (Hagaoth) and called it *Mapath ha-Shulhan* (The Table Cloth). In these additions which are quite extensive, Isserlis set forth the Franco-German views of Jewish law. Wherever he saw Karo opposing such views, he immediately corrected him by deviating from his decision and offering another. Isserlis paid special attention to customs (Minhagim). There are hundreds of customs, popular ways of conduct included in his *Mapah*. The expressions "And this is the custom in these countries," and "Thus we conduct ourselves" abound in the book. Isserlis raised many *Minhagim* to the status of laws, believing that every custom has roots in the life of the people. At times, he followed a custom even when it opposed the law, though he could not find any special reason for it.[3]

There is a prevailing opinion that the *Mapah* of Isserlis or the glosses and additions of the *Ra-Maa* imparted a tone of severity and rigorousness to Jewish law, and that the burden of the law would have been lighter had the code been left as it was issued from the hands of Karo. This opinion is only partially true. It is true that on the whole there are more severities (Humoroth) than leniences (Kuloth). Yet the excess of the former over the latter is not as great as is usually maintained. In general, as one scholar aptly observes,[4] the Spanish codifiers were more lenient in the dietary and kindred laws (Isur we-Heter), while the Franco-German codifiers always took the more rigorous view in such matters. But in laws affecting the relation of Jews and gentiles, such as food and wine prepared and handled by the latter and certain phases of the Sabbath law, the Germans were inclined to be more lenient while the Spanish scholars leaned towards rigorousness. Isserlis reflects, therefore, in his additions, the German view both in its rigorousness and leniency.

Besides, there are many leniences which he himself introduced and of special importance is a certain principle for decision of the law. This principle is the one which allows the rabbi to pronounce a lenient decision in a matter of law, when the usual one would involve a considerable loss (Hefsed Merubah). It is a very pliable principle and makes much for the mitigation of the law in a large number of matters, as it is entirely left to the rabbi to decide what

[3a] On this, see Tshernowitz's elucidating essay in ha-Shiloah, V. 2.
[4] Tshernowitz's, Ibid, p. 400.

constitutes "a considerable loss." It is for him to determine whether a small loss would not be considered a considerable one if it affected a poor man. Thus, this principle which was established by Isserlis helped to introduce a great amount of leniency in the decision of laws. The *Ra-Maa* displays also a certain liberality in matters of opinion and attitude to the sciences and other branches of knowledge besides Rabbinics. Karo who was a mystic was very rigorous in such matters. Thus he prohibits the reading of books of history and secular literature on the Sabbath, while Isserlis allows the reading of this literature if written in Hebrew. He likewise allows the use of the astrolabe (an astronomical instrument) on the Sabbath, showing in all such decisions his enlightened attitude towards science and investigation.

The *Mapah* of Isserlis made the *Shulhan Aruk* complete, and henceforth it was gradually accepted as the final authoritative code, though even then not without a struggle.

61. RABBI MORDECAI JAFFE (The Lebush)

As stated, the *Shulhan Aruk,* even after it was completed by Isserlis, still had to struggle for some time for final acceptance as the authoritative code of Jewry. Small wonder, then, that contemporary scholars in Poland who, for one reason or another, found fault with the Karo-Isserlis code, thought best to try their hand at codification and compiled their own codes. The most important of these scholars was Rabbi Mordecai Jaffe. (1530-1612.)

Rabbi Mordecai was born in Prague but went to Poland to study where he attended the academies of Luria and Isserlis, thus having the two great Rabbinic scholars of the generation for his instructors. He later returned to Prague and established his own academy. In the year 1561, on account of the persecution of the Jews in Bohemia, he left the country and went to Italy where he devoted himself to various studies including philosophy and astronomy. After a stay of ten years, he returned to Poland and held successively the post of rabbi in the largest Jewish communities, such as Lublin, Kremenetz, Grodno and Posen. During his stay in Poland, Rabbi Mordecai displayed great activity in the communal affairs of this center of Jewry and is said to have been instrumental in making "The Council of

Four Lands" (Vaad Araba Arátzoth), a permanent and authoritative institution.[5]

Rabbi Mordecai Jaffe, like his teacher Moses Isserlis, was a versatile scholar as he was interested in other branches of knowledge besides Halakah. Among his works, there are commentaries on the *Guide* of Maimonides, on the astronomical portion of the Mishnah Torah (dealing with the calendar) on the *Ricanti,* a famous Kabbalistic book (Sect. 114) and finally a supercommentary on Rashi's commentary on the Bible. All these show the diversity of his scholarly interests. But like all the Polish scholars, his strength lay in the field of Rabbinics and on the works in this field his fame rests.

These works are the *Five Lebushim* (Garments) which constitute his code. Mordecai Jaffe named all his works, ten in all, *Lebushim* in allusion to Esther (VIII, 15) where it is said, "And Mordecai went out from the presence of the king in royal apparel of blue and white and with a great crown of gold and with a garment of fine linen and purple." And since his name was Mordecai, he adopted the name *Lebush* as a title for his books and called each work by this name qualifying it by the adjectives in the verse. Thus one of his works is called *Lebush Malḳut* (Garment of Royalty), another *Lebush Teḳheleth,* etc.

The history of the code of Rabbi Mordecai is a very interesting one. While yet a young man, he planned to compile a code which would give the decision of the law briefly and clearly, but during the time that he was arranging the material, Rabbi Joseph Karo published his *Beth Yoseph.* At first, he rejoiced at it greatly, admiring Karo's erudition and skill. However, after examining it carefully, he found that it did not serve the purpose as its discussions were too lengthy. Jaffe then planned to prepare a digest of the *Beth Yoseph,* but before he completed his work, Karo himself published the *Shulhan Aruḳ.* When this work came to his hand, he was again disappointed, both on account of its brevity and because of its disregard of the views of

[5] The Council of Four Lands was the supreme tribunal and the highest administrative organ of the entire Polish Jewry. All matters affecting the relations between the Jews and the government, such as the fixation of the amount of taxes to be paid, the distribution of these among the communities, as well as cases of adjustment between the communities proper were brought before it and its decision was final. The members of the council consisted of representatives, both laymen and rabbis, of the four provinces, large Poland, little Poland, Galicia and Vohynia and hence its name. The council met several times during the year when fairs were held. Its exact date of origin is not definitely known, but it is surmised that by the middle of the sixteenth century it was already in existence. It later extended its scope of activity to all phases of Jewish life. It was dissolved by the Polish government in 1764.

German authorities. He then set out to prepare a complement to it, and again he was thwarted by the fact that his teacher Isserlis had already done so. However, upon examining the completed work, he still found it unsatisfactory on account of its brevity and decided to return to his work.

The *Lebush* was intended by the author as a compromise between the lengthy *Beth Yoseph* and the too brief *Shulhan Aruk*. It follows the same order of arrangement as the latter and is accordingly divided into the four divisions of that book, except that to the first division, the *Orah Hayyim,* two *Lebushim* are devoted. His method is both to state the decision briefly and also to indicate the derivation of the law from the Bible through the subsequent sources. He does not, however, quote the sources verbatim, but merely gives the gist of the opinions they contain. Besides this principal contribution, he introduced many deviations in the decisions where he differs with Karo and Isserlis. In general, he like Isserlis, paid great attention to customs, but still, at times, he rejected many of them which in his opinion, were founded on ignorance. Wherever possible, Rabbi Mordecai supplied the reasons for many laws and decisions, and as he was also a student of the Kabbala, he drew upon it frequently for explanations of practices and customs. In this, he was unlike his teacher, Isserlis, who though himself a Kabbalist, did not inject its teachings into the Halakah.

The *Lebush* is well organized and written in excellent style. On account of its qualities, it was considered authoritative by the contemporary scholars, and for a time, it looked as if it might supplant the *Shulhan Aruk* as a code. But it was not to do so: first, scholars found errors in its decisions and quotations; second, the single authority of Rabbi Mordecai Jaffe could not outweigh the combined authorities of Karo and Isserlis. Accordingly, the popularity of the *Lebush* began to wane after a short while, and the *Shulhan Aruk* came into its own. Soon a number of great scholars began to write commentaries on the *Shulhan Aruk,* and thus placed the seal of added authority upon it.

C. Code Commentaries

62. *INTRODUCTORY*

As was noted several times, the making and compilation of codes did not stop for a moment the continuous literary activity in the field of Rabbinics. On the contrary, it served as a stimulus for a fresh activity which resulted in the writing of new works which contained refutations of the decisions of the codes or additions to these decisions, or commentaries which explained the codes themselves. As there were many codes compiled, and as the number of scholars in all Jewries who wanted to distinguish themselves in some species of literary activity was quite large, it follows that an excessive number of commentaries on codes were written during the generations. In fact, there is hardly a code even of the unimportant ones which was not ornamented by four or five commentaries. The more important codes were commented upon by many times that number. Thus, we have one hundred and eighty-six commentaries extant on the Code of Maimonides alone,[6] and undoubtedly many more were lost or are still lying hidden in manuscript.

However, of this mass of literature, there are a few works which rise above the mediocre status of commentaries and deserve special attention even in a brief survey of this field of literary activity, both on account of their special merit as well as on account of their authors. These particular commentaries were singled out by the printers of the codes to be included in the editions and are thus part of the code literature. Moreover, most of these commentaries are really important Rabbinic works themselves, and very often served either as a basis for new codes or as authorities for later scholars for decisions differing from those of the codes.

63. *COMMENTARIES ON THE CODE OF MAIMONIDES (Mishnah Torah)*

The Mishnah Torah, both on account of its importance and because of its excessive brevity in stating the decisions, received great attention at the hands of the commentators. The first important commentary on that code was written by Rabbi Shem Tob Abraham Gaon of Spain, a disciple of Solomon ben Adret under the name of *Migdal Oz* (A Strong Citadel). There was a double purpose to his work, first, to supply the sources of Rabbi Moses' decisions and show how he derived them from the Talmud and other books, second, to refute the objections of Rabbi Abraham ben David (Raabad) to the code. The book is, therefore, of great value as Rabbi Shem Tob opens up for us the treasures of this great code and shows us Mai-

[6] A Jellinek in his *Kuntres ha-Rambam*.

monides' way of reasoning in matters of law. It has also an added value from the fact that Rabbi Shem Tob corrected many errors in the text of the Mishnah Torah, for he possessed a copy corrected by Maimonides himself. Yet with all its qualities, it is brief and insufficient, and left enough room for the commentators who followed.

The second commentary is one by a contemporary German scholar Rabbi Meir ha-Cohen, a disciple of Rabbi Meir of Rothenburg, by the name of *Hagaoth Maimonioth* (Maimonidian Glosses). This work is limited only to those parts of the code which deal with the laws practiced after the destruction of the Temple. In his work, Rabbi Meir at times explains the text, and at times, supplies reasons for the decisions of Maimonides. His main purpose, however, was to add to the decisions of Maimonides the opinions of the Franco-German scholars. Especially numerous, in the *Glosses,* are the decisions of the teacher of the author, Rabbi Meir of Rothenburg. The work of Rabbi Meir ha-Cohen was held in great esteem by the later codifiers who incorporated some of his decisions and views in their own codes.

Another excellent commentary on the code was written about the same time by Don Vidal di Tulusha of Spain under the name of *Magid Mishnah* (The Informer of the Mishnah, an allusion to Zechariah IX, 12 and to the name of the code Mishnah Torah). This is a real commentary as the primary aim of the author was to explain the meaning of the words of Maimonides. He, of course, paid great attention to the stating of the sources and to the refutation of the objections raised by the opponents of Rabbi Moses. Having been a great admirer of the logical system of Maimonides in the arrangement of the code, Don Vidal endeavored to show the student its value and comprehensiveness. He, therefore, prefaced his commentary on each section with a short introduction devoted to the explanation of the logical inherence of the various groups of Halakic statements contained in that section, their sequence and order of precedence. He believed that if we understood correctly all the details of the arrangement of the code, many of the objections raised against some of the decisions would disappear and difficulties would be cleared up. The style of Don Vidal is terse and concise, and unnecessary scholastic discussions are avoided. Later codifiers quote the commentary frequently and speak of the author with great reverence, usually by the name of *ha-Rab ha-Magid* after his commentary.

Of the life of Don Vidal, we know practically nothing except what is told to us by Isaac Barfat (Sect. 67) in his Responsa that he was the colleague of Rabbi Nissim Gerundi. We can thus conclude that he flourished in the second half of the thirteenth century. There is no other work ascribed to him. The commentary is his only literary monument.

The fourth and probably the best commentary is the *Keseph Mishnah* (literally, Double Silver)[7] after Genesis XLIII, 12 and with allusion to the name Mishnah Torah by Rabbi Joseph Karo. Karo was a great admirer of the code and he was anxious to make it accessible to all, to point out the sources of the Halakoth, to refute objections and to explain every difficult passage. He was, at first, moved to compose his own commentary for the reason that Don Vidal's did not cover the entire code as parts of it were either lost or not completed, and he, therefore, intended to comment on only the omitted parts. However, after beginning his work, he found that the *Magid Mishnah,* with all its excellent qualities, was not sufficient to a complete understanding of the text. He, therefore, decided to cover the entire code.

Karo's *Keseph Mishnah* is quite an extensive commentary and embraces all the phases of explanation indicated above. However, its length is variable. On the missing parts of Don Vidal's commentary, it is lengthy and detailed, on the other parts it is shorter and is devoted to the elucidation of points either not touched upon by Vidal or erroneously or insufficiently explained by him. Karo constitutes himself a champion of Rabbi Moses and strives with all his skill to defend his views against all objections raised by Abraham ben David as well as Rabbi Meir ha-Cohen, the author of the *ha-Gahoth Maimonioth.* In doing so, he endeavors to defend the views of the Spanish codifiers against those held by the Franco-German scholars.

Besides these four most important commentaries, there are three more printed with the text, the first a partial commentary by Rabbi David Ibn Abi Zimra (Sect. 69), the second the *Lehem Mishnah* (Double Portion of Bread or the Bread of the Mishnah, allusion to the name) by Rabbi Abraham di Buton (1560-1606) of Salonika, and the third, the *Mishnah le-Melek* (The Viceroy, i. e. it serves to explain the words of the king, the scholar) by Rabbi Judah Rusanis

[7] Karo, however, explains the word Keseph not as silver, but as derived from the root Kasof, i. e. to desire, and the meaning therefore is "double desire" or "great desire" to understand the words of Maimonides.

(1557-1627). The first is an extensive commentary as Ibn Abi Zimra wrote his work before Karo. The nature of the second is variable for the following reason. When di Butan began his work, he was unaware of Karo's commentary, and he, therefore, wrote extensively, but after covering the first two books, the commentary reached him, and he changed his method, writing down such comments as were not included by Karo. The third is more in the nature of a *Tosofoth,* i. e. glosses, additions, and novellae to the commentaries of the predecessors.

64. COMMENTARIES ON THE TUR

The number of commentaries on the code of Rabbi Jacob is also large, though they are not as numerous as on that of Maimonides. The most important which are joined to the text in all editions are four in number. The first is Karo's *Beth Yoseph,* but as noted above, it is only a commentary in name, for in reality, it is a code in itself. Yet, inasmuch as it follows the order of the *Tur* and quotes the sources of the laws, it throws light directly and indirectly upon many passages of the text.

The second commentary is the *Darkē Moshe* (The Ways of Moses) written by Rabbi Moses Isserlis. It was originally intended as a real commentary on the text, but meanwhile the *Beth Yoseph* appeared and there the tendency to disregard the views of the German codifiers was in great evidence. Rabbi Isserlis, who considered himself the champion of these views, turned his commentary into a polemic work, as the *Darkē Moshe* is devoted more to combating the views of Karo than to the explanation of the Tur. In this work Isserlis laid the foundation of his later complement to the *Shulhan Aruk*. He defends there vigorously the decisions of the German codifiers and also raises the folk customs to the status of laws, a principle which he carried out with more persistency in his later work. Isserlis, however, paid some attention to the text of the *Tur* proper and explained difficult passages and supplied the sources of its statements.

The third commentary is the one by Rabbi Joshua Falk (d. 1614), a contemporary of Rabbi Meir Lublin and a disciple of Rabbis Luria and Isserlis. His commentary is really a double one, as it is divided into two parts, one named *Perishah* (commentation) and the other *Derishah* (investigation). The names indicate the character of the parts. In the first the author really explains the text offering various interpretations, some excerpted from other commentaries and some his own. In the second part, he supplies the sources for the statements of the *Tur* and offers proof by keen discussion for his own interpretations of the text where they differ from those of Karo and Isserlis. In addition, Falk wrote glosses to Isserlis' commentary on the *Tur,* adding some new rules and decisions not mentioned by Rabbi Jacob, Karo or Isserlis. The fine arrangement of his commentary which separated the element of explanation from that of scholastic discussion, its brevity and conciseness, and the mental keenness displayed in its remarks made it a valuable contribution to the exegesis of the code.

The fourth and last important commentary is the *Beth Hadash* (The New House) by Rabbi Joel Jaffa or, as he is better known, Sirkis (1570-1641). He was one of the leading rabbis of his generation and occupied rabbinical posts in important Jewish communities, among them that of Brest and Krakow. Rabbi Joel belonged to that class of rabbis who were not entirely satisfied with the *Shulhan Aruk* as a code, and it was his intention to bring back the *Tur* as the code of authority. But in order to accomplish this, the *Tur* had first to be commented upon properly as Karo's work was insufficient, and Falk's had not yet reached him. He, therefore, composed his own commentary which is both sufficient and extensive. Sirkis' primary purpose was to explain the text in detail, and he carried out his purpose completely. He not only explains the statements of Rabbi Jacob but analyzes them into their constituent parts. He also explains the statements of the authorities quoted in the text. In addition, Rabbi Joel who possessed a critical faculty for discovering faulty readings in texts, as evidenced by his glosses to the Talmud, also did much to correct the text of the Tur. He spared no effort in examining old manuscripts and editions until he succeeded in establishing the correct readings. His corrections have helped much toward the understanding of the text, as many a difficulty in meaning was removed by these improved readings. The commentary *Beth Hadash* (abbreviated Bah) made the *Tur* an open book accessible to all students.

65. *COMMENTARIES ON THE SHULHAN ARUK*

As pointed out, all efforts on the part of the opponents of the *Shulhan Aruk* to prevent its acceptance as the authoritative and final code were not successful. On the contrary, as years went by, its use became more prevalent. One of the important factors in the acceptance of the *Shulhan Aruk* was the fact that great scholars who did recognize its value began to write commentaries on it a few decades after its appearance, and thus put their seal of approval upon the text. The number soon began to multiply, so that in the course of time, the *Shulhan Aruk* became the book most commented upon next to the Code of Maimonides. However, in this case, as in that of the other standard codes, the number of important commentaries are few and these will be surveyed.

The first of such commentaries was written by Joshua Falk, the commentator on the *Tur* under the title *Sepher Meiroth Ainaim* (The Book Which Enlightens the Eye) better known by the abbreviation *Sema* the initials of the three words. It is intended, as the name indicates, to enlighten the student in the understanding of the text. And it really deserves its name, for it covers all phases of exegesis. It supplies both the sources of and the reasons for each decision, explains almost every expression of the text of both Karo and Isserlis and finally, also gives the correct readings of Isserlis' glosses and clarifies them. Falk also added some new rules of his own which he indicated by an asterisk to show that they do not belong to the *Shulhan Aruk* proper. To complete his work, he also added a new detailed table of contents of the part he commented upon instead of the brief one composed by Karo. However, this splendid commentary was not completed, as only the first part of it, that on the *Hoshen Mishpat* appeared. Had Falk completed his commentary on all the four parts, it is possible that the later commentators could well have afforded to spare themselves the trouble of composing their works.

But since Falk had not written any commentaries on the other books, there was a need for further commentation which was soon filled by the works of the great scholars who ultimately became the expounders of the *Shulhan Aruk*. These were Rabbi David ben Samuel ha-Levi (d. 1667) and Sabbatai Cohen (1622-1663). Rabbi David was born at Ludmir, Volhynia and early in life distinguished himself as a great scholar. As a result, the famous Rabbi Joel Sirkis (Bah) of Krakow offered him his daughter in marriage. He later held the post of rabbi in several Jewish communities including that of Ostroh where formerly Luria and Edels served as spiritual leaders. During the persecutions of Chmelnicki in the years 1648-49, Rabbi David together with a number of other rabbis fled to Germany. But after wandering about for several years, he returned to Poland and became the rabbi of Lemberg where he died. Rabbi David conducted academies in all the cities where he resided and these were attended by hundreds of students who later became rabbis themselves. Thus, his authority was of great weight among the scholars of his generation, a fact which explains the wide acceptance of his commentary.

He named his commentary *Ture Zahab* (Golden Rows, in abbreviation Taz) under which name Rabbi David is so often quoted. It covers all the four parts of the *Shulhan Aruk,* but the character and the value of the commentaries differ. The most important is the one on the part named *Yore Dea.* It is this commentary, printed during his life time in 1616, on which his fame rests.

The purpose of Rabbi David's work seemed to have been a double one. He states in the introduction that since after the appearance of Karo's code, many rabbis arose who wrote their own works and differed in their decisions, the very purpose of that code had been defeated for there was again confusion and indecision. He, therefore, intended to bring about unanimity once more in decision of the law through his commentary and furthermore to reestablish the authority of the *Shulhan Aruk.* He carried out both purposes. He explains the text, indicates the sources and defends the decisions of the code from all refutations, thus establishing its authority. But he also devotes much space to quoting the opinions and the views of Luria, Falk and Sirkis, the opponents of Karo and Isserlis, and compares them with those of the latter, analyzing and testing their arguments, and ultimately arriving at the final decision. Thus, it is not a plain commentary but really a work containing both interpretations of the text and additions to it. The *Taz* is written in a pilpulistic manner and contains lengthy scholastic discussions, yet on account of its great merit, it was accepted in all schools. The next in importance is Rabbi David's commentary on the *Orah Hayyim,* but it falls much below the one on the *Yore Dea.* It is of a more scholastic nature, and deals less with the text than with the discussions upon the opinions of the sources which underlie the *Shulhan Aruk.* Rabbi David is here more of a critic of the opinions of the various code writers than a commentator. Still, even here, he explains and expounds the text many times, and as usual, endeavors to arrive at the final decision, and also adds some new laws not contained in the Code. His commentaries on the parts of the *Hoshen Mishpat* and *Eben ha-Ezer* are fragmentary, and are primarily collections of discussions on things related to the subject of the text. These commentaries were printed many years after the author's death and were only joined to the *Shulhan Aruk* because of the authority of the *Taz* on the *Yore Dea.*

The other great commentator, Rabbi Sabbatai was the wonder of his age. When a mere youth of twenty, he was appointed a member of the Jewish court of the famous community of Wilna. During the persecutions of the years 1648-49, he emigrated to Germany and was appointed rabbi of the community of Helishau in Moravia, where he died at the age of forty-one. Rabbi Sabbatai wrote his commentary on the *Yore Dea* at the age of twenty-four and named it *Sifthē Cohen* (abbreviated *Shakh,* the Speech of the Cohen, an allusion to his name and to the expression in Malachai II, 7, "The lips of the priest guard knowledge"). It was printed in the year 1646, the same year the *Taz* issued from the press.

The commentary testifies to the great scholastic skill and keen mental acumen of the author. It aimed to interpret the text, decide between the opinions of Karo and Isserlis and to defend both of them from the attacks of the opponents. In order to carry out his first aim, Sabbatai quotes and explains the sources on which the decisions of the code are based, and also scrutinizes minutely every expression of the text so that every statement becomes clear. As for the second purpose, he endeavors to smooth out the apparent differences between Karo and Isserlis and bring their views into harmony as much as possible. Great energy is devoted by him to the defense of the *Shulhan Aruk*. He quotes the opinions of the later authorities (Ahronim) who differed with the code, criticizes them and thus removes their objections, though he himself differs at times from both Karo and Isserlis. His commentary is thus, like the *Taz,* a great work in itself which excels the former by its brilliancy, logical acumen and scholastic keenness.

When the *Shakh* appeared, Rabbi David the author of the *Taz,* saw that a great rival to his own commentary had arisen and looked at it askance, especially since its author was a mere youth. The other scholars also disregarded it at first for the same reason, and Rabbi Sabbatai's commentary was in danger of being pushed aside. He then composed a special work by the name of *Nekudoth ha-Keseph* (Points of Silver) devoted entirely to the refutation of the opinions of the *Taz.* This new work displayed the great scholarship of Sabbatai and the rabbis took notice of the new star which had arisen on the horizon of Rabbinic scholarship. Rabbi David, on the other hand, did not deign to enter into an open polemic with his young antagonist, but added a few pages to his commentary wherein he refuted the arguments of the author of the *Shakh* without mentioning him by name, merely stating, "some say" or "some ask." However, henceforth, the *Shakh* took its place beside the *Taz,* and in time even took precedence over it and these two became standard commentaries on the *Shulhan Aruk*.

Rabbi Sabbatai also wrote a commentary by the same name on the *Hoshen Mishpat,* but it does not bear the same characteristics. It is not a real commentary, for that work was practically done by Rabbi Falk (Sema). It is rather a work of criticism of the opinions of all the codifiers, including those of Karo and Isserlis. There is exceptional scholastic skill displayed in it, and the erudition shown is astounding. It was, therefore, greatly admired by students, but when they were in need of a commentary they turned to the *Sema* of Falk.

Among the more important commentaries on the other two parts of the *Shulhan Aruk* may be mentioned first, the *Magen Abraham* (The Shield of Abraham) by Rabbi Abraham Abeli Gumbiner on the part known as *Orah Hayyim.* Rabbi Abraham was the rabbi and head of a community at Kalisz, one of the leading communities of Poland and ranked high among the scholars of the day. His work is a real commentary as it is primarily devoted to the explanation of the text, but like the others, it also contains some additions in decisions and customs. It was accepted by the scholars of the day and is, therefore, considered even in the present day a standard work on all questions of ritual and festival laws, while the *Taz* is relegated to a secondary place.

The second is the *Helkath Mehokek* (The Portion of the Law-Giver) on the fourth part of the Code called *Eben ha-Ezer* by Rabbi Moses Lima (d. 1651). His work filled a real need, for up to his time, this part of the Code had been neglected, and except for the fragmentary work of the *Taz,* no commentary was written on it. Rabbi Moses' commentary is an extensive and detailed one and primarily expounds the text. The third commentary is the *Beth Samuel* (The House of Samuel) on the same part of the Code by Rabbi Samuel ben Uri of Fürth (fl. 1640-1690). This work is a kind of supplement to Lima's, devoted more to discussions on points of law related to the text rather than to the explanation of the text itself. Yet, inasmuch as the author displays great erudition in his discussions and keen analysis of the sources, his work throws new light on many passages of the text and was therefore greatly esteemed by the scholars.

With the composition of the standard commentaries on all the parts of the *Shulhan Aruk*, the code of Karo and Isserlis received its final authorization and became the ultimate compendium of Jewish law followed by the entire Jewry. This, however, did not prevent later scholars from continuing to write commentaries and *novellae* to the code. The fertile Rabbinic mind always possesses enough ingenuity to add something new to the works of its predecessors, be it a new interpretaion of the meaning of their statements or the raising of objections to their decisions and removing them or the deduction by analysis of new decisions. Accordingly, the compiling of commentaries and additions to the code was constantly increasing, but only a few of these received recognition and were joined to the text.

Of these later commentaries, the most important are several which bear the same name *Beēr Heteb* (A Good Explanation) and are of similar character, but were written by different men. The most popular is the one composed by Judah Ashkenazi, dayan of Tiktin (fl. 1700-1740). It covers the first three parts of the code, i. e. *Orah Hayyim, Yore Dea* and *Eben ha-Ezer*. The fourth part, the *Hoshen Mishpat* dealing with civil law was commented upon by his son-in-law, Moses Frankfurt. Another commentary of the same order and which later received the same name was composed by Zechariah Mendel of Krakow, covering the parts of *Yore Dea* and *Hoshen Mishpat*. There are a few more such commentaries. The general characteristic of these is that they form a digest of the contents of the standard commentaries and are brief and concise. This quality contributed greatly to their popularity and many smaller editions of the code contain only the *Beēr Heteb*.

Other less important commentaries are the *Peri Hadash* by Hezekiah da Silva (c. 1700), *Peri Megodim* (Sweet Fruit) by Joseph Teomim, a school teacher of Krakow, and *Pithē Teshubah* (The Gates of Responsa) by Abraham Hirsh Eisenstadt. All these are more or less supercommentaries on the standard ones. Finally, there is a work which deserves to be mentioned, though it is not a commentary. This is the *Beēr ha-Golah* (The Well of the Exile, an allusion to the fact that the author was then a refugee) by Moses Rivkash of Wilna (1600-1660). This work is a register of the sources from which the statements of the text were drawn. It is primarily limited to the task the author set for himself, but here and there, it contains also glosses, readings and short notes where certain objections raised by commentators are refuted.

D. Responsa

66. *CHARACTER OF THE RESPONSA OF THE PERIOD*

The commentaries on the Talmud and the codes hitherto surveyed with all their extensiveness and voluminousness formed after all only the lesser part of the Rabbinic literature produced during this period. The larger portion of it is occupied by the Responsa. Almost every rabbi of importance whether in France, Spain, Germany, Italy, Poland or elsewhere considered it his duty to write a book of Responsa. The number of such books of collected Responsa which appeared in print reaches to several thousand, while those that are still in manuscript will undoubtedly equal if not exceed that number. And still, this mass of legal literature is only to a small degree theoretical and scholastic, for on the whole, it was called forth by the exigencies of life. In the life of the Jews of the Middle Ages wholly permeated by religion as it was and where the scrupulous observance of the Law was the paramount question, inquiries were bound to spring up daily to which the dry codes could not afford an immediate answer. Life is always ahead of codified law and Jewish life is no exception. Secluded though it was, it displayed considerable variety. In most of the European and Eastern countries, the Jews possessed inner autonomy which empowered them to regulate their own social, communal and judicial affairs in addition to their religious observances. Besides, their relations to their neighbors and to the governments, the persecutions and exiles also contributed to the complexity of that life. Hence, it is quite reasonable to assume that the greater part of the Responsa were actually written in answer to inquiries regarding cases which occurred and which pointed to new phases of life not taken account of by the ordinary codes. The answers had to be deduced by the respondent scholar by analogy and analysis, either from the codes or directly from the Talmud.

We must, however, note a difference in the relation of these Responsa collections to the codes in accordance with the age in which they were written. The earlier collections written before the final codes, the *Tur* and *Shulhan Aruk* which were accepted as standard contain much simpler matter, i. e. queries to which the inquirer could have found an answer in any well compiled code, were such available. The later collections were primarily limited to questions of a complicated nature, the answer to which was not found explicitly in the codes. Sometimes because a decision could not be reached on account of difference of opinion among codifiers, the respondent was called upon for a decision. The nature of the Responsa varies with the character of the inquiries. In the case of the simpler inquiries, the answers are likewise simple and brief, and in the case of the complex ones, the answers are similarly complicated, lengthy and display much scholastic ingenuity.

From all that has been said, it becomes clear that the Responsa performed a double function, inasmuch as they were both a basis for and a supplement of the codes. Many of the decisions of the earlier authorities in their Responsa were later incorporated by the compilers in their codes. On the other hand, the decisions of the later scholars covering cases not found in the codes were considered as precedents by still later scholars who were guided by them in similar cases. The Responsa, however, are of interest not only to the Rabbinic scholar, but to the historian as well. These collections of inquiries and answers reflect Jewish life during the Middle Ages in all parts of the world to its fullest extent in all its phases and manifestations. The Responsa teem with inquiries touching upon the economic, family, social and communal life of the Jews, and are thus a veritable mine of information upon the daily life of the Jew and his conduct, both religious and social. It is to be regretted that this source has not been exploited sufficiently by writers on Jewish history, who could, on the basis of the Responsa, reconstruct a fair picture of Jewish life in the past.

On the whole, there is a certain sameness to this large mass of collected Responsa which arises from the similarity of Jewish life in the various Jewries. But there is also variety in them where considerable difference in the types of life existed. The Responsa of this period (from the 12th to the 18th centuries) can, therefore, be subdivided into two epochs, those written in the first three centuries, i. e. up to the end of the fifteenth, and those written subsequently. Each of these epochs exhibits two types of Responsa. In the first epoch, these are the Spanish and the Franco-German, and in the second, the Responsa hailing from the East and those penned in the West, i. e. Germany and Poland. In the former type, the life represented is more varied and many-colored. The wide inner autonomy the Jews of Spain and the East possessed is reflected in the exceptional large number of judicial cases dealt with in the Responsa, in the severe punishment meted out by the judges upon offenders against Jewish law and in the excellent form of communal organization described there. The freer type of life carried on by these Jews is manifested in other ways among which is also the frequency of infringements upon morality, cases of which are described in the Responsa. The latter type of Responsa, on the other hand, exhibits the more secluded life of the Jews of Germany and Poland, their restricted rights, the persecutions and exiles. Cases arising from these conditions abound. The Responsa teem with questions of taxes, special levies, cases of conversion and cases of women whose husbands were killed during the persecutions (Agunoth), who petitioned for permission to remarry.

The difference in the degree of intellectuality of the various Jewries is also evident in these types. The Spanish-Eastern Responsa contain many inquiries of a non-Halakic character, namely concerning historical matters, theological and philosophic opinions, explanations of Biblical verses or meaning of Talmudic terms and some mathematical problems. The German-Polish collections are limited primarily, with few exceptions, to cases of law.

As in the preceding chapters, our review will be limited to a small number of collections of Responsa written by the great authorities and possessing exceptional merit and value.

67. *SPANISH RESPONSA FROM THE TWELFTH TO THE SIXTEENTH CENTURY*

The most important Responsa collections of the thirteenth century are those of ben Adret and Rabbi Asher. True, there is a collection of Responsa ascribed to Nahmanides bearing the name *Sheiloth u-Teshuboth l'Rabenu Moishe bar Nahman* (Responsa to Inquiries by our Teacher Moses ben Nahman), but careful perusal shows clearly that with the exception of five or six Responsa, the entire collection belongs to ben Adret. Nahmanides, therefore, can not be taken into consideration as a respondent.

Of the two collections, the first is the more voluminous, the more extensive and all-embracing. Ben Adret was considered the greatest scholar of his day and his name was widely known throughout Jewry. Inquiries, therefore, were addressed to him from all parts of the world, including Palestine. His Responsa collection is divided into five parts, of which the first part alone contains twelve hundred and fifty-five answers. Adding to these five parts the pseudo-Nahmanides' collection which belongs to ben Adret, the number of Responsa reaches to well over three thousand. The inquiries touch on all phases of law, religious, family and civil. The last two phases are exceptionally well represented. Almost one-half of the Responsa is devoted to cases of civil law and communal affairs. This part supplies much information concerning Jewish life in Spain. We learn of the various kinds of businesses the Jews were engaged in, of the regulations and statutes fixed by the elders of the communities and of kindred matters. Thus, we see that Jewish life was well regulated by the community leaders, that they fixed the price of commodities (R. 590), determined the curriculum of the schools, banned the study of certain books (R. 417), passed regulations regarding the validity of promissory notes and many more things. We also learn that although Jewish life was, on the whole, superior morally to that of their neighbors, yet there were occasional breaches of family morality, but we note that these breaches were severely punished.

The Responsa of the *Rashba* contain a large number of non-Halakic inquiries. There are a considerable number of questions asking for explanations of certain contradictory statements either in the Bible proper, such as between verses in 2 Samuel, XXIV and I Chronicles XXI (R. 12), or between statements in the Talmud and the Bible. Again, some ask the meaning of verses or passages in the Aramaic translation of Onkelos. There are a number of highly interesting theological inquiries, such as regarding the relation between the performance of precepts (Mitzvoth) and their inner meaning and intention (Kavanah), others regarding the role destiny plays in human affairs, or whether the cures for sickness mentioned in the Talmud are effective, and whether some should not be subsumed under *Darke ha-Emori* (i. e. The Ways and Superstitions of the Amorites, prohibited by the Bible). There are also some philosophical inquiries, such as the question of the contradiction between the theory of the indestructibility of the world taught by the philosophers, and the opinion expressed in the Talmud that the world must come to an end (R. 9), questions on Providence and others.

In all his answers to such complicated questions, ben Adret gives his opinion at great length, defending tradition against philosophy. He does not, however, disparage the teachings of philosophy. On the contrary, he pays his respects to them but claims validity for tradition which is a supplement to the Bible. He admits that many verses of the Bible can not be taken literally, that they have to be interpreted, but that we must place upon them the interpretation of tradition. In general, ben Adret endeavors to the best of his ability, to deal with these vexing problems in a rational manner, circumscribed by tradition.

We have in this collection several valuable historical documents bearing on the second polemic against the works of Maimonides (Ch. X, Sect. 154). Numbers 414-417 contain the letters sent out by a number of scholars with ben Adret at their head to the communities of Spain against the study of philosophy, condemning the allegorical interpretation of the stories of the Bible, and to these is added the ban (Herem) published by them against the study of philosophy by any one younger than twenty-five years of age. Number 418 contains the long and masterful defense of the study of philosophy by Yedayah Bedersi (Ch. III, Sect. 29). This apology is of great literary value both on account of its style and content. The method of ben Adret in his Responsa differs from that in his code and *novellae*. Here with few exceptions, he is brief and answers the inquiries directly without unnecessary lengthy scholastic discussions.

The collection of the Responsa of Rabbi Asher is a considerable one, though not as voluminous by far as that of ben Adret. It must contain between twelve and fifteen hundred Responsa. It is divided into one hundred and eight small groups called *Kelallim* (K'lal in Hebrew meaning a general subject). The Responsa in each of these *Kelallim* deal with only one subject. Rabbi Asher, like ben Adret, was well known throughout Jewry, and the inquiries came from many lands. His Responsa, like those of the former, cover all phases of Jewish law and the greater part of the book is devoted to civil and communal law. Unlike ben Adret, Asher's Responsa are limited only to Halakic matter and contain no exegetical and theological discussions. Rabbi Asher, hailing from Germany, was a strict Talmudist and knew little of secular studies. Once in anger at an inquirer who insisted that the knowledge of logic was necessary in order to render a fair decision in a certain case, he exclaimed that he was thankful to God he did not engage in any secular studies. (K'Lal LV, 8.)

The Responsa of Asher strongly reflect the conditions of Jewish life in central and southern Spain. In that part of the country the Jews had an extensive autonomy and special privileges were conferred upon them by the government. Rabbi Asher, being the rabbi of Toledo, the largest Jewish community, was looked upon by the government as the chief Jewish judge, and his judicial powers which he utilized to the fullest extent were very wide. We learn from the inquiries that the Jews administered capital punishment in certain severe offences with the tacit consent of the government. In the case of an informer who repeatedly injured the interests of the community and was secretly killed by its agents, Asher decides that all the members must bear the expense incurred by that action, for regrettable as the act was, it was of benefit to the entire community (K'lal 6, R. 21).

Rabbi Asher was at first astonished on his coming to Spain to see the Jews exercising the power to punish malefactors either by death or mutilation. In time, he approved of these measures, and in his zeal for law and morality consented to and even urged such punishments. In a case of blasphemy, where a Jew blasphemed God in Arabic and was arrested through the agency of Judah Ibn Vakar, the financial agent of Don Juan, the inquirer asks what is to be done with the culprit. Asher decrees that his tongue be cut out. (K. XVII, R. 8.) In the case of an adulteress who was turned over by Don Juan to Ibn Vakar for judgment, the latter, after deciding to punish the sinner by mutilating her face, asks Asher's consent to the judgment. This is given with commendation.

This severity in punishment should, however, not be taken as a sign of harshness of character, but is to be considered as a mark of zeal for the preservation of the good name and dignity of the Jewish religion, namely that it should not be considered lightly in the eyes of the gentiles who acted in similar cases with much greater severity.

From Asher's Responsa, we also learn of the wonderful organization of the communities, how they fixed their statutes, how they levied taxes for charity and in what orderly fashion they conducted their affairs. We also glean some facts concerning the state of morality among the Jews. It was, on the whole, very strict and was enforced, as we have seen, but there were also cases of infraction. Thus, there were cases where bigamy was practiced if the first wife was childless after a period of ten years. This was done with the tacit consent of the community since the Spanish Jews did not accept the ban of Rabbi Gershom against bigamy (Vol. I, Ch. X, Sect. 141). At other times, we note Rabbi Asher denouncing very strongly the practice of certain men of marrying in one place and then again in another city, and urging a ban against them (K. XLIII, 8). In general, it can be inferred that bigamy while not infrequent, was mainly limited to cases where the wife was childless. In other cases, it was suppressed by the communities. Asher endeavored to stamp out all laxity of morals in one form or another. In answer to an inquiry as to what was to be done with an addict to gambling who foreswore the playing of cards before the leaders of the community but broke his oath, Asher responded that he should be fined a large sum of money, and if necessary, be chastised bodily (K. XI, 9).

From all this, we can infer that Jewish life in Spain during the thirteenth century was exceptionally well organized and that the communities took great care of the welfare of the individual members in all its phases, economic, spiritual and moral. These endeavors are all recorded in the Responsa of the period and thus serve as first hand documents of the history of Jewish life, besides being of value as an important part of Rabbinic literature.

The fourteenth century produced a number of Responsa collections, both small and large. To the smaller collections belong the one by Rabbi Nissim Gerundi, the famous commentator on Al-Fasi's Compendium. The number of Responsa extant is only seventy-seven and they deal with the usual subjects, and likewise reflect the Jewish life of the period. One case shows us the economic straits in which the large Jewish community of Barcelona found itself in the second half of the fourteenth century. An inquiry tells that this community was forced to borrow money and had to give a silver vessel as security. Not having a vessel of its own, it turned to one of its members, asking for the loan of the desired pledge, and as a result of this action, litigation arose. Another collection is that of Judah ben Asher (d. 1349). It contains several hundred brief Responsa by the author and also a number of Responsa by other scholars of the generation.

The first of the large collections of Responsa is by Isaac ben Sheshet Barfat, usually known as *Ribash,* i. e. Rabbi Isaac ben Sheshet (1326-1408). Rabbi Isaac was one of the leading scholars of the day, a pupil of Rabbi Nissim Gerundi and a friend and colleague of Don Hasdai Crescas, the famous philosopher. He lived for some time in Barcelona as a private citizen refusing to act as rabbi, but after some informers brought an accusation against him and Hasdai Crescas which resulted in their arrest, he left the city and accepted the post of rabbi at Saragossa. From there, he went to Valencia, the city of his birth. Meanwhile, the great massacres broke out, in the year 1391, and Rabbi Isaac together with many more Jews left the country. He settled in Algiers, North Africa, where he was accepted by that community as their rabbi. Later, he was appointed by the sultan as the chief rabbi of the entire district. In his old age, he resigned his post, turning it over to a younger scholar, Simon Duran.

Ribash's collection contains five hundred and eighteen Responsa, dealing with all phases of the law. This collection is the most important of his Halakic works, for we only possess some of his *novellae* to two tractates of the Talmud. It is in these Responsa where his great erudition is displayed, for *Ribash,* unlike his predecessors, wrote his Responsa at length, basing his decisions on proofs from the sources. His decisions were considered authoritative and a number of them were incorporated in various codes. The Responsa of *Ribash* reflect the turbulent conditions of the time and depict the life of the Jews in Spain as well as that in North Africa. We find many inquiries there which deal with cases of Marranos and their relations with the Jews, a result of the forced mass conversion in the year 1391. There is also a number of Responsa containing historical data concerning the settlements of the Spanish refugees in northern Africa. Many of the Responsa tell of the personal tribulations of Barfat and of the attacks he sustained from his opponents in the several communities in which he lived.

His Responsa, like those of ben Adret's, contain non-Halakic matter, such as explanations of Biblical verses and Agadic passages and a few philosophic questions, among which there is one on the compatibility of God's prescience with the freedom of the human will. *Ribash,* though not a philosopher, was liberal in his views and asserts that it is permitted to study the sciences, but warns against the study of Aristotle and advises not to engage in it. He speaks, however, with great respect of Maimonides and even of Gersonides. Yet he charges the latter with perverting Maimonides' statements on some important matters.

The last collection of the century was the one by Rabbi Simon ben Zemah Duran (1361-1444). Rabbi Simon was born in the island of Majorca where he studied under Rabbi Vidal Ephraim, a great Talmudist and mathematician. A few years before the massacre of 1391, he left the island and emigrated to Algiers, where he was first a judge in the court of Rabbi Isaac ben Sheshet and later succeeded him to the chief rabbinate. Rabbi Simon was one of the last Sephardic scholars whose knowledge was many-sided, embracing philosophy and the sciences besides Halakah. From his teacher Don Vidal Ephraim, he acquired a mastery of mathematics which he put to good use in solving calendar and other mathematical problems affecting certain Halakic subjects. He was deeply interested in religious philosophy and wrote several philosophic and theological works. His investigations extended also to history, to which he devoted the fourth part of his *Magen Aboth* (Sect. 80), and grammar.

His collection is divided into three parts and contains in all eight hundred and eleven Responsa. As he was the chief rabbi of an important district, thickly populated with Jewish communities, and as he was one of the leading scholars of the day, inquiries poured in from many scholars and communities on all subjects of Jewish law. His Responsa, therefore, reflect, like those of the preceding scholars, all conditions in Jewish life. The question of the Marranos and their relations with the Jews occupies in his Responsa a more prominent place than in those of *Ribash*. The non-Halakic element in them is considerable on account of his versatility. Thus, we have a number of mathematical Responsa bearing on the calculation of the area of a circle and a sphere, some calendar calculation problems, several historical Responsa where Duran displays his knowledge of Jewish history in fixing the dates and succession of the Gaonim and other scholars. There is also a considerable number of Responsa dealing with grammatical questions, especially with the vocalization of words, and Duran evidences his mastery of Jewish grammar, daring even to refute Kimhi, the master grammarian. A few Responsa deal with Kabbalistic questions. Finally, there are several (Pt. I, 144-148), defending the rabbis for accepting a salary from the congregations. It seems that in Duran's days, although the custom had been in practice for some time, it was not altogether legitimatized and still needed some defense.

68. *GERMAN AND ITALIAN RESPONSA (1200-1500)*

The German and French scholars were, as we have seen, engaged primarily in the compilation of codes or commentaries on codes in which they included many Responsa. Consequently, there are not many such collections left by scholars of these centuries. Those that are left, however, are of great importance.

Of these, the first in rank is the collection of Responsa by Rabbi Meir of Rothenburg (Sect. 55). Rabbi Meir was, as noted above, the leading scholar of his day; his Responsa therefore are numerous and deal with a great variety of subjects. Many of them, however, are not included in the collection which bears his name, but are incorporated in the writings of his great disciples. Thus, the *Mordecai,* the *Hagoth Maimonioth* and the Compendium of Rabbi Asher (Sect. 55) contain hundreds of Responsa by Rabbi Meir. The collection proper consists of one thousand and twenty-two replies to inquiries of which the larger part belong to him, for as in the case of other early collections, this one also contains a considerable number of Responsa by earlier scholars, such as Jacob Tam and Samson ben Abraham, and some by Rabbi Gershom, the Light of the Exile.

The collection of Rabbi Meir deals to a great extent with questions of religious law in its several phases, but there is also a considerable number of Responsa covering the various forms of civil law, which as usual, reflect the conditions of Jewish life. We note there many inquiries concerning cases arising from the lending of money on interest to gentiles, one of the chief occupations of the Jews in Mediaeval Germany. The echo of the persecutions and suffering on account of restrictions and expulsions is heard in many of the Responsa dealing with cases of forced conversions, heavy taxation and kindred matters. The inner life of the Jews is reflected in many ways. Especially interesting is a number of Responsa concerning the pawning and sale of books which show the high value placed upon books by these poverty-stricken Jews. Likewise, the large number of inquiries regarding the relations of teachers of children to the parents who engage them, including the questions of salary, duties of office and other matters proves to us the high position education held in Jewish life. The inquiries covering commercial cases indicate that the Jews of Germany during the thirteenth century, were engaged in the export and import business carrying their commerce to other lands. A single Responsum concerning the stealing of a slave from a Jew by a fellow Jew shows that in spite of the numerous restrictions placed by the Church upon the buying of slaves by the Jews, some managed to own and possess slaves.

The collection contains a number of documents dealing with various statutes (Takonoth) enacted by great rabbis and assemblies of rabbis. Thus, they give a list of the *Takonoth* by Rabbi Gershom, by Rabbi Jacob Tam, by an assembly of the rabbis of France and Germany in 1320 and by a still later assembly. These institutes are of great importance, as some of them, especially those concerning family life, are still in effect.

The fourteenth century produced a number of great scholars who undoubtedly wrote books of Responsa, but for one reason or another, few of them were left. All that we know about such activity is gleaned from references by later authors to collections of Responsa by Rabbi Menahem of Meisburg, by Samuel ben Aaron of Shitzstadt and by others. All these collections are lost with the exception of a few Responsa of Rabbi Menahem which were joined to a later work of Rabbi Jacob Weil.

From the fifteenth century scholars, however, we possess a number of collections. The earliest of these is the one written by Rabbi Jacob ha-Levi Möllin, known as *Maharil* (d. 1427, Sect. 53). This great scholar, expert on Jewish customs, was considered the authority in his generation, yet the number of Responsa left by him is not large. The collection contains only two hundred and five Responsa. They deal primarily with religious laws, but a considerable number cover also civil and family cases. These throw no special light upon the state of Jewish life in the fifteenth century as they discuss ordinary conditions. There is, however, one Responsum justifying the practice of a superstitious custom expressly prohibited in the Talmud, which shows the state of mind of the Jews of Germany at that time.

A quite important collecion of Responsa is the one by Rabbi Jacob Weil (d. about 1456). He was a disciple of Rabbi Jacob Möllin, and after the latter's death became the authority in the Rabbinic world. His collection contains one hundred and ninety-three Responsa discussing various subjects of Jewish law. Cases of communal affairs occupy an important place in the collection, for many communities turned to him to straighten out their affairs. Rabbi Weil used his authority to allay differences of opinion and establish peace and order in Jewish life. His Responsa are written in a brief manner without unnecessary discussion, except on certain occasions. His decisions were accepted by succeeding scholars and many of these were incorporated by Isserlis in his additions to the *Shulhan Aruk*.

A work of high value is the *Terumath ha-Deshen* by Rabbi Israel Isserlin (d. 1460). The name signifies literally the separation of the ashes, and its peculiarity is explained first by the fact that *Deshen* amounts numerically to three hundred and fifty-four, the number of Responsa in the collection, and secondly by the excessive humility of the author. He probably wanted to indicate that he considers his

Responsa only as ashes on the altar of learning, as the phrase is applied in the Talmud to the clearing of the ashes from the altar.

The subjects dealt with in this collection are varied, civil and family law being well represented. Jewish life is fairly depicted there and several Responsa show that in spite of oppression, life was not all gloomy in the Mediaeval ghetto but that occasionally it was brightened by dancing and merriment. Thus, we find an inquiry narrating the following case: A rented a girdle from B for the purpose of ornamenting himself at a wedding dance. A girl asked him for the loan of the girdle, which he agreed to do on condition that she consent to betroth herself to him in exchange for the favor. She consented, and the inquirer wants to know whether the betrothal is valid. At other times, we note the great poverty existing in the Jewish communities. An inquiry deals with the fact that several communities were forced to use one Ethrog on the Feast of Tabernacles on account of lack of funds. The Responsa of Isserlin were considered by later scholars as authoritative and were quoted by codifiers.

A fourth collection in this century is that of Rabbi Israel Bruna (1400-1480). He was a disciple of Israel Isserlin and Jacob Weil and was a renowned scholar of the day. His life, however, was full of misfortune. First, he was exiled from Brünn and thereupon settled in Regensburg or Ratisbon. But soon after his settling there, he was attacked by a resident scholar Rabbi Anschel, who though not the official rabbi objected to Israel's functioning as one. A controversy broke out in which many rabbis took part. Israel's teachers, Weil and Isserlin, defended his rights. When the quarrel quieted down, he was thrown into prison by the emperor as a pledge that the Jews would pay their crown taxes. He was released on bail but was soon imprisoned again on a charge of a blood accusation made against him by a converted Jew. He was later freed but the community was soon involved in similar false accusations, and all the Jews were arrested and imprisoned for a number of years.

Yet this turbulent life did not prevent Israel from writing Responsa in considerable numbers. The collection consists of two hundred and eighty replies to various inquiries mostly dealing with questions of religious law and only a small portion discussing civil law. In Israel's Responsa, there is reflected the rigorous piety of Mediaeval German Jewry, which expressed itself in scrupulous observances of small matters and customs. Most of the replies relate to such scruples, and on the whole, Bruna enjoins their observance, and like his teacher, places a high value upon customs. There is, however, one curious Responsum which indicates a certain laxity in regard to card playing. A correspondent asks whether a man who has vowed not to play cards may appoint an agent to play for him (R. 124)? Bruna does not permit the appointment, as the agent stands in the place of the man and the vow is thus not observed. From the serious tone of the inquiry and the reply, it is evident that card playing at the time was frequently indulged in among the Jews of Germany, and though it was not approved of by the rabbis, no serious efforts were made to stop its practice.

Turning to Italy, we note that Halakic learning declined in that country during a period of two hundred years, that is from the middle of the thirteenth to the middle of the fifteenth century. Hardly any book of importance was left to us by an Italian scholar in all these years. Only with the second half of the latter century, a revival of Jewish learning set in, and for a few centuries thereafter, Italy became once more a great center of Rabbinic learning which made important contributions to that branch of literature.

The revival, however, was not of native origin. It was primarily due to immigrant scholars who flocked to Italy from many lands, inasmuch as the position of the Jew there was comparatively better than in other countries. This migration of individual scholars coupled with the settlement of a large number of exiles from Spain and Portugal raised the intellectual level of Italian Jewry and made the revival of learning possible. The immigrant scholars were well received by their native brethren, who offering them Rabbinical posts in important communities, gave them an opportunity to continue their studies. As a result, we have a number of collections of Responsa of great value and merit.

The most important of these is the collection by Rabbi Joseph Kolon (1410-1480). This rabbi had a checkered life and career. His place of birth is not definitely known. It seems, however, from numerous references in his Responsa to decisions of well known French rabbis that he was born in that country, and that in his youth he wandered from city to city with his father. He lived later in Chambery, province of Savoy, but was compelled to leave the city in the general expulsion of the Jews from that province. He then settled in Italy, where at first he established an elementary school for Jewish children at Bologna. Yet, even in this period, his fame spread, and in spite of the fact that he did not occupy a rabbinical post, inquiries came to him from distant cities and his authority was willingly accepted. He later became rabbi of Mantua where he established an academy, which was frequented by students hailing from all parts of Italy and even from other lands. On account of a quarrel between him and his colleague, Judah Messer Leon of the same city, he together with the latter was ordered by the Duke to leave Mantua. He then settled in Pavia where he served as the rabbi of the community until the day of his death.

Kolon possessed a strong personality wielding his rabbinical authority with great dignity. He was a man of truth, and though otherwise very modest, when he believed that a religious principle had been violated either by a rabbinical colleague or a community, he minced no words and chastised the offender severely. It mattered little whether the offence against morality, religion or good conduct was committed in his own city or in a distant country. In his zeal for truth, he endeavored to carry his authority to all parts of Jewry. Thus he wrote a severe letter to the Jewish community of Wirzburg, Germany, reprimanding them for mistreating their rabbi. He interfered in the quarrels between Israel Bruna and Anschel whom the former put under ban unjustly. In spite of the fact that Bruna was a leading scholar, Kolon ordered him to rescind the ban. Again, when misinformed by evil-minded persons that Rabbi Moses Kapsali (1400-1495), chief rabbi of Constantinople, rendered certain incorrect decisions in matters of family law, he immediately wrote to the heads of the community calling upon them to remove their rabbi from his post as he had proved himself undeserving of it. It later turned out that the information was false and Kolon apologized profusely to Kapsali and ordered his son, in his testament, to travel to Constantinople and apologize in person.

Kolon's work, consisting of one hundred and ninety-seven long Responsa, reflects Jewish life in Italy in a general rather than a particular way. We note there the poor state of the rabbinate in that country, namely that many had assumed the title of rabbi without deserving it. We also learn that the rabbis were but too prone to excommunicate people for any slight offence against them. Kolon fights this indiscriminate banning and declares that there is hardly one in the generation who is worthy of the rights and privileges conferred by the Talmud upon a Talmid Hakham and it is only such a man who may allow himself to excommunicate any one for an insult to his honor. He also expresses his opinion that pilpul, i. e.

scholastic dialectics, is not the primary quality which makes for scholarship but that being versed in Halakah is of greater importance (R. 169).

In his decisions, he followed as a rule, the more severe opinion and respected custom greatly. He says in one Responsum, that if a custom is well established (R. 54) and accepted even the prophet Elijah can not change it. Yet, he made a distinction between customs and fought against irrelevant ones. Thus, he decides that there is no basis for the practice by pious Jews of not adopting the dress of the gentiles (R. 88). These views are liberal for a fifteenth century rabbi. Among his Responsa, there is one which throws light upon the profession of medicine among the Jews. It deals with the case of a medical corporation established by four physicians and later dissolved by the action of one of them. (R. 182.) From this, we learn that the number of physicians was excedingly large and that they had to combine in order to avoid competition.

The Responsa of Kolon were considered authoritative and his decisions were frequently quoted by codifiers.

Another collection of Responsa produced in Italy in the first half of the sixteenth century was one by two immigrant rabbis, Judah Mintz (1408-1509) and his grand-daughter's husband, Meir Katzenellenbogen (1482-1565). Judah Mintz was born in Germany at Mayence where he studied under famous scholars. On account of the expulsion of the Jews from that city in 1461, he settled in Padua, Italy, where he served as rabbi for a period of forty-seven years. He was also engaged in the study of the secular sciences, and is said to have taught philosophy at the University of Padua where, according to one source, his picture was hung in the halls of that famous institution. He was recognized as one of the leading scholars of that generation and his Responsa were very numerous. But due to the sacking of the city immediately after his death, all his writings were destroyed and only sixteen Responsa were saved which were published by Meir Katzenellenbogen together with his own collection.

Rabbi Meir Katzenellenbogen hailed from Prague where he studied under Jacob Polack (Sect. 46) founder of the pilpulistic system of study. He then went to Italy, studied under Mintz, married the daughter of Abraham Mintz, son of Judah, and succeeded his father-in-law in the rabbinate of Padua. Katzenellenbogen's fame spread to many lands nad his decisions were sought in Poland as well as in

Italy. It is for this reason that many of his Responsa are included in the works of other scholars.

The joint work is small as it contains ninety Responsa of Katzenellenbogen and sixteen of Mintz. It covers cases representing all phases of Jewish law and reflects to a certain degree the particular life of the Jews in Italy. From one Responsum of Mintz (R. 5), we learn that due to the influence of the environment there was in certain strata of Jewish society a laxity of morals. From another, we note the spread of the custom in the Jewish ghettoes of celebrating the festival of Purim by masquerade balls and carnivals. Mintz upon being interrogated on the question, sanctions the custom. Katzenellenbogen dates his Responsa according to the months of the general calendar, i. e. fifth of June or December, though he retains the Jewish year. In one of his replies, he takes issue with Rabbi Elijah Kapsali of Crete who wanted to prohibit the people of his community from reading the prophetic portion of Jonah on the Day of Atonement in Greek translation and not in the original Hebrew. Katzenellenbogen urges them to continue this custom. All this shows that the enlightened Italian environment influenced these rabbis in their views and forced them to make some concession to life.

Responsa Literature of the Second Period (1500-1750)

69. *COLLECTIONS OF RESPONSA BY EASTERN SCHOLARS*

As was noted above, the sixteenth century marked both the rise of a new center of learning in the East and a revival of the study of Rabbinics among the exiles of the Spanish Jewry who settled in Eastern lands. This century witnessed a remarkable phenomenon, almost unparalleled in the history of any national literature, namely the exceptional literary productivity of a group of people who but a few decades ago had been rudely torn from their ancestral homeland and transplanted into an entirely different environment. This productivity went on, as observed in previous chapters, in many branches of literature, but it was especially prolific in the field of Rabbinics. It is, therefore, not to be wondered at that the Responsa collections left by the numerous scholars of this new center during the period is exceedingly great.

We must, however, not forget that this Eastern center was not entirely devoid of Jewish learning even before the Spanish immigrants arrived. There was always some considerable intellectual activity among the Jews of Greece and those of the Aegean Islands. We had occasion to refer to scholars hailing from those parts, especially from Constantinople. This indigenous literary activity increased during the second half of the fifteenth century after the conquest of Constantinople by the Turks, which began a new era of freedom for the Jews of those parts. At that time, we meet in European Turkey scholars whose activity is worth while recording.

The greatest of these scholars was Rabbi Elijah Misrahi (1450-1525). Misrahi was a native of Constantinople and studied under Rabbi Elijah ha-Levi of that city. He also devoted himself to the study of secular sciences, especially mathematics and astronomy in which he attained great proficiency. He was first engaged in teaching Talmud and mathematics, but after the death of Moses Kapsali was appointed chief rabbi of Turkey. During his occupancy of the office, he brought about closer relations between the Rabbanite and the Karaite communities of the capital, and he decided in his Responsa that Rabbanite scholars might impart instruction to Karaites in Talmud and other Jewish studies, thus opposing his colleagues who issued a ban prohibiting such action.

Misrahi wrote many works covering various branches of literature; an extensive supercommentary on Rashi's commentary on the Pentateuch; a commentary on the *Semag* (The Code of Moses of Coucy), a commentary on Ptolemy's Almagest; the standard work on astronomy of the Mediaeval Ages; several books on mathematics and a collection of Responsa. The last work contains one hundred and thirty-eight Responsa dealing with various subjects of Jewish law. The type of life of the Jews under the Turkish regime is well reflected in them. We note the wide autonomy that the Jewish communities enjoyed and the great authority of the rabbi who was also the general assessor of taxes for all communities and the go-between between the Jews and the government. In the Responsa, there is also reflected Misrahi's liberal attitude towards the sciences, the Karaites, and his aversion to the recent Kabbalistic theories and their newfangled customs which they attempted to foist upon the people.

Probably the most important collection of the entire sixteenth century was the one by Rabbi David Ibn Abi Zimra (abbreviated Radbaz), (1464-1574). Ibn Abi Zimra was born in Spain but on account of the persecutions, he left the country before the exile and settled for a time in Fez, North Africa, whence he soon migrated into Egypt. He spent over forty years as a rabbi of the community of Cairo, and after reaching old age, resigned his position and went to Jerusalem where he died at the unusual age of one hundred and ten years.

Ibn Abi Zimra was considered the leading rabbi of his day, both on account of his great learning and on account of his position as chief rabbi of a well organized Jewry. His wealth added to his prestige. It was on account of his position that he was able to abolish the counting of years according to the antiquated Seleucid era (Vol. I, p. 9), to which the Egyptian Jews still clung and substitute the era of creation adopted by all other Jews. He wrote a number of commentaries on the Code of Maimonides and other works, but his chief literary contribution was the large Responsa collection. It can be said that he was, like ben Adret in his day, the fountain head of wisdom to which people from all parts of the East turned in order to quench their thirst for Rabbinic knowledge.

It is surmised that he wrote more than three thousand Responsa of which only about thirteen hundred were preserved. These are divided into four parts. They deal with numerous cases representing all phases of life and law. The life typified there was the life of Jewry in Eastern lands with all its peculiarities. Thus, from the numerous inquiries touching upon family life, we learn that the custom of marrying two wives was quite prevalent among the Jews of the East who did not subscribe to the prohibition of Rabbi Gershom against bigamy. A number of Responsa deal with proselytes and a considerable number with slaves and their emancipation, which prove that the Jewish law concerning the emancipation of slaves was still in practice. Very interesting is his long Responsum concerning the relation between the Rabbanites and the Karaites. There were quite large communities of Karaites in Egypt and their relations with the Rabbanites seem to have been friendly. There were also cases of intermarriage between members of these two factions as evidenced in the inquiries. Consequently, two different opinions arose among the rabbis. One inclined to leniency, aiming to bring about closer relations between these two branches of Israel, the other more severe, insisted upon complete separation allowing no mixing between the two even when a Karaite wished to embrace Rabbanism. Ibn Abi Zimra adopted a somewhat more lenient course, though severe enough. He allowed intermarriage between Rabbanites and Karaites when the latter embraced Rabbanism officially. He did, however, contrary to the view of Maimonides, prohibit the circumcision of Karaite children on the Sabbath and the imparting of instruction in Talmud to them but permitted the teaching of the Bible. His reason for the distinction between the Talmud and the Bible was that the sect would later scoff at the teachings of the former. He explained his departure from the lenient attitude of Maimonides towards the Karaites by asserting that they had changed for the worse since that time.

The collection, like those of the earlier Spanish scholars contains many non-Halakic Responsa. These are explanations of Agadic passages, answers to queries, such as why Jonah fled from God and whether the resurrected dead will die again, discussions concerning the freedom of the will, prophecy and other subjects of a theological nature. Very characteristic is his liberal attitude concerning dogmas. He decides that one who denies a dogma because of his erroneous philosophy is not an apostate, for we find in the Talmud that a certain Hillel who denied the coming of the Messiah[8] was only mildly rebuked by his colleagues and was not considered an apostate.

The disciple of Rabbi Abi Zimra, Rabbi Bezallel Ashkenazi (d. 1530) famous as a collector of the commentaries of the early scholars (Sect. 45) also left a book of Responsa. It contains only forty-one replies to inquiries dealing mostly with cases of civil and family laws. Ashkenazi differs in his style of Responsa from his teacher. Whereas the latter is brief and limits himself to the question in hand, the former follows the scholastic pilpulpistic method, and deals with each case at greaet length, quoting numerous sources and analyzing each quotation.

The contemporary and colleague of Abi Zimra, a member of his court in Cairo, Rabbi Moses Al-Ashkar known by the initials *Maharam* Al-Ashkar (1460-1535), likewise left an exceptionally valuable collection of Responsa. Al-Ashkar was born in Spain and studied at Zamora under Rabbi Samuel Valencia. Together with the rest of the Jews, he left that country during the expulsion of 1492 and settled for a while at Tunis, North Africa. From there, he migrated into Egypt where he spent many years as *dayan* of the community. In his old age, he settled in Jerusalem where he spent his declining years.

Al-Ashkar corresponded with the greatest scholars of his time, including Elijah Misrahi and inquiries were sent to him from all parts of the Turkish empire, as he was considered a great authority on Rabbinic law. He was distinguished by an exceptional love of truth,

[8] Sanhedrin, 99a.

championing it with great zeal and sparing no one. This quality in his character brought him much trouble as he acquired many enemies. Al-Ashkar knew Arabic perfectly and made great use of Rabbinic books in that language. Like all scholars of that time, he also engaged in the study of the Kabbala, but at the same time did not forsake the study of philosophy, especially that of Maimonides which he defended vigorously against attackers.

The collection contains one hundred and twenty-one Responsa, most of which deal with cases of family law, such as the question of *Agunahs* or cases arising from irregular betrothal (Kidushin). In general Al-Ashkar was very lenient in the case of *Agunahs,* endeavoring to find ways and means to free these unfortunate women and to allow them to remarry. This endeavor on his part involved him in many controversies with famous scholars of his day.

Al-Ashkar steered clear of the pilpulistic method, and as a rule went to the first sources, either the Talmud or the early authorities. Maimonides was his greatest authority from whose decisions he seldom dared to deviate. Maimonides was also his standard in matters of opinion and when one criticized his views, Al-Ashkar rose in defence of his beloved teacher. Thus in a long Responsum (R. 117) which amounts to a fair-sized booklet, he directs a scathing criticism against Shem Tob ben Shem Tob's work, *Emunoth* (Beliefs) which contains severe strictures of the views of Maimonides.

Al-Ashkar defends Maimonides' conceptions of resurrection and immortality endeavoring to show how they correspond with the beliefs of pure tradition. He finds, however, great difficulty in defending the statement that many stories of the Bible where the actions of angels are described merely relate to visions and not to real occurrences. Finally, he states that Maimonides was a believer in the Kabbala and ascribes to him a book by the name of *Megillath Setorim* (Secret Scroll), where he is supposed to have confessed that Kabbala is a higher study than philosophy, and that greater things can be accomplished by means of that science than by means of physics.

The style of Al-Ashkar is, on the whole, terse and concise, except that he usually prefaces his Responsa with a paragraph or two in ornate style and rhymed prose. This afforded the vehicle of expression for his poetic spirit as he also wrote poetry, and five of his sacred poems are appended to the Responsa.

The numerous Palestinian scholars of this generation produced many books of Responsa of which a number are of great value. The first of these is one by Rabbi Jacob Berab (1474-1541). Berab was born in Spain and left the country during the expulsion, sojourning temporarily in North Africa. From there, he went to Palestine and settled in Safed. Berab, influenced by the Messianic aspirations of the generation, conceived a great idea, that of renewing official ordination (Semikah) in Jewry,[9] with the ultimate view of re-establishing the Sanhedrin. This idea, which had it been carried out, would undoubtedly have established authority in Israel, found at the time great opposition on the part of the scholars of Jerusalem, chief of whom was Levi ben Habib. On account of the quarrel that broke out as a result of the proposed plan, Berab was forced to flee Safed for fear of being seized by the government on a charge brought against him by informers, and he settled in Damascus.

Berab's collection contains fifty-six Responsa to inquiries from many rabbis in Palestine, Egypt and Turkey. They deal with various phases of Jewish law.

A more important work is the one by Berab's antagonist Levi ben Habib (1480-1546). Rabbi Levi was also born in Spain at Zamora. After the expulsion, he fled together with his father, Jacob, the author of the Agadic collection *Ein Jacob,* to Portugal where he was forced to accept Christianity. He later escaped to Turkey and settled at Salonika, residing there for about thirty years as the head of an academy. He then left for Palestine, stayed for some time at Safed, and finally settled in Jerusalem where he occupied the prominent position of chief justice of the Jewish court.

Habib's book contains one hundred and forty-four Responsa dealing mostly with religious and family law. Rabbi Levi was a great

[9] The right of ordination was held during Tannaitic times by the head of the Sanhedrin. The patriarch, the head of that august body, often with the consent of its members and in certain exigencies even without it, possessed the power to ordain officially deserving scholars and confer upon them the title rabbi. The recipient of the title was then considered an expert judge (Dayan Mumhah) holding the right of jurisdiction in all cases. With the disappearance of the Sanhedrin as an institution, ordination was automatically abolished. None of the subsequent scholars during the generations, no matter how great, were considered expert judges. At the end of the fourteenth century, Rabbi Meir ha-Levi of Vienna found it necessary in order to improve the state of the rabbinate and to prevent undeserving people from assuming that office to institute a quasi-ordination which was called by the old name of *Semikah.* This, however, meant only that the scholar "ordained" possessed sufficient knowledge to exercise the functions of rabbi, but in no wise conferred upon him the privileges of old. This kind of ordination is still practiced to-day.

The real intention of Berab was to reestablish the Sanhedrin. But since every member of that body must be a really ordained rabbi, it was necessary to resuscitate, therefore, the ceremony of ordination in order to accomplish the ultimate purpose. He believed, of course, that the reestablishment of the Sanhedrin would hasten the coming of the Messiah.

controversialist, and many of his Responsa contain controversies against the decisions of other scholars, some of them the greatest of the generation. They reflect some curious aspects of Jewish life in the East. Especially is there to be noted the large number of inquiries concerning vows pronounced by various people, of which a peculiar case holds our interest. A certain man during a severe illness promised a quarter of his body to the prophet Samuel. He got well, but on account of poverty, he could not go to the grave of Samuel located near Jerusalem to fulfill his vow. The inquirer wanted to know whether that vow could be annulled. This case shows clearly the superstitious practices the Jews adopted from their neighbors, the Mohammedans, who vowed parts of their bodies to their saints and then redeemed them.

Among other things there is a number of long Responsa discussing the questions of the seven year cycle (Shemitah) and the calendar, where Rabbi Levi displays great mathematical and astronomical knowledge and also establishes rules for the calculation of the calendar. He even demonstrates his calculations by figures and tables. There is also appended to the book a separate pamphlet (cuntras) on the *Semikah* controversy wherein Rabbi Levi justifies his view against Berab.

A valuable collection of Responsa was left by another member of the Safed center, Moses ben Joseph di Trani (1490-1570), known in abbreviated form as *Mabit*. Rabbi Moses, a descendant of the famous di Trani family of Italy which produced such scholars as Isaiah the Elder and the Younger (Vol. I, Sect. 148) was himself born in that country. In 1525 he emigrated to Palestine and settled at Safed where he presided at one of the academies.

The collection is a voluminous one, is divided into two parts and contains eight hundred and forty-one Responsa. Di Trani was a distinguished scholar even in that age, and inquirers sought his opinion on many cases of law. The Responsa of Trani mirror the complicated Jewish life of the period. They deal with private as well as with communal life. We find a number of cases regarding contracts between rabbis and their communities, picturing the state of the Rabbinate at the time; inquiries concerning business affairs, indicating the important role the Jews played in export trades; cases of charity, bequests and statutes and ordinances of Jewish communities. One such ordinance has historical value. It was passed by several Turkish communities such as Salonika, Brussa and others not to send their wares to the port of Ancona, Italy, but to Pesaro. This act was passed at the instigation of Donna Gracia Nasi as a reprisal against the pope who expelled the Marranos from Ancona, a papal city. The Jews of Turkey wanted to help their brethren who were invited by the duke of Pesaro to settle in the city by transferring their trade thither. However, some merchants deflected from the agreement, and Trani was appealed to and asked to decide whether they could be forced to adhere to the ordinance. He decided that from a pure legal standpoint, they could not be forced to comply, if by the change of the trading port a financial loss accrued, but he appeals to their sense of Jewish loyalty not to desert their brethren in need.

His son, Joseph di Trani (1558-1639), was likewise a renowned scholar of his day. He lived for a large part of his life in Safed, and later, while visiting Constantinople to solicit support for the academies in Palestine, he was offered the Rabbinic post of that community. He accepted the offer and held the position for the rest of his life.

Joseph Trani's collection is divided into three parts and contains about five hundred Responsa to inquiries addressed to him from all parts of the Turkish empire. His decisions were considered authoritative by scholars and frequently quoted.

The other important books of Responsa by Eastern scholars of this period are two small collections by Joseph Karo (Sect. 58), one under the title of *Abkat Rochel* (The Dust of a Spice Dealer) and Responsa (Teshuboth), collections by Rabbi Samuel di Modena (1505-1589), Joseph Ibn Leb and Moses Alshik. Samuel was rabbi of Salonika and a student of Levi ben Habib, Joseph was his fellow student and colleague, and Moses, a resident of Safed, was a disciple of Karo and one of the few ordained by Jacob Berab after he introduced the official *Semikah*.

70. *THE RESPONSA OF THE POLISH SCHOLARS*

The period from the fifteenth to the eighteenth centuries was one of intensive productivity in the field of Rabbinic literature in Poland. It follows, therefore, that the number of collections of Responsa left by the scholars of the time is considerable, for every important scholar had to pronounce upon numerous cases of law that came to his attention. But as in previous surveys, we will have to select the most authoritative and outstanding collections.

The first in order of time of composition is the one by Solomon Luria (Sect. 46). However, it is not a large one, as it contains only one hundred and one Responsa, which deal mostly with phases of religious law, with only a small part devoted to civil law, the latter dealing mostly with cases of libel. These cases are of great interest, as they show Jewish life to have been so well organized that no one could issue a false rumor injuring the character of a man or woman without being punished. Luria is very severe in his judgments, for not only does he exact a public apology from the libeler, but frequently orders corporal chastisement for the offender.

The Responsa hold for us a still greater interest in revealing the character of Luria himself. This severe and austere scholar appears in his replies as a man of independent character who champions truth without respect to authority. Thus, he decides with rather great liberality for his time that the covering of the head does not constitute a sign of piety, and that one may even study the sacred books with uncovered head, if he finds the wearing of a hat inconvenient for one reason or another (R. 72). Luria was also interested in history, and a long Responsum of his deals with the succession of the Franco-German scholars and possesses considerable historical value. He was likewise interested in grammar. In another of his Responsa printed in the collection of Moses Isserlis, he chides the latter for being careless in his writing and committing many grammatical mistakes. On the other hand, he disparages the study of philosophy and reproaches Isserlis for quoting Aristotle in support of an opinion which affects a legal decision.

The second collection is that of Isserlis (Sect. 60). It contains one hundred and thirty-two Responsa dealing with various phases of law. Among his correspondents are Solomon Luria, Joseph Karo, Meir Katzenellenbogen of Padua and others. It includes also a number of Responsa by other scholars. The life reflected in the inquiries and replies is the usual Polish Jewish life of his day. The main interest of the book lies in the fact that the character of Isserlis himself is revealed there. We note his love for philosophy and investigation, his admiration for Maimonides' *Guide* and his attitude towards the Kabbala. Against Luria's attack on Jewish philosophy he launches a vigorous defense for its study. And though he admits that it is not fitting that Rabbinic scholars study Aristotle's books in the original, since some of them contain erroneous opinions, he maintains that the views quoted by Maimonides in the *Guide* are correct and agree with Jewish tradition. He concludes by saying that he would rather flee from the study of the Kabbala than from the study of philosophy, as one may be misled more by the former than by the latter (Resp. 7).

Rabbi Meir Lublin (Sect. 47) also left a collection which contains one hundred and forty Responsa. Lublin, one of the leading scholars of the day, had many inquiries addressed to him on cases affecting civil and family law. His replies mirror Jewish life in Poland to a greater extent than the other collections. We hear in them the echo of the turbulent times in the many *Agunah* cases, where women ask permission to remarry on the ground of imperfect testimonies that their husbands were killed in the wars. From a Responsum concerning an ordinance enacted by two communities to defend their members against accusations by informers at public expense, we learn that informing was a frequent phenomenon in Jewish life. Likewise, other angles of Jewish life are illuminated by the Responsa. As for Lublin himself, he seemed to be interested only in Halakah. Other studies hardly existed for him. One curious discussion concerning the case of a woman said to have been consorting with a devil shows the naive state of his beliefs.

The book of Responsa by Joel Sirkis (Sect. 64), the author of the commentary *Beth Hadash* on the *Tur,* contains one hundred and fifty-eight Responsa embracing all phases of law. Like the collection of Lublin, it tells of the events of the time. We hear of accusations made against individuals and communities, of many *Agunah* cases, and of sufferings incurred by the Jews on account of the wars between the Poles and the Russians, or as they were then called, the Muscovites. An interesting fact to be gleaned from the book is that the Jews, though not obliged to serve in the army, still participated in active war service. In one Responsum, there is a testimony in the case of an *Agunah* where it is told that eleven Jews participated in a certain battle with the Muscoivtes, and one of them, Berakah with the rank of an officer, was killed in the engagement after performing heroic deeds.

The moral tenor of the Jewish communities can be guaged from another Responsum (43), which deals with an inquiry by the heads of the community at Kalisz concerning the following case: A Jew was accused of desecrating the image of Jesus, and while he was led to his execution, he turned over his purse containing the image to the beadle of the community. The authorities looked for the beadle but he had fled the city. They therefore demanded that the community turn him over to justice, as otherwise they would impose penalties upon it. Sirkis was asked for a decision whether they should comply with the request of the authorities or suffer the consequences. His answer was as follows: If the beadle himself received the purse, he should be surrendered to the authorities, as he did it on his own responsibility, but if he received the purse from the hands of a second person and not from the martyr himself, the heads of the community should rather suffer the punishment than hand the beadle over for torture.

Rabbi Zevi Hirsh Ashkenazi (1668-1711), a leading scholar of his day, usually known as Hakham Zevi, left a fine collection of Responsa. Rabbi Zevi was a son of a Polish scholar, Rabbi Jacob of Wilna, but his family emigrated to Moravia and thence to Hungary. He studied in Salonika and Constantinople, where he received the title of Hakham. He then returned to the home of his father, which was in the city of Ofen. During the siege of the city, his wife and only child were killed by a bomb, whereupon he left for Serajevo in Bosnia where he became rabbi. When this city also was besieged, Zevi fled the country, and after many wanderings, settled at Altona, married the daughter of the rabbi, and ultimately succeeded him in office. He was subsequently invited to become chief rabbi of the German community of Amsterdam. There he was involved in a quarrel with the Portuguese community regarding the famous propagandist of Sabbatianism, Nehemia Hayyun (1660-1726), and as a result, he went to London, and thence to Poland, the Mecca of all scholars, where he accepted a call as rabbi at Lemberg, spending the rest of his life there.

Zevi made a name for himself as a doughty fighter against Sabbatianism, that is the pseudo-Messianic movement which swayed various Jewries for over a century. It misled many scholars and wrought much mischief in many Jewish communities. As a clear-headed man, he foresaw the evil consequences of this movement and endeavored to check its spread.

There are one hundred and sixty-eight Responsa in the collection of Zevi to inquiries addressed to him from all parts of Jewry. On account of his wanderings and his serving as rabbi of many communities both Ashkenazic and Sephardic, Zevi was known throughout the Jewish world and his correspondents hailed from the East as well as from the West. Most of the Responsa deal with pure religious law but a fair proportion cover cases of civil and family law. Of the inquiries affecting Jewish organized life, are to be noted several coming from the Portuguese communities in Altona and Hamburg which passed ordinances forcing members of the congregations who moved to nearby cities to continue paying their dues to the old congregations. We see in this a struggle on the part of the disintegrating communities to maintain their integrity in the face of changing conditions.

A curious inquiry is the one coming from the heads of the Sephardic community of London. These ask Zevi to pass an opinion on the statement made by their rabbi, David Nieto, in a sermon that God and nature are one. Some people interpreted this as an inclination to Pantheism and accused the rabbi of free thinking. He in turn explained that he meant by his statement that the order of nature and Divine Providence are identical, in other words, that God is the cause of the activities known as nature. Zevi responds that the statement of Nieto as he interpreted it is in perfect accord with Jewish tradition and that he should be commended rather than reprimanded. Another Responsum throws light upon the attitude of Zevi to the Kabbala. This fighter of Sabbatianism, though he saw the evil accruing to Jewry from excessive devotion to mysticism, yet never doubted the efficiency of practical Kabbala. He discusses seriously the question whether a homunculus (Golem) created by the means of Kabbalistic incantations can be counted as a tenth man to complete a quorum (Minyan) for prayer and other purposes. He decides, however, in the negative. (Resp. 93.)

Of the Responsa collections of the eighteenth century which are very numerous, the most important and most popular among scholars is the one entitled *Noda bi-Yehuda* (Known in Judah) by Ezekiel Landau (Sect. 49), rabbi of Prague. Landau was the leading scholar of the generation and the inquiries addressed to him were very numerous. The book contains eight hundred and fifty-five Responsa divided in two volumes. It is arranged systematically, each volume being divided into four parts in accordance with the parts of the *Shulhan Aruḳ*. The collection reflects to an extent Jewish life in that century, especially the parts dealing with family and civil law.

Though Landau properly belongs to the beginning of the modern period, little can be detected in his replies of the first pulsations of modern Jewish life except perhaps in two things. First, there is a Responsum about shaving the beard with a powder (which is permissible) on *Hol-Moed* (i. e. the intervening days between the first and second holidays on Passover and Feast of Tabernacles), from which it appears that the custom of shaving the heard had already spread among certain strata of the people. Second, there is quite a number of Responsa concerning infractions of marital chastity by Jewish women which can probably be interpreted as a sign that the spirit of lax morality of the latter part of the eighteenth century penetrated even through the walls of the ghetto.

The method of Landau is the Scholastic one, his Responsa are very long and display great erudition, fine skill of analysis and keen-mindedness. His decisions enjoyed great authority among the scholars of the entire nineteenth century. They were treated as a text and many leading scholars of the last generation wrote glosses and *novellae* to them which are printed together with the collection in later editions.

Of the other books of Responsa produced during the seventeenth and eighteenth centuries we may mention *Emunoth Shemuel* (The Trust of Samuel) by Rabbi Aaron Samuel Kaidonover (d. 1696) who was born in Wilna and held Rabbinical posts in Fürth and Frankfurt on the Main. Then we have the *Sheiloth Yaabetz* (The Inquiries of Jaabez, abbrev. for Jacob Emden ben Zevi) by Jacob Emden (1696-1776), the famous opponent of Jonathan Eibeshitz (Ch. X) and the *Ponim Meiroth* (Shining Face) by Rabbi Meir Eisenstadt (d. 1774) who was rabbi in a number of Jewish communities and ultimately in Eisenstadt, Hungary.

E. Methodology

71. *WORKS ON METHODOLOGY AND TALMUDIC ENCYCLOPAEDIAS*

This prolific period in Rabbinic literature produced also a number of works on the methodology of the Talmud and even of the post-Talmudic literature, especially the codes. The earlier books on methodology which were surveyed in the first volume (Sect. 160) were mostly short treatises on the history of tradition and were limited primarily to an account of the work of the successive bearers of tradition, i. e. the Tannaim and Amoraim. In addition, they also stated a few rules for deriving Halakic decisions from the expansive and vast Talmudic discussions. Here and there they also explained some Talmudic terms. But they did not treat the subject of methodology adequately. They neglected to explain the hermeneutic rules (Midoth) by means of which Halakoth were derived by the Tannaim; they likewise omitted to give the terms and rules used and invented by the Amoraim which form the very warp and woof of the Talmud.

These deficiencies were made up by the methodological works of the post-classical period. These books, which began to be written by Franco-German scholars are comprehensive treatises on the subject covering every phase. The scholars, who delved in the depths of the "Sea of the Talmud," exposed its mysteries and discovered the intricate methods of Talmudic discussions. Their works are, therefore of great value.

72. *BOOKS ON METHODOLOGY*

The first book in this field is the *Sepher Keritoth* (The Book of a Love Covenant, i. e. the author made a covenant of love with these studies) by Rabbi Samson of Chinon, France (1300-1350), one of the younger Tosafists. It is an all-comprehensive work and is divided into five parts which are subdivided into portals (Shearim).

The first part called *Botē Midoth* (The Divisions of the Rules of Interpretation) deals with the thirteen hermeneutic rules of Rabbi Ismael (Vol. I, Sect. 43), which as an enlargement of the seven rules of Hillel are the basis of all motivated Tannaitic Halakah. Each rule is discussed in a portal in an extensive manner in all its phases and applications. The second part is devoted to those rules which apply only to laws relating to Temple service. The third discusses the thirty-two rules collected by Rabbi Eliezer, the son of Jose the Galillean, a Tanna of the fourth generation, and applied primarily in the interpretation of verses for Agadic purposes. The fourth deals with the history of the Tannaim and Amoraim and also states the rules for decision between the opinions of the authorities of the Talmud. The fifth part is of great importance, as it is devoted to the deduction of new rules applied by the Talmudists in their interpretation of the Bible in addition to the standard ones, and to an extensive elucidation of the methods and terminology of both parts of the Talmud. The first portal of this part is devoted to the new rules of interpretation, the second to the methods and terminology of the Mishnah and Baraitoth, the third to the methods, terminology and peculiarities of the expression of the Gemarah. This portal throws light upon many a knotty passage in the Talmud by clarifying the peculiar expressions and likewise helps to understand the complicated Talmudic discussions by supplying the key to their methods.

Rabbi Samson undoubtedly used earlier sources, and in fact, declares in his preface that he did not invent the contents of the book himself. Unfortunately, he did not indicate the sources which he used. We do, however, know that in the historical part, he followed the *Seder Tannaim we-Amoraim* and the latter of Rabbi Sherira Gaon (Vol. I, Sect. 190). The style of the book is rather difficult and in many places not clear. This is due to the fact, in most cases, that the book is only a first draft and was never revised by the author. Because of this, we find many lacunae, abbreviated expressions and even incorrect statements and quotations. The last, of course, may be due to errors of copyists. However, with all these defects, the *Keritoth* served as the foundation for all those who continued the work in methodology.

Almost contemporaneous with Samson of Chinon, Menahem ha-Meiri (Sect. 43) wrote his commentary on Aboth, *Beth ha-Behirah* (The Chosen House) which contains an introduction dealing with the history of tradition and its bearers. In a logical and orderly manner, he discusses the leading men of the generations from the time of Adam to the giving of the Torah, and from that to the exile. Beginning with Ezra, he describes the scholars and the heads of the Sanhedrin to the destruction. The generations of the Tannaim, he begins with Johanan ben Zakkai and counts five generations. This is followed by an account of the Amoraim, five generations of Saburaim, the Gaonim and the leading scholars who succeeded them to his own day. The book is interspersed with valuable philosophic remarks concerning the rise of religions in the world, prophecy, tradition and similar subjects. He displays a fine historical and critical sense in his discussions on the nature of the Mishnah, Baraitoth and the Tosephta, as well as in his characterization of the Gaonic period. A digest of this work was later prepared by Isaac de Lates under the name *Shaare Zion* (The Portals of Zion).

The second complete methodological work was written by Rabbi Joshua ha-Levi of Talmisan, North Africa, by the name of *Haliḳoth Olam* (The Ways of the World, i. e. the world of Jewish law and religion). In his preface, the author tells how he came to write the book. He fled his native country on account of persecutions that broke out there in 1467 and went to Castile. On arriving in Toledo, he found a patron in Don Vidal ben Labi, and at the latter's request, wrote this book in order to instruct him in the ways of the Talmud.

It is divided into five portals which are subdivided into chapters.

The first portal or section deals with the nature of the Mishnah, its divisions and orders, the generations of the Tannaim and Amoraim, and the pseudonyms of scholars. The second one discusses in great detail the terminology of the Gemarah, the third the methods of the Mishnah, the fourth the thirteen rules of hermeneutics. The fifth is devoted to a statement of the rules of decision of the Halakah.

Rabbi Joshua, of course, utilized to a great extent the *Sepher Keritoth,* but improved upon it. The main improvement consists in the orderly and logical arrangement of the material and in the clearness and simplicity of style. These qualities made the book accessible to any intelligent student who wished to acquaint himself with the method and ways of the Talmud. Of special value is the second portal which gives in a systematic way and detailed manner the terms and methods used by the Amoraim. It is more comprehensive than the part of the *Keritoth* dealing with the same subject. The *Haliḳoth Olam* was translated into Latin in 1634 by the famous Christian scholar Constantin L'Empereur of Holland.

An older contemporary of Joshua ha-Levi who contributed to the science of methodology was Rabbi Isaac Kampanton (b. 1463) of Spain. Rabbi Kampanton was one of the leading scholars of the day, and his contemporaries speak with great reverence of his numerous writings. But of all his works, only a small pamphlet of about twelve leaves is left, called *Darḳē ha-Gemarah* (The Ways of the Gemarah). It is, though small, of great value, for it is a work written both by a Talmudic scholar and an excellent logician. Kampanton was the first to place Talmudic methodology on a scientific basis, as he uses rules of logic and its terminology in his elucidation of the ways of the Talmud.

His students followed up the work of the master and several of them composed their own works on methodology. The first was Samuel de Serillo who wrote a book by the name of *Kelale Shemuel* (The Rules of Samuel) discussing the hermeneutic rules of the Talmud. The second Samuel Valencia wrote a special treatise on the single rule of interpretation (Midah), *Kal-we-Homer,* i. e. inference a fortiori.

Later Spanish scholars continued the work of their predecessors in this field. Among them was also the famous Joseph Karo, author of the *Shulhan Aruḳ* (Sect. 58) who composed a treatise called *Kelale ha-Gemarah* (The Rules of Gemarah) which was supposed to be a supplement to Joshua ha-Levi's *Halikoth Olam,* and contains numerous original observations on the various devices used by the Amoraim in their Halakic discussions.

A short treatise on the rules of interpretation and methods of the Talmud, as well as on the rules employed by the codifiers was written by Rabbi Hayyim Benveniste (1603-1673) and was added as an appendix to his book, *Sheyorē Kenesseth ha-Gedolah,* a supplementary volume to his *Kenesseth ha-Gedolah.* Like his great work, which is primarily a compilation of decisions from many books, the rules and observations of this treatise are mostly collected from other works, interspersed with original remarks.

The most comprehensive work, though by no means the most scientific one on the subject of Rabbinic methodology and terminology is the *Yad Malachi* by Rabbi Malachi ha-Kohen (fl. middle of eighteenth century). The book is divided into three parts. The first called *Kelalē ha-Gemarah* is devoted to a survey of all the possible rules, terms and expressions used in the Talmudic discussions. This covers about three-fourths of the book, and the subjects are arranged alphabetically. The author, however, does not use any scientific method in arranging his material, but merely follows the order of the letters of the first word of the rule or term. If the first letter of the first word is *He* it is subsumed under that letter, if a *Daleth,* under that one. As stated, it is very detailed, the first part containing six hundred and sixty-seven rules and terms, covering almost every technical rule or expression of the Talmud. The author made use of all previous works in the field but selected the opinions he approved. At times, his own definitions of terms differ from those of his predecessors. As a rule, the articles are brief, but occasionally he indulges in a long discussion when refuting some opinion of former scholars. Some of these discussions are of great value for the understanding of the Talmud. Thus, article 663, is a long discussion on the authenticity of Halakic statements transmitted by disciples in the name of their masters. He analyzes at great length the attitude of the Amoraim to such traditions, the conditions of their veracity, namely, how and when such statements were utilized as proof for decisions and when they were not, as well as all other phases of this important subject. A number of such lengthy discussions are found in the book.

The second part, called *Kelalē ha-Poskim* (Rules Employed by Codifiers) gives all the rules and observations which throw light upon the methods used by the great codifiers in their works. The codes treated in this part begin with those of the Gaonim and end with the *Shulhan Aruk*. These observations are of great merit as they help to understand many peculiarities in the manner of decision and style of such codes as those of Al-Fasi, of Maimonides, the *Tur* and the *Shulhan Aruk*.

The third part is called *Kelalē ha-Dinim* (Rules of Decisions). It contains explanations and definitions of famous legal maxims and accepted laws. It is arranged, like the first part, in alphabetical order.

We can not close our survey of Rabbinic literature of the post-Classical Mediaeval period without mentioning a work, which, on account of its comprehensiveness and thoroughness is one of the outstanding productions in this long period of literary activity. This is the Rabbinic Encyclopaedia, *Pahad Yitzhak* by Isaac Lampronti (1679-1756).

Lampronti was born at Ferrara and studied at Mantua under Abraham Sarari. He later went to Padua and studied medicine and philosophy at the famous university. On returning to his native city, he was appointed as the head and rabbi of the academy, which work he performed gratis, his occupation being the practice of medicine in which he achieved distinction.

The *Pahad Yitzhak* is a unique work of its kind. The author undertook to arrange in alphabetical order all subjects discussed in Talmudic and Rabbinic literature in order to select the proper views and opinions stated on the subjects. He gives not only the Talmudic sources, but quotes also in proper order, the views of the codifiers and very frequently those of the important Responsa writers. When a certain article deals with a legal case which was a subject of controversy among the rabbis in his time, he incorporates all the Responsa bearing on that case, written by contemporary scholars. In this way, the Encyclopedia contains also a large number of Responsa.

Although it is primarily a Halakic work, yet it contains a number of articles of an Agadic and homiletic character. The work is exceedingly valuable as a reference book, for almost every subject in Rabbinics is quoted there, and references are given to the places where each is discussed in the Talmud, codes and Responsa. Lampronti also gives biographical and historical data concerning the lives and times of the Tannaim and Amoraim, as well as lexicographical explanations of terms and expressions used in the Talmud.

Only six volumes of this great work, up to the letter *Mem,* were printed during the author's life time. The rest remained in manuscript, and were only published during the years 1864-1874 by the society *Mekitze Nirdamin* which was founded in Germany for the purpose of publishing such works of older authors, which for one reason or another were left in manuscript form.

CHAPTER V

PHILOSOPHY, THEOLOGY AND ETHICS

73. *GENERAL OBSERVATIONS*

The philosophic literature of the post-Classical period differs from that of the preceding one in a number of respects. Unlike other branches of literature, it is not merely a continuation of what has gone before, but possesses a depth and intensity which had not been attained even by great thinkers of the Classical Age, in fact, a real character of its own which injects into Jewish philosophy a note of originality. True, this period did not produce another Maimonides who welded the philosophic and theologic teachings into a system, and it is also true that a great part of the philosophic literature under discussion consists of commentaries upon the book containing that very system. But even these very commentaries contain not only explanations but numerous additional discussions which throw a new light upon the same problems discussed by Maimonides and the older thinkers. They are original philosophic works which deal with the old problems in a newer, broader and deeper way. There is, for instance, Gersonides who in his book, The Wars of the Lord, deals, it is true, with fewer problems than Maimonides, but in a more thorough and scientific manner. Again, there is Hasdai Crescas who dared not only to criticize the teachings of the master Maimonides, but even to challenge the fundamental principles of Aristotle himself, and there are numerous less conspicuous workers in this field whose labors added a new note to Jewish thought.

This difference in the character of the philosophy of the post-Classical period was to a large extent brought about by two factors, the change of language and the extension of the philosophic horizon. In fact, the first factor can, to a certain degree, be said to have been the cause of the other. The language of Jewish philosophy of the first period was Arabic, that of the second Hebrew. The reconquest of Spain by the Christians and the removal of scientific and philosophic study from Spain to Provence in the thirteenth and fourteenth centuries made that change necessary. When Arabic ceased to be the spoken tongue of the Jews, Hebrew took its place as the language of philosophy and science, as no other was available.

The task of converting Hebrew into a medium of expression of philosophy and science was not an easy one, new terms had to be coined, new meanings placed upon old words, and verbal forms expanded and moulded into flexible usages. This task was first undertaken by Judah Ibn Tibbon (1120-1190), who emigrated to Provence from Spain. He was followed in this work by his sons and many others, about whom we will have more to say. Judah began his work by translating the books of Saadia, Bahya and Judah ha-Levi, thus satisfying the craving of the Jews for these studies. His son Samuel completed the translation of the works of the Jewish philosophers by rendering into Hebrew the *Guide of the Perplexed* by Maimonides.

Once the gates of philosophy were thrown open to the large number of intellectuals who read only Hebrew, a taste for this study developed among the scholars and a desire for a deeper draught of the waters of the fountain of wisdom arose in the hearts of many. The demand called forth a feverish translating activity which continued for many years in Provence and Italy. As a result, almost the entire philosophic literature was translated into Hebrew and made available to the seekers of wisdom.

This made the study of philosophy both popular and comprehensive. No more was the coveted wisdom limited to the few who were acquainted with Arabic, but every intellectual Jew who wanted to enter "the garden of philosophy" could easily gain access to it through the numerous translations of the books of Aristotle, Al-Farabi, Ibn Sina (Avicenna) and the famous commentaries of Ibn Roshd (Averroes). Consequently, the number of students increased and many were those who, wishing to gain the title of philosopher, tried their hand at composing treatises upon one phase of philosophy or another, and thus increased the literature on the subject.

On the other hand, those who evinced a real interest in philosophy and were bent on delving deeper into its mysteries could now satisfy their heart's desire. The wide literature on the subject covering every phase gave them an opportunity to obtain a comprehensive view of all the problems without having recourse either to Greek or to Arabic, and thus were enabled to add their own contribution to philosophic study.

The comprehensiveness and intensity with which philosophy was studied during this period brought about an extension of the sphere of its literary discussion to include problems which were hitherto little touched upon. Logic and psychology afford good instances of such extension. In the entire Classical period, only two books were written by Jewish authors on the subject of logic, and these of an elementary character only (Vol. I, Sect. 164), while the latter age produced a veritable literature on the subject, consisting mostly of commentaries or compendia on the works of Aristotle and his Arabic followers, and a few original works. The subject of psychology, likewise, though germane to the metaphysical theological problems with which Jewish philosophy concerned itself, was hardly touched upon by the older thinkers. At best, they devoted to it only a chapter or two in their general works, and there is scarcely a single work devoted exclusively to this subject. The situation changed from the twelfth century on. The translation of Aristotle's *De Anima* together with the commentaries of Averroes opened a new vista before the Jewish thinkers and the question of the soul and its destiny henceforth assumed great prominence in Jewish thought. This was manifested in a number of treatises devoted to a discussion of the soul, its essence and its faculties. That these discussions were brought in relation with the theological and ethical problems of immortality, freedom of the will and human conduct goes without saying. And just as these problems received a broader and deeper elucidation by the later thinkers, the other problems of philosophy, such as the metaphysical and physical problems of time, space and the creation of the world, as well as the theological problems of God's prescience and human freedom likewise received a more intense treatment at their hands. Even aesthetics which was entirely strange to the early savants received some attention from a later philosopher of the sixteenth century, Judah Abrabanel.

Another characteristic of the philosophy of the period is its thoroughgoing rationalism. The older thinkers aimed primarily to prove that the teachings of the Bible are compatible with those of philosophy and the result was a mutual adjustment. Not only did they adjust the Bible to philosophy, but philosophy to the Bible. The savants of the later period were more bent on rationalizing religion and conforming it to the teachings of Aristotelianism than on the vindication of the truth of the former and proving its compatibility with the principles of the latter. They were so saturated with the spirit of the thought of the age that it never occurred to them to doubt the validity of its principles. And if the Bible apparently did not enunciate the very same teachings current in philosophy, it had to be interpreted in such manner, forced or not forced, as to state them. Hence, there arose a school of allegorists who interpreted a large part of the Bible in an allegorical manner, so as to make it speak of matter and form, movement and rest in good Aristotelian fashion. Some of these thinkers were even ready to yield on the question of *creatio ex nihilo,* creation from nothing, which was defended so vigorously by the earlier philosophers, and to concede to matter some kind of eternal existence saving the principle of creation by devious means.

However, this inclination towards rationalism is not manifested throughout the entire period, but is really limited to its first half. At the end of the fourteenth century, a reaction set in and conservatism became dominant. But in reality, with the end of that century, real philosophic investigation terminates. Those thinkers who come after that time were either commentators or mere gleaners in the field of thought.

Finally, there is to be noted the influence exerted by the Jewish philosophy of the period upon the scholastic thought of the age. The extent of that influence has not been fully investigated as yet. But it is fairly well established that in the transmission of Aristotelianism and the accumulated Arabic philosophic and scientific investigations from the East to the West, the role played by Jewish scholars was of great importance. Not only were many of the Latin translations of the works of Averroes, Avicenna and of others made from the Hebrew translations, and not only were the works of Jewish philosophers translated into Latin, but these scholars helped to spread the philosophic teachings by personal contact with the leaders of Christian thought.

With the removal of the center of Jewish Scholastic activity from Arabic speaking countries to Provence and Italy, the thinkers had to adapt themselves to new conditions and to a new language, and they did so accordingly. It did not take long for Latin to become current among the Jewish savants, and a number of them even helped to translate books, either directly from the Arabic or from the Hebrew, into that language. As a result, the currents of Jewish and Christian thought mingled, and the former influenced and helped to shape the trend and form of the latter. Almost all the leading Scholastic philosophers, William of Auvergne, Alexander of Hales, Albertus Magnus, Thomas Aquinas, Duns Scotus, Roger Bacon and others acknowledge in their works the influence of the teachings of Jewish thinkers upon their systems.[1] Even in the Renaissance period, we can still detect traces of Jewish teachings in the thought of the age which acted as a leaven and quickened the formation of a new conception of the world and life.[2]

Thus, the Jewish philosophy of the period, though written primarily in Hebrew did not remain the islated expression of a group, but became a contributory stream which helped to swell the general current of thought and carry it to further progress.

74. *TRANSLATIONS*

As noted above, the work of translation played an important part in the development of Jewish philosophy; it will therefore, not be amiss to give a brief survey of this activity.

First, as to the extent of the literature translated. It is well known, in spite of the fact that Aristotle was the central axis round which Mediaeval thought turned, no Greek original text of his works existed during a large part of the Mediaeval Ages, and a knowledge of his philosophy was derived entirely from translations. It was the Syrian scholars who acted as transmitters of Aristotelian teachings and who introduced them to the Arabic world during the seventh and eighth centuries by translating the works of Aristotle, as well as portions of the writings of other philosophers, from the Greek into Syriac, and from Syriac into Arabic. Many were the workers in this field, but most distinguished among them were Honein ben Ishak and his son. It was not long before all the genuine works of Aristotle, as well as a number of spurious works ascribed to him were translated into Arabic. To these were added also the *Isagoge* of Porphyry (an introduction to Aristotle's works on logic) and the commentaries of Alexander of Aphrodosias and Themestius and excerpts from other peripatetic philosophers.

These translations served as a basis for a whole philosophic literature which was gradually produced by numerous Arabic thinkers. These Arabic scholars commented on the works of Aristotle, abridged them, wrote compendia of the various sciences, and paraphrased single books. Of the most important Arabic philosophers were Al-Kindi (d. 863), Abu Nazar Al-Farabi (d. 950), Ibn Sina or Avicenna

[1] On this see Jacob Guttmann, Die Scholastic des Dreizenten Jahrhunderts in ihrem Beziehungen zum Judentum. Breslau, 1902.

[2] M. Waxman, The Philosophy of Don Hasdai Crescas, p. 45.

(d. 1037), Abu Hamid Al-Gazali (1058-1111), and finally, the greatest of them all, Ibn Roshd or Averroes (1126-1198). Each of these wrote numerous works centering around the teachings of Aristotle, both commentaries on his works and abstracts and compendia of parts of his system, as well as independent works of their own. In time, as the literature of the commentators and expositors grew, the original translations of the Aristotelian books were set aside and were less used so that, as a result, many of them were lost. The older Jewish thinkers, however, must have had access to the original translations and studied them together with the commentaries of Al-Farabi and Avicenna, and later with those of Ibn Roshd.

It was primarily the books of these philosophers which were translated into Hebrew, and it was from these that the Jewish scholars drew their knowledge of Aristotle, for we find comparatively few translations into Hebrew of the Arabic versions of Aristotelian books without the commentaries, only two or three of such works being extant. We must not, however, conclude that the philosophers had a garbled idea of the views and opinions of Aristotle, for the commentaries and compendia of the Arabs were written with great pains and effort to reproduce the teachings of the great master in as exact a manner as possible. Besides, the commentaries always contained a large part of the text, and one species even the entire text, so that as a result, little was missed.

The number of the books translated from the Arabic into Hebrew in the field of philosophy alone besides that of the sciences is so large that the mere enumeration of their titles would cover many pages. We will, therefore, have to limit ourselves to the most important works. We will begin with those of the last of the commentators of Aristotle, that of Averroes, for it is his works that practically constitute the Aristotle of the thirteenth century, known both to Jews and to Christians alike.

Averroes, considered in his day the greatest commentator of Aristotle, spent a life time in the study of the works of the great master and wrote commentaries on all his works with the exception of the Politics, the translation of which either did not reach him, as he says, or as some aver, was not translated at all into Arabic. Instead of this, he made an abstract of Plato's Republic which deals with the science of the State. His works on Aristotle are of three kinds: (1) Compendia of the various books where Averroes presents the contents of the works in his own words and his own order without quoting the text; (2) middle commentaries where the text is quoted to a large extent but not completely; (3) long commentaries where the text is completely given, and the commentary takes each word into consideration. In Hebrew, this kind of commentary was called *Aruk*, i. e. Long or *Perush Al-ha-Milah* (Commentary according to the Word).

All these three types of works were translated into Hebrew. Thus there is a translation of the entire Organon, which includes all that Aristotle had written on logic, his books on physics, of the Metaphysics and other works. As a rule, there are several translations of almost every book. And so, the entire works of Aristotle according to Averroes were translated and retranslated into Herbew. As Averroes' works, in the latter part of his life fell under the ban of the fanatical Almohades, rulers of Spain, many of his original Arabic books were lost, and are only found in Hebrew translations which present to-day the most complete set of his works, and many of the Latin translations were also made from the Hebrew. Averroes' commentaries and the text, as said, covered almost all works of Aristotle. There are, however, two exceptions, the *Meteora* of Aristotle, a book on the meteors translated by Samuel Ibn Tibbon directly from the Arabic text without any commentary and the *Ethics* which was translated from the Latin by Don Meir Alguadez (c. 1400).

Besides his numerous commentaries on and compendia of Aristotle's works, Averroes wrote independent works of his own, many of which were also translated into Hebrew. The most important are: *Quesita in Libros Logicae Aristotelis* (Dissertations on questions connected with the Organon), *De Substantia Orbis* (Dissertations on Physics), *Epistola de Connexione Intellectus Abstracti cum Homine* (Dissertations on the Union of the Human Intellect with the Active Intellect of the World), and finally, the *Destructio Destructionis* (The Destruction of the Destruction, Heb. ha-Polath ha-Hapola), a polemic book written against the famous book of Al-Gazali, The Destruction of the Philosophers (Sepher ha-Hapolah). The *Destructio Destructionis* was very popular among the Jews, as it defended philosophy and was translated twice, first by Kalonymos (14th century) and later anonymously. The first Latin translation of the book was also made by the famous Jewish translator Kalonymos ben Kalonymos.

Al-Farabi was the next favored author of the Jews. The earlier philosophers studied his works assiduously, and quoted him extensively. Maimonides speaks of his teachings in the highest terms of praise. It is not to be wondered at then that his books were preferred by the translators and most of them were rendered into Hebrew. The most important of these are his Compendium of Aristotle's Organon (*Kitzur Mi-Kol MleKeth ha-Higoyon*), The Book of Principles, (*Sepher ha-Hathholoth*) dealing with the principles of existence and containing also an appendix on the principles of politics and *On the Intellect and the Intelligible.* The last named work was translated into Hebrew several times under three diverse titles: (1) *Sepher ha-Seḳel we-ha-Musḳoloth,* (2) *Beseḳel ubi-Musḳol* (On the Intellect and the Intelligible), and (3) *Maamar be-Mahuth ha-Nefesh* (A Book on the Essence of the Soul).

Abu Hamid Al-Gazali was another favorite of the translators who rendered into Hebrew almost all his works. The most popular of these were (1) The Tendencies of the Philosophers, a kind of compendium of philosophic opinions of which two Hebrew translations exist, one by Isaac Ibn Albalag (end of the 13th century) entitled *Deoth ha-Pilisufim,* and the other by Judah Nathan (1350) by the name of *Kavanoth ha-Pilisufim* (The Intentions of the Philosophers); (2) the famous *Thafoth Al-Falasifatu,* the Destruction or the Refutation of the Philosophers. Gazali, though well versed in philosophy was more inclined to acknowledge the authority of religion over that of human reason, and entertained great skepticism regarding the principles of philosophy. This skepticism which he expressed in that work with great skill made a deep impression on his contemporaries as well as on succeeding generations. Yet, in spite of the popularity of the work, it was not translated into Hebrew until the beginning of the fifteenth century. It was about 1413 that Zerahya ben Isaac ha-Levi, a disciple of Hasdai Crescas undertook to translate it into Hebrew under the title of *Hapolath ha-Pilisufim.* The translation was done at the request of the patron of letters, Don Vidal Benveniste Ibn Labi Besides these two important works, several other books of Gazali were translated at various times into Hebrew.

Avicenna (Ibn Sina) seemed to have been, of all the great Arabic philosophers, the least favored among the translators. The reason for it might have been the fact that he was frequently attacked by his successors and his theories were repeatedly refuted. But whatever the cause of the slight interest the translators took in his work, the result is that of his numerous philosophic works, only two were rendered into Hebrew. These are *On the Heavens and the World*

(Sepher ha-Shomayim we-ha-Olam) translated by Moses Melgueil (c. 1250) and the *Al-Najah,* a short encyclopædia of the sciences of physics and metaphysics. The last work was translated by Todros Todrosi (1330-1340) under a queer title *ha-Tzolath ha-Nefesh.* Literally, it means the saving of the soul, but it is to be understood rather as meaning the refuge or salvation of the soul, inasmuch as the study of the sciences affords that salvation.

Most of these translations from the Arabic were done during the thirteenth century and some during the fourteenth. However, as years passed by, the knowledge of Arabic among the Jews diminished while that of Latin increased. It was then that translations from that language began to appear. It is to be noted that in spite of the fact that the Christian philosophers whose works were rendered into Hebrew were all dignitaries of the Church, which as we know, was to a large degree responsible for the sufferings of the Jews, this fact did not prevent the scholars from studying their works assiduously and translating them into their own tongue, so as to spread among their brethren the truths they believed to have found in those writings. The current maxim found so frequently in Mediaeval writings, "Accept the truth no matter whosoever pronounces it," adequately expresses the attitude of these scholars towards truth and knowledge.

The earliest of the translations from the Latin was the book of Adelard of Bath (1120) entitled *Questiones Naturales,* containing a series of dialogues between an uncle and his nephew touching on various problems of nature. The translation was made by Berakhya ha-Kakdan (Sect. 159) under the title *Dodi We-Neḳdi* (Uncle and Nephew). The version was recently edited and translated into English by Sir Herman Gollancz. There followed then numerous translations from the works of almost every Scholastic philosopher of importance. Thus, we have Hebrew translations of two books by Albertus Magnus (1193-1280), namely his Commentary on Aristotle's *De Anima* and the *Philosophia Pauperum,* an introduction to the physics of Aristotle. This work was translated into Hebrew by Abraham Shalom ben Isaac (1495) under the title of *Kizur ha-Pilusufia ha-Tibith* (A Compendium of the Philosophy of Nature). Thomas Aquinas, the great Scholastic, seemed to have found favor with the translators for no less than nine of his works were rendered into Hebrew, among them two of his commentaries on the books of Aristotle, the Metaphysics and the *De Anima* and a work on the Ideas (named erroneously in Hebrew, Maamar ha-Hemshalim). Of the works of other philosophers rendered into Hebrew we find those of Boetius, Raimundus Lullus, Duns Scotus, Vincenz of Beauvais and of many lesser lights. Boetius' famous work, *De Consolatione Philosophiae,* (The Comfort of Philosophy) was translated twice, and even given a euphuistic title, *Menahem Meshib Nafshi* (Lamentations, I, 5).

The center of this activity was, as mentioned, Provence. It was there where the cultures of the East and West mingled, that such work could have begun and developed. Thither came a number of Jewish immigrants from Spain who were conversant with both Arabic and Hebrew, and these acted as the transmitters of the treasures of knowledge stored in the works written in Arabic both by Jews and Moslems, and made them accessible first to their brethren and ultimately to the great world. The moving spirits in this useful literary activity were the members of the Tibbon family, Judah, Samuel and Moses, father, son and grandson. However, others soon followed in their wake, the guild of translators kept on increasing, and later even spread to other countries, especially to Italy where they were often encouraged in their work by royal patrons of learning. Thus, for two centuries, the thirteenth and fourteenth, the scholars of Provence were feverishly busy translating a philosophic and scientific literature from one language into another.

Judah and Samuel devoted themselves primarily to the translation of Jewish works written in Arabic. It was Moses who was the initiator of the great undertaking of "Introducing the beauty of Japhet (Greek wisdom in Arabic garb) into the tents of Shem." He was the translator par excellence, the number of works he rendered into Hebrew amounting to over a score, among them several commentaries and compendia of Averroes, Themestius' commentary on the Metaphysics, Al-Farabi's Book of Principles and many other works of various philosophers. Jacob ben Abba Mari Anatoli (1200-1250), son-in-law of Samuel Ibn Tibbon upheld the tradition of the family and rendered many works into Hebrew noted among which are Averroes' Middle Commentary on the first Five Books of Logic of the Organon and his long commentary on the *Analytica.* Anatoli's fame as a translator reached Frederic the Second of Naples who was a great patron of learning, and he invited him to his court where he was engaged in cooperation with Christian scholars in translating Arabic works into Latin. Another member of the Tibbon family,

Jacob ben Makir-Tibbon (1230-1312), known as Don Profiat was also engaged in this work. To him belong the translations of Averroes' Compendium of Logic entitled *Kol Mlekheth ha-Higoyon* (The Entire Work of Logic), the nine books of Averroes' Commentary on the *De Partibus Animalium* and the *De Generatione.*

Of the other leading translators, the most outstanding is Kalonymos ben Kalonymos (1287-1337) of Provence. He, like Anatoli, was later invited by Robert of Anjou to Italy, to cooperate in the work of translation into Latin, where he translated Averroes' Destruction of the Destruction into that language. The number of the books translated by him into Hebrew is considerable and includes several books of Averroes' Commentaries on the Organon, the Commentaries on the Physics, Metaphysics and other books, and also Al-Farabi's work on the Classification of Sciences. (Bemispar ha-Hokmoth.) Other noted laborers in this field were Todros Todrosi of Arles (c. 1300-1350), a very prolific worker, Zerahya ben Isaac (1250-1300), Zerahya ben Shealtiel Gracian (1270-1290), Samuel ben Judah Marsili (first half of fourteenth century) and Isaac Albalag (14th century). Besides these, there was a large number of other scholars who contributed their share to this type of literary activity, sometimes attaching their names to their works, and sometimes giving them to the world anonymously.

The work of these translators forms a valuable chapter in the history of Jewish literature, for not only did it enrich it in content and ideas, but it also contributed greatly to the development of the Hebrew language. It was due to the work of these scholars that Hebrew became a vehicle of expression for philosophic and scientific ideas. True, none of the translations display great skill in the mastery of the language and are often full of Arabisms and awkward expressions. It is also true that there was little unity in the creation of a scientific terminology and that each author differed considerably from the others in the use of that terminology. But with all these shortcomings, the work of these translators is of permanent value for it laid the foundation of a scientific and philosophic Hebrew style.

75. *COMMENTARIES*

In the wake of the activity of translation, there followed another literary activity which is akin to it, but possesses more individuality and opportunity for self-expression, and that is the writing of commentaries on the translated books. Commentary writing was an important species of intellectual endeavor in the Mediaeval Ages, as the commentaries of the great Arabic philosophers, Avicenna, Al-Farabi and Averroes testify. In fact, these were not mere commentaries aiming to explain obscure words and doubtful expressions, but often original works which contributed to the deepening of the subject matter discussed. It is not to be wondered at then that these commentaries themselves, especially those of Averroes became the subject of numerous supercommentaries, and thus a considerable literature of this type was produced in Hebrew during the thirteenth, fourteenth and fifteenth centuries.

The commentaries, in general, can be divided into two classes, (1) those on books written by Arabic philosophers, and (2) those on the books written by Jewish philosophers. Of the latter class, there is practically one book on which the commentators concentrated their attention, and that is the *Guide* or the *More Nebukim* of Maimonides. For several centuries, this book was the Bible of Jewish philosophers and was assiduously studied and analyzed, so that all philosophic study during this period bears a direct or indirect relation to this book. As for the commentaries on the books of the gentile philosophers, there was a special predeliction for the books of Averroes on account of the importance attached to them, yet we find a large number of commentaries on books of other philosophers.

Of the leading commentators on the books of the Arabic philosophers, the first is the famous philosopher, Levi ben Gerson (1288-1344) who was exceedingly active in that direction. He wrote supercommentaries on most of Averroes' commentaries on the books of logic, on his compendium, and the middle commentary on the physics, on the compendia of the *De Coelo* and the *De Anima,* on his commentaries on the *De Animalibus** (Baale Hayyim), *De Generatione,* the *Parva Naturalia* and the *De Sensu* (ha-Hush we-ha Muhosh, i. e. on sense and things sensed), and he also commented on the book *Meteora* (Ototh ha-Shomayim) translated from the Arabic without the commentary of Averroes.

The second one is Moses of Narbonne, known as the Narboni, who wrote supercommentaries on the middle commentaries of Averroes on the Physics and the *De Coelo,* and also commentaries on the Tendencies of the Philosophers (Kavonoth ha-Pilisufim) by Al-Gazali, and the philosophical romance of Ibn Tophail, the Letter of

* Gersonides supercommentary was translated into Latin by Jacob Mantinus and was incorporated in the Latin version of Averroes' works, published in 1521.

Hai ben Yaktan (Iggereth Hai ben Yaktan). Of the other commentators, the better known are Joseph ben Shem Tob whose commentaries on the *Isagoge* of Porphyrys and on the Ethics of Aristotle are extant, Shem Tob ben Joseph (1461-90) who explained the Physics and the *De Anima,* Isaac Albalag from whom we possess a commentary on the Physics, and Judah ben Jehiel Messer Leon of Mantua who left us a commentary on the books on logic by Aristotle in Averroes' rendering.

From what has been said about the place The *Guide* of Maimonides occupied in the schools of Jewish philosophy, it can be easily inferred that the commentaries on that book were numerous. But not all of them were preserved, and even of those that were preserved only a limited number attracted the attention of the scholars and the students, so that they were ultimately printed either together with the text or in separate books. Of these, the earliest was the *More ha-More* (The Guide of the Guide[3]) by Shem Tob Ibn Falaquera. In his preface, the author states the motive for the writing of this commentary which is the following: The study of philosophy, says he, is useful to those who are prepared for it, but dangerous to those who have not the preliminary education. But even those whose understanding is mature and who have had some preparation in this science are liable to err and misinterpret the words of Maimonides, because of insufficient acquaintance with the philosophic sources upon which he drew. To supply this knowledge is the purpose of Falaquera in his commentary.

The work is divided into three parts (1) the commentary, (2) a summary of the contents of the first fifty-seven chapters together with short notes explaining some difficult passages, and (3) several chapters containing corrections of Samuel Ibn Tibbon's translation. The commentary which occupies the largest part of the book is not what one usually understands by that word, as it is primarily a compilation of excerpts of statements of various Arabic and Jewish philosophers on the subjects dealt with in the chapters of the *Guide.* These statements very frequently elucidate the meaning of the passages in the work, and at times, introduce a new note in the entire discussion of the subject. Of the excerpts quoted, a large part is taken from

[3] This is the literal translation, but Shem Tob interprets the second *More* as meaning the rebellious or misguided, i. e., that his commentary intends to correct the opinions of those who misinterpreted the Guide.

the writings of Averroes. They are so numerous that Falaquera does not quote him by name but by the title "The scholar referred to."

The spirit of the commentary, unlike those later ones, is very conservative. Falaquera is inclined to see in the views of the Arabic philosophers, not excluding the radical Averroes, an agreement on many points with the views of Jewish tradition. He even takes exception to the statement of Maimonides that all that Aristotle said regarding things in the sub-lunar world (the technical name for the earth and life on it) is true without doubt, and says that it is greatly exaggerated. On the other hand, he agrees with him in his remark that Aristotle had no positive proof for his assumption of the eternity of the world, but merely plausible arguments. Falaquera proves his point from the very language of Aristotle regarding this matter, which carries a slight ring of uncertainty.

The second commentary was written a century later by Joseph Ibn Kaspi (1280-1340) of Argentiers, the Bible exegete and philosopher (see Sect. 17). It is really a double commentary consisting of two parts, each complete in itself and bearing two different titles, *Amudē Keseph* (Pillars of Silver) and *Maskioth Keseph* (Mosaics of Silver) respectively. The first part contains explanations of the simpler parts of the *Guide,* while the second aims at probing the secrets contained in some passages which are intended only for the initiated and the select. The commentary is distinguished by keen analysis and a free spirit.

Kaspi belonged to a group of Provence Jewish philosophers who did not hesitate to draw the consequences from their philosophic principles, even at the risk of coming into conflict with tradition. His radicalism is especially evident in the *Maskioth.* Thus, in his remarks on Chapter XIII, Pt. II of the *Guide,* where Maimonides asserts his opposition to the principle of the eternity of the world, he expresses himself as seeing no necessity for believing in creation *De Novo,* and that this belief is no dogma in Judaism. Again, in his commentary on Ch. XXIX, Pt. II and Ch. XXVII, Pt. III, he outlines briefly and rather subtly his allegorical interpretation of the first chapters of Genesis, according to which the story of the creation is not to be taken literally, but merely as symbolic expressions of certain philosophic theories and principles (see Sect. D of the chapter). However, wherever he is not inclined to be extremely radical, his remarks are illuminating, and many of them were incorporated in later commentaries.

The third important commentator on the *Guide* is the philosopher Moses ben Abba Mari of Narbonne. He, like the previous commentators, felt that Maimonides had failed to give the premises on which his conclusions were based and thus his words were misunderstood. He aims, therefore, to supply the deficiency and also to point out some philosophical shortcomings of the master's views, where they do not agree with the more developed opinions of the later philosophers, especially with those of Averroes with whose teachings Maimonides was not sufficiently conversant. He endeavors to reveal to a certain extent the "secrets" contained in the *Guide,* though with great caution.

Narboni's commentary is permeated, like Kaspi's, with a free spirit, for he belonged to the same group of liberal thinkers. However, he is not as outspoken as Kaspi and his remarks are veiled and are very often ambiguous. Thus, in his comments on Ch. XXVII, Pt. II of the *Guide,* where Maimonides asserts that the world, though created, is not destructible, he remarks ironically that in asserting that the world is eternal in the future though created in the past, the master met Aristotle half way, "As if such things can be settled by a compromise in a court of justice." He means to imply by these words that it is impossible to accept the compromise of Maimonides, and that if we assume that the world is created, we must also assume its destructibility, and vice versa if we assume its indestructibility we must also assume its existence from eternity. He was not, however, able to conceal his free ideas from the students, and the more conservative thinkers of the successive generations looked upon his work with suspicion, though they copied from it extensively.

These commentaries, however, are not really commentaries in the strict sense of the word, as they are intended more for the deep student who wishes to delve in the mysteries of philosophy, but they do not satisfy the needs of the ordinary student who wants to understand the plain meaning of words and passages in the *Guide.*

To fill this need was the aim of the later commentators. Of these, the first was the grammarian and student of philosophy, Profiat Duran, known under the pen name of Ephodi (d. 1396). His commentary is complete, covering every chapter, but it is very brief as he limited himself to short notes explaining every difficult expression and elucidating the meaning of those passages which needed clarifying. About a century later, another commentary was produced by Shem Tob ben Joseph (d. 1488) with the same intention, that is to make the *Guide* accessible to the ordinary student. This commentary is an extensive and detailed one, and in fact, too extensive, as many of his explanations are unnecessary being too obvious. He himself recognizing this deficiency apologizes for it by stating that even the easier passages of the book need the attention of the student, and to call forth that attention is what he aimed at by his notes. Shem Tob had before him the commentaries of his predecessors and he utilized them to a great extent, excerpting whole pages from the works of Kaspi and Narboni and numerous passages from Ephodi, but he very seldom mentions them by name.

Yet, with all the extensiveness of Shem Tob, there was still room for another commentator to add his own explanatory notes to those of his predecessors. This commentator was Asher ben Abraham, surnamed Bunyan Crescas. He confesses in his preface that he is not certain whether he has fathomed the meaning of those passages upon which he comments, yet he hopes that he will be of great help to the young students. His notes are brief, but on the whole illuminating. These last three commentaries, though they fall behind the older ones in depth and philosophic penetration, were yet, on account of their simpler character, more current and popular with the students, and for this reason, they were repeatedly printed with the text, while the former remained for a long time in manuscript as separate works.

Partial commentaries on selected passages or chapters of the *More* were written by many scholars. Of the most outstanding of these, the first is the commentary on the twenty-five propositions which form the introduction to the second part of the *Guide* by Hillel of Verona, (Sect. 77); second, the extensive commentary of Don Isaac Abrabanel on Chs. I-LV, Pt. I and Chs. XXXI-XLV, Pt. II, Ch. I, Pt. III and a separate treatise called *Shomayim Hadashim* (New Heavens) on Ch. XIX, Pt. II. The character of the commentary will be discussed in connection with the exposition of the philosophy of Abrabanel. We possess also a Kabbalistic commentary on the Guide entitled *Sodoth ha-More* (The Secrets of the Guide) by the famous mystic Abraham Abulafia (see Sect. 106). In this commentary, Abulafia attempts to reconcile the teachings of Maimonides with those of the Kabbala.

76. LOGIC

On account of the many commentaries on Aristotle's works of logic, the compendia of the same and the supercommentaries written by Jewish scholars, very few independent works on logic were composed during the period.

There were, however, several men who found it necessary to add to this mass of literature translated from Arabic and extensively commented upon some works of their own, and wrote short treatises on the subject of logic. The first of these was Joseph Waspi who wrote a compendium of logic for his son under the name of *Zeror ha-Kespeh.* The author is quite conscious of the fact that Al-Farabi and Averroes preceded him in this work, still he believes that his book, on account of its brevity, will be of some use to his contemporaries who wish to acquire the elements of logic without great labor and much expenditure of mental energy. He further believes that a knowledge of the principles of science will help towards an understanding of the meaning of the Holy Scriptures. With this aim in view, Kaspi included in his compendium only the contents of the first six books of Aristotle's Organon, omitting the Topics, the Poetics and the Rhetoric, believing that the contents of these books would contribute little to the exegesis of the Bible.

The second one was Levi ben Gerson who, after writing a critical supercommentary on a number of Averroes' commentaries on several books on logic, wrote a book entitled The Right Syllogism (ha-Hekesh ha-Yashar). This work contains his strictures both upon Aristotle's and Averroes' views of the structure of the various syllogisms and gives an exposition of his own views. It drew upon itself the attention of the gentile scholars and was immediately translated into Latin, under the title: *Liber Syllogismi Recti.*

A third writer on logic was Joseph ben Moses Kilti of Greece, a scholar who lived at the end of the fourteenth century. He wrote the book, entitled *Minhat Yehudah* (The Gift of Judah) in honor of another scholar, Judah ben Jacob Ibn Eter of Spain, hence its name. The work presents the contents of the entire Organon, including the Poetics and Rhetoric.

77. PSYCHOLOGY

As noted above, the problem of the soul, which in the Classical period occupied only a secondary position in Jewish philosophy, became very prominent during the post-Classical Age. The reason for this importance is to be sought in the great influence exercised by the teachings of Averroes upon Jewish thought. Averroes devoted excessive attention to the problem of the soul which was left open by Aristotle on account of the ambiguity of the language he employed in his statement on the subject. There arose, therefore, many differences in the interpretation of the words of the master among his principal commentators, Alexander of Aphrodisias and Themistius. The Arabic commentators, whose view of Aristotle's teaching was colored with Neo-Platonic conceptions, injected into this question still greater diversity. The result of all this was Averroes' theory of the soul and intellect known as the *Unitas Intellectus*.

The theory which concerns itself with the intellect and not with the lower parts of the soul is briefly as follows: Aristotle, as known, spoke in his description of the soul, of parts, faculties or even of three souls, which are the vegetative, the animal and the human. The first includes those powers and forces which regulate the activities of nutrition and growth of the body common to man, animals and plants. The second embraces the activities of sensation, perception and movement which are common both to man and animals. The third, soul or reason, is peculiar to man alone. The first two parts or souls, he taught, are intimately connected with the body and disappear with its death. It is the third alone which is immortal. He further taught that the third part contains two elements, the active and the passive which ulimately came to be known as the active and the passive intellects.* He did not, however, say much more about the nature and character of reason and its ultimate destiny. Hence, there arose the different interpretations. Regarding this intellect, Averroes says that not only is it bipartite but tripartite. It consists of the material intellect, the acquired (Sekel ha-Nikne) and the active. The material intellect is a disposition in the soul to perceive ideas and concepts aroused by the association of the universal Active Intellect (Sekel ha-Poel), a separate intelligence which rules the sublunar world, with the soul of man. In the course of its activity, the material intellect acquires more and more concepts and ideas so that it becomes the acquired intellect. When it reaches the highest degree of perfection, it then becomes active and unites with the Active Intellect of the world after the death of the individual.

* Aristotle himself called the second element νοῦς παθητικός, i. e., passive reason, but the name νοῦς ποιητικός, i. e., active reason for the first is according to Zeller found only in later writers.

Averroes thus reduced the immortality of the soul to a minimum in depriving it of the individuality of the person, and making it consist merely in the ultimate unity of the active reason of the individual with the Universal Intellect. That such a theory threatened to undermine some of the fundamental principles of religion in general and of Judaism in particular, such as beliefs in immortality and reward and punishment in the hereafter, goes without saying. Jewish philosophers found themselves, therefore, in a difficult position. On the one hand, there was the authority of Averroes, the great interpreter of *the philosopher,* (the name applied to Aristotle in the Mediaeval Ages), and on the other hand, the question of how this theory could be accepted without making a breach with religion. Hence, there arose the great interest in the problem of psychology, which was expressed either in separate works entirely devoted to the problem or by giving to it prominent space in their general works on philosophy.

The first book dealing exclusively with psychology is the *Tagmulē ha-Nephesh* (The Reward of the Soul), by Hillel ben Samuel of Verona, Italy (1220-1295). Rabbi Hillel went to Spain in his youth to be instructed both in Talmud and philosophy. He spent three years at the academy of Jonah Gerundi at Barcelona as he relates in his book, and simultaneously studied philosophy and science with other masters. He later returned to his native country and lived in Ferrara and Forli where he was engaged in the practice of medicine. Hillel had a knowledge both of Arabic and Latin, and was probably the first Jewish philosopher who made extensive use of philosophic and scientific books in Latin, even translating them into Hebrew. He was a prolific writer, engaged in translations, the writing of commentaries and in the composition of original works. He translated several medical works from the Latin, among them a book on surgery, and also the famous book *Liber De Causis,* a pseudo-Aristotelian work. His commentary on Maimonides' twenty-five propositions was noted above. Of his own works, not all were preserved in their entirety; some of them are extant in a fragmentary state, from which we can see that they dealt with theological and philosophical questions. His main philosophic work is the *Tagmulē ha-Nephesh* on which his title as a philosopher rests.

This book is divided into two parts, the first dealing with the philosophical side of the problem of the soul, namely, defining its essence and functions, and the second with the theological phase, namely of the soul's reward and punishment. In his introduction, the author explains the purpose of the book, saying that the reader will derive a double benefit from the discussion of this problem. First, that since the soul is the thing by means of which man becomes what he is, it is not meet that we should remain ignorant of our very human essence. Second, if one should possess an erroneous conception of the soul, he is liable to continue in his error, and arrive at similar wrong conceptions of the universe, angels and even God Himself. It is, therefore, his purpose to put forth a clear conception of the soul and thus set men right in their concepts of spiritual things. He does not, however, lay claim to much originality, inasmuch as he admits that he collected his material from many books dealing with the subject, but he reserves for himself the right to reject those opinions which do not stand the test of truth, for the search of truth is his aim.

The first part of the book is subdivided into seven sections, proving various propositions concerning the soul. In the first section, Hillel proves the existence of the soul as an entity distinct from the body by a number of proofs of which we will quote one. We see, he says, that natural bodies are of various grades. Some take food, grow and reproduce while others, like stones and minerals, do not discharge these functions. We must, therefore, assume that the functions performed by the former do not arise from the fact that they are bodies, for stones are also bodies and are endowed with all the properties that the definition of a body involves. It is to be concluded then that there is a different principle, not the body itself, which supplies this perfection to the first class of beings not possessed by the other class. This is the soul. He next proves that the soul is a substance, not an accident nor a property. It is not an accident, for an accident is that, the destruction of which does not cause the destruction of the object in which it resides, while the body cannot exist as a living body without a soul. Further, accidents may pass from one genus to another, thus color is found in man, animals, plants and minerals, while the soul is found only in the first three genera. It is not a property, for properties may exist in things sometimes in potentiality, and sometimes in actuality, while the human soul is always an actuality for without it, the body is but a corpse. It is, therefore, a substance, and substances again are either corporeal or incorporeal. The soul is not a corporeal substance, for a body is divisible, changeable and subject to motion, but the soul is not susceptible to any of these things as will be proved, hence it is not a corporeal substance.

True, we speak of the soul as ascending or descending, but these expressions are only metaphorical, an assertion which he proves at length in accordance with the Aristotelian conception of locomotion. The objection to the unchangeability of the soul, arising from the fact that man passes from one emotion to the other, e. g. from joy to sorrow, he meets by saying that these emotions are not inherent in the soul as such. They are primarily due to bodily humours, and the soul is only affected by the mixture of these humours, so far as it is united with the body. In its own nature, it is not subject to emotions. The union of the soul with the body is to be understood as the union of form with matter, namely that it supplies the perfection to the latter.

The indivisibility of the soul is proved by Hillel in the following manner. If the soul is divisible, we have to assume either that each part possesses all the powers of the whole, or that the whole contains an inseparable sum of the powers of the parts. In the first case, we arrive at an absurdity as we posit a multiplicity of souls; in the second, we must say that the divisibility is only potentially so and not actually. However, since every force in the potential must sometimes become actual, which is not the case with the potential divisibility of the soul, it follows that it is not even potentially divisible. He next defines the soul as an emanated formal substance which subsists through its own perfection and occupies the fourth place in the order of spiritual beings, namely after the universal Active Intellect. The order he refers to is the usual one posited by the Arabian and Jewish philosophers, namely (1) God, (2) the Separate Intelligences, (3) the Active Intellect, (4) the Soul. The ultimate source of emanation is, of course, God who works through the mediacy of the intelligences. He now comes to the crucial question which is the relation of the soul to the Active Intellect and the description of the essence and activity of the human intellect, the higher part of the soul.

But before attending to this question, he digresses on a discussion of Averroes' theory of the unity of the soul which posits that there is one universal soul and that the individualizations in men are only due to the association of that soul with the various human bodies. Hillel is inclined to accept this theory, but in a modified form as will soon be evident. He then resumes his description of the intellect, dividing it, like Averroes, into three elements; the *hylic* or the material, the acquired and the active, described above. He further agrees with Averroes that the material intellect is acted upon by the universal Active Intellect, which action helps it to realize its powers and become an active intellect in itself. This is accomplished by the process of conception, the more the material intellect conceives ideas and universals, the more active it becomes, and continues to rise in the degree of conception until it is able to conceive the Active Intellect itself and thus be united with it. All this is discussed by Hillel at great length and with many proofs which we have omitted on account of their technicalities.

Thus far, he agrees with Averroes, but when he comes to the question what the relation of the intellect is to the human soul, he disagrees with him. Averroes taught that the intellect is neither a part of the soul nor its form, but merely an immaterial substance coming from the Active Intellect which is united with the soul during life and is released after death, going back to its source and retaining none of its former individuality. That could not be accepted by Hillel. He, therefore, endeavors to prove by a series of arguments that the intellect is a part of the soul, and what is more, that it is the very form of the soul and thus directs all its forces, even that of the perceptive and of feeling and growth. Yet, this form is not lost with the death of the body, though the lower parts of the soul, like all other forms, disappear with the destruction of the matter with which they are connected. The intellect is eternal, and being the form of the soul of the individual, it retains all its individuality and is thus subject to reward and punishment.

In the second part, our author takes up the question of reward and punishment after death. He proceeds, at first, to lay down a general proposition that both reward and punishment are not of a corporeal but of a spiritual nature. He offers many reasons for this assertion, one of which is as follows: If the soul, as proved, is incorporeal, immaterial and a formal substance, how can it be affected by corporeal punishment, for all corporeal action implies the permeation of the influence of the agent in all parts of the patient, but a spiritual substance has no parts. Further, were the reward and punishment corporeal, why separate the soul from the body? Would it not have been better if the good were rewarded and the wicked punished while living, so that they would thus serve as an example to others?

He then shows how man can reach a happy state after death. God, says Hillel, provided man with the means to attain his goal, that is the intellect with which He endowed him. Here he gives a more detailed account of the stages of that intellect. The first is the material intellect which is prepared to receive the ideas and conceptions. The second, the acquired intellect, i. e. the sum of the ideas man acquires through life, and the highest is the active intellect when man is able to conceive the universal Active Intellect. The acquired intellect consists of two parts, the speculative and the practical, that is one that is devoted entirely to contemplation, and the other which busies itself with doing things. The practical part is again divided into the cogitative and the technological. The first is the power by means of which man decides upon actions, estimates their propriety and justification, the second is the power which endows man with skill for the arts. The practical reason is, of course, associated with the imaginative faculty, for without it, no action or art can be carried out. We must not, however, think that these two parts of the acquired intellect differ in essence. In reality, the speculative and the practical elements are one in essence, and differ only in their objects, as the objects of the former are the true and the false, and the objects of the latter are good and bad.

We must also not conclude that the development of the acquired intellect is alone sufficient to cause man to obtain righteousness. The other forces of the soul must cooperate, especially those of the will and the emotions, and it is, therefore, meet for man to train all his faculties, even that of sensation, i. e. his five senses, to the service of the Lord.

After stating his general conception of the nature of reward and punishment, Hillel proceeds to describe it in more detail and to meet the objections that may arise to the view from many passages in Talmudic literature which apparently speak of material kinds of reward and punishment. He devotes a good deal of space to explaining the Talmudic passages, which speak of *Gan Eden* (Paradise) and the *Gehinom* (Hell) in rather gross terms, by employing the usual devices of allegory and parable. He concludes that these descriptions were primarily meant for the masses who will neither be induced to do good nor deterred from committing evil by spiritual reward and punishment, but are in need of more material promises or threats. In reality, we are to understand that the reward of the righteous is the rise of the soul to a high degree of contemplation, and the punishment of the wicked consists in this that their souls will be conscious of their low and degraded state and this consciousness will cause them great pain and suffering. Hillel makes a number of digressions to explain Talmudic passages dealing with these questions and also discusses the question of resurrection and the world to come. He is, however, not clear on the last named subjects, for while he constantly asserts that the soul is eternal, he states in connection with resurrection that the wicked will rise and be punished by being condemned to destruction, namely that their souls will be destroyed. But then the question arises, how can the soul be destroyed? This inconsistency is the result of an attempt to bring into complete harmony the views of a radically inclined rational philosophy with the various views expressed in the passages of the Talmud and Midrash, without discerning which passage is authoritative and which is not.

In an appendix to the *Tagmulē ha-Nephesh,* Hillel discusses the question of free will and human choice of action as well as its compatibility with Divine prescience. He approaches the question from a new angle hardly touched upon previously, that is, the difficulty we meet in explaining why one chooses the doing of good and the other of evil. The difficulty is greater, of course, if we assume with Averroes that the nature of the soul is one with all men. But it is not removed even if we assume that there is a separate soul created for each man. In that case, we will have to assume that either all souls were equally created good or that only some were good and some bad. In the first instance, the difficulty is evident, for if they were all good, whence the difference in choice of action; in the second instance, the question arises, if some people were originally endowed with bad souls, then again they have no choice in their actions.

In proceeding to solve this difficulty, Hillel points out that it is inherently connected with the famous problem of the compatibility of the freedom of the will with Divine prescience, namely, how can we say that God knows things in the future and yet assert that man is free to act as he chooses? God's knowledge must be correct, the human action must then be in accordance with his foreknowledge, and if on the other hand, the action be different than His foreknowledge, then His knowledge is incorrect. He offers the following solution to this ancient problem. There are, he says, three principles of existence, form, matter, and non-being. These have three corresponding attributes, the necessary, the possible and the impossible. The first refers to form, for it is active, the second to matter since it is potential, the third to non-being. Since man is compounded of matter and form, the attributes of necessity and possibility are pertinent to him. Necessity is the principle of his existence and essence; possibility belongs to accidents which befall him and is the principle of his ability to choose. Since these two principles are inherent in the very nature of man, God does not change that nature nor does His foreknowledge of human action change it, but He conceives every human action as a possibility. True, He knows beforehand which side of the possibility will be realized, but the knowledge does not affect the possibility, just as the fact that the carpenter knows how to make a table from boards of wood does not necessitate the converting of the boards into that table, for they also may be made into a chair or a chest. Should we assume differently, then we would have to conclude that either God is unjust for He thus changes the nature of the possible into the necessary, or that His conceptions are false, i. e. the action is possible in nature, and yet He conceives it as necessary.

Since it has been established that possibility is the principle of choice of action, the original problem may also be solved, though it may still be asked why some men possess inclination to do good and some to do evil, since all men possess possibility of action. Hillel then makes a distinction between the choice of good and that of bad. The cause for the former, says he, is essential as it arises from the speculative and the practical intellect, that of the latter is accidental. There is really no essential cause why man should be wicked, but it arises through a series of accidents. At one time or another, things happen to men which weaken their mental resistance to temptations. We can, therefore, understand the reason why some men are good and some are bad, though their souls may be of one nature. Those who choose the evil path do so because of a series of accidents that caused changes in their souls.

But here one may ask, why then should the wicked be punished if their choice of evil is accidental. To this Hillel answers that these accidents are preventable, for were man to use his intellect, he could avoid them. That there are some flaws in this reasoning is evident. He, however, was neither the first nor the last who failed to give a complete solution to this most difficult problem in Jewish religious philosophy.

ii. SHEM TOB IBN FALAQUERA

The second treatise devoted solely to psychology is the *Sepher ha-Nephesh* (The Book of the Soul) by Shem Tob Ibn Falaquera. It is a small book divided into twenty brief chapters, but covers the subject completely and gives a clear conception of the psychological science of the day.

In the introduction, the author states that he wrote this brief treatise on the soul for his own use as a manual for reviewing his psychological studies, as the knowledge of the soul leads to the knowledge of God. He quotes in this connection the famous maxim ascribed to Mohammed (though Falaquera ascribes it to certain hermits), "Man, know thy soul and thou wilt know thy creator," and concludes, therefore, that the science of the soul precedes the science of the Deity.

Before proceeding to describe the soul and its faculties, the author devotes three brief chapters to the proof for the existence of the soul, to the medium of activity of its powers and to its definition, respectively. He offers only one proof for the existence of the soul, one which was also stated by Hillel ben Samuel, namely, that since only some bodies have the power of conception, it follows that this power is something different than the body, for otherwise all bodies would have possessed it. He posits a certain kind of air as the bearer of the medium for the powers of the soul by means of which they affect the various organs of the body. The soul is to be defined as the highest perfection or *entelechy* for a natural organic body. Falaquera says that he is careful in defining the soul as the highest perfection, and not as the form of the body, though in reality, it is the form of the latter, for the term *form* may include accidents such as shape and size, but perfection denotes things essential.

Adopting the Aristotelian conception of the soul as a tripartite one, consisting of the vegetative, animal and human parts or souls, he begins to describe each part. The vegetative soul possesses the powers of nutrition, growth and reproduction. The first power preserves the equilibrium of metabolism in the body; the second is a higher degree of perfection, inasmuch as it converts the excessive amount of food unused for making up the daily waste of the body into an increase of the organs. The third is the further perfection of the power of growth, and its instrument of activity is the balance of unused food left after the process of growth is completed. He concludes that the purpose of the nutritive power is the preservation of the body, that of growth its perfection and that of procreation the perpetuation of the genus, for God has endowed every being with the love for continuation of existence.

To the animal soul belong the following powers: the vital, that of sensation, of imagination and of memory, and these he proceeds to describe. The vital power he describes as the instinct for self preservation, namely the instinct to follow what is good for the organism and avoid what is injurious to it. He gives a fairly correct account of the five senses, noting that sound arises from the vibration or the movement generated in a hard body when struck by another body, and that air is the medium through which it is carried to the ear. He is aware that smell is generated through a gaseous or smoky vapor detached from the odoriferous body and carried through the air to the nostrils. Touch is properly described by him as containing four different kinds of sensation, hard and soft or pressure, wet and dry, hot and cold or temperature, and that of roughness and smoothness. He is also aware that the entire skin is the organ for tactual sensation. He speaks in the fashion of his time of a common sense (sensus communis) which is an internal and not an external sense. The function of the common sense is to coordinate the sensations of the other senses into one perception. It is practically the faculty of perception which Falaquera calls the common sense.

He then discusses the other powers of the animal soul, namely imagination and memory. The first, he says, operates with the materials prepared by the common sense or perception, and combines different perceptions into imaginary representations. It differs both from sensation and from the ideation of the intellect, for the data of the sensations are correct, while those of the imagination are not always so. Again, with the intellect we can conceive abstract ideas while the imagination can never conceive anything abstract, as its representations are always corporeal and individual things. In discussing memory, our author distinguishes between mere memory or retention and remembrance. The first, he says, is possessed by any animal which is able to retain a perception after the external stimulus has ceased to operate, the second is peculiar only to man, for it consists in an effort to recall by means of thought forgotten images or representations and review them. This power is a complex one for in addition to the power of recalling, there is also a judging or discerning power which decides what image or representation is exactly the one sought for. This discussion of the animal soul is completed with a brief chapter on the emotions.

Falaquera proceeds to describe the human soul or intellect. He adopts the Averroistic division into *hylic* or material, acquired and active intellects. The first is called material for its likeness to matter, inasmuch as it is a disposition ready to assume any form. The acquired intellect consists of two sets of ideas, one of which, according to Falaquera came by Divine help, namely, the axioms and the first principles, e. g. that the whole is larger than the part and similar notions, and the other is acquired by the process of reasoning. This intellect when applied to pure knowledge is called theoretical and when applied to matters of conduct, practical. The active intellect is the highest degree the human soul can attain. It is reached when the intellect is able to conceive the highest ideas without effort or travail.

Falaquera proves briefly that the human soul is incorporeal for it is not connected with the body and remains after its death. The first is proved by the fact that while the senses are weakened after exertion such as the impairing of vision or hearing due to a strong stimulus from a powerful light or from an extremely loud sound, the intellect, on the contrary, is strengthened by exertion, for after one has succeeded in conceiving high ideas, he conceives lower ones more easily. Again, the sensations weaken after man has reached mature age, while the intellect, on the other hand, grows stronger at that period. To the objection that the fact that the intellect is unable to function when the body is sick would prove its dependence on the latter, the author replies that while the intellect is a separate substance, yet it is related to the other powers of the soul, such as the senses, imagination and emotion, and when these are impaired, the intellect is unable to concentrate upon higher things. It is for this reason that when the body is sick and the other powers of the soul are distorted, the intellect can not perform its function properly. Since the intellect is incorporeal, it follows that it is not destroyed with the body, and hence immortal.

The book closes with a fine summary of the contents of the preceding chapters and with two additional brief chapters which describe the opinions held by various philosophers regarding the soul and the influence exerted upon it by the universal Active Intellect. Falaquera, like Hillel, believes that the universal Active Intellect brings out the *hylic* intellect of man from potentiality into actuality, and turns it successively into the acquired and active intellects, and like him, he asserts that at death, the immortal part of the human soul connects itself in some way with the Universal Intellect. The uniting with that Intellect is not given in detail, for Falaquera carefully avoids in this manual any discussion of theological questions and limits himself entirely to psychological matter. In general, it can be said that the author carried out his aim admirably, for it really gives a clear outline of that science as far as it was known in his day.

A. Philosophy

78. *LEVI BEN GERSON*

Levi ben Gerson, or Gersonides, was not only a commentator on philosophical works written by others, but a deep thinker who made an important contribution to Jewish philosophy during the post-Classical period. His chief philosophical work is the *Milhamoth Adonai* (The Battles of the Lord), a work which occupies a distinguished place in philosophic literature alongside of the *Guide* of Maimonides. With Gersonides, the current of Aristotelianism in Jewish philosophy which began with Abraham Ibn Daud (Vol. I, Sect. 172) reached its climax. Maimonides was a close follower of the Stagirite, but whenever the teachings of the former clashed with those of the Bible, he gave precedence to the tenets of the latter. Not so Gersonides; he drew from the philosophic teachings their ultimate conclusions and if they did not entirely agree with the Bible, he twisted the words of the Scriptures in all possible ways, so as to force them into some kind of an agreement with philosophy, strained as the interpretation might be. Consequently, the philosophy of Gersonides is of a more radical nature than that of Maimonides, and therefore, it did not enjoy the popularity of the latter, for it was always suspected of containing dangerous heresies. In fact, a later scholar of great piety ingeniously remarked that the book should not be called the Battles of the Lord but the Battles with the Lord.

The *Milhamoth* does not, like the *Guide,* contain a complete system of Jewish philosophy but only an extensive discussion of a number of metaphysical problems which have a bearing on religious questions. Gersonides, though he believed like Maimonides, that religion and philosophy can be brought into complete harmony, nevertheless was more interested in philosophy than in theology. He omitted, therefore, a number of problems which heretofore occupied a prominent place with the philosophers who preceded him. Thus, he does not attempt to prove the existence of God, nor define the nature or the concept of the Godhead, neither does he enter into a discussion of revelation, reward and punishment, resurrection and other kindred problems. He does discuss the problems of the attributes of God and the nature of prophecy, but in a rather brief and incomplete manner. The main problems with which he is concerned are the world order, the soul of man, the relation of God to these two, and finally that of creation. These are discussed very extensively, especially those of the soul and creation, which occupied an important place in the thought of the time.

The work is divided into six books some of which are subdivided into several parts, and these into chapters. The first book is devoted to the discussion of psychology and the immortality of the soul. The second deals with the dreams and divinations touching also partly on prophecy. The third discusses the problem of God's foreknowledge of events and that of the freedom of man. The fourth takes up the question of Divine Providence. The fifth which describes the world order, namely the heavenly bodies and their relation to the sub-lunar world, was originally divided into three parts, the first of which, entirely devoted to astronomy, is omitted from all editions of the *Milhamoth.* The second part contains a partial study of the nature of the stars, spheres and the intelligences moving them, and the third discusses God's relation to the spheres, the roles of the universal Active Intellect and the Divine attributes. The sixth book is an extensive treatise in two parts on the problem of the eternity of the world and creation, one of which deals with the physical-metaphysical aspect of the problem where all arguments pro and con concerning creation and eternity are stated. In the other, the author attempts to reconcile his views with the teachings of the Bible and also discusses the question of miracles and prophecy.

Not all the parts of the books of the *Milhamoth* were written simultaneously; thus the first part of Book VI was written twelve years earlier than the rest of it and only later incorporated in the work. Nor are the ideas contained therein given in a systematic order, as some of the principal theories are treated in more than one book. It will, therefore, be necessary for us in giving a brief survey of the philosophy of Gersonides to deviate from the order of the books given by the author and adopt a system of our own, and furthermore, on account of the abstruseness of the arguments, we will have to omit them and only give succintly the results reached by Gersonides in his reasoning.

According to Gersonides, God is the only fundamental being in existence. All other beings acquired existence from Him and He is the ground and order of perfection of all beings throughout all time. As stated, he does not attempt to prove the existence of God, but assumes it as an established fact, relying on the arguments of his predecessors. Unlike Maimonides and his followers, Gersonides refuses to accept the theory of homonymity, namely that there is only a likeness in name, between the attributes when applied both to God and man. Nor does he believe that these attributes should all be taken negatively. He believes that the attributes are applied both to God and man in different degrees of perfection, that is, to God in the highest degree and to man in a smaller measure.

The positive attributes are then, according to our philosopher, existent, living—by the last is to be understood the quality of perfect conception of reasoning—one, active, eternal, potent, good and righteous. The first three attributes are, of course, the primary ones, two of which are incorporated in the *Shema* recited every day, namely, "Hear, O Israel, God our Lord, God is one," where His existence and unity are emphasized. The other five are really included in the concept *active,* that is His relation to the world. Since He is the source of whatever goodness, righteousness, potency, and eternity all other beings possess, it follows that He is active, good, righteous, eternal and potent par excellence. It is, of course, understood that all these attributes are predicated of God in an infinitely higher way than of other beings, and that they do not impair His unity for they are only phases of one being.

From God, we pass to the world. The cosmology of Gersonides is the Aristotelian modified by the Arabic philosophers and infused with Platonic and Neo-Platonic elements. He does not discuss in detail the manner of creation, namely whether it was by a direct act of God or by a series of emanations. It seems that he really advocates a kind of combination of both, though he speaks constantly of the emanation of His power and perfection, but of this later.

The universe is, on the whole, divided into two unequal parts, the world above the moon, and the world below the moon, or the sublunar world. The world above the moon consists of a series of spheres which move the planets and the stars. Besides the spheres of the planets, there is also the sphere of the fixed stars. As each planet has more than one sphere, the number of spheres is much larger than the planets. It had been variously fixed by Aristotle and his followers, and according to Gersonides, the number is sixty-four.

The worlds of the spheres and the sublunar one differ in the matter of which they are composed. The matter of the first world, called ether is pure, imperishable and unchangeable, while that of the second consists of the four elements, namely fire, air, water and earth which undergo a constant series of combinations and disintegrations, thus bringing about the process of generation and decay.

The heavenly bodies are the recipients of the emanation of God's perfection so that they are living and rational beings. The universal nature of each sphere is called a separate intelligence or the spirit and the mover of the sphere. These spheres and their movers control and guide all the events and happenings in this sublunar world. It is they and their movers that cause, by reason of the various changes in their own movements and positions, all the multifarious changes in the sublunar world. Each sphere and its mover has a specific task to perform and the spirit of that sphere conceives only a part of the order of this world, namely, the one resulting from its own activity. In addition to the conception of that part of the order, it conceives, of course, the First Cause or God. Yet, though they appear to be separate in their totality, they form a unified whole, for they help and perfect each other. The order of existence, as a whole, in its various ramifications is conceived only by God and one other being, namely the universal Active Intellect (Sekel-ha-Poel).

The universal Active Intellect is, in reality, the same that Aristotle called the world soul. But while in the system of the Stagirite, the world soul plays rather an insignificant part, it assumed under the guise of the new name and through the influence of Neo-Platonism great importance in the schools of the Arab philosophers and consequently also among the Jews. We have had occasion more than once to refer to it, but did not stop to define it. This intellect is, according to Gersonides, the result of all the activities and influences of the heavenly bodies. These bodies, as mentioned, direct the changes and events in the sublunar world, but each of them directs only a part. However, from the combined emanation of all their conceptions, there results an Active Intellect which coordinates and harmonizes all activities. The intellect, while only an emanation of the spheres and their movers is, nevertheless, higher than they. In the totality thus effected, there is an all-embracing quality, for the Active Intellect conceived the entire order in the sublunar world and thus becomes its moving spirit.

This Intellect differs from God, inasmuch as its activity and conceptions are limited to the sublunar world, whereas God comprehends the entire universe. The role of the Active Intellect is all embracive, as it performs numerous functions. It guards the order of the sublunar world, it gives form to the sublunary things and preserves their existence, and acts as the most important factor in the process of human knowledge. This, of course, brings us to the discussion of the nature and character of the human soul.

We are now able to pass on to the discussion of the soul to which Gersonides devotes many pages. He opens his discussion on the question by stating the three views of the commentators of Aristotle regarding the master's conception of the human soul. Gersonides limits himself primarily to that and does not touch on the other parts of the soul denominated the vegetative and the vital. Alexander of Aphodisias, the first commentator said that the passive or material intellect has the soul or a part of it for its subject and resides therein, and that this intellect is merely a capacity and possesses no substantiality of its own. Consequently, it perishes together with the lower soul. Themisius, on the other hand, taught that this passive intellect of which Aristotle speaks is an independent spiritual substance which is imperishable, and is only associated with the other parts of the soul during life. Averroes taught as we have already seen, that the passive or material intellect is merely an individualized form of a part of the universal Active Intellect which is thus associated with the soul of each man.

Gersonides then analyzes all the three views at great length and finally, proposes his own, which is as follows. He agrees with Alexander that the passive intellect is the potentiality for developing pure thought, residing in the sensitive and feeling soul, namely that which possesses the faculties of sensation, perception and imagination. But here, he parts company with Alexander. His view on the further development of that intellect differs considerably from that of the latter. This potentiality or capacity is developed during human life into actuality by the help of the Active Intellect, and gradually there is built up in the human mind a stock of ideas and conceptions of universal import and character. This actualized reason is called the acquired intellect. This intellect is a variable one dependent upon the capacity of each individual. The more a man progresses, the more he discovers the unity and order in this world; and were it possible for him to conceive all universals in their completeness, he would see them all united into one. This, however, is impossible, as that is the function of the Active Intellect. What man can do, therefore, is to strive to unite as much as possible with that Intellect and thus unite indirectly with God.

This acquired intellect of man undoubtedly contains elements of a perishable character, inasmuch as it is mixed up with the sensuous part of the soul. But it has also elements of pure thought generated by the influence of the Active Intellect, and these are imperishable and immortal.

It is, therefore, in this way that we conceive the immortality of the soul. The more a man strives to develop his acquired intellect to conceive the universality of things and the unity of the order of the world, the nearer he approaches the universal Active Intellect and the better he understands God. Consequently, the sum total of his thoughts on these exalted subjects remains immortal. Yet, this immortality is an individual one, as the acquired intellect of one man differs from that of another.

The ascendency to higher and higher levels in this scale of knowledge constitutes, according to Gersonides, the purpose and happiness of human life. This happiness is heightened after death, for the intellect is then freed of the defectiveness accruing to it by the association with the body and is able to unite all concepts into one whole. It is, however, understood that no new conceptions are acquired after death, for conceptions are acquired by means of the senses and other faculties of the soul which perish with death. But the conceptions that man had acquired during life become clearer and furnish him constant and unchanging pleasure.

What has gone before leads us to the solution of the vexing problems of the compatibility of God's prescience of events with human freedom, and that of Divine Providence. These problems are solved by Gersonides in the following manner. He agrees with Maimonides that God's knowledge is totally different from that of man, but rejects his assertion that He knows also the particular things and happenings in this world. He scrutinizes this assertion and shows the difficulties it involves, especially its relation to human freedom. He, therefore, says that God knows Himself, and through that knowledge, He knows the entire order of the universe, since He is the principle of it. He knows then the things from their general and unified aspect, and consequently, also the particulars from their side of unity, but he does not know these particulars in their infinite ramifications. This solves also the question of the existence of possible action on the part of man in spite of God's foreknowledge. Possible events have two aspects, they may be preordained in one way, and possible in the other. From the aspect of the general order of events, they are determined, but from the aspect of human choice, they are indeterminate. God knows these things, namely human action so far as they are possible, but He does not know which side of the possibility will be realized. It must, of course, be understood that when we say that possible things are determined, it only means that their possibility is determined by the general order preserved in this sublunar world by the Active Intellect, but not their realization. In this way, human freedom is saved by Gersonides.

Gersonides differs from Maimonides also in his theory of Providence. While the latter excepts the human species from the general established order and that of natural law and extends to it a special Divine Providence, Gersonides includes also the individuals of the human species under that order and does not accord the species as a whole that kind of special Providence. He does admit, though, differentiation in regard to Providence among the individuals of the human species. This differentiation is based on his conception of the world order and the influence of the Active Intellect on the human soul. The order in the sublunar world was, as we have seen, established by God and is preserved and regulated by the heavenly bodies, whose activity is controlled by the Active Intellect. Hence, there arises the difference among human individuals; the higher one rises in intellectual endeavors and the more concepts of reason he acquires, the closer he is to the Active Intellect and thus to God, and consequently more Providence is extended to him. In fact, we have here the idea of a special Providence reintroduced in a modified form.

This special Providence consists not in the performing of miraculous deeds in behalf of the recipient but in the fact that the intellectual man, who is also the righteous, is, through the Active Intellect, the recipient of information concerning impending events. And thus being informed beforehand of future occurrences, he escapes the evil or attains the good.

This possibility on the part of man to have a foreknowledge of coming events plays an important part in the system of Gersonides. He believes in foreknowledge through dreams and divinations, and of course, in prophecy. Prophecy is also a species of foreknowledge except that it is of a higher kind and must have a prerequisite preparation in intellectual conception. Prophecy is a kind of emanation from God through the mediacy of the Active Intellect, and since it is dependent on preparation, it is of many degrees in accordance with the stage of ethical and intellectual preparation of the man. Moses, possessing the highest type of such preparation, was the greatest prophet.

Gersonides applies also this theory to the solution of the problem of injustice in this world. He analyzes at great length the various opinions contained in the Book of Job and concludes that the view of Elihu is the right one. It is as follows: The order established by God through the mediacy of the heavenly bodies is intended, on the whole, for the good. It is, therefore, no injustice if the wicked are also recipients of the good, since it follows in a general way. Likewise, the evil befalling the righteous comes through the necessary order of events when they become lax in their righteousness and the special Providence is removed from them. At times, evil befalls them as a warning that they have begun to turn from the way of God. Thus, there is a way of escape open to the righteous man, that is by turning back to God, he will attain the special Providence which is expressed either in the forewarning by the Active Intellect of coming evils or by pointing a way to the good. On the other hand, the wicked are left to the order predetermined by the heavenly bodies and do not escape the evil. Gersonides feels, however, that this theory is not sufficient to explain all cases and adds therefore, that the real good is after all the happiness of the soul, and that the real evil is the loss of that happiness. In this case, the accruing of both good and evil to the righteous is only relative. He further adds that sometimes God does show a special Providence to the righteous by bringing upon them a lesser evil in order to forestall a greater one impending over them through the general order. Likewise, sometimes He brings evil directly upon the wicked, both as a punishment and as a means to save the righteous. This last method belongs, however, to the miraculous which is not frequent.

Gersonides, as stated, incorporated his essay on the question of creation at the end of the book, thus leaving the most difficult question to the last. He goes into it at great length, analyzing all the Aristotelian arguments for the eternity of the world and finding them faulty. He comes to the conclusion that the world was created in time and by the will of God. There remains, however, the question whether it was created from something or from nothing. The difficulties in the way of assuming creation *ex nihilo* as other Jewish philosophers had done, being many and insurmountable, Gersonides adopted the Platonic theory, i. e. creation out of chaos. He says that creation was out of chaos or formless matter, and that the creation in time was due to the imperfection of that matter which was not as yet ready to be created or formed. He stands thus almost alone in the entire history of Jewish philosophy in assuming such a radical solution to the vexing problem of creation, but he was of a daring nature.

In concluding the book, the author devotes several chapters to the reconciliation of his philosophical views with the teachings of the Bible. In order to effect this reconciliation, he uses the allegorical and symbolic method of interpretation of which mention has already been made above (Sect 18). He also states there his view of miracles which is inherently connected with that of creation, and which likewise was discussed above in connection with his commentary on the Pentateuch.

Gersonides can be said to be the last Aristotelian in Jewish philosophy. With him, the dominance of the Stagirite in Jewish thought ends. The nexet stage in Jewish philosophy is no mere blind subjection to the theories of this great master, but one of criticism of his views and opinions.

79. *HASDAI CRESCAS*

Hasdai ben Abraham Crescas (1340-1410) was the first philosopher who dared to criticize the very fundamentals of Aristotelianism, the system which dominated the schools of thought of both East and West for a period of eight hundred years. He hailed from Barcelona, Spain, and was a descendant of one of the noblest Jewish families in Catalonia. He was a great Talmudic scholar, an ardent student of philosophy, and in addition, also wealthy. All these qualities gave him prestige among his brethren both in Spain and other countries. Though he never occupied any official rabbinical position, he rendered decisions in legal matters and his word was law to many Jewish communities. Even the gentile world esteemed him greatly, and he was often consulted on matters of state by the king of Aragon, James the First.

As a result of a conspiracy, Crescas was accused before the king and was thrown into prison together with some of the notables of Catalonia, among whom was also his aged teacher, Rabbi Nissim Gerundi (Sect. 44). He was ultimately released on bail. The persecution of the year 1391, which brought ruin and desolation to most of the Spanish Jewish communities, did not spare Hasdai. In the massacre of Barcelona, his only son was killed. He then removed to Saragossa and spent the rest of his life in philosophical study.

The work on which the fame of Crescas as a philosopher rests is called the *Or Adonai* (The Light of the Lord). It was originally intended to be a part of a larger work, for Crescas wanted to imitate Maimonides and write a comprehensive work embracing the entire content of the Jewish religion, both the practical and the theoretical phases. The first part which was supposed to be called *Ner Mitzvah* (The Light of the Precept), as he tells us in the introduction, was intended to be a compendium of all the laws in the manner of the Code of Maimonides but with citation of sources and explanations. In the second part, he intended to deal with the theoretical side of religion, to enunciate dogmas, to establish the principles of religion in accordance with philosophic principles, and to clear these principles from all doubt which had arisen since the days of Maimonides. Crescas, however, later decided to change the order of the parts, for he came to see that a clear comprehension of the theoretical side of religion should rather precede the discussion of its practical phase than follow it. He therefore composed the *Or Adonai* first with the intention of following it up with the Compendium. It seems, however, that due to the turbulence of the times, the project was not completed and the *Or Adonai* is the only part of the work left.

As may be seen from the purpose of the work, it is intended to give a complete statement of the principles of the Jewish religion and is accordingly all-embracing, dealing with all questions of Jewish philosophy and theology. In fact, it was supposed to supplant the *Guide* of Maimonides and correct its assertions and conclusions on important questions of faith and dogma. However, it is not the statement and the formulation of the principles of Judaism contained in this work which make for its great importance, but it is primarily the attempt to correct the opinions of Maimonides which imparts to the book its value. Crescas was not only a philosopher but a critical philosopher. He saw the weakness of some of the fundamental points of the Maimonidian system, and undertook to uncover it. He was, however, not satisfied with limiting himself to the views of Maimonides, but went to the very source of this famous system, namely the works of Aristotle. He thus became not only the critic of Maimonides but of Aristotle himself.

Crescas undertook this work of criticism in defense of religion, or as he says, in order to clarify the conception of the dogmas of Judaism. But what had happened to other critics of philosophy before him also happened to him, namely that his criticism of the philos-

A page from Hasdai Crescas' Or Adonai
(Spanish Ms. Adler collection, Jewish Theological Seminary, N. Y.)

ophy of others ulimately led to the formulation of new philosophic concepts of his own which surpassed in depth and originality the philosophic opinions of the preceding thinkers. The contribution of Crescas to Jewish as well as to general philosophy is a double one, a keen criticism of the fundamentals of Aristotelianism, which ultimately brought about the freeing of the European mind from the shackles of an antiquated view of the cosmos, and the restatement of some philosophic concepts which likewise exerted great influence upon the thinkers that followed him.

As the *Or Adonai,* in spite of its philosophic value, is primarily a work of dogmatics, it is, therefore, arranged in accordance with the scheme of dogmas the author intended to enunciate. The work is divided into four books (Ma'amarim) which are subdivided into parts (Kelalim) and these again into chapters. The first book deals with what the author calls the great underlying principle of all religion (ha-Shoresh ha-Gadol), namely the existence of God and the proofs for such existence. Crescas does not call the belief in the existence of God a dogma, for it is the very basis of all religion, as without it we can speak neither of religion nor of dogmas . It is in this book which occupies about a third of the entire work that Crescas launches his criticism against the principles of the Aristotelian conception of the universe. The second book is devoted to the elucidation of the dogmas of faith which are, according to him, six; namely, (1) God's knowledge of the events and happenings in the world; (2) His Providence; (3) His potence; (4) prophecy; (5) freedom of the will; (6) the existence of a purpose in the universe. Here he analyzes the theories of his predecessors on these subjects, especially those of Maimonides and Gersonides and develops his own views.

The third book contains a description of the true beliefs or secondary dogmas, of which the creation of the world is one. It is especially his view of creation which attaches importance to this book. The last book is a collection of thirteen brief discourses on various subjects. The main subjects discussed are, whether the world is destructible or not; whether there exists one or many worlds; whether the heavenly bodies are living and rational beings or not; and whether they have control of the affairs of men or not? Among other questions discussed are the efficacy of amulets and charms, the existence of demons, the transmigration of souls (Gilgul Nefashoth), and the conception of Paradise and Hell.

In giving a brief survey of the philosophy and theology of Crescas, we will have, of course, to omit his critical and analytical arguments, which are too complicated and abstruse to reproduce and limit ourselves to a statement of his views. He begins, like the preceding Jewish philosophers, with the proof of the existence of God. But before he does that, he devotes the greater part of the first book to a criticism of the proofs of the existence of God offered by Maimonides. As it is known, Maimonides proves the existence of God not through the creation of the world like Saadia and Bahya, but bases it directly upon certain propositions of physics, twenty-five in number, culled from the various Aristotelian works. The basis of all these propositions is the impossibility of the existence of an infinite in any form, neither as body or force, nor as infinite space, nor as an infinite number of causes. Crescas attacks many of these propositions and by a chain of keen analytical arguments, shakes the foundations of the Aristotelian cosmology and establishes the probability of the existence of infinite magnitudes and of infinite space. He thus paved the way for the modern conception of the universe, and hence the importance of his criticism.

After he disposes of the validity of the proofs of Maimonides for the existence of God, he offers his own proof which is as follows: Whether there is a finite or an infinite series of causes and effects, but as long as the series is given and all things in the universe are caused, we do not find in nature a thing that is absolutely necessary of existence. This is impossible, for if all beings were possible of existence, i. e. they may exist and they may not exist, there must be some power that calls forth existence, so as to overbalance the possibility of non-existence. It follows, therefore, that there is a being necessary of existence, and this being is God. The proof has an original ring to it, and its value was recognized by Spinoza who quotes Crescas by name and lauds his proof.

He then passes on to the attributes of God, and here too he takes issue with Maimonides' conception of the attributes. Like Gersonides, he objects to the former's theory that the attributes we apply to God are absolutely unlike those we apply to men, and that they are only negative and do not express the essence of God. Crescas contends that the attributes are essential and positive. It is true that the essence of God is inconceivable in its totality, and it is also true that as far as our conception is concerned, we can not give the attributes a positive content, for that would determine God, but in regard to

God Himself, they are surely positive, and He can be described by them. As to the number of attributes, Crescas does not differ with Maimonides. They are existent, living, potent, one and willing. In regard to unity, Crescas explains that he means by it only simplicity, for numerical unity can not be proven philosophically, but is only a matter of revelation. This remark, however, should not be taken seriously, for from Crescas' own definition of God, this kind of unity can likewise be deduced, but he merely uttered it for the sake of argument.

A fine contribution to the theory of attributes is made by Crescas in his adding one more essential attribute to God, and that is joy and happiness. According to Aristotle, the joy of the Godhead is not an attribute but a result of His being eternally contemplative to the highest degree. He was followed in this by Maimonides. Crescas criticizes this view, for says he, joy and pain with men are only a result of their overcoming obstacles or being thwarted by them. But since God has no obstacles in His knowledge, He can, therefore, not be said to have joy in contemplation, and therefore, says Crescas, this Divine happiness is a concomitant result of His love, which is essential to His being. God is voluntarily the cause of all things, and since we know that existence is good, it follows that insofar as He is voluntarily the cause of being, He is voluntarily good. The continuation of the existence of beings is the continual emanation of His goodness. It is evident, then, that insofar as God continues to emanate His goodness voluntarily, He loves this emanation, and it is this action permeated with love, which is described as joy or happiness. It is essential to God, for it is inherently connected with His being the cause of things. This then is the high conception of Crescas' *Amor Dei,* the Love of God.

Crescas' treatment of the problem of God's knowledge of events and happenings in this world is very interesting. He deals with it at length, and analyzes the theories of Maimonides and Gersonides, and ultimately rejects them and offers his own view. He is more lenient towards Maimonides' view and even defends it against the objections of Gersonides, but he severely criticises the latter's theory. Against the solution of Gersonides which states that God knows the particular only through the unified general order of things but not through their side as particulars, and that God knows the possible events as possible but not which side of the possibility will be realized, Crescas raises many objections of which we will quote a few.

If we accept this theory, says Crescas, we really attribute to God imperfections, for if God does not know the particulars as particulars, it follows since the number of particular things is infinite, that He possesses ignorance in regard to the infinite. The relation of God's knowledge to His ignorance is, therefore, as the finite to the infinite, for the number of things that He does know, according to Gersonides, is only finite. Again, if God does not know beforehand which side of a possible event will be realized, it follows that He does not know which side was realized even after its occurrence. Were He to know of the accomplished event, a change in His knowledge would be implied, since before the occurrence of the event, He knew it only as possible, and after it, as actual. Should we, however, agree, in order to obviate a change in His knowledge, to such a possibility of ignorance on His part, it would follow that God is ignorant of the greatest part of human history, which is, of course, absurd. It is evident, therefore, that the theory of Gersonides must be abandoned. Crescas' own view is that we must draw a distinction between the knowledge of God and ours, His being casual and ours derivative. By His knowledge and will, things acquire existence, while our knowledge is derived from existing things by means of the senses and imagination. This essential difference removes all difficulties raised by Gersonides against God's knowing the particulars. God does not attain perfection by His knowledge of them nor does He need sense and imagination in order to know them, for it is His knowledge that causes the existence of things, and the particulars also acquire their existence through His knowledge.

As to the main problem of the compatibility of the existence of the possible with God's prescience, Crescas says that God does know beforehand which way the possible will be realized, yet that does not change the nature of the possible, for things may be necessary in one way and possible in another. This really implies abandoning to a certain extent the freedom of the will and he really does so. But in order to understand his full conception of the subject, we must first discuss his theory of Providence.

As for Providence, Crescas posits that it extends also to individuals, yet it is not entirely uniform. It is in some respects generic and universal, and in some ways individual. The general Providence is seen in every existing being, in its composition, natural tendencies, organic function, mental powers, and so forth. These forces may vary according to the genus and species but are alike in every individual of that species. We see, therefore, that natural laws are taken in as a part of Providence. The human species is an example of the extension of both general and special Providence since it is endowed with reason. It is general for every individual participates in it alike, and it is special for it is only for that species alone. The particular Providence consists in rewarding and punishing man for following or not following an ethical and religious life. This kind of Providence is in complete relation to the degree of perfection of the individual and is arranged and determined by God's eternal will. Crescas then emphasizes in contradiction to the view of the Aristotelians who related Providence to contemplation, that the perfection he speaks of is the ethical-religious perfection of man.

The problem of injustice is inherently connected with the question of Providence and Crescas grapples with it accordingly. After analyzing the views of the predecessors, he says that the real good is not the material good, nor is the real bad the material evil, but both are of a spiritual nature. The practice of virtue brings about the acquisition by the soul of a tendency and inclination to virtue and the more a man practices virtue under adverse circumstances, the greater the degree of his perfection. It follows then that when the righteous suffer, it is really for their own good, for by this, their perfection increases and their inclination to do good is deepened which is real good. His solution of the other horn of the dilemma, namely why the wicked prosper is not as happy as the first one. He resorts to the usual methods of his predecessors, such as those proposed by Gersonides, namely that the good accruing to the wicked comes from the determination of the order of things by the heavenly bodies, or that it serves as a means for his ultimate punishment, and finally, that the good befalling the wicked leads to spiritual evil of the soul.

Crescas then returns to the question of free will. It is an important dogma and must be clearly established. After a long review of the arguments for and against the existence of the possible, he concludes that the possible exists in some aspects and in some it does not. It exists only in regard to itself but not in regard to its causes, that is man thinks he is free to choose and acts accordingly, but in the long chain of events, his action can be considered necessary. He admits that the very endeavors and exertions of energy on the part of man are some of the mediate causes in the chain of causality and thus help to determine the actions of man. Religion, according to him, does not object to such a conception, for the precepts and commandments were given to us in order to spur us on to the exertion of our will in the proper direction, which in itself becomes a cause for the proper kind of activity. Reward and punishment follow from observance or non-observance of the precepts as natural effects follow from their causes. His example is the fact that a man is scorched by fire even when the touching is accomplished without any wilfull inclination. Similarly, though man's actions may be necessitated in the long run, yet he should be punished or rewarded for their performance. We see thus that Crescas admits a good deal of determinism in human actions and believes that man's free will is primarily based first on the fact that he really does not feel the force of the causal chain and thinks that he is free to act, and second, that his own inclination is a link in the chain of causes. This view was followed by many philosophers. That such a view of limited freedom does not affect the prescience of God is clear, for His knowledge is above time, and He knows beforehand in whichever way man may act, though there is still some room for the possible insofar as human endeavors and attempts are factors in the decision of the act.

We pass then to the question of the purpose as manifested both in human life and in the universe. As for the first, there are three possible ends, which may be considered as the goal of human life (a) perfection of morals (b) contemplation and (c) happiness which may be either material or spiritual. Crescas scrutinizes them all and finds some of them wanting. Material happiness can not be an end for it is temporal, and spiritual happiness may then be regarded as the hypothetical goal. But what does this happiness consist of? It can not be identified with the perfection of morals, for these are merely a means to an end, that is to attain perfection of the soul. Again, its contents can not be contemplation as the followers of the peripatetics asserted, for their view is full of contradictions. Here the author launches a number of criticisms against this theory, the gist of which is the following: If, as the rationalists say, the increase of intellectual concepts is a means to the happiness of the soul, why do we need precepts and commandments of God? Mathematics and conceptions of physics are also of an intellectual character, and those who conceive them should likewise attain immortality. Secondly, if according to their theory, the acquired intellect which is the only thing immortal is a separate substance from the soul, it does not agree with reason nor with Divine justice that reward and punishment should be meted out to a being (i. e. acquired intellect) which had little to do with the soul of the man who followed or transgressed the precepts. This theory is then untenable. The question still remains what then is the content of happiness?

Crescas then advances his own view, namely that love of God is the final end which leads to spiritual happiness. To understand this concept clearly, we must have a glimpse of Crescas' theory of the soul and consider two more points in connection with it. The soul, he asserts, is the form of the body, a spiritual being and is potential in regard to the conception of ideas. It is the form of the body, for we see that on its departure, the body disintegrates just as things without form do. Again, it is spiritual, for it possesses powers which are not dependent on the senses. It is capable of reasoning, for it is the subject or bearer of the reasoning power which is related to the body by means of the soul. This conception is a great deviation from the view of the peripatetic philosophers, for according to this view the immortality of the soul embraces not only the acquired intellect but the soul as a whole, and this idea will play its part in the concept of purpose.

Turning to the other points, Crescas posits three propositions, first, that God loves the good, for existence is good and He continues to cause it constanly. Second, since causality is all through His will, it follows that the love of the good is an essential conception of His perfection. Third, that love and desire for a thing are not proportionate to the intellectual vigor employed in conceiving that thing. The result of these propositions is as follows: God loves the highest good for His perfection is the highest, and similarly, it is true that the higher the good loved the higher the degree of perfection one attains in loving it. It is evident that since God is the highest good, the love of Him is necessary for the perfection of the soul. And since we also know that the intensity of desire and love is independent of the reasoning power, and further that the soul is the only thing immortal, we reach then the ultimate conclusion that the perfection of the soul consists in the love of God and varies according to its intensity, and hence it is the end of human life. This concept, however, should be understood to mean primarily the love of the good, for God is good and thus it serves as a basic ethical principle. We still have to define the other aspect of purpose, namely the Divine purpose in the world. This can be placed in syllogistic form. The will of God is to do good. Existence or reality is goodness. Hence, the universe carries its own purpose within it.

The final link in the chain of Crescas' philosophy is his theory of creation. In it, the will of God plays an important part. As usual, he scrutinizes at length all arguments for the eternity of the world, and justly criticizes Gersonides for positing the eternal existence of primal or formless matter. He proposes his view which is in a way a compromise. Creation, says Crescas, must be conceived as having been accomplished through will, not through emanation. He does not say how matter was brought about, but attempts to overcome the difficulty of how the manifold of existence could come out of God who is simple, by saying that existence as a whole is good, and from this angle of its basic quality of goodness it is simple. And since God is the principle of goodness, he could produce the world, for God is good and reality is good, and thus like produced like. This is, of course, a partial solution, for the question still remains, how was matter produced? There is yet a greater difficulty which is the following. If creation was through will and will is eternal, how could we assume the novelty of the world, i. e. creation at a certain time? On the contrary, it must have existed from eternity for there was no obstacle to His will. To this pertinent question, he gives only an evasive answer. He admits at first the possibility of a series of worlds continually having been created and destroyed. But he does not insist on this assertion and takes refuge in tradition. In brief, he stops short of his own conclusions. With the theory of creation, the philosophic aspect of Crescas' view ends.

Turning to Crescas' theology, or more exactly to his dogmatics, we see that here as well as in his philosophy, he introduced a note of originality. He divides the dogmas, on the whole, into two classes, primary and secondary. The first he calls fundamental doctrines of Judaism without which the entire Torah can not exist (Pinoth Torioth), and the second, true beliefs (Emunoth Amitioth), the denial of which makes one a heretic (Min). He has still a third class which he calls rational opinions. To the first class belong the six dogmas enumerated above. The second class, he subdivides into two divisions, (a) beliefs independent of special precepts, and (b) dependent upon special precepts. To the first belong (1) *Creatio De Novo*, (2) immortality of the soul, (3) reward and punishment, (4) resurrection, (5) immutability of the Torah, (6) the special prophecy of Moses, (7) the belief in the answer of the oracle consulted by the high priest (Urim we-Tumim), and (8) the coming of the Messiah. To the second belong (1) efficacy of prayer and priestly benedictions,

(2) the value of penitence, (3) the importance of the Day of Atonement and the holidays.

The whole system of his dogmatics is undoubtedly a peculiar one and differs greatly from that of Maimonides as well as from that of other Jewish philosophers. First, he does not count, as noted, the belief in the existence of God as a dogma. He calls it the great basic principle but not a dogma. It is difficult to understand the reason for this omission. Second, he excludes resurrection, the coming of the Messiah, the eternity of the Torah, the special character of the prophecy of Moses from the class of dogmas placing them in the class of true beliefs in contrast to Maimonides who does consider them as such. Third, he includes as secondary dogmas such beliefs as the veracity of the oracle and the efficacy of prayer, which none of the Jewish dogmatists had ever done before nor has he been followed in this matter. Fourth, he includes purpose or love of God as a dogma.

It would take us too far afield to discuss the question comprehensively. It will suffice to say that the reason for all these peculiarities is to be found in two things. The first is Crescas' emphasis on the importance of emotion and action in religion rather than speculation as held by the peripatetic philosophers. The second is, as Dr. David Neumark suggests,[4] our author's polemic tendency against Christianity. Crescas wanted to show that many of the principles which Christianity boasts of as being its own innovations, are really found in Judaism. Hence, his placing as a dogma of first importance the love of God, and as secondary dogmas, penitence and the belief in the mediacy of the priests, beliefs which Christianity emphasizes and considers as her own contributions to religion.

Of the views which Crescas holds regarding the true beliefs some deserve notice. He differs in his conception of prophecy both from Maimonides and Gersonides. It is, he says, primarily caused by an influence from God Himself (not by the Active Intellect as Gersonides avers) upon the human reason. Again, the would be prophet need not be, as Maimonides states, a highly intellectual person but he must be distinguished by his deep love of God and great zeal for preaching the truth to others. His love of God must be very intense and he must strive with all his heart to unite with Him. That this striving is attained by means of observation of the precepts goes without saying.

[4] See his book *Ikkarim* (Dogmas), Vol. II, pp. 173-76.

In regard to immortality, Crescas believes that the entire soul remains immortal and retains its full individuality. The reward and punishment after death, he pictures like Maimonides and Hillel ben Samuel, as spiritual, namely that the soul of the righteous enjoys complete conception of the Godhead, and the soul of the wicked feels pain at the lack of this conception. *Gan-Eden* and *Gehinom* (Paradise and Hell) are only symbols for this kind of reward and punishment. The souls of some of the wicked are also temporarily divested of their qualities, so that this punishment is spoken of in the Talmud as a kind of destruction of the soul.

Interesting is also his view of resurrection, for while he sides with Meir Abulafia against Maimonides in saying that people will live forever after resurrection, he can not overcome the difficulties in the way of an actual resurrection of the same body after it is disintegrated into its elements. He, therefore, proposes a compromise and explains that resurrection will be accomplished by an act of creation of new bodies for the still existing souls. When the souls will be placed in the bodies, they will resume their reminescences and thus revive the old individuality. This view is rather a unique one, for most philosophers had avoided describing the resurrection and the traditional theologians took it plainly as a miracle. In conclusion, we can say that though Crescas often arrives at results which are at variance with his own premises and his inconsistencies are numerous, yet his teachings are valuable to us, as they are the expression of a great mind grappling with the basic problems of reality, life and religion.

80. SIMON BEN ZEMAH DURAN

Simon ben Zemah Duran, rabbi at Algiers, the great Talmudic scholar and Responsa writer whose works in the field of Rabbinics were discussed above (Sect. 67), also made some notable contributions to Jewish philosophy and theology, especially to the latter in his several works on the subject. He wrote a philosophic commentary on the book of Job under the name of *Oheb Mishpat* (Lover of Justice), a book wherein he defends Maimonides against attacks of Crescas entitled *Or ha-Hayyim* (The Light of Life), and finally, his chief philosophical work *Magen Aboth* (The Shield of the Fathers).

It is this book in which he primarily expounded his philosophical and theological ideas. It was intended as an introduction to the treatise of *Aboth,* and is divided into four parts, three dealing with the fundamental dogmas of Judaism and with the philosophic problems they involve in their broadest interpretation, while the fourth is devoted to the recounting of the succession of the bearers of tradition. This part is usually printed as a separate treatise, and its historical value will be discussed in its proper place. (Sect. 128). It is the *Magen Aboth* proper that we are concerned with at present.

The main contribution of Duran to Jewish philosophy and theology consists in his introducing a new order in the fixation of Jewish dogmas. Being an ardent follower of Maimonides, he accepts all his views, and deviates very little from his theories except occasionally when he either follows Gersonides, or introduces his own modifications. He, therefore accepts also the number of dogmas of the former, namely thirteen, but believes that they can be really reduced to three principal ones including by their very definition the others which are merely the unfolding of the main concepts. He believes that he found this scheme in the first *Mishnah* of the eleventh chapter of the treatise Sanhedrin. This *Mishnah* reads, "All Israel shall have a portion in the world to come, as it is said (Isaiah Ch. LX, 21), 'And thy people are all righteous, they shall forever inherit the land.' But these shall not have a portion in the world to come, one who says resurrection is not mentioned in the Torah, or who asserts that the Torah was not given from heaven, or the *apikoros,* i. e. he who denies the existence of God."

Here then, says Duran, we have the three dogmas of Judaism, taking them in reverse order which is really the order of their importance: The existence of God, Divine origin of the Torah and reward and punishment, of which resurrection, mentioned in the *Mishnah,* is the most complete expression. Again, taking the three dogmas in their fullest unfolding, we see that they necessarily contain all the thirteen articles of Maimonides. Thus, if we prove philosophically the existence of God, we must necessarily conclude that He is one, incorporeal and eternal. Again, the Divine origin of the Torah implies first a belief in prophecy, for without prophecy as a medium between God and man, how could such origin be imagined; second, it implies a belief in the *sui-generis* character of the prophecy of Moses, as this is stated in the Torah proper. Finally, this dogma involves *eo ipso* a belief in the eternity and immutability of the Torah, for how could a Divine command be changed? Further, we can not maintain the dogma of reward and punishment without presupposing God's knowledge of things in this world and His Providence. But if we turn to the Jewish people and observe their great suffering, we must conclude that their reward will not be complete unless the promised coming of the Messiah and the resurrection at the end of days be realized. We have then exactly the thirteen articles of Maimonides.

To the further elaboration and to the substantiation of these dogmas and their enfolded concepts by philosophic speculation, Duran devotes the greater part of the *Magen Aboth*. The scheme of the dogmas is the scheme of the division of the book. The first part which he calls the Portion of God (Helek Adonai) is devoted to the proofs of the existence of God and the dependent concepts. It is subdivided into five chapters dealing with the existence of God, His unity and incorporeality, His eternity and attributes. The second part called The Portion of Our Oppressors (Helek Shosenu) discusses the Divine origin of the Torah in four chapters, dealing with prophecy, peculiarity of the prophecy of Moses, Divine origin of the Torah and its immutability. The fourth chapter which is primarily a polemic treatise against Christianity and Mohammedanism is usually omitted from the editions of the book and printed separately under the title *Kesheth u-Magen* (Bow and Shield). The third part called the Portion of Jacob (Helek Yacob) takes up in four chapters God's knowledge of things in the world, Providence and reward and punishment together with the inherent problems of freedom of the will and injustice, the coming of the Messiah and resurrection.

Had Duran applied himself to his subjects, the book would have been of much smaller proportions, but he introduces a multitude of extraneous subjects, such as a discussion of the *Merkabah* of Ezekiel, the vision of Isaiah, Kabbalistic interpretations of certain subjects and similar things. Especially voluminous is the third part. It contains an extensive description of the physiology of man and animals with special attention to the process of reproduction, a detailed discussion of human psychology, and other subjects of the same nature.

In his philosophy, Duran shows hardly any originality. It is primarily based on the theories of Maimonides with a fair admixture of those of Gersonides, where his views do not run contrary to the orthodox tendency of the author.

In general, Duran agrees with Maimonides in all his principal theories, but being more conservative, he deviates from the latter's teachings in a number of points. The following are to be noted:

He rejects Maimonides' assertion that at the revelation at Sinai, the Jews heard only a voice pronouncing the first two commandments but not the distinct words which were only heard by Moses, and avers that all the Jews heard the words of the Commandments. He also differs with both Maimonides and Gersonides in regard to Providence. The two asserted that the special Providence extended to man depends entirely on the intellectual capacity of man. Duran rejects this view and says that it applies to all men irrespective of their degree of intellectuality. This view is based on his conception of the soul. The soul is a form separate from matter, like the form of the angels. It was created by God at the time of the creation of the world and existed before the birth of man. It is, therefore, in the same relation to God as the separate intelligences, the movers of the spheres. His view of prophecy is a mixture of those of Maimonides and Gersonides. Like the former, he says that it is an emanation from God to the intellect and the imagination of the chosen man, but adds, like the latter, that it comes through the medium of the universal Active Intellect. He agrees with both that the prophet must be a man of high intellectual attainments and rich imagination.

The special character of the prophecy of Moses is explained by him to consist in the fact that it was not accomplished by the mediacy of the universal Active Intellect, but that Moses himself attained the degree of the Active Intellect.

In general, the tendency of Duran is to reconcile many opposing views, and philosopher though he was, he also followed the mystic teachings of the Kabbala. He identifies the mover of the first sphere with the angel Michael of the Bible and Metatron of the Talmud and mysticism, and the universal Active Intellect (Sekel ha-Poel) with Gabriel and Sandalphon of the Talmud.

Duran, though not an original thinker, had a wide knowledge of the philosophic and scientific literature of his day, especially of physics and medicine, as he was a physician by profession. His physiology and psychology contained in the third part of the *Magen Aboth* is of considerable value in philosophic and scientific literature. He describes the subjects he discusses with a skill which gives evidence of his mastery of the facts, and here and there, he offers an original explanation which clarifies the matters discussed. His *Magen Aboth* is, therefore, a useful epitome of the main philosophic and scientific subjects which held the interests of intellectual men of his time.

81. JOSEPH ALBO

Contemporary with Simon Duran there was another Jewish philosopher who devoted much attention to the problem of dogmas in Judaism. This was Joseph Albo (1380-1444), the disciple of Hasdai Crescas. He was born in the city of Monreal, Spain, and as it seems spent a great part of his life there. In addition to his being proficient in Rabbinics, philosophy and science he mastered also several languages, for he knew besides Hebrew also Spanish and Latin, and was a physician by profession. Though he held no official Rabbinical position, he was known as a famous teacher in his time, and his inclination to preaching and homiletics is reflected in his philosophic works.

As an outstanding scholar and spiritual leader, he was compelled to participate in the famous religious disputation held at Tortosa in the year 1413-1414 at the command of King Ferdinand of Aragon and Pope Benedict, the XIII. At this disputation, the Jewish representatives had to face the convert Geronimo de Santa Fe (Joshua ha-Lorqui) and refute his arguments drawn from the Talmud, both that the Messiah had already come and that Jesus is that Messiah. The disputation lasted for a long time and apparently Geronimo did not succeed in convincing those present of his contention. The Pope angered by the unfavorable results persecuted some of the Jewish disputants and as a result, Albo had to forsake his native city and settle at Soria where he composed, at the request of his friends, the *Ikkarim* (Dogmas).

Albo, though a disciple of probably the most original Jewish philosopher, Hasdai Crescas, did not inherit his master's originality nor his depth of thought. His contribution to Jewish philosophy is of no special value, for in his discussion of all the problems which have a philosophic aspect, he follows in the main either Maimonides or Crescas and adds only a point here and there for the sake of elucidation. His importance lies primarily in the field of dogmatics. And though it is claimed that even in this field he borrowed his main thesis from Duran, namely that of reducing the dogmas of Judaism to three principal ones, no impartial judge can deny him originality in the manner of classification, analysis and elucidation of the conception of Jewish dogmas. After all, even Duran can not claim complete originality for his reduction of the dogmas to three such statements for as we have seen above, it is already found in the Mishnah. It is not always the mere formula which is of importance but the explanation and the philosophic interpretation of the formula that is of value. And in this direction, Albo displayed great skill and keen analysis.

The work of Albo was actuated by the exigencies of the time. The first half of the fourteenth century was a trying time for Spanish Jewry. On the one hand, great pressure was brought upon them by Church and government to abandon their religion and embrace Christianity; religious disputations were frequently arranged and eloquent Christian preachers visited the synagogues and delivered their fiery sermons in denunciation of Judaism. On the other hand, Jewish renegades loosened upon their former brethren a mass of propaganda literature, intended to weaken their belief in the faith of their fathers. As a result, confusion arose in the minds of many Jews and willingly or unwillingly, they began to doubt some of the principles of their religion. A clear pronouncement of the principles of Judaism and its fundamental dogmas was then necessary. All previous attempts in this direction were, either on account of the brevity of the treatment of the subject or on account of the lack of clearness of method, insufficient for the purpose. To satisfy this need, Albo wrote his *Ikkarim*. His purpose was really a double one, first, to fix and standardize the dogmas and principles of the Jewish religion, and second to prove that almost all the principles of religion are not only compatible with philosophic conceptions but are also clarified by these conceptions. In both these things, he succeeded to a great extent.

The *Ikkarim* is divided into four books or sections, each dealing with a specific subject. The first containing six chapters is devoted to a detailed discussion of the character of Divine religion in general, differentiating it from conventional and natural religions, and fixing the principal dogmas of that religion together with the principles that are derived from them. He comes to the conclusion that the Divine religion which, in his case, is Judaism has three fundamental dogmas, (1) the existence of God, (2) the Divine origin of the Torah or revelation, (3) reward and punishment, and that each of these dogmas has a number of roots or subsidiary beliefs which are inherent in and contained within its conception. The other three books provide lengthy expositions of these three dogmas in which philosophic substantiation for their validity is offered, the subsidiary principles evolved and an interpretation of many Biblical verses and Talmudic passages in a philosophic manner are given. In these expositions, the author discusses at length all the philosophical and theological problems with which his predecessors have busied themselves, and states or rather restates the solutions in a clear and popular, though not concise manner. There are good reasons to believe that the first book was originally written as a separate treatise and much earlier than the other three books. Albo himself states at the end of the first book that the fixation of the number of dogmas and the subsidiary principles was his original purpose, but at the request of his friends, he added the three other books for the purpose of the explanation of the dogmas and their derivatives philosophically.

Albo begins his discussion of dogmatics by a criticism of the lists of dogmas laid down by Maimonides and Crescas. The first, he says, did not really define properly the word principle, or dogma (Ikkar), for this word denotes a fundamental principle upon which a thing depends for its very existence, and without which such existence can not be represented. Now in Maimonides' list of dogmas, there are a number which are not of this nature. As an instance, he cites the belief in the coming of the Messiah which Maimonides counts as a dogma, yet we find a Rabbinic authority denying this principle,[5] and no one ever thought of calling him an apostate. Again, Crescas defined the word *Ikkar* more carefully, but even his list is not perfect, for his six primary dogmas are not peculiar to Judaism alone, and his secondary ones are not all principles of a wide connotation, but in some instances contain only single precepts. It is necessary, therefore, he concludes to devise a new scheme of dogmas.

He, therefore, posits the three principles mentioned above, existence of God, revelation, reward and punishment as fundamental to a Divine religion. These principles, however, have to be defined and unfolded. When this is done, another series of principles called roots (Sheroshim) may be evolved or particular dogmas subsumed under the general. These particular dogmas define and determine the character of an individual religion in distinction from other Divine religions if such there be. But in order to determine accurately what are really fundamental dogmas and what particular dogmas each of them subsumes, we must define the nature of Divine religion.

Looking upon life in general, we see that the beasts of prey as a rule live separately. Other animals may be, at times, gregarious, but this gregariousness is not absolutely necessary to their life. The human species, on the other hand, is social by nature and group life is a necessary condition for its existence. Group life must of necessity

[5] Sanhedrin, 99a.

have a set of laws and customs which should regulate the conduct of the group and preserve its integrity. This includes the primitive law against murder, theft and robbery which we may call natural law or religion. In order, however, that the group may develop and progress, another set of laws is necessary which we call conventional law, usually instituted by a king or judge, and to which all people agree. This kind of law provides for security of business transactions and fixes the principles of the lower morality. But God, in His desire to endow man with real happiness, that is the happiness of the soul and wishing to further his progress in that direction causes His spirit or His emanation to rest upon one man, and this man institutes the higher law or religion. This we call Divine law or religion.

On comparing the conventional and Divine religions, we see the immense superiority of the latter over the former. The former, as said, can not improve the human soul, nor can it even fix the higher morality, for since the founder of that law is a man, he can not fix an eternal standard for morality, and its concepts are subject to change. Again, investigating the principles of both laws, we find that those of the conventional law are freedom of the will and purpose, for no king can make a law without assuming the possibility of man to choose his actions and without aiming at a certain purpose. The principles of the Divine law are, existence of God, revelation and reward and punishment, for without these, we cannot conceive it as Divine. If there is no God, there is no Divine Law, likewise if there is no revelation, we can hardly call it Divine, and finally, if there is no reward and punishment, there is no purpose to that law, for if it can not improve the soul that it may attain immortality, it has no superiority over the conventional law. Albo, thus substantiated by the definition of the Divine law, the three fundamental dogmas, and by comparing it with the conventional law eliminated Crescas' two dogmas, freedom and purpose, relegating them to the substratum of religion in general, since they are also the principles of the conventional law.

We are now ready to discuss the derivative dogmas. One who does not believe any of these three primary dogmas has no share in Divine religion, but he must also agree to the derivative principles, for otherwise he is a heretic. These principles are eight in number. Under existence of God are included (1) His unity, (2) incorporeality, (3) His not being in time, and (4) freedom from defects. From revelation there are derived three, (1) God's knowledge of events,

(2) prophecy, (3) authenticity of God's messenger. Under reward and punishment is included Providence. Albo calls one of the derivative dogmas in the first group, independence of time and not "first in existence" *(Kadmon)* as Maimonides had done, in order to include also eternity of existence. Again, freedom from defects includes all the usual attributes either bestowed upon Him or negated of Him, for should we attribute to Him an improper attribute or vice versa deny Him a proper one, He is defective. The derivative dogma, knowledge of events, is included by him under revelation and not under reward and punishment as Duran had done, for the reason that were God not to know the happenings in this world, how could He cause prophecy or revelation?

We must also note that Albo, in distinction from Duran and Crescas, does not consider the peculiarity of the prophecy of Moses, nor resurrection, nor creation, either first or secondary dogmas. He took the meaning of the word dogma strictly as such, without which religion would fall, and therefore counted only those to be first or even secondary dogmas which are absolutely inherent in the fundamental principles. Consequently even if one does not believe in the superiority of the prophecy of Moses or in resurrection or in *creatio ex nihilo,* he is still not a heretic. He did not, however, mean to disparage the value of these beliefs, for he says that every Jew is obliged to believe in six more doctrines of a third class which he calls *Branches* (Anafim). These are (1) *creatio ex nihilo,* (2) *sui generis* nature of the prophecy of Moses, (3) immutability of the Torah, (4) the capability of even one precept to perfect the human soul, (5) resurrection, and (6) the coming of the Messiah. The one who does not believe in these branches is a sinner but not a heretic, nor is he excluded from a portion in the world to come.

We have thus surveyed briefly Albo's logical classification of the dogmas and his analysis of their meaning. We must, however, note his general substantiation of the principles which are the fundamentals. One of the principles, that is the existence of God, is substantiated by philosophy, the others by experience and *consensus omnium.* Our ancestors, Adam, Abraham, Noah and others had experienced revelation, prophecy and reward and punishment in their own lives. This experience has been handed down by tradition which can not be doubted. Again, the very act of the revelation at Sinai was a mass experience, accepted by everybody as a fact, hence, its veracity. It is for this reason that Albo omits to include the belief in the *sui generis* character of Moses among the dogmas, for the authenticity of his message was verified by the mass experience of entire Israel. It is this experience which is of the utmost importance in revelation and not the miracles Moses performed.

In this, as well as in many other statements, is revealed the rationalistic tendency of Albo. Thus he tells us that while every Jew must accept the three fundamental principles even if he does not entirely conceive them rationally, the secondary dogmas must be based upon reason as much as possible. Moreover it is a duty to investigate the principles of a religion for only then one will attain to real belief. Furthermore, if one philosophizes and derides one of the dogmas because he does not consider it as such and believes he can prove his assertion, he is not a heretic. A heretic is one who admits that the Torah laid down a real dogma, and yet denies it. There is, says Albo, perfect freedom for every Jew to investigate the dogmas of his faith and interpret the Bible in accordance with his opinion. The reassertion of the freedom of research by Albo at a time when philosophic study in Jewry was already in its decline was of special importance to the students of the day.

In conclusion, it may be added that the *Ikkarim* is written, on the whole, in a clear and popular style, and the discussions are interspersed with many fine homiletic remarks which attracted the readers. It is for the many fine qualities which the book possesses that it became one of the most popular philosophic works ever written by a Jewish scholar.

82. *DON ISAAC ABRABANEL*

Don Isaac Abrabanel, the famous statesman and Bible exegete (Sect. 20) also wrote a number of philosophic works and although he contributed little that was new to philosophic thought, yet his works deserve notice in a survey of Jewish philosophic literature. Abrabanel was not only a prolific writer but one with a tendency to deal with questions at exceeding length and great detail. Conciseness and brevity were not among his many virtues. He, therefore, devoted entire books to the discussion of single problems, and as a result, his works in the field of Jewish philosophy and theology are considerable.

The most important of them are, (1) *Atereth Zekenim* (The Crown of the Elders), a discussion of the problem of Divine Providence, (2) *Miphaloth Elohim* (The Works of God) where the question of *creatio ex nihilo,* miracles and prophecy are discussed; (3) *Rosh Amanah* (The Foundation of Belief), a work on dogmatics; (4) two commentaries on the *Guide* of Maimonides, one called *Shomayyim Hadashim* (The New Heavens) covering Chapter XIX, Pt. II of the Guide, and the other covering Pt. I, Chs. I-LV, Pt. II, Chs. XXXI-XXXVIII,, XLII-XLV, and Pt. III Ch. I, and (5) Answers to Philosophic Questions addressed to him by Rabbi Saul ha-Cohen. He also wrote three works on the coming of the Messiah where all questions connected with this great event are discussed at great length. They bear a general title *Migdol Yeshuoth* (The Tower of Salvation), and also individual titles, namely (a) *Mayenē ha-Yeshuah* (The Fountains of Salvation, Isaiah XII, 3), (b) *Yeshuoth Meshiho* (The Salvation of his Anointed Ones, Ps. XVIII, 8) and (c) *Mashmia Yeshuah* (The Announcer of Salvation, Isaiah LII, 1). The first is an interpretation of the eschatological chapters of the Book of Daniel; the second an explanation of the Messianic passages of the Talmud and Midrashim with special emphasis upon the refutation of the Christian interpretation of these passages advanced by the convert Joshua ha-Lorqui; the third elucidates the Biblical passages of Messianic import.

Besides these works, Abrabanel wrote several more books dealing with philosophic questions, but they were lost and are only known through his own reference to them in his other works. In addition, many of his philosophic views and opinions are scattered in his commentaries on the Bible and in his commentary on the tractate *Aboth* bearing the name *Nahlath Aboth* (The Inheritance of the Fathers).

The range of Abrabanel's knowledge of the philosophic literature was exceedingly wide. Not only was he versed in the entire Jewish philosophic literature, but he was also well read in the works of the Arabic and scholastic philosophers. As a statesman in countries which had a large Arabic speaking population, he must undoubtedly have known the language, and most likely read some of the philosophic works in that language. That he knew Latin and was acquainted with the works of the leading Scholastics, we know from the numerous references to them in his books. He is even said to have translated a work by Thomas Aquinas into Hebrew. As a result of this versatile and all-embracing knowledge, his own books contain complete statements of all views and opinions concerning the questions discussed, and are of great importance in tracing the history of the development of the philosophic problems and their solutions.

His method in the philosophic works is similar to that which he uses in his exegesis (Sect. 20). First he states a series of doubts and arguments against a certain theory or view which he wants to prove or maintain and then proceeds to meet them one by one. It is the same method used by Crescas in his *Or Adonai,* and is akin to the pilpulistic or dialectic method used by the keen-minded commentators on the Talmud, (the Tosafists Vol. I, Sect. 145). Abrabanel is very exhaustive in his method, omitting hardly a single statement ever made by a philosopher against a particular view or theory. Thus he helps us greatly to clarify our conception of the problem under discussion.

Abrabanel's attitude towards philosophy can be briefly described as that of one who is first a believer, then a philosopher. He, of course, admits that it is our duty to conceive and understand the principles and merits of our faith philosophically, but when philosophy clashes with religion, he is always ready to forsake the former for the sake of the latter. He represents thus the extreme conservative tendency in Jewish philosophy. On the whole, he is a follower of Maimonides and defends him vigorously against all those who attacked him, especially against Crescas. Yet, he follows Crescas in a number of points where Maimonides seems to him too rationalistic.

He differs with Maimonides and partly follows Crescas in the question of Divine Providence, prophecy and miracles. He rejects the theory of the rationalists that Providence is graded according to the degree of intelligence of the recipient and that the higher a man is in the scale of intellectuality, the greater is the special Providence accorded to him. He is especially severe against Gersonides who asserts that Providence is effected through the mediacy of the universal Active intellect. According to him, Providence is exerted by God directly upon three chosen representatives of the three divisions of the universe, i. e. the world of separate intelligencs, the spheres, and the sublunar world. In the first division it is the first intelligence which receives from God the direct influence and is in constant contact with Him. In the second, the first sphere or heaven is moved by God Himself, and in the third, the people Israel is under the direct Providence of God. All other nations receive the Divine Providence through the mediacy of the heavenly bodies. As for the individuals of that people, Providence does not depend upon the degree of intellectuality, but is primarily an act of grace by God. Abrabanel sees also special importance in Palestine which is the only land, in his opinion, where men can attain real happiness. In all this can be seen, of course, the influence of Judah ha-Levi and partly of Crescas, but the original conception of the direct Providence bestowed upon Israel is already found in the Talmud,[6] and Abrabanel merely gave it a quasi-philosophic aspect by comparing Israel with the two representatives of the other divisions of the universe.

Abrabanel likewise rejects the rationalist theory of prophecy according to which one must possess a high degree of intellectuality and a powerful imagination as prerequisites to his receiving the gift of prophecy. He believes that prophecy is a direct influence from God, not as Gersonides averred that it comes from the universal Active Intellect, nor as Maimonides asserted, through the mediacy of that Intellect, and this influence illuminates the mind of the recipient without any preliminary preparation of intellectuality and strength of imagination. The only prerequisite of the prophet, according to Abrabanel, is his purity of morals and pious conduct. In this, he undoubtedly follows Crescas whose similar theory of prophecy was noted above.

Nor is Abrabanel satisfied with the theory of miracles of the rationalists which tries to explain their occurrence by saying that God had placed at creation a power in the very nature of things that at certain times such events should occur. He is especially severe with Gersonides who says that the passage in Joshua X, 12-14, telling of the stopping the sun in its course and other passages in the Bible relating similar miracles are not to be taken literally, but in a modified form. Abrabanel is against any attempt to minimize the importance of miracles. In this he is entirely in accord with the view of Nahmanides and other conservative teachers.

Probably the most important of his works on philosophical-theological questions is the *Rosh Amanah,* his book on Dogmatics. In this book, he undertakes to defend Maimonides' scheme of dogmas against all those that subsequently criticized it, especially against Crescas and Albo. The importance of his work, however, does not lie in the fact that Abrabanel develops his own theory of dogmas, or improves that of Maimonides, for on the contrary, he asserts at the end of the book that as far as he is concerned, there are no dogmas in Judaism at all, but one must believe in the entire Torah with all its precepts and commandments. It may, however, be assumed that this statement was only made to appease some of the zealous spirits in Israel who

[6] B. Sabbath, 156a.

objected to the enunciation of dogmas. The main value of the book consists in Abrabanel's lucid exposition of the whole subject of dogmatics as it was developed from Maimonides to his own day. His own analysis of the arguments of Crescas, Albo and others against Maimonides, as well as his skillful defense of the dogmatic scheme of the master form a real contribution to the study of Jewish dogmatics.

83. JUDAH ABRABANEL

Don Isaac Abrabanel's love of philosophy was intensified and deepened in that of his son, Judah Leon Medigo (1470-1530). Judah was the eldest son of Don Isaac, having been born during the former's residence in Lisbon, Portugal. Together with his father, he fled the country and settled in Toledo where he married and had two sons, Isaac and Samuel. At the expulsion, while making preparations to sail with his father for Naples, he sent his son Isaac with his nurse to Portugal for a temporary sojourn. The king, who bore the Abrabanel family a grudge, ordered the detention of the child and later baptized him. It seems that Isaac never rejoined his father, and Judah mourned the loss of his son all his life, though for a time, he kept in contact with him. We possess a Hebrew poem written by the father when the son was twelve years old in which he pours forth his plaint over the vicissitudes of his life and especially over the forced separation from his son, and finally urges him to return to the fold and become worthy of his ancestry. Whether the son fulfilled his father's request or not is not definitely known.

Judah himself sojourned in Italy. First he was employed as physician to the Spanish governor of Naples, and then he settled in Venice and occupied himself with the practice of medicine, study of philosophy and writing of Hebrew poetry. He must have been very skilled in medicine and acquired a great reputation for proficiency, as the surname Medigo, the physician, indicates. His chief philosophical work written in Italian under the name of *Dialoghi D'Amore* (Dialogues about Love), was later translated into Hebrew by Judah di Modeno* under the name *Vikuah al-ha-Ahabah*. It enjoyed considerable popularity among the Italians as it was one of the first books on philosophy written in the vernacular, and it saw five editions in twenty years. It was later translated into French, Latin and Spanish, but unfortunately was not very popular among the Jews, probably on account of its secular content, and it was not published until 1871. Yet, it has interest for the history of Jewish thought, for though it deals primarily with subjects outside of the usual circle of ideas of Jewish philosophy, it still has a Jewish note to it, and its central idea, the definition and description of the all-inclusive love of God, most likely exerted some influence upon the formation of the concept of the *Amor Dei* of Spinoza.

The book is divided into three dialogues between Philo, (the lover), and Sophia (wisdom), called in Hebrew *Hobeb* (lover) and *Naama* (pleasant). The first dialogue opens with a discussion of the distinction between love and desire, and goes on to define the various kinds of love, such as love of the pleasant, of the useful and the proper, and also touches upon the distinction between human and Divine love. In the second dialogue an attempt is made to show how love is the principle dominating all existence and how this principle operates in the human, animal and even in the inanimate world. In this connection, an analogy is made on a large scale between man, the *microcosm* and the universe, the *macrocosm*.

The third dialogue which covers the largest part of the book deals with a multitude of subjects. It describes the *Amor Dei,* the love of God and shows how it permeates the entire circle of existence, defines the concept of beauty and the beautiful, states the doctrine of the ideas of Plato, and discusses the soul and its activity. The dialogues are profusely illustrated with stories from Classical mythology which in the manner of the spirit of the Renaissance are allegorically interpreted to contain a philosophic meaning.

It is impossible to give a succinct account of the ideas embodied in the book as it is not written in a systematic philosophic way, but in the dialectic manner of the Platonic dialogues, where different subjects are connected loosely like links in a chain. We will only give the gist of the underlying idea. This is that love which is primarily spiritual and intellectual is the principle permeating the entire universe in two ways, from God to the lowest beings, and from those beings through the entire chain back to God. God, who is, as the philosophers say, the knower, the known and knowledge all in one is also the lover, the beloved and love. Because of this love, He created the world which reflects the Divine beauty. The love of God continues to permeate the semi-circle of existence, namely from God to the world of intelligences, thence to the spheres, and then to the sublunar world to the lowest being there. In this semi-circle there is a constant descent of both the love of God and Divine beauty or perfection. The love is expressed in the fact that it continues the existence of all these beings and helps them to attain their perfection. When the bottom of the semi-circle is reached, that is the *hylē,* formless matter, then the ascent begins, the *hylē* loves the forms of the elements, these love or desire the forms of the minerals and plants; the animals also love the higher forms and finally man loves the intellect which by constant ascent returns to God who is the ultimate beloved, and the circle is completed.

Abrabanel, though speaking of beauty and of pleasure as being the purposes of love gives to both concepts an intellectual content. Real beauty is the intellectual beauty reflected in the plan and harmony of the world and the origin of which is God Himself. Physical beauty is only a shadow and copy of the intellectual beauty, and on seeing a beautiful person, we are pleased because the soul recognizes in him the reflection of Divine beauty. The good of the soul is, therefore, the ascent from the contemplation of the physical to the conception of the intellectual beauty. The pleasure of love is the uniting of the lover with the beloved, and since man loves God and strives to unite with Him, he experiences great pleasure in the striving as well as in the conception of such a union. We can note in this theory the foreshadowing of Spinoza's *Amor Dei Intellectualis.*

Abrabanel, in the course of his discussion, touches on a number of Jewish subjects. He discusses creation and makes a feeble attempt to defend *creatio ex nihilo,* but he really seems to be inclined to accept the Platonic theory of the eternity of formless matter, and creation consists in the introduction of order and form in that matter which is a view identical with that of Gersonides. He speaks of the special prophecy of Moses and offers an allegorical interpretation of the story of creation of man in the good style of Jewish allegoric philosophers. Thus, Judah Abrabanel with all his immersion in Classic philosophy and his own contemplation of the beautiful and the harmonious has not omitted the Jewish note from his thought.

84. BARUCH SPINOZA

The famous philosopher, Baruch Spinoza (1638-1677) was, as is well known, excommunicated by the elders of the Portuguese Jewish community of Amsterdam, and was thus declared to be outside the pale of Jews and Judaism. Yet, without questioning the justice of this act, we can righlty assert that no similar ban can be passed against the writings of that philosopher to exclude them from a place in Jewish literature, no matter how broadly or narrowly we may define the term. It is true that the philosophy of Spinoza in its main teachings can hardly be considered a Jewish system of thought and in some points can even be said to be antagonistic to the fundamental principle of Judaism, that is the pure spirituality of God. Nevertheless, its origin is undoubtedly rooted in the teachings of the Mediaeval Jewish philosophers and especially in that of Crescas.[7] Furthermore, the entire system of Spinoza runs quite parallel to the other systems of Jewish thought in form if not in content. As such, an exposition of his philosophy in the light of its Jewish origins should certainly be included in a survey of Jewish literature. However, the complexity of his thought and the technical nature of its teachings prevent us from following the Spinozistic system in its winding mazes. We will limit ourselves to the elucidation of one point in Spinoza's system which will prove its probable derivation from a criticism of the solutions offered by Jewish philosophers to the problem of creation.

As we have noted in the course of our survey of Jewish philosophy, the problem of creation was found by all thinkers the most difficult to solve, and in their attempts at a solution which should harmonize in some manner with the teachings of the Bible, they either abandoned the principles of philosophy and sought refuge in tradition, or made half-way concessions to the eternity of matter. Thus, Gersonides assumed the eternal existence of a formless matter, and limited creation to the forming of the world out of this primal matter. Crescas, criticizing Gersonides' theory propounded his own, which, if drawn to its conclusions really involves eternal creation and a continuous existence of a series of worlds. But even his theory is hardly satisfactory, for the question of how matter came from the all spiritual God was not solved.

It is, therefore, my belief that Spinoza, after meditating upon the insoluble difficulties in connection with the problems of creation and the origin of matter as presented by the Jewish philosophers, resolved to try a different solution, namely to include matter or extension as an attribute of God and thus solve the riddle. He thus posited his fundamental doctrine that God is identical with the universe and that His two attributes or manifestations conceived by us are thought and extension or matter. In this wise, he escaped both the Aristotelian

[7] On this point, see Manuel Joel, zur Genesis der Lehere Spinoza's; M. Waxman, The Philosophy of Don Hasdai Crescas, N. Y., 1920; Baruch Spinoza's Relation to Jewish Philosophic Thought and to Judaism, J. Qu. R. N. S., Vol. XIX, No. 4 and David Neumark's splendid essay, Crescas and Spinoza.

dualism of positing two eternal principles, God and the world, and the difficulties connected with creation. The doctrine itself, as indicated, is antagonistic to Judaism, and henceforth his system develops in another direction, though he keeps up the form of Jewish philosophy by discussing some of its main problems, such as freedom of the will, immortality and the love of God, endowing the concepts with an entirely different content than that given to them by Jewish philosophy.

But while we could dismiss the philosophy of Spinoza with such a brief notice not even mentioning his famous work the Ethics, wherein this philosophy is contained, we can not dispose in this manner of his theology and the *Tractatus Theologico-Politicus* which embodies it. This work is intimately connected with Jewish teachings and bears a close relation to the dogmatics of Crescas, and furthermore, some of the theories propounded there exerted an influence upon the theories of later Jewish thinkers. It deserves, therefore, a more detailed discussion.

The *Tractatus Theologico-Politicus* was one of the few books which was published during Spinoza's life time, in 1670. For fear of persecution, it was published anonymously and the place of publication given as Hamburg though actually printed in Amsterdam. It contains twenty chapters dealing with such subjects as prophecy, miracles, election of Israel, the interpretation of Scriptures, dogmas of faith, delineation of the constitution of the Hebrew Republic, and finally with the authority of the state in religious matters and the right of every man to freedom of thought. To the question of the interpretation of the Scriptures, Spinoza devotes seven chapters and offers a searching and thorough examination of the composition of the books of the Old Testament, based on historical and literary grounds furnished by he Scriptures themselves. He was thus practically the founder of modern Biblical criticism.

The purpose of Spinoza in writing the Tractatus was, as he declares in the introduction, to defend freedom of thought on the one hand and to prove, on the other hand, that religion and its authorities, which, according to him, are the rulers of the states and not the priests and ministers, have a right to dictate to individuals what opinions they should hold or not hold. He does this by proving that religion and philosophy operate in two entirely different spheres. The province of the former is that of good and bad, namely moral action, while that of philosophy is true and false. Religion is not a matter of speculation but of revelation and common sense and its dogmas do not need any philosophic grounding. It therefore, does not need to concern itself about philosophy and can leave it well alone, and hence philosophers should have freedom of thought.

This is the main purpose, for it is stated explicitly by Spinoza in the introduction, but I believe and every careful reader of the *Tractatus* will agree that Spinoza had also another motive for writing this book, namely, to vindicate himself against those who excommunicated him and placed him beyond the pale of Judaism. He wanted to show that the Judaism, in the name of which they spoke was not the real Judaism as given by Moses and intended by him to have eternal validity, and further that Judaism is expressed primarily in moral not in ceremonial acts. He endeavors, therefore, to show that not only is the entire Rabbinic law a mere fiction but even the Biblical laws expressly stated in the Pentateuch no longer have authority even for the Jews themselves, for they were given only in order to maintain the supremacy of the Jews and their well being as a body politic. With the cessation of Jewish political life, ceased also the validity of these laws and there remained only the moral laws of the Scriptures which every one should observe.

To prove these theses, Spinoza undertakes an examination of the Scriptures in the widest sense, namely of their contents, teachings, and the principles of belief enunciated there, and on the basis of this examination, attempts to establish his conception of religion and determine its proper province. He opens his book with a discussion on prophecy and the character of the prophet. At the very outset, he indicates clearly his intention to prove that religion is absolutely distinct from speculation. Differing both with Maimonides and Crescas, he declares that imagination is the only characteristic of prophecy, namely that the prophet must have a most vivid imagination which can be easily impressed or affected by objects even while awake. He does not say explicitly why prophecy comes to some men and not to others, nor whether it is by the will of God or not, but we can infer that he considers the prophets as media of the expression of God's will. He is quite conscious that imagination can not always be relied upon with certainty as it may be deceptive, and he, therefore, says that the true prophecy was always supplemented by a sign. It follows, of course, that many of the utterances of the prophets were not true but mere vagaries of their minds. He further adds that the minds of the prophets were disposed to justice and to goodness which is another proof for the certainty of their utterances. The prophets saw things in accordance with their individual intellectual opinion, capacity and temperament. If the prophet was of a higher intellectual attainment and of a gentle nature, his prophecy was of a higher nature and he spoke of hope, victory and peace. If, on the contrary, his intellectuality was of a lower degree and he was of a harsh nature, his prophecy assumed a grosser form and a darker hue.

Revelation in general was made by visions, but Moses was an exception, inasmuch as he actually heard a voice of God which was created for the special occasion. In all these assertions Spinoza both follows the Jewish philosophers and differs from them. He allows the superiority of the prophecy of Moses, and even assumes with Maimonides and others that there was a special creation of a voice, but does not accord to Moses, as they do, the exceptionally high intellectuality and the immediate conception of the Divine. Even he had a mediate conception, that is through the voice. The only one to whom he does allow such a high conception is Christ, for "He communicated with God in the way of mind with mind."[8] He adds, however, that he derives this opinion from the New Testament. That Spinoza in this as in many other things made an excessive concession to caution, for fear of being persecuted, goes without saying, as not in vain did this great hermit inscribe on his seal ring the single word *Caute,* beware. The whole purpose of the two chapters on prophecy and the prophet becomes clear, which is to show that the promulgators of the Scriptures were men who were not endowed with deep reasoning power, but merely with a strong imagination, disposed to goodness and justice and that their teachings were intended for practical purposes only. Moreover, these prophets expressed themselves in a language and manner which was adapted both to their personal moods and to the capacity of their hearers. From all this, it follows that the Scriptures contain eternal verities, but of a limited and practical nature, and not of a high philosophic order.

He next takes up the questions of the election of Israel and whether prophecy was peculiar to Jews only. He comes to the conclusion that prophecy was not limited to Israel and champions the case of the gentile prophet Balaam against the rabbis. He also avers that the election of Israel consisted not in the fact that they excelled any other nation in intellectual attainments or in moral conduct, but in that they

[8]Tractatus, Eng. Tr. Ed., Trübner, p. 39.

were a practical nation, and "conducted the business that bears upon security of life more successfully, and that they overcame great dangers, especially by the outward aid of God."[9] By the words, "aid of God" is to be understood the special constitution given to them for the good of their body politic and its security which was meant for them alone and for no other nation. That this view of the election of Israel is distorted by personal feelings of the propounder and is contradictory to the Scriptures and even to logic will be pointed out in more detail later.

As a result of his conception of prophecy and the election of Israel, he comes to the conclusion in the following two chapters, (IV, V), that the concept Divine Law connotes that law which regards solely the highest good or true happiness, that is the knowledge and love of God. It is in harmony with the law of nature, namely the moral law, which is universal and common to all men. It follows, therefore, that the historical narratives in the Scriptures have no special bearing upon the universal laws, and they were related merely as a concession to the human mind and especially to the Jewish mind which could not conceive things otherwise except in a tangible form. Again, all the ceremonial laws stated in the Scriptures were given for the Jews only as a means to the safety and security of the body politic. They have, therefore, as indicated, no general validity for the rest of humanity nor even for the Jews after the loss of their state. In this way, Spinoza delivered his intended blow against those who excommunicated him from the fold of Judaism.

After a short chapter on miracles, he proceeds to elicit the true principles of faith or the dogmas. This he claims can be accomplished only by a true interpretation of Scriptures and examination of its content. He devotes a chapter (VII) to the method of interpretation of the Bible where he takes issue with Maimonides for his forced method of interpretation. He comes to the conclusion that the Scriptures can be understood only by the Scriptures alone and that no other form of interpretation is true. But in order to use this method rightly, we must have an historical knowledge of the composition of the books and their development. To this he devotes five chapters (VIII-XII).

After examining the various changes which the Scriptures went through and coming to the conclusion that they had been tampered with by many hands, especially by the Pharisees, he singles out some

[9] Ibid, p. 75.

doctrines which he believes to be the true teachings of the Bible. These then are the dogmas of a universal religion. Before presenting his dogmas, Spinoza gives a general definition of faith. "Faith is nothing but this, to entertain such thoughts of God, as if wanting, obedience to Him is witheld; and obedience given, adequate thoughts of God are implied."[10] We see clearly his tendency to make the entire religion a matter of obedience and action not speculation and knowledge. The dogmas follow:

(1). God, the supreme being, the just, the merciful exists and is the example of a true life. He who knows not God or believes not that God exists can not obey Him.

(2). God is one. No one doubts but this belief is absolutely necessary to the highest devotion, admiration and love of God; for devotion, love and reverence arise from the idea of supreme excellence in one over all.

(3). God is omnipresent and all things lie open before Him. Were He held not to see all, doubts might arise of the impartiality of His justice, or His justice might even be altogether denied.

(4). God has sole dominion, is right in all things, uninfluenced by aught beyond Himself; He acts and wills of His own sovereign pleasure and peculiar grace.

(5). The worship of God consists, and obedience to Him is shown in justice and charity alone.

(6). All who obey and worship God in this way are saved.

(7). God forgives those who repent of their transgressions.

To the last dogma, Spinoza gives a special Christian coloring by adding that "He who believes that God in the plenitude of His grace and mercy forgives erring man and is moved thereby to a greater love and reverence towards the Supreme, indeed knows Christ."[11] But all this is merely another concession to the dominant religion which Spinoza made not of his inner inclination but out of caution.

The dogmas themselves, in spite of Spinoza's assertion that he elicited them out of the Bible by a very laborious and original method, are really taken, as Dr. Neumark has shown, from Crescas.[12] The first two, the existence and unity of God are what Crescas calls The Great Principle, (ha-Shorosh ha-Gadel), except that Spinoza omitted

[10] Ibid, p. 252.
[11] Ibid, p. 256.
[12] Essays in Jewish Philosophy, p. 301ff.

to state the speculative arguments of the former and substituted the more practical ones. The third and fourth, God's knowledge, dominion and right in all things correspond to the first three fundamental dogmas of Crescas, namely knowledge, Providence and potence. The latter's fourth and fifth dogmas, prophecy and free choice are omitted and the principle of obedience is substituted by Spinoza. In the sixth dogma, that of people being saved, there is a pale reproduction of two of Crescas's secondary dogmas called by him true beliefs, namely immortality and reward and punishment, though Spinoza does not make clear in what "being saved" consists. The seventh dogma that of repentance, which, Spinoza says in his explanation, brings to a love of God is likewise taken, minus its Christian addition, from Crescas who counts repentance, *(Teshubah),* as a true belief and connects it with the purpose of man's life which is love of God.

The enunciation of the dogmas of faith which define the character of religion enables Spinoza to establish clearly the complete severance of philosophy from religion which he does in the fifteenth chapter. He is then ready to carry out his other purpose, to determine the functions of government in its relation to the control of religion. After defining the scope of natural and civil rights and describing the origin of authority as arising from the tacit compact by which the individuals transferred their rights to the sovereign power—this is principally the theory of Hobbes—he attempts to put limitations upon the power of government. For this purpose, he draws a picture of the constitution of the Hebrew Commonwealth (Ch. XVII). In this chapter, he describes it as an autocracy where God was the ruler to whom the Jews transferred their rights. In this Commonwealth, religion and state were completely united. He notes its good points and advantages, and says that it could have existed forever if not for one peculiar circumstance. This was the anger of God, who wilfully gave the Jews laws which ultimately brought ruin to the state. Here Spinoza shows himself less the philosopher than the polemist. On the basis of a verse in Ezekiel Ch. XX, 25, he constructs his theory that God in His anger gave the Jews laws which brought about the destruction of their state. The theory is entirely imaginary, for no reason is adduced for the manifestation of anger from the time of the foundation of the state. It is entirely dictated by the suppressed hatred of the philosopher for his former brethren.

From the constitution of the Hebrew Republic, Spinoza draws political lessons for his own day. He concludes that the ministers of religion should limit themselves to teaching but not to lawmaking, that authority even in matters of religion should rest with the state and that democracy is not always a boon. He seems to favor a monarchy but does not entirely commit himself on the subject. He finally closes with a passionate appeal for freedom of thought. Man, says he, in the compact by which he transferred his rights to the power of the state has not divested himself of all rights, and the right to think is one of these. Since religion has little to do with speculation, it follows that though the state possesses full authority on religious matters, it has no right to control the expression of thought on the part of its subjects. Thus, the book full of original ideas and also of original defects, ends.

To the most prominent defects of the book, due to the author's bias against the Jews, belong the theories of the election of Israel and that of the downfall of the Jewish state. In spite of Spinoza's constant insistence on his interpreting Scripture from the words of Scripture only, he has hardly done justice to this method in his above-named theories. The Bible is full of references to the election of Israel because of their moral excellence, and yet Spinoza asserts that this election consisted merely in giving them a set of laws intended for the safety of their body politic. He did not even trouble to explain why God should have been more interested in the safety of the Jews than in that of other nations. Such is the power of prejudice that it blinds even clear-headed philosophers.

That the theories of Spinoza exerted some influence upon later Jewish thinkers goes without saying. For the present, it will be sufficient to point out that Moses Mendelsohn in his Jerusalem, borrowed from Spinoza the entire conception of the Jewish Theocracy, which he turned to good use in defending Jewish rights, though he did not mention the name of the author. The theory that the validity of the laws ceased with the destruction of the state, also exercised some influence upon the views of the radical leaders of the Jewish Reform movement, but this matter will be discussed later.

85. MINOR PHILOSOPHICAL AND THEOLOGICAL WORKS

During the second half of the fifteenth century, we note among the Jews of Spain and Italy a movement of reaction against the study of philosophy, the leaders of which believed such study to be injurious to religion. The opposition found expression in the work of Shem Tob ben Shem Tob (d. 1430), who in his book *Sepher Emunoth*

(The Book of Beliefs) delivered a vigorous attack against the opinions of Jewish philosophy and also against the philosophers themselves, not sparing even Maimonides. He was, of course, not alone in the field as many agreed with him.

This reaction naturally called forth a counter movement on the part of those who were faithful both to philosophy and religion. They endeavored to show, as many of their predecessors had done, that philosophy is not antagonistic to religion, but there is a new note in their defence. They really attempt to draw a line between the two and define the province of each. They assert that the study of philosophy is helpful toward a better understanding of the principles of faith, but concede also that there is a large province of religion wherein philosophy does not enter and where man must rely on faith alone.

In this so called "reconciliation literature," there are, as might have been expected, various tendencies. Some authors are inclined to give philosophy a wider scope, and some, on the contrary, want to limit its function. The most important of such works are those of Abraham Bibago (d. 1472), Joseph ben Shem Tob (d.c. 1460) and Elijah del Medigo (1463-1498).

Abraham Bibago lived in various cities in northern Spain and was widely versed in the entire philosophical and scientific literature written both in Arabic and Latin. He wrote commentaries on the second Analytics, Physics and Metaphysics of Aristotle and on some of Averroes' medical works, as well as a number of treatises on philosophical and theological subjects. Of these, the most noted is the *Derek Emunah* (The Way of Faith).

The work is divided into three books which are subdivided into portals or sections. The first deals with Divine knowledge and Providence, the second with the nature of the intellect, the purpose of life, of religion and of philosophy. The third book is devoted to the enunciation of the principles of faith, discussion of miracles, creation and ethics. In this work, Bibago appears as a thinking believer, one who endeavors to follow a middle course between extreme rationalism and irrational faith, and while he admits the necessity of philosophic study, he limits its application in matters of religion. He also wrote several other treatises under various titles dealing especially with the question of creation, where he defends "creation from nothing" against the Aristotelian view of the eternity of the world .

Joseph ben Shem Tob, the son of the opponent to philosophy, Shem Tob ben Shem Tob, wrote commentaries on the *De Anima* and the

Ethics of Aristotle and on the Treatise on the Material Intellect by Ibn Roshd and also on a similar treatise on The Intellect by Alexander of Aphrodosias. Besides, he composed a number of other works on various subjects.

His *Kabod Elohim* (The Honor of God) is primarily devoted to a delineation of the relation between philosophy and religion. He begins with a discussion of the highest good in life, and quotes a number of passages from the Ethics of Aristotle and from the Republic of Plato which state that the highest happiness is contemplation. This view, says he, had been accepted by Jewish philosophers, and since the Torah also speaks of human happiness, they had, therefore, concluded that the ways of philosophy and those of the Torah are one. As a result, they endeavored to find in the Torah the teachings of philosophy, which attempt caused them to misinterpret the Torah. He rejects this view and proposes a middle way. There is no doubt, he says, that Aristotle is right in asserting that the purpose of human life is the perfection of both morals and intellect, and that the first is only a means to the second. But, on the other hand, we who believe in the Torah assert that the performance of the precepts leads to real happiness, and that this happiness is connected with immortality, while that of Aristotle in no way promises a life after death. Where then is the reconciliation? This, he says, consists in the fact that both the Torah and philosophy agree that there is a purpose in human life, which purpose is realized by exercising the best qualities that are in man as man, namely by acting and thinking nobly. But they differ in the definition of what constitutes noble action and thought.

In general, there are two kinds of happiness, one which pertains to man as a natural and social being, and a higher one which God has bestowed upon the Jews through the Torah. This kind of happiness is Divine. To obtain the first kind, reason is sufficient, but for the attainment of the second, we have need of the precepts of the Torah. He finally takes up the question of the usefulness of the study of philosophy and admits that it leads to the perfection of man as man, though to the perfection of the Jew, the Torah is all sufficient. Yet he says there is no doubt that one who is perfect both in intellectual endeavor and in religious matters is a higher type of man than he who is perfect in one way only. And further, the one who attained the human or intellectual perfection is likely to attain Divine or religious perfection in a better way than he who lacks the former attainment. Joseph thus found some usefulness for the study of philosophy even from a strictly religious point of view.

Rabbi Elijah del Medigo, a descendant of a noble Jewish family was born on the Island of Crete. He later settled in Padua, Italy, where he taught philosophy at the university of that city, and was teacher and friend of the famous philosopher and mystic Pico di Mirandola. Elijah wrote a number of works on philosophical subjects in Latin, among them treatises on the Unity of the Intellect, the Essence of Existence, and Concerning the First Mover. He also composed several Hebrew works, of which only one is extant, the *Behinath ha-Dat* (The Examination of Religion). The work was written in the year 1491 at the request of his disciple Saul Ashkenazi. It is logically divided, although not actually, into three parts. In the first, he discusses the relation between philosophy and religion. He believes that the two have separate provinces and do not oppose each other. It is true that the basic principles of religion agree with the truth of philosophy, e. g. the beliefs in the existence of God, His unity and incorporeality. But there are also other principles, such as prophecy, reward and punishment and the possibility of miracles which can not be substantiated by logical and philosophic method, and yet we are bound to accept them on the basis of religious injunctions only. In his insistence that the basic principles of religion must agree with logical or axiomatic truth, he frankly states that were the Torah to assert the corporeality of God or any other attribute which is contrary to the fundamental principles of reason, it would not have been our duty to accept such assertions, nor would we have been punished for disavowing them. The reason which God Himself implanted in us can not possibly subscribe to such beliefs.

In the second part, he discusses first briefly the Thirteen Articles of Maimonides and then devotes himself to the matter of the interpretation of the Torah. This interpretation says the author, has two phases, one relating to the law, and one to opinion. As for the first, there is undoubtedly a general agreement, for the Talmud and Codes are accepted by all Jews. The minor differences in the decisions of the laws arise from the fact that we have no authoritative legal body to give ultimate decisions. But as for the second kind of interpretation, that is in opinions and views derived from the Bible, there are great differences. Some think that every word in the Torah contains secrets and mystic teachings, and some take the words of the Bible in a plain way, and others again interpret the Scriptures so as to make them agree perforce with the views of philosophy. Elijah rejects both extreme methods, but is especially severe against the Kabbalists, the representatives of mystic interpretation. He frankly doubts the authenticity of the Zohar and the ascription of its authorship to Simon ben Yohai. He ends the discussion on interpretation with a few remarks on the Agada and asserts that we are not bound to accept its statements, when they contradict logical truth or data of experience.

In the third part, del Medigo propounds the question whether there are reasons for the precepts of the Torah. He believes that undoubtedly there are, for the Bible itself offers explanations for some of its precepts, and what is predicated of a part may be predicated of the whole. Maimonides was, therefore, right in his attempt to offer reasons for a great part of the Mitzvoth. He further believes that the knowledge of the reason or the meaning of a precept will prompt one to perform it. Yet we must know that Judaism insists upon action and not on mere belief or the knowledge of the intention of the precept. However, it is not always advisable, says del Medigo, to disclose the reasons for which the precepts were commanded. In this matter, we must, he asserts, proceed cautiously and only such explanations as will not cause any misunderstanding should be written down. With these remarks, Elijah closes his treatise, on the Examination of Religion. He himself presented a good example of caution, for undoubtedly, his views were more radical than those he cared to reveal.

B. Ethics

86. INTRODUCTORY

We noted in the preceding survey of Jewish philosophy during the post-Classical period that philosophic thought had not slackened in Jewry, and while no attempt was made to build up complete systems, yet the representative thinkers made important contributions towards a wider understanding of the very same problems with which the philosophers of the earlier generations busied themselves. The same, however, can not be said with respect to the ethical teachings of these times. For reasons which were discussed elsewhere (Vol. I, Sect. 174), Jewish philosophers did not deem it necessary to treat the problem of ethics in he same philosophical manner as they treated the other problems which engaged their attention. But while in the Classical period, we do find a few books devoted to the evolving of the philosophical theory of human conduct, this period is practically devoid of such works.

This, of course, does not mean that there was a paucity of ethical works. On the contrary, there was great productivity in the field of ethical literature, and the number of books dealing with the proper conduct of the Jew reaches into the hundreds. But all these writings are primarily practical, outlining the conduct which a religious Jew should follow, and emphasizing certain virtues which man must acquire in order to fulfill his duties to God and the Torah. Nowhere is there an attempt made to establish rules and principles. The entire literature is permeated with the pietistic spirit according to which the Torah and its Commandments are the only source of right living. As a result, the line of demarcation in this literature between homiletics and ethics is hardly noticeable, and the content of quite a large number of these books consists of interpretations of Biblical verses and Agadic passages in an ethical pietistic manner. In fact, most of the ethical books remind us of the Agadic collections of old and the productivity of this literature can be fairly well considered a continuation of the Agada, just as the Rabbinic literature of the period is a continuation of the Halakah. The latter kept on amplifying, extending and broadening the practice of the laws, while the former continued to amplify and deepen the spirit of these laws and make them an important factor in the life and conduct of the individual.

Yet, as most of the ethical books, at least in the first half of the period were written in Spain and the Provence, they were not entirely left without the influence of Jewish philosophy. This infiuence is noticed both in the content and in the arrangement of the material. It seems that almost all the writers of these books were acquainted with the works of Maimonides, Saadia and Bahya and also with those of other philosophers. A considerable number of excerpts from their writings found their way into the ethical books, though the sources are seldom given. More often, thoughts and teachings derived from the books of the philosophers are given in the language and the style of the ethical writers themselves, which proves that some of these teachings became the common property of every Jewish scholar. Likewise, psychological observations and scientific remarks upon the nature of man and things abound in these books, which again shows to what extent the content of the philosophic and scientific literature of the period became a part of the intellectual equipment of every Jewish savant, even the most pious.

The influence of philosophy is noticed to a still greater extent in the logical and methodical arrangement of the books. Almost all books written by Spanish and Provence authors are arranged in accordance with a well defined plan and scheme. They represent quite a contrast in this matter with the famous "Book of the Pious" (Sepher Hasidim Vol. I, Sect. 176), the typical example of the German ethical school which represents a mere compilation of disjointed maxims and injunctions.

The absence of the real speculative element in these books, however, by no means reflects upon the purity of their teaching. Like the Book of the Pious, they breathe the most exalted type of ethics. They are permeated with the noblest spirit of the love of God and man, and inculcate right living and conduct with a glow of religious piety and emotion which is hardly paralleled in any ethical literature of the world. Their purpose was not so much to teach the fulfillment of the Commandments as to purify the human soul and make it an instrument of realization of the will of God in this world. Hence, the greater insistence upon the virtues which affect the relations of man to man rather than upon those which lead to pious conduct in purely religious matters, though these were by no means neglected.

87. *ETHICAL LITERATURE FROM THE THIRTEENTH TO THE SIXTEENTH CENTURY*

The earliest of these books was the *Shaarē Teshubah* by Rabbi Jonah Gerundi (d. 1263). He was a great Talmudic scholar and wrote some commentaries on the Compendium of Al-Fasi (Sect. 43). He distinguished himself, however, by his piety more than by his learning, and was called by his generation Rabbi Jonah the Pious (ha-Hassid). He wrote besides the *Shaare Teshubah* also two other ethical treatises, the *Iggereth ha-Teshubah* (The Letter on Penitence) and the *Sepher ha-Yirah* (The Book of Piety or Reverence). The *Shaare Teshubah,* however, is the most important.

The book is divided into four portals. The first is devoted to a definition of repentance and an explanation of its principles, the second to a description of the various ways by which man should arouse himself to penitence, the third to a classification of the precepts and the punishment meted out for their transgression, and the fourth contains a discussion of the conditions of forgiveness. In the long detailed discussions of penitence to which the first section is devoted, there is no attempt made to base it on psychological grounds or to prove that man is free to repent, for this is taken for granted. The author inculcates primarily the great necessity of penitence and analyzes its constituent elements. He gives their number as twenty among which he enumerates repentance for evil acts, sorrow for the past, worry on the part of the sinner lest the act be repeated, shame and humility of heart and others. After stating the elements of penitence, he describes in the second portal the means by which a man should arouse himself to penitence. The means, according to the author, is self examination, and the times when this should be emphasized are six. A man is to examine himself and be aroused to penitence when (1) he suffers tribulation; (2) in old age; (3) when he listens to penitential sermons; (4) when he studies the Bible; (5) during the ten days of penitence between New Year and the Day of Atonement; (6) and finally, every day, for one does not know his end, and, therefore, the thought of the day of death should serve as an incentive.

Great skill is shown by Rabbi Jonah in his classification of the precepts and the degrees of severity of punishment attached to their transgression. It is all-inclusive and very detailed and makes no distinction between purely religious sins and moral transgressions; both classes are equally condemned, and in a way, the moral lapses even more severely. The catalogue begins with transgressions of Rabbinic injunction and ends with those sins for which the transgressor forfeits his position in the world to come. The author is very strict with those who separate themselves from the community and do not observe its enactments passed from time to time. Such enactments, he says, are made for the purpose of strengthening Jewish social life and religion, and thus sanctify the name of God. If one refuses to obey them, he disparages the name of God. He strongly condemns the sins of lying and flattery, analyzing them into many classes. He includes under the first the vain boasting of a man of qualities which he does not possess or the exaggeration of the details of an event which one witnesses. Though these things may not injure anyone, they are considered falsehoods, and one is warned not to indulge in them, for they will ultimately pervert his soul. Under flattery are included also such slight offences as abstaining from reproaching evil doers for their acts, or merely honoring the wicked for the sake of peace. Such is the rigorous way of conduct Rabbi Jonah inculcates. On the whole, there is a noble spirit of piety and morality permeating the book which sets up a standard of life at times difficult to follow, yet an ideal worth striving for.

ii. The second ethical book written at the end of the thirteenth century was the *Kad ha-Kemah* (A Jar of Flour, i. e. substance of truth) by Bahya ben Asher, the commentator on the Bible. In this book, the subjects are arranged alphabetically and are treated briefly though quite adequately. The articles include, besides strictly ethical subjects, such as humility, purity of heart, patience and others, also some that bear on principles of religion and ceremonies. Thus the letter Aleph includes an article on belief (Emunah), the letter Heth on Hanukah, *Pe* on Purim, *Shin* on the Sabbath (Shabath) and so on. However, in the treatment of all these articles, the strictly ceremonial or legal side is omitted and the religious and ethical phases emphasized. Bahya, on the whole, like rabbi Jonah, treats the subjects from a purely religious point of view without attempting to find a speculative basis for the virtues he wishes to inculcate. Yet here and there, he makes an exception and endeavors to give to his ethical teachings a philosophical aspect. Thus when speaking of the great sin of robbery, he says that one who robs his fellow man not only commits an ethical wrong, but even denies the very principles of faith, namely the existence of God, which assertion he proves as follows. We know by philosophic reason that this world has a creator who is one and the very source of truth, for the harmony of the various parts of the universe testify not only to the unity of the Creator but to His truthfulness, as truth is identical with perfection. It follows, that man who is created by this God should strive to be like Him and act in accordance with truth so that he might approach God and be exalted. The one who acts contrary to this principle estranges himself from God and sinks lower in the scale of being. Therefore, the one who commits robbery in any form, even if he only evades the payment of taxes due to the community by denying the real status of his wealth, denies indirectly the existence of God by showing through his action that he despises truth which is the essential attribute of God.[13] In this statement, we see an attempt to find a philosophic basis for human conduct.

Such remarks are scattered throughout the book. Thus, when speaking of the severity of the sin of desecrating the name of God (Hillul ha-Shem), he makes it obligatory upon every Jew to conduct himself in strict justice to every one, for not only is the Jew who transgresses any of the social laws guilty of breaking that particular law, but he also commits the grave sin of desecrating the name of God.

[13] Kad ha-Kemah, Article *Gesel,* p. 18, a-b.

It is known, says Bahya, that the religions and the laws of other nations are derived from our Torah, and since the civil laws are the very foundation of our religion, it follows that when the nations see that we do not observe them we degrade the honor of the Torah and desecrate the name of God.[14] He is equally zealous for the name and honor of the Jewish people and believes that Jews ought to conduct themselves as a model nation, and that each individual is responsible in his conduct for the honor of the entire nation. Moreover, such exemplary conduct will ultimately bring about redemption. Here he offers a very interesting reason for the dispersion of Israel which reminds us of the mission theory propounded by the founders of Reform Judaism. To my mind, says Bahya, one of the reasons for the dispersion of the Jews among the nations was that they should instruct the various peoples in the beliefs of the existence of one God and of His Providence in the world.[15] To Bahya, however, the realization of the mission was a means for redemption, not an end in itself, for the sooner we complete our purpose, the sooner will we be gathered from dispersion.

The book is replete with keen homiletic interpretations of Biblical verses and Agadic passages, and also with a number of excerpts from the writings of Saadia and Maimonides. The Kabbalistic teachings to which Bahya was inclined, inject a mystic strain in the work. The style of the book adds to its otherwise fine qualities. It is light, elastic and on the whole, makes pleasant reading.

iii. The fourteenth century produced a number of ethical books, the most important of which may be considered to be the *Sepher ha-Yasher* (The Book of the Righteous) by Zerahyah ha-Yevani (The Greek) hailing from a city in Greece (d.c. 1394). It was erroneously ascribed by the printers to the Tosafist Jacob Tam, because he wrote an Halakic book under that title (Vol. I, Sect. 146). However, it is now definitely established that Zerahyah was the author of the book. Of his life little is known, but from the book it is evident that he was philosophically inclined and was well versed in Jewish philosophic literature. In fact, he states in his introduction that the value of the precepts and the laws of the Torah is ascertained by the testimony of two witnesses, first by reason, second by the prophets, thus placing the testimony of reason first. Yet, this inclination to philosophy did not by any means diminish Zerahyah's piety, and the book

[14] Ibid, Article *Dinim* (Laws), p. 246.
[15] Ibid, Article *Geulah,* p. 21b.

is permeated with the spirit of deep reverence for God and the Torah which is prevalent in all the ethical books of the period.

In explaining his motive for writing the book, the author begins with a complaint against his contemporaries who have forsaken the path of religion and morality and are engrossed in the pursuit of riches, honor and pleasure. He, however, includes himself among the rest of the generation and says that he, like them, was addicted to the pursuit of the vanities of this world, and as a means for his own salvation, he wrote this treatise, aiming to direct his soul towards the proper worship of God and the right conduct. He hopes, though, that because his book differs from the previous works on ethics by its popular treatment of the subject, it will also exert some influence upon others.

The *Sepher ha-Yashar* is divided into eighteen portals or chapters. The first one which is called the Secret of Creation of the World (Sod Briath ha-Olam) serves really as the foundation of all the following chapters, inasmuch as it supplies the speculative basis for the central conception of the book, which is the worship of God (Abodath Adonai). Of the others, six chapters are devoted to a definition and description of that worship (Chas. II-VI and XIII) four to penitence (VII-X), and seven to related subjects, such as the world to come, the remembrance of the day of death, the distinction between the righteous and the wicked, and similar matters.

Zerahya seemed to have taken Bahya Ibn Pakudah, the author of The Duties of the Heart, as his model and was greatly influenced by his teachings. Like him, our author bases his ethical system on the recognition of the greatness of God through observation of the wonders of the universe. It is for this reason that he opens his book with the chapter on the secret of creation. The secret, or rather the purpose, consists in this that God in creating the world thereby perfected His name. Not that God, in any way, lacked perfection before creation, but the term God would have no meaning unless there were created certain things recognizing Him as such. It follows, therefore, that the more men strive to act in likeness to God, the more they testify to the perfection of His work and thus sanctify His name. Hence, the worship of God constitutes at least one of the purposes of creation, and by carrying it out in the proper way, we do His will. The next step is to understand how that worship can be attained.

In the exposition of the content of worship, the author at first lays down two conditions which make real worship possible. These are: (1) the possession of a kind heart, for one who is good to men will also do good in the eyes of God, (2) the belief that only God is perfect, and that all other things are defective. Out of these conditions, there is generated the love of God which constitutes a cardinal element in His worship. Love alone, however is not sufficient; it needs, on the one hand, reverence or fear of the Lord to complement and strengthen it, and on the other hand, wisdom, in order that the love be expressed in the proper action. Without wisdom, man does not know how to fulfill the will of God. To love, reverence and wisdom two more elements must be added to make the worship of God complete and all-inclusive. These are, reason and belief. By reason is meant the attaining of the higher conceptions of God and His essence which is a matter of cultivation and training. As a result of reason, there comes true belief which though not always confirmed by reason is yet based on it, for since some of the elements of belief agree with reason, we must conclude that the part not substantiated by it is likewise true, even if due to the imperfection of our mental capacities, we are unable to conceive its rationality.

We have then, five elements in the proper worship of God, namely, love, reverence of God, wisdom, i. e. practical knowledge, reason and belief. These five complete each other, for there can not be love without reverence, nor reverence without love. Again, without reason which supplies the basic conception of God, real love can not arise, nor can it be applied without wisdom, and finally, belief, which is a strong conviction of the truth of the Torah and the precepts contained in it, adds the necessary vigor to all the other elements.

After completing the theoretical side of his ethics, the author turns to the practical phase of the subject and discusses the ways and means by which one can cultivate the proper worship of God. He enumerates thirteen obstacles which man must remove from his path of right conduct. These comprise indulgence in pleasure, anger, flattery, laziness, arrogance, bad company, lack of faith, mockery, false science, envy, impatience, parsimony and unbelief in the final judgment. He discusses each of these obstacles and offers advice how to overcome them. The author next describes the way a man can train himself in the worship of God, and then turns to the other important subject of the book, that is, penitence.

In his view of penitence, Zerahya is greatly influenced by Maimonides. Like him he considers the righteous who have never sinned higher than the penitent, and interprets the famous Talmudic maxim,

"The real righteous do not stand where the penitent stand"[16] to mean simply that the former are not classed together with the latter, and not as it is usually explained that the righteous do not attain the degree of worth of the penitents. This was not a popular view in an age when *Teshubah* was the main subject of most of the ethical books. He deals with penitence in a general way describing briefly its conditions and the proper times for its performance. The book closes with a few brief chapters on diverse subjects such as self-examination, the vanity of the pleasures of this world, and the necessity of bearing in mind the day of death. These chapters are permeated with a spirit of asceticism in the manner of all writers of the day.

iv. Another ethical book produced towards the end of the century was the *Menorath ha-Maor* (The Lamp of Illumination) by Israel Ibn Al-Nakawa of Toledo, Spain. Of the life of the author, little is known except that he died the death of a martyr during the massacre of 1391. The book was originally intended to be a much larger one and included, as the author tells us in the introduction, besides the chapters on ethics, also a compendium of the ritual laws, but for some reason, this plan was not carried out and we have only the ethical chapters.

The work opens with a poem in honor of the Torah and is followed by the introduction. In it, Nakawa tells us the circumstances which impelled him to write the book. Contemplating the greatness of the Torah and tradition, a desire arose in him to write a work of his own, in order to add something to the great tradition of Israel. He hesitated for a time to carry out his plan, but in an exalted moment, experienced a vision in a dream and heard a Divine command bidding him to enter upon the work without delay. Moreover, a lighted lamp was shown to him, and this suggested the title. He further tells us that he drew his material from the entire Jewish literature, from the Bible down to his own day, and gives a list of the sources, the majority of which are the various Agadic books and compilations. We find among them also several Midrashim which are now lost and his excerpts are the only passages preserved.

The *Menorath ha-Maor* is divided into twenty portals which deal with various subjects bearing upon practical phases of the ethical and religious life. There seems to be no particular order followed. Nakawa himself says that he did not emphasize any particular virtue or

[16] T. B. Berakot, 34.

precept, not knowing whether there is any difference in the rewards for precepts performed. He selected, however, the most important virtues for discussion. Thus he begins with a long chapter on charity, followed by others on prayer, on meekness, on penitence, on the study of the Torah, and on the observance of the laws. These are followed by chapters on loving-kindness, on the Sabbath, on honoring parents, on the duty of marrying, on training of children, on love of fellow-men, on abstaining from slander, on keeping a secret and on general good manners. In short, he practically covers all phases of life, of the individual, of the family and of man in society.

There is, on the whole, little originality in the book, nor is there the least attempt made to form any theories regarding virtue or otherwise. It is primarily a compilation of hundreds of beautiful maxims regarding the practice of the various virtues discussed, culled from numerous sources and arranged in order. There is, however, great skill displayed in the weaving together of these sayings in one flowing text. There is also a fine subdivision of the main subjects into sections. Thus, the chapter on charity deals first with charity in general, its value and importance, then with various forms of charity, chief of which is hospitality, then with its distribution, classes of persons to receive help, methods of collection, and finally, it describes the qualities of the giver. The same method is pursued in the other chapters.

It seems that for a few centuries, the book of Al-Nakawa was read and studied by many, for we find extensive excerpts from it in later ethical works and numerous references to it by authors. In a later age, it was supplanted by others and forgotten. It was edited only recently from a manuscript in Oxford, the only one in existence and published with notes and introduction by Dr. H. G. Enelow.

v. Of the numerous ethical books produced during the fifteenth century the earliest was an anonymous work entitled *Orhoth Tzadikim* (The Ways of the Righteous). It was also known by the name of *Sepher ha-Midoth* (Book of Ethics or Virtues). The author most likely hailed from southern Germany and his book reflects the method of the German moralists.

The aim was entirely a practical one, namely to instruct man how to train the forces of his soul with which he is endowed in such a way that his actions tend towards the good. Man possesses five powers, says the writer. These are the five senses which are the sources of all action and even of thought, as all thought has its origin in the senses. It is through the use of the senses that the various qualities which the heart or the soul possess are strengthened or weakened. It is, therefore, through training in their proper use that man may acquire the good qualities and avoid the bad ones. But even the acquisition of good qualities or virtues will not lead man to the right path of conduct, unless he possesses in addition the fear of God (Yirath Shomayyim). "Fear of God," says the author, "is the bond which joins the virtues into one harmonious whole, and is like the thread which holds together a string of pearls. The moment you loosen the thread, the pearls scatter, and likewise if you are lax in the matter of the fear of God, the virtues will become ineffective. And when man possesses virtues, he is likely to observe the Torah and its precepts, for the Torah is dependent upon the improvement of the qualities of the soul."[17] It was then for the purpose of teaching the improvement of the qualities of the soul and to inculcate the fear of God that the book was written.

It was this view which influenced the arrangement of the material in the book. It is divided into twenty-eight chapters, twenty-five of which deal with virtues and vices, and three with penitence, Torah and the fear of God. The first twenty-five chapters are grouped in pairs, namely one deals with a certain vice and the other with its opposite virtue or vice versa. Thus, the first chapter discusses pride, the second meekness, the third shamefacedness, the fourth arrogance, the fifth love, the sixth hatred, and similarly the other qualities of the soul are grouped. There are a few exceptions, such as regret, envy or the vice of the evil tongue, to which the opposite can not be easily found, and these are treated singly.

The ethics taught in the book are entirely practical, and given in the form of advice to the reader. The whole tenor of the work reminds us of the Book of the Pious by Judah ha-Hassid (Vol. I, Sect. 176). Like Judah, our author teaches the ways of deep piety and noble conduct in the highest degree.

Here are a few examples of the teachings. Speaking of meekness, he says, "Be modest in thy dealings with men of all stations under all circumstances. In matters of business, conduct thyself not only justly but in the most equitable manner. Especially meek shall thy conduct be towards those who are dependent upon thee, such as thy servants or the poor whom thou supportest. The one who is humble towards widows or orphans or strangers and suffers patiently even their abuse

[17] Orhoth Tzadikim, Introduction.

is the real meek man." Discussing the vice of cruelty, he says, "Be merciful towards the non-Jewish servants; do not load them with work and do not treat them lightly either by hard words or by striking them. Even when you reprimand them, let it be in a mild manner and listen patiently to their complaints." The treatise is replete with such noble ethical injunctions and every chapter bristles with them.

Besides the Book of the Pious, the author drew also extensively upon Bahya's Duties of the Heart, the ethical portions of he *Rokeah* by Eleasar of Worms and other books by German Jewish authors. The chapter on Remembrance is primarily a reproduction of chapter III in portal VIII of the Duties of the Heart, and the chapter on Penitance is a condensed form of the discussions of the *Rokeah* on the subject. The book is profusely illustrated with moral stories and parables culled from many works. All these qualities made it very popular, in spite of the anonymity of the author, and it was widely read and studied and even translated twice into the Judaeo-German vernacular.

88. ISAAC ABOAB'S LAMP OF ILLUMINATION

The most outstanding ethical book of this period is undoubtedly the one written by Isaac Aboab of Toledo (d. 1492), during the second half of the fifteenth century and named, like the work of Al-Nakawa, *Menorath ha-Maor* (The Lamp of Illumination). The author was one of the leading Talmudic scholars of his day and wrote many works, including a commentary on the *Tur,* the code of Jacob ben Asher (Sect. 55), supercommentaries on the commentaries of Rashi and Nahmanides on the Pentateuch and books of homilies. The work by which he is most remembered is the *Lamp of Illumination*. At the time of the expulsion from Spain, he went at the head of a delegation to Portugal and obtained from the king permission for the exiles to settle temporarily in that country. He settled in Lisbon, but shortly after his arrival there, he passed away.

However, though we have definitely ascribed the authorship of the *Lamp* to Isaac Aboab of the fifteenth century, it is only fair to state that this is not the unanimous opinion of Jewish scholars. For a long time, it was commonly accepted that this particular Isaac Aboab was the author of the book and the earlier Jewish historians and bibliographers, such as Ibn Yahya and others all agreed in this view. The first one to doubt the authorship of the *Lamp* by this Aboab was the famous eighteenth century bibliographer, Hayyim David Azulai (Sect. 145). He was followed by the great Jewish scholar, Leopold Zunz, who in a very learned essay on the subject[18] turned this doubt into a certainty and came to the conclusion that the *Lamp* was written by an earlier Isaac Aboab who lived about 1300, and that the time of its composition was about 1320.

Yet in spite of Zunz's great mastery of Jewish learning, his conclusion can not be accepted and later Jewish scholars have reverted to the earlier opinion and decided that the Isaac Aboab of the expulsion was the author of the book. It would take us too far afield to reproduce the arguments that were advanced pro and con of the theory, yet a few facts may be indicated which point definitely to the second Aboab—if there ever was a first—as the author of the *Lamp*. The first is the great popularity of the book, for we know that it was popular not only during the later generations, but even during the life of the author himself. His disciple, Abraham Zacuto (Sect. 129), in his *Yuhasin* refers to it in a manner which indicates that the *Lamp* of Aboab was well known to everybody. It is more reasonable to assume, therefore, that the author of this book was one who was greatly revered in his time and who was otherwise distinguished as a scholar in many fields of learning, than to assert that he was one who was unknown except by this work alone, and who lived two centuries before. In fact, we see that Nakawa's *Lamp* which closely resembles Aboab's was completely forgotten, though it was written only at the end of the fourteenth century.

Second, as we will see, there is not only the community of name between the two *Lamps,* Nakawa's and Aboab's, but also common material which indicates that one author borrowed from the other. Had Nakawa borrowed from Aboab, as would be the case if Aboab lived in 1300, then Nakawa would most likely have referred to him, as he gives a list of all his sources, while on the other hand, Aboab does not. Besides, Nakawa tells us, that the *Menorath ha-Maor* was suggested to him by the vision of a lamp which could not have been the case had he borrowed the name together with some of its contents from a popular book. The case is different with Isaac Aboab. Nakawa's treatise was little known, and when he conceived the writing of a book which was to resemble that of Nakawa's but on a larger scale and with an entirely different arrangement, he did not

[18] Die Ritus der Juden, pp. 204-210.

hesitate to adopt the name of an earlier work. Besides, the plan of the division of Aboab's book is more appropriate to the name *Menorah,* for it is arranged in seven branches like the candelabrum of the Tabernacle.[19] So much for the authorship.

The purpose for which the author undertook his task was, as he explains in his preface, to supply instruction in matters of practical religion and ethics which should be accessible to everyone, even to those who are not versed in the Talmud and Codes. He was moved to write the book, because he saw that this phase of instruction was neglected. The scholars were busy either in pursuing legal dialectics or in compiling codes. The Agada with its multifarious teachings, as well as other studies which tend to improve the soul were disregarded by all, and to remedy this defect he composed his book. He felt, however, that it would not be proper to deal only with Agada and neglect Halakah entirely; he therefore, as he tells us, also wrote a popular code under the name of *Aaron ha-Eduth* (The Ark of Testimony). We do not know what became of the other work, whether it was completed or not.

The *Menorath ha-Maor* is divided into seven books, each of which is called a Light or Candle (Ner), subdivided into sections (Kelal), and these into parts, and then into chapters. The division seems to be a very elaborate one indeed, yet it was done on logical principles and there is fine cohesion in all its parts. The arrangement is based, according to the author in his introduction, on the three all-embracive principles of conduct embodied in the verse 16 Ch. XXXIV of the Psalms which reads, "Turn from evil and do good, seek peace and pursue it." Here, then, we have three principles, to avoid evil, to do good and to pursue peace. Now the avoidance of evil has two phases, not to desire and not to speak evil. The doing of good has three phases, first the observance of the precepts which is conducive both to right conduct and to the health of the body, the second the study of the Torah which leads to truth and to the improvement of the intellect, and the third, the ways of penitence, for there is none who does not sin and have need to return to the right path. The third principle again has two phases, namely the seeking of the ways of peace and love, and the acquisition of meekness, a state of the soul which leads to peace and love. Hence, we have seven parts of the ethical and religious life, which together make an harmonious whole.

[19] For other arguments see Enelow's introduction to the edition of Nakawa's Menorath ha-Maor, pp. 20-23.

It is these seven parts or subjects which are treated by Aboab in The Seven Candles or books. The first book deals with the avoidance of passion and is subdivided into three sections describing the principal human passions, envy, love of pleasure and honor. The second book is devoted to the evils arising from the power of speech. It contains ten sections (Kellalim) dealing with mockery, falsehood, flattery, slander, insult, vain or useless speech, quarreling, excessive hilarity, mentioning the name of God in vain and speech which causes the desecration of the Holy Name. The third describes the observance of the precepts which embrace the entire life of the Jew both as an individual and in relation to the family and fellow man. In its ten sections, it deals with circumcision, training of children, prayers, Sabbath and festivals, marital life, charity, honoring parents, dispensing of justice and a few kindred subjects. In all these discussions, very little of the actual law concerning these matters is given, but it is primarily the inner meaning of the precepts which is explained and emphasized. The purpose of Aboab was to impart sanctity to the religious life so as to prevent it from becoming mechanical and perfunctory. The fourth book, which takes the Torah as its subject, discusses it in four sections, on the duty of study, its method, its reward, and honor due to scholars. Penitence is the theme of the fifth book, and its three sections deal with the ways and days of *Teshubah* as well as the conditions of forgiveness. To the pursuit of love and peace, the sixth book is dedicated, and the cultivation of good manners and a life of peace is discussed in its two sections. The last book treats of the various phases of humility and meekness, both as a virtue of the soul and as expressed in speech and conduct. We see thus the wide field of life and conduct which the *Lamp* of Aboab illuminates. In fact, it embraces every action, speech and thought of man.

The method and the content of the work resemble to a great extent that of Nakawa's *Lamp*. The instruction is imparted largely through excerpts of beautiful statements and maxims drawn from all Agadic sources, as well as from other books, skillfully arranged under the respective headings of the subject. This is, however, no patch work, for these sayings are woven into discourses which flow freely and smoothly, and are introduced with the author's own remarks, and often interspersed with them as well. There is no doubt that Aboab made considerable use of Nakawa's work and borrowed from it a great many quotations, especially those which are drawn from Midrashim now lost, but he did not always make the same use of them, and they are at times quoted under different though closely related headings.

In general, Aboab's sources are more extensive than Nakawa's; he did not limit himself to those of Agadic books, but drew also upon philosophic and exegetic works. He had a strong inclination for philosophy and though the *Lamp* treats of conduct from a religious and pious point of view, yet many a time, there is an attempt to inject a philosophic note in the discussion. Aboab is anxious to obtain the agreement of the philosophers to certain views. Frequently, we meet with a statement, "This is the decree of the Torah and the philosophers do also agree in that." Aristotle is often quoted in support of an ethical or religious opinion. Of the Jewish philosophers and scholars, Maimonides is, of course, the most frequently cited. Next to him, Isaac Ibn Latif, the mystic philosopher, is the beloved authority of our author. But use is made also of the writings of Ibn Ezra, Jacob Anatoli and others.

Aboab was also inclined to mysticism and its strain is quite in evidence in the *Lamp*. It is, however, of the philosophic type. Thus, he attempts to explain the inner meaning of the precepts of the fringes (Tzitzith), phylacteries and that of circumcision by mystic reasons, saying that the phylacteries point to the existence of a higher world, i. e. that of the intelligences, the *tzitzith* to the existence of the middle world, i. e. that of the spheres, and circumcision to the existence of the lower world with its passions, namely, that the performance of the act causes the curbing of passions. Similarly, he finds that the four kinds of plants which we take during the Feast of Tabernacles symbolize the four elements; thus the Ethrog (Apple of Paradise) symbolizes by its color the element of fire; the Lulab by its height that of air; the willow branch that of water as it grows near it; the myrtle that of earth, for it is the lowest of the trees. Such interpretations of ceremonies and precepts are numerous with him. Their purpose was to deepen the meaning of the performance of the precepts and raise them to a higher level.

The book is illustrated with many beautiful parables and stories culled from the extensive Jewish literature, one of which we will quote here.

Speaking of penitence, Aboab tells the following story taken from a lost Midrash. Once a number of men departed on a sea voyage, and a strong wind carried their boat to an island. The island was very beautiful to look upon. It was well watered and its stately trees bore all kinds of sweet fruit; the ground was covered with luxuriant foliage and many colored flowers, while bright-hued birds fluttered cheerfully among the trees. It seemed a very paradise to the sea-weary passengers of the boat. The travelers were, however, divided in their opinion into five parties. One group refused to leave the ship and land on the island for fear that meanwhile a wind may come and carry the ship away, and they would be forced to remain there for the rest of their lives. The second did land on shore for a while, ate the fruit of the trees and returned immediately to the ship. The third group stayed on the island for a longer time, but when the wind came and the sailors made ready for departure and signalled them, they heeded the signals without delay and returned. The fourth tarried for a still longer time on the island, ignored the signals and even the hoisting of the sails and the raising of the anchor. But when the ship began to leave, they rushed to the sea, waded into it and climbed aboard. The fifth group was so engrossed in eating the fruit of the trees and enjoying the pleasures the island afforded that they did not notice the departure of the ship. When winter came and they remained without shelter and food exposed to the bitter cold and the attacks of the wild animals, they mourned greviously at their short-sightedness, but to no avail, and ultimately perished on that island.

The meaning of the parable is simple. The island is the world with its apparent pleasures, and the travelers the people. The first group are the totally righteous who cling to good actions—the ship of refuge—and do not pursue the pleasures of the world; the second are the men who follow pleasures in their youth but repent immediately; the third those who repent in old age—when the signals come; the fourth those who repent before death; the fifth are those men who miss the last chance and die unrepentant and are punished in the other world.

The *Lamp* of Aboab, on account of its many qualities was one of the most popular ethical books. It was printed many times and provided with commentaries, and to make it accessible to the women, it was translated into Judaeo-German.

89. *ETHICAL WORKS FROM THE SIXTEENTH TO THE EIGHTEENTH CENTURY*

The second epoch of the post-Classical period is marked, as is well known, by a spirit of rigorous piety and unquestioned belief in all teachings of tradition. Added to this, there is also the influence of the Kabbala, which by this time had taken a strong hold upon Jewish life and colored almost all literary productions of every type. It is small wonder, therefore, that an age like this should be productive in the field of ethics and the teaching of practical religion. However, most of these books are really not ethical treatises but compilations of maxims and Talmudic passages, interpreted homiletically and arranged in the form of homilies or commentaries on Biblical books. There are only a few outstanding books which deserve to be mentioned either on account of their intrinsic value or on account of their popularity. Yet these books like the others, though devoted primarily to the instruction of good conduct are devoid of speculation, thus reflecting the spirit of the time.

i. The earliest of such books was the *Reshith Hokmah* (The Beginning of Wisdom) by Elijah di Vidas (d. 1518). The author was a disciple of Moses Cordevero (Sect. 117), the famous Kabbalist who settled in his old age at Safed, the center of mysticism at the time, and his entire work is permeated with the mystic spirit and the teachings of the Kabbala. In fact, more than half of the content consists of quotations from the Zohar and other Kabbalistic books.

The *Reshith Hokmah* proper is divided into five portals (Shaarim) or sections which are subdivided into chapters. They deal with the fear and love of God, penitence, holiness and meekness respectively. There are five more sections describing the observance of the precepts, dealings in business, training of children, dispensation of justice and good manners in general. But these are not of the authorship of di Vidas. They, like the appendices containing the text of a Midrash called *Hupath Eliyahu Rabba* and several other compilations of Agadic ethical maxims, were copied from Al-Nakawa's *Menorath ha-Maor.*

The title of the book is taken from Psalms CXI, 10, "The fear of the Lord is the beginning of wisdom," and accordingly, the author treats of fear or reverence of God first, though he considers worship from love a higher degree of religiosity. He is conscious that not every one can attain to complete love of God which is the highest stage of perfection of the soul, but every one if he assumes the existence of a God can revere and fear the Creator. Fear of God is, therefore, the key to all religion. It is, however, more applicable to the prohibitive precepts (Lo Taasē), while love is mainly applied in the performance of affirmative precepts, *(Asē)*. The titles of the sections are of broad connotation and deal with a multitude of subjects embracing the entire ethical and religious life. Thus, under "the Fear of God" are included trust in Him, and honor of God and the Torah; under love, the prayers and benedictions are treated, as they express love of God. Likewise, under holiness, a large part of religious and ethical conduct is included, for it is by this conduct that man can attain to holiness.

Besides the quotations from the Zohar, the author draws upon Bahya's Duties of the Heart, the *Rokeah* and many Agadic books, chiefly the *Tanna dibe Eliyahu* (Vol. I, Sect. 87). The book contains also texts of two other small Midrashim which the author copied from manuscripts, one the *Masseketh Gehinom* (A Tractate on Hell) containing a vivid description of the various divisions or circles of hell, and the other *Hibut ha-Keber* (The Sufferings in the Grave) describing the punishment inflicted immediately after burial. These must have been late pseudo-Midrashim of unknown date.

ii. The other work is the *Shebet Musar* (The Rod of Instruction) by Elijah ha-Kohen of Smyrna. It contains fifty-two chapters, dealing with various phases of ethical and religious conduct. It is of a more popular nature than the *Reshith Hokmah* and appealed more to the masses. It was, therefore, reprinted many times and was found on the book shelf in every pious Jewish home.

90. *MINOR ETHICAL WORKS*

Besides the above mentioned books, there appeared a number of smaller works on ethics and practical piety which for one reason or another did not gain popularity and were either left in manuscript form or were printed once and forgotten. They should, however, be mentioned in a survey of this type of literature.

To these belong (1) the *Sepher ha-Metzoref* (The Book of Refinement) by Berakhya ha-Nakdan (see Sect. 158), the famous fabulist. The book contains an introduction and thirteen chapters dealing with such subjects as sensualism, taming of the passions, justice, treatment of the unfortunate and the poor, pursuit of honor, hope, the soul and its immortality and the like. The book is extant only in manuscript. (2) A work entitled *Begidath ha-Zman* (The Treachery of Life) was written in the middle of the fifteenth century by one named Rabbi Mattathias and treats, in rhymed prose, the problem of old age, the suffering of the righteous and the prosperity of the wicked. It ends by urging complete trust and confidence in the justice of God. (3) Towards the end of that century (c. 1460-1480), Moses ben Eliezer wrote his book on ethics entitled The Garden (*ha-Gan*) which is divided into seven sections, corresponding to the seven days of the week. It was intended that the reader should peruse one section each day.

Of the other works composed during later centuries, we may also mention (4) the *Marpe Le-Nefesh* (A Cure for the Soul) by Abraham Zahlon (d. 1595), (5) The *Sepher ha-Hayyim* (The Book of Life) by Hayyim ben Bezallel, the brother of the famous Rabbi Liwa of Prague, creator of the homunculus *(Golem),* and finally, (6) the popular work *Kab ha-Yashar* (The Measure of Righteousness).

The last named book was written by Zevi Hirsh Kaidonower (1705) both in Hebrew and Judaeo-German. It contains one hundred and two chapters, the numerical equivalent of the word *Kab* (Kuf—100, Beth—2), dealing with various subjects of ethical and religious conduct. There is no particular order of arrangement and no sequence between the chapters. Some subjects are repeated at times and on the whole, the book resembles a string of isolated articles more than chapters of a well-planned work. The *Kab ha-Yashar* reflects the gloomy, rigorous and mystic spirit of the seventeenth century Polish Jewry. It is replete with quotations from the Zohar and stories about demons and transmigrations of souls *(Gilgulim)* and similar superstitious beliefs current in that age. Yet, the ethics it teaches is pure and the virtues it inculcates are noble and exalted.

Much ethical teaching is also contained in the various commentaries on the tractate *Aboth* of the *Mishnah*. Almost every scholar of note found it necessary to write a commentary on this treatise. Besides those of Rashi, Maimonides and Bertinoro (Sect. 45), we possess commentaries by Menahem ha-Meiri (Sect. 43), Simon Duran, Joseph Ibn Nehemias, Joseph Yabetz, Moses Almoshnino, Judah Lirmah and others. Rabbi Samuel di Usida, resident of Safed in the sixteenth century and a disciple of Isaac Luria, the famous Kabbalist, wrote a commentary on the treatise entitled *Midrash Shemuel* which consists primarily of excerpts from numerous preceding commentaries. He thus preserved many passages from works which are no longer extant.

91. ETHICAL WILLS AND TESTAMENTS

The post-Classical period of Jewish literature is exceptionally rich in that species of ethical treatises, known as Wills and Testaments which were intended by the writers to impart instruction to their children in the conduct of life. Almost every scholar of note thought it his duty to leave to his children in addition to a portion of the goods of this world also some spiritual legacy, and the number of such testaments is accordingly considerable. We will, therefore, limit ourselves to such treatises which are important either on account of the fame of the writer or the excellence of instruction as well as the reflection of the conditions of life which they contain.

The earliest of such productions during this period are the ethical epistles of Moses ben Nahman (Sect. 42) or Nahmanides. As it is known, Nahmanides left Spain in 1267 for Palestine where he spent his last years. From there he kept up an active correspondence with his children, and several of his more lengthy epistles were left to posterity. The first is an epistle addressed to his oldest son, Nahman, in which he enjoins him to lead an ethical life. The letter reflects the deep piety and noble religious feeling of Nahmanides. He warns his son especially against the vices of anger and pride, for these are the sources of all sin, and admonishes him to acquire the virtue of humility. In teaching him the importance of this particular virtue, Nahmanides makes the following fine remark which reflects the pure love of fellow men. "Every man should seem in thine eyes as one greater than thyself. If he be wise or wealthy, it is thy duty to show him respect. If he be poor and thou the richer, or if thou be wiser than he, bethink thee in thy heart that thou art the more guilty, he the more innocent. If he sin, it is from error; if thou sin, it is from desire."[20] After completing his praise of the virtue of humility *(Anavah)*, the author urges his son to think of the presence of God, to study the Torah and to pray with religious fervor and without admixture of other thoughts.

The second epistle was sent to his younger son, Solomon, who seems to have been an official at the court of the king. It deals chiefly with the value of chastity. Nahmanides warns his son not to be en-

[20] Hebrew Ethical Wills, Ed. I. Abrahams, Vol. I, Phil., 1926, p. 97.

snared by the glamour of court life but to cling to purity of conduct. He also gives him a few rules of religious practice, namely to pray three times daily, to be careful in reciting the blessing before and after meals and always have with him a correct copy of the Pentateuch which he shall study diligently. Above all, he admonishes him to trust in God, for he says, "Know that thou art not master over thy works, nor hast thou power over thy hand, but everything is in the hand of God to do as He wills."

A very interesting testament is one written by the great Talmudic scholar, Asher ben Yehiel (Sect. 43). It is a fair sized treatise and bears various titles, such as *Sepher ha-Hanhagah* (The Book of Conduct) and *Orhoth Hayyim* (The Ways of Life). It is divided into two parts, the first, containing twenty-three sections, deals with various things, and especially with giving the tithe of all income for charity, the second containing one hundred and thirty-two short sections is devoted to general ethical and religious conduct. Rabbi Asher tells his children first to be amicable to all people, not to injure them in any way, whether in matters of money or by words. He next admonishes them to honor God, to trust rather in Him than to rely on the "broken reed" of human support, or to make gold their hope. He further warns them against evil speech and advises in general to weigh the words they utter, saying, "Esteem the utterance of thy money as of less import than the utterance of thy words."[21] Continuing to instruct his children in the art of life, Asher makes these remarks, "Look not at him who is above thee in riches but at him who is below. Turn thine eyes to thy superior not to thy inferior in the service and fear of God. Never be weary in making friends, but consider a single enemy as one too many."[22] He ends by admonishing his successors to be careful to give charity every day, though the sum be small and to observe the practice of tithe giving if they be rich, and further that they pay special attention to prayer. "Know," says he, "that prayer is the service of the heart. If thy child address thee and speak not from his heart, art thou not angry? How then shalt thou, insignificant man, act in the presence of the king of the universe?"[23]

Of an entirely different character, though permeated with noble sentiments of ethical duty and rational piety is the testament of the

[21] Ibid, p. 120.
[22] Ibid, p. 121.
[23] Ibid, p. 124.

philosopher and scientist, Joseph Ibn Kaspi (Sect. 75). The little treatise known by two names, *Sepher ha-Musar* (Book of Morality) and *Yore Deah* (The Teacher of Knowledge) was written by Kaspi in his fiftieth year (1332) during his wanderings in Spain in search of knowledge. It was addressed to his youngest son, Solomon, at Tarascon, Provence, who was only twelve years old at the time.

The work is divided into twenty short chapters and aims to present to his son a way of life which is pious, rational and ethical, and also a conception of Judaism which insists both on observance of the precepts and on pure belief in its principles. In the first four chapters, Kaspi tells of the fundamental principles of Judaism, that is to believe in one God and to love and fear Him as well as of the great importance of practice in Judaism, namely, the observance of the precepts. He illustrates the necessity of both belief and practice by drawing attention to the nature of man. "Know," says he, "that man is compounded of body and soul, and that the rational faculty which belongs to the soul is partly practical, partly speculative. Neither of these can exist without the other just as the soul can not exist without the body. For this reason, the Commandments are divided first into those which affect the well-being of the body and those which affect the well-being of the soul, and secondly, into the practical and the speculative."[24]

But while the observance of the precepts is of great importance, it is not necessary for every one to master the entire legal literature, so that he may be able to decide all ritual questions. He can, on occasion, consult the specialists of the law. It is different, though with matters of belief, according to Kaspi. Every Jew must not only believe in the principles of Judaism but understand them by means of proof and logical reasoning. He, therefore, urges his son to attain this conception of Judaism through study of the philosophical books, especially the Metaphysics of Aristotle and the *Guide* of Maimonides. The study of these books, however, he advises him to reserve for a more mature age, namely after he reaches twenty. For the present, he outlines the following program of education. For two years until the age of fourteen, he should devote his entire time to the study of Bible and Talmud. From fourteen to sixteen, he recommends the pursuit of diverse studies, namely to devote some time to the review of what he had previously studied, but the greater part of the time,

[24] Ibid, p. 133.

he should give to mathematics and ethics. For the study of the former, he recommends Euclid's Elements, Al-Fragani's Astronomy, and Ibn Ezra's book of Numbers; for that of the latter, the Book of Proverbs, Ecclesiastes, The Sayings of the Fathers with the commentary of Maimonides, also the first book of his Code and Aristotle's Nichomachean Ethics. During the following two years, namely from sixteen to eighteen, he urges him to divide his time between the study of Jewish law and logic. He recommends for the former, the Compendium of Al-Fasi, the Codes of Maimonides and Moses of Coucy (Semag) and as for logic, he promises to compose for him a compendium of that science. The next two years, Kaspi advises to devote to the study of physics, besides the continuance of the previous studies and from twenty on to enter upon the study of philosophy and theology.

The second half of the book, from chapter XI to XX is devoted to a defense of the study of philosophy against those men of his time who considered such study heretical and incompatible with complete observance of the Jewish religion. Kaspi shows that not only is philosophy not antagonistic to religion but that it really offers proof for the truth of its principles, and that many of the philosophical books are only an exposition and justification of the precepts of the Torah. In these chapters, he admits that the study of the Talmud and the Codes is of great importance, but he polemizes against those who say that this should form the only subject of interest to Jews. He claims that only the rabbis should specialize in the decision of the law, but that other people may deem the study of the nature of God or His attributes as important as a decision concerning a point of the dietary laws. As for rules of conduct in other ways of life besides study, Kaspi among other things urges his son to marry a woman of good family, beautiful in form and character, but not to pay any regard to money, and especially warns him against greed and pursuit of wealth. He even concludes the epistle with a four line poem against this vice containing a pun on his name Kaspi (Silver) which reads as follows:

From thy yearning after thy silver comes thy wrath
Never does this care leave thee, till it make an end of thee.
Yet, will it be thy comrade when thou goest to thy grave?
Or will it be a help unto thee in the distress that then befalls?[25]

[25] Ibid, p. 161.

The testament of Judah ben Asher (1270-1349), who succeeded his great father in the rabbinate of Toledo is of great interest from many points of view. Besides the ethical instruction it imparts, it also contains a number of important historical data. It is logically divided into three parts, though not actually so. In the first part or introduction, Judah tells of his own life, relates certain episodes of his childhood, his wanderings from Germany to France and other countries, the ultimate settlement in Toledo and of his succession to the position of his father. With humility, he tells us that his knowledge is not great, for on account of defective eyesight, he was unable to study, and that he accepted the rabbinical position with reluctance.

The second part contains the ethical instruction proper. He admonishes his children first of all to fear God and think Him present always, and warns them not to indulge in the pleasures of the body. "For though," he says, "food to man is like oil to a lamp; if it have much it shines, if little it is quenched, yet it is sooner extinguished by redundancy than by deficiency of oil." He next urges them to study the Torah assiduously, and not to think that its knowledge will come to them without travail as a heritage from their ancestors. He especially urges his sons to study the Bible with commentaries and the Hebrew grammar, and not to neglect these studies as he had done in his youth. After this, he turns to conduct in life and inculcates the avoidance of the four cardinal vices, lying, scoffing, flattery and slander. As an illustration of the importance of the virtue of truthfulness, he tells a pointed story. There was a sinner who upon regretting his evil deeds, came to a sage and asked for an easy road to repentance. The latter answered, "Keep thyself from lying." The man went out gleefully thinking that he will be able to continue his former conduct and yet be considered righteous. He planned a theft, according to his wont, but then he bethought himself; if any one inquires whither goest thou, if I tell the truth, I shall be caught; if I answer falsely, I shall transgress the order of the sage. And thus it was with all offences, and as a result, he became completely reformed.

He further warns them to beware of pride and to honor all men, for thus they will be honored themselves. He illustrates the value of his virtue by another beautiful story. A sage was asked, "Why dost thou honor all men?" He replied, "I have never come across one in whom I failed to recognize superiority over myself, therefore have I shown him respect. Were he older, I said he has done more good than I; were he richer, I said he has been more charitable; were he younger, I said I have sinned more; were he poorer, I said he has suffered more; were he wiser, I honored him for his wisdom; were he not wiser, I said his fault is the lighter."[26]

The third part tells of the management of his finances and contains an elaborate scheme for the distribution of charity. Judah figures up the entire sum he received as compensation from the community as rabbi during the twenty-three years and expresses his desire that this sum be entirely spent for charity and the support of the Torah. He deducts from it a tenth which, in accordance with the custom in the Asheri family, he had already given to charity, and as a return for the other nine-tenths of his salary spent for the support of his children, he dedicates his library to the use of students. Of the rest of his estate, he leaves for each of his children only one hundred gold pieces and assigns two thousand pieces to be used in business of which both the principal and profit should be applied towards a dowry for his youngest daughter, Dora. The residue he dedicates as a foundation fund for the support of any of his children who should devote himself to scholarship, or in case no child of his own did so, to the support of any other scholars. The testament also contains an agreement entered into by the children and grandchildren of Asher to maintain the ancient custom of the family of giving tithes from all income for charity.

We have also a testament by Jacob ben Asher, the famous author of the Code (Sect. 57). It is primarily devoted to injunctions concerning carefulness in observance of ceremonies, but it is also permeated with a spirit of deep piety together with noble spirituality. Among the points to be noted in this testament are Jacob's urgence to love God to the degree of being ready to undergo martyrdom if necessary, to study the Talmud assidiously but not waste time in casuistry, and finally, not to heed dreams or omens but trust in God implicitly. On the last point, Jacob is very detailed. He asks his children not to inquire of fortune tellers nor to cast lots nor attempt to pry into the future in any other manner, for the resort to such means is due to a lack of faith in God.

Very charactersitic of the type of life of the Jews of Germany in the fourteenth century and of the noble sentiments prevailing among them is the testament of Eliezer ben Samuel ha-Levi (d.1357) of Mayence. Eliezer ha-Levi was neither rabbi nor head of an academy

[26] Ibid, Vol. II, p. 178.

but an ordinary scholarly layman, and Israel Abrahams rightly characterizes his testament as an expression of "The Ideals of the Average Jew." He admonishes his children to observe carefully their daily prayers, to study every day, to deal honestly with all people, gentiles and Jews alike, to talk sparingly, to give a tithe of their wealth to charity, and in general not to refuse the request of any poor man. His daughters he enjoins to be modest and to honor their husbands. He further entreats his children, sons and daughters, to live in large Jewish communities so that their children may obtain the proper Jewish education. The children must get instruction in the Torah, Eliezer says, even if the parents be compelled to solicit the money for tuition from others. He continues to impart instruction in all ways of life, namely to prepare early for the Sabbath, and not indulge in card playing nor in dances nor in any other frivolities. He enjoins them to be tolerant and humble; not to be quarrelsome and to seek peace even at the expense of suffering a loss of money or an insult; not to pursue wealth and to be content with what they possess. He finally advises his descendants to eat and drink moderately, to conduct the household expenses in orderly fashion, for according to a wise saying, "Method in expenditure is half a sufficiency"; and to dress in nice and clean clothes as well as to keep their houses clean. He concludes the testament with several personal requests, not to deliver any funeral orations for him, to wash his body in a scrupulously clean manner, just as he himself used to do on Friday afternoons before going to the synagogue, and to bury him at his father's side. Regarding the last request, he remarks, "If the space be a little narrow, I am sure that he loves me well enough to make room for me by his side." These words are undoubtedly naive but express a deep elemental human sentiment.

Equally characteristic of the type of life led by the Jews of the South of Europe in the fourteenth and the fifteenth centuries is the ethical will of a layman of the Provence, Solomon ben Isaac. The will is divided into two parts, the first containing a list of regulations which he drew up for his own conduct, and the second a number of instructions to his children. Among the regulations which he observed were the following: not to eat before he has studied one page of the Talmud as long as he enjoys good health; not to eat at one meal more than one course of meat or not more than two courses altogether; not to swear by the name of God; not to curse any man in His name; and to rise every night to praise the Almighty and to supplicate for His mercy.

For an omission of any of these or other rules laid down by him, Solomon fixed a penalty either in the form of giving an extra sum for charity or in abstaining from drinking wine or eating meat on that day. He also ordered for himself the distribution of charity, namely to give for this purpose one peseta from all purchases he makes for the household if price of such amount to ten ducats. Again, for every bird or a load of wood to give a peseta (pashut) if the price be one ducat. He also determined that if he should live to see his sons married he would urge them to give one percent from the dowry they receive to charity. These and other rules he lays down for his children to follow.

In the second part, he enjoins the sons that each always have a table in his house with a volume or two of the Talmud on it, so that he may read it when he comes home. Further, he asks that they be modest, merciful and charitable, that they train their children in the study of the Torah, and that each strive that at least one of his descendants devote his whole life to study.

From the sixteenth century on, we note in the testaments that have come down to us the influence of mystic or Kabbalisic teachings. The most important wills written during these centuries are those of Abraham, Jacob and Sabbatai or Sheftal Hurwitz. Abraham was the father of Isaiah Hurwitz, the famous Talmudic scholar, Kabbalist, and author of the *Shenē Luhoth ha-Brith,* (the Two Tablets of the Law), and Sheftal the son of the latter, (d. 1660). Jacob, the writer of one of the testaments was the brother of Isaiah. The testament of Abraham bears the title of *Yesh Nohalin* (Some Inherit) borrowed from the name of the eighth chapter of the Talmudic tractate *Baba Bathra,* dealing with the laws of inheritance. He writes in the opening lines as follows: "Some inherit and bequeath their children wealth and property. I have nothing to offer but a rule of righteousness and guidance in the fear of God." He then goes on in eighteen chapters to instruct his children in all the details of life. His teachings are permeated with a spirit of asceticism and mysticism but tempered with sentiments of piety and ethics.

Jacob did not really write a separate testament but merely lengthy glosses and additions to that of his father's will. These glosses amount to fifty-two and at the end, he tells his children to read both testaments, his and his father's twice a year on the eve of the New Year and the eve of the Day of Atonement.

Sheftal's will is a more elaborate affair. It consists of an introduction and twenty-nine sections. In the introduction, he tells the story and the genealogy of his family both on his father's and mother's side. He apologizes for this act and says "I did not give these details out of pride to show of what great men I am a descendant but because in these turbulent times (the period of 1648, Cossack persecutions), it is meet that you should know definitely to what family you belong." He then continues to outline a way of life, warning against all vices, anger, envy, hatred and slander, and urges the practice of the virtues of peace and generosity, and especially the giving of tithe for charity. He finally draws up a course of study for the sons. He admonishes them to study for study's sake *(Torah Lishmah),* to be versed in the *Mishnah,* and to know the twenty-four books of the Bible with commentaries, to learn *Gemarah* with the commentary of the *Tosofoth,* and master the Hebrew grammar. Only after they have attained a thorough knowledge of the Talmud, Bible and Codes, does he advise them to turn to the study of the Kabbala.

A number of such ethical wills have been preserved for us from the eighteenth century. The earliest of these are two testaments, one by Jonah Landsofer (Scribe of Sacred Scrolls) written in 1710, and the other by his contemporary and friend, Moses Hassid. Landsofer lays down as the great principle in life, "That the purpose of man's creation is the service of God." He says further, "Of that service, the root is fixed in man's innermost being with the heart as the watchman over it. Prayer in the highest sense is this heart service, a complete absorption which no preoccupation invades." He advises his children to recite several extra prayers in Judaeo-German which should contain supplication for those needs which are most urgently felt. It is this special emphasis on prayer which presages some of the Hassidic teachings.

Moses Hassid's will is permeated by the Kabbalistic teachings of Isaac Luria (Sect. 118). He emphasizes the observances of ritual ablution and prayer and warns against a state of gloom, all in accordance with the theories of Luria whom he quotes frequently.

Examples of all-embracing piety expressing complete subjection to God and of noble love for fellow beings are two testaments hailing from the latter half of the century, one by Alexander Sueskind (d. 1794) and the other by Joel ben Abraham Shemariah (d. 1799). The first on account of his acceptance of the vicissitudes of life with an attitude of *Gamzu le-Tobah* (This, too, is for good) was nicknamed like an early Tannaitic sage, *Ish Gamzu.* His will bubbles with optimism. He tells his children to accept the kingship and lordship of God with joy and glee, and that they should be ready to undergo martyrdom cheerfully. He further mentions his own practices which should serve them as a pattern, namely that he always thanked God with great joy for all happenings, good or bad. Next to the love of God, he says is the love of man which he admonishes them to observe with the utmost care at all costs and sacrifices.

Joel ben Abraham Shemariah who lived in Wilna was a scholarly layman. His testament breathes the purest type of ethics. He emphasizes only two precepts *(Mitzvoth),* love of fellow man and the sanctity of the Sabbath. Regarding the first, he says, "It was oft my way at assemblies to raise my eyes and regard those present from end to end, to see whether in sooth I loved every one among them, whether my acceptance of the duty to love my fellow man was genuine. With God's help, I found indeed that I loved all present. Even if I noticed one who had treated me improperly, then, without a thought of hesitation, without a moment's delay, I pardoned him and forthwith I resolved to love him. If my heart forced me to refuse my love, I addressed him with spoken words of friendship until my heart became attuned to my words."[27] Such a remarkable passage breathing the purest love of fellow man is hardly paralleled in the ethical literature of the world.

To this century belong also the testaments of Israel Baal Shem Tob, founder of Hassidism, and Elijah, Gaon of Wilna, but these will be discussed later in connection with the delineation of their characters.

C. Philosophic Exegesis

92. *GENERAL REMARKS*

The species of literature known as philosophic exegesis, which had already made its appearance in the Classical period (Vol. I, Sect. 179), had developed to a much greater extent during the period under discussion. The spread of philosophic ideas among the masses of intelligent Jews necessitated a new kind of interpretation of the Bible in accordance with the intellectual ideas in vogue. Accordingly, there

[27] Hebrew Ethical Wills, Ed. I. Abrahams, Vol. II, p. 346.

arose people who specialized in this particular field and composed works which dealt exclusively with this kind of interpretation.

We must, however, distinguish between two kinds of philosophic exegesis, one of a simple and systematic nature and the other of a complex and loose character. To the first type belong the commentaries on the Bible, such as those of Gersonides and Abrabanel and others which aimed primarily to explain the Scriptures in a systematic and orderly manner but also to inject, whenever necessary, a philosophic interpretation of a certain passage or parts of the Bible (Ch. II).

To the other type belong books, the primary aim of which is not to explain the Bible chapter by chapter, but either to interpret such passages as in their plain meaning contradict philosophic views concerning certain subjects, e. g. creation, so as to remove the contradictions, or to elicit certain philosophic truths from the Bible itself. This kind of exegesis is topical by nature and borders more on homiletics than exegesis. In fact, the contents of the works were originally delivered as discourses in synagogues and later collected in books. This was to a great extent stimulated by the use of similar methods in the Church during the thirteenth century. The forced interpretation of many parts of the Old Testament by the Scholastics found its echo in the synagogue.

The underling motive of all these books was the striving of every philosopher in Jewry from Philo on to harmonize the teachings of the Bible with those of philosophy. Yet, there were great differences between these harmonizers and consequently between their methods. Some there were whose philosophy exceeded their piety, and who did not despise any means, even twisting and distorting the passage of the Scriptures in the most atrocious manner in order to make the Bible conform to their views. Some were more moderate and affected a middle course, while some were more pious than philosophic, and their aim was to elicit the philosophic truths of the Torah and show that they conduce to happiness and enlightenment. But even to accomplish this more moderate aim, a good deal of interpretation had to be done and much energy had to be spent in order to make the words of the Bible say things different from the plain meaning. Consequently, allegory was used by all three classes of interpreters in different degrees. The extremists applied alleogry to a great extent, at times disregarding the *Peshat* entirely, saying that certain passages have only an allegorical meaning. The others used allegory as an aid to an understanding of the Bible, merely saying that it has different possible meanings. This, however, was an axiom with all interpreters, mystics as well as rationalists. It is even stated in the Talmud (Yer. Talmud, Sanhederin Ch. IV) that there are forty-nine phases to the Bible, and later Agadic sources increased them to seventy.

The structure of these books is not only topical but loose. Being of homiletic origin, the preachers or the holders of the discourses did not limit themselves to the Biblical passages to which the topic of the discourse was attached but interpreted also other passages found in the Scriptures either in prophetic books or the Hagiographa. Very often, they connected their interpretations with Midrashic passages and endeavored to prove that the Agadists held the same views. Thus the line between exegesis and homiletics was entirely obliterated.

Many of the books of the more radical type of philosophic exegesis were lost and are known only by excerpts or through statements by their opponents regarding their teachings. The works of the other type are too numerous to be discussed in detail, and we will, therefore, limit ourselves to a few important specimens of this literature.

93. SAMUEL IBN TIBBON'S EXEGETIC WORKS

The earliest of the works on philosophic exegesis during the thirteenth century was Samuel Ibn Tibbon's book *Yiḳowu ha-Mayyim* (Let the Waters Be Gathered). The book deals with the problem of creation and aims to interpret the first chapters in Genesis. It was inspired by a question asked of the author by a fellow philosopher. The question touches upon the nature of the two elements, water and earth and is as follows: Since we know according to the physics of the day that each element strives towards its appointed place, such as fire towards the upper regions and earth towards the downward, and that the lighter element is always above the heavier, why then do not the waters cover the entire surface of the earth, and how can there be any dry land? This question which was a frequent subject of discussion with the Arabic philosophers troubled Ibn Tibbon for a long time. Of course, he was aware that from the point of view of the Bible, it could be answered simply that God changed the nature of the elements and ordered the waters to recede even against their nature, as it is said, "Let the waters be gathered" (Gen. I, 9). But upon analysis, it is not so simple as that. We assume that God fixed the order of nature; how then was it disturbed right there and then? The answer to this question really involves a complete explanation of the process of creation which is told in a cryptic manner in the first chapter of Genesis. Ibn Tibbon sets out to do so, but he is involved in many difficulties, for chapter CIV in Psalms offers a different view of the order of creation. This chapter is then explained. Again, passages in Midrash *Bereshith* (Genesis) *Rabba* offer some difficulties. Furthermore, the question of angels is inherently involved with that of creation, for the angels or the separate intelligences had some part in the creation of the world. This question leads to the explanation of the visions of Isaiah (Ch. VI, 1-10) and of Ezekiel's *Merkabah*. Thus, the author is involved from topic to topic and from interpretation to interpretation. The result is that the questions of creation, function of angels, Divine Providence and even the question of Job are discussed and explained, while the original question is almost lost sight of, though not entirely neglected. We have then a book of twenty-two chapters dealing with Divine subjects instead of an answer to a question which could be condensed into a chapter or two. But this was really the aim, namely the discussion of many problems and the exposition of numerous passages. The question served the author as a pretext for offering his various discussions. In this book, Ibn Tibbon makes a moderate use of allegory.

94. *THE ALLEGORISTS*

We do not know the exact time of the origin of the school of exegetical allegorists, nor who was the founder of that school, but we do know that during the second half of the thirteenth century, there existed in Provence a school of Jewish philosophers who interpreted the Bible in an extreme allegorical manner. In the few works that are left to us by authors who were supposed to belong to that school, the tendency to allegory is quite in evidence, but not in the extreme measure described by the opponents of the allegorists.

The movement aroused great opposition in pious circles and caused the issuance of a second ban against the study of philosophy by Solomon ben Adret (Sect. 42) as well as a division in Jewry. The polemic literature which was produced as a result of this strife will be discussed in the proper place (Ch. X). Here we are only interested in the method of exegesis of these allegorists.

From the writings of the opponents, we learn both of the numerous adherents of the school as well as the content of their exegesis. These exegetes concentrated their attention primarily upon the narrative part of the Bible and allegorized it completely. They were not satisfied with interpreting the first chapters in Genesis allegorically, such as the story of the fall, to say that the snake symbolized passion, and the woman, matter or the passive intellect, while Adam stands for reason, but they extended their allegorical exegesis also to the historical part. Thus they are reported to have interpreted Abraham and Sarah as symbolizing form and matter, Isaac and Rebecca the active and passive intellects. Some said that the twelve sons of Jacob stand for the twelve constellations, others that they symbolize the forces of the soul. Thus, Leah represents the faculty of sensation and feeling, her six children the five senses and the common sense. Again the battle of the four kings against the five (Genesis, Ch. XIV) is explained as a battle of the various forces of the soul. Even the life of Moses did not escape their allegorization. By Bathya (daughter of Pharaoh) is meant the active reason which drew Moses out from the river of errors; Jethro, his father-in-law who has seven daughters again represents reason, and the seven daughters are the seven sciences. They even extended their explanation to some of the miracles and the vestments of the high priests. They attempted to rationalize the stopping of the sun by Joshua, and the oracle of the *Urim we-Tumim* borne by the high priest by saying that he put in his vestment an astrolabe and was thus able to observe the conjunction of the constellations and foretell the future. These and many more things are quoted in their name. It is not known definitely whether the allegorists really believed that the passages in the Bible meant nothing else but these allegories, or that they considered them as another phase of the meaning of the passages besides the plain meaning of the words.

The only book of the school extant is the *Malmad* (The Pointer) by Jacob Anatoli, the famous translator (Sept. 74). It is a collection of discourses arranged according to the portions of the week, where passages from each portion are topically explained in a philosophic manner. The extreme allegorical method is absent, and ethical teachings are elucidated. The book was held in some esteem, for Isaac Aboab quoted it in his *Lamp.* It is interesting to note that though such extreme allegorization undoubtedly was very harmful and aroused great opposition, no attempt was ever made by the opponents to put under ban the writers of such books. There was certainly a fair measure of freedom of thought given in Spanish and Provence Jewry to writers and scholars during the thirteenth century.

95. *ISAAC ARAMA'S AKEDAH*

Probably the most important book of philosophic exegesis is the work by Isaac Arama (1440-1505), entitled *'Akedath Yitzhak*, literally the Sacrifice of Isaac, but the title was used by the author in the original linguistic sense of the root *Akad* (to bind) and meaning The Compilation of Isaac. Isaac Arama was a famous Talmudic scholar and preacher of his day. He first lived at Zamora in the province of Leon, Spain, but later was invited to occupy the rabbinical post at Tarragona in the kingdom of Aragon where for some time he headed an academy. There, influenced by the practice of Christian preachers to hold learned and philosophic discourses, he began to do likewise, and it is these sermons which form the basis of this work. From Tarragona, he was called to Kallatayud in the same kingdom where he stayed until the expulsion. It is not definitely known whither he went after he left Spain, but it is surmised that he settled together with other exiles at Salonika, Turkey, and that he died there.

In the introduction Arama states the motive for the writing of the book and its purpose. There are many commentaries on the Bible, he says, but all these do not satisfy the need for the proper understanding of the contexts of the Torah. They deal mostly with the explanation of words and passages and merely give the plain meaning of the stories and precepts. They do not bring out the full teachings of the Bible in a philosophic light. The need for such understanding, he continues, is especially urgent in this country (Aragon) where the Christian preachers, many of them very learned, expound the doctrines of their faith as well as the words of the Bible in a philosophic and scholarly manner, and the Jews who often listen to their preaching, desire that their rabbis should do likewise. He, therefore, undertook to remedy this defect by writing the *'Akedah* which aims to draw out the deeper meaning of the precepts, as well as those of the narratives.

He tells us that he devoted many years to the preparation of the work as he had studied all the previous commentaries, had delved into the mysteries of the Midrashic passages which explain the Bible, had also sifted the books on philosophy both moral and political, and selected such doctrines as he deemed proper. These he included in his discourses and joined them together with his own remarks into one harmonious work.

Each discourse in the book contains two parts, one the discourse proper where stress is laid upon the general thought or doctrine deduced from the passage or portion of the Bible, and the other which aims to explain the meaning of the section in an exegetical way. The first is called *Drishah* (Discoursing), and the second *Prishah* (Commentating). The lines between the two, however, are not drawn fast, for sometimes the exegesis does not follow the discoursing but is included in it. As the book was primarily arranged according to discourses, it is divided into one hundred and five portals or chapters, each containing a complete discourse. These portals follow the order of the weekly readings of the Bible (Sidroth). To readings from the earlier parts of Genesis and Exodus more than one discourse is devoted, but the readings from the later parts of these books as well as those from the other books are, as a rule, included in one discourse. The discourses are topical, that is, a certain passage is selected containing a topic for discussion and this is expounded and analyzed at great length until the teaching is brought out clearly. Weekly readings which offer more than one topic for discussion contain, as said, several discourses.

The method usually followed by Arama in the exegetical part of the discourse and at times even in the entire discourse is like the one used by Isaac Abrabanel in his commentary on the Bible (Sect. 20), namely the placing of a series of doubts or difficulties at the beginning of the chapter, and then, in the process of explanation, solving them one by one. The general method of the book is the homiletic one, that is, subjects are joined to each other not in a strict scientific manner but in a loose way; not only are the Biblical passages placed at the head of the discourse expounded, but many other passages in the Bible are involved as well as Midrashic statements which come within the purview of the discussion. Likewise, subjects which are ancillary to the main topic are elucidated and explained, and as a result, the discourse is often expanded to the size of a small book. This however does not impair the value of the work, for the wealth of exegesis, information and elucidation does not bewilder the skillful student who knows how to pilot his way through the intellectual labyrinth.

The discourses deal with topics of great value for the understanding of religion and ethics in general and Judaism in particular. Arama who was inclined to philosophy endeavors to present the teachings of Judaism in a philosophic light as much as possible, but never at the expense of religion. To him, the truth of the Torah comes first, that of philosophy second. He believes like many Jewish scholars that there are several phases to the meaning of all parts of the Torah including the narratives, and he, therefore, interprets the stories allegoricolly. But the allegorical interpretations by no means vitiate in any way the truth of the plain meaning of these narratives. This view enabled him to enlarge the scope of his topics and discuss subjects of great importance for all classes of Jews, the liberal as well as the deeply pious. Some of his discourses deal with the definition of the soul (in connection with the creation of man), with the symbolic meaning of paradise and the four rivers (Gen. II, 8-15) which point to the faculties of the soul and its activities, with the harmony between the world (Macrocosm) and man (microcosm), which two he believes to be like two musical instruments attuned to one scale. Other discourses treat of the necessity for man to be diligent in his work, as otherwise the Divine Providence extended to him will be deficient; with the conception of prophecy; with the idea that life according to the Torah must be based upon a happy family life and the observance of justice in the state; with freedom of the will; with the value of the Sabbath and many other problems.

His view of the Sabbath deserves to be summarized. Arama derives from the Sabbath his theory of dogmas. There are, according to him, three fundamental dogmas in Judaism: belief in the creation of the world, in the Torah, in the world to come, i. e. reward and punishment. All three are included in the Sabbath. It teaches creation, for it signifies the cessation of God's creative act and it follows that it must have begun. It further teaches us the value and validity of the Torah by the fact that the Sabbath is set aside as a day of spirituality devoted to the study of the Torah, and finally, it symbolizes the world to come, for just as the Sabbath is the day of rest which comes at the end of a week of work and constant movement, so will the world to come be the great day of rest following the life of man which is full of change and constant motion. This world to come will be the real and true *Sabbath*.

Arama illustrates the teachings of Judaism by many parallels from general ethics, science and politics which show his wide reading and great versatility of knowledge. The *Akedah* enjoyed great popularity during the ages, and was drawn upon by generations of preachers for philosophic data and religious teachings.

Chapter VI

SCIENCE

96. *GENERAL FEATURES*

The post-Classical period in Jewish literature which, as we have seen, was distinguished by great productivity in the field of philosophy and theology, was likewise noted for a prolific literary activity in the field of science. In general, the lines between philosophy and science were never drawn fast, either in the ancient or in the Mediaeval world, as there was no tendency towards specialization, and research and investigation on the part of the savants included the entire scale of the various kinds of knowledge. The Greek philosophers were also mathematicians, and Aristotle was not only the greatest philosopher but the father of several sciences, notably that of zoology. The leading Arabic philosophers were likewise profound scientists, such as Avicenna who was considered throughout the entire Mediaeval period the master of medicine. In fact, the term philosophy was interpreted to connote all types of knowledge systematically arranged, and the various sciences were considered only as branches of philosophy, thus, physics was the philosophy of nature, and medicine a branch of physics.

The Jewish philosophers were, of course, no exception. They, like their Mohammedan or Christian colleagues included the sciences in their range of study, and as a result, we find that the same people who were famed as philosophers also shone as leaders of science and enriched the scientific literature with their works just as they had done in the field of philosophy. And when the great activity of translation began, and the masters of both languages, Arabic and Hebrew undertook, in response to popular demand, to transfer the accumulated knowledge of the Arabs into Hebrew, it was not limited in its scope, but included all branches of knowledge. The same hands which busied themselves with translating the philosophic works of Aristotle or Averroes also translated books on astronomy, mathematics and medicine written either by the same authors or by others. It was not long, therefore, before the number of books in Hebrew which deal with the various sciences had increased until it reached into the hundreds covering every field of human knowledge.

The scientific activity, however, grew not only in extensiveness but also in intensity, for the spread of knowledge brought about a deeper and more penetrating insight into its principles. Not only were the Jewish scientists active as translators of Arabic books, but also as commentators of these works, and ultimately as writers of original treatises on the same subjects. It must be admitted though, that with the exception of a few works by Gersonides and Jacob ben Makir which were really contributions to the astronomy of their day, the originality of the other books written by Jews on the various sciences is not very great. Most of them consist of restatements of the theories and principles current in the general works of the day.

The sciences that flourished mostly among the Jews during the period were mathematics, astronomy and medicine. The first two were cultivated both from a pure scientific motive and for a religious purpose, for they were closely connected with the fixation of the calendar, and the determination of certain problems discussed in the Talmud. It is true that by the beginning of the thirteenth century the calendar was well fixed, and any further discussion of the subject was quite unnecessary, yet the Jewish scholars were not satisfied with a mere set of data, but wanted to investigate the very principles upon which the calculation of the calendar was based. A knowledge of astronomy and of mathematics was considered not only an ornament for an accomplished scholar but a very necessity. Hence, there arose the great interest in these sciences and the multiplicity of books on the subjects. Medicine was studied primarily for a practical purpose, for, as is well known, the Jews served as physicians to kings and popes, and medicine was the most favored profession among them. Yet, in spite of that, the Hebrew medical literature offers very few books which can be considered a real contribution to that science.

The lack of originality, however, can be explained to a certain extent by the fact that even the general scientific literature displays very few works of an original stamp. Almost the entire science of the period, from the twelfth to the fifteenth century, consists in constant restatements by the Christian scholars in bulky Latin volumes of the theories of the Arabic savants of an earlier generation, with some additions of their own. The Jews, therefore, could hardly do better.

The principal reason, though, for the absence of real contributions to science among them is the fact that they lacked permanent institutions dedicated to the cultivation of such knowledge. With the possible exception of a Jewish medical college at Montpelier in the Provence, the existence of which is surmised by some scholars, the Jews had no universities. Study was primarily done in an individual and auto-didactic way. It is only from the fifteenth century on that we have any record of Jewish students attending general universities. If we add to this the insecurity of their position, the constant expulsions and massacres to which the Jews were subjected, we should rather wonder at what had been accomplished than demand still greater things from these lovers of knowledge who left us an extensive literature in all branches of science while working in the shadow of death and persecution.

The value of this literature and the contribution of the Jews in the Mediaeval Ages to the progress of science should, however, by no means be minimized. It formed a very important link in the scientific literature of the world. Through it passed the wisdom of the East to the West and vice versa the knowledge of the West to the East, for many were the Latin works of European scholars that were rendered into Hebrew and thus carried to the farthest corners of the world. It brought the Jewish mind to the cognizance of the great world, as many of the Hebrew books were translated into Latin and thus became a part of European civilization.

The centers of the scientific literary activity during the first two centuries were like those of philosophic literature: Provence, Italy and northern Spain. In the later period, that is from the fifteenth century on when it began to decline, it had no particular center, but sporadic efforts at scientific productivity were made in many countries, Germany, Austria, Turkey, Poland, and chiefly Italy. Most of the translations made during the earlier period were made from the Arabic. But soon the scholars of Provence and Italy and even of Spain became conversant with Latin, and translations from that language began to appear and gradually increased until they finally equaled those made from the Arabic. The works of Italian scholars and those of the later period were primarily influenced by the European sciences, especially after the Renaissance. It is to be noted, however, that though the Copernican system gradually gained ground during the fifteenth century and was finally accepted after the time of Galileo, it did not produce the corresponding change in Jewish astronomical literature. With the exception of Joseph Solomon del Medigo, a disciple of Galileo, most of the other scientists still clung to the Ptolemaic or geocentric conception of the universe, and even del Medigo hesitated about accepting the new view though he was quite conversant with its principles. Such is the power of tradition.

The following survey can not, of course, enter into an analysis of the content of the books nor even give an adequate conception of the very extensive branch of literature but merely mark its high lights and the most prominent books.

97. *TRANSLATIONS*

The activity of translation went on, as stated, for almost two centuries, and during this time at least, all the important scientific books in Arabic and a good portion of the unimportant ones were rendered into Hebrew. Likewise, an exceedingly large number of Latin books was translated and made accessible to the Hebrew reader. It seems that the work of translation was not coordinated. Each scholar exercised his own judgment in the selection of the books for translation, and as communication between the scholars of the various countries or even between those residing in the same country was not regular, it often happened that the same books were translated several times either by contemporaneous scholars or by savants of different generations. It is thus that we possess, as a rule, several translations of the standard books in the sciences of mathematics, astronomy and medicine.

The leading translators of the scientific books were the same men who carried on the work of translation in philosophy. Moses Ibn Tibbon, Jacob ben Makir, Jacob Anatoli, Kalonymos ben Kalonymos and also lesser lights rendered great service in translating one standard scientific book after another.

In the three leading sciences, mathematics, astronomy and medicine which occupy the bulk of the mass of translated scientific literature, we have the following classical works.

(i) Mathematics and Astronomy

Of the works of Archimedes, we have the book "Concerning the Sphere and Cylinder," translated by Kalonymos ben Kalonymos under the name of *b'Kadur we-be Itztavana* and his Measurement of the Circle, translated anonymously entitled *be-Meshihath ha-Agulah.* Of Euclid's Elements, we have several versions, the principal one being by Moses Ibn Tibbon. Almost all the versions bear the titles *Yesodoth* or *Sheroshim Shel Iklidas* (The Elements or Principles of Euclid, Iklidas being the Arabic form of Euclid). One of the versions, however, bears the name *Mishnoth Iklidas.* Besides the Elements, there are also translations of his Data and his Optics. The first was translated by Jacob ben Makir and is entitled *Sepher ha-Matanoth* (Book of Data). The translation of the second is an anonymous one. To the works of pure mathematics, we have to add the translation of an algebra composed by a leading Arabic mathematician, Abu-Kamil Schadja. It was rendered into Hebrew by Mordecai Finzi (d. 1375) under the title *Tahbuloth Hokmat ha-Mispar* (Schemes of the Science of Numbers).

The number of books dealing with astronomy and its various phases is exceedingly large. The most important of these are, first the Almagest by Ptolemy, the Bible of the astronomers in the Mediaeval Ages, translated by Jacob Anatoli, second the various compendia of this book as well as an introduction to it. The same Anatoli translated two compendia of the Almagest, one by the Arabic astronomer, Al-Fragani (883) and one by Averroes under the titles *Yesodoth ha-Tekunah* (The Elements of Astronomy), and *Kitzur Almagest* (The Compendium of the Almagest) respectively. Moses Ibn Tibbon rendered into Hebrew, Geminus' *Isagoge* or introduction to the Almagest under the name *Hokmath ha-Kokabim* (The Science of the Stars). A similar work by the famous Arabic astronomer, Al-Bitrugi (Al-Petragius) was also translated by Ibn Tibbon and entitled *Hokmath ha-Tekunah* (The Science of Astronomy). Jacob ben Makir rendered into Hebrew the astronomical works of Ibn Al-Heitam and that of Costa ben Luka on the Globe, naming them *Sepher ha-Tekunah* and *Sepher ha-Galgal* (The Book of the Construction and the Book of the Globe) respectively. Kalonymos ben Kalonymos translated several books of Ptolemy and three works of Al-Kindi, namely on Nativity, an astrological work (Iggereth be-Molodoth), on Moisture and Rain (Iggereth be-Lahuth Ube-Matar) and on the Causes of Rain (Iggereth ha-Geshem). To the most famous books translated from the Latin belongs the popular *Sphera Mundi* (The Sphere of the World), a text book on spherical astronomy written by John Hollywood (d. 1256). The book was translated by Solomon ben Abigdor (1378) under the name of *Mareh ha-Ophanim* (The Aspect of the Spheres). At the end of the book, there is a figure of the globe with a short commentary on its construction. The translation was in great demand by the Hebrew students of astronomy and was later supplied with notes and commentaries.

(ii) Medicine

The Jewish scholars were, of course, greatly interested in the translation of medical works into Hebrew, but it seems that the interest in this particular science was not as keen as that in mathematics and astronomy, and the numbers of translations is not, therefore, as large as in the field of the former sciences. Yet, there is hardly an important book in the medical literature of the entire Mediaeval period, in Arabic or in Latin which was not translated into Hebrew. The greatest attention was, of course, given to the medical classics, the works of Hippocrates, Galen, Rhazes and Avicenna.

Almost all the works of Hippocrates known to the Arabs were rendered into Hebrew by various men. Among them are the books (a) on Diagnosis (ha-Kdomath ha-Yediah) most probably by Nathan ha-Meati of Italy; (b) on Severe Diseases (Hanhogoth ha-Holoyyim ha-Hadim); (c) on Air, Water and Places (be-Avirim Meimoth We-ha-Arozoth) both by Meati; (d) and the *De Foetu* (Sepher ha-Uber) by an anonymous scholar. The well known aphorisms of Hippocrates which were already commented upon by Maimonides (Vol. I, Sect. 201) were translated several times during this period under the title *Pirke Abukrat* (The Chapters of Hippocrates).

Galen was another favorite of the Jews. Practically all his works are found in Hebrew. Chief of these are his summary of medicine called *Ars Parva* (ha-Measeph le-Kol ha-Mahnoth), translated anonymously; (b) the Book of Diseases and Symptoms; (c) On Medicines, translated by Zerahya ben Isaac of Rome; (d) The Book of Crisis, rendered by Bonna Solomon Rocca of Barcelona; (e) On Blood Letting (Sepher ha-Hakoza), translated by Kalonymos ben Kalonymos. There are also several compendia of Galen's works on a number of medical subjects which were composed by Alexandrian physicians and were rendered into Hebrew from the Arabic under the title *Sepher ha-Kebutzim* (The Book of Compilations). The work contains seventeen small treatises on all phases of medicine.

Of the works of the Arabic physicians those of Avicenna occupy the leading place. His Canon of Medicine, which was considered the standard medical text book during the Middle Ages, was rendered into Hebrew several times by various scholars. The chief translations are first that of Nathan ha-Meati of Rome, entitled *Sepher ha-Kolel* and the second by Zerahya ben Isaac of the same city. The first is found complete in five books, but of the second, only the first two books are extant. A digest of the Canon made by Avicenna himself, and known as the Small or Short Canon was translated by Moses Ibn Tibbon under the name of *ha-Seder ha-Kotan*. There are also several other works of Avicenna rendered into Hebrew. Of the other Arabic medical writers, we must note the several translations of Averroes's treatise, *Kuliat* on general medicine, rendered by an anonymous scholar under the titles *Miklol* and *Sepher ha-Kolel Be-Refuah,* and the Hebrew renditions of a number of works by the celebrated physicians, Rhazes (Al-Razi) and Avenzohar. Among the translated works of the last two authors of special importance are the Book on Pediatrics (Meholi ha-Naarim) by Rhazes and the Dietetics by Avenzohar (Sepher ha-Mezonoth). The medical works of Christian physicians are also well represented in this translated scientific literature. The translations from the Latin began to increase from the fourteenth century on, but there are also earlier ones. Among the very early ones, may be counted the rendition by the philosopher, Hillel ben Samuel (Sect. 77) of a book on surgery by Bruno di Lungobucco under the title *Sepher Keritoth* (from the Heb. *Karoth,* to cut).

98. ENCYCLOPAEDIAS

Before we proceed to survey the more or less original contributions made by Jewish scholars to scientific literature in its various branches, we must note a number of books, which though they contain little original matter and consist primarily of compilations from either Arabic books or from Hebrew translations of these books, contributed much to the diffusion of knowledge among the Jews. These books aimed to give a summary or an epitome of the entire scientific knowledge of the day, and are therefore, encyclopaedic in character.

The earliest of such works was the *Midrash ha-Hokmah* (The Search of Wisdom) by Judah ben Solomon Cohen (b. 1219) of Toledo. Judah was a disciple of the famous Rabbinic scholar Meir Abulafia, and like him, was inclined to mysticism and rigorous religious views, but at the same time, he mastered the science of his day and was highly proficient in Arabic. In fact, the encyclopaedia was originally written by him in that language and later translated by himself into Hebrew.

The book is divided into two parts, each of which has several appendices dealing with theological and exegetic subjects. The first is devoted to logic, physics and metaphysics, giving brief abstracts of the contents of the works of Aristotle on the subject. The epitome of logic is incomplete as it covers only the contents of the *Isagoge* of Porphyry, the Categories, the *De Interpretatione* and the First Analytics (on syllogisms). The survey of physics is more extensive as it includes not only the Physics proper but also the other Aristotelian books on the subject, such as the *De Coelo,* On Generation and Decay, On the Senses, and the *De Anima* (psychology). The summary of metaphysics is exceptionally brief and is really limited to a number of excerpts from Aristotle's work on the subject together with some of the comments of Averroes.

The second part dealing with mathematics and astronomy begins with a survey of Euclid's Geometry, followed by an abstract of the Almagest and Al-Bitrugi's (Al-Petragius) book on astronomy, concluding with an abridgement of Ptolemy's System of Astrology. The appendices or separate treatises deal with explanations of certain passages from Genesis, Psalms and Proverbs, with the secret meaning of the letters of the alphamet and with a philosophic interpretation of parts of the Bible. Of the value of the sciences in general, the author says that they serve only as a means to a better understanding of the higher wisdom found in the Bible. Aristotle, says he, wanted to explain the higher spiritual world by means of investigation of the two lower worlds, namely the sublunar and that of the spheres; the prophet, on the other hand, devoted himself to a knowledge of the spiritual world and conceived the other worlds from the point of view of that knowledge. We can, therefore, utilize the sciences only as a means of developing our powers of understanding, but can not fully conceive the spiritual world without the help of tradition.

ii. Another work of this kind is the *Deoth ha-Pilisufim* (Opinions of Philosophers) by Shem Tob Falaquera (Sect. 77). It is, however, more of a philosophic nature and includes only the sciences contained in the works of Aristotle. The book is likewise divided into two parts, the first one dealing with physics and the second with metaphysics. In the first, a survey of all Aristotelian works on natural sciences, including those on minerals, plants and animals is given. The second part contains an abstract of the metaphysical theories of Aristotle and his commentators. Falaquera was, as we know, very well versed in the entire philosophic and scientific Arabic literature, and his abstracts are, therefore, in accordance with the views of Averroes and all other followers of Aristotle. Falaquera also wrote another book called *Reshith Hokmah* (The Beginning of Wisdom), which is an introduction to all sciences as well as philosophy. Falaquera frankly admits in his preface that he has compiled the contents of the book from the works of others, yet he used the material very dexterously and succeeded in giving a general conception of the entire knowledge of the age in a brief and concise manner. In the introduction which is written in rhymed prose, Falaquera discusses the three popular conceptions of happiness. The first is that of bodly well-being, the second, skill in the conduct of life and adaptation to conditions, the third is the acquisition of wealth. He proves that all three do not constitute real human happiness, for the first two kinds are not the peculiar share of man, as the animals excel him in strength and some even in the art of life, and as for the third, it is not stable but subject to vicissitudes. Real happiness consists, therefore, in the perfection of the mind. It was for the people who seek for such happiness that he wrote the book in order to show them the way to wisdom.

The book is divided into three parts: the first describes the nature and the character of the moral qualities; the second contains the classification of sciences and their description; and the third deals with proving that philosophy is the only means of obtaining happiness. The first part is really a short treatise on morality, and in fact, he calls it *Iggereth,* i. e. an Ethical Epistle, and it was placed at the beginning for the reason that one who wants to acquire wisdom must first perfect himself in ethical conduct. He, therefore, discusses briefly first habit, the chief means for the acquisition of virtue, then the classification of virtues and the Aristotelian theory of the golden mean, which is the primal character of virtue.

The second part occupies the main body of the book and is divided into nine sections, some of which are subdivided into several chapters. The first section states the purpose of the outline of the sciences, and the use the student can derive from such an outline. The second and third deal with language, the former explaining its origin and the latter describing the science of linguistics. It is a very concise statement of the principles of grammar and the classification of the words in a language, but an accurate one. The fourth section is devoted to the origin of the sciences, tracing the steps in the development of knowledge from the inaccurate and legendary stage to the accurate and descriptive one. Logic is treated in the fifth section, where in five chapters its definition, use, terms and the classification of its parts are adequately described. The sixth section takes up the classification of the mathematical sciences and their description. The seven chapters of the section deal with arithmetic, geometry, astronomy, optics, music, mechanics and the devices of experimentation respectively. Physics is treated in the seventh section, and metaphysics in the eighth, while the ninth speaks of politics and the sciences of law and forensics.

The third part is divided into three sections, the first expounding the uses of philosophy and its application, and the other two containing abstracts of the philosophies of Plato and Aristotle. These abstracts contain sketches of the works of these philosophers and a very brief survey of their contents. The work, as a whole, presents the outline of all knowledge in a very able and skillful manner, so that the reader is able to obtain a general concept of the scope of the various sciences and of the subjects with which they deal. It must be admitted, though, that the sciences are not all treated alike. More space is given to the description of the so-called mental sciences, such as logic, metaphysics and philosophy than to the mathematical and natural ones. This can, of course, be explained by the fact that the author was more interested in this type of studies than in those relating to pure science.

iii. A quite important encyclopaedic work is the *Shaarē ha-Shomayyim* (The Gates of Heaven) by Gerson ben Solomon of Arles. Regarding the time of the author, opinion is divided. Some scholars believe him to have lived in the first half of the thirteenth century and the book to have been composed in the year 1240. Others believe him to be the father of Levi ben Gerson, but in the opinion of Steinschneider, this Gerson could not have lived earlier than the middle of the fourteenth century, as some of the excerpts he quotes are taken from Hebrew translations done in that period.

The book is divided into three parts which are subdivided into sections. The first part is devoted to physics and other natural sciences such as mineralogy, botany, zoology and the physiology of the human body. The second part deals with astronomy, giving extensive excerpts from the Almagest, Al-Fragani's Book on Astronomy as well as from the works of Avicenna and Averroes on the subject. The third has theology for its theme and contains primarily excerpts from the works of Averroes, of Maimonides and the *De Anima* of Aristotle. It contains at the end a glossary of scientific terms and a detailed table of contents. The work which consists almost entirely of excerpts from numerous Greek and Arabic treatises testifies to the wide knowledge of the author of the philosophic and scientific literature of the period. But this by no means proves that he was versed in the Arabic language, as all of his citations are taken, as he himself states in the introduction, from works translated into Hebrew. The wealth of material collected by Gerson testifies to the extent of the translated literature which existed in his day.

The *Shaarē ha-Shemayyim* was very popular through the ages, and served as a source of information in scientific matters to generations of Jewish scholars. On account of its popularity, it was reprinted several times.

iv. The last attempt at compiling a work of an encyclopaedic character was made by Meir Aldabi of Toledo (c. 1360). It is entitled *Shebilē Emunah* (The Paths of Faith) and contains ten sections called *Netibim* (Roads) subdivided into chapters called *Shebilim*.

The book bears a popular character, inasmuch as it contains a mixture of mysticism and philosophy, superstitious belief and scientific data placed side by side without any attempt to distinguish between them. The purpose of the author was, as he states in the introduction and as the name testifies, to show that philosophy and science if rightly interpreted only help to strengthen faith. Yet, there is no systematic attempt made to carry out the purpose, as on the whole, emphasis is primarily laid on the supplying of information. Aldabi does not give, like the other encyclopaedists, abstracts of certain books except short quotations, here and there, but he gives a connected statement of facts in a flowing style, as if he wrote the entire book himself. Yet we know that he borrowed long passages from previous works of this kind, especially from Gerson's Gates of Heaven.

The plan of the book is as follows: The first section treats of God and gives in a brief manner the proofs for His existence, unity and incorporeality, as well as a description of the attributes. Being inclined to mysticism, Aldabi weaves into the philosophic discussion some Kabbalistic teachings and reveals a few secrets concerning the meaning of the names of God. The second section contains four chapters, the first of which endeavors to prove the creation of the world from nothing. The other three are devoted to a description of the earth, its division into zones, its habitable parts, the movement of the spheres in general and that of the sun and moon in particular. After treating of God and the world, he devotes the rest of the book to man. The third, fourth and fifth sections treat of the body of man. The third section deals with prenatal conditions that are to be observed, the fourth with the anatomy and physiology of the body, and the fifth with hygiene. The last section is a lengthy one, containing ten chapters which give a complete description of the various phases of hygiene and their adaptation to the ages of man from infancy to old age. This section contains also an alphabetical table of fruits and vegetables which should be used in the diet after proper preparation. The sixth section is devoted to psychology, and the seventh to what the author calls the hygiene of the soul or the proper conduct of man in life. The last three sections take for their subject three dogmas, namely the beliefs in oral law, in reward and punishment in the hereafter, in the coming of the Messiah and the resurrection respectively. On all these very important theological questions Aldabi hardly expresses an original opinion but is well satisfied with quoting excerpts from various authorities, both rationalists and those inclined to mysticism. Only very seldom does he endeavor to reconcile the two sets of excerpts. Yet with all the defects of his work, it served as a source of information in scientific matters through the generations, and judging from the numerous times it was reprinted, it must have been a popular book.

99. *ORIGINAL WORKS ON ASTRONOMY AND MATHEMATICS (1st period, 1200-1450)*

The deep interest shown by Jewish scholars in the sciences of astronomy and mathematics was not limited to translations of works on these subjects from other languages, but also expressed itself in the production of a more or less original scientific literature. This literature first began in the compilation of commentaries on the standard works translated. Thus, we have a number of commentaries on Euclid's Elements, among them one from Levi ben Gerson and one by the famous Rabbinic scholar, Elijah Misrahi (d. 1523). The Almagest was commented upon by Samuel ben Judah from Marseilles, Elijah Misrahi and others. Moses Almosnino wrote a commentary on the Hebrew translation of the *Sphera Mundi* entitled *Beth Elohim* (The House of God). There is also an anonymous abstract of the translation of the *Sphera Mundi* called *Sepher ha-Galgal* (The Book of the Sphere) with additional notes by later authors.

From commentaries, the Jewish scientist passed over to original works. The first of such works was one by Levi ben Gerson entitled *Sepher ha-Tekunah* (Book of Astronomy). It was originally incorporated in his *Milhamoth* (Sect. 78) and formed the first part of book *V* of that work. The printers, however, omitted this part from the work, as it is really a separate book in itself. It is found complete in manuscript but was never printed. Yet, it is of great value and was extensively used in the Mediaeval Ages. It consists of one hundred and thirty-six chapters and opens up with general observations on astronomy. He then gives a description of a new instrument which he invented for astronomical observations which he calls *Megaleh Amukoth* (The Revealer of Profound Things). This part was translated into Latin by order of Pope Clement VI under the title: *Tarctatus Instrumenti Astronomie*. The rest of the book is devoted to a criticism of the Ptolemaic system, the astronomy of Al-Bitrugi, the exposition of his own views and to corrections of the theories of these two astronomers. Gersonides had also written an arithmetic under the name of *Sepher ha-Mispar* (The Book of Numbers).

The contemporary of Gersonides, Jacob ben Makir also invented an astronomical instrument, known as the new quadrant, which is described in a book named *Robah Israel* (figuratively meaning Israel's quadrant), in which name there is a play upon the words taken from Numbers XXIII, 10 and indicating the name of the author, for Israel is another name for Jacob. The invention, as well as the book were well received by the scientists of the time and the latter was translated into Latin immediately after its appearance under the title *Tractatus de Novo Quadrante*. The quadrant itself was named *Quadrans Judaicus*.

Another contemporary who lived in Spain, Isaac ben Joseph Israeli (first half of fourteenth century), wrote a comprehensive treatise on astronomy and calendar calculation, named *Yesod Olam* (The Foundation of the World). Israeli was a disciple of the great codifier, Rabbi Asher ben Yehiel (Sect. 55) and composed the book in honor of his teacher in order that he and his disciples might conceive clearly the principles of calendar fixation and calculation But as this is impossible to attain without a general conception of astronomy, Israeli gave an abstract of that science, and also as much mathematics as necessary for a student in astronomy to know. The book contains five sections. The first deals with that part of mathematics which serves as an introduction to the science of the stars. It contains a few chapters on the principles of arithmetic and numbers, and then forty-two propositions culled from the fields of geometry and plane and spherical trigonometry. The second section is devoted to a description of the world and contains besides the elements of astronomy, also chapters on physical geography, that is, on the zones and climes of the earth. The third describes the movements of the sun and the moon, the calculations of their positions at various times and eclipses. In this section, Israeli devotes a few chapters to the exposition of the theory of Al-Bitrugi which deviates much from that of Ptolemy.

The fourth section is devoted to the discussion of the principles of calendar fixation. The author describes at length the principles on which the Jewish calendar is based, gives an exposition of the two theories of the length of the solar solstices (Tekufa) one ascribed to the Amora Samuel and the other to Rab Ada bar Ahbah, which affect greatly the calendar calculations, and also explain a number of Talmudic passages bearing on the calendar. The section contains also a chapter on the Mohammedan and Christian eras and another one on Jewish chronology where he gives a brief historical survey of the chain of tradition, i. e. the succession of the leading scholars from the days of the Great Assembly to Asher ben Yehiel. The fifth section instructs the student how to compose a calendar giving all the necessary rules for the purpose. It also contains a large number of tables for calculating the time of the birth (Moled) or rise of the new moon each month, the dates of the solar solstices and the solar and lunar cycles. The work is illustrated by a considerable number of figures. The *Yesod Olam* enjoyed great popularity among Jewish students of astronomy and was considered a standard book on calendar calculation.

Much effort was spent also by Jewish scholars in improving and editing the various systems of astronomical tables. The tables prepared by Ptolemy were found defective by later astronomers and improvements and additions were constantly made by them. From time to time, new sets were issued either by individual astronomers or by groups. The most important of these were the tables of the Arabic astronomer, Al-Tabbani (776), the Toletan tables fixed in the year 1080 by a group of astronomers among whom there were said to be several Jewish scholars, and the Alfonsine tables prepared by a conclave of astronomers at the behest of Alfonso X, King of Spain, in the year 1252. It is asserted that the presiding officer at this meeting of scientists was a Jew by the name of Isaac ben Sid, who is said to have been a cantor.

These sets of tables were translated into Hebrew, commented upon and often reissued with additions. Many books were written by Jewish astronomers containing tables with descriptions for their use. Of such books the most noted were the Tables of Gersonides, of Jacob Poel (1361) and Jacob ben Makir, whose work *Luhoth* (Tables) was translated into Latin under the name of *Almanach Prophatii,*—Prophatius being the surname of Jacob. Other authors who compiled such tables and incorporated them in their larger works on astronomy were Immanuel ben Jacob of Tarascon, in the Provence, whose book *Shesh Knofaim* (Six Wings) was considered a standard work, and Isaac Ibn Alhadib (The Hunchback) of Castile (1300-80) who wrote the *Orah Selulah* (The Trodden Path). The first book describes the solar and lunar movements and is divided into six treatises each called *Kanaf* (A Wing). The tables at the end of the book bearing the title *Kanfe Neshorim* (The Eagles' Wings) are based on those of Al-Tabbani's set. The second one is primarily a work on chronology and the tables are used as the apparatus by means of which historical dates are determined.

German Jewish scholars, though devoting themselves primarily to Halakah and Rabbinics did not, however, remain entirely unaffected by the great scientific activity going on in the neighboring country of Provence, and some of them were attracted by its lure. Thus, we have several mathematical and astronomical works composed by German savants. Meir Shapira wrote an arithmetic entitled *Biur Darke ha-Heshbon* (An Explanation of the Ways of Arithmetic) divided into seven chapters where he gives an exposition of the principles of that science and also a collection of problems for practice in their solution. He also wrote a commentary on Immanuel's Six Wings. His son, Isaac, wrote a book on the comets and on the conjunction of Saturn and Jupiter. Another book on arithmetic was written by Joseph ben Moses Zarfati also hailing from northern France and probably a contemporary of Meir and Isaac Shapira.

100. THE SECOND PERIOD (1450-1700)

With the beginning of the fifteenth century, the center of scientific literary activity was transferred, like the activity in other fields from Spain and the Provence to other countries, first to Italy and Turkey, then to Germany and Poland. But, before the expulsion,

Spain produced a great scientist in the person of Abraham Zacuto whose works on astronomy and mathematics were considered authoritative in his time, and were consulted by the navigators of the age of discovery. Zacuto distinguished himself as an authority in the sciences of astronomy and mathematics while yet a young man and was recognized by his gentile colleagues as such. He acted as professor of astronomy in Salamanca, the leading university of Spain, for a number of years until the expulsion. Together with his teacher, Isaac Aboab, he settled for a time in Portugal, where he was appointed by King Manoel I as the royal astronomer and cartographer, and it was upon his advice that the expedition of Vasco di Gama for the exploration of new lands was sent out. The discoverer used Zacuto's astronomical tables as well as his perfected astrolabe. When the Jews were expelled also from Portugal in 1496, Zacuto sojourned for several years in North Africa and ultimately settled in Turkey where he died in the year 1520.

Zacuto's chief work in astronomy is one called the *Hibbur ha-Gadol* (The Large Treatise or Almagest) which contains a complete set of astronomical tables and calculations. These tables were written in Hebrew and Spanish (in Hebrew script) and were later translated into Latin under the title of *Expositio Tabulorum*. The Tables of Zacuto were held in great esteem by his contemporaries and were used not only by Vasco di Gama but also by Columbus on his voyage of discovery. His other works included writings on the principles of astronomy in Arabic and the famous book on Jewish history, the *Yuhasin* (Book of Genealogies) which will be discussed in the proper place.

During the sixteenth century, many Jewish scholars, some of them authorities in Rabbinics, were engaged in the study of mathematics and astronomy, especially the latter, since it had great bearing on the fixation of the calendar. The results of their studies were incorporated in numerous treatises on the subjects. These scholars, as said, hailed from many countries, but Italy was the center of scientific activity, and those scientists who were born and educated in other countries came thither to acquire a scientific education.

Of the scholars whose scientific works deserve to be noted either on account of their intrinsic worth or their popularity, we will mention a few. The first is Matthias de Lacrut (1530-1550) who was born in Poland and later came to Italy, where he studied science and philosophy at the university of Bologna. He wrote a commentary on

Solomon Ibn Avigdor's translation of the *Sphera Mundi* (Sect. 97) but is primarily known for his own little book *Zel ha-Olam* (The Image of the World). This work is not original but an elaboration of a French treatise by the name of *L'Image du Monde* by Gossouine. Matthias, however, dressed it in a Hebrew garb and changed the contents in a way that it appears as if it were entirely his own. It contains three parts, subdivided into a number of short chapters or portals. The parts, however are not devoted to the description in a scientific manner of one subject in its entirety but each one treats popularly of a number of subjects. Thus, the first part discusses the purpose of creation, the seven sciences, the sphericity of the earth, the movement of the stars and similar things. The second part is devoted primarily to a geographical description of the earth and the wonders of distant lands, especially India under which name he includes the greater part of Asia. This part contains also some paragraphs on the phenomena of rain, snow and hail. The third treats of the moon, eclipse of the sun and diverse things. The book has little scientific value, for the author draws upon antiquated sources, and there is no reflection of the new science of the day. His description of the parts of the earth still speaks of three continents, though America was discovered three or four decades before the work appeared, and it is full of grotesque stories about the wonders of distant lands. Yet, it was quite popular and served as a source of information for some scientific data to the Jews who knew no other language but Hebrew.

The other sixteenth century scientist whose work is of great importance and value is Rabbi David Gans (1541-1613). David Gans was a native of Prague who distinguished himself in many fields of intellectual endeavor as a Rabbinic scholar, scientist and historian (Sect. 132). He was a disciple of the codifier, Moses Isserlis in Rabbinics and was in close touch with the astronomers, Johannan Kepler and Tycho Brahe, and for the latter, he translated a book on the Alfonsine tables from Hebrew into German.

His chief work on astronomy is the *Nehmod we-Noim* (The Desirable and the Pleasant). In his introduction, after repeating the assertion so often made by Jewish scholars that the sciences were originally developed by the Jews but that they were forgotten by them on account of the exile, he gives a survey of the history of astronomy from the earliest times to his own day. He does not fail to mention the names of the Jews who wrote on that science, and also emphasizes that the Egyptians, Babylonians and Pythagoras borrowed their knowledge from the Jews. He states that Abraham and Solomon were very proficient in the science of the heavens. He speaks of Copernicus in the most excellent terms, praising him as the greatest scholar of the age and calls his work a miracle of knowledge. Yet, he does not subscribe to his theory and says of it that it was already known to the ancients and was rejected by them. This attitude can be explained partly by the influence of Tycho Brahe who was a great opponent of the Copernican revolution and partly by the piety of the author who could not accept the view of Copernicus since it contradicts Biblical passages. He concludes the introduction by stating the reasons which moved him to write his book. First, because astronomy teaches us the greatness of the handiwork of God. Secondly, it offers proof for the existence of God; thirdly, the science of calendar calculations is based on its principles; and finally, since the gentiles seeing that the Jews are devoid of science have contempt for them, this knowledge will raise the honor of Israel in the eyes of the nations.

The book itself is divided into twelve parts which are subdivided into three hundred and five small sections. It covers the entire science of astronomy as well as physical geography and all closely related subjects. The first two parts discuss seriatim the nature of the four elements, the spheres and planets as a whole, explain the form of the universe on the mechanical sphere which resembles it and describe the ways used for determining the celestial poles and the altitude of the sun. The third part deals with the earth, its continents, its division into three hundred and sixty degrees of longitude and latitude, and finally gives an alphabetical table of the longitudinal and latitudinal locations of a considerable number of cities. The fourth, fifth, sixth, seventh and eighth parts are devoted to the discussion of the position of the zodiac, movements of the sun and the moon and the resultant measurements of time, namely the month, year and the day as well as the changes of the seasons. The ninth, tenth and eleventh deal with eclipses, movements of the other five planets and the use of the quadrant for determining the altitude of the sun and the celestial poles. The twelfth part discusses diverse subjects, such as the comets and other matters.

Gans, on the whole, displays great knowledge of his subjects, and though he rejects the Copernican system, makes use of all the other changes and discoveries in the field of his sciences. Thus, in describing the earth, he speaks of eight continents, adding to the three known continents, New Guinea, the Arctic and the Antarctic, North and South America, the latter of which he calls Peru. He describes these new lands according to the best knowledge of his day, for he is aware that New Guinea is an island, but says that on account of its extent, the geographers of the time decided to call it a separate part of the earth or a continent.

A number of other scholars have also written books on astronomy which dealt especially with the calendar. Some of them were commentaries on earlier works. The codifier, Mordecai Jaffe wrote a commentary on Abraham bar Hiyya's work, *Zurath ha-Aaretz* and a book on the calendar incorporated as one of the *Lebushim* (Garments) in his great code called *Lebush* (Sect. 61). Isaachar Ibn Susan (1539-1575) of France wrote another book on the calendar by the name of *Ibbur Shanim* (The Intercalation). Calendars for many years, some running for a century and longer were issued by many scholars. They were provided with rules for calendar-making and notes on the solar and lunar movements and are thus part of the scientific literature of the century.

101. JOSEPH SOLOMON DEL MEDIGO

The interest in science on the part of the Jews did not slacken during the seventeenth century, and we have a number of scholars who left treatises dealing with various phases of the sciences. But the greatest of them all was Joseph Solomon del Medigo (1591-1655) or as he was known in his time *Yashar* of Candia (Yashor being the Hebrew initials for Joseph Shlome Rophe). Del Medigo was one of the peculiar and most interesting personalities in Jewish history during the latter period of the Middle Ages. His range of knowledge was so extensive that it included practically all sciences in addition to deep and wide erudition in Rabbinics and Jewish mysticism; and just as his knowledge was diversified, so was his character. At one time, he is engrossed in mysticism and writes a multitude of Kabbalistic treatises, and at another time, he disparages the secret wisdom and calls it superstition and its study a waste of time. At another period of his life, he abandons the sciences, and devotes himself to the study of the Talmud and codes, and at still another, he minimizes the value of the Talmud and extols that of science. The meanderings of his spirit fitted in closely with the vicissitudes of his life which was a checkered one and full of change.

Joseph Solomon del-Medigo

Joseph Solomon was born in Candia or Crete and was a descendant of a very noble and scholarly family which produced many great men, among the mthe notable Elijah del Medigo (Sect. 85). His father, Elijah, himself a great Rabbinic scholar gave him an excellent education in Rabbinics, and hired tutors to instruct him in Greek, Arabic and Italian. At the age of fifteen, he entered the university of Padua and studied astronomy under Galileo, and also medicine and philosophy. At the age of eighteen he graduated from the university and returned to his home in Crete. There he married and spent a few years, but his restless spirit did not permit him to remain at home very long. He soon began to travel, visiting Egypt first, where he met the great scientists of the land. With one of them, Ali Ibn Rahamdan, an Arab, he held a public debate and issued victorious, and at the request of another scientist by the name of Jacob the Alexandrian, he wrote a book on mechanics.

From Egypt, he went to Constantinople, where he was initiated by Jacob Ibn Nehemias into the mysteries of the Kabbala. Thence, he went to Poland where he was engaged as a physician by Prince Radzivill and remained in that country for some time, mostly in Vilna, Lithuania. However, life in that country which was very backward and devoid of interest in scientific studies did not suit the temperament of del Medigo, and he took his wanderer's staff again. For some time, he held rabbinical positions at Hamburg and later at Amsterdam in the Sephardic communities of these cities, and ultimately at the age of sixty-six, he decided to go to Palestine to spend his remaining days. On the way to Palestine, he stopped at Prague where death overtook him.

Del Medigo, as stated, was very prolific and versatile in his writings. The number of volumes he claims to have written amount to twenty-eight. Many of them contain special treatises on different subjects. Of these, two works were encyclopaedias of sciences and one an outline of science. Of the encyclopaedias, the one called by the rather exotic name *Bosmath Bath Shlomeh* (Bosmath, the daughter of Solomon, figuratively speaking the spicy work, the spiritual child of Solomon, name of author) was considered by del Medigo the best of all his works. It dealt with geometry, astronomy, optics, logic, ethics and also physiognomy and other sciences. Unfortunately, the book so greatly extolled by the author, was lost and we are unable to judge its merits. Seven of his works dealt with algebra, geometry and astronomy and one of them *Mayan Ganim* contained originally ten treatises on various phases of science including a book on mechanics, but only part of these are extant. One of his works, *Refuoth Tēalah* (Medicinal Cures) was devoted to medicine. The rest are works on Kabbala, commentaries on several of Ibn Ezra's books, Arama's *Akedah,* translations of some of the works of Philo, of the Aphorisms of Hippocrates and an introduction to logic. A large number of these books, however, were either lost or are still in manuscript. Only five of his scientific books or parts of books and four of his Kabbalistic works were printed. Still, the few scientific works that saw the light are sufficient to prove del Medigo a master of the sciences of his day.

These five scientific works, though separate treatises, are really parts of one book called *Elim* or *Mayan Ganim,* the composition of which as well as the name have a history of their own. A Karaite scholar by the name of Zerah ben Nathan of the city of Troki, hearing of the fame of del Medigo, began to correspond with him asking to be instructed in science. His first letter was unanswered, but Zerah being anxious to hear from the master sent a second letter accompanied by a present. Meanwhile he made the personal acquaintance of Moses Metz, a disciple of del medigo and this stimulated the desire of Zerah to hear directly from the former. He finally sent a third letter, containing definite questions and problems to which he sought answers. There are twelve sections in the letter called by Zerah in his euphuistic style *Wells,* i. e. the main problems and seventy brief questions, mostly paradoxical called *Date Trees,* corresponding to the number of wells and palms the Jews found at Elim, one of the stations on their journey through the desert (Exodus XV, 27). Hence, the book, embracing both questions and answers, is called *Elim.* Most of the problems are of a mathematical nature, but they contain also some that deal with other matters. Thus in Well *V,* Zerah inquires regarding demons, incantations, dreams, use of amulets, mystery of physiognomy and similar things. In Well IX, he is anxious to know of other esoteric sciences, especially of alchemy. The same can be said about the seventy briefer questions. To this epistle, del Medigo answered first in a long letter, where he informs him of his opinion of the Kabbala, followed by a sketch of the main lines of Jewish Mediaeval literature and a list of his own works. Later, he wrote the *Mayan Ganim* consisting of thirteen treatises, intending to answer in full all the comprehensive problems

Tobias Katz
(Reproduced from Levinson's Tubia ha-Rofē)

and questions of Zerah, but of which only the five parts of the *Elim* were printed. These are as follows:

The first part contains the letter of Zerah, an epistle of Moses Metz to Zerah wherein he tells him about his master and the works he wrote and discusses a number of mathematical questions, as well as several epistles to scholars by del Medigo himself. These letters deal with the questions of the veracity of the senses, the study of medicine, and some mathematical problems. The second part called *Sod ha-Yesod* (The Secret of the Foundation) deals with spherical trigonometry and solves many of its intricate problems. The third part called *Hukoth Shomayyim* (The Laws of Heaven) discusses astronomy. It contains a commentary on a number of chapters of the Almagest of Ptolemy and discussions on the determination of the altitude of the sun and the longitude and latitude of places according to the course of the stars. There is also an appendix which contains a table of the latitude and the longitude of the most important cities of the world.

The fourth part designated *Geburoth Adonai* (The Power of God) is primarily a description of the universe, especially the planets, stars, and constellations in accordance with the opinion of the astronomers from Ptolemy to his own day. He lays special emphasis on the new discoveries from the time of Copernicus to his own, but he does not decide whether the views of Copernicus are the right ones though he quotes them. He devotes much space to the distance of the various planets and stars from the earth, as well as their magnitude, and discusses the methods of the calculations of such measurement. The fifth part named *Mayan Hathum* (The Sealed Well) is intended to answer the seventy paradoxical and problematical questions of Zerah. It deals with a variety of subjects, mathematical, astronomical and optical. In this book, the author shows to a full extent the great versatility of his knowledge in the entire field of science in all its divisions. The knotty problems of Zerah are solved one by one with skill and dexterity. It is interesting to note that in this work, del Medigo throws out a suggestion which were it carried out to its ultimate conclusion would have led to the discovery of the telegraph centuries before it was actually invented.

102. TOBIAS KATZ AND HIS MAASE TUBIA

One of the interesting scientific works produced at the end of the seventeenth century was the *Maasē Tubia* (The Work of Tobias) by Tobias Katz (1552-1729). The interest lies not so much in the originality displayed by the author as in the encyclopaedic character of the work and the popular manner in which it was written. Tobias was born at Metz, Alsace, where his father, Eliezer took refuge when fleeing from Poland from the persecutions of Chmelnicki. When he was quite young, he lost his father, and left then for Poland in order to prepare for the Rabbinate, but observing the poverty and low state of Polish Jewry, he decided to leave the country and study medicine. He attended first the university at Frankfurt on the Oder where he was admitted by special recommendation of the Elector of Brandenburg and later went to Padua, Italy. There, through the protection of the physician, Solomon Congliano, he succeeded in entering the famous university of that city and obtained in the year 1683 the degree of doctor of medicine. He returned to Poland for a short time and practiced his art, but later settled in Constantinople where through the help of Israel Congliano, a brother of Solomon, he obtained a position as court physician, which position he held during the reign of five sultans. In his old age, he realized his life's desire and settled in Jerusalem spending there the rest of his days.

The author tells us in his introduction that during his stay at the university of Frankfurt on the Oder, the professors of the school very often drew him and his Jewish fellow student Gabriel into religious discussions. During these disputes the scholars often taunted Tobias that the Jews were devoid of science and secular wisdom. He then vowed not to rest until he had written a book in Hebrew on the sciences, so as to show the nations that Jewish literature also possesses books of a scientific nature. This vow he carried out during his stay in Turkey by writing his *Maasē Tubia.* It was finished in Constantinople in 1701, and later printed in Venice in 1708 with an introduction by Tobias' friend and patron Solomon Congliano.

The *Maasē Tubia* is, as said, encyclopaedic in character and is intended to impart information on all sciences from philosophy to medicine. But inasmuch as Tobias was a physician by profession, he treats the last science with more skill and precision and at greater length than the others. The work, as a whole, is divided into three parts which are subdivided into treatises and chapters. The first part includes the entire field of knowledge except medicine to which the other two parts are devoted.

The first part contains five divisions, four of which deal respectively with the spiritual or the upper world, the heavens or the world of the spheres, the earth or the lower world, and man or microcosm, and the fifth with a number of physical problems. In the first division, the subjects usually dealt with in Jewish philosophy are discussed, such as, proofs for the existence of God, His unity, eternity and incorporeality, the existence of angels, the immutability of the Torah, the Providence of God, reward and punishment and the question of the Messiah. The author adds to the analysis of all these important questions hardly anything of his own, but reproduces the proofs, arguments and theories found in the books on Jewish philosophy, especially in the Ikkarim of Albo. He even quotes a number of passages verbatim from this book without mentioning the source.

The second division gives in thirty chapters a rapid survey of the entire sciences of astronomy and physiography, describing first both the Ptolemaic and Copernican theories of the universe, then the spheres, the sun and the moon, the fixed stars, the comets and the natural phenomena of rain, snow, hail, and kindred matters. All this is done not in a strictly scientific way but in a popular manner. Tobias is, on the whole, very conservative in his views and is very wroth against Copernicus for his theory which contradicts a number of statements of the Bible, and for this reason he rejects it and clings to the Ptolemaic system.

The third division devoted to the lower world or the earth is very deficient from a scientific point of view. It only contains a few chapters dealing with its spherical form and its division into zones, continents and degrees. The rest describe certain wonderful things found in the world, such as the Chinese wall, the quinine plant and other trees and plants with peculiar properties, including the coffee tree. Similarly, the fourth division deals with the microcosm in an extremely popular and semi-scientific manner. It does not give the anatomy of man nor his physiology for these are reserved for the other two parts dealing with medicine. It is limited to a short review of physiognomy, i. e. expression of the human face by means of which the character of men can be diagnosed and to a few stories about the existence of human freaks in various parts of the world. The fifth division called *Yesodē ha-Olam* deals with the four elements and certain physical phenomena connected with them. He still believes in the existence of only four elements. Although he is aware of a few more elements considered by the chemists as such, he doubts the truth of their views. He instructs his readers in a number of physical facts, such as the existence of a vacuum, the principles of the pump, a kind of crude thermometer and other things. The book has a considerable number of drawings which serve as illustrations of the instruction imparted. The medical parts of the book are of greater scientific value than the encyclopaedic, and these will subsequently be discussed.

103. MEDICINE

Although as noted above, the original medical literature in Hebrew is not proportionate to the exceedingly large number of Jewish physicians, it is yet a considerable one. The first attempt at original work in medicine was expressed by the commentaries and compendia of the Canon of Avicenna. Thus, Moses Ibn Tibbon and Solomon Ibn Jaish wrote commentaries on the Canon. Nathan ha-Meati (1279-1283) wrote a compendium of the same work. Meshullam ben Jonah, a Spanish physician (2nd half of the 13th century) wrote a compendium in two parts of the medical works of the celebrated Abou'l Qasim entitled *Sepher Hefetz ha-Shalem* (The Book of the Perfect Desire). The first part treats of the theory and the second of the practice of medicine. Of the writers who wrote original works on one or more medical subjects, mention should be made of Solomon ben Joseph Ajub (1259-1265) of Beziers whose treatise on hemorrhoids, was considered authoritative in his time. He also wrote a book on prescriptions entitled *Sar ha-Mashkim* (Royal Cup Bearer). Another one, Johanan Yarhoni (c. 1300) composed a treatise on the colors of urine (Mareoth ha-Shetan) where he discusses the various colors of the urine as symptoms of diseases. Abraham ben David Kaslavi (1322-1329) of Perpignan made a great reputation as physician by writing several medical works, the first, *Maamer be-Kadahath Dibrioth* (A Treatise on Pestilential Fevers), a second one, *Mekalkel Mahla* (The Care of Disease) and the third *Ale Raanan* (Fresh Leaves). Meir Alguadez, physician to Henry III of Castile (1405) wrote a book on prescriptions in Spanish which was later translated into Hebrew by his disciple, Joseph ha-Cohen under the title *Mekitz Nirdamim* (The Revival of the Slumberers, i. e. the sick). Finally, to the fourteenth century belong Judah ben Jacob who composed a work on hygiene under the name *Hanhogath ha-Brioth,* and Elijah ben Judah who is said to have written in 1418 a book on gynecology in the form of a dialogue called Jacob and Dinah. Dinah asks the questions and describes the diseases and Jacob offers the cure. It is not, however, certain wheher it is an original book or a translation.

The number of Jewish physicians during the sixteenth and seventeenth centuries was exceptionally large. In almost every country, there flourished many Jewish medical men who enriched the science of medicine with their works. Not all of them, however, wrote in Hebrew. Some employed the language of the country or Latin as the medium of expression, but some were faithful to the tongue of their fathers. To the former belong Amatus Lusitanus (1511-1562) and Zacuto Lusitanus (1575-1642). The first was born in Spain, studied at Salamanca and became a famous practitioner. But his fame as a physician did not protect him from falling under the ban of the inquisition, and for fear of being seized by it, he left Spain and for a time sojourned in France and Italy. During his stay in the latter country, he received an invitation from the king of Poland to become the court physician which invitation he declined and chose rather to settle in Salonika and practice there among his brethren. Lusitanus left a large number of medical treatises in Latin which were considered of great value and merit by the scholars of his time. The most important of them was his history of medicinal cures during seven centuries entitled *Curiationum Medicinalium Centurias Semptem.*

The second, Zacuto Lusitanus was born at Lisbon, a descendant of a famous family, his great-great-grandfather being Abraham Zacuto, the celebrated astronomer (Sect. 100). Zacuto practiced medicine in Portugal for twenty years. But as all Marrano Jews, he was in constant fear of the Inquisition, so he finally decided to leave the counry and settle in Amsterdam. There he took an active interest in Jewish affairs and was a leader of the Portuguese community. His numerous works on medicine gained for him a great reputation among physicians of many countries, who corresponded with him on medical matters. Zacuto, as said, did not write in Hebrew but a successor of his, Jacob Zahlon (see below) quotes in a Hebrew treatise on medicine a long excerpt from a work of Lusitanus containing rules of conduct for a physician. The rules reflect the purity of soul and the high regard Zacuto had for the profession as well as his deep insight into medicine, and some of them deserve to be quoted as an example of a Jewish conception of the art of healing. These are the following:

The physician should first of all be pious. He should be well dressed. He should not be talkative nor parsimonious and should not insist on his fee. He should not be vain nor envious. He should admit his mistakes and accept cheerfully the censure of his elders. He should possess good sense and be well disposed. It is best that he study every subject thoroughly, buy rather few books but good ones and peruse them carefully. He should refrain from making false promises and undertaking to cure the incurable. He should neither make light of an illness nor exaggerate its condition and should be willing to consult with other physicians. The principal aim of the physician should be to cure the patient, but he should consider the difficulties and dangers of the cure. At times, he should entertain the patient with pleasant conversation. In giving counsel, he should follow the rules of medicine and observe closely the workings of nature. In general, the physician should assist nature, for it is the most important factor in health. He should observe closely the strength of the patient, particularly the condition of his brain, and should be very careful in giving medicine to the young and the very old as both are weak, and take great care in the treatment of infants. Such are some of the golden rules of Zacuto, the physician.

Among those who contributed to the medical literature in Hebrew during this period are Benjamin Musafia (1606-1675) of Hamburg, Hayyim Bohmer of Poland (1669), Jacob Zahlon (1630-1693) of Italy and Tobias Katz. The first wrote a book containing medical aphorisms culled from the Holy Scriptures, and the second a medical treatise entitled *Luah ha-Hayyim* (The Table of Life) where a system of hygiene is discussed. This book was translated by Wagenseil into Latin. The works of the last two were of greater importance and deserve somewhat longer description.

Zahlon wrote a large treatise on medicine called *Ozar Hayyim* (The Treasure of Life) where he discusses in great detail all diseases and their cures. In the introduction, the author tells us of the great value of the science, quotes as said, the rules of conduct for physicians from Lusitanus and adds some of his own, among them an injunction that the physician should not prolong his visits unnecessarily and that he should not charge a fee to the poor nor to relatives and friends. In the last case, however, he allows him to accept a fee if there is a possibility that the friend will refrain from calling him otherwise.

The *Ozar* is divided into thirteen books, each dealing with a separate phase of medicine. The first treats of hygiene and dietetics, the second, of fevers and their cures, the third, of the pulse, the colors of urine and the condition of the tongue, the fourth, of poisons and their cure. From the fifth to the tenth book, the author describes all diseases of the body, giving first the diagnosis of disease (Book V) and then the diseases of the head, eyes, ear and nose, followed by those of the chest and the stomach. Book ten deals with external diseases, and eleven and twelve with women's and infants' illnesses. Book XII is devoted to mental diseases but was omitted in printing on account of an ailment to which even an all-knowing physician could not offer any cure, namely a shortage of funds. The subjects are treated in the form of questions and answers which method added, of course, to the popularity of the book, but on the other hand, the names of the medicines are all given in Italian limiting its use to those conversant with that language.

The last two parts of the *Maasē Tubia* are, as stated, devoted to medicine. In the part which is called *Olam Hadash* (A New World) the author covers briefly the entire field of the science of medicine. He divides medicine into three branches, physiology, pathology and therapeutics and divides his work accordingly into three sections. In the first one which he calls *Eretz ha-Hadashah* (The New Land), he discusses the structure of the body, its state of health and diseases, gives the rules of diagnosis by the pulse and the color of urine and also devotes some chapters to hygiene. The second section denominated *Beth Hadash* (The New House) treats of pathology. He compares the human body to a house and discusses the diseases of the various parts accordingly, beginning with the head or the top of the house and ending with the feet or the foundation. Tobias is almost the only physician of the century who describes in detail a certain skin disease peculiar to Poland which was also frequent among the Jews of that country and was known as *Pelica Polonia.* The third section called *Mishmar ha-Bayith* (The Guard of the House) discusses the cures of disease and various medicines. The part named *Gan Naool* (The Closed Garden) discusses diseases peculiar to women and their cure, and its second division closes with an appendix containing a list of herbs and fruits used in medicine together with their application for medicinal purposes. The book contains several fine drawings among them two bearing on the human anatomy.

On the whole, Tobias displays a thorough acquaintance with the medicine of his time and knows of Harvey's discovery of the circulation of the blood, but he is still addicted to the Mediaeval terminology and speaks of the humours and the animal spirit which has its seat in the heart and the psychic spirit located in the brain and similar things. Tobias' book marks the last important scientific contribution to Hebrew Mediaeval literature. With the beginning of the eighteenth century, the production of scientific literature in Hebrew practically ceases.

Chapter VII

THE KABBALA

104. INTRODUCTORY

The mystic literature of the second period of the Mediaeval Ages presents a reverse aspect than that of other branches of literary activity. While the latter display, on the whole, a decline in the quality of their productions as compared with those of the preceding period, the former, on the contrary, attains during the same portion of time, Classic height and splendor. The best and most typical books on mysticism were written during these centuries, and that form of expression of the Jewish genius, which hitherto formed only a small current in the stream of Jewish literature, began from the thirteenth century on to increase and swell until it reached enormous proportions and exerted great influence upon the character of Jewish life up to the end of the Mediaeval period. It fermented, as one acquainted with Jewish history knows, numerous Messianic stirrings among the Jewish masses and gave rise to great popular movements of which Hassidism is the most typical example.

Mysticism, during the period under discussion, not only received a fresh impetus for productivity but also assumed a new name. The teachers of the new esoteric doctrines were no more satisfied with the modest names, *Torath ha-Nistor* (Secret Teachings) or simply *Sodoth* (Secrets), which were in vogue in the earlier epoch of mysticism (Vol. I, p. 383) but gave to their teachings the name *Kabbala* (Tradition) by which appellation it is henceforth known. By this they meant to indicate that their doctrines, though not widely known and though not mentioned in the Bible nor in the Talmud, were yet handed down from man to man during the ages, down to the first Kabbalists at the beginning of the thirteenth century. In fact, several of the early Kabbalists state explicitly that their teachings are passed over in silence both by the Bible and the Talmud but that the devotees of the secret lore (Baale ha-Abodah) received some intimation of them by oral tradition.[1]

The Kabbalistic tradition traces the origin of the Kabbala to Isaac the Blind (period of activity 1190-1200), the son of Abraham of Posquiers, the great Talmudic scholar and opponent of Maimonides (Vol. I, Sect. 150). Some sources, however, ascend two generations and declare David, the father of Abraham, the first teacher of this doctrine, while one source gives the following chain of transmission of this mystic teaching, Isaac the Nazarite, his disciple Jacob the Nazarite, succeeded by Abraham ben David, who in turn taught the Kabbala to his son Isaac the Blind. It is to be noted that in all these cases, the real transmitter o fthe secrets is the prophet Elijah. All sources agree that it was he who imparted the instruction and only differ as to who was the first recipient of this lore, whether Isaac the Nazarite or David or Isaac the Blind. Yet, though these men are named the founders of the new mysticism, little is left of their teachings or writings with the possible exception of Jacob the Nazarite to whom a small mystic work is ascribed by some scholars (see below). The real development of the Kabbala begins with Azriel, the disciple of Isaac the Blind.

The fact that the early Kabbalists name as the founders of the theory persons who preceded them only by a generation or two and coupled with the phenomenon that during the two centuries (the 11th and 12th) which separates the earlier and later currents of mysticism hardly anything was produced in that field, gave rise to many speculations as to the place of origin of the Kabbala. Zunz believes that the seat of the mystic teachings was Palestine, and from there it was transmitted to Italy and southern France and thence to northern Spain and Germany.[2] Jellinek and others assert that the home of the Kabbala was Babylonia and thence it spread to Spain and Germany. In fact, there is a recorded tradition in the name of Eleazar of Worms (d. 1238), a German Kabbalist, that a certain mystic Abu Aaron of Babylonia came to Lombardy at the end of the ninth century, and finding there the scholar and *Paitan* Moses ben Kalonymos, instructed him in the secret lore.[3] This tradition was considered for a time legendary and the very existence of Abu Aaron was doubted. But the recently discovered historical Chronicle of Ahimaatz (Vol.

[1] Ma'areketh Elohuth, ed. Mantua, Ch. VII. p. 82.
[2] Gottesdienstlichen Forträge, p. 404.
[3] Joseph Solomon Del Medigo in Mezareff Le-Hokmah, ed. Amst. 1631, p. 145.

I, Sect. 191) written in southern Italy, in the year 1054 corroborates the tradition, as it speaks of the arrival of Abu Aaron from Bagdad to Bari in the second half of the ninth century and describes him as a miracle worker versed in practical mysticism. Graetz sees in the Kabbala a reaction against the spread of Aristotelian philosophy among the Jews which reached its climax through the influence of Maimonides. The late Dr. Neumark, while conceding the influence of Palestinian teachings upon German mystics endeavors to explain the Spanish-Provence type of Kabbala as a mere accentuation of the mystic element contained in the teachings of some of the Jewish philosophers, such as Saadia, Bahya and others.

Each of the theories cited, undoubtedly, does not contain the whole truth and does not explain sufficiently the rise of such a complicated system as that of the Kabbala. However, each one contains a part of the truth and by a combination of these parts, we may probably arrive at the proper explanation of the rise and origin of the new current of mysticism.

Our starting point in the solution of this problem is, that in spite of the claim that the founders of the Kabbala received their teachings by revelation through Elijah, which meant to indicate the sudden rise of the system by inspiration, the Kabbala is in reality an intensive development of the immature theories contained in the earlier mysticism and is a continuation of that current in Jewish thought and literature. In fact, we can find all the elements of the former phase of mysticism also in the Kabbala except that here they are both intensified and magnified to a considerable degree, and hence the complexity of its teachings.

As we pointed out in the survey of the earlier phase of mysticism (Vol. I, p. 383), that doctrine contained three main elements of prime importance and two subsidiary ones, which though mere results of the first three, yet served as factors in the development of the system. These are, first, the questions clustering around the *Merkabah,* i. e. the manifestations of God, His attributes and His relation to the world on the one hand, and the problems grouped around the question of creation, on the other hand. The second is the hypostatization of the Torah, making it together with its letters an eternal, or at least, the earliest being, as well as an instrument in the creation of the world. The third is the power attached to the names of God and those of the angels. The fourth is the extensive development of the belief in angels and the theory that they are the powers of God and the mediators between Him and the world. The last element is the conclusion drawn from the foregoing theories or elements, namely that since the letters of the Torah were the instruments in the creation of the world, and the names of God and angels possess peculiar powers, and the angels are the mediators between God and the world, it follows that by the proper use of these letters and names, one can work miracles and perform wonders. It is this theory which was especially cultivated in Germany. All these five elements of earlier mysticism are retained in the Kabbala in their entirety, and with the exception of some esoteric doctrines concerning the human soul and an extensive and rich symbolism, it contains hardly anything new. But in order to understand more clearly the nature of the Kabbala as well as its relation to earlier mysticism, we have to go into a further analysis of the first principles of the system and repeat partly in substance what was said on the subject in Volume I.

Mysticism, like Jewish religious philosophy, grappled with two problems. First, assuming that God is exalted above all being and that His essence is beyond all conception, how can we reconcile His relation with such a gross materialistic world as ours? Second, how could such an exalted Being ever create a material world, and whence did matter come? The solutions offered to these vexatious problems both by philosophy and mysticism are akin in principle, and in reality, the latter borrowed some of its most fundamental principles from the former and was influenced by it throughout its entire course of development. But because of its different methods of approach and essentially different outlook upon things, mysticism arrived at entirely divergent results.

The general character of the solution offered by mysticism to the above stated problems can be comprised in one word, mediation. By this is meant, as far as the first problem is concerned, that the relation between God and the world is carried on by mediators. On this principle, all currents of opinion in the doctrine agree. The difference arises in the nature of these mediators. One asserts that they are angels, another avers that they are merely powers embodied in the letters of the alphabet, while a third names them only attributes (Midoth), and both hypostatizes and endows them with peculiar power and force. The same solution was also applied to creation, namely that it was accomplished through mediators.

But here the question arose, whence the mediators? Are they created beings or do they constitute a series of emanations? On this point, there was undoubtedly a difference of opinion among the early mystics. The propounders of the theories that the letters and names of God served as instruments in creation and symbolize certain powers of God, as well as those who relegated all power to the angels, most likely kept aloof from the doctrine of emanation. They believed that the powers symbolized by the letters and names as well as the angels were created by God and endowed by Him with certain functions in the conduct of the world. This seems to be the underlying idea of the early mystic literature described in Volume I, section 181. But there were always restless spirits in Judaism who did not find such explanations sufficient to clarify all the complicated problems, and they turned to the more profound solution, that of emanation.

The theory of emanation which found its clearest expression in the system of Plotinus was not an innovation of his but merely perfected by him. Some of its teachings were afloat in the Oriental world of thought long before his time, and of course, were not unknown to Jewish sages. It is, therefore, most probable that the secret teaching designated by the Mishnah as *Maasē Bereshith* contained among its various teachings also some form of the doctrine of emanation.[4] However, little is left us of that particular doctrine from the time of the Tannaim to the end of the Gaonic period. The doctrine, however, continued to be cultivated, for it appears in a rudimentary form in the *Book of Creation* (Sepher Yetzira) described in Volume I, section 182.

The other current of mystic thought which speaks of mediators of various kinds kept on developing at an enormous pace, as is testified by the great mass of early mystic literature. In this literature, much emphasis is placed upon the powers symbolized by the combination of the letters of the alphabet and those of the various names of God, as well as on the development of a complete system of an heirarchy of angels and a classification of their functions.

The first attempt to combine both currents of mystic thought was made by the author of the *Book of Creation*. There, as pointed out in our survey of its teachings, much is made of the value of the letters of the alphabet and of the names of God and their combinations and permutations. But the theory of emanation is also stressed

[4] On this point, see Dr. Neumark, Toldoth ha-Pilisofia Be-Yisroel, Vol. I, pp. 55-76 and the author's Brochure, Ben Zoma, Ch. III.

and the ten Sephiroth[5] considered as ten emanations are mentioned there for the first time. True, the emanation theory is given in this book in its most rudimentary form and in an indefinite manner, yet it is contained there even if not fully developed.

The *Book of Creation* which appeared about the end of the ninth century, most likely in Palestine, but spread also to other Jewish centers, such as Babylonia, North Africa and Italy, gave undoubtedly a fresh impetus to the development of mysticism. However, this development went on in a secret way, as no authoritative book on the subject is found from the appearance of the *Sepher Yetzira* to the end of the twelfth century. The fragments containing Kabbalistic teachings and ascribed by later Kabbalists to various Gaonim as excerpts of larger works written by them are most likely spurious. The works themselves from which these fragments are supposed to be taken were never discovered. The *Sepher Yetzira* itself received quite a good deal of attention by the leading scholars of the tenth century. Almost simultaneously, Saadia Gaon in Babylon, Isaac Israeli in North Africa and Sabbatai Donolo in Southern Italy wrote commentaries to the book. But with the exception of the last one who retained in his commentary the mystic character of the book, the other two endeavored to introduce into it their own philosophical ideas rather than to expound the mystical doctrines really contained therein.

We must therefore, look for the continued development of mysticism during the three centuries, from the tenth to the twelfth, to less open channels of literary activity which found expression in small booklets of a pseudepigraphic character. This activity was undoubtedly carried on in Palestine, the home of mysticism and of its earlier literature, but it spread also to Babylon, and during the tenth century and later, both countries became centers of mysticism. In fact, the evidence for the existence of such activity in the latter country and of its literature comes to us from references in the Responsa of the last Gaonim. Hai Gaon (969-1037) speaks of a number of booklets of a mystic character bearing such exotic names as the Sword of Moses, the Lord of the Torah (Sar ha-Torah) and similar ones. The same source gives also the type of the mysticism cultivated. The inquiry which called forth this Responsum from Hai, contains a request addressed to the Gaon by several leading Babylonian scholars to enlighten them concerning the miracles and wonders performed

[5] For the meaning of the word Sephiroth see Vol. I, p. 393, also below.

by certain mystics through the use of various combinations of the letters of the holy names of God. From this, as well as from the Responsum itself which gives a few excerpts from the esoteric books mentioned we can see that those elements in mysticism were cultivated which emphasize the value of the combinations of the letters of the holy names and attribute great power to the angels, while the speculative side of mysticism contained in the theory of emanation was neglected. It was destined to rise later in other counries.

The letter combination and angelogical types of mysticism which ultimately gave rise to practical Kabbala (Kabbala Maasit), inasmuch as the mystics claimed to be able to perform miracles by manipulation with the names of God and angels, were pursued, as said, from the tenth to the twelfth centuries both in Palestine and Babylon and from these two centers they were brought to southern Italy. There is certainly truth in the tradition quoted above of the arrival of Abu Aaron from Bagdad to that country and of his imparting instruction in the mysteries to Jewish scholars there. But as Italy, during this period, was in close communication and under the influence of Palestine, it is reasonable to assume that it also contributed its share of influence to the development of mystic teaching in the former country. That the letter combination type of mysticism was brought over to Italy as early as the tenth century can be seen from Sabbatai Donolo's commentary on the *Book of Creation,* written at that time, which emphasizes extensively the letter and Divine name elements in the book, and passes over in silence the emanation theory, for Donolo speaks of the Sephiroth as symbolizing physical elements.

Side by side with the type of letter mysticism, there continued to be cultivated the angelogical variety of mystic teachings which was already found in the earlier books, the *Otioth di Rabbi Akiba* and the *Hekaloth* group, in a fair stage of development (Vol. I, Sect. 181), and ultimately these two types amalgamated into one. We can not describe the method of amalgamation nor determine its exact time, as the ways of the development of mysticism during the eleventh and twelfth centuries are difficult to follow. We only know that by the end of the twelfth century and through the thirteenth, a fully developed practical Kabbala is revealed for us in Germany. Its most typical representative is Eleazar of Worms. He, as stated, traces the tradition of mysticism to Italy and to Abu Aaron who instructed Moses ben Kalonymos in its lore. This Moses who, according to Eleazar's version was the father of the Kalonymos family of *Paitanim,* was transported by Charles the Bald to Germany at the end of the ninth century. It seems that mysticism was for a long time the private heritage of this illustrious family until Eleazar himself, one of its descendants, began to publish its teachings. He had a few disciples who followed his type of mysticism to a certain degree, notable among whom was Abraham di Colonia (Koln). This phase of the Kabbala which may be designated the German Kabbala and which, as we have shown, is really a descendant of the Palestinian-Babylonian mysticism of Gaonic times, flourished only for a short time during the thirteenth century. It was soon superseded by the other phase which bears the name of speculative Kabbala (Kabbala Iyyunith) that had its rise in the Provence and attained its zenith in Spain. In fact, the former was not really superseded but absorbed by the latter, for the more perfect type of Kabbala, the Spanish one typified in the *Zohar,* is really an amalgamation of all elements though the emanation theory always remains its central teaching.

105. GERMAN TYPE OF KABBALA

We have thus far endeavored to trace the relation of the various phases of the Kabbala and especially the German type to the earlier mysticism. It remains for us to say a few words about the character of this type before we turn to the more important current of later mysticism, the speculative one. As was pointed out, two distinct elements are to be found in this particular variety of the Kabbala, namely the mystic power attached to the names of God and to the letters of the alphabet on the one hand, and the exceptional role played by the angels in the creation of the world and its conduct on the other hand. Both of these elements are of ancient origin, for we find them expressed in a simple and rudimentary form in the Talmud and Midrashim. In the earlier mystic literature, we find two distinct types of books, the *Otioth di Rabbi Akiba* and similar works, which emphasize the first element and the *Hekaloth* group which deals primarily with the second, i. e. angelology. Yet no fast line can be drawn between these two sets of books, for we find references in the first group to the power of angels and their functions, especially to that of *Metatron* the Archangel, and likewise is the theory that the letters were instruments in the creation of the world mentioned several times in the second group. From this we can see clearly that earlier mysticism really united in its teachings both these phases.

The author of the *Book of Creation*, however, had almost entirely omitted the theory of the power of angels as there is only a single reference to it and developed instead the letter and Divine-name mysticism into a system. Not only does he speak of the letters of both the names of God and of the alphabet as having been instruments in creation but he also discusses their division and their various combinations. By figuring out that there are two hundred and thirty-one permutations to each letter of the alphabet when joined with the other twenty-one letters, he opened a wide way of speculation on this subject. Accordingly, the letter mysticism began to develop extensively after the appearance of the *Book of Creation.* The gist of this teaching is that since the letters of the Divine names and those of the alphabet possess a mystic power of creating things, it follows that any one who is acquainted with the secret of combining these letters or with the manipulations of their various permutations can also perform wonders as well as penetrate into the secrets of wisdom. Moreover, the mystics were not satisfied with the mere permutations of the letters but employed other devices also, such as the numerical value of certain letters, (Gematria), e. g. if the numerical value of any word happened to equal the numerical value of any of the known names of God, that word also was considered a holy name. A second device was the *Notaricon,* i. e. if the initials of the words in a certain sentence spelled a Divine name or equalled in numerical value any of the names of God, the sentence acquired special significance. A third device is the substitution of the letters of the alphabet one for the other, namely the alphabet is divided into any number of groups and each letter of one group is substituted for the corresponding letter of the other group. We will cite a few examples of the well known systems of substitution. The first is the *At Bash* where the letters placed at the beginning of the alphabet exchange with those placed at the end, thus, the *Aleph* with the *Tau,* the *Beth* with the *Shin,* etc.; the other is the *Al Bam* where the letters are likewise divided into groups of eleven each, and the *Aleph* exchanges with the *Lamed,* the *Beth* with the *Mem,* etc.

As a result of the employment of all these devices, the number of Divine names increased a hundred fold. Almost any word or verse in the Bible could be made to yield holy names and acquire peculiar significance. In other words, the entire Bible became one mystic text full of secrets (Sodoth) and esoteric teaching. In fact, Nahmanides states explicitly in the introduction to his commentary on the

Pentateuch that he is in possession of a true tradition that the entire Pentateuch consists of the names of God provided you know how to divide and arrange the letters properly. These peculiar manipulations of names and letters were greatly amplified when the current of letter and number mysticism was joined with the current of angelogical mysticism. These above stated devices when applied to the names of angels increased their number manifold and correspondingly the number of secrets and esoteric doctrines. And this brings us to the subject of angelology.

The existence of angels is spoken of in the Bible numerous times but nowhere except in the Book of Daniel, parts of which belong to the Maccabean age, are they mentioned by name. It seems that this namelessness signifies indefiniteness of conception, for the Biblical term *Malak* simply means messenger. Accordingly, in many passages where this term is mentioned, it may be interpreted to mean a prophet who was sent by God with a special mission, and the Rabbis in the Agada interpret some passages in this manner. In many passages, however, the term *Malakim* and especially *Seraphim* actually indicates supernatural beings with fiery-winged bodies as in Isaiah Ch. VI, 2-4. But still in the pre-exilic Biblical books, no specific function is assigned to those angels. It is only in the post-exilic times, when through external influence as well as through certain inner spiritual conditions, a whole system of angelology began to shape itself, that we begin to hear of name-bearing angels who assume definite functions. Thus in Daniel, Ch. VIII, 16 we read of an angel *Gabriel,* a compound of *Geber,* man, and *El,* a name of God, who is called so according to verse 15, because he appears in human form. It may also be that the name was given him because he functions on occasions when power is needed, the compound *Geber* should then be related to *Geburah,* strength. Again, we find in the same book X, 13 and XII, 1 the name of an angel Michael (Heb. Mi-Ko-El, i. e. who is like God) who is called in the first verse "One of the first princes" in the hierarchy of heaven, and in the second reference, he is assigned a special function, namely to take care of the Jewish people.

We note then in the Book of Daniel the beginnings of an angelic hierarchy of mediators between God and the world. The further steps of this development are noted in the Apocalyptic and pseudepigraphic books where the number of angels is constantly increased and new names signifying different functions appear. The early

Agada also contains some phases of this new development of the angelic hierarchy. We find in the Talmud a number of names of angels some of which are Hebrew compounds and some are even borrowed from Greek and Latin. Under the influence of the Philonian Logos (Vol. I, Sect. 180) and other mystic teachings which were prevalent in the Oriental world in the first century, there rises to a place of exceptional importance in the current of early Jewish mysticism, an angel by the name of *Metatron* (for meaning of the name see Vol. I, p. 381). He becomes the real mediator between God and the world. In some Agadic passages, he is merely spoken of as an angel, but in others, he is designated as *Sar ha-Olam* (The Prince of the World), which shows that he is commissioned with the supervision of its conduct. In this way, the power of mediation of the angels reached a high degree. The Tannaim of the second period, noting the development of the tendency of magnifying the power of mediation of the angels and fearing that it may ultimately undermine the pure conception of monotheism, especially the idea of the direct Providence of God, attempted to check its growth. Thus, Rabbi Joshua ben Hanania taught that angels do not exist forever but are created and pass away; and still more, that every day a new group of angels come into being and as soon as they sing the praise of God, pass through the river of fire called *Di-Nur* and are consumed.[6] Even *Metatron* himself was not spared, and on one occasion, he is said by the Talmud to have been the recipient of a severe and undignified punishment.[7] All these statements were made with the intent and purpose of representing the angels as mere beings created by God, subject to His will and disposition, who serve as messengers to perform a certain act, not as meditors with extended or full powers.

However, this check by the official spokesman of Judaism was not really effective. The current of mysticism continued to flow in its channel, and in the literature produced by its representatives, the angels kept their place of importance as mediators and even multiplied and increased. As was described in the first volume (Sect. 381), both groups that of *Aleph-Beth* Midrashim ascribed to Rabbi Akiba and the *Hekaloth* group ascribed to Rabbi Ishmael developed a complicated hierarchy of angels and assigned to them great power as mediators.

[6] Bereshit Rabba, Ch. LXXVIII, sect. 1.
[7] T. Bab. Hagega, 15a.

The place of *Metatron* is raised even higher. In the *Otioth Di Rabbi Akiba,* he is credited with possessing, like God, seventy names and is even called the smaller or lower God (YHWH ha-Katon). This appellation is full of significance and was bound to bear some mystic fruit.

The theory which raised *Metatron* to the highest mediator or rather as the plenipotentiary of God as indicated by the above appellation, was secretly developed by the mystic school during the centuries until it was revealed for us in fuller form in the Provence and Germany at the beginning of the thirteenth century. As it is known, one of the purposes of Jewish philosophy was to purify the conception of God, and consequently explain all anthropomorphisms of the Bible. This tendency must have affected also the mystics and they attempted to solve the problem in their own way utilizing the role of mediator played by *Metatron* or another angel, called *Sar ha-Ponim* (The Prince of the Presence) for that purpose.

The earliest reference to such an attempt by a mystic sect in Babylonia, during the tenth or eleventh century, to solve the problem of anthropomorphism in the Bible, we find in the work of the Arabic writer Shahrastani (fl. at the end of the 11th century), in his Religious and Philosophic Sects. In this work, he describes a Jewish sect by the name of *Makariba* (according to Jellinek, the name is derived from *Merkabah,* i. e. The Mystic Chariot) and says of them, "They believe that God spoke with the prophets through the mediacy of a certain angel whom he chose from among all his creatures and made him His plenipotentiary in this world. They further say that the descriptions of God found in the Bible refer to this angel for it is impossible to describe God in any form. They assert that it is the angel who spoke to Moses from the thorn bush and elsewhere, as God can not possibly exchange words with man."

References to the *Kerub ha-Meyoo'hod,* the special cherub who wields all power in the world are also found in Gaonic lore. But while in these writings, the doctrine is in a rudimentary form, it is fully developed by the Kabbalists of the twelfth and thirteenth centuries. Two thirteenth-century Kabbalists quote Abraham ben David as saying, "The Agadic remark that God puts on phylacteries and similar statements refer to the *Sar- ha-Ponim* (The Angel of the Presence), or perhaps there is one higher than he who is emanated from the highest cause and possesses the highest power. It is this angel that appeared to Moses and to Ezekiel, in the form of a man sitting on the chariot, as well as to all the other prophets. The Cause of Causes however, never appeared to any man in any way, and this is the secret of creation."[8] We do not exactly know what Abraham ben David means by the words "secret of creation," but it is sufficiently clear that the theory of a mediating angel was carried by him very far and to a point where he assumes almost all the functions of God's rule in the world. Finally, the German Kabbalist, Eleazar of Worms wrote a special book by the name of *ha-Kerub* or *ha-Kabod* where he develops fully the theory of the ruling angel. According to him, the *Kerub* practically rules the world, while God, the Cause of Causes, is hidden beyond any cognizance. This then is the zenith of the angelological current of mysticism. It must be admitted, however, that this extreme tendency in angelology was not accepted by all Kabbalists. The others were satisfied with multiplying the number of angels and assigning to them various functions. Even Rabbi Eleazar of Worms who speaks of the plenipotentiary angel does not mean to make him the only mediator but merely places him at the head of a great hierarchy of subordinate angels.

The joining of both the letter and the angelological currents of mysticism into one system made the esoteric doctrines still more complicated. To the numerous combinations and devious methods used by the mystics in regard to the names of God and the letters of the alphabet there were added, as stated, more devices which were applied to the names of the angels. As a result, the names of the angels multiplied, for each one received more than one name, for by turning the letters of the principal name in various ways, a number of appellations were obtained. In this way, almost every text of the Scriptures and of the prayers could be made to produce names of angels, and hence, the number of secrets (Sodoth) contained in the Scriptures as well as in the prayers became very numerous. In fact, special books were composed by the Kabbalists for the purpose of revealing the secrets of the prayers. One of such books *Sodoth ha-Tephilah* (The Secrets of Prayer) was written by Eleazar of Worms. And, moreover, even special prayers to angels were composed asking them to intercede on behalf of the supplicant. This was done in view of the fact that some angels are supposed to function as the bearers of the prayers bringing them to the attention of God.

[8] Quoted in Ma'areketh Elohuth, Ch. X, p. 157, also by Isaac of Acco in his Meirath Enayyim at the beginning of the weekly portion of *Bo*.

All these teachings were not developed for a mere theoretical purpose but had a practical ring to them. For if we assume that there is a supernatural power attached to the combination of the letters of the Divine names and also that the knowledge of the private names of angels imparts to the possessor a power over that angel, it follows that the use of such combinations and names will bring definite positive results. Thus, in order to cure the sick all that one need do is to write a formula containing certain names of God or the names of angels whose function it is to bring disease upon man and order the illness to disappear by these very names. Such formulas were really invented for all events in human life and even in nature. Hence, the excessive use of amulets (Kameoth) and charms. The matter is, however, not so simple, for in the occurrence of events, several powers participate. For instance, as every event takes place in time and as time is divided into seasons, months, weeks and days, and each of these divisions is supervised by a separate angel, we must, therefore, implore not only the angel whose function it is to supervise that particular event but also the angels who have charge of that division of time in which the event occurs. The amulets, therefore, must contain a number of formulas. We can not, of course, go into the mazes of this particular trend in mysticism which employed various ways and devices in order to attain the desired ends. The above can only serve as an illustration of the workings of the method.

This then is the character of that phase of Kabbala which was cultivated during several centuries in Babylonia, Palestine and ultimately brought into Italy and Germany. The typical representative of this phase of the Kabbala is Eleazar of Worms, who in his fifteen Kabbalistic works embodies all these teachings. He deals with letter and number mysticism, with angelology and with the practical use of the results of the theories. It is from this school that the *Sepher Raziel* emanated, where we find numerous formulas for the fulfillment of all needs of life. There we find instructions how to succeed in business, to escape enemies, to find buried treasure, and even how to pass through fire and not be injured or how to wade through deep water and not be drowned.

We must understand, however, first, that these teachings were not limited to Germany, as they were known also in France and Spain, and second, that not even all German Kabbalists emphasized the various elements of their teachings alike. Some laid more emphasis on the letter combination theory and some stressed the angelological phase. What is important for us to know is, that those two elements are found in all systems of Kabbala and play a great part even in the speculative phase which is the standard type. It is for this purpose that we have gone at length into delineating these elements or phases of mysticism. To dwell, as many writers on the subject have done, merely on the speculative phase of the Kabbala, would lead to a misunderstanding of the entire nature of this form of Jewish thought as expressed in its leading works, especially in the *Zohar* and principal post-Zoharitic mystic books. The later type of Kabbala, though containing a good deal of speculative matter is, after all, not philosophy. It absorbed also the other phases of mysticism which we may designate the irrational ones and blended them together with the speculative into one complicated system.

106. SPECULATIVE KABBALA (Kabbala Iyyunith)

When undertaking to delineate the development of the speculative current in Kabbala which appeared at the beginning of the thirteenth century in Provence, the investigator in this field of Jewish thought finds his task exceedingly difficult. The origins of this doctrine are not so easily traced to the teachings of early mysticism as those of the other current. It is true that the later Kabbalists ascribed some mystic works to some of the Gaonim where the doctrine of the Sephiroth—the central doctrine of the speculative Kabbala—is taught and expounded, but as pointed out, these works are spurious. We will, therefore, have to look elsewhere for its origins.

The only link which unites the speculative Kabbala to the earlier Gaonic mysticism are the few Mishnoth (sections) in the first chapter of the *Book of Creation* where the theory of the Sephiroth is cryptically and enigmatically taught. It is clear that the Mishnoth gave the speculatively minded mystics the starting point for the development of their system. Yet, there is a great distance between the Sephiroth theory of the *Sepher Yetzira* and that of the Kabbalists. In spite of all later interpretations by mystic scholars who endeavored to put their own ideas into the words of that book, one can clearly see that the Sephiroth of the *Sepher Yetzira,* with the exception of one, are primarily physical elements, while those of the Kabbala are spiritual forces. Further, creation according to that book was accomplished by means of letter combinations and the names of God and not by a series of emanations and Divine influences as the speculative Kabbala teaches. It must be admitted though that there is reference to emanation in the *Sepher Yetzira,* inasmuch as the ninth Mishnah in Chapter I teaches the emanation of the first Sephirah, namely the spirit of the living God or the *Holy Spirit* (Ruah ha-Kodesh). But this is done in a rudimentary form. It is evident that other influences were at work to convert this elementary teaching of the Sephiroth emanation of the *Book of Creation* into the complicated system of the later Kabbalists.

We are unable to trace the stages in the development of the Sephiroth theory or to describe definitely all influences that shaped and moulded it. But a deeper study of the Neo-Platonic current in Jewish philosophy, namely the systems of Gabirol and his followers will reveal to us at least one of the sources of these influences. We find many parallels between the teachings of Ibn Gabirol and to a degree also those of Bahya Ibn Pakudah in his work *Toroth ha-Nephesh,* and the later Kabbala.

Ibn Gabirol teaches in his *Mekor Hayyim* (Fons Vitae), as described in the first volume (Sect. 167), the creation of the world by a series of emanations of substances which became more material the further they are removed from the first source. He speaks of the Divine will which flashes through the universal matter and unites it with the universal form acting as a force which binds the entire universe into one. True, he does not make clear whether universal matter and universal form were created by Divine will or emanated from God, but the will itself is a kind of emanation hypostatized by him, and Gabirol clearly states that the mediate substances between God and the sublunar world were emanated from the first two. Further, that the mediate or the simple substances, as he calls them, are: the universal intellect, the universal soul and the universal nature. Again, Bahya in his *Toroth ha-Nephesh* (The Doctrines of the Soul) teaches that there are three worlds besides the lower world; namely the world of intellect, the world of the soul and the world of nature (Olam ha-Teba).

To all these teachings, we find corresponding theories in the Kabbala. It teaches that the Sephiroth emanated one from the other, and that they act as mediators between God and the world. It makes the will of God play a role in the universe similar to that described by Gabirol, sometimes under the same name of will (Hephetz, or *Reutha* in Aramaic) and sometimes under the name of influence (Hashpaha). It also adopted the same division of the mediators into intellect, soul and nature in its triad division of the Sephiroth (see below). As for Bahya, it was most likely his classification of the entire existence into four worlds which served as the prototype of the Kabbalistic four world theory, namely the worlds of *Aziluth* (Emanation), *Beriah* (Creation), *Yetzira* (Formation) and *Asiyya* (Action). In fact, even this idea may be traced to Gabirol for he, according to Ibn Ezra, was the first to see in Isaiah Ch. XLIII, 7, the allusion to the mystery of the world, the very same verse from which the Kabbalists derive the existence of three out of the four worlds they posit. In addition, Gabirol's comparison of the expansion of the will of God in matter to the penetration of the rays of light in the air, became one of the fundamental symbolic expressions of the Kabbala.

From all these, it can evidently be seen that Gabirol's system and similar views of Jewish Neo-Platonic philosophers served as a leaven to ripen and develop the theories of the speculative Kabbala, primarily the Sephiroth theory which is its central doctrine. It is, of course, understood that these teachings can only be considered one source of the development of the Kabbalistic doctrines, and that there were undoubtedly a number of other factors at work which brought about their shaping and moulding. There was certainly influence exerted through some channels upon these teachings by Moslem mysticism known as Sufism and by other non-Jewish esoteric systems. But what interests us is that these teachings were gradually developed from the rudimentary Sephiroth theory of the *Book of Creation* into the full system which began to find expression in the early Kabbalist literature. We can not assign a definite reason why the Kabbala appeared just at the time it did, since there is no doubt that some of its principal teachings were known a long time before. But there is some truth to the assertion often made by Jewish scholars that the rise of the Kabbala at the end of the twelfth century was primarily due to a reaction in Jewish life and thought against the spread and dominance of the Aristotelian philosophy. The Kabbala, though some of its speculative teachings dissent from the fundamental view of Judaism in a greater degree than the doctrines of philosophy, is mainly permeated by a deep religious emotion and spirit of piety. Its appearance and rise, therefore, represent the struggle of religious emotion against a dry rationalism.

However, whatever the reasons for the rise of the new current of mysticism might have been, the fact is that from the end of the twelfth century to the beginning of the fourteenth, we note a feverish literary activity in the field of mysticism, which culminating in the appearance of the *Zohar,* gradually developed that system of thought known as the speculative Kabbala or simply Kabbala. We will briefly trace the development of the principal stages of that system as reflected in its literature from its rise to the *Zohar.*

The first Classic work of the Kabbala is the *Masekheth Azilut* (The Tractate on Emanation). It belongs most likely to the twelfth century and was written either by Jacob Nazir himself or by one of his disciples. In this work, we note the sproutings of the most important elements of the Kabbala and its deviations from both the philosophic and the ordinary views of Judaism. First, it introduces the element of emanation in the creation of the world; second, it teaches for the first time the existence of four worlds: that of emanation, creation, formation and action. Third, it refers to the doctrine of concentration of God's light at the beginning of the process of creation, from which there emanated both light, the primal matter of the world, and darkness, which the book considers a positive element and the origin of gross matter. Finally, the author develops the doctrine of the Sephiroth, and gives them their standard names which are indicative of their functions. These ten Sephiroth are not, as in the *Book of Creation,* the four elements and the points of space but spiritual forces, both the instruments in creation and hypostatized attributes of God. The author, however, does not develop the theory of emanation fully, and does not reject creation entirely. (For details see below.)

The next stage of development of the doctrines of the Kabbala is to be seen in the book known as the *Bahir* (Clearness). According to the opinion of most of the Jewish scholars, it is the work of a disciple of Isaac the Blind, often called the father of the Kabbala. It does not bear his name, but in the usual way of the Kabbalists to give their work a pseudepigraphic character, it is ascribed to Nehunya ben ha-Kanah, a Tanna of the second generation, who is mentioned in earlier mystic literature as a transmitter of the esoteric teachings.

In the *Bahir,* the outlines of the doctrines delineated in the Tractate on Emanation are expanded and assume a fuller form. The existence of the world, or at least some element of it, before the process of creation described in Genesis, is asserted. It is not made clear though whether actual or potential existence is meant. The later Kabbalists interpreted it as a potential existence, for to assume an actual existence would have meant to posit the eternity of the world. The Sephiroth theory is further expanded. Out of the primal light which is called the Hidden Light (Or ha-Ganus) and also *Kether Elyon* (The Highest Crown) the other two Sephiroth emanated, *Hokmah and Binah* (Wisdom and Understanding). These three represent the head, and out of them emanated the seven lower Sephiroth. The Sephiroth are the powers of God through which He manifests His Being and not merely instruments. Through them the world had arisen and through them it is conducted, maintained and stabilized. The *Bahir* introduces also a great part of the symbolism which plays such an important role in the Kabbala, especially the symbolism centering around the human form. The human form is, according to the Kabbala, a reflection of the manifestations of the God-head and is often called *Adam Kadmon,* (First or Original Man, see below), and much is made of this theory in the entire mystic literature. The *Bahir* begins to develop this view and draws comparisons between the Sephiroth and the organs of the human body. There are in the book also the beginnings of the uniting of the two currents in mysticism, namely the doctrine of the combination of letters and the emanation theory. The author symbolizes the Sephiroth by certain letters of the alphabet and claims that they are also expressed by letters in God's names. Finally, we meet there in a rudimentary but fairly developed form the important doctrines of the sexual dualism existing in everything (the male symbolizing the active and the female the passive principle) and the value of their unification (Zivug). The *Bahir,* therefore, represents the second stage of the Kabbalistic theories in a considerably expanded form but still far from complete.

Another step in the development of the Kabbalistic theory is made in the work of Rabbi Azriel (d. 1238), the disciple of Isaac the Blind. Azriel left three Kabbalistic works, (1) a *Commentary on the Ten Sephiroth,* (2) a *Commentary on the Song of Songs,* and (3) a *Commentary on the Sepher Yetzira.* He utilizes to a great extent the philosophic method in his explanation of the theories and is the clearest of the Kabbalist writers. The gist of his teachings is as follows: Of God we know only what He is not, but not what He is; all that we can say of Him is that He is the *En-Sof* (Unlimited), a term often employed in Kabbala but first used by Azriel; He is all-embracing, and all being is potentially in Him. From this cardinal principle follow the other principles of his teaching, namely the potential eternity of the world and the character of the Sephiroth. The world, according to him, was potentially eternal in God, and creation meant a bringing out from the potential into the actual or an outflowing and an emanation. This creative emanation was in the form of a series of degrees from the infinite to the finite, from the spiritual to the material.

This transition was accomplished by means of the Sephiroth which are both infinite and finite. They are infinite, insofar as they receive constant influence from God, and finite insofar as He by His will may diminish the flow of that influence. They were emanated and not created. They are ten and yet one, for God is their source and their power is contained in Him. Likewise, each higher Sephirah contains the powers of the lower ones, and consequently they are enfolded one in the other and all in God. As an illustration of the simultaneous unity and diversity of the Sephiroth we may cite the flame, sparks and the color of the fire which are all one though they appear different. The Sephiroth were emanated at different times. The first Sephirah which contains the powers of the rest existed always potentially, and likewise the second. The other Sephiroth which were used in the creation of the world were emanated before creation. Yet their late emanation indicates no change in the will of God, as their powers were contained in the first two which existed potentially from eternity. Finally, Azriel teaches that every Sephirah as well as every being and thing contains two powers, an active and a passive (male and female), for by the unity of these powers, they testify to the unity existing in the universe. He also adds to the symbolism of the Kabbala by employing a scheme of colors which represent the various Sephiroth.

The final stage of development of the speculative mystic theory in the pre-Zoharite Kabbalistic literature is represented by the *Ma'arekheth* group of works. To this belong the *Sepher ha-Temunah* and the *Ma'arekheth Elohuth* (The Divine Order) itself and several others. The first of the two is by an unknown author, and inasmuch as the Tanna, Rabbi Nehunya ben ha-Kanah is given as the supposed author, it is pseudepigraphic, though some scholars ascribe it to Rabbi Perez Cohen. The second is of indefinite authorship. Both were written about the end of the thirteenth century. In the *Temunah,* the Sephiroth are definitely described as inherent forces in God flowing out of Him in a natural way. Their relation to God is said to be like the relation of the organs to the body as a whole.

In this book, we find also clearly expressed the idea of a double emanation, the positive and the negative. From the three higher Sephiroth, two series of emanations descended, each consisting of seven members, one incarnating all that is good and beautiful, the other representing strictness, rigorousness and ultimately evil. By positing this double emanation, the Kabbala attempted to explain the origin of evil.

In the *Ma'are*k*eth* which is a large work consisting of fifteen chapters, the first seven called *Maara*k*oth* (Orders) and the last eight *Shearim* (Portals), all the various strands of the Kabbalistic theory are woven together into a connected whole. The special contribution of the book consists in the increased symbolism of the Sephiroth theory. The author quotes a multitude of names by which each Sephirah is known, each signifying a different function. He also introduces the tripartite division of the Sephiroth, namely into the right, left and middle groups (see below). He develops the two important teachings of the Kabbala, the likeness of the order of the Divine powers of the Sephiroth to the human body (The First Man or the Adam Kadmon theory), and the erotic motive, namely the functions of the male and female elements in being and their unification (Zivug).

We have thus surveyed briefly the stages of the speculative Kabbala as they progressed during the thirteenth century and prepared the way for the appearance of the *Zohar.* We are now prepared for a more systematic exposition of the theories of the Kabbala as embodied in the *Zohar,* the standard work of the entire system which embraces all elements and phases, the rational as well as the irrational. But before undertaking the exposition, we must take account of another smaller current in thirteenth century mysticism and also discuss briefly the extent and nature of symbolism in the Kabbala.

Besides this larger current of speculative Kabbala centering around the Sephiroth, there was also another one which clung to the letter and number type of mysticism. The representatives of this current were Abraham Abulafia of Toledo (1240-1300) and Abraham of Cologne (2nd half of the 13th century), the disciple of Eleazar of Worms. Abulafia though he does not reject in his numerous Kabbalistic works the Sephiroth theory entirely, yet minimizes its value. He even criticizes some of the Kabbalists for making the Sephiroth a part of the essence of God or identifying them with Him. To him they are more the symbols of God's powers which He manifests at will than actual emanations. Abulafia lays prime importance upon the combinations of the letters of the alphabet, and especially upon those of the names of God. He develops a complicated system of combinations and permutations of letters and believes that by means of these it is possible for the initiated to attain to the knowledge of all wisdom and hidden secrets, and even prophecy. As a matter of fact, he calls his Kabbalistic system the prophetic Kabbala.

Abraham of Cologne does not go as far as Abulafia in his minimizing the value and character of the Sephiroth, but in his *Kether Shem Tob* (The Crown of the Good Name, i. e. the Divine Name), he attempts to reconcile between the theory of the Sephiroth and the type of letter mysticism and combine them into one. The booklet is devoted entirely to the name of God, i. e. the *Tetragamaton* and its substitutes. He endeavors to show how the letters of the Divine name both by their form and by their numerical value symbolize the Sephiroth and their functions and point to other phenomena in the creation and conduct of the world. Abraham of Cologne also knows of the likeness of the order of the Sephiroth to the human form; and draws the usual parallels. He likewise uses the color scheme employed by the Spanish-Provence Kabbalists to indicate the functions of the Sephiroth.

Though this current was a minor one in the teachings of the Kabbala, yet its influence was not lost and some of its doctrines were incorporated in the summing up of the entire system which is embodied in the *Zohar*. There we find all elements of mysticism thrown together in an unsystematic manner, for though one phase may predominate, yet all other phases are also found there in a more or less chaotic form. It is this peculiar nature of construction which makes it so difficult to understand the book and to comprehend its theories.

ii. Symbolism

If the theories of the Sephiroth and that of emanation, the development of which we outlined, are the soul of Kabbala, then symbolism and figures of speech can be said to be its body. Without a conception of the many-hued symbolic language in which this esoteric teaching attempts to convey its ideas, one can hardly comprehend its nature and character. All symbols, as was already pointed out (Vol. I, p. 384), are meant to be a bridge between the limited human mind and high abstract conceptions. They represent an attempt to clutch at ideas which are otherwise inexpressible by human language and make them more comprehensible by means of more familiar figures and notions. It follows, therefore, that the higher the ideas, the more delicate and refined the conceptions which underlie a system of thought, the more extensive and the more complicated is the symbolism employed by the teachers of that system. It is especially so when that system aims to appeal primarily not to the mind but to the human heart and to the imagination as is the case with mysticism in general and with the Kabbala in particular.

The great source of symbolism in Kabbala is the doctrine of the special value of the letters of the alphabet and those of the Divine names. From this doctrine, it follows that every letter is a symbol of some power or force, and not only the letter as a whole, but its form and shape and even its various parts all have some significance. If we add to this the innumerable combinations, mutations and substitutions employed by the initiated in letter and number mysticism, we can easily grasp to what extent the number of symbols increased and multiplied. Another source of symbolism is the doctrine of the Sephiroth. The Sephiroth which are in essence abstractions of the Divine powers manifested in the world, could not in this pure form be grasped even by the intelligent. They have functions, and functions must be described by names. But the moment they were named they were already hypostatized, for a name first of all has more than one meaning, and secondly it consists of letters which can be combined and permutated. The circle thus widened, for each of the Sephiroth assumed several names and these again acquired new meanings and significations which were represented by new symbols. Each letter in the Divine names was, therefore, made to symbolize by its form and shape a certain Sephirah.

Again, in order to give a more concrete form to the arrangement of the Sephiroth and their functions, the analogy between their order and the form of the human body was introduced. This theory known as the *Adam Kadmon* theory was already referred to before and will be discussed later. In the course of the development of the Kabbala, the analogy was worked out in detail, a correspondence was found between the various Sephiroth and the organs of the body, as well as the different parts or faculties of the soul. The names of the organs were consequently transferred to the various Sephiroth in order to denote the correspondence, and thus a new path of symbolism was opened. Likewise, the symbol of light which is the most fundamental and most ancient symbol for representing the manifestations of God's presence already used in the Bible, Agada and early mystic literature, was elaborated by the Kabbalists into a number of phases and gradations. As a result, they introduced a color scheme to designate the differences between the Sephiroth, their functions and influences.

Still another source of intensive symbolism was the figurative designation of the two forces in being, the active and the passive, by male and female, and the importance attached to their union, temporary or permanent. The erotic motive was thus introduced and a wealth of symbols ensued from its application. As the principle of dualism was also applied to the Sephiroth, some of them are, therefore, denominated masculine and some feminine with all the complicated expressions that these appellations imply.

There are quite a number of other sources of symbolism, but they are too intricate to reproduce. We will now take for the sake of illustration, one or two examples of the development of certain symbols which will give us a glimpse into that exotic growth of the peculiar language of the Kabbala. Thus, the first Sephirah, by the fact that it is the first and the beginning of all the others was given the name *Kether* which designates that it is the crown or top of the system. But *Kether* also means crown in another sense, namely one which rests on someone's head, hence the name implies also the notion of a head, which in turn implies the figure of an entire body, hence the origin of the entire concept of the *First Man* and the whole analogy implied by that concept which was referred to above. Moreover, there is no reason why the first Sephirah should not also be called head (Resha) and accordingly, it is called so. But the second Sephirah, *Hoḳmah* (Wisdom) is inevitably connected with the brain which is in the head, and is therefore, also entitled to be called head. To make a distinction between the two, i. e. *Kether* and *Hoḳmah,* the former is called *Resha Hivra* (The White Head). The adjective *white* denotes that *Kether* includes all kinds of influences, just as white light contains all lights and colors.

Again, since the first Sephirah, according to some Kabbalists, existed potentially from eternity and the other Sephiroth were emanated later, it is called *Atiḳ Yomim* (The Ancient of Days), an expression borrowed from Daniel, Ch. VII, 9. Further, since the Sephiroth represent phases of Divine manifestation and the first Sephirah is a source of the others, it is meet that when speaking of the Sephiroth in terms of the organs of the human body, it should be called *Ariḳ Anpin* (The Long Face) and all the others *Zeir Anpin* (The Small Face).

Following the analogy of the human body and calling the first Sephirah head, the channels of influence emanating from it are, therefore, appropriately called hairs, and thus a whole symbolic doctrine developed called the Doctrine of the Hairs (Torath ha-Searoth) which dealt both with hairs of the head and those of the beard.[9] Such examples could be multiplied many times, but these will suffice to show us how complicated that symbolism is. In the course of the ages, it became more complicated and entangled, as each symbol was surrounded by a secret (Sod) and made a special subject of study. And furthermore, the symbols ceased to be means of expression for ideas but became ends in themselves and thus deviated the teachings of the Kabbala into channels entirely different from its original intended path. They became grossly anthropomorphic in spite of the pure conception of the God-head they originally came to impart. Likewise, the erotic motive became too prominent and complicated and this brought dire results. Yet the exalted teachings of the Kabbala were not entirely lost in the mass of symbolism and gross figures of speech. They always shone forth and exerted a noble influence upon the higher class of the devotees of mysticism. It is to the elucidation of these teachings as briefly and as clearly as possible that the next section is devoted.

B. Teaching of the Kabbala

107. THE THEORY OF THE SEPHIROTH

In the center of the Kabbala stands the theory of the Sephiroth. According to it, God is entirely unknown, His essence can not be conceived, and all that we know of Him is that He is unlimited and infinite. He is, therefore, denominated the *En-Sof* (The Endless), or in the flowery language of the *Zohar,* The Hidden of all Hidden (Setimah di Setimin). But God must, in spite of all this ,reveal and manifest Himself both to the world and to the mind of man. The first is related to God either in being His handiwork or emerging from Him in some way, and this relation must have some form of conceivability and some media through which the relation is conveyed. Again, the mind of man must also have some manifestations of God, for without any attributes Divine existence amounts to nothing.

[9] Reference to the hairs of the God-head is already found in Daniel, Ch. VII. 9, where it is said of the Ancient of Days, "And the hair of his head was like the pure wool."

To overcome this difficulty, the Kabbala teaches that there are between the En-Sof and the world ten Sephiroth[10] which are both manifestation of His substance and media of His will. It is by means of these that the world came into being and is preserved, ordered and governed. As manifestations of God, each of the Sephiroth expresses the Divine substance in a different way or aspect, which in the language of the Kabbala is called *Partzuf* or *Anpin* (Face). As attributes, they correspond to the ten names of God found in the Bible.[11] They also correspond to some attributes enumerated in I Chronicles, XXIX, 11 where it is said, "Thine, O Lord, is the greatness and the power and the glory and the victory (Netzah), and the majesty, for all that is in the heaven and the earth is Thine; Thine the kingdom, O Lord, and Thou art exalted as head above all." It seems that also the names of most of the Sephiroth were borrowed from this verse. The names of the ten Sephiroth are: *Kether* (Crown), *Hokmah* (Wisdom), *Binah* (Understanding), *Hesed* or *Gedulah* (Kindness or Greatness), *Geburah* (Power or Strength), *Tiphereth* (Beauty or Glory), *Netzah* (Might or Victory), *Hod* (Splendor or Majesty), *Yesod* (Foundation), *Malkuth* (Kingdom or Kingship). We can readily see that six out of the ten names are taken from the verse quoted above.

We have described the Sephiroth both as manifestations of Divine substances and media of His will which is in a way a synthesis of various opinions, for there is really no complete agreement on the subject. The view maintained by Menahem Recanti is that the Sephiroth are totally different from God and are only His instruments of work. They arose as a result of a shrinking of the light of God, and it is His will which works through them, and this permeation of His influence is called *Aziluth* (Emanation). Another view is offered by David Abi Zimra which on the other hand, identifies the Sephiroth with the God-head, namely that they express the very substance of the *En-Sof*. Cordevero disregards both these opinions and offers his own, which is really a compromise between the two. God, he says, is present in the Sephiroth but is also above them. He is unknown and indefinable, but they are emanated and from a certain

[10] Many suggestions were offered as to the derivation of the word Sephirah, two of which seem to be the most plausible. One traces it to the Greek word σφαῖρα, i. e., a sphere, and the other the Hebrew root ספר to count. According to the last interpretation, Sephirah means a number or rather one of the numbered forces. See Vol. I, p. 393.

[11] For the enumeration of the Divine names see Zohar, Pt. III, p. 11b.

aspect can be defined. We are, therefore, to distinguish in them two phases, an inner one and an outer one. The inner phase which is really the light of God flashing through the Sephiroth is simple and indivisible. The outer phase or the Sephiroth proper are the garments of that inner light of the soul, and hence arises the difference in the activity or the spread of the light of the *En-Sof*. There is a certain limitation to the Sephiroth which is indicated by the various names they bear. The inner light passing through the vessels, i. e. the Sephiroth, though itself simple and one, assumes different aspects in accordance with the quality of the vessel through which it passes. Cordevero likens the process to water which passing through vessels of various colors assumes a different color in each vessel, while in reality, the water remains colorless. In this way, Cordevero wants to combine both theories and say that the Sephiroth are both manifestations of the substance of God and His instruments. The soul of the Sephiroth is an expression of the Divine substance, while the bodies of the Sephiroth are instruments of the God-head.[12]

Yet the concept could not be complete unless we further analyze the term *vessel* or *body* applied to the outer phase of the Sephiroth. The Sephiroth have no positive reality, they merely represent the limits which God set for the outflowing of His light in order that it may be seen. This brings us to the process of emanation of the Sephiroth and the theory of the concentration of the Divine light, known as *Tzimzum*. The reason for the assumption that they were emanated and not created is clearly stated by one of the early speculative Kabbalists. He says, "The infinite is perfect, and the first thing caused by Him must likewise have been perfect. This could be accomplished through emanation which is a more perfect power than creation. Furthermore, since the Sephiroth act as the media of God's power and they supply sustenance to all things without diminishing their own power, they must receive that power through emanation which is constant. If they had been created, their power would have been exhausted, as a created thing maintains no continual connection with the Creator."[13]

The beginnings of the process of emanation the Kabbalists have veiled in language mysterious in form and content, which describes it as the concentration on the part of God by Himself. The texts say, "When the Hidden of all Hidden wanted to reveal Himself, He

[12] Pardes Rimmonim, p. 18a.
[13] Rabbi Azriel in his commentary on the ten Sephiroth, p. 5a.

concentrated His light on one point, called the Primal Point (Nekudah Rishonah),"[14] and that point is the first Sephirah. Through the concentration, they aver, an empty space was created which they call *Avir Kadmon* (Primal Air) which was after all not a complete vacuum, but retained vestiges of the Divine Light. This primal air or space has not been sufficiently explained by the Kabbalists, but most likely it was the source from which the physical world was emanated.[15]

With the emergence of the first Sephirah, the process downward continued. Out of the first Sephirah the others were evolved, the higher one containing the power of the lower and serving as their cause and source. Yet though we speak of ten different Sephiroth bearing different names, we must consider them, as stated above, a unity, for they are contained one in the other and all in God.

We have now a general outline of the hierarchy of the Sephiroth. But before we proceed to discuss in detail their various functions, we must clear up certain points connected with their emanation. The theory of emanation caused a good deal of perplexity to commentators and interpreters of the Kabbala. It involves certain contradictions. The logical consequences of such theories are that if the *En-Sof* exists eternally, it follows that the Sephiroth were emanated from eternity, for emanation means an outflow which is more or less an automatic process. Again, if the Sephiroth exist eternally, it would follow that the world which is the result of their activity also exists eternally. Such assumption would undoubtedly contradict the traditional Jewish teachings, and therefore, the Kabbalists, at least most of them, shrank from drawing the logical consequences. Only a few daring spirits asserted that Sephiroth existed potentially always. The majority speak of the emanation of Sephiroth in time, and moreover, in different times. Thus Azriel teaches that the first two, i. e. *Kether* and *Hokmah* existed potentially always, while the others were emanated before the creation of the world. Cordevero says distinctly, "There was a time when the Sephiroth were not emanated."[16]

This proves distinctly that the Kabbalists of the type of Cordevero overlooked the incompatibility of their teaching with the plain mean-

[14] Zohar, Pt. I, 2a.

[15] The concept of "Concentration" (Tzimtzum) is a very difficult one to understand, for how can we speak of concentration in an infinite. It can only be said to have been formulated as an attempt to explain the origin of emanation or the rise of the differentiation out of the undifferentiated. The explanation, however, is not a logical but symbolic one.

[16] Pardes Rimmonim, p. 25c.

ing of the word emanation (Aziluth) for they assumed an emanation in time and by the will of God. However, even these mystics conceded a kind of potential existence of the Sephiroth before actual emanation. Thus, Cordevero endeavors to explain the pre-existence of the Sephiroth in the God-head before revelation by a parable. A granite stone, says he, when struck by iron emits sparks of fire, but the fire was not really in the stone except in a certain potential way. Likewise, the Sephiroth before emanation were all one and so intensely united with the essence of God that they actually did not exist.[17] We see in this an attempt to reconcile contradictory elements, namely to assert the emanation of the Sephiroth and yet say that it was in time and through will. Emanation is, of course, interpreted to mean the emergence from a state of non-being into a state of being.

There is still another point bearing upon the Kabbalistic conception of the Sephiroth which needs to be clarified before the resumption of our task, the description of the Sephiroth. We must always bear in mind that no matter what philosophic or speculative aspect this doctrine might possess, it was never presented in any logical or scientific form. It is given to us in the high and warm colors of Oriental symbolism, and quite often the plastic and representative element of symbolism overshadows the original thought underlying the teaching, so that the kernel of speculation is lost in the exotic husk of symbolic language. Again, symbolism, as a rule, has a tendency to prolific reproduction and excessive multiplication, for as pointed out above, the symbols in time become not a means of conveyance for ideas but ideas in themselves, and as such give birth to a new set of symbols intending to convey and clarify the original, and thus the cycle increases and widens.

For this reason, the later Kabbala, the Zoharitic and especially the post-Zoharitic presents to the student a veritable jungle of symbols which baffles penetration and prevents one from getting at the underlying ideas of this great mass of literature. Thus, the Sephiroth which symbolize certain powers or expressions of God in His relation to all existence, became through the numerous symbolic means applied to them separate entities to whom special prayers were offered, and were endowed with numerous functions and multitudinous relations to each other and to the world. As a result, the doctrine became complicated and assumed an entirely different aspect from what its original propounders meant to give to it. Even the

[17] Ibid, Portal 5, Ch. IV.

clearest minded among the Kabbalists, Moses Cordevero for instance, could not extricate himself from the weight of symbolism, and though he constantly insists upon the purity of conception of the God-head and the Sephiroth, he frequently relapses and talks in the gross symbolic language of the other Kabbalists which borders upon a sensual anthropomorphism. Bearing these points in mind, we will continue the account of the Sephiroth.

The first Sephirah *Kether*, is often called a point (Nekudah), or the Hidden Point (Nekudah Setima), or the Simple Point (Nekudah Pshutah). All these appellations mean to indicate that this Sephirah is still unknown and is all-embracing. It is, speculatively speaking, a mode of pure being. On account of its being the first, it is also called *Saba or Atiḳa* (The Old One) or *Atiḳa Kadisha* (The Holy Old One) or *Atiḳ Yomin* (The Ancient of Days, a name borrowed from Daniel, Ch. VII, 9) and again, on account of its position (see below) it is called *Resha Hivra* (The White Head) and also *Ariḳ Anpin* (The Long Face). These various names indicate the exaltedness of its position and the fact that in it all conceptions are united. The symbolic names merely approach a conception which is inexhaustible.

Out of *Kether,* the absolute principle of being, there came forth two other principles which are apparently opposite but in reality inseparable. These are *Hoḳmah* (Wisdom) and *Binah* (Understanding). With these two, there enters the principle of dualism which, according to Kabbala, runs through the entire universe and which it chose to denominate masculine and feminine phases of existence. This theory was already expressed in the *Booḳ of Creation* and greatly elaborated upon in the *Zohar.* The last book lays down a principle saying, "At the time when the Holy Aged One wanted to give definite form to all existence, He formed things in two phases, that of masculine and feminine. All things exist in these two forms."[18] Masculine and feminine are in reality symbols for the active and passive phases of existence. But the application of these two names introduced, as noted above, the erotic element in this mystic teaching which had far reaching consequences as evidenced by the role played by the term *Zivug* applied to the union of these two elements, the same as applied in Hebrew to the marital union of male and female.

According to this theory, therefore, *Hoḳmah* represents the mascuilne and *Binah* the feminine element. They are consequently denominated *Aba* and *Ima* (Father and Mother) respectively. From their

[18] Zohar, Pt. III, p. 290a.

union proceeds the son, *Daath* (Knowledge), which though a product of these two was never considered a separate Sephirah. *Kether, Hokmah* and *Binah* are the first triad which represents the intellectual powers of the world of thought (Olam Muskal). We must not forget, however, that *Kether* represents pure being, and there is, therefore, an identification of being and thought.

The other seven Sephiroth are called *Sephiroth ha-Binyan* (The Sephiroth of Construction) because it is primarily through these that the world was created and is conducted. They are likewise divided into triads. The second triad consists of *Hesed* (Kindness), which is masculine, *Geburah* (Power) which represents the feminine element, and *Tiphereth* (Glory) which unites both elements. *Hesed* is also called *Gedulah* (Greatness) and *Geburah* is also denominated Din (Justice). This triad represents the moral qualities and forces or the *Olam Murgash* (World of Emotions).

The third triad consists of *Netzah* (Might or Victory) masculine, *Hod* (Splendor) feminine and *Yesod* (Foundation) which unites them both. This triad represents the dynamic aspect or the *Olam ha-Mutba,* the world of nature and its forces, *Netzah* typifying extension and growth, *Hod* reproduction and *Yesod* uniting both. The last Sephirah is *Malkuth* (Kingdom) which stands by itself for it is really no separate attribute but represents the harmony of all other Sephiroth, and receiving their influences transmits them to other links in the chain of existence. It is through the mediacy of *Malkuth* that the Sephiroth act upon the world, and hence its great importance. It is because of its role of mediator between the Sephiroth and the other worlds that it is also denominated *Shekinah,* signifying the presence of God in creation.

In addition to this system of triads, there is another arrangement of the Sephiroth into triads due to their positions. But before describing this second order of triads, we must say a few words regarding the theory of the First or Primordial Man (Adam Kadmon). This theory which plays such an important role in the *Zohar* and the later Kabbala is rarely found in the mystic works of the earlier period. Of course, God Himself is pictured in the Bible in the human form (Cf. Isaiah VI, 1; Ezekiel I, 26; Daniel, VII, 9); but these anthropomorphic expressions need interpretations and were accordingly interpreted by commentators and philosophers. On the whole, they have little to do with the concept of the Primordial Man of the Kabbala. Some of the mystical books of the earlier period of the type of the

Shiur Komah (Measure of Height, Vol. I, sect. 181) depict God in the form of man and describe in grotesque manner, the proportions of His limbs. But this strange description is to be construed, as was pointed out (Vol. I, p. 391), as a crude and inadequate attempt to express the greatness of God in human terms. At any rate, in none of these books is the term *Adam Kadmon* mentioned or referred to.

We will have to trace the origin of the doctrine of the Primordial Man to the teachings of Philo. There, we find both the term, as well as similarity of content. Philo calls the Logos the first emanation and the first born son of God. Further, he says that before the lower man was created, there was emanated the idea of man which is the true man, the Primordial Man, whom he sometimes calls the second Logos. Here we see an attempt to endow certain emanations with the form and likeness of man. The term Primordial Man, however, is also found in the teachings of some of the gnostic sects who applied this term to God Himself.

Through some channel, the Philonic use of the term had reached the founders of the Kabbala and they adopted it and developed it along the same lines. The fundamental idea is that man is a microcosm reflecting in his form the great world. Therefore, all manifestations in the universe, spiritual as well as material, must have assumed the human form, and as the first of these manifestations was the emanation of the Sephiroth, hence they are the Primordial Man. Says the *Zohar,* "Before the Holy One, blessed be He, created any form in the world, He was one without form or likeness. But after He made this form of the *Merkabah* (Divine Chariot described by Ezekiel) namely of the Heavenly Man, He Himself is expressed in that form and is called JHVH."[19] From these as well as from many other quotations in the *Zohar,* it can be seen that the term Primordial Man applies to the sum of the Sephiroth, the system of the emanations as a whole. The theory, however, was subjected to further development by the later Kabbalists especially by Isaac Luria (see below) known as the *Ari* who initiated a new epoch in the teachings of the Kabbala. Luria reverted more to the Philonian conception of the Logos as the first emanation and the all-embracive mediator. According to him and his followers, the *Adam Kadmon* is the first emanation which preceded the emanation of the Sephiroth, and the Sephiroth are the body of the Primordial Man. These Kabbalists developed a very complicated scheme of Sephiroth and multiplied

[19] Zohar, Pt. II, p. 42b.

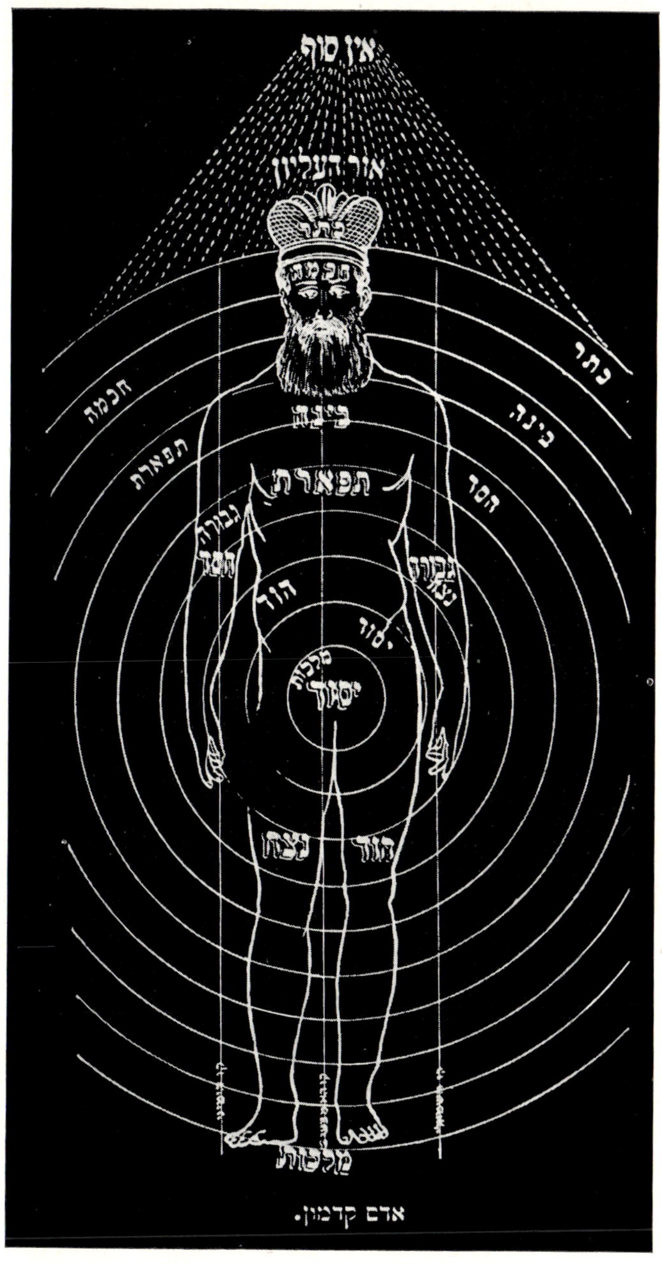

The position of the Sephiroth arranged in the form of the Primordial Man.

(Reproduced from Ginsburg's The Kabbalah, London, 1865)

their number by four times ten, namely asserting that there are ten Sephiroth in each of the worlds. However, we can not enter into all these exotic teachings and we will return to the position of the Sephiroth as affected by the view of the *Zohar* of the Primordial Man.

According to that view, the first Sephirah *Kether* corresponds to the head as a whole, the second *Hokmah* to the right, and the third *Binah* to the left side of the head. (Another version has it that *Hokmah* corresponds to the brain and *Binah* to the heart.) The fourth Sephirah *Hesed* corresponds to the right arm, and the fifth, *Geburah* to the left; the sixth *Tiphereth* to the chest or torso; the seventh and eighth Sephiroth, *Netzah* and *Hod* correspond to the right and left legs respectively; the ninth *Yesod* to the genital organ; and the tenth *Malkuth* to the soles of the feet. As a result of these symbolic positions, we have a second system of triads; the first consisting of *Hokmah, Hesed* and *Netzah* form the Right Column (Amudah di-Yemina); the second *Kether, Tiphereth* and *Yesod* the Middle Column (Amudah di-Metziuta); and the third comprising *Binah, Geburah* and *Hod* the Left Column (Amudah di-Smolah). The Right Column denotes the more active Sephiroth which signify the expansion of power, and hence the more merciful; the Left Column represents the more passive Sephiroth which connote concentration of power, and hence the more stern; and the Middle Column contains the most important Sephiroth, each of which represents the unity of the other two members of the triads. This figure of the positions of the Sephiroth is often called by the Kabbalists the Tree (Illan).

There are many other figures representing the Sephiroth. Some mystics represent them as a series of concentric circles, others merely in groups of three in the form of the Hebrew vowel Segol thus ˙.˙ and still others in the form of a large Aleph. But the idea underlying all these representations is the same, namely, the one outlined above.

The Sephiroth have, besides position, also certain colors by which their action is symbolized. Like all other symbols used by the Kabbalists, the color scheme is an attempt to indicate the various activities attributed to the Sephiroth, as well as the nature of the concepts by which we represent each of them. There are quite some differences among the Kabbalists in regard to the various colors to be assigned to the Sephiroth, but the following scheme of Cordevero seems to be the adopted one.

The color of the first Sephirah *Kether* is black, which signifies that its light is hidden beyond conception, for it is exalted above all beings. However, some Kabbalists assign to it the pure white color which signifies the form of *Kether* when it reveals itself into activity, for then it is symbolized by the strong glamor of white. They call it then by the term employed in Ezekiel I, 22, "The Terrible Ice" (ha-Kerah ha-Nora). The color of *Hokmah* is blue or rather light blue (Tkeleth), for it is a color which can easily be changed into other colors, denoting the influence exerted by this Sephirah upon the others, as wisdom is the source of activities. *Binah* is said to possess the color of deep green like that of grass. This color is given to it because it is the color of all fruit before ripening, and likewise *Binah* is the immediate channel through which the influence passes to the other Sephiroth of construction.

The color of *Hesed* is white and that of *Geburah* is red. These two colors signify two opposite characteristics, white symbolizing mildness or mercy, and red sternness and justice, which correspond to the activities of these two Sephiroth. Light yellow is the color of *Tiphereth,* for this color has, in addition to the red and green, also an element of white, and this Sephirah, according to the Kabbalists, harmonizes both *Hesed* and *Geburah*. *Netzah* and *Hod* are represented by the color of white tinged with red and vice versa by red tinged with white. This indicates that in the first, the element of mercy is predominant while in the second that of justice. Reddish yellow is the color of the ninth Sephirah *Yesod,* as it receives its influence from *Tiphereth* and *Netzah* and *Hod,* and thus reflects all the colors of these three Sephiroth. *Malkuth,* being the harmony of the other nine Sephiroth and acting as the medium of their activities is represented by all colors or by white in the sense that it unites all colors. In concluding the subject of the graphic symbolization or the color scheme of the Sephiroth, we may remark that these colors which were originally used only as means for expressing the activities of the Sephiroth in time assumed, as all other symbols of the Kabbala, great importance and received a special function in the application of the mystical teachings in practice.

The Sephiroth, though ten in number, form as stated, one unity, for they are all connected with one another. Their activity is made still more unified by the theory advanced by the Kabbalists that each Sephirah really reflects all the other Sephiroth and is only differentiated from the others by the predominance of the particular element which imparts its name to it. As an example we may take the Sephirah *Hesed*. It, according to this theory, possesses the powers of all the other Sephiroth, but that of mercy is predominating and constitutes its peculiar individuality. This, of course, conduces to unity of action, for each Sephirah acts upon the other through a correspondence of similar phases in both. Thus, for instance, when the Sephirah Crown influences Wisdom through the particular mode which is denoted by the name Crown, Wisdom, the recipient of the influence, turns towards the former that phase which reflects the mode or power of Crown. Again, when the influence emanated by Crown is of the mode of Wisdom, it acts through its own phase of wisdom on the corresponding phase in the other Sephiroth, and thus the procedure goes on. It follows, therefore, that there are many forms of activity to each Sephirah.

The means of conveyance of the influence from one Sephirah to another is called *Tzinor* (Pipe, Canal). It is described thus by Cordevero: "When a lower Sephirah wishes to receive influence from a higher one, it must turn towards it a lighted face, in order to cause the light in the upper Sephirah to shine and radiate its activity. The light emitted from the lower Sephirah together with the one emitted by the upper one as a response to the stimulus is called the *Tzinor* (The Canal) of influence."[20] Through it, the power of one Sephirah is conveyed to the other. There are twenty-two of such *Tzinoroth,* as some Sephiroth, e. g. Crown, Wisdom, etc. have three canals, and some only two and a few only one. The general principle in the exertion of influence and the activity of the Sephiroth is that there must be a simultaneous desire on the part of both the lower and the upper, or the patient and the agent, that such influence be exerted. The desire of the higher Sephirah to exert influence is called *'Itharutha di-le-Ela* (The Arousing from Above), and the desire of the lower Sephirah to receive the influence is called *'Itharutha di-le Thatha* (The Arousing from Below). Quite often no activity is carried on by the higher Sephiroth unless there is an incitement or arousing by the lower ones.

This doctrine of the double incitement to activity had far-reaching consequences in the Kabbalistic teaching. Not only was it applied to the mutual influence exerted by one Sephirah upon another, but to the conduct of the affairs of the world by the Sephiroth as well. There must always be an incitement in the world below in order

[20] Pardes Rimmonim, p. 32c.

that they act in the proper way. This incitement or arousing ('Itharutha) is, of course, the conduct of man. Hence the extraordinary importance attached to human action. If man acts properly, he arouses the Sephiroth to action, to the exertion of more light and influence, and consequently of more good to the world. If on the other hand, he acts improperly, the activity is slackened, the *Tzinoroth* (canals of influence) are stopped and the world is left to its own natural fate, or what is worse, the powers of sternness and strict justice come into action and evil ensues.

This exertion or secretion of influence (Shepha or ha-Spaah) is very often denoted by the mystics by the erotic names of *Zivug* or *Yihud* (both signifying union in an erotic sense). They frequently speak of the *Zivug* or *Yihud* of two Sephiroth, and while undoubtedly they mean to indicate by the terms the strong desire on the part of these two for giving and receiving influence, yet the use of the terms coupled with designating the one Sephirah masculine and the other feminine, or husband and wife, gives to the whole doctrine an anthropomorphic aspect.

Although this union occurs with all of the pairs of the opposite Sephiroth, yet there are two pairs which are more active and from whose union many activities take place. These are *Hokmah* and *Binah* and *Tiphereth* and *Malkuth*. The first two are called father and mother (Aba we-Ima). Their importance consists in the fact that they represent thought in the active and passive phases, which form the basis of all order in existence. It is from them that the other two triads of Sephiroth which represent the worlds of morality and nature, were emanated. The act of emanation is represented symbolically to have occurred by a union of the father and mother. Of the other pair, Tiphereth is of exceptional importance. It is a central Sephirah harmonizing the forces of the moral world, i. e. mercy and justice and dominates the triad of Sephiroth representing the world of nature. It is, therefore, a center of activity. *Malkuth* receives the influence of all the Sephiroth and transmits it to the world below. It is, therefore, through the union of the two which are likewise represented as husband and wife, or bridegroom and bride, that most of the things taking place in the world occur. In general, these two Sephiroth, on account of their great activity, have many names. Thus, *Tiphereth* is called King (Malka), Holy King (Malka Kadisha) and also *Tzadik* (The Righteous). Likewise, *Malkuth* being the transmitter of the activity of the Sephiroth and the mediator between them and the other worlds and possessing many functions, is also denoted by various appellations. Besides those mentioned above, it is called *Matronita* (Princess) and Eve (Hava), both indicating its character of being a recipient. For the same reason, it is called Moon (Yareah) for it receives its light from the other Sephiroth. In like manner, the other Sephiroth have many names too numerous to recount.

All that has been said about the teachings of the Kabbala in regard to the Sephiroth are in effect only the outlines of these doctrines. The actual teachings stated in the enormous mass of Kabbalistic books are complicated and ramified, as each point is magnified beyond all proportion. Thus, the theory of union between the opposite Sephiroth is developed in an amazing way by the later Kabbalists. They discern various phases in the union in different ways, so that the discussion of this subject alone occupies many pages in their books. Besides, highly erotic coloring is given to the entire discussion of the union of the Sephiroth, which coloring produced bad effects during periods of mystic enthusiasm expressed in Messianic movements.

However, even what was said, indicates sufficiently the great metamorphosis which took place in the teachings of the speculative Kabbala which began with pure philosophic conceptions and ended with their conversion into a complicated hierarchy, endowed with gross anthropomorphic qualities. It is true that some Kabbalists have repeatedly asserted that the anthropomorphic terminology employed is a mere symbolic garment. But many there were also who took the symbols for the real thing and were misled and even misled others. Such is the power of misused symbolism.

108. THE FOUR WORLDS

As we have seen, the purpose of the Kabbalists in positing the existence of the Sephiroth was to explain the relation between the Infinite (En-Sof) and the world of matter by making them the mediators between the two. But the distance between the En-Sof and the world of matter is so great that the Sephiroth alone which are highly spiritual powers or mere expressions of the substance of God, are not sufficient to fill the gap. There must be some links in the chain of being which affect its gradual thickening or materialization. A theory had been advanced, therefore, by the early Kabbalists (see above p. 353) that the Sephiroth represent only one world, that of

Aziluth (Emanation), and that in addition, there are three more worlds, that of *Beriah* (Creation), *Yetzira* (Formation) and *'Asiyah* (Action).

It was already noted (above p. 354) that this theory was first advanced in the *Maseketh Aziluth,* and there the existence of the last three worlds is supported by a verse in Isaiah. We wish, therefore, to turn to the description of the worlds themselves. The world of *Beriah* contains the throne of God or the *Merkabah.* The Kabbalists enveloped the concept of the throne in a cloud of mystical terms so that it is really impossible to ascertain its exact meaning. But it can safely be inferred that it connotes a group of forces more manifest and more revealed than the Sephiroth. In fact, they speak of ten steps of the throne, and at times, of ten wheels (Galgalim). According to this source, *Maseketh Aziluth,* there dwell also in that world the souls of the righteous.

The world of *Yetzira* contains ten orders of angels which are presided over by *Metatron.* At times, it is called the world of *Metatron.* Metatron, as is known (Vol. I, p. 381; Vol. II, p. 347) is called in the Talmud, The Prince of the World (Sar ha-Olam), i. e. of the lower or sublunar world, and is therefore, the direct agent who comes in contact with it and supervises its activities through the orders of the angels as well as through the spheres. Here we can see one more reason for positing the existence of the four worlds, and that is the incorporation by the speculative Kabbala of the doctrine of angelology. Room had to be found in the new scheme of things for the angels, and thus a separate world was given to them. According to the source quoted above, the world of *Yetzira* contains also the souls of ordinary men.

The world of *'Asiyah* is the world of matter and contains the nine spheres and the lower world. This, however, is the view of the most authoritative exponents of the Kabbala, but the *Tractate Aziluth* differs on this point. According to it, *'Asiyah* still contains a number of lower orders of angels.

These worlds, as we have seen, are divided into ten grades or parts. These divisions are sometimes called also by the name Sephiroth, and accordingly, there are ten each in *Beriah,* in *Yetzira* and in *'Asiyah.* Cordevero explains that by using these terms, the Kabbalists do not mean to assert that there are actually Sephiroth in the other three worlds, but merely that they spread their influence and light also through the other worlds.

The underlying conception of the doctrine of the four worlds is that *being* in its various ramifications is one great unity. The breath of God permeates them all. The worlds or the great divisions of existence are all manifestations of the will or power of God. They all have one source, the *En-Sof,* and the difference between them is due to the distance from the source. The further a link is from its origin, the grosser and more material it becomes. But in all of the links, the light of the Sephiroth, the first emanation flashes through. In general, we have to recognize not only a descending movement but also an ascending one. When materialization reached its lowest point in the grossest element—earth, an ascending movement set in, expressed by a desire on the part of all things to return to their origin. Thus, the kingdom of plants represents a step higher than that of minerals, that of the animals another step, and that of man still another. Man himself represents many stages and expressions of that desire, and finally, the process is completed in the return of the souls of the righteous to the source. This theory will help us in a degree to understand the Kabbalistic concept of creation which is very obstruse.

109. CREATION

The problem of creation, though it constitutes one of the fundamental problems of the Kabbala to which its teachings are supposed to offer a solution, was dealt with in an unsystematic way by it. It is usually referred to in symbolic terms and in very enigmatic language and has to be inferred from the theories of the Sephiroth and that of the four worlds.

In general, it can be described as a modified emanation. When the process of concentration (Tzimtzum) took place (see above p. 364), the Primal Point (Nekudah Rishonah) was revealed, and this point or the Sephirah Crown constitutes a kind of primordial substance from which the long chain of existence developed through the world of the Sephiroth and the other three worlds, link from link. As stated, there is in this chain both unity and difference, the difference being proportionate to the distance of a certain link from the source. It is through this gradual process of emanation that matter was evolved. The Zohar, as well as the other Kabbalistic works do not explain the process of creation in detail, but in their usual symbolic style speak of it in pictures and figures. Thus, says the Zohar, "When the Hidden of the Hidden wanted to reveal Himself, He first created a point, enveloped it in an image and then covered Himself with a rich and luminous garment."[21] The point is the first Sephirah, the image the sum of all Sephiroth, the garment the world. In another place, the process is referred to in more detail, though still in enigmatic language. Says the Zohar, "From the first point on, there proceeded a series of emanations which permeated one another and one was clothed by the other so that the emanations became garments to one another, and thus finally the world was formed."[22] This cryptic and picture language gives us a glimpse into the Kabbalistic concept of creation. The farther a link was in the series, the heavier a garment it became, and the last links became the various grades of matter. Matter arose, according to this conception, from the inevitable conditions inherent in a thing created. Everything which is created is more limited than the power which creates it, and when the chain of created things is long, it follows that the farthest links shall have more limitation and become grosser.

I have called the Kabbalistic conception of creation a modified emanation for the reason that it does not posit emanation pure and simple. Such kind of emanation would imply that the emanated things existed from eternity, and would deny creation altogether. This, however, does not seem to be the case, in spite of the fact that some of the modern interpreters of Kabbala as well as some of the Kabbalists themselves, are inclined to accept this view, for all sources speak of creation and describe a time when the Sephiroth were not in existence. Cordevero says explicitly, "There was a time when the Sephiroth were not emanated."[23] We must, therefore, assume that the primal substance (the first Sephirah) was emanated by the will of God, and thence the process continued by itself. This view undoubtedly diverges greatly from the traditional view of creation from nothing. Some Kabbalists, in order to avoid a break with tradition have, therefore, interpreted the word *"Nothing"* (Ayin) to mean something which is inconceivable. And since the first point or the Sephirah *Kether* is often called by the Kabbala, *Ayin,* on account of the fact that it is hidden and beyond conception, the mystics believe that they still teach the traditional view of *creatio ex nihilo,* namely that the world (The Yesh) was created from the primal substance, i. e. *Kether* which is called "Nothing" or *Ayin.*

[21] Zohar, Pt. I, p. 2a.
[22] Ibid, p. 20a.
[23] Pardes Rimmonim, p. 25c.

To this theory of creation, there is attached another concept concerning creation which completes the former view and intends to explain the rise of evil in the world, a thing which the Kabbala as well as Jewish philosophy found difficult to account for. This is the doctrine of the earlier worlds. According to this view which is found in the oldest parts of the *Zohar,* such as the *Saphra di-Zenuita* (The Book of Secrets) and the *Idra Rabba* (The Great Assembly), God created a number of earlier worlds but these were destroyed. Their destruction was caused by the fact that they did not possess the proper form and image which is that of the Primordial Man (Adam Kadmon). As seen above, it is this form containing the two elements, namely those of masculine and feminine or the active and the passive, which is considered by the mystics to be the proper form for existence. They call it in their language the *scale* or the *balance* (Mathkela). As long as this *scale* was not introduced the worlds could not exist. These earlier worlds are called figuratively by a number of names, such as *Sparks* (Nitzotzoth), the *Earlier Kings* and finally the *Kings of Edom.* This last appellation is very peculiar and arises from the fact that the whole theory is introduced as a strange commentary to otherwise simple verses in Genesis XXXVI, 31-43. In these verses, there is a recital of the names of the Kings of Edom who ruled before a king arose in Israel. The *Zohar* interprets this passage in an enigmatic way, saying that the Kings of Edom denote the older worlds, while Israel is a symbol for the perfect world.

These worlds, however, were not totally destroyed but continued to exist in a passive way. Their destruction or in the Zoharitic figure "The Death of the Kings" merely represents a low state of existence, a state of pure femininity, sternness, without the mildness of *Hesed.* Hence these worlds or "Kings" are the source of evil and are often called *Klipoth* (Husks), a name employed by the Kabbalists to denote the powers of evil. The underlying idea of it all is the Platonic one that matter is evil. Matter, therefore, carries evil with it and the powers represented by the early kings are degrees below the matter of the world. It is in this way that the Kabbala explains the origin of evil in the world. There are undoubtedly many contradictions in it, for it is impossible to grasp fully how from a principle which is all good—God—evil should ultimately be evolved, even if the chain of emanations should extend to infinity. But these contradictions are not the share of Kabbala only. They belong likewise to philosophy and to all other attempts at systematic explanations of the relation between God and the world.

However, no matter what speculative explanations of the origin of evil, the Kabbala might offer, in practice it incorporated in its theories all the irrational teachings about evil and its incarnate powers, the demons of the earlier mysticism. It adopted the entire system of demonology current in the earlier literature of this kind, and even classified and graded the various kinds of demons or angels of destruction (Malakē Habalah). It made the world of evil a counterpart of the world of good, carrying through a correspondence between the number of grades of demons and those of angels, such as assigning to both ten orders and positing various other similarities. In all these teachings, there are undoubtedly influences from sources extraneous to Judaism, but these influences date from a much earlier period than the one in which the Kabbala arose. In general, it can be said that the Kabbala had taken earlier material and merely amplified it, and at times even elaborated it in his own peculiar way. Its chief contribution consists not only in drawing a parallel between the worlds of evil and good, but in unifying them. It calls the world of evil the left or hind side (Sitra di-Smola or Sitra Ahra) meaning by these names that even this world reflects the power of God. In fact, it teaches that even the *Klipoth* contain sparks of holiness (Nitzotzoth Shel—Kedushah), a theory which resulted in important consequences. To go into more details about the Kabbalistic system of evil, its powers, the demons and their grades and orders would carry us beyond the limits of the work.

110. MAN

We have already noted both in regard to the Sephiroth and in regard to creation what important role was assigned by the Kabbala to the form of man which they call the image of the Primordial Man (Adam Kadmon). It readily follows that the Kabbala should place an equally high value upon the earthly man, his nature, character and strivings. And in fact, it did so. Man, as is known, holds a high position in all spiritual expressions of Judaism, in the Talmud, Bible and Agada. But in the Kabbala, he attained his highest position. According to it, he is the very purpose of the entire creation, for does not his form represent the perfect form of the universe in being *"its scale or balance"* as the mystic doctrine teaches us?

But man is even more than that, he is a real microcosm reflecting in the structure of his body the structure of the universe. In fact, the idea that man is a microcosm is already found in the early Agada,[24] but the Kabbala intensified it and carried out the comparison between the body of man and the universe in great detail, and moreover, in its usual mystic way it derived from this comparison certain suggestions how to read the destiny of man from his external appearance. In other words, the Kabbala endeavored to develop a science of physiognomy.

The skin, says the *Zohar,* can be compared to the firmament which covers many things. And like in the firmament, the stars and planets in their formation and combination display certain signs by means of which the initiated can learn secrets, so does the skin possess such signs which reveal to those who know how to read them the secrets concerning the character and future of man.[25] These signs are, of course, the lines that cover the face and the palms of the hands and the formation of the nails. The passage continues to give the interpretation of these signs into which we can not enter. What is important for us is that the Kabbala placed such value upon the body of man that it attached importance even to the smallest details.

However, no matter how important the human body may be, the soul of man is of still greater importance, and the Kabbala accordingly devotes to it considerable attention. According to its teachings, the soul of man corresponds in its parts to the divisions of the Sephiroth and is inherently connected with three of them. The soul, as is well known, consists of three parts, *Neshamah* representing the intellect, *Ruah* the spirit, the seat of good and evil or of the moral qualities, and *Nephesh,* the animal soul which is closely connected with the body and directs its higher activities.[26] They, therefore, correspond exactly to the three triads of the Sephiroth which represent the worlds of intellect (Olam Muskal), of morality (Olam Murgash) and of nature (Olam Mutba) respectively (Sect. 107.) Each of these parts has its source in one of the Sephiroth as fololws: *Neshamah* in *Hoḳmah, Ruah* in *Tiphereth,* and *Nephesh* in *Malḳuth.*

To these three primary parts of the soul, the Kabbalists added two more making five altogether. The fourth part is the Spirit of Life (Ruah ha-Hiyyuni or Haya) which has its seat in the heart and from there spreads through the entire body. The Spirit of Life seems to

[24] Aboth Di-Rabba Nathan, Ch. XXXI.

[25] Zohar, Pt. II, p. 76 a-b.

[26] This division of the soul is both Platonic and Aristotelian and was adopted bv Jewish philosophers.

be lower than the animal soul or *Nephesh*. According to Cordevero,[27] the former is the dwelling place of the latter, for the *Nephesh* is more spiritual. The function of the Spirit of Life is the organization of the lower activities of the body,[28] while the *Nephesh* supervises the higher functions including that of sensation. The fifth part is the form or image of the body named *Tzelem* (Image) which according to the mystics has a kind of separate existence even before birth, nay even before the union of man and woman which brings about this birth, takes place. In a philosophical way, this *Tzelem* means the individualized idea of the body of each man, but the mystics hypostatized it into separate existence. The *Zohar* even says that this image is present at the union of man and woman and the body of the child is formed in this image.

The soul, according to the Kabbala, is pre-existent, and as said, its highest part has its source in the Sephirah *Hokmah,* and according to the view of other mystics (above p. 374) the souls dwell in the upper worlds, namely those of the righteous in the world of *Beriah* and those of the others in that of *Yetzira.* The bringing about of its descent is, therefore, made a function of the activity of the Sephiroth. According to the Zohar, at the descent of the soul into the body, a union between the Sephiroth *Tiphereth* and *Malkuth* (Beauty and Kingdom) occurs and by means of that union, the descent takes place.

This union of the Sephiroth which represents the uniting in activity of the two elements, the masculine and the feminine (p. 372) necessitates a union of these very elements in the soul itself. In fact, the Kabbala teaches that all souls in their pre-existent state consist of masculine and feminine elements. When the time comes for the descent of the soul, it is split in two, the masculine half descends into a male child and the feminine half into a female child. Later in life when the time of marriage arrives, these two are again united.[29] This kind of marriage is called the proper marriage, but not every man meets with such good fortune. The mating of the souls depends on the deeds of the man. If he is worthy, he obtains as his life partner the woman who possesses the second half of his soul and is his real *Bath Zug* (Mate). If he is unworthy, he marreis any woman.

[27] Pardes, Rimmonim, Sect. XXXI, Ch. IX.

[28] In fact, Cordevero and many other Kabbalists do not consider the Ruah Hiyyuni a part of the soul at all, but merely the seat of Nephesh.

[29] Zohar, Pt. I, p. 91b. There is a similar allegory told by Plato in the symposium, but his version is rather a crude form of that allegory.

The allegory, of course, is a beautiful one, but the practical realization of its idea undoubtedly involves difficulties and contradictions. Yet its proper importance is not lessened by this fact, for it enhances the value of marriage. In fact, in the Kabbala marriage has become not only an act of performance of the functions of the body, but and maybe primarily so, that of the soul. To obtain the right kind of *Zivug,* i. e. matrimonial union, a man must prepare himself spiritually and morally for that purpose.

The soul, as it descends from the upper worlds where it originated must by necessity return to its source, and hence the importance of right conduct in human life. The world is a school for the soul where it is repeatedly tried, and by these trials it is elevated and perfected. The *Zohar* compares the sojourn of the soul of the righteous on earth to the sojourn of a king's son in a country far away from the royal palace. The prince was sent thither for special training, but when the training was ended, the king sent the queen after him and she brought the prince back to the palace.[30] Likewise, when the time for the departure of the righteous from this world arrives, a union of the king and queen occurs again, i. e. the Sephirah *Malkuth* unites with the king, the Sephirah *Tiphereth,* and the soul is thereby returned to its source.

In connection with all these views of the pre-existence of the soul and its sojourn on earth, the Kabbala has introduced an exotic teaching into Judaism which ultimately became one of its important doctrines. This is the doctrine of metempsychosis or transmigration of the souls (Gilgul, from the verb galgal, to roll, i. e. the souls roll on to another body). This teaching was quite well known in Oriental religions, especially in Brahmanism, and it was also adopted by some Jewish sects in Gaonic times,[31] but was never sanctioned as a doctrine until the Kabbala came and incorporated it in its teaching. The underlying idea of all the various shades of the theory of transmigration of souls is the attempt to reconcile many contradictions in the belief in God's absolute justice in his dealings with man. Without going into details of the origin of this doctrine and its application to life, we will only note one of its aspects. Of the two phases of the problem of Job, namely why the wicked prosper and the righteous suffer, the doctrine of transmigration at least attempted to offer a solution to the latter one. The righteous that suffer possess souls

[30] Zohar, Pt. I, p. 245b.
[31] See Saadia Emunoth Deoth, ed. Warsaw, p. 160.

that had sinned in a previous existence and are, therefore, expatiating their former sins.

The Kabbala applied this theory in a similar, though not identical way. The soul, it asserts, must return to its source in a pure state, but if in life, it was spotted with sin, it must be purified by being sent down again into another body. Sometimes the soul must go through several migrations until it is purified.

Allied to the idea of transmigration is the idea of *'Ibbur* (Pregnancy) which means that at times an additional soul is given to a man in order to help him to improve his way in life. At another time, it is done by God as an act of grace. When two souls are not able to attain perfection separately, they are united in one body so that by joint efforts they may attain the end. The name *'Ibbur* is given to this process for the reason that often one of the souls is of a higher type and acts as a mother to the weaker one, which is in relation to it as the foetus to the mother. This theory is practically an innovation of the post-Zoharite Kabbalists. With them the views of the transmigration and the doubling of souls assumed an enormous role. According to Luria and his followers, the souls of all men must undergo the process of migration after death, those of the wicked in order to perfect themselves (Tikkun), while those of the righteous may descend into bodies again for the benefit of the weaker souls. The later mystics developed these two doctrines into a system with practical consequences. They claimed to be able to drive out the extraneous soul of the wicked which entered the body of a living person and provide it with other means for obtaining the necessary perfection. In late mystic parlance, this act is called "the expelling of the Dybbuk" (Dybbuk being the name for the migratory soul on account of its clinging to the body of another man). They also claimed to be able to endow any man with a higher soul, and in general, they asserted that the great men of later generations possess as additional souls those which had belonged to famous and pious men of former generations. They averred that they can recognize by merely looking at the face of a person whose soul he possesses in addition to his own.

From all what was said about the soul of man, its course, destiny and return to its former dwelling, it can be easily inferred that man's activity in this world exerts great influence upon the activity of the Sephiroth in the world in general. We have already noted that the activity of the Sephiroth needs stimulation from the lower world

(Itharutha di le-Thatha) and that the canals (The Tzinoroth) through which their influence descends are aroused to action by a desire manifested in the recipients of that influence. Man who is composed both of body and a soul, i. e. matter and spirit, is the proper medium through which these two worlds unite. It is he who supplies the stimulus to the activity of the Sephiroth, and it is he who manifests the desire to unite with the higher powers. His actions, therefore, if they are good, stimulate the influence of these powers and increase blessing in the world. On the other hand, if they are sinful, the influence is retarded, for the *Tzinoroth* (canals) are not aroused, and as a result, blessing in this world is diminished and evil is strengthened. Hence, the righteous man (The Tzadik) assumes, according to the Kabbala, such an important role in the world. Not only does he himself possess power, but he also ennobles and raises the whole world through the rise of his own soul.

We have thus outlined the principal teachings of the speculative Kabbala concerning the important subjects of God, the world and man. It is necessary though to bear in mind that while the views presented in this outline are undoubtedly contained in the doctrines of the mystics, they are not always presented in the Kabbalistic writings in a coherent and connected manner. On the contrary, these grains of speculative thought have to be extricated with difficulty from a mass of ideas, views and teachings, which to say the least, are irrational. As already noted, the standard Kabbala, i. e. the main current of mysticism which began to flow from the thirteenth century on and continued to increase through the ages, though called speculative, in reality incorporated all the irrational elements of the earlier mysticism as well as some of those of the German Kabbala. Like the other mystic currents, it concedes great power to numbers and letters and operates with their combinations even to a greater degree than they did. In short, the Kabbala is an unsystematic synthesis of all the elements of mysticism which ever found expression in Judaism, and as such, one should not attempt to characterize it by one of its phases or aspects. It contains undoubtedly philosophic elements, but it is not merely a philosophy, as it includes much more. It can best be compared to a wide stream where different currents flow side by side, and though often intermingled, yet preserve their distinct colors and peculiarities. In order to understand it more fully, we must take into consideration not only the teachings just surveyed but also the more or less irrational elements which predominated the earlier type of mysticism spoken of in the first section of this chapter.

This heterogenous character of the Kabbala brought about also great variety in the types of its literature, for every Kabbalist was free to exercise his predilection for a certain element of the teachings. Some who were philosophically inclined, emphasized the speculative aspect, while others who were more mystical than philosophical, stressed the irrational elements. Each one, of course, presented his view as the teaching of the Kabbala. The teachings presented in the survey are those of the standard or Classical type as embodied in the *Zohar* and according to the interpretations of the best commentators. The later Kabbala, from the time of Luria on, introduced many changes and alterations. But all these changes consist primarily in matters of teachnique, i. e. in increasing and complicating the symbolism of the Kabbala and in the stressing of certain elements of the teachings. Whatever is new in these theories will be discussed in the following section in connection with the literature of that period.

C. The Literature of the Kabbala

111. GENERAL FEATURES

Kabbalistic literature, like other phases of Jewish literature has its Classical and post-Classical periods. The first lasted for little over a century, from the last quarter of the twelfth to the beginning of the fourteenth and terminated with the appearance of the *Zohar*. (c. 1300.) The second extended from the fourteenth to the end of the eighteenth, and to some extent, was continued after that time. The literature of the two periods can be further subdivided into various types, namely the pre-Zoharitic and the Zoharitic of the first period, the pre-Lurianic and the post-Lurianic of the second.

The works of each of these periods are distinguished by special characteristics. Those of the Classical are noted for their originality of content, Agadic style and anonymity of authorship. Those of the second period bear mostly the character of compilations, commentaries and collections of interpretations of the teachings embodied in the works of the Classical period. However, the Kabbalistic books produced from the sixteenth century on, which reflect the influence of the Lurianic type of Kabbala do display a certain amount of originality. With very few exceptions, the works of the post-Classical period bear the names of their authors.

The task set for themselves by the authors of the Kabbalistic books of the Classical period determined the character of their works. They were developing a new view of the world and life, and filled with this vision, they struggled for expression and grasped at every symbol, which brought them nearer to their aim, hence their originality of content, and the flashes of thought as well as the flights of poetic expression with which their works are marked. Again, those authors wanted consciously or unconsciously, to pass off this new view as a very ancient one, as one that dates from antiquity but was hidden from humanity until revealed. Hence they could not attach their names to their works, and these were given to the world either anonymously or as pseudepigraphic productions. In fact, most of the Kabbalistic works of the Classical period are ascribed to authors of the Tannaitic period, such as Simon ben Yohai (Zohar), Nehunya ben ha-Kana (Bahir), Rabbi Ishmael or others.

Partly on account of the supposed authorship and partly because in general, the line of demarkation between Agada and mysticism was not as yet drawn fast, the style and method of these books is completely Midrashic. The fundamental views of the Kabbala, like that of the Agada, are that all wisdom is contained in the Bible, that the Bible has more than one meaning and that the most important meaning is the hidden one. Hence, it was the task of these mystics to evolve all the secrets of their teachings from the text itself by all possible methods of the Agada and also by the more developed methods of the early mystics. (Sect. A of this chapter.) The works consist, therefore, of mystical homilies on verses of the Bible, and at times contain also pure Agada. The name Mystic Midrashim would in reality be a very appropriate one for these books, and in fact, the *Zohar* is often quoted as *Midrash di Rabbi Shimon ben Yohai.* The language of the Classical Kabbalistic books is in most cases that of the Agada, namely Hebrew mixed with Aramaic. However, in many of the books, Hebrew predominates and their style resembles that of the younger Midrashim (Vol. I, Ch. VI). The *Zohar* or rather the Zoharitic books, however, are written almost entirely in Aramaic.

The works of the second period possess almost none of these characteristics. The nature of their content which is, as said, primarily interpretative made all these devices unnecessary. The authors usually explain the teachings of the Kabbala, and either quote from the early works to support their view or take a passage as a text for interpretation in order to evolve from it a particular view or doctrine. It must not, however, be concluded that the great mass of Kabbalistic works of the second period are all commentaries on earlier works. Nay, on the contrary, some works do contain much originality, for they contributed greatly to the development of the doctrine of Kabbala. Likewise, many of the ideas that these books teach are evolved by the authors from verses in the Bible by the same methods of the earlier Kabbalists, but not in the manner of the first group of works. The later writings are discourses on the Kabbala, and the mystic interpretation of the verses come as a part of the discourse. Even when the Kabbalistic work is called a commentary on the Torah or any other book of the Bible, it is primarily a collection of mystic comments and not a systematic work of exegesis. The language of the books of the second period is almost invariably the usual Rabbinic Hebrew employed during the Middle Ages, seasoned with the peculiar flavor of the simile and the parable so common in the Classical Kabbala. As in the previous surveys, we will note only the most outstanding works.

112. THE EARLY KABBALISTIC BOOKS

As we already had occasion to point out the principal teachings of the important Kabbalistic books of the pre-Zoharitic period (cf. above sect. 309), we will limit ourselves to the more external literary characteristics of these works.

i. The first Classical work which, as stated above, was the *Masekheth Aziluth* (Tractate of Emanation), was written according to the opinion of Jellinek and his followers during the second half of the twelfth century either by Jacob Nazir himself or by one of his disciples. There is no doubt that the opinion is correct to a great extent, for there are many signs which point to this late date of composition. However, the style and other evidences may point also to an earlier date, namely the Gaonic times.[32] It is therefore, not improbable that the book is composed of two strata, an older and a younger one. The older one contains pure Agadic matter and the younger the Kabbalistic elements.

The book consists of ten sections, a number of which begin with the usual Midrashic formula, "Patah," i. e. "one opened the discourse." The names of those who conducted the discourses are Elijah,

[32] L. Ginzberg, Article Cabbala, Jewish Encyclopaedia, Vol. III, p. 459, ff.

Yaareshya, Zechariah and Yeruham, the sons of Joseph. We know of no Tannaim or Amoraim by these names, but they are mentioned in I Chronicles Ch. XIII, 27. In *Shemoth Rabba* (Large Midrash to Exodus) Ch. XL, however, these names are said to be different appellations of the prophet Elijah. It is, therefore, suggested by Jellinek[33] that the author purposely ascribed the discourses to these men to make people believe that the teachings contained there emanated from the prophet Elijah himself who, according to the Kabbalists, imparted the secrets of the Kabbala to the initiated. The suggestion seems very plausible but not entirely convincing, for the name Joseph, the father of the four men carrying on the discourses, is not mentioned in Chronicles or in the Midrash. On the contrary, in the verse in Chronicles, Yeruham is the father of the other three and not their brother. It may, therefore, be said that the names were chosen by the author at random to give his utterances an appearance of hoary antiquity. The language of the *Maseketh Aziluth* is almost pure Hebrew like those of the younger Midrashim and the Kabbalistic doctrines are still in the first stage as pointed out above.

The second Kabbalistic book, the *Sepher ha-Bahir,* is likewise pseudepigraphic. It is ascribed to Rabbi Nehunya ben ha-Kana, but was most likely written by one of the disciples of Isaac the Blind at the beginning of the thirteenth century. The signs indicating the late date of its composition are unmistakable. Of the many such evidences, we will quote one and that is the quotation by the *Sepher ha-Bahir* of the maxim of Abraham Ibn Ezra that, "Letters are like bodies and their meanings like souls." This maxim is nowhere mentioned in Jewish literature previous to Ibn Ezra and is undoubtedly taken by the Bahir from the former's commentary on the Pentateuch. The name *Bahir* is given to the book because it begins with a homily on the verse of Job, XXXVII, 21, "And now men see not the bright light (Or Bahir) which is in the heavens." Jellinek sees in the beginning of the book a reference to Isaac's blindness who saw not by physical light but by a brighter light which is heavenly.

Yet though the book was written as late as the date assigned to it, in style and manner it is made to resemble the Midrashic books. On the whole, it is a collection of Agadic and mystic interpretations of a number of verses of the Bible taken mostly from Genesis, but a considerable number also from other books of the Pentateuch. These verses from the Torah are the basis of the discourses, but in the

[33] A. Jellinek, Auswahl Kabbalistischer Mystic, Introduction, pp. 1-2.

course of development of the discourses, verses from other Biblical books are also interpreted. Besides Rabbi Nehunya, other sages take part in the discussion, all of them bearing the names of certain Tannaim. The discourses are often carried on in the form of a dialogue and are written in a fine Hebrew style with a tinge of Aramaic. The *Bahir* employs to a great extent the Mashal, i. e. the parable. Almost every passage is illustrated by a parable. To the outline of the teachings of the book given above, we may add that the *Bahir* is the first Kabbalistic work which attempted to assign mystic reasons for many of the precepts of the Torah. This attempt might have been aroused by a desire to counteract the influence of Maimonides who in the third part of *More Nebukim* offered rational reasons for the precepts. The Bahir spread among the mystics immediately after its appearance and its antiquity was hardly questioned. Isaac ha-Cohen of Geronna, a Kabbalist, who flourished only a few decades later, writes of the book as an ancient document imported by the mystics from Palestine into Germany and thence transmitted to the initiated of Provence.[34]

To the Apocryphal books of the early Kabbala belongs also the *Sepher ha-Temunah* (The Book of the Image) which is likewise ascribed to Nehunya ben ha-Kana. It was most likely written by an anonymous author at the end of the thirteenth century. It consists of three sections and deals primarily with the forms of the letters of the alphabet and their connection with the Sephiroth. This represents an attempt to connect the two elements in Kabbala, that of letter mysticism and the doctrine of the Sephiroth. The contributions which the book makes toward the development of the theories of the Kabbala were already noted above.

ii. Of the non-Apocryphal Kabbalistic works which appeared before the *Zohar,* the earliest and the most important are those of Rabbi Azriel called also Ezra (1160-1238). Rabbi Azriel who was born in Spain went to the Provence to study under Isaac the Blind, and on his return to his country initiated a number of his followers, among whom was also the famous Moses ben Nahman, in the new mysteries. His influence on the development of the Kabbala was exceedingly great, as he gave the doctrines he taught a philosophic coloring which made them more attractive to the philosophically-minded people.

The works of Rabbi Azriel are (1) *Perush ha-Derashoth* (The Commentary on Homilies), explanations of Agadic passages; (2) a

[34] A. Jellinek: Beitrage zur Geschichte der Kabbala, Pt. II, p. 64.

commentary on the Pentateuch; (3) commentaries on the *Book of Yetzira;* (4) on Canticles; (5) the *Sepher ha-Miluim* (The Book of Consecration) on the Kabbalistic doctrine; and (6) the *Perush Eser Sephiroth* (Commentary on the Ten Sephiroth). Only three of his works are extant, the commentaries on *Yetzira,* Canticles and the Ten Sephiroth. The others are known only by excerpts in later Kabbalistic works. The commentary on the *Book of Creation* was, however, published in the editions of the book under the name of his disciple Nahmanides, but internal evidences of the work show definitely that it belongs to Rabbi Azriel. His most important work is the Commentary on the Ten Sephiroth, the outline of which teachings was given above (p. 356). The book is in the form of a dialogue between a teacher and a pupil. There are twelve such dialogues consisting of questions and answers. The first two are devoted to two fundamental theses of philosophical theology, namely that there is a God guiding the world and that God is infinite and incorporeal. The others are devoted to the proving of the existence of the Sephiroth and the description of their essence, character and order. The twelfth dialogue is longer than all the rest and cites proofs for the teachings from verses of the Bible. It is an attempt to show that all Kabbalistic teachings are grounded in the Bible and are not mere inventions of the mind. Azriel, like the author of the *Sepher ha-Bahir* devotes much space in his works to the mystic reasons for the precepts (Taame Mitzvoth). And if we will assume with Jellinek that the works of Azriel precede the authorship of the Bahir, he was the first mystic to do so. But this assumption seems to be unfounded.

The disciple of Azriel, Moses ben Nahman, the great Talmudist and renowned Bible commentator, is also known as a Kabbalistic teacher, but it seems that he wrote no special work devoted particularly to mysticism. His Kabbalistic views are to be gathered from remarks interspersed in his commentary on the Pentateuch, as well as in other works, such as the *Shaarē ha-Gemul* (The Portal of Reward), a treatise on reward and punishment and the *Derashah,* a discourse on the qualities of the Torah. Two works were, however, ascribed to him, one the above mentioned Azriel's commentary on the *Book of Yetzira* and the other, the *ha-Emunah we-ha-Bitohon* (Faith and Trust). After examination, though, scholars came to the conclusion that these works did not emanate from the hand of Nahmanides.[35]

[35] A. Jellinek, Ibid, p. 40.

The last important work of this group is the *Ma'arekheth Elohuth* (The Divine Order or System) of which teachings we already had occasion to speak. The authorship of the book is not quite definitely established. Zunz and others ascribe the work to a certain Peretz ben Isaac ha-Kohen who lived at the beginning of the fourteenth century. This would, of course, make the *Ma'arekheth* a post-Zoharitic work, and this seems improbable as there are in it no traces of those elements in the Kabbala which are peculiar to the *Zohar*. Moses Cordevero ascribes the book to Todros Abulafia who died in 1283, which would make it a product of the second half of the thirteenth century. But though the authorship can not be definitely determined, it is almost certain that it was composed before the appearance of the *Zohar*. The author, though he for one reason or another, conceals his name, does not at all endeavor to make the book appear pseudepigraphic. On the contrary, he speaks in a personal manner and quotes other Kabbalists by name. Among the mystics he mentions are Nahmanides, Abraham ben David, Eleazar of Worms, and a certain Rabbi Isaac, his teacher. Were the *Zohar* known to him which most likely would have been the case if it had already appeared, he would undoubtedly have quoted it.

The book, as pointed out above, develops the mystic theories in a more systematic way than the previous books, and its relation to some of them, especially to the *Bahir* is like that of a commentary to a text. In addition to the mystical teachings developed by the author, there is also a philosophic element in the work. The first two sections are devoted to an enunciation of the dogmas of Judaism and to the elucidation of the concept of God. In these sections, the author shows himself well versed in the Jewish philosophy of his day and his arguments are largely based on the theories of Maimonides.

Of the other Kabbalistic works which appeared before the *Zohar,* are to be mentioned first those which reflect to a great extent the other current in Kabbala, namely that of the German type. To these belong the works of Eleazar of Worms and Abraham Abulafia which, as described above, are primarily based on letter mysticism, second the *Kether Shem Tob* of Abraham di-Colonia which is an attempt to combine both elements, namely the letter mysticism and the Sephiroth theory and third the several works by Joseph ben Abraham Gikatilia (1248-1300).

Gikatalia was a very fruitful writer and left us a number of treatises. The more important of these are the *Ginath Egoz* (The Garden of Nuts), *Shaarē Ora* (The Portals of Light) and the *Sepher ha-Nikud* (The Book of Punctuation). Gikatalia can be considered to be a faithful follower of Abulafia. He endeavored to introduce his teachings in the Kabbala and made much of the theory which attaches great importance to the letters of the alphabet and to those of the names of God. He even developed it further than Abulafia. His *Shaarē Ora* is a treatise on the ten names of God, and the *Sepher ha-Nikud* deals with the mystic interpretations of the vowels and accents.

The works of Isaac Ibn Latif (1228-1290) of Toledo represent a distinct current in Kabbalistic literature. Latif was both a philosopher and a mystic, and this combination is reflected in his works. He is a very prolific writer and left a number of books of which the outstanding are *Ginzē ha-Melek* (The Treasures of the King), the *Zurath Olam* (The Form of the World) and the *Shaar ha-Shomayyim* (The Portal of Heaven). In all these works, the teachings of philosophy and Kabbala intermingle.

According to Latif, the world was created by the eternal will of God out of nothing. It is because of this that the world is finite, for it was so determined by His will. So far speaks the philosopher, the follower of Maimonides, but henceforth he parts company with philosophy and turns to the path of mysticism. It is not after all the material world which was created by the primal will of God, but only the first created being for there must be mediators between God and the lower world. The first created being is an absolute simple entity and is the ground of all existing things. In this process of emanation, the further a being is in the scale of existence, the more material it becomes. Thee number of separate intelligences is ten, and these are the Sephiroth. The intelligences or Sephiroth were the mediators through which the lower worlds were created. Latif divides all existence in three groups or worlds, the world of intelligences, the middle world, i. e. the world of the spheres and the world of nature embracing all bodies in existence. And if we add the first created being which is the source of all these worlds, we really have four worlds corresponding to a certain extent to the system of the four worlds of the Kabbala, though differing from it in important points.

Latif's views thus represent an attempt to limit the teachings of the Kabbala and to guard that they deviate not from the fundamental doctrine of Judaism, namely creation. He accepts emanation and existence of the Sephiroth, but he limits the process by positing a first created being. He employs also to a great extent the symbolism as well as the method of interpretation of verses and the style of the Kabbala.

The final links in the pre-Zoharite Kabbalistic literature are the works of Moses de Leon (1250-1305) the very same man who was instrumental in bringing about the appearance of the *Zohar* and who is often spoken of as its author. Moses was born in Leon, Spain, but led a wandering life, sojourning for periods in different cities. He was deeply immersed in the study of the Kabbala and possessed an encompassing knowledge of the entire field of mysticism. He also possessed a facile pen and the ability to write in a style which is brilliant but not clear. He is the author of a number of Kabbalistic works—his reputed authorship of the *Zohar* can not be definitely established as will soon be evident—but only one is extant in print. This is the *Shekel ha-Kodesh* (The Holy Shekel). The teachings embodied in this work are, on the whole, almost identical with those of the *M'aareketh*. In his other works we meet with almost all the elements of the Kabbala embodied in the *Zohar*.

113. THE ZOHAR

The *Zohar* or rather the group of mystical works which go by that name, can fairly be described as the Bible of the Kabbala. It is the very corner-stone of the entire mystic movement, which after its appearance became a potent factor in Jewish life for six centuries or more. It is the axis around which the great mass of subsequent Kabbalistic literature turns. All later books either use its passages as a basis for further development of the mystic teachings or merely explain various parts of this great work.

The influence of the *Zohar* was heightened to a certain extent by the quaint mode of its appearance, which was and still is a mystery. As is well known, the Zohar is a pseudepigraphic work supposed to have been composed by the Tanna Simon ben Yohai with the assistance of an assembly of sages initiated into the secrets of mysticism. It was revealed to the world at the end of the thirteenth century through the agency of the Kabbalist, Moses ben Shem Tob de Leon.

According to de Leon's own story, the book was hidden in a cave in Palestine, the very same cave, in which, as told in the Talmud,[36]

[36] Talmud B. Sabbath, 33b.

Simon and his son Eliezer hid for thirteen years, and there Moses ben Nahman, on his arrival in the Holy Land discovered it. He sent the book to his son in Catalonia, but a wind carried it away and brought it to a certain place in Aragon whence it fell into the hands of Moses de Leon. The way this most remarkable book made its appearance is indeed exceptional. Yet it seems that the supposed miraculous revelation of the *Zohar* did not greatly affect its acceptance by contemporaries as a genuine work of Simon ben Yohai, though as we will soon see, there lacked not doubters of its authenticity even at that time. However, as time passed, its authority grew and for a number of centuries hardly anyone dared to question the antiquity of the *Zohar*. Only from the sixteenth century on, we begin to hear voices of doubt which intimated that the *Zohar* is not a genuine work but a composition of later date and that de Leon himself is probably its author. During the nineteenth century, the question of the authorship of the *Zohar* became a point of controversy among scholars to such a degree that practically a fair-sized literature was created around this question. Yet in spite of the fact that the problem has been discussed extensively, it can not be said to have been definitely solved, for though most of the authoritative scholars are inclined to consider the *Zohar* a complete pseudepigraphic work and de Leon to be its author, there are some who still defend the antiquity of, at least, some parts of it. It must, however, be understoo dfrom the outset that in the controversy around the *Zohar,* the story of its revelation played rather an insignificant part. Most of the arguments against the authenticity and antiquity of the book are based primarily on the heterogenous character of the book itself which presents many contradictions and anachronisms. As the question of the authorship of the *Zohar* is not merely a matter of literary curiosity but really throws light upon the nature and character of this work, we will give a brief survey of the arguments involved in the controversy in their historical setting.

The first historical document, containing evidence of a suspicion of the lateness of the *Zohar,* which arose in the minds of some immediately after its appearance, was written by a contemporary of de Leon, Isaac of Acco. This document was originally recorded by Abraham Zacuto, the author of the historical chronicle *Yuhasin,* and was inserted in the first edition of the book printed in Constantinople in the year 1566. Subsequently, however, editors have deleted this passage, but in 1850, an English Jewish scholar, Filipowsky, issued a new edition of the book from a manuscript in the Bodlean library where this account is found in a more extended form.

In this account, Isaac who was himself a Kabbalist, tells us that in the year 1305 he came from Acco in Palestine to Spain with the purpose of ascertaining the origin of the *Zohar*. The reason for his undertaking such a journey was that he had been greatly impressed by the book but had found there suspicious passages, namely that while the entire book was written in Aramaic (in his words the language of the Jerusalem Talmud) some passages were written in Hebrew. He concluded, therefore, that certain parts were forged. On coming to Spain, he inquired of the mystics regarding the manner of the revelation of the *Zohar* and most of them recounted the miraculous story of de Leon. Others, however, asserted that the book was not composed by Simon ben Yohai but by de Leon himself, who acting as a medium[37] to a heavenly power, wrote these wonderful secrets through inspiration, but in order to obtain a higher price for the work, ascribed it to Simon ben Yohai. Isaac then immediately went to Valedolid to meet Moses de Leon himself. The latter told him that he does possess the ancient manuscript at his home in Avila and will show it to him on his arrival there. On the way to Avila, Moses took sick and died. When Isaac arrived there, a relative of the deceased told him that he is certain that Moses never had any manuscript. He corroborated his statement by the testimony of the wife and daughter of Moses himself which had been given on the following occasion. The family of Moses having remained destitute after his death, and on hearing of this, a rich man Joseph de Avila who wanted to obtain the original copy of the *Zohar* offered the widow large sums of money and promised to take her daughter as wife for his son if she would let him have the coveted manuscript. Mother and daughter then testified that Moses never had a copy, and that he distinctly had told them that he himself had composed the book and ascribed it to Simon ben Yohai so that he might get a high price for his work. Isaac then continues to tell of his meeting later with the mystic Joseph, the son of Todros Abulafia, who assured him

[37] Medium or automatic writing, as it is called to-day by psychical research men, is the term applied to writing which is supposed to be done either by dictation or under the inspiration of a supernatural agent or the spirit of a dead person. In this process, the writer does his work not on his own initiative but is entirely subjected to the will of the agent. Often he is not even conscious of what he is doing and has no inkling of the content. In the last case, the writing is strictly automatic. Numerous cases of such writings are recorded both in Mediaeval literature and in modern works on psychical research.

that Moses really possessed an ancient manuscript, for upon request, he immediately furnished a second copy of a part of the *Zohar*. Isaac remarks that the proof was not convincing for Moses might have left with him a copy of his own work so that he could have easily recopied it. He, however, later met a disciple of Moses who gave a more favorable testimony.[38] Here the narrative breaks off and we can not ascertain the nature of that testimony. But from the opening sentence as well as from the fact that Rabbi Isaac himself quotes the *Zohar* under the name of *Midrash Jerushalmi* (A Jerusalem Midrash), in a book which he wrote subsequently, we can conceive that the testimony was convincing to him.

We quoted the document at length for the reason that it is of great importance both on account of the close relationship between those that testified to the forgery of the *Zohar* and the author and also because of the fact that the controversy began immediately with the appearance of the book itself. This testimony is employed by most of the scholars, who believe Moses de Leon to be the author of the *Zohar,* as one of the strongest arguments for their case. We will, however, see subsequently, how much veracity it contains. One thing is clear, that the document left little impression upon the contemporaries of Isaac as well as upon the succeeding generations, as for two centuries not a dissenting voice was heard, and almost all sages in Jewry avowedly believed in the authenticity of the *Zohar*.

Towards the end of the fifteenth century, there first arose the voice of the philosopher and Classical scholar Elijah del-Medigo (see Sect. 85) who declared openly in his book *Behinath ha-Kabbala* (The Test of Tradition) that the *Zohar* was not written by Simon ben Yohai. He argued that the facts that the Talmud and the Gaonim knew not of the *Zohar* nor of its teachings, that it appeared at such a late date and that it is full of historical anachronisms, such as making later Amoraim the companions of Simon ben Yohai, prove conclusively his assertion.

Half a century later, the countryman of del-Medigo, Judah Leon de Modena (1571-1648) made a vigorous attack upon the Kabbala in general and the *Zohar* in particular in his book *Ari Nohem* (The Roaring Lion). He went deeper into the subject but still in a general way. A century later, Jacob Emden, the indefatigable contender against the gross abuses of practical Kabbala and the adherents of false Messianism, wrote his famous critical work, *Mithpahat Spharim*

[38] Yuhasin, ed. Filipowsky, pp. 88-89.

(The Wrapper of Books). There he advanced two hundred and eighty arguments which prove by numerous citations of the contradictions, anachronisms and incorrect statements contained in the various parts of the work, that the *Zohar* as a whole could not possibly be of ancient origin, and that the greater part of it was written by Moses de Leon, and that several smaller sections were composed even later than his time. He does, however, concede antiquity to some small fragments of the book.

Emden's arguments were mostly incorporated by the critics of the nineteenth century, such as Samuel David Luzzato, Adolph Jellinek, Heinrich Graetz and others, and as they added some of their own, the arguments against the authenticity of the *Zohar* are too numerous to reproduce. We will, therefore, cite only the most important of them, which are the following: (1) The gross anachronism in the names of the teachers mentioned certainly points to a later date of composition. Among the initiated are also Rab, the first Babylonian Amora, Rab Hanuna Saba, his disciple and others, who lived generations after Simon ben Yohai. (2) The Zohar knows of the existence of the vowels and accents, calls them by name and makes them the basis of mystic interpretations. These vowels and accents were invented by the Massorites whose work was completed at the earliest in the ninth century (Vol. I, Sect. 92). Moreover, one part of the book uses the term *Master of Dikduk* (Grammar), a term first coined by Dunash ben Labrat at the end of the tenth century, and also that of *Tenuah Gedola* (long Vowel) a term not used in Jewish literature before Joseph Kimhi, who introduced the division of the vowels into long and short.

(3). The Zohar made great use of the works of Jewish philosophers of the eleventh and twelfth centuries. It borrowed their terms, phrases and ideas. Thus, it speaks of the *Ilath ha-Iloth* (Cause of Causes), the four elements (Arba Yesodoth), the animal soul (Nephesh ha-Behemith) and similar terms peculiar to Jewish philosophy which were not used before its rise. Moreover, it describes the qualities of the four elements in the distinct Aristotelian manner. Again, it cites the expression, "a donkey carrying books" to denote a man who knows many books but does not master their contents in an intelligent way, an expression first found in Bahya's *Hobboth ha- Leba-*

both.[39] It incorporated the idea of Judah ha-Levi that the Jews are among the nations as the heart in the body, namely the central seat of the spiritual life force. It even employs some theories in physics expounded by Maimonides.

(4). The *Zohar* deviates in many things from the Talmud in matters of law and knows of many later differences in legal interpretation. It mentions the custom of putting on two pairs of phylacteries which arose as a result of the difference between Rashi and his grandson Jacob Tam regarding the arrangement of the Biblical passages placed in them. It knows of the custom of reciting the *Kol Nidrē* on Yom Kippur night which is not older than the eleventh century.

(5). There are also a number of linguistic evidences which prove both its late origin as well as the unacquaintance of the writers of the *Zohar* with the very language they were employing. Thus, the *Zohar* uses the word *Esnoga* for synagogue, and in its usual exotic way derives it from the two Hebrew words *Esh Nogah* (A Bright Fire). But the word is merely the Portuguese equivalent for synagogue. Likewise, the word *Dormita* used in the *Zohar* for sleep can not be explained on the basis of any Semitic language, except as one borrowed from Romance languages. Moreover, the Aramaic language in which the work is written has many deviations from all types of Aramaic whether Biblical or that of the Babylonian or Palestinian Talmud. It indicates rather an endeavor at imitation than the natural use of a language by men accustomed to speak that tongue as would have been the case if the authors were really Tannaim. In addition, there are evidences of attempted translations from the Hebrew which led to errors. Thus, the *Zohar* uses the Aramaic verb יזיף which means to borrow in the sense of accompany. This error can be only explained on the basis that the writer had in mind the Hebrew word לוה which means both to accompany and to borrow, and on translating it into Aramaic stumbled on the first equivalent. Of such misuses of Aramaic words, there are many examples in the *Zohar*. Besides these mistranslations, there are also many incorrect quotations from the Bible and the Talmud.

(6). Finally, there are prophecies in some parts of the book, especially in the *Additions* (Tikkunim) which inform us that the *Zohar*

[39] True, the expression is not original with Bahya, as it is first found in the Koran, Sura LX. But at any rate it could not have been used by Simon ben Yohai and his contemporaries.

will be revealed around the year 1060 (1300 C. E.), and also various Messianic dates are given all of which fall in the sixth millenium. All these things go to prove that there was a conscious effort on the part of the authors to make people believe in the antiquity of the book by including prophecies regarding the date of its appearance.

This array of arguments which is only a small part of the entire number of proofs advanced by scholars, makes a good case for the late date of the composition of the *Zohar* and also for the claim that its birth place was Spain. We still have to show that the author was Moses de Leon himself. The *Zohar,* argue critical scholars, is not only a work of the thirteenth century but was actually composed by the same Moses de Leon who revealed it to the world. The evidence of this assertion is not only the above quoted testimony of his wife and daughter cited by Isaac of Acco, but numerous parallel passages found both in the other works of Moses and the *Zohar*. The parallels run so close that even an error in a quotation from a verse in Psalms XLVI, 9 found in a passage in the *Rimmon* (Pomegranate) of de Leon is duplicated in an identical passage in the *Zohar*. Besides these parallels, there are many references in the *Zohar,* plain and veiled, to a Moses who will arise at about the beginning of the sixth millenium of the Jewish era and will reveal this great work. All these evidences, conclude the scholars, point unmistakably to the fact that Moses de Leon is the author of the *Zohar*.

However, in spite of the array of arguments for the late date of the *Zohar* and its authorship by Moses de Leon, there are quite a number of scholars who insist both upon the antiquity of the work, at least of some parts of it, and that Moses de Leon was not its author. Their arguments can be summarized as follows: First, the language of the *Zohar* which is Aramaic of the Palestinian dialect, proves its antiquity. They say that such an acquaintance with this dialect which should enable one to write a group of works in it, could not have been possessed by any scholar at the end of the thirteenth century. It must, therefore, have been written at a time when the dialect was spoken. Second, there is a Kabbalistic work by the same Moses de Leon called *Sepher ha-Shem,* which is written in Hebrew and contains many teachings of the *Zohar*. That the same man should have at first forged a book in Aramaic, and then given a part of it in Hebrew sounds improbable, for he might have feared discovery. Third, on general grounds, it seems impossible that one man whose life was rather short and who passed his days in wandering should have been able to accomplish such a forgery on so grand a scale.

To these arguments which were advanced by the great expositor of the teachings of the Kabbala, Adolph Franck, modern students of the Kabbala, added several more.[40] They use the very same arguments advanced by the opponents, namely the parallel citations in the Hebrew works of de Leon as a proof that he did not compose the *Zohar.* Their main argument is that all these passages found in de Leon's works are introduced by him in such a way which shows that they are quotations from secret books. In fact, he quotes a *Midrash Yerushalmi* (Jerusalem Midrash) numerous times. These quotations are given verbatim in the Aramaic dialect and are found in the *Zohar.* This proof, however, is not convincing, for one may argue that he forged the *Zohar* early in life and copied in his other works passages from it before he revealed it to the world, and in order to obviate this possible objection, the champions of the antiquity of the book buttress their claim by the fact that some difficult expressions of the *Zohar* were unintelligible to Moses himself just as they are to us. This, they say, would prove that Moses copied these passages from an old book, unless we should assume that he was extremely shrewd and had used these devices with a definite purpose to mislead the people.

Finally, they adduce proofs from quotations of passages from the *Zohar* found in the works of other authors, who though living in the thirteenth century were older than Moses. These quotations are found in the Kabbalistic work *Ozar ha-Kaḇod* by Rabbi Todros Abulafia. The value of these quotations depends entirely on the fixation of the year when this Todros died. Graetz believes that Todros died in the year 1304 which would invalidate the proof entirely, for by this time the *Zohar* was already published and he might easily have copied from it. But there are statements to the effect that Todros died in the year 1283 and undoubtedly wrote his book five or ten years earlier. This date has, of late, been definitely established and the fact gives the matter an entirely different aspect, for the *Zohar* was not published until the end of the century. Besides, the Kabbalist Joseph Gikitalia (above p. 390) quotes in his book *Shaarē Ora* (The Portals of Light) passages found in the 'Idra Rabba (The Large As-

[40] On this see G. Shalom in publications of the Institute for Jewish Studies at the Jerusalem University, Vol. I, No. III, pp. 16-28.

sembly), an important part of the *Zohar* and introduces them by the formula "Our sages of blessed memory said," a formula exclusively used for quotations from Talmudic or Agadic books. Gikitalia wrote his work earlier than Moses de Leon, for in a work written by the latter in 1293, he already quotes the *Shaarē Ora.*

It must be admitted that these last arguments though plausible are not entriely convincing, for if we assume that Moses de Leon wrote the *Zohar,* it is reasonable also to assume that he had not compiled it in a short time, for it would take many years to compose a work of such magnitude. It is, therefore, quite probable that being engaged in this work for a long time, he might have shown parts of it to Todros much earlier than the publication of the *Zohar,* and that the latter included some passages from these parts in his own book, for de Leon dedicated a book to Todros and thus came in frequent contast with him.

In general, all these arguments do not intend to prove the antiquity of the *Zohar* but merely that some of its parts were known before its publication, and therefore, de Leon can not be said definitely to be the author of the *Zohar,* but might have been its editor. However, these assertions may be true though not on the grounds of these later proofs but on the basis of the arguments quoted above by Franck, though his conclusions are untenable.

Weighing the arguments on both sides of the question, we may conclude that the arguments against the antiquity of the *Zohar* and its authenticity as a work emanating from the school of Simon ben Yohai have an overwhelming preponderance in their favor. It is different, though with Moses de Leon's authorship of the *Zohar.* To assume that he wrote the entire *Zohar* and published it as an ancient work is highly improbable. Against such an assumption stand the two arguments of Franck, namely the use of the Aramaic language and the fact that the forgery of the entire work is too much for one man.

We are, therefore, inclined to accept the solution offered by Jacob Emden in a greatly modified way. Emden believed that certain parts of the *Zohar,* namely the smaller collection consisting of the *Saphra di Zenuita* (The Book of Secrets), the two *'Idroth, Rabba* and *Zuta* (The Large and Small Assemblies) and other passages really emanated from the school of Simon ben Yohai, though not in the present form. They were edited, he says, by a later hand in Gaonic times. The other parts called *Sitrē Torah* (The Secrets of the Torah) and the *Tikkunim,* he assigns to the thirteenth century and avers that they were written by de Leon, while the third part, such as the *Midrash ha-Nealam* (The Hidden Midrash) he assigns to even a later date.

We believe that Emden is right in assuming the earlier existence of certain parts of the *Zohar,* but with this difference that we can not determine definitely which are the parts, nor can we ascribe any part of it to Simon ben Yohai. The reason for this assertion is as follows: The Talmud and Midrashim contain many references to Tannaim and even Amoraim who engaged in the study of mysticism, and there are numerous passages wherein their teachings are recorded. In all these passages, the name of Simon ben Yohai is not mentioned even once, nor is there a single mystic statement attributed to him. It is, therefore, impossible to assume that Simon ben Yohai engaged in this study to such a degree. Were the case so, a reference to his teachings would certainly have been found in the Talmudic and Midrashic literature among the many Agadic statements attributed to him.

The earlier parts or fragments of the *Zohar* were merely pseudepigraphic works written probably during late Gaonic times (9th and 10th centuries) in Palestine. We have seen (Vol. I, Sect. 181) that there were many mystical pseudepigraphic works, such as the *Hekaloth* group, the *Otioth di Rabbi Akiba* in earlier times, and the *Maseketh Aziluth* and the *Bahir* in the twelfth and thirteenth centuries. There is no reason why we can not assume that there were other pseudepigraphic works ascribed to Simon ben Yohai written at about the time stated above. They usually circulated under the name *Midrashim* and when written in the Palestinian dialect, they were called *Midrash Yerushalmi,* the name under which even the *Zohar* is often quoted. These small works were undoubtedly much simpler in their teachings and did not contain the higher speculative elements found therein in their present form, which were added later. It is with these materials that Moses de Leon worked. He incorporated them in his work and added much of his own. And since these works were written in Aramaic, we may reasonably assume that Moses de Leon wanting to present the entire work as having emanated from the school of Simon ben Yohai wrote the additional parts also in Aramaic, so as to make it appear unified. He did not always succeed and some parts of the *Zohar,* such as the *Midrash ha-Nealam* are written in Hebrew mixed with Aramaic. This part was, probably, as Landauer suggested long ago, his first attempt and he was not as yet skilled in the Aramaic dialect. His skill improved with practice.

There is no doubt that Moses de Leon whether he was the writer of the greater part of the *Zohar* or mere editor, possessed great skill, for it required talent to piece together materials from different Midrashim and add new material and yet give the entire heterogenous work a character of unity. The *Zohar* group of works, in spite of the heterogenuity, confusion and extensive repetition, retains the stamp of unity. It must be admitted, however, that this unity is only of a general nature and is expressed more in the unity of the teachings than in that of the form, for the *Zohar* consisting of various parts and supplements presents an incomplete set of works, the final welding of which was probably prevented by the sudden death of Moses de Leon.

We do not claim absolute certainty for the hypothesis put forth by us, but merely assert that it is very probable that Moses de Leon was both writer of a large part of the *Zohar* and editor of the earlier incorporated parts. To determine exactly the sections contributed by de Leon himself, as well as to define with a degree of accuracy the earlier pseudepigraphic fragments incorporated therein, would require a minute examination of the entire *Zohar* literature which for the present is still a desideratum.

114. THE CHARACTER OF THE ZOHAR

The group of Kabbalistic works which make up the *Zohar* literature is divided into three separate books which were printed at different times. These are the *Zohar* proper, the *Zohar Hadash* (The New Zohar) and the *Tikkunē ha-Zohar* (The Explanations or Additions to the Zohar). However, what we call the *Zohar* proper is by no means a homogenous work but a heterogenous one. It contains the largest number of the parts of the group. It consists of (1) the *Saphra di-Zenuita* (The Book of Secrecy), a booklet of only three pages which is considered the source and nucleus of the entire *Zohar;* (2) the *'Idra Rabba* (The Large Assembly); (3) the *'Idra Zuta* (The Small Assembly); (4) the *Zohar* to the section *Bereshith,* i. e. the first section of Genesis, which has peculiar characteristics though a part of the entire Midrash of the *Zohar;* (5) the *Midrash Zohar* to the Pentateuch; (6) the *Sitrē Torah* (The Mystersies of the Torah); (7) the

Ra'aya Mehemna (The Faithful Shepherd); (8) the *Midrash ha-Nealam* (The Hidden Midrash); and (9) the *Rasa di Razin* (The Secret of Secrets).

All these are really separate works of large or small quantity and are as such distinguished in all editions of the *Zohar*. The pages which they occupy bear the respective titles. They, of course, possess different characteristics.

The *Saphra di Zenuita* is, as said, the very source of the entire *Zohar* and is written in a most enigmatic language. It is frequently quoted in the other parts as a text and extensively commented upon. This little booklet can be compared to the anonymous portions of the Mishnah (Stam-Mishnah) for no names of the revealers of the secrets are given there and no other books are quoted or referred to. It consists of five short chapters.

The *'Idra Rabba* is called thus because it contains the teachings revealed at an assembly of initiates presided over by Simon ben Yohai. This original group of ten initiates are the leaders of the discussions in the entire series of the *Zohar* works. They were Rabbis Simon and his son Eleazar, Aba, Judah, Yosē bar Yakob, Isaac, Hiskia bar Rab Hiyya, Yosē and Yesa. The *'Idra Rabba* is primarily a commentary to the *Saphra di Zenuita,* although it contains many other additions. In the printed editions, it is inserted in the section of *Naso* in the Book of Numbers, and extends for eighteen pages or folios (127-145).

The *'Idra Zuta* contains the teachings supposed to have been revealed by Simon ben Yohai immediately before his death, and the number of initiates was smaller, for three of the original group had already departed from this world. It is principally an addition to the *'Idra Rabba* and expounds the teachings given in the former. In the *'Idra Zuta* the *Saphra di Zenuita* and the *'Idra Rabba* are quoted as texts and also other books are mentioned there.

The *Zohar* to the Bereshith section of Genesis, though really a part of the entire mystic Midrash to the Pentateuch has its own peculiarities and it is probable that it was originally a separate book written prior to the entire Midrash. It is also a kind of extensive commentary to the *Saphra di Zenuita* and together with the introduction, it is a considerable work, for as we know, the question of creation was the center of Kabbalistic teachings, and raised much discussion. There were different versions to many of its passages and these versions were partially incorporated in the *Tikkunē ha-Zohar* which likewise deals mainly with the problem of creation.

The *Midrash Zohar* to the Pentateuch which forms the bulk of the book contains discussions of a philosophical, theological and Agadic nature together with mystic teachings. It is arranged in the form of a Midrash basing the discussions and comments on the verses of the sections of the Pentateuch. Like the Midrash, many of the discourses have introductions of short homilies which begin with the usual word "Patah," i. e. one opened the discourse." In a number of sections, the Agadic element exceeds the Kabbalistic, but in others the mystic element predominates. In general, there is little system in the *Midrash Zohar,* for teachings of different character are thrown together and secrets of mysticism are inserted in the middle of pure Agadic passages.

The *Sithrē Torah* is a collection of passages which deal primarily with mystic teachings regarding the soul, angels, the secrets of the letters and the name of God. It seems that these are fragments from a larger work and represent the incorporation of the older elements of the esoteric teachings, namely letter and Divine name mysticism. There are hardly any references in the *Sithrē Torah* to the Sephiroth theory. These passages are found in the printed editions only in four sections of the Book of Genesis, namely those of *Noah, Lek̨-Lek̨a, Va-Yera* and *Va-Yetzē.*

The *Ra'aya Mehemna* (The Faithful Shepherd) is a work which intends to explain the meaning of the precepts in a Kabbalistic way. It is of considerable size, as passages under this title are found in all the four books from Exodus to Deuteronomy. The author endeavors to find a hidden meaning almost in every precept (Mitzvah). He uses in this connection an extensive symbolism and finds correspondence in the various rituals to the *Merk̨abah,* to the Sephiroth and other elements of the world of the Kabbala.

The *Midrash ha-Nealam* deals primarily with allegorical interpretations of verses and passages in the Book of Genesis. Its teachings center around the problems of the soul and its destiny in the hereafter, namely the various phases of eschatology. It contains also much Agadic matter and employs frequently the *Mashal* form of illustrations. Linguistically, it differs from the rest of the *Zohar* group in that it is written in Hebrew with an admixture of Aramaic, while the other parts are written almost entirely in Aramaic. There are, however, pure Aramaic passages even in this Midrash which harmonize poorly with the rest of this work. They seem to be quotations from other books. In fact, the *Midrash ha-Nealam* designates frequently passages with the title *Our Mishnah* (Masnitin) or prefaces them with the words "Our rabbis taught" (Tanu Rabanan) which is the usual designation in the Talmud for a quotation from a *Baraitha.* All these characteristics aroused the suspicion of readers as to its authenticity even in early times as evidenced from the words of Isaac of Acco quoted above. The *Midrash ha-Nealam* is found in the printed editions of the *Zohar* under separate titles in the sections *Va-Yera, Hayē Sarah* and *Toldoth.* Large fragments of it, however, are also contained in the *Zodar Hadash* on Genesis.

The *Raza di-Razin* is a small booklet of ten folios contained under that title in the *Yithro* section of Exodus. It is devoted primarily to the problem of physiognomy and develops an entire system of signs and features by means of which the character of a man can be determined and his future foretold. Different versions of some of its parts are found in the *Tikkunim* and the *Zohar Hadash.* In some of the editions of this latter work, however, these versions go under the name *Sithrē Torah.*

The Tikkunim which are printed separately are a collection of seventy additions to the *Zohar* in the *Bereshith* section of Genesis. They are called so because they are further explanations to the teachings given in that part of the *Zohar.* The word *Tikkun* which is derived from the Aramaic root *Taken* meaning to improve or to repair, is used in the language of the *Zohar* in the sense of to explain or to add, hence, *Tikkunim* means explanations or additions. It was undoubtedly composed after the *Zohar,* for in several of its sections, the book is quoted by that name, and it is even stated there that Simon ben Yohai foretold that the *Zohar* will be revealed at the beginning of the sixth millenium.

The *Zohar Hadash* consists of three different parts. It contains first of all, additions to the *Zohar* on different sections of the Pentateuch as well as various recensions of passages contained in the old *Zohar.* Second, it includes large fragments of the two mystic works *Midrash ha-Nealam* and *Raza di Razin.* Third, it comprises three small *Zohar Midrashim* to Canticles, Ruth and Lamentations. The last Midrash is denominated *Midrash ha-Nealam* and was most likely taken from that work.

Viewing the various parts of the *Zohar* literature from the aspect of the particular teachings they impart, we can say that while they do not disclose a systematic development of these teachings, there is an evident sequence in their arrangement. Their sequence in the teachings is undoubtedly connected with a chronological sequence in the appearance of the separate parts. The *Saphra di Zenuita* (The Book of Secrecy) which, as stated above, is the nucleus of the *Zohar* most likely appeared first. We have reference in the Responsa of Solomon ben Adret (Sect. 67) to a certain mystical book which appeared in his days under the name of *Plioth ha-Hokmah* (The Wonders of Wisdom) and was supposed to contain revelations made by an angel to a precocious youth at Avila. Ben Adret denounced the new-fangled teachings as well as the prophecy of the youth and issued a warning against the new mystic current. Scholars are inclined to identify the *Plioth ha-Hokmah* with the *Saphra di-Zenuita,* and claim that its name and character were changed after the denouncement of ben Adret. The mediacy of the youth was dropped and the book was given a complete anonymous character, as no name of teachers are mentioned there, not even that of Simon ben Yohai.

In the teachings of the *Saphra di-Zenuita*, the Sephiroth theory is only referred to in a veiled way and never stated explicitly. It emphasizes particularly the teachings of the emergence of the first point in the process of creation, i. e. the hidden point, or in the language of the more explicit Kabbala, the first Sephirah, the theory of the Primordial Man and especially the theory of the union of the two elements of existence, that of masculine and feminine, in brief, the *Zivug* theory. It opens with a statement concerning the worlds which were created and destroyed before this world came into being, because they did not possess the right balance of the two elements and then goes on to speak of the importance of their union. It also devotes a considerable space to the delineation of the form of the *Adam Kadmon* in connection with the relation of the canals of influence (Tzinoroth) to the various attributes of God, which canals are symbolized by the hairs of the head and beard of the Primordial Man.

It is evident though that the theory of the Sephiroth, even if hardly mentioned in this book, is after all the basis of all its teachings, for they are intimately connected with it. The *Saphra di-Zenuita* was written with the purpose of making the teachings as enigmatic as possible to show that they need further explanation, and in fact, these explanations come in the other parts.

The *'Idroth* purport to explain the *Saphra di-Zenuita* and develop its teachings in a more systematic way. Here, Simon ben Yohai and his companions are introduced and more explicit reference to the Sephiroth given, but even in the *'Idroth,* there is no complete statement of this important teaching of the Kabbala. They must have been written immediately after the *Book of Secrecy.*

The *Zohar* to the first section of Genesis followed the *'Idroth.* It further develops the theory of the beginning of the process of creation and connects it more closely with the Sephiroth.

The *Ra'aya Mehemna* which deals with the symbolic and mystic explanation of the precepts is evidently earlier than the Midrash of the *Zohar* on the other books of the Pentateuch, for it came to complete the first cycle of *Zohar* writings. The mystic explanations of the precepts is the final link in a mystic conception of Judaism, the greatest part of which was outlined in the previous works. It contains, however, later additions, for it refers to the entire *Zohar* and even tells of its discovery.

The *Midrash ha-Zohar* is the largest work in the group. Here all other teachings, including the theory of the Sephiroth, find complete development, though not systematically. In general, this work is a mixture of Kabbala, Agada, theology and philosophy, and the mystic teachings are interspersed among the others. It deals extensively with all theological problems, such as the fixation of the dogmas of Judaism, freedom of the will, reward and punishment and others. It is possible that the authors of this work utilized to a great extent Agadic material, and had interwoven there the mystic teachings.

The *Midrash ha-Nealam* is devoted especially, as stated above, to the question of the soul in connection with eschatological problems, but employs allegory to a very great extent. It is undoubtedly one of the later works in the group but it may also contain earlier parts. In its allegorical teachings, it was certainly influenced by the methods of the philosophical allegorists (Sect. 94), whose interpretations of Biblical passages precipitated in the thirteenth century the opposition to the study of philosophy. Thus, the *Midrash ha-Nealam* explains the death of Sarah and the mourning of Abraham for her in Genesis XXIII, 2 to mean the death of the human body and the mourning of the soul over its loss; Sarah and Abraham stand for the body and the soul, and *Kiryath Arba,* the city in which Sarah died represents the four elements of which the body is composed. This interpretation is only a slightly changed version of the interpretation of the allegorists that Sarah and Abraham represent matter and form. The allegoric interpretations of this Midrash are tinged, of course, with mystic colors.

The *Tikkunim* contain little that is new in their teachings, except that they enlarge and develop some of the theories found in the other works. They especially develop the symbolism of the forms of the letters of the alphabet and even of that of the vowel points and the accents. Many interpretations are based on the symbolic meaning of these forms as well as of their names.

Of the general features of the *Zohar,* besides that of the peculiar language in which it was written, are the references to earlier works, the poetic nature of many of its passages, and its acquaintance with and the use of the science of the day.

The *Zohar* quotes a number of books as sources for its theories. These are *Saphra di Adam* (The Book of Adam), *Saphra di Shlomē Malka* (The Book of King Solomon); *Saphra di Hanok* (The Book of Enoch); *Saphra di Hamnuna Saba* (The Book of the Aged Hamnuna); *Saphra di Yesa Saba* (The Book of the Aged Yose); *Saphra di Agadata* (The Book of Agada); and *Saphra di Bene Kedem* (The Book of the Children of the East). In addition, there are many discourses given in the name of a *Saba,* an aged sage and also in the name of a youth, Yenuka. It is not known whether the books quoted were really some pseudepigraphic works which served the authors as sources, or mere fiction and were quoted in order to give an impression that the teachings expounded are derived from ancient sources. Most likely, some of these books were current in the circles of the mystics during the ages and did contain a part of the teachings incorporated in the *Zohar.* But as for the youth, the *Yenuka,* there is no doubt that it is the same precocious child in whose name the first version of the *Saphra di-Zenuita* under the name *Plioth ha-Hokmah* was originally revealed. While his name was removed from that book, it was retained in the other parts, and the passages attributed to him were written by the author himself.

The language of the *Zohar* is not only strong and powerful but highly poetic. Figures of speech and similies abound. Picture and symbol are the very warp and woof of every mystic literature and the *Zohar* is the most typical of its kind. Thus the Large Assembly ('Idra Rabba) begins with this characteristic poetic passage "The days are short, and the supervisor of the tasks is insisting on their completion. The call goes forth daily, but the reapers of the field are few (reapers of the field is an appellation of the initiates). Those that are already among the rows of the vineyard do not observe their way and do not know whither they go. Therefore, gather you initiates to the assembly chamber dressed in armor, swords and spears in your hands, prepared for the great event."[41] In a description of the Sephiroth and the relation of the other Sephiroth to the first one, *Kether,* the Zohar says as follows: "The first Sephirah is the unfailing source, and from it there issued forth a bubbling well, that is *Hokmah,* and then He (God) made a large basin called *Yam* (sea) i. e. *Binah,* which is filled with water flowing from the well. This *Yam* overflows into seven other vessels or channels which are the seven lower Sephiroth. And when the master breaks the vessel, the water flows back to the source and they remain broken vessels without water."[42] By this is meant that the other Sephiroth derive their very existence and essence from the constant influence of the first Sephiroth which flows through them.

The *Zohar* borrowed poetic expressions from the great poets. Like Gabirol, it calls the abode of the souls the nest of the birds. With Harisi, it terms the body the garment of the soul, and uses many other similar expressions. In general, light and color play an exceptional role in the *Zohar* literature. Their symbolic uses are applied in innumerable ways. The very processes of emanation and creation are represented by the flashing of light with its multifarious rays. However, all that was said and quoted is only a small particle of the mass of poetic expressions found in this peculiar group of books where poetry and flights of imagination are cardinal elements in their makeup. It is in a great measure due to these elements that the *Zohar* exerted such an influence upon generations of scholars and students, both Jews and non-Jews.

The author or the authors of the *Zohar* made extensive use of the natural sciences as they were known at the time. There are many physiological passages which bear evidence to a fair acquaintance with the functions of the organs of the body. There are also a number of scientific maxims quoted in the various parts of the work, among them the famous Aristotelian maxim, "Nature does not make any leaps" (Natura saltum non facit). Very remarkable is the passage in the *Zohar* which discloses a knowledge of the rotation of the earth around the sun. It is quoted in the name of the book of Rabbi Hamnuna Saba and reads as follows: "The earth revolves in a circle like a ball; some of the inhabitants are below and some above. All the creatures differ in their looks in accordance with the change

[41] Zohar, Pt. II, p. 127b.
[42] Ibid, p. 42b.

of the climate. There are places on the earth where there is light when the opposite places are in the dark. In other words, there is day in one place when there is night in another. There is one place where the day lasts for almost the entire twenty-four hours, except for a very short time of darkness."[43] Here we have almost all the elements of the modern astronomical view of the world; the sphericity of the earth, its rotation on its axis, the antipodes, the changes of the length of the day, and the influence of climatic conditions upon the races of men. Yet we must not consider that the author of this passage was a percursor of Copernicus, for the essentials of the latter's theory were known in antiquity, but the view of the earth's rotation was discarded and superseded by the Ptolemaic system. The author of the passage might have learned it through Arabic sources which recounted the various ancient theories about the world. At any rate, all the other facts show a wide acquaintance with astronomical data.

It remains for us to say a few words about the name *Zohar* applied to this group of works, though it is not the only name by which it is known. Some of the earlier Kabbalists call it by the simpler name *Midrash di Rabbi Shimon ben Yohai* and some by the name *Midrash Yehi Or* as the words *Yehi Or* are contained in the opening sentence of the work. But the name *Zohar* is the most widely known and quoted. In fact, it is called so in the book itself in the *Ra'aya Mehemna* (Zohar Pt. III, p. 153a) and several times in the *Tikkunim*.

The name is given to it by the authors not only because it enlightens the reader in the study of the secrets of the Torah, but primarily because of the opening paragraph with which the *Zohar* begins. It quotes the verse in Daniel XII, 3: "And they that be wise shall shine as the brightness (Ke-Zohar) of the firmament; and they that turn many to righteousness may be as the stars for ever and ever." It then goes on to interpret the verse in various ways, among which are also that *Zohar* symbolizes the secret teachings, and the *Maskilim* (the wise) are the initiates and the *"Mazdike ha-Rabim"* (they that turn many to righteousness) are the instructors who impart these holy teachings to the students. It follows then that the book which contains these mystic doctrines shared by all these wise men should be called *Zohar*, and hence its name.

The *Zohar* was first printed in Mantua, in the year 1560, in three volumes. In the same year, it appeared at Cremona in a second

[43] Zohar, Pt. III, p. 10a.

זה השער לי"י

ספר הזהר

על התורה מהקדוש האלהי
ר' שמעון בן יוחאי ז"ל עם סתרי
תורה ומדרש הנעלם ותוספתא
על קצת פרשיות עם מור' מקום
הפסוקים. ופי' המלות בסוף
הספר. הודפס והוגה עם רב
העיון ע"י הצעירים עמנואל בכמ'
גבריאל יצ"ו מקורפלי ממשפחת
בנאלוקי. ואברהם יצ"ו בכמ"ר
משלם ז"ל ממודינא.

פה מנטובה

תחת ממשלת מעלת אדונינו הדוכוס
גוליילמו גונזאגה יר"ה וסדרו
ע"י השותפים ה"ה הסופר כה"ר מאיר יצ"ו
בכמ"ר אפרים ז"ל מפדובה
ויעקב בכמ"ר נפתלי הכהן ז"ל מגאזולו

Title page of ed. princeps of the Zohar, Mantua, 1560
(Copy in possession of the Jewish Theological Seminary, New York)

edition to which is appended the decision (Pesak) of Isaac de Lates, Rabbi at Pesaro, where he authorizes the publication of the book and argues against those who believed that it were better that it remain hidden in manuscript as such things should not be allowed to be disclosed. The Cremona edition contains some additional matter which could not be fitted in, in any of the other parts, and therefore, the editors placed it at the beginning of the book and called it *Hak-damah* (The Preface or Introduction). Since then the *Zohar* appeared in many editions, of which the most important are those of Sulzbach prepared by the gentile Kabbalist Knurr Von Rosenroth, author of the famous work, *Kabbala Denudata,* in the year 1664 and of Amsterdam in the year 1805. Almost all editions retain the division into three volumes and the pagination of the Cremona edition. The first volume contains the *Zohar* to Genesis, the second to Exodus, and the third to Leviticus, Numbers and Deuteronomy.

115. KABBALISTIC LITERATURE OF THE FOURTEENTH AND FIFTEENTH CENTURIES

With the appearance of the *Zohar,* the Kabbala began to spread to other countries outside of Spain and the Provence. As a result, the adherents of the new mysticism increased, and its teachings began to penetrate into life and literature. But this penetration was not accomplished without difficulties and struggle. On the one hand, the Kabbala had to overcome the opposition of both the Rabbinic scholars who looked askance at these new-fangled teachings and of the philosophers who saw in it a dangerous enemy. On the other hand, it had to consolidate, clarify and interpret its own theories, and make them apply to the various phases of religious life and thought.

The Kabbalistic literature of the two centuries following the appearance of the *Zohar* possesses therefore, little originality. It is devoted either to the interpretation of the *Zohar* and other mystic works or to the defense of the Kabbala. On the whole, there are few outstanding books produced during this period. These are the following: During the fourteenth century, we meet first the works of the Italian mystic Menahem Reccanti (c. 1320), the *Taamē ha-Mitzvoth* (The Meaning of the Precepts) and his *Perush al-ha-Torah al-Dereḳ ha-Emeth* (The Commentary on the Pentateuch in the True Way). In the *Taamē ha-Mitzvoth,* he offers mystic reasons for the observance of the precepts in the manner of the earlier Kabbalists.

He is the first to quote the *Zohar* under various names, and excerpts numerous passages from it. His commentary on the Pentateuch is likewise permeated with the spirit of the new teaching and is really the first of its kind. It also contains a large number of citations from the *Zohar* and the *Bahir* and other works together with their interpretations. The second important Kabbalistic production is the *Brith Menuha* (The Covenant of Rest) by Abraham ben Isaac of Granada (end of the 14th century). It deals primarily with the names of God and the angels, the mystic value of their letters and vowels. Another attempt was also made in the middle of the century by Abraham Ibn Wakar to effect a reconciliation between the Kabbala and philosophy. He wrote a short treatise on the elements of the Kabbala where he endeavors to give the mystic teachings a philosophic aspect.

Among the noted mystic productions of the fifteenh century are the commentaries of *Ziuni* and *Zeror ha-Mor* (A Bundle of Myrrh) on the Pentateuch, that of Moses Botarel (d. 1409) on the *Book of Creation* and the *Minhath Yehuda* on the *Maareketh* as well as the independent works of the *Sepher ha-P'liah* (The Book of Wonders) and the *Sepher Emunoth*. The authors of the *Zenui* and the *Zeror ha-Mor* are Menahem Zion of Speyer, Germany, and Abraham Saba respectively. They applied the doctrines of the Kabbala to the interpretation of the Torah, but Botarel's commentary on the *Yetzira* is distinguished by its numerous quotations from unknown Kabbalistic works which he ascribes to Gaonic authors, but are in reality pseudepigraphic. The *Minhath Yehuda* was written by Yehudah Hayat of Spain toward the end of the century, and while it is primarily a commentary on the early Kabbalistic work, *Maareketh ha-Elohuth* (Sect. 112), it contains also some original views and interpretations of the theories of the Kabbala. Hayat was considered an authority by the later mystics and his *Minhath Yehuda* was frequently quoted by subsequent authors.

The *Sepher ha-P'liah* is the work of an unknown author who sometimes calls himself Kana and sometimes Elkanah ben Yeruham of the family Rom. He claims to be a descendant of the mystic Tanna Nehunya ben ha-Kanah to whom the *Bahir* and other books are ascribed. It is primarily a compilation of excerpts from numerous Kabbalistic works dealing with the problems of creation and emanation. It contains also polemic matter against the Talmudic scholars who refuse to recognize the primacy of the Kabbala. The *Sepher Emunoth* is by Shem Tob ben Joseph Ibn Shem Tob (d. 1430), the father of the philosopher Joseph ben Shem Tob, the commentator of Maimonides' *Guide*. Shem Tob devotes his book to the defense of the Kabbala attacking vigorously the teachings of the philosophers especially those of Maimonides. He then develops his own view of the fundamentals of Judaism from a Kabbalistic standpoint. The *Emunoth* contains a good deal of information about the development of the Kabbala, for he quotes numerous excerpts from works supposed to be written by famous Gaonim, which however, are not authentic and belong to the class of pseudepigraphic works.

116. THE LATER KABBALISTIC LITERATURE (from the 16th to the 18th centuries)

With the expulsion of the Jews from Spain and the downfall of the Kabbalistic center there, mysticism turned toward the Orient in search of a new center. It did not take long and a new Kabbalistic center arose in Palestine, in the city of Safed, which exceeded in influence the previous ones, those of Provence and Spain.

Both time and place were favorable for the revival of the Kabbala, the spread of its teachings and the rise of its prestige among all the Jews of the world. The times were turbulent, and the great suffering which the Sephardic exiles scattered in many lands were undergoing, had inclined many of them to take refuge from the miseries of a cruel world in the quiet recesses of mysticism. Besides, these sufferings engendered in the hearts of the exiles the hope of redemption, to the approach of which the very miseries testified, for according to the Talmud, great suffering must precede the arrival of the Messiah, and they are even called the "birth pangs" of the Messiah (Heblē Moshiah). Messianism was, therefore, in the air and the delving into mystic teaching was considered by many sages both a necessary preparation for the great event and also a means for the determination and calculation of the coveted end of the exile, the *"Ketz."*

Not less effective was the stimulus of the place. Palestine, the holy land, the ancient home of mysticism was conducive not only to further cultivation of the Kabbala but to a complete immersion in its secrets on the part of the students. The very fact that a considerable number of Jewish scholars had settled, early in the sixteenth century, in Palestine and most of them in Safed, was considered by many a beginning of the approaching redemption. This in turn, attracted other scholars to follow suit and likewise settle there. The large number of scholars who gathered in Palestine in general, and Safed in particular, during the first half of the sixteenth century not only made that city a center of both Talmudic and Kabbalistic learning, but gave to the teachings emanating from it complete authority in the eyes of all Jewry. It was thus that the new Kabbala going forth from Safed was speedily and unequivocally accepted by all Jewish settlements.

About the middle of the sixteenth century, there gathered in Safed such a galaxy of scholars and mystic sages that was hardly ever witnessed by Jewry. Among these were the aged David Abi Zimra (Sect. 69), the famous Joseph Karo, author of the *Shulhan Aruk,* Solomon Alkabetz, the author of the Sabbath Hymn *Lekah Dodi,* (Come My Beloved), Moses Cordevero and many others. All these scholars were devoted Kabbalists. Karo even published a book by the name of *Magid Mesharim* (The Preacher of Righteousness), supposed to contain revelations made to him by a special agent whom he called the *Magid* (Preacher). During this time, Safed was also visited by the famous mystic and enthusiast said to have proclaimed himself as the forerunner of the Messiah, Solomon Molcho, who died as a martyr in 1532. All this made the air of Safed replete with Kabbalistic teachings and many were the mystic works produced during the time.

117. MOSES CORDEVERO

Of the numerous Kabbalists who made Safed their center of activity, Moses Cordevero (1522-1570) was the most erudite and prolific author. He was born in Cordova, Spain, and later settled in Safed where he became a disciple of Rabbi Joseph Karo. There he became interested in the study of the Kabbala and devoted himslf to it with all the fervor of his great soul. After acquiring exhaustive knowledge of all the devious ways of the mystic teachings and mastering the entire literature of the Kabbala, he began to write his own works, and although he was a very young man at the time, his books were accorded recognition by the older Kabbalists and spread to all parts of the world.

Cordevero was a productive writer, and the number of his works is considerable. Besides six or seven volumes containing his own views on the Kabbala, he wrote a long commentary on the entire group of works of the *Zohar* under the name of *Or Yakar* (A Precious Light). His great contribution to the study of the Kabbala, however, consists primarily in his systematization of its teachings in an orderly and masterly way. He was well acquainted with Mediaeval Jewish philosophy and having acquired its methods and its logical way in the presentation of a subject applied them to his own works. He thus became the expositor of the Kabbala. The crown of his works is the *Pardes Rimmonim* (The Garden of Pomegranates). It contains his complete Kabbalistic teachings and deals practically with every phase of the Kabbala. It consists of thirty-two portals (Shaarim) which are subdivided into two hundred and seventy chapters. As Cordevero's views are based on the doctrines contained in the *Zohar* and other Kabbalistic works, we have in the *Pardes* a complete system of the Kabbala, and this work has served all students as a trusty guide in its complicated mazes. We must, of course, discount a personal bias of interpretation, but on the whole, he aimed correctly.

The value of the book is greatly enhanced by its clear style and logical presentation of the subject matter. The style of Cordevero has in it nothing of the abstruseness of the other Kabbalistic works. On the contrary, it is easy to understand and special pains are taken by the author to popularize every difficult subject. He uses profuse illustrations which elucidate the most difficult points. Cordevero does not attack philosophy, but on the other hand, endeavors to bring some of the teachings of the Kabbala in harmony with those of philosophy.

His other works, such as the *Elima Rabbata* (The Large Elim)[44] and the *Shiur Komah* are practically digests of the *Pardes* with some additions. He also wrote a book by the name of *Or Nearab* (The Mixed Light) where he vindicates the importance and the great value of the study of the Kabbala. Cordevero had a large number of disciples in Safed, and many followers in all parts of the world who continued to expound his views after him.

118. ISAAC LURIA ASHKENAZI

Cordevero left many disciples after him, but there was one among them whose name and fame far outshone that of his master, and whose teaching not only superseded those of his instructor but left a lasting mark upon the further development of the Kabbala. That disciple was Isaac Luria Ashkenazi (1534-1572) or as he is known,

[44] It is called so after the place Elim mentioned in Ex. XV, 64, where the Jews rested on their march in the desert. That place had twelve wells and seventy date trees. Cordevero's book adopted a division of sections which are represented by wells of water and seventy chapters symbolized by date trees. (See sect. 101.)

the *Ari* (abbreviation for Ashkenazi Rabbi Yitzhaki).[45] Luria was born in Jerusalem, but due to stressed family conditions caused by the early death of his father, he was taken by his mother to Cairo, Egypt, to be brought up in the house of his uncle Mordecai Francis. There he studied under the famous Talmudic scholar David Abi Zimra (Sect. 69). At the age of fifteen, he married the daughter of his uncle and immediately afterward began to devote himself to the study of mysticism. His zeal for that study was so great that it affected his whole conduct. He began to lead an extreme ascetic life and became a visionary, saying often that he had been visited frequently by Elijah who revealed to him the secrets of mysticism. Finally, he decided to settle at Safed in the year 1570. At first, he became a disciple of Cordevero and led a quiet life, but soon one of the Kabbalists of the city, Hayyim Vital Calabrese found out his great knowledge of the Kabbala, and he immediately became his disciple and set out to reveal the *Ari* to the world. It did not take long and the name of Luria became famous throughout Jewry, for Vital was a very skillful manipulator and used all means to herald the name of his master and his own along with it. The *Ari*, however, did not enjoy his newly found fame for long, for he died in 1572 during the pestilence which raged in Safed that year, only a short time after settling there. His real fame and influence though began to grow after his death.

Of the authentic teachings of Luria we know very little, for he left no books written in his own handwriting. We have only one short statement in his own name quoted in the *Etz Hayyim* of Vital, where he refers to Cordevero as our master and teacher. All that we know of the system of Luria is derived from the numerous writings of Vital.

Hayyim Vital Calabrese (1543-1620) was a man of heterogenous character and possessed many contradictory qualities. He was a visionary and a dreamer but also seemed to have had a practical sense and a passion for honor and fame. He tried many things in his life, among them also the study of alchemy, but on the whole, he was not successful in his attempts except in the revealing of the *Ari* to the world. Immediately after the death of the latter, Vital together with a few of the other disciples set out to tell the world of the greatness

[45] This particular abbreviation was chosen for the reason that it also means lion, a title which signifies greatness and also because it may be read Adonenu Rabbi Yitzhak, i. e., our master Rabbi Isaac.

of their master. They told such wonderful tales about him that many became anxious to obtain his works . Vital then announced that he is the sole possessor of the teachings of the *Ari* and that he has many manuscripts which contain notes of these teachings. He received large offers of money for permission to copy the manuscripts, but apparently refused them. However, his brother Moses copied six hundred folios and sold them to a rich Kabbalist. These were later published with Hayyim's consent under the title *Etz Hayyim*. After Vital's death, more of his works were published, among them the *Otzroth Hayyim* (The Treasures of Hayyim), the *Sepher ha-Gilgulim* (The Book of Wanderings) ascribed to the *Ari* himself and also the *Sepher ha-Hesyonoth* (The Book of Visions), a kind of autobiography where Vital magnifies the greatness of his master but still more his own (Sect. 141).

It is from these books as well as from a few others that were edited and published by the son and friends of Vital that we have to derive the teachings of the *Ari*. And though Vital is not above suspicion of having mixed up some of his own confused ideas with those of his master, yet on the whole, they must be authentic. These teachings in contradistinction to those of Cordevero are given in a most unsystematic way and in a confused manner and are made still more complicated by an abstruse style.

It will be out of place to enter here into a more detailed analysis of the views of the *Ari* and we will give only a few of the general features. We have already pointed out above (p. 368) the *Ari's* view concerning the Primordial Man, that he considers it a separate emanation prior to the Sephiroth, and we may add that he identifies it with the *Kether*. According to him, though, *Kether* is not among the ten Sephiroth. In place of it, he counts *Daat* (Knowledge) as a Sephirah. Another important doctrine of his speculative view is the theory of the "Breaking of the Vessels" (Shebirath ha-Kelim). By this is meant that the Sephiroth which are called *Kelim,* vessels or instruments, because of the influence of God streaming through them, were once broken. But not all the Sephiroth, only the last seven which received their influence from the first three were broken on account of the excessive light which rushed through them. The light then returned to the first three Sephiroth, but sparks (Nitzotzoth) were scattered through the universe and mixed with things of evil. Hence it is the duty of the righteous man to redeem these sparks and to return them to their sources, or as he calls it to afford them a

Tikkun (Redemption or Correction). The third doctrine is the development of a new theory concerning the canals of influence or *Tzinoroth* by means of which the Sephiroth act. He introduced a complicated and abstruse system of phases of the activity of the Sephiroth which he calls *faces* (Partzufim). These *Partzufim* assume a number of coverings (Malbushim), and thus the symbolism of the Kabbala is greatly increased and ramified. He also laid excessive stress on the other phases of symbolism, especially on the erotic aspect. In the Kabbala of the *Ari,* the erotic element plays an exceptionally undue role.

Turning to the practical aspect of his teachings, we note therein several elements, the principal of which is his inclination to asceticism. Luria resuscitated some of the principles of the German Kabbala which insisted on the practice of asceticism as a means of purification of the soul. Accordingly, he taught that man is to enjoy life as little as possible and is to devote himself to the study of the Torah and its secrets. He was himself a master of such practice. This, however, was subservient to his great desire for the redemption of the world which to him centered around the redemption of Israel and the coming of the Messiah. In fact, he believed himself, according to his followers, to be the Messiah ben Joseph who is supposed to precede the real Messiah. All this was derived from a theory which is only referred to occasionally in the Kabbala, but which the *Ari* developed extensively. According to it, the soul of Adam contained the souls of all future generations. They were originally all good, but after the fall, good and bad elements were mixed in them, hence the good souls contain sparks of evil, and on the other hand, wicked souls contain sparks of good. When the separation will be completed, then the world will be redeemed and the Messiah will come.

To this purpose, Luria expanded the Metempsychosis view (Gilgul) of the Kabbala, as well as its theory of impregnation of souls. ('Ibbur.) As stated above (Sect. 110), according to the Ari, almost every soul must migrate through other bodies in order to get rid of the particles of evil. If it is an exceptionally good soul, it enters the body of another man and impregnates the other soul in order to help it along in the struggle for the good.

Applying his theories to life, the *Ari* taught the necessity of fasting, praying, and the purifying of the body by ablutions. He is said to have performed many wonderful things, among them driving out evil souls from the bodies of men or women, affording them other means of correction (Tikkun), and divining at a glance the identity of the secondary souls of men which came to their help. His disciples claimed that they had acquired the secrets from him and were able to perform similar things and even promised to endow others with the same ability if they would follow their teachings.

Thus the Kabbala of the *Ari,* consisting of the grafting of certain peculiar elements upon the old teachings and joining both with a distinct outline of a way of life, was launched by Vital and his associates upon a mystically inclined Jewish world, and it spread rapidly. Its great success may possibly be attributed to the above stated fact that it combined imagination and enthusiasm with a distinct practicality of conduct. To this, we may also add as a factor in its success the hope of redemption which the Kabbala held out before its adherents as the ultimate aim of all efforts.

119. THE POST-LURIANIC LITERATURE

The *Ari* type of the Kabbala, on account of its complicated and abstruse form of construction, was amenable to many interpretations and elucidations. And since it put its mark on the entire mystic literature of two centuries, it follows that the literary productivity of mysticism was very great during the period. In fact, Kabbalistic books run into the thousands. The countries which produced most of this literature were Italy and Poland.

Of the numerous Kabbalist writers in Italy who were active during the second half of the sixteenth century and the first half of the seventeenth, we will mention the Talmudic scholars Azaria de Fano (d. 1620), Joseph Solomon del-Medigo, Abraham Herrera (d. 1639) and Moses Zacuto (Sect. 36). De Fano was first a follower of Cordevero, and his earlier work *Pelah ha-Rimmon* (Half a Pomegranate) is practically a digest of the *Pardes Rimmonim,* but later he became a follower of Luria and his *Asarah Mamoroth* (Ten Statements) bears imprints of Luria's influence. Herrara's *Shaar ha-Shomayyim* (The Portal of Heaven) is written in the spirit of rationalism and is close to the teachings of Cordevero.

Del Medigo, on the other hand, scientist and skeptic though he was, was attracted by the teachings of Luria. His Kabbalistic works comprise the *Sheber Yoseph* (The Supply of Joseph), the *Metzoref Le-Hokmah* (The Purification of Wisdom), and the *Nobloth Hokmah* (Unripe Fruit of Wisdom). In these, he defends the Kabbala against the attacks of Elijah del-Medigo and others and teaches its various phases in the manner of Luria.

Of the works of the Polish Kabbalists during the period, the most outstanding are the *Megale Amukoth* (Revealer of Secrets) by Rabbi Nathan ben Solomon Shapiro (d. 1633) rabbi at Krakow, the *Shenē Luhoth ha-Berith* (The Two Tablets of the Covenant) by the famous Talmudic scholar and ethical teacher Isaiah Hurwitz (1570-1630), rabbi of the communities of Frankfurt, Posen, Prague and Krakow and the *Shefa Tal* by his son Sheftal Hurwitz (1650). Shapiro and Sheftal Hurwitz follow the teachings of Cordevero, but Isaiah Hurwitz who completed his work in Palestine fell under the influence of the Kabbala of the *Ari* which is evident in his work.

Of the three works mentioned, the most important is the *Shenē Luhoth ha-Berith* usually called in abbreviated form *Shaloh* (initials of the words). It exerted great influence upon the life of the Jews of Eastern Europe and helped more than any book to introduce the Kabbala in daily religious life. It is really not a mere book on the Kabbala but a kind of encyclopaedia of the teachings of Judaism. It was written by Isaiah as a manual for his children before he left for Palestine but as said, it was not finished until after his arrival there. The work consists of two parts, the first one dealing with the teachings of Judaism and the second, a Kabbalistic commentary on the Pentateuch. The first part has a very complicated arrangement. It is generally divided into three divisions, the first called *Asarah Mamoroth* (Ten Discourses), the second *Asarah Dibrayah* (Ten Commandments), and the third *Asarah Hilulim* (Ten Praises).

The first division takes up in ten long chapters the theoretical principles of Judaism, the unity of God, His Providence, worship of God, purity of heart and holiness, and the destiny, election and duties of Israel. These are the general outlines, but in reality, there are a variety of subjects discussed, and even some decisions on important parts of the law are given when such affect the conduct of man and are conducive to the attainment of holiness.

The second which is the body of the book deals with the performance of the precepts under three aspects, the legal, mystical and ethical. The author divides the precepts into classes which he prefers to name after the tractates of the Talmud, such as *Hulin, Sabbath, Pesahim* and others. In each tractate, he groups certain laws which resemble that name, while each section contains three parts in accordance with the aspects treated. The legal aspect or the code proper is called *Ner Mitzvah* (The Precept Is a Light), the mystical, where the precepts are explained according to the Kabbala, is called *Torah Or* (The Light of the Torah), and the ethical where he deals with the ethical import of every precept and its observance, *Tokhahat Musar* (Chastisement of Instruction). The third division is a short digest of the *Hoboth ha-Leboboth* of Bahya with some modifications. The second part of the book also contains the two aspects *Ner Mitzvah* and *Torah Or*. In the first, the author states briefly the number of precepts found in each section of the Pentateuch, and in the second, he comments on the section in Kabbalistic manner.

Hurwitz through his work, which is a combination of a code and Kabbalistic treatise influenced religious life, for he introduced many customs in the ritual and in the observance of other laws which have no basis otherwise except in the Kabbala, and because of his authority they were accepted by a great part of Jewry. Due also to his influence, some Kabbalistic prayers were incorporated in the prayer book.

Of the later Kabbalistic literature, we will only mention two introductions to the teachings of the Kabbala. The first is the *Shomer Emunim* (The Guardian of the Truth) by Joseph Irgas (1685-1730) of Italy, and the second is the *Pithē Hokmah* (The Doors of Wisdom) by Moses Hayyim Luzzato. The first is written in the form of two dialogues between an opponent of the Kabbala and a Kabbalist. The second consists of one hundred and thirty-eight short sections, in each of which a certain point is briefly stated and then explained by a larger commentary.

The greatest expression of the influence of the Luria type of Kabbala upon life is, of course, embodied in the movement of Hassidism, but of this later.

Chapter VIII

KARAITE LITERATURE

120. *GENERAL CHARACTERISTICS*

The Karaite literature of the post-Classical period shows on the whole, like that of the Rabbanite, a decline in the character of the quality, but unlike the latter, also a decrease in the quantity. This phenomenon is undoubtedly inherently connected with the general decline of the Karaite movement. From the twelfth century on, we note a constant ebbing in the life of this sect, the number of Karaite communities keep on decreasing and the zeal for propaganda slowly dying out, though here and there, it spurts forth in the form of a literary attack against some Rabbinic doctrines but with a much weaker force than hitherto displayed.

The causes for such decline in Karaism seem to have been the remarkable strength of the Rabbanites expressed in the vigorous literary productivity during the three centuries (9th-12th) on the one hand, and the secular influence of the environment which resulted from the geographic distribution of Karaite settlements, on the other hand. Against the illuminating display of intellectual activity in all fields of literature on the part of the Rabbanite scholars, poets and philosophers, the feeble efforts made by the Karaites, even during the Classical period, were put into the shade and made any further continuance of literary activity by them dependent on the productions of the former. Again, the fact that most of the Karaite settlements were situated in Mohammedan countries, where persecutions were not frequent and where they shared a language and a mode of life in common with the general population, weakened their resistance to the influence of the external environment. The Karaites having separated from their brethren the Rabbanites, and having been deprived of the advantages of an age-long tradition, formed a small and weak minority in a large Mohammedan world, and could not, therefore, withstand the attraction exerted by the Mohammedan religion and culture as well as that of the larger Jewish group, the Rabbanites. As a result, many Karaites became converts to Islam, while many others returned to the fold of Rabbanism. For the first fact, we have the testimony of a Karaite scholar, himself a convert, Abu Nasr Samuel ben Abbas, and for the second, the report of *Estori ha-Parkhi* (Sect. 137) in his work *Kaftor we-Ferah,* that an entire Karaite community in Egypt joined the Rabbanites in the year 1313. Conversions of small groups and individuals were undoubtedly more numerous. As a consequence of these continuous deflections, Karaism weakened and deteriorated.

We must note though that from the twelfth century on, new Karaite centers not situated in the East rose into prominence. These were the Byzantine, the Crimean, and later from the sixteenth century on, the Lithuanian. Yet this fact by no means signifies any contradiction to what was said above. Of these three new settlements, the Crimean was situated in a Mohammedan country; the Byzantine, though ruled up to 1453 by a Christian power, was yet too near the East not to be influenced to a great extent by Arabic traditions; and the Lithuanian was only a small offshoot of the Crimean. Second, it is really the activity of these settlements, especially those of the Byzantine and Lithuanian which lay to a certain degree outside of the influence of the East which saved Karaism from extinction. As we will see, it is these very countries that formed the literary centers during the entire post-Classical period, and only a small portion of Karaite literature was produced in the other lands where Karaism had formerly grown and blossomed.

The general traits of the Karaite literature during the post-Classical period are first, the extensive use of Hebrew as a medium of expression; second, the conciliatory tone towards the Rabbanites; third, its dependence upon the literary productions of the latter; and finally, the lack of originality and the display of a tendency to eclecticism. The fact that the main centers of intellectual activity during the period were situated in countries where Arabic was no longer a spoken language forced the Karaite writers to adopt Hebrew as their literary tongue. In fact, the change began in the twelfth century when Byzantium became a seat of Karaite learning. As a result, a large number of works were written in Hebrew. Only during the thirteenth and fourteenth centuries, do we still meet with a number of works written by Eastern authors in the once favored Arabic tongue. As the centuries progress, literary productivity in Arabic dwindles down to an insignificant quantity.

The overwhelming intellectual achievements of the Rabbanites during the Classical period compelled the Karaites to pay, though involuntarily, respect and homage to their opponents. We do not meet, therefore, any more in the writings of the Karaite scholars of the post-Classical period the rabid and aggressive tone of strife manifested in the earlier works. The Rabbanite sages are referred to with dignity and when their ideas are refuted, it is done on scientific grounds and not as a polemic duty. But moreover, the Karaites were really attracted by the literature of their opponents and impressed by their scholarship. The Rabbanites, on their part, feeling secure in their strength, feared no more the weak enemy and displayed a friendlier feeling towards the Karaites and even instructed them in Talmud, codes, Bible, exegesis, and other subjects. The closer intercourse between the two factions necessarily brought the weaker under the influence of the stronger. It thus happened that the Rabbanite philosophers and poets became the masters and authorities to the Karaites, and their works models of imitation. It is in this way that the Karaite literature practically became a dependency of that of their opponents.

However, with the best efforts made by the savants of the sect, their literature did not rise to a high level of original productivity. With the exception of two writers, the two Aarons, the works of the others are primarily of an eclectic nature. They consist principally of imitations of older works or of a jumble of excerpts of such writings with some additional material, or at the best, of interpretations and comments of their teachings. Still, we do find at times a book that strikes a new note unheard before in the rather monotonous literature of Karaism.

The scope of the Karaite literature during the period had, on the whole, remained in the same bounds determined by the writers of the former generations. It had been only slightly widened to include other subjects which were not dealt with before. As was pointed out in our survey of the Classical period (Vol .I, Ch. XIII), the Karaite literary productivity expressed itself primarily along three lines, namely, in works on Bible exegesis and the science of the Hebrew language, compilation of legal manuals or Books of Precepts (Sepher Mitzvoth) and treatises on philosophy, and added to this also some compositions of liturgical poetry.

The same favored subjects were cultivated by the writers and scholars of the period under discussion with the exception that from the sixteenth century on, we note on the part of the Lithuanian savants, an interest in history and in polemics, not against their brethren the Rabbanites but against other religions. This new trend was brought about by external pressure. Christian scholars became interested in the history of the sect and turned to its leading scholars for information. They then found it necessary to present to the world a connected story of the origin and teachings of the religion they confessed together with some defense of their tenets, and hence the historical and polemic activity.

A. The Eastern and Byzantine Centers

121. MINOR WORKS

There was considerable literary activity going on in both the Eastern and Byzantine centers of Karaism during the thirteenth century, and we have a number of works hailing from that time, written in both Hebrew and Arabic with the former predominating. Many of them are, however, anonymous. To these belong two Books of Precepts, four philosophical treatises, a book on the calendar and several small dictionaries and compendia of grammar for school use. All of these works, with the exception of the lexicographical and grammatical, were written in Hebrew.

Of the Books of Precepts, one is a work of importance, for its author shows a wide acquaintance not only with the laws of his sect but also with philosophy and science. He endeavors to explain the precepts in a rational way and uses philosophical terms. He hailed from Byzantium as is evident by his use of Greek words in a considerable number.

The first of the four philosophical works entitled *'Iḳrē ha-Emunah* (The Dogmas of Faith) enunciates the ten Karaite dogmas in a brief manner, an attempt which was undoubtedly inspired by Maimonides' fixation of dogmas. The second entitled *Sepher ha-Mor* (The Book of Myrrh) is a more elaborate affair dealing with God and His attributes, creation, prophecy and kindred subjects. The author follows the philosophy of the Karaite savants but knows also Maimonides and speaks of him with great respect and love. The other two are *Shealoth U-Teshuboth* (Inquiries and Responsa) containing discussions on the unity of God and creation in dialogue form and the *Mofeth ha-Ahduth* (The Proof for Unity), an essay on the proofs for Divine unity.

Among the writers whose works are left to us, the following deserve to be noted:

i. Jephet the physician, named Abu'l-Hassan Al-Barquomani, who lived in Alexandria about the middle of the thirteenth century, wrote, besides a medical treatise, also a polemic work in Arabic entitled *Sepher Teshubah* (The Book of Refutation). In this work, he reproduces all the arguments against the Rabbanites made by the earlier scholars and attacks especially the anthropomorphic Agadic passages in the Talmud. He does, however, speak favorably of Maimonides, and in general, speaks of the Talmud and Talmudists without acrimony.

ii. Al-Fadhl, who is usually quoted by his successors as *Mu-Allimun Al-Fadhl,* i. e. the teacher Al-Fadhl, and who lived in Cairo about the end of the thirteenth century is known primarily for his compilation of the prayer book (Siddur) which became the standard one among the Karaites. It is really an important work, for it contains not only a collection of prayers and liturgical poems, but also decisions regarding all matters of liturgy and the conduct of public worship besides formulas of texts of marriage and divorce documents. The *Siddur* can thus be called a code of the ritual laws and customs. There is also appended to it a number of discourses on the dogmas, on the unity of God, on the sciences and other subjects. The decisions of the laws of the ritual, as well as the discourses are written in Arabic. There is also extant an Arabic commentary by Fadhl on the Song of Moses (Deut. Chs. XXXII, XXXIII).

iii. A contemporary of Al-Fadhl, Israel ben Samuel Al-Moghrebi who also lived in Cairo was a judge of the Karaites there, and is, therefore, called ha-Dayan. The name Al-Moghrebi (The Westerner) indicates that he was born in North Africa, but must have migrated to Egypt in his youth, for nothing is mentioned of his activity in his native land. Israel was a prolific writer and wrote most of his books in Arabic. The most important of his writings are (1) a book on the calendar entitled *Seder Inyan ha-Ibbur* (The Order of Intercalation) in Hebrew; (2) The Book of Doctrines in Arabic (Kitab Al-Amanat) where he discusses the articles of faith in connection with his commentary on the Decalogue; (3) a treatise on the laws of slaughtering of animals also in Arabic but of which Israel himself made, in the year 1306, an abstract in Hebrew under the title *Hilkoth Shehitah;* and (4) his great work, the *Kitab Al-Murshid* (The Book of Guidance), a Book of Precepts.

Al-Moghrebi was considered by his successors an authority on law and his books are frequently referred to, especially the *Book of Precepts.* Israel in his last named book, when dealing with the question of prohibited marriage ('Arayoth), joins with the two earlier savants, Joseph Al Basir and Yeshuah ben Yehudah in reforming the complicated marriage system known as *Rikkub* (Vol. I, p. 404). He carried his reforms further than they did and abrogated some prohibitions on marriages between people of distant relationship. The legal authorities of later generations relied on his decisions against the earlier authorities.

iv. To the thirteenth century, belongs also the greatest Karaite poet Moses Darai, the physician. His residence was Cairo, but he must have wandered around for some time, for he visited Jerusalem, Damascus and other cities. A great controversy arose in the last generation among Jewish scholars about the period of this poet. Simha Pinsker, the pioneer writer on the history of the Karaites who first introduced Darai's Diwan in Jewish literature, placed him in the ninth century, and because of the similarity between some of Darai's poems and those of Gabirol, Halevi and Moses Ibn Ezra's, he made them imitators of the former. His theory was proved altogether untenable on many grounds, and it was definitely established that Darai lived in the middle of the thirteenth century. The reference in his poem to Jerusalem held successively by the Mohammedans and the Christians points undoubtedly to this time, besides many other proofs.

The imitator then was Darai and not the great Rabbanite poets. He borrowed extensively from them not only single expressions but whole lines and even complete stanzas which he modified to a certain extent. Yet he was not without talent, for he was a prolific poet and his Diwan contains hundreds of poems, many of which possess great merit. Darai was one of the few Karaite poets who wrote, besides sacred poetry, also on secular subjects. Like his models, the Rabbanite poets of the Classical period, he composed poems on love, wine and friendship and wrote epigrams, many of which are pointed and witty. In this last endeavor, he seemed to have been greatly influenced by Ibn Ezra.

122. *AARON BEN JOSEPH*

The greatest Karaite scholar and writer of the thirteenth century was undoubtedly Aaron ben Joseph (1250-1320), usually called Aaron, the first, to distinguish him from his namesake Aaron ben Elijah (Sect. 123). He made a name for himself in all the fields of Karaite literary productivity, namely exegesis, philosophy and legal interpretation, and also tried his hand at composing sacred poetry. He was born in the Crimea but left it at an early age and wandered about in search of learning, which he undoubtedly obtained in a great measure. He was well versed in the Mishnah and Talmud and studied with great avidity the works of Ibn Ezra, Maimonides and Nahmanides, and is even said by a later Karaite historian, to have delved in the mysteries of the Kabbala. He ultimately settled in Constantinople where he practiced medicine, for his surname is ha-Rofē, the physician.

Aaron wrote commentaries on the Pentateuch, on the Prophetical Books and on the Hagiographa, a short Hebrew grammar entitled *Klil Yofi* (Perfect Beauty) and compiled a prayer book in which he incorporated many of his poems. But it is primarily on his extensive commentary on the Pentateuch named *ha-Mibhar* (The Selected Commentary) that his fame rests. It is this work which contains not only Aaron's exegesis but also his religious philosophy and legal interpretation. He seemed to have taken Ibn Ezra and Nahmanides as his models, especially the former. There is an evident effort on his part to imitate Ibn Ezra both in his style which is cryptic and terse and partly in content. But on the other hand, he also opposes his views.

Aaron's method in exegesis is a rationalistic one. He says in the introduction to the *Mibhar* that truth and falsehood do not become as such by the authority or lack of authority of the person who utters them but are to be determined by their intrinsic quality. He, therefore, does not hesitate to depart from the views of his predecessors and adopt at times the inerpretations of the Rabbanites if they contain the truth. The philosophic views contained in the *Mibhar* are briefly as follows:

Like all Jewish philosophers, Aaron teaches the creation of the world by the will of God, though he seems to be inclined to assume the Platonic view of the pre-existence of formless matter or *hylē*. This will, however, is not a separate quality of God, but identical with His essence. Likewise, we are to understand all attributes not as separate qualities but as expressions of the essence of God. Regarding angels, he rejects the Rabbanite view as well as the Karaite that they exist in a certain form or that they were created before the world, and that God took counsel with them at the creation of man. The words in Genesis I, 26, "Let us make a man," he explains not as Rashi, Ibn Ezra and other commentators as referring to the consultation with the angels, but as a metaphorical address by God to nature, which laws operate in the life of man as in all other things. Angels then are separate intelligences which emanated from God.

Concerning prophecy and prophets, he says that with the exception of the visions of Moses those of the other prophets were mental representations of the imagination or dreams. He, therefore, explains the visit of the angels to Abraham (Gen. Ch. XVIII), the wrestling of the angel with Jacob (Ib. XXXII) and the speech of Balaam's ass (Numeri XXII) as having occurred in dreams. Moses alone saw a revelation of a vision and heard a voice, both of which were, of course, especially created for that purpose.

Aaron enunciates clearly the doctrines of the freedom of the will and explains the words of the Bible that God hardened Pharaoh's heart (Exodus X, 1) not to yield to the request of Moses to free the children of Israel, to mean merely that Pharaoh remained obstinate, but not that God actually interfered in the freedom of his action in order to mete out greater punishment upon him. Several Jewish philosophers, among them Maimonides, have explained it in the last named manner, but Aaron would not have God deprive man of freedom in any way.

Very peculiar is his conception of the soul. According to him, it is dependent upon the body, and he localizes the faculties of the soul in certain parts of the brain the functioning of which is stimulated by the passing of the blood through these parts. On the whole, he presents rather a material view of the nature of the soul, though at the same time he speaks often of its immortality.

His exegesis proper is distinguished by a freedom of interpretation. He clings, on the whole, to the Karaite mode of explanation of the legal part of the Bible and endeavors to refute the opinions of the Rabbanites. But whenever necessary, for one reason or another, he deviates from the views of his predecessors, and at times even adopts a Rabbanite opinion. His decisions on legal matters, as said, vary often from those of the earlier Karaite scholars. Aaron also shows great skill in pure exegesis of the verses of the Bible by displaying a keen linguistic sense which penetrates into the meaning of the text. The commentaries on the other books of the Bible are not as elaborate as the *Mibhar* but are likewise distinguished by attention to *Peshat,* as well as by the rational spirit pervading them.

Aaron, as stated above, tried his hand at poetry, but in the many poems which he composed, we can see a mastery of the language but not real poetic spirit. Most of these are of a didactic nature, and the noted among them are those which deal with the contents of the weekly portions of the Pentateuch. In these poems, he gives a rhymed summary of the story and the legal ethical teachings of each portion. They served as models of imitation for both Karaite and Rabbanite poets. The style of Aaron, while rich and varied, is rather hard and difficult and on account of this, his poems were provided with commentaries by later writers.

123. AARON BEN ELIJAH

The fourteenth century contributed its share to the literary productivity of the Karaites. Both centers, the Eastern and the Byzantine, brought forth a number of scholars who left their mark on the intellectual development of Karaism. The most important of those whose sphere of activity belongs to the East was Jephet ben David Ibn Zag'hir ha-Rofē (d. 1345) of Cairo. He was a disciple of Israel ha-Dayan, and like his teacher wrote a Book of Precepts in Arabic. It is a detailed work, divided into ten large sections which are subdivided into numerous chapters. It covers the entire field of Karaite Halakah and deals in an especially elaborate manner with the question of prohibited marriages ('Arayoth). Like his teacher, Jephet was inclined to leniency on this question and is quoted together with him by later scholars as an authority whose decisions are to be relied upon against the views of the older savants. The work was later translated into Hebrew.

To Jephet belongs also the honor of writing the only book of Responsa extant in Karaite literature. Unfortunately, only a fragment of the work is preserved and from this we have to infer the nature of the entire book. It seems that it was intended to be a commentary on the Pentateuch in the form of lengthy Responsa to certain inquiries. Jephet displays in his discussion a keen analytic mind and an acquaintance with the casuistic method of the Rabbinic scholars.

However, Jephet, and the other writers of the generation were overshadowed by the intellectual activity of one of their contemporaries, Aaron ben Elijah (1300-1369), called Aaron the Latter (ha-Ahron) to distinguish him from his predecessor, Aaron ben Joseph. Aaron was born in Nicomedia, a city in Asia Minor, which was at the time under Byzantine rule, and where there was an important Karaite community. It is not definitely known where he received his education. He mentions in his work the names of three of his teachers, Judah, his uncle on his mother's side, Moses, later his father-in-law, and one by the name of Joseph of whose literary attainment little is known. His education, however, was a thorough one. He mastered the entire Karaite literature, was well acquainted with the works of the Rabbanites and must have been versed in the Arabic language and knew some Greek.

Like his namesake Aaron ben Joseph, Aaron ben Elijah distinguished himself in the three great branches of intellectual productivity, philosophy, exegesis and legal discussion; but unlike him, he did not concentrate his contribution in a single work but wrote three separate treatises in each of these fields. These are the *Etz Hayyim* (The Tree of Life) in philosophy, the *Gan-Eden* (The Garden of Eden) in Halakah and the *Kether Torah* (Crown of the Torah) a commentary on the Pentateuch, in exegesis. Of the three works, the *Etz-Hayyim* is the most important, and we will turn our attention to it first.

The first Aaron strove to be the Karaite Ibn Ezra, and the second Aaron aimed at becoming the Karaite Maimonides. We, therefore, notice in his Magnum Opus, the *Etz,Hayyim,* both a conscious and an unconscious imitation of the *More Nebuḳim*. He not only quotes the Rabbanite philosopher numerous times by name, and refers to him many times anonymously, but the entire book is dependent on the *Guide* both in the scope of the subjects it embraces and in its contents. Rabbi Moses ben Maimon is the central figure of the work, for Aaron quotes his opinions either for the pupose of adopting them as the right view or for the purpose of refuting them. Yet, it would be wrong to assume that the *Etz-Hayyim* is a mere abridgement of the *Guide* with some additional notes. On the other hand, it possesses some features which make it a real contribution to Jewish philosophy and of great interest to the student of that science even today. First is its completeness, for like Maimonides, Aaron strove to give a complete system of religious thought, of course, from the Karaite point of view, and the effort is well carried out, though not in the masterly manner of the former. Second, the great amount of informaion the work contains concerning the views of the philosophers of the *Kalam* (Vol. I, Sect. 161), as well as of those of other Eastern sects make it valuable for the student of human intellectual development. Third, Aaron's own philosophical position as that of a mediator between the theories of the Kalamitic philosophy followed by the early Karaite and Rabbanite thinkers and the Aristotelianism of the later Jewish philosophers is not without interest.

The *Etz-Hayyim* differs in arrangement from the *Guide,* for while Maimonides begins with interpretations of the anthropomorphic expressions of the Bible followed by the theory of the attributes and the criticism of the *Kalam,* and then takes up the proofs for the existence of God, Aaron reverses the order. He begins with the proofs for the existence of God, follows it up with interpretations of the anthropomorphic expressions and then takes up the question of the attributes. This order undoubtedly seems more logical but as was explained (Vol. I, Sect. 173) Maimonides had his reasons for following the seemingly illogical order.

In the exposition of his proofs for the existence of God which occupies the first fourteen chapters of the book, Aaron reverts to the earlier method introduced by Kalamitic philosophers and followed also by Jewish thinkers both Karaite and Rabbanite such as Saadia and others. This method is an indirect one and consists first in proving that the world was created and then drawing the necessary conclusion that consequently, there is a creator. But before really producing his proofs, he draws a sketch of the views of both the Aristotelians who believe in the eternity of the world and of the Mutakallimin who advocate creation. He also cites their proofs for the existence of God, namely the direct proof from motion and the indirect from creation. As these depend upon the various conceptions of the nature of bodies, he also gives a short account of the physics of the two systems. The Aristotelian view that all bodies consist of matter and form is too well known and needs no exposition, but the Kalamitic theory of bodies is rather a peculiar one and needs a short explanation. The Kalamites believed that the basis or the substance of bodies consists of atoms floating in the void which in their single state have no magnitude. These atoms when they unite assume magnitude and are the bearers of numerous other accidents or qualities. The accidents are constantly changing and according to the view of the more orthodox of the Mutakallimin both they and the atoms are constantly created by God. Their view is then that bodies consist of atoms and accidents or qualities which are constantly changing.

Maimonides devoted much space to the exposition of the theory of the Kalamites and to its refutation. Aaron attempts to defend the Kalamitic theory from the attack of Maimonides, and though he does not accept it, yet claims some scientific motive for its formation. He then advances some criticism against the opinion which maintains the eternity of the world and also against Maimonides, who though he did not accept this view, yet formulated his proof for the existence of God in accordance with it. Finally, Aaron produces his own proof, which he says, is valid according to both views of the nature of bodies. He says, whether all bodies are composed of matter and form or of atoms and accidents, as long as one of these constituents, namely, either form or accident is constantly changing, we are forced to assume that it originated in time, for change or dissolution in time means also origin in time. And since bodies can not exist without that particular constituent, they also had their origin in time or in other words, the world was created. There is, of course, one other alternative possible, namely that things had created themselves but this is disproved by a series of arguments. There remains, therefore, one conclusion that the world was created by a creator. God's incorporeality follows from the nature of the proofs, for were He corporeal, He would be composite like all bodies and would need a creator. This proof is really not new, for we find it in Saadia and in all early Jewish and Arabic philosophers, but there are some new angles in the detailed exposition given to the deduction, as well as in the critical remarks directed against the method of Maimonides.

After establishing the existence of God, His incorporeality and creation, Aaron devotes forty-six chapters to the explanation of the anthropomorphic terms found in the Bible. The material is largely borrowed from Maimonides. He is, however, careful to inform us that Karaite scholars had preceded Maimonides in this matter, and that he follows mainly their views, adding some of his own, so that we should not consider him a mere copyist. Yet, notwithstanding this apology, the close resemblance between the explanations given in the *Guide* and those in the *Etz-Hayyim* afford us sufficient grounds to assume that the latter are imitations of the former.

Having proved to his satisfaction that the Bible like philosophy teaches the incorporeality of God and that the anthropomorphic expressions are only methaphors, he takes up the question of the unity of God which must be elucidated before discussing the theory of attributes. He analyzes the concept of unity and finds that it contains three distinct meanings, namely (1) simplicity as opposed to compositeness, (2) the unity of His essence and (3) His uniqueness, namely that He is the only being necessary of existence and that there is no other. The first phase of unity is in reality derived both from the concept of incorporeality and from the definition "necessary of existence," for otherwise His existence would depend upon the composition of His substance as a cause. The second phase is inherently connected with the theory of attributes and is deferred for later discussion. As for the third phase, he adduces a number of proofs that there is only one God and no other, all of which were quoted by the earlier Jewish philosophers, Saadia and Bahya.

The gist of Aaron's theory of attributes is as follows: God is one in essence, but as we primarily conceive Him through His actions, He can be described by five attributes which are: omnipotent, omniscient, living, acting by will and existent. These attributes, Aaron says, by no means indicate any multiplicity in God's essence, for they really indicate one thing. He proves this in the following way. Life consists in the power of perception, hence living is identical with omniscience. Again, acting with will means performing the right action whch involves true conception. Nor is potence different from knowledge as far as God is concerned, for His activity consists primarily in thought, and hence His omnipotence consists in an all-embracing knowledge. Likewise is God's existence not distinct from His essence, for with Him they are one, since there is no other cause for His existence except His essence. These attributes, Aaron asserts, to be positive and essential, that is they describe the essence of God. He is not unmindful of the criticism levelled by Maimonides against such an assumption but he says that the solution of Maimonides by declaring these attributes negative, namely, that "wise" means not ignorant and so forth, does not improve the situation. A negaive attribute really connotes the same thing as a positive, for when we say God is not ignorant and mean by it that no kind of ignorance can be applied to Him, we really say that He is all-wise. There is no *tertium quid* between these two terms, and if we deny the one, we necessarily assert the other. The case being thus, it is more proper to speak of positive attributes as the Bible does. He does admit though that when we call the attributes positive and essential we do not really know their essence, for as they are identical with the essence of God, they really can not be known. By observing God's actions, we must conclude that such attributes must exist, but know no more.

In going over to the problem of Divine Providence, Aaron discusses two points which serve as important factors in the formation of his theory on the subject. These are the attributing to God, in contradistinction to Maimonides and others, a kind of sense perception and the question of the nature of good and evil. In regard to the first, he says, that while it is true that God does not perceive things by means of corporeal organs, nevertheless He knows of them, for it is not possible for the creator of the sense organs not to possess such a perception.

As for the nature of good and evil, Aaron refutes the Kalamitic view that good and bad acts should be considered as such not by their own character but in respect to the will of the one who commanded them, and rejects likewise the view that evil is merely a negative thing, namely the absence of good, an opinion held by Maimonides, and he then propounds his own view. In acts of good and evil, Aaron says, we are to distinguish two kinds, those that are performed by men and those that are brought about by God. The character of the first is determined both by convention and purpose. People consider an act good if it is done for the purpose of increasing human welfare, and on the contrary bad, if it is injurious to that welfare. This, of course, affords latitude in the determination of the character of an action, for certain acts which are in themselves bad may become good if the purpose for which they are performed is good, as for instance, the amputation of a leg in order to save the body. Concerning the second kind, namely the acts brought about by God, he says that they are all good and that the evil is only a seeming one. The evil is brought upon us either as a punishment, or for the purpose of avoiding the occurrence of a still greater suffering.

Aaron is now ready to develop his view of Providence. He differs with Maimonides who asserts that special Providence extends only to the human species but believes that it extends to all species. Nor does he find difficulty in asserting that God knows both the general and the particular things, differing with those who maintain that He knows only the former and not the latter. The holders of this view claim that we can not ascribe to Him a knowledge of particulars, for such knowledge arises from sense perception and God has none. Aaron, however, asserted that He does possess such perception, and hence His knowledge of particulars is as perfect as of general things. He agrees with the view of Maimonides that God knows beforehand the way a man will act and that yet this knowledge does not impair human freedom nor the nature of the possibility of man's action.

The question of Providence is inherently connected with reward and punishment, with the problem of the suffering of the righteous and the prosperity of the wicked, and our author devotes his attention to these matters. On the whole, he says little that is new in the solution of these problems. The prosperity of the wicked and the suffering of the righteous are due either to their previous good and bad deeds, or in the case of the wicked, the good accruing to them is for the purpose of punishing them more severely later; and in that of the righteous, the evil befalling them is either for the purpose of bestowing a greater reward, or a chastisement of love with the intention of ennobling their character. In the last manner, he says, are to be explained the trials of Abraham and Job. In the interpretation of the meaning of the Book of Job, he diverges greatly from the view of Maimonides and follows in the main the Karaite opinion.

In the discussion of the question of reward and punishment, our author stumbles upon a problem unknown to Rabbanite thinkers but frequently met with in Karaite philosophical discussions, that is the question, are the animals compensated for their suffering? From the point of view of complete Providence which says that even individuals of the animal species are included in the Divine scheme, the question arises then why should God's justice not be applied also to them? The Mutazilia (a branch of the Kalamites) maintained that animals are really rewarded for their suffering. Aaron rejects this preposterous view, but overcomes the difficulty by saying that the life of the animals is an act of grace on the part of God, and it is by His will that they were given to man for food, hence there is no wrong in slaughtering them for that purpose. He then passes over to the questions of the purpose of the world, prophecy, the character of the Torah and the nature of the precepts. Regarding the first, he says, that while we can not assign a definite reason for the purpose of the entire universe and must leave it to the wisdom of God, we are to assume that man is the purpose of the sublunar or the lower world, as he came into being last at the end of creation. The other two parts of the universe, namely that of the spheres and of the intelligences have undoubtedly their puroposes but we do not know them. Aaron endeavors to find a kind of general purpose or rather reason for the creation of the universe which is God's goodness. The world is good and God enjoys doing good. This idea is already found in Saadia's *Emunoth* (Vol. I, Sect. 166).

If man is the purpose of the lower world, it follows that God in His goodness should assist man to attain his destiny. This was done by giving him the Law and endowing some individuals of the species with the gift of prophecy. The discussion of prophecy comes, therefore, next in order. Like Maimonides, he surveys the views of prophecy held by various thinkers and in general follows the outline of the *Guide* in the entire exposition of the nature of prophecy and the classification of the degrees of prophets, but makes obvious changes so as not to appear a mere copyist. Thus while Maimonides insists upon three qualifications for the prophet, namely intellectual excellence, high ethical conduct and the perfection of the faculty of imagination, Aaron emphasizes the first two only, leaving out the third element. He refers to it, though, in the course of the discussion, but in an indirect manner, so as not to show his dependence upon the *More Nebukim*.

Our author teaches together with all other Jewish philosophers, the superiority of the prophecy of Moses. While other prophets had their messages given to them in dreams or visions, Moses received his when awake and in the clearest manner. From the *sui generis* nature of Moses' prophecy, there follows the perfection of the Torah as well as its immutability. Aaron assigns the perfection of the given Torah as the reason why the Karaites refuse to accept the oral law or the tradition of the Rabbanites. This tradition, he claims, changes the Torah, inasmuch as it adds to as well as detracts certain things from its contents and thus assumes its imperfection which is impossible. The narrowness of such an objection is evident and might with equal force have been applied to the Karaite interpretation as well.

The precepts of the law have, of course, a purpose since the law was given to man as a means of perfecting his soul. But the precepts consist of two classes, one rational and the other merely imperative (Toryoth), and while the purpose of the first class is evident, that of the second is not so obvious. Aaron, therefore, comes to the conclusion that the precepts of the second class are disciplinary measures, namely that by fulfilling them, man is trained to perfect himself in the carrying out of the rational commandments.

The last ten chapters of the book are devoted to the question of reward and punishment in the world to come, which is, of course, connected with the question of the immortality of the soul. Aaron is, however, brief on this subject. The soul, according to him, is created but exists before the body. The reason for it is that the soul is a self-subsisting substance and is not dependent upon the body for its existence. It is also immortal, for since it is the cause of knowledge, an immaterial thing, it must itself be immaterial and hence not subject to decay. Reward and punishment in the world to come follow from these premises, for if the soul is immaterial and immortal, its reward must likewise be immaterial which can not be carried out in this world. It follows also that the more perfect a soul is the greater is its reward. But he does not deny, like some Jewish philosophic rationalists, reward to the non-intellectual ones, for as long as they observe the laws the purpose of which is to elevate the soul, they will share in the world to come.

He finally discusses the nature of reward and punishment and attempts to define the meaning of the terms "world to come" (Olam ha-Ba), resurrection (Tehiyat ha-Metim) and Paradise (Gan-Eden). He gives the various views on the subject held by different theologians but the entire discussion is confused. He himself seems to believe in resurrection in the literal sense. As regards the determination of the status of man, whether he should be rewarded or punished, Aaron adopts the Rabbinic standard, namely that man is judged in accordance with the majority of his actions. If these were good, he is classed as righteous, if evil as wicked. The book closes with a discussion of *Teshubah* (Repentance) which gives the ten steps necessary for attaining its completeness. In this enumeration, there is an evident influence of the *Treatise on Penitence* (Shaare Teshubah) by Rabbi Jonah Gerundi (Sect. 87).

Judging the philosophic work of Aaron ben Elijah as a whole, we can say that while it displays little originality and is greatly dependent upon the *Guide* of Maimonides, yet as a complete enunciation of Karaitic religious philosophy it is of great value. Aaron, while differing from the views of the earlier thinkers of his sect, still defends their principal tenets with great skill and ability. The *Etz-Hayyim* can be said to be an attempt at a reconciliation between the two currents of religious philosophy, that of the earlier Kalam and the later Aristotelian, which was carried out in a fairly successful way but found no followers.

The second great work of Aaron is his Book of Precepts called *Gan-Eden,* and he distinguishes himself in the field of law as in the field of philosophy, for his legal book is probably the best of the Karaite codes. But even here Maimonides was his model, for the *Gan-Eden* is an imitation of the *Mishnah Torah* as the *Etz-Hayyim* is of the *Guide.* Aaron however, did not, like Maimonides, include in his code a survey of beliefs in ethical teachings, but limited it merely to the law, for the former phase, he claims, was sufficiently covered by the philosophic work. Yet even the *Gan-Eden* is not without the influence of philosophic theory. In the introduction, the author gives a kind of rational background to the entire work. He enumerates seven Karaite dogmas, which are the following: Belief in existence, unity and incorporeality of God, creation, God's Providence, the conduct of the world by the will and wisdom of God, reward and punishment, the veracity of prophecy and authenticity of the Torah. He then adds that all the precepts were given for the purpose of inculcating these dogmas, and accordingly he prefaces each section containing a group of precepts with a philosophic statement of their purpose and value.

The *Gan-Eden* covers the entire Karaite Halakah and is divided into thirty-four sections which are subdivided into chapters. The subject matter is logically arranged and, as it seems, according to the division of the laws into those relating to the life of the individual, the life of the family and that of society. He takes up first the laws dealing with the calendar, the Sabbath and the festivals. This is followed by a section on prayer, on the slaughtering of animals which includes other dietary laws, and finally on regulations of purity and impurity. The family laws come next.

In two extensive sections, one named *'Aroyoth* and the other *Seder Nashim,* the prohibited marriages and the laws of marriage and divorce are stated in detail. The other sections are devoted to civil law. Of all the sections of the book, those on the civil law are the briefest and most uninteresting, and exhibit in a marked degree the poverty of Karaite communal life and how little Jewish law was applied to it. The most important sections of the book are the *Dinē Shehitah* (Laws of the Slaughtering of Animals) and the *'Aroyoth*

(Prohibited Marriages). These two were also published separately, the first under its proper title and the other named *Zofnath P'aaneah* (Revealer of Secrets).

The *Gan-Eden* more than any other Karaite code shows its dependence upon Rabbinic law. Involuntarily many Talmudic interpretations of the law and regulations are incorporated. Here and there attempts are made to derive regulations direct from the text as in the case of people disqualified as witnesses on account of their conduct. This, however, is only a show of independence. In reality, the regulations are borrowed from the Talmud. There are also polemic discussions against Rabbanite scholars, especially against Saadia and Ibn Ezra, but those are carried on without hatred.

The commentary on the Bible called *Kether Torah* (The Crown of the Law) is, like Aaron's other two outstanding works, an important contribution in the field of exegesis. It pays great attention to the philosophic and the legal interpretation of the verse, but it does not neglect the exegetic phase, namely, that of explaining linguistically and grammatically the meaning of words and passages. Especially valuable is Aaron's lengthy introduction, where in the manner of Ibn Ezra, he gives a detailed exposition of the various methods of exegesis employed by previous commentators, as well as the fundamental principles of difference in the interpretation of the Bible between the Rabbanites and the Karaites. The introduction together with some excerpts of the commentary itself were translated into Latin.

In conclusion, we wish to say a few words about the Hebrew style of Aaron ben Elijah. It is, on the whole, more lucid and plastic than that of the earlier Karaite writers and bears undoubtedly marks of influence of the style of the great Rabbanite writers. Yet it still retains the stiffness of the Karaite manner of writing, and the frequent use of peculiarly coined words often obscure the meaning of passages.

Taking into consideration the great achievements of Aaron ben Elijah in all the three fields of Karaite learning, it is not to be wondered at that the succeeding generation of his sect hailed him as the teacher *par excellence* and referred to him with admiration and love.

124. THE FIFTEENTH AND SIXTEENTH CENTURIES

The works of Aaron ben Elijah denote the high water mark in the Karaite literature of the post-Classical period. What was produced during the two following centuries, the fifteenth and the sixteenth, was considerable in quantity but mediocre in quality. Most of these productions were of a compilatory and eclectic nature. The writers busied themselves with excerpting from the works of the earlier scholars to which they added some opinions of their own. Yet even this period was not entirely barren. There were a few men who rose above the level of general eclecticism and made some important contributions in their respective field. That field was primarily the one of legal discussion.

The fields of exegesis and religious philosophy were comparatively neglected. In the latter one, we hardly find a single work of importance even of the character of a comprehensive compilation, and in the former, we meet with a number of commentaries mostly of a popular nature. However, as a compensation for lack of interest in philosophy, we notice an increased attention to matters of science and as a result a number of scientific books appear. This interest in science was mainly stimulated by contact with the Rabbanites. The great Rabbanite scholars, Mordecai Komtino (14030-1500) and his disciple Elijah Mizrahi (Sect. 69) who distinguished themselves not only as Talmudists but also as scientists had a number of Karaites as students and instructed them both in sacred and secular subjects. These, in imitation of their masters, extended the scope of their literary activity to include some subjects of science in which they were particularly interested.

i. Of the leading writers of the period, the first is Samuel Al-Moghrebi, the Westerner, or as he is usually known, Samuel ha-Rofē ben Moses ha-Dayan of Cairo (1350-1420). As his name indicates, he was born, like his predecessor Israel who held the same position and bore the same surname, in North Africa and migrated in his early youth to the East. His main work by which he is primarily known is his large and comprehensive treatise on law written in Arabic and named *Al-Murshid* (The Book of Guidance), or *ha-Meyashar* in Hebrew.

The purpose of the book is, as stated by the author in the introduction, to clarify the opinions of the earlier authorities and arrive at definite decisions in matters of law. It is divided into twelve sections dealing with all phases of Karaite law. The one on prohibited marriages, *'Aroyoth,* is like in all codes of the sect, especially extensive. He sides in this very complicated question with those who took a more lenient view and follows primarily Israel ha-Dayan and his disciple Jepheth. He relies on them against the early authorities. Samuel's code was considered authoritative by the Karaite communities of the East and his decisions were followed by them. The work was translated into Hebrew in the year 1722 by Samuel ha-Cohen of Damascus.

Of his other works there are extant (1) a commentary on the Pentateuch in the form of questions and answers; (2) an introduction to the portions of the Pentateuch called in Arabic *Mukadamat* containing short homilies and poems to each portion; and (3) a book on the calendar called *Kitab Al 'Ibbur* which was later translated into Hebrew.

ii. Another writer of the sect whose contributions in the field of exegesis is of some importance, is Abraham ben Judah of Constantinople (1420-1450). He wrote a commentary on the entire Bible entitled *Yesod Mikra* (The Foundation of the Scriptures). It is a popular work intended as a manual for teachers. Yet it is executed with great skill, for it contains the best of the comments of the earlier exegetes. On the whole, Abraham follows the *Peshat* method, but some books, he interprets in a rationalistic-philosophic way. Thus, the Book of Canticles he explains as an allegorical discussion between the Active Intellect and the soul. In his commentary on Daniel and Ezra, he renders the Aramaic portions of the book into Hebrew.

This Abraham was the founder of a family of writers and copyists of earlier works, who were known by the surname Tishbi which originated with Elijah the son of Abraham. Elijah copied the work of an earlier namesake *Hiluk ha-Karaim v'ha-Rabanim* (The Division between the Karaites and the Rabbanites) which was discussed in Vol. I, sect. 186 and which was for a time ascribed to him. The grandson, Judah ben Elijah, completed and annotated Abraham's work. The son of Judah, Joseph Tishbi, wrote several works on calendar calculations and a supercommentary on a part of the *Mibhar* of Aaron ben Joseph.

iii. Elijah Bashiatzi (1420-1491) can be justly considered the most important scholar and writer of the period. He was born in Adrianople, where his father and grandfather were the spiritual leaders of the Karaite community. His education was a thorough one in all branches of Jewish lore. He completed his studies in Constantinople under Rabbanite scholars, among them Mordecai Komtino who introduced him to the study of the sciences. In the year 1460, at the age of forty, he succeeded his father as Haham of the community of

Adrianople and there he composed his great legal work, *Adereth Eliyahu* (The Mantle of Elijah) on which he labored for thirty years, but which left unfinished was completed by his colleague, Caleb Afendopulo.

Bashiatzi had in addition to the scholarly motive also a personal reason for composing his new code or legal compendium. His father and grandfather had shown, during their occupancy of the position of Haham, great leniency in interpreting the Sabbath laws, for which they were severely attacked. Elijah therefore undertook to show in his work that deviations are allowed if the later scholars find that their predecessors had erred in the derivation of the laws from the Biblical passages.

The scholarly reasons which induced him to write the new legal work were, as he states in his introduction, the lack of clarity of the decisions found in earlier works. The differences of opinion between authorities and the low state of scholarship among the Karaites of his day, made it impossible for the people to know the law. He expected to obviate all these difficulties in his own code by a careful sifting of the material and a systematic arrangement of the contents of the laws, as well as by the indication of the Biblical sources from which each regulation is derived. He follows the old Karaite arrangement of the subject matter by taking up groups of laws in the established order, but is careful to state the precepts, both the affirmative *(Asē)* and the prohibitive *(Lo-Taasē)* involved in each group.

Bashiatzi, as mentioned, displays in his *Adereth,* a spirit of independence and does not hesitate to differ in his decisions from the accepted Karaite opinion and even, if necessary, to side with the Rabbanites on certain important matters. We will cite one example of his independent spirit. One of the important differences between the Karaites and the Rabbanites is the interpretation of the precept, "Thou shalt not seethe a kid in its mother's milk." (Ex. XXIII, 19; XXXIV, 26; Deut. XIV, 21.) The Talmud interprets this to include first, not only the prohibition of boiling the flesh of a young goat in its mother's milk, but the flesh of all domestic animals which are eaten; second, not only the boiling in their mother's milk, but in milk in general; and thirdly, not only the boiling but also the eating of flesh and milk together and even to enjoy its use in any way. The Karaites agreed in most of these points but stressed the words "its mother's milk" and said that the prohibition extends only to the boiling and eating of the flesh of animals in or with their mother's milk only, but not if the milk comes from another animal. This leniency was accepted by all Karaites, but Bashiatzi decides in favor of the Rabbanite view and prohibits the eating of meat and milk together in general.

The *Adereth* contains fourteen sections beginning with the calendar and followed by a discussion of the laws of the Sabbath, the festivals, prayer, laws of purity and impurity, of marriage and divorce, prohibited marriages, circumcision and of mourning in consecutive order. The sections are subdivided into many chapters, and sometimes an account of special importance are given also in several parts. Thus, the section on prayer contains three parts. The first deals with the conception of God, the honor due Him and the ten dogmas; the second describes the two forms of the worship of God, namely, the one which is expressed by the performance of the precepts which Bahya calls *Hoboth ha-Ebarim* (The Duties of the Organs) and the other by the observance of those precepts enjoined upon the heart and mind (Hoboth ha-Lebabboth); it also discusses the principles of ethics. The third part is devoted to the laws of prayer proper. The *Adereth,* after having been completed by Afendopulo was received with approval by the Karaite scholars and great authority was given to its decisions. It was later provided with commentaries by several scholars. Of the other works of Bashiatzi, we may note (1) his *Sepher Keli-ha-Nehoshet,* a treatise on the construction of the astrolabe and on various astronomical and astrological problems, and (2) the *Melitzah ha-Mitzvoth,* a poem on the six hundred and thirteen precepts in imitation of such poems by the Rabbanites known as *Asharoth.*

iv. A prolific writer of the 15th century was Caleb Afendopulo, (1430-1505) the brother-in-law of Elijah Bashiatzi. He was born in Adrianople, but his home seems to have been Belgrade. He spent a great part of his literary efforts in improving, completing and annotating the works of others. Thus, he added two sections to Bashiatzi's *Adereth* and made a detailed table of contents to Judah Hadassi's Encyclopædia *Eshkol ha-Kofer* (Vol. I, Sect. 186) and to Aaron ben Elijah's *Etz-Hayyim.* Of his own numerous works, the most noted are (1) the *Gan ha-Melek* (The Garden of the King), (2) the *Sepher 'Asara Maamoroth* (A Book of Ten Discourses), and (3) the *Sepher Mathematica.* The first is a treatise on physical, mathematical and chronological problems consisting of twelve sections, each of which includes many chapters. The second contains discussions on a number of subjects, but in reality was intended as a commentary on the one hundred and nineteenth Psalm. It was a Karaite custom to study portions of that Psalm, on the afternoons of the seven Sabbaths between Passover and Shebuoth, and for this purpose the long chapter is divided into seven parts, each of which is read and discussed on a different Sabbath. Caleb accordingly divides his commentary into seven sections. Yet it is not a commentary in the proper sense of the word, but a group of discourses. He finds in the Psalm proofs for the Karaite teachings and mystic references to philosophic and scientific principles. In general, the book contains discussions on the meaning of the laws, the nature of God and His attributes and the dogmas. The short commentary on Canticles appended to it explains the book as an allegorical dialogue between God and Israel. The third is a text book for the study of the science of numbers. He wrote also several booklets on legal subjects, each of which he named *Iggereth* (An Epistle) and a longer and complete commentary on the Book of Canticles where he follows the same allegorical method indicated in his shorter work on the book.

v. The last of the noted writers of this period was a youthful author, Moses ben Elijah Bashiatzi (1554-1572). He was the grandson of Elijah Bashiatzi and was endowed with a remarkable literary gift in his early youth. At the age of sixteen, he is said to have written several works. Being desirous of obtaining as much learning as possible, he travelled for a few years in the East and stayed for some time in Egypt where he explored the famous Karaite libraries in the city of Cairo. Unfortunately the life of this precocious youth was cut short by sudden death which overtook him in his eighteenth year.

He managed, however, to accumulate a great stock of knowledge in his short life which, as displayed in his works, amounted to a mastery of the entire Karaitic literature from Anan down to his own day. His most important work is the *Matē Elohim* (The Staff of God) which deals with the motives, history and nature of the Karaite schism. It is divided into four sections, the first describing the antecedents of the Karaites. Here he makes the assertion that the Karaites recognize a part of Talmudic tradition as that belonging to their ancestors, for they followed the Shammaite school, while the Rabbanites adopted the teachings of the Hillelites. In the second section, he enumerates the names of the Karaite bearers of tradition from Moses to the Nasi, Boas the Second, which is supposed to oppose the accepted Rabbanite line of the bearers of tradition. There is included in this section also an essay on the early sects of the Sadduceans and Boetusians where the author rejects with contempt the oft-made assertion by the Rabbanites that the Karaites are the spiritual heirs of the Sadduceans. The third and the fourth sections deal with the rules and principles of interpretation of the Bible and with the relation of the six hundred and thirteen precepts to the Decalogue respectively.

Moses also wrote two other works dealing with legal questions and a book on dogmas and the principles of belief. In all his works, however, there is little originality, for they consist of quotations from earlier authors. Their value lies primarily in the citations from such works which were lost and of the nature of which Bashiatzi's excerpts are the only source.

Besides these leading Karaite writers and scholars of the period there was a host of others of lesser importance. Of these, the following deserve to be mentioned: Judah Gibbor (fl. 1500-1540), his son, Elijah, Moses Zarudi (fl. 1575-1625), and Moses and Joseph Bagi (end of 16th and 1st quarter of 17th centuries). The first wrote many works, among them the *Minhath Yehuda* (The Gift of Judah) a rhymed abstract of the contents of the Pentateuch and a philosophic work named *Moed Katan* (The Lesser Feast). The second is primarily known for his commentary on the famous astronomical work of Immanuel ben Jacob, *Shesh Knofaim* (Sect. 99). Zarudi was a prolific writer and is said to have written ten books on various subjects of which the *Mitzvoth Moshe* (The Command of Moses) on the calendar and *Yemin Moshe* (The Right Hand of Moses) are the outstanding. The other two were likewise very productive, each producing several works, of which the noted are the *Mitzvoth Moshe,* a large and comprehensive book of precepts by Moses Bagi, the *Kiriya Neamanah* (The Faithful City), on the differences between the Karaites and the Rabbinites and the *Sapha Berura,* an extensive philosophic work by Joseph Bagi.

With the works of these writers and scholars, the literary activity of the Eastern and Byzantine Karaite centers practically comes to an end. Of the two, the Byzantine center especially contributed several fine chapters to the literature of the sect. But as the centuries passed, the activity kept on diminishing until it ceased completely.

125. THE CRIMEAN AND THE LITHUANIAN CENTERS

The settlement of the Karaites in the Crimean Peninsula is a very old one, though the date of its origin can not be definitely determined. The Karaite scholar, Abraham Firkowitz, had endeavored in the fifties of the last century by a series of documents, tombstone epitaphs and epigraphs on ancient Scrolls of the Torah to prove that there were Karaite communities in the Crimea as early as the end of the eighth century. Moreover, he even claimed that the Crimean Jews were descendants of the ten tribes and thus endeavored to prove that Karaism was the original form of ancient Judaism. The evidence looked imposing enough and some Jewish scholars were misled by it, but on close scrutiny its spuriousness became evident, and more clear thinking scholars completely rejected the Firkowitz theories regarding the Karaites in the Crimea. However, be that as it may, one thing is certain that in the second half of the twelfth century, there were many members of the sect living in the peninsula. For this we have the testimony of the traveller Petahia, written in the last quarter of that century (Vol. I, Sect. 196), that he found in the Crimea a large number of Karaite communities. Most likely, the first *Karaim* came to the peninsula from Baylonia through the Caucasus, and with their noted zeal for propaganda, succeeded in converting a number of the native Jews who lived there in the time of the Khazars, who in their ignorance could not well distinguish between the Rabbinism they had hitherto adhered to and the teachings of the new settlers. Rabbinism, however, was not entirely destroyed in the Crimea, for there remained many Jews who clung to their ancient form of faith.

The relations between the Karaites and the ruling people, the Tartars, were on the whole friendly, and the conditions for the development of the sect favorable. Accordingly, the communities flourished and increased, synagogues and schools were built, and it was not very long before the Crimea became one of the noted centers of Karaism in Europe. A large number of documents of various kinds testify to the active religious and communal life of that center from the twelfth century on. Many names of scholars who either resided in the peninsula or who were born there but later went to Byzantium to be educated are mentioned in the works of Karaite authors, from which we learn that there was considerable intellectual intercourse between the Crimean and Byzantian centers.

From the Crimea the Karaites spread to Lithuania and Poland. Their first settlement in Lithuania undoubtedly took place in the last quarter of the fourteenth century when the Lithuanian prince, Witowt (1350-1430), brought from his raid on the Crimea a hundred families of Karaim and settled them at Lutzk, Wolhynia. Later, many more emigrated from their old home and settled in various Lithuanian and Polish towns. There were many communities in a number of cities but the principal ones were those of Troki near Wilna in Lithuania and the above mentioned Lutzk. These two cities formed the main seats of learning of the sect, and it is from there that the largest number of scholars hailed. The Karaites enjoyed the same privileges as the Rabbanite Jews in Poland and were at times even given special rights. As a result, the communities flourished during the fifteenth and sixteenth centuries. However, as compared to the large number of Rabbanites who resided in the Polish kingdom, the sect formed only a small minority and was subjected to the former in the fixation and collection of taxes and the conduct of relations between the Jews and the government.

126. THE LITERATURE

Taking in consideration the favorable condition under which the Karaites in the Crimea and Poland lived, it was but natural that they should have developed a considerable intellectual activity. In fact, the bibliographer, Simhah Lutzki (see below), gives long lists of scholars and savants who lived in these two countries. Yet, the literary output of this period is a comparatively meager one and displays little originality. Of the centers which contributed to the literature of the period, the one in Lithuania and Poland is the most productive, for on the whole, we meet with very few Crimean authors, as the life there was isolated and of a primitive character. The situation was different in Poland.* There the Karaites came in contact with the Rabbanite literature and to a certain degree with the culture and literature of the Poles. This contact stimulated their efforts in various directions. Another impetus towards literary activity was the interest taken by Christian scholars in the history and teachings of the secet. These scholars directed their inquiries to Karaite savants, and the latter were forced to give accounts of their origin and doctrines.

As a result of these causes, we note a broadening of interest on the part of the Lithuanian and Polish Karaite writers, for, while they continued to write Books of Precepts and Biblical commentaries or

* From the end of the fourteenth century. Lithuania was a part of the Polish Kingdom.

supercommentaries, they also began to devote themselves to other subjects. We have, therefore, a number of historical and scientific works. Still with all this, only a few of the writers attained prominence so as to deserve a description in a general survey. We will, therefore, select the most outstanding.

i. The first and probably the most important writer of the period was Isaac ben Abraham Troki (1533-1594). We know little of the events of his life except that he obtained an intensive and extensive education not only in Karaite and Rabbinic lore, but also in secular subjects. He mastered besides Hebrew also Polish and Latin and was well read in the theological literature written in these languages.

Poland was in the sixteenth century a place of refuge for many members of the liberal Christian sects which arose then in western Europe, such as the Socinians, the Arians, and other anti-trinitarians. Lutheranism also spread there to a certain degree among the petty nobles. As a result, theological discussion was fashionable in certain social circles, and Isaac who seemed to have been on friendly terms with nobles and priests was greatly interested in them and was often drawn into such discussions as a defender of Judaism. He mastered a great part of the Christian literature, had a thorough knowledge of the New Testament, and read the works of the Socinian Simon Budni and other controversialists of the day, as well as all other books on Christianity he could find.

Armed with all this knowledge, Isaac determined to write a treatise in defense of Judaism and its teachings against all attacks of the Christians. This apologetic work he named *Hisuk Emunah* (The Strengthening of Faith). It is an excellent apologetic and polemic work, executed with great skill and ability displaying a thorough knowledge of the subject.

The book is divided into two unequal parts. The first, containing about three-quarters of the entire work, is devoted largely to apologetics refuting all arguments advanced by the Christians against Jews and Judaism, but includes also some polemic matter. The second is entirely polemic and points out the contradictions and errors found in the New Testament, from the synoptic Gospels to the Apocalypse of John. In forty-three of the fifty chapters of the first part, Isaac answers the general Christian complaints against the Jews for their refusal to acknowledge Jesus and his teachings and refutes the proofs from the Old Testament for his Messiahship. He relies chiefly on the Scriptures and draws his ammunition from the arsenal of Biblical learning. His arguments are clear and concise, and are distinguished by keenness of mind and are often tinged with irony.

Thus, Isaac points out the failure of Jesus to qualify as the Messiah of the prophets. He was not of the Davidic descent, for since the Christians say that Joseph was not the father of Jesus, it follows that he could not have descended from David, for the genealogy given in the New Testament is only of Joseph but not of Miriam. Nor was he the man of peace the Messiah is supposed to be, for Jesus said, "Think not that I come to send peace on earth, I came not to send peace on earth but a sword." (Matthew X, 34.) On another occasion, Isaac upbraids the Christians for their taunt against the Jews that God forsook them because they refused to accept Christ and that their bitter lot is only a result of that refusal. First he points out that since the most Christian nations of the day had for a long time refused to accept Jesus and persecuted his followers, how then can we assume that God chose them after the perpetration of all these acts? Second, he asks ironically, "Does justice really rule in the world? Do all the righteous prosper? Are the Mohammedans followers of the true religion? Why then taunt the Jews for their misery?"

In his refutation of the Scriptural proof for the coming of Jesus, Isaac is thorough and complete. He discusses all the proofs seriatim, beginning with certain verses of Genesis and ending with those of Zechariah. He displays a fine exegetic and linguistic skill in the interpretation of the verses and quotes the works of the Rabbanite savants, Isaac Arama and Isaac Abrabanel.

The author is equally keen and ironic in his attack against the teachings of Christianity and shows their impracticability. Thus, he says Judaism tells us to give only a tithe for charity while Jesus said we should give all we possess, a thing which no one will carry out. Again, Jesus taught that one should turn the other cheek when smitten, yet he himself complained bitterly when he was struck, (Gospel of John, XVIII, 23) and Paul cursed the man who smote him (Acts XIII, 10). Isaac attacks the doctrine of original sin and charges the Christians with changing their own law by not obeying its dictates. He defends the immutability of the Torah and proves it from the New Testament itself. The book, on the whole, is a very able apology of Judaism and also a keen polemic work. We may add that the value of *Hisuk Emunah* is enhanced by its light and flowing style which contains none of the hard features of the Karaite writings.

The *Hisuk Emunah* was left unfinished by Isaac and was completed from the author's notes and edited by his disciple, Josepeh Malinowski. For fear of the censor, it was not printed but circulated in manuscript form. Curiously enough, it was first printed by a Christian scholar who was unfriendly to the Jews, Johann-Christoff Wagenseil, with a Latin translation under the name of *Tela Ignea Satanae,* i. e. The Fiery Darts of Satan. He also appended a short refutation of its main arguments. Since then it was printed many times. Besides the Latin translation by Wagenseil, there are several renderings into other languages, into Spanish by Isaac Athaas in 1621, and into Judaeo-German, or Yiddish, by an annoymous translator in 1705.

The book made a great impression in the Christian world, and several books were written by theologians to refute its arguments, one by the German scholar Jacob Gusset which even bears a Hebrew title, *Shemesh Zedakah* (The Sun of Righteousness). On the other hand, the free spirits of the eighteenth century welcomed it, and Voltaire speaks of it with praise.

ii. The disciple of Isaac Troki, the above-mentioned Joseph Malinowski (1570-1640), was a prolific writer. He composed an abstract of the treatise on the laws of slaughtering of animals by Elijah Bashiatzi and a *Sepher Minhagim* (A Book of Customs) containing the order of the synagogue ritual and several commentaries. He is, however, primarily known for his long didactic and philosophic poem *ha-Elef Leka.* The name is borrowed from Canticles VIII, 12 and is applied to the poem because it contains one thousand words each beginning with a He (ה). It discusses the mysteries of life and the dogmas, and was greatly valued both by Karaites and Rabbanites.

iii. Zerah ben Nathan Troki (1595-1663) was the disciple of Joseph Malinowski. He is known for his correspondence with the scientist Joseph del Medigo. His letters which touched on many problems, physical, mathematical, medical and theological, were incorporated in del Medigo's treatise spoken of above (Sect. 101). From the nature of his numerous inquiries, we can see that Zerah's range of knowledge was very extensive. He was interested in the Kabbala, and from one of his letters to Menasse ben Israel, we learn that he also studied the works of Philo. However, besides his letters to del Medigo, Zerah is not known to have composed any other works.

iv. A leading Karaite writer of the seventeenth century was Mordecai ben Nissan of Kukisoff. His most famous work is the *Dod*

Mordecai (The Friend of Mordecai), a treatise on the origin and history of the sect. The fame of the work, though, does not rest on its contents but on the circumstances which called forth its composition which are as follows:

A Christian scholar, Jacob Trigland, professor of theology at Leyden, Holland, being interested in the Karaites, addressed a letter written in classical Hebrew to the Haham of the community of Karaites at Lutzk, wherein he propounded four questions concerning the history and literature of the sect. The first question consists of four parts: (1) Whether the Karaites and Sadducees are identical except that the former do not deny the immortality of the soul as the latter had done? (2) Whether the Karaites existed as a separate sect during the time of the Second Temple? (3) Whether the origin of the sect is to be traced to Anan who created the schism on account of his thwarted ambition to succeed his uncle in the Patriarchate? (4) If the Karaite sect had already existed in the time of the Second Temple, are there any definite proofs for such an assertion?

As to the second question, Trigland states that he found a letter said to be written by Menahem, a Karaite, to Akillas the proselyte, a student of Saadia Gaon, and he inquires whether this Akillas is identical with Aquila, the translator of the Bible into Greek or with Onkelos, the Aramaic translator of the Pentateuch?

The third question concerns itself with the identity of the *Sepher ha-Mitzvoth* of Aaron ben Elijah with a book called *More Aaron*.

The last question is whether the text of the Bible of the Karaites is any different from that of the Rabbanites, and whether the sect possesses definite views concerning the time of origin of the vowels and accents?

The letter of Trigland was turned over by the leaders of the Lutzk community to Mordecai ben Nissan for an answer, and he composed the *Dod Mordecai* for that purpose. It is a small treatise of twelve chapters, each fancifully connected with the name of a son of Jacob. In the first chapter which is called *Matē Reuben* (The Tribe of Reuben, the first son of Jacob) he merely restates the questions. Of the rest, eight chapters are devoted to the four divisions of the first question. The gist of his answer is as follows. The Karaite schism dates not from Anan but from the time of Simon ben Shotah, head of the Sanhedrin during the time of Alexander Jannaus, the Hashmonean King. According to Mordecai, it was Simon who originated Rabbanism, while his colleague Judah ben Tabbai and his followers remained faithful to the old traditions which are that of Karaism. In other words, the Karaites are really older than the Rabbanites and are by no means identical with the Sadducees who originated a hundred years earlier than the time of Simon ben Shotah. The proof he adduces for this assertion is a statement by Judah ha-Levi in his Kuzari at the end of the third section. There, ha-Levi says, "That in the time of Simon ben Shotah, due to the disturbances caused by the rift between the Pharisees and the king, the Karaites joining with others who denied oral tradition, struck root."[1] Ha-Levi then goes on and differentiates distinctly between the Karaites and the Sadducees. Mordecai, as other scholars of his sect, while rejecting the first statement of ha-Levi, that the Karaites joined forces with other opponents of oral law, emphasizes the second statement that they differ from the Sadducees.

No matter how flimsy the foundation of his assertion of the antiquity of his sect may seem to the critical reader, Mordecai felt justified in his answer to the first part of Trigland's first query. But as for the second, whether the Karaites already existed as a sect in the time of the Second Temple, he felt a bit uneasy. He was, of course, forced to assert their existence, and found proof in two statements, one by Josephus and the other by the Church father, Epiphanus, both quoted by Asarya de Rossi in his *Meor Enayim* (Sect. 144) The first speaks of a fourth sect, that of Judah the Galillean, and the second mentions a sect called *Zedukim* who were different from the Sadduceans and were called so because they followed righteousness (from Zadik, righteous). It is, therefore, says Mordecai, safe to conclude that the Karaites are identical with this sect mentioned by Epiphanus. This supposition is his answer to the second part of the query, but to the latter's demand for more satisfactory evidence, he apologizes that on account of the loss of the ancienet books through exile and their destruction by the enemies, he can offer no more authentic proofs. From all that was said, it follows, of course, that Anan ben David was not the founder of the sect but only a great teacher. Nor did he strive for the patriarchate. It was another Anan, a son of Sheftia who lived at the time of the redaction of the Mishnah who participated in the quarrel about the patriarchate.

To corroborate his view, Mordecai gives a list of Karaite patriarchs from Zerubabal down to 1640. The list is a typical example of his

[1] Kuzari, sect. 3, par. 65.

ignorance of history, for it is full of anachronisms, and besides, many of the names of earlier patriarchs are Rabbanites who for one reason or another were converted by him to Karaism. The only thing that can be said in his favor is that he copied the list together with many of his arguments from earlier writers.

The other three questions he answers briefly. He knows little about the Menahem referred to by Trigland, but points out the anachronism implied in making Akillas or Onkelos a pupil of Saadia. As for the identity of the two, he quotes Azarya de Rossi on the subject. Mordecai supplies the information regarding the book of Aaron ben Elijah and also some additional data about other books. About the text of the Bible, he says that the Karaite text is the same as the one of the Rabbanites and he also believes, like many Rabbinic scholars, that the vowels were given at Sinai. This, he says, is the opinion of the savants of his sect.

We can readily see that there is little originality in this treatise. The only valuable features in it are the long excerpts he quotes from other works and the information he supplies about some of the books in his possession. Mordecai also wrote another book named *Lebush Malkuth* (Royal Garment with reference to Esther IX, 15, where it says, "And Mordecai went out dressed in royal garment") on the differences in the interpretation of a number of laws between the Rabbanites and Karaites. In addition, he composed a Hebrew grammar and some liturgical poems.

v. A contemporary of Mordecai was another Karaite savant, Solomon ben Aaron Troki. He performed a service for his sect similar to that of Mordecai. The Swedish Oriental scholars were at the time, like those of the Dutch, greatly interested in the Karaite teachings. One of these scholars, John Poppendorff, the rector of the university in Riga, visited the Lithuanian communities of the sect in the year 1697 and invited Solomon, who was wise in learning but young in years, to lecture at the university of Upsala on Karaism. The young scholar who also knew Latin accepted the invitation and delivered the desired lectures.

He was also asked by the Swedish government through its representative to give a short resume of the origin of the Karaites, their tenets, and their differences with the Rabbanites. For this purpose, he composed a small Hebrew treatise named *Apiryon* (The Canopy). It consists of twenty-four short chapters and an introduction where the origin of the schism is given in the same manner as stated by

Mordecai, but in a very concise form. In the book proper, he expounds clearly and briefly the Karaite ceremonial observances during the entire year with special reference to the festivals and the liturgy. He also states the principal beliefs and the dogmas of the sect. Mordecai ben Nissan saw this and expressed his disapproval of its brevity. But notwithstanding the latter's strictures, the *Apiryon* is an excellent resume of both the principles and practices of Karaism and gives a lucid concept of its essence.

Solomon was a prolific writer and wrote several other works, among them a large book by a similar name, *Apiryon Shlomeh* (The Canopy of Solomon with reference to his name and Canticles Ch. IV, 9). The work consists of two parts, the first dealing with the law and the second containing a polemic against Christianity. The second part is a recast of an earlier controversial work called *Migdal Oz* (A Tower of Strength). The *Apiryon* contains also a chapter on the education of children wherein he outlines a program of instruction. Another controversial work of his against the Rabbanites is entitled *Lohem Shearim* (Warfare at the Gates) and presents the arguments in the form of a dialogue between the representatives of the two factions in Jewry. A manual of Hebrew grammar by the name *Raḳ we-Tob* (Tender and Good) completes Solomon's literary activity.

vi. Abraham ben Yeshua Yerushalmi was a noted Karaite writer of the eighteenth century. He was born, as his name indicates, in Jerusalem around 1675 and received there an extensive education in the entire field of Jewish knowledge. He mastered thoroughly both the Karaite and Rabbinic lore. On account of a pestilence which raged in his native city at the end of the century, he left the country and settled at *Tchufut* Kalē in the Crimea. There he completed in 1712 his important work on religious philosophy and dogmatics entitled *Emunah Omen* (The True Belief).

The work possesses a number of very interesting points and not the least of them is the author's relation to Rabbanite learning. Not only does he display great erudition in Talmudic and Rabbinic literature in all its phases, Halakic, Agadic and philosophical, but he also speaks with the greatest reverence and praise of the great Rabbanite teachers. His estimate of Maimonides can compare favorably with that of the Rabbinic disciples of the master, and Ibn Ezra is to him the great exegete. Even when he champions the cause of Karaism against its opponents his tone is mild and calm.

In the introduction, Yerushalmi states that a treatise on Karaite religious philosophy must deal with the following four subjects: (a) the veracity and Divine origin of the Mosaic law; (b) its immutability; (c) the establishment of the truth of Karaite teaching against the Rabbanite view; (d) and the investigation whether a Jew should occupy himself with sciences, whose teachings contradict some of the tenets of religion? Accordingly, the work is divided into four sections, each devoted to one of these subjects. But while the other subjects are dealt with briefly, the proving of the superiority of Karaism is dealt with at length. In general, the author enunciates his teachings in a clear logical manner and the entire work is permeated with a rational spirit.

vii. The last of the Karaite scholars of the Mediaeval period was Simha Isaac Lutzki, i. e. of Lutzk in Wolhynia. He was born at the beginning of the eighteenth century and spent a great part of his life in his native city. It is there also where he began his literary activity. But in the year 1750, he settled at Tchufut Kalē in the Crimea where he continued to act as teacher and Haham for the rest of his life.

Lutzki was a prolific writer and he left a large number of works. He began as a copyist of ancient works, then turned commentator and finally emerged as author. Of his commentaries, the most noted is the one on the *Etz-Hayyim* of Aaron called *Or-Hayyim*. His own leading works are (a) the *Arba Yesodoth* (The Four Elements), (b) *Meirath Enayim* (The Light of the Eyes), (c) The *Sepher Tapuah* (The Book of the Apple) and the *Orah Tzadikim* (The Path of the Righteous).

The first book is a collection of four discourses on the four fundamentals of religion, namely the creation of the world, the existence of God, His holiness, spirituality and unity. The second is a book of law in two parts, the first called *Ner Mitzvah* (The Light of the Commandment) dealing with the precepts proper, and the second, *Ner Tzadikim* (The Light of the Righteous) on the differences between the Karaites and Rabbanites. The third is a Kabbalistic book discussing the *Maasē Merkabah* and *Maasē Bereshith* and the numerical combinations of the letters of the name of God. Lutzki, who according to his own confession, read few of the Kabbalistic works, is an ardent mystic and defends vigorously the antiquity of the Kabbala. The *Orah Tzadikim* is a small treatise dealing with the much discussed subject of the origin of the Karaim. It is divided into three parts *(Shevilim).* The first discusses the history of the schism; the second gives lists of the bearers of Karaite tradition; and the third is a bibliography of the most important Karaite works alphabetically arranged.

Lutzki repeats in the first part of his treatise much of what Mordecai had said in his works. He revives the theory advanced by Kirkisani and Elijah ben Abraham, author of the *Hiluk* (Vol. I, Sect. 186) that Jeroboam ben Nabat, founder of the kingdom of Israel, was also the founder of the Rabbanite sect. That, though, does not prevent him from saying that Simon ben Shotah was an additional founder of Rabbanism. He claims that the Karaim during the Second Temple were called *Zedukim* which name he derives from *Tzadik,* and yet they are not identical with the Sadducees. All such statements testify to his ignorance of historical facts. His bibliography of the Karaite literature, though not exact, is valuable, for it supplies important information, and it is for this work that Lutzki is primarily known.

With the end of the eighteenth century, the Karaite settlements in Poland began to dwindle and literary activity ceased. The few scholars who arose among the Karaites in Russia during the nineteenth century will be noted in the proper place.

Chapter IX

HISTORY, GEOGRAPHY, TRAVEL AND AUTOBIOGRAPHY

127. INTRODUCTORY REMARKS

The historical and geographical literature of the Jews during the second period of the Middle Ages greatly surpasses that of the former period both in quantity and in quality. This statement, however, applies only to the literary productivity in this field from the fifteenth century on. During the first two centuries of this period, with the exception of a few chronicles giving the succession of the generations of scholars, hardly any work of real historical value was produced. It is with the end of that century that works on history began to appear in considerable numbers. Especially fertile in this type of books was the sixteenth century, for most of the works on the past life of the nation were composed in that span of time.

The reasons for the special interest evinced by Jewish scholars in the life story of their people during that century were the expulsion of the Jews from Spain in 1492 and the establishment of new Jewish centers in the East on the one hand, and the influence of the general Renaissance of letters and science on the other hand. The breaking up of an old established center of Jews and Judaism engendered in the hearts of many savants a fear, lest the descendants of the scattered exiles ultimately forget the former glory of their ancestors and the great achievements of their famous men, and they, therefore, endeavored to fix these things in their memory by supplying them with written records of the deeds and works of past generations. In addition, the great calamity that befell the Spanish and Portuguese Jews, which in spite of its severity, had not annihilated that Jewry but had even spurred its members on to new achievements in other lands and climes, stimulated some chosen spirits to chronicle also the sufferings of the Jews in general during the centuries. They wanted to show by these records and narration of events that the Jewish people will continue its existence in spite of all persecutions.

The general revival of letters which reached its height in the sixteenth century could not pass by the Jews. The new discoveries made during the century, the voyages made by travellers to ancient lands, which broadened the horizon of men and aroused their curiosity had their effect also upon the children of the ghetto. They were still secluded, but here and there, in Italy and elsewhere, the barriers were broken and contact between Jewish scholars and the general world was established. The new learning made its way among the children of Israel and many among them studied assiduously not only their own lore but also the languages and the literature of their neighbors. In their desire to help their brethren in the increase of knowledge, they imitated the scholars of other nations and wrote histories of a more comprehensive nature where they narrated not only the events in the life of their people but also those which transpired in the life of other nations. Others devoted their books entirely to the life of other peoples, and still others wrote of the world, gave a description of the earth and its inhabitants and of the new discoveries.

The causes for the rise of historical literature during the period determined in a certain measure its nature and character. The two outstanding features of this form of intellectual activity which raised its quality above that of the Classical period are its scope and method. The later historians were not satisfied with merely recording the names of scholars of the generations gone by, though this was still an important part of their work, but gave a connected narrative of events which transpired in the entire Jewish history, and as a rule, included also a sketch of universal history, thus widening the scope of their work to include both the Jews and other nations.

As to method, we note a great improvement in the method of treatment of the historical material. With the exception of a few early chronicles which still give the events in a confused manner, the other books follow a systematic division into periods and epochs and treat their material in orderly sequence. Some even have chronological tables and indexes of names and events appended at the end of their books.

This endeavor to introduce a scientific method in the arrangement and the ordering of the historical material did not, however, raise the level of the works to that of real histories. The critical spirit is still absent and no serious attempt is made to sift the facts and ascertain the truths. Credulity is prevalent, legends are recorded as facts and folk tales are taken at their face value. As a result, the narratives contained in all these books constitute a mixture of fact and fancy, and great caution is to be exercised by the modern historian who uses these books as sources, in order to separate the kernel of fact from the chaff of imagination. Yet there is at least one work which forms an exception to the rule and which is permeated by a real scientific spirit. This is the *Meor Emayim* of Azarya de Rossi. In it, the author blazed the way for a new evaluation of Jewish history and laid the foundation of historical criticism.

The desire to record the past deeds of their nation which animated the Jewish scholars of the age did not always express itself in complete delineation of the story of the Jews but often found satisfaction in merely recording the history of the Jews of one country, or even in narrating the events of a certain persecution or any other event which had taken place in a single community. Others found it useful to record the histories of the towns in which they were born or resided. As a result, we have a considerable number of sectional histories which reflect bits of Jewish life and serve as sources of information for the historian.

An important feature of this entire literature is the excessive emphasis it lays upon the life stories of the great men and their literary activity. As in the histories of the Classical period so in the histories of this age, the great man and his work forms the center of the narrative around which all other facts and data cluster. Next to the great man, suffering and persecution occupy the important place, and form another axis around which Jewish history revolves. Whether such methods are satisfactory is of course greatly to be disputed, but under the peculiar circumstances of Jewish life, the result could hardly have been different. As was pointed out by us, (Vol. I, p. 420) a people in exile, living in a scattered state and lacking a united national life can not produce any real history. Learning and suffering seem to be the unifying threads of its variegated life, and hence they must form the background of a great part of its history.

The works which we subsume under the title geography are, in this period, as in the preceding one, primarily tales of travel. Of geographical books proper, there are only a few, while the tales of travel, on the other hand, are numerous. Most of them, however, consist of descriptions of journeys to the Holy Land. Palestine was always a subject of great interest to the Jews, and books describing its nature and character, the life of the people and the location of the graves of the great men and saints were read with avidity. But these tales of travel or itineraries contain really more than descriptions of Palestine, for they tell also of the countries adjacent to it and the places through which the traveller passed. In addition they lay special emphasis upon the description of Jewish life in these localities, and thus serve as sources not only of geography but of history as well.

Next to Palestine, the tales of travel to distant lands, such as India, Arabia or parts of the newly discovered world occupy an important place. These tales had a peculiar interest for the people, for besides satisfying the ordinary curiosity for miraculous events occurring in far distant places, they invariably told wonderful tales about the ten tribes, the existence of which was placed in different parts of the world. These stories inflamed the imagination of the people and raised their hope for redemption, a hope which was prevalent during the sixteenth century, the age of Messianic movements.

The itineraries are, on the whole, well written and give the events of the journey, as well as the description of places in a connected manner. Many of them give a wealth of details, display keen observation and form pleasant reading.

A valuable addition to this type of literature are several books of autobiography and personal memoirs. Biography, as such, was really unknown in Mediaeval literature. The works passed as biography were in reality collections of legends and tales clustering around the lives of the saints, and Jewish literature is no exception in this matter. In the period under discussion, there began to appear a number of stories full of miracles and legends about the lives of martyrs and saints. These stories destined primarily for the masses were written mostly in the vernacular of the German-Polish Jews, the Judaeo-German, and will be noted in the proper place. But of a real biography, we have no record. On the other hand, we have several autobiographies written during this period both by scholars and laymen. They are of exceptional interest, for they reveal to us not only the daily life of the writers but also the life of the people at large in their intimate relations. They constitute a novel and most welcome feature in Mediaeval Jewish literature.

A. History

128. CHRONICLES

Of the group of works which due to their form are designated Chronicles, there are two kinds, literary and general. The first deals almost entirely with the succession of the bearers of tradition and their works, while the second has a wider scope and includes also general events. Most of these chronicles, however, were not written originally as separate works but as parts of larger works on Agada or Halakah.

i. The earliest of such chronicles belonging to the first class is the historical introduction affixed by Menahem ha-Meiri of Perpignan to his commentary on the treatise *Aboth,* named *Beth ha-Behira* (The Chosen House), composed in 1287. The work was already described above (p. 186) and we may add here that he carries the lists of scholars and their works to his own time and thus lengthens the chain of the bearers of tradition of Jewish law and learning. An important feature of the work is, that the author hailing from the Provence was thoroughly acquainted with the accomplishments of the Franco-German scholars and he, therefore, gives extensive data about their personalities and activity.

ii. A similar introduction to an Halakic work by the name of *Kiryath Sepher* was written by David de Estella of Spain in the year 1320. It contains little new except that it adds one more short link to the long chain of the history of tradition.

iii. A more valuable introduction is the one written by Isaac de Lattes to his work *Shaare Zion* (The Portals of Zion), composed in the year 1372. The work, as a whole, deals with various subjects relating to the history and the order of the oral law, and the introduction is, therefore, more embracing and exact. De Lattes had used the chronicles of Menahem ha-Meiri as his source, but is detailed and pays greater attention to the literary history of Provence. His data on this particular phase are especially valuable, for he hardly omits the name of any scholar of Provence. His chronicle served as a source to later historians and bibliographers in their treatment of the development of Jewish learning in that country.

iv. The last of such literary chronicles is the introduction of Menahem ben Zerah to his code entitled *Zedah la-Dereḳ* (Provision for the Road) written in 1374. It is primarily a digest of the previous chronicles but contains a few data of his personal biography which constitute its chief value.

There are three chronicles which belong to the second class, inasmuch as they deal both with general events and with biographical and literary data.

i. The first of these is the Chronicle of Joseph ben Tzadik of Arvalo, Spain, which is incorporated as a chapter in his book on the ritual, *Zeker Tzadik* (The Remembrance of the Righteous). The Chronicle begins with the creation and ends with the year 1487. Taking into consideration that it covers such a long period of time, it is exceptionally brief in the recording of events. The author divides the entire history into six divisions, namely according to the millenia of the Jewish era and notes in each only the outstanding men and events. He is more detailed in the period from the close of the Talmud up to his own time. Here he gives not only events that occurred in the Jewish world but also some of the important ones that took place in the life of other nations. The critical spirit is entirely absent and the Chronicle contains anachronisms and strange reports and even contradictions. In one place, the author asserts that Rome was founded by Romulus in the time of David, and that the former, fearing the latter, signed a peace treaty with him. Later he assigns the founding of Rome to the time of Hezekiah about 725 B. C. E., a date which is very close to the one set by the Romans themselves. He decides, though being aware of the correct date of the birth of Jesus, that, after all, the Talmudic tradition is the right one and that Jesus lived in the time of Alexander Januaus, and was born about 87 B. C. E. Besides there are a number of errors in the dates of important events.

The *Book of Tradition* by Abraham Ibn Daud (Vol. I, Sect. 193) undoubtedly served as the main source of this chronicle up to the year 1161, but for the period following that date he employed various records. The chronicle of Joseph ben Tzadik was in turn used as a source by later writers who unfortunately copied its errors along with the true facts. Its chief value lies in the full data it supplies regarding the lives and activities of the Spanish scholars during the fourteenth and fifteenth centuries.

ii. A more extensive chronicle, though not as complete since it covers a much shorter period, is *The Book of Tradition* (Sepher ha-Kabbala) by Abraham ben Solomon of Torrutiel in Spain. The book is intended as a supplement to Abraham Ibn Daud's *Book of Tradition* written in 1161, and covers the period from that date to the year 1510.

The Chronicle is divided into three portals (Shearim) which are devoted to various subjects. The first portal deals with the lives of such scholars, who though they preceded Ibn Daud, were not recorded by him. These are mostly Franco-German savants of whom the former had no knowledge. The second chronicles the activities of the great men in Israel from the middle of the twelfth century to the death of Rabbi Isaac Campanton (Sect. 72), i. e. to the year 1463. The final section embraces a number of subjects, namely a sketch of the history of the Spanish kings from 1250 to Ferdinand and Isabella, a brief record of events in Spanish-Portuguese Jewry during that period with special reference to the persecutions, and finally a description of the expulsions both from Spain and Portugal and the subsequent settlement of the exiles in Morocco.

In the first two sections, the author evidently used the chronicle of Joseph ben Tzadik as a source, for in certain places he seems to have copied from it verbatim. He does, however, add many more details and is especially inclined to embellish the lives of his favorites with legends. He also gives a fuller list of the literary productions of the great men and is even careful to give the date of the composition of important works. In the third section, he is entirely independent of Joseph's Chronicle and gives a fair account of the happenings during the period. His narrative is especially valuable for the description of the expulsions and the resulting events. He speaks of these matters as an eye witness and as one who himself lived through these tragedies. Of great importance is his brief but strong invective against the upper strata in Spanish Jewry during the years immediately preceding the expulsion. He claims that the great majority of the higher classes had forsaken the ways of their fathers and in their pride had imitated the conduct of the gentiles. He considers the expulsion almost a just punishment for their sins, for he says, "That only the poor clung to the oral law." There is undoubtedly great exaggeration in this statement. On the other hand, there is much truth in his other assertion that only a few of the leading Jews of Spain went into exile and that the majority of them chose rather to embrace Christianity than to take the wanderer's staff. He is especially bitter against Abraham Senior, the chief rabbi of the Jewish communities in Castile and the colleague of Isaac Abrabanel in the management of the royal finances. Abraham condemns him as one who influenced many others to follow his example and pronounces curses upon the entire family.

iii. The third chronicle is the *Dibrē Yoseph* (The Words of Joseph) by Joseph ben Isaac Sambari of Egypt, written in 1673. The work is primarily devoted to the history of the Jews in the Eastern countries, especially to that of Egypt, but he incorporates also reports on other famous Jewish scholars, such as Abraham ben David, the antagonist of Maimonides, Nahmanides, Rashi and others. There is an absolute lack of method and arrangement in the book, inasmuch as the author speaks of Nahmanides before Ibn Ezra, and commits other similar errors which testify to a complete lack of arrangement. It seems that the part of the chronicle which deals with men who lived and events that occurred in countries other than those of the East, represents merely a collection of stray notes which were for some reason incorporated in the book. The part devoted to the Jews of the East, if disentangled from the extraneous matter, seems to have some definite plan in its narrative. It begins with an account of the origin of the office of the *Nagid,* i. e. head of the Jewish communities in Egypt. We are told that it was instituted in the year 985 at the request of the wife of the Sultan, the daughter of the Caliph of Bagdad, who wanted to have an office established in Egypt similar to that of the exilarchate in Babylonia. This is followed up with the story of the life of Maimonides, interspersed with descriptions of the Jewish institutions in Egypt, especially of the synagogues in Cairo and also narratives of certain events in the life of the Egyptian Jews. He then narrates the subsequent history of the Jews of that country to the end of the fifteenth century, the time of the expulsion from Spain. From there on, the narrative includes the events that took place in the life of the Jews of the entire East, with special reference to the settlement of the Spanish exiles in the various cities of the Turkish empire. The work closes with a number of lists of the scholars and rabbis who resided in the cities of Alexandria, Cairo, Salonika, Constantinople, Aleppo and Damascus.

Sambari's narrative is extensive and detailed. He loves to embellish the lives of his heroes with legends and curious anecdotes, and he even quotes excerpts from their works.

Of especial value for the history of the Jews in Egypt in particular and that of the East in general are his detailed narratives about certain persecutions which occurred in the former country, and the full lists of scholars who lived in the above-mentioned cities or settled there after the expulsion. Sambari must have used the chronicle of Abraham ben Solomon to a certain extent, but he evidently had access to other sources, for some of the biographical details he supplies about the lives of Isaac ben Shesheth of North Africa and Abraham Zacuto are not found in other works known to us. Our author is a Kabbalist and he repeats the story often told by mystic writers that Maimonides in his old age turned Kabbalist. He even claims to have seen a small mystic treatise of Maimonides which he sent to his famous pupil, Joseph Ibn Aknin (Vol. I, Sect. 160). It is to be regretted that Sambari's chronicle came down to us in a mutilated state for many pages are missing and many passages are incomplete. But even in its present state and with its confused arrangement, it is of importance for the Jewish historian as a source which contains many data not found in any other place.

129. THE BOOK OF GENEALOGIES OF ZACUTO

The first of a series of works on Jewish history composed during the sixteenth century is the *Sepher Yuhasin* (The Book of Genealogies) by the famous astronomer Abraham Zacuto (Sect. 100) written in 1505. The primary purpose which Zacuto had in mind when writing his book was to present a clear and amplified account of the history of Jewish tradition and its bearers. He was not satisfied with the outline of the succession of the Tannaim and Amoraim given by Maimonides in the introduction to his code, for he claimed that it was incomplete and contained errors and omissions. Nor was he pleased with the *Book of Tradition* by Abraham Ibn Daud on account of its brevity. He wanted to delineate the characters of each of the Tannaim and Amoraim as fully as possible and supply all data found in the extensive Talmudic literature about their lives and activities. He believed that a work of this nature has not only historical but also religious value, inasmuch as in the decision of a point of law, the knowledge of the time of those who pronounced the opinions is of great importance. According to the rules of legal decision, the opinion of a disciple, if it opposes that of his master is invalid, but again this rule operates only until a certain period. From that period on, the rule is reversed and the opinions of the later scholars are held more valid.

It was, therefore, Zacuto's main interest to elucidate the period of Jewish history beginning with the Great Assembly and ending with the close of the Talmud. But as he felt that such a work would not be complete, he carried the history down to his own days and included also the record of all important events in Jewish life. He further appended a sketch of universal history from creation to the end of the fifteenth century.

The *Book of Genealogies* is arranged according to a well defined plan, and the material is treated in accordance with a definite method. It is divided into five sections called, *Maamarim,* the first two of which are devoted to the history of tradition, the other two to the history of men and events from the close of the Talmud to his time, and the last to universal history.

In conformity with the purpose of the work, Zacuto devotes his main attention to the first two sections, and consequently they occupy about three-quarters of the book. The first section opens with a brief sketch of Jewish history from Adam to Simon the Just, the last of the Great Assembly. From then on, Zacuto concentrates on the bearers of tradition and their activities, mentioning only briefly the political events. He narrates the lives and deeds of the leading scholars of seven generations before the destruction of the Temple and of the four generations of Tannaim after that, to the close of the Mishnah. The author is very scrupulous in his work, for he determines painstakingly the exact time of each scholar, the teachers who instructed him and the number of his disciples, as well as his relations to his colleagues, his methods of teaching and all other appertaining data. He quotes extensively from Talmudic literature to substantiate his views, and in the discussion throws light upon many points in connection with that literature. In order to complete the history of the Tannaitic period, he finally treats again of all the Tannaim in a brief alphabetical series of articles which include all names omitted in the general narrative.

The second section is devoted to the history of the Amoraim. The method of treatment is the alphabetical one, and here as in the first section, the author displays the same scrupulousness and care in dealing with his subject. The period presents great difficulties, for the number of Amoraim is very large and their sayings are scattered in the many volumes of the two Talmuds, the Babylonian and the Palestinian. But the zeal and great knowledge of the author overcame the difficulties, and he produced a clear account of the succession of the Amoraim as well as of their sayings and views.

The third section covers the generations of the Saburaim, Gaonim, and the early history of the Jews in Spain. Zacuto follows, according to his own statement, the *Book of Tradition* of Abraham Ibn Daud and his account of the period is very brief, as he adds little that is new. The fourth section treats of the following period of Jewish history in a very succinct manner. He is careful to note all the great men and their important works but gives very few data about their lives. Of the events that occurred during the period only those that took place in Spain are recorded. He even fails to mention the Crusades and the Black Death persecution in the year 1348.

This section, however, contains a valuable historical document. This is the letter of Isaac of Acco, spoken of above (Sect. 113), where that Kabbalist tells of the efforts he made to ascertain whether the *Zohar* was really an authentic ancient mystic book composed by the Tanna, Simon ben Yohai or was written by Moses de Leon himself.

The fifth section contains, as said, a sketch of universal history. The entire period of history is divided by Zacuto into ten epochs. The first five epochs follow Jewish land marks, the first from Adam to Noah, the second from Noah to Abraham, the third, fourth and fifth from Abraham to David, from him to the exile and from that to Alexander. The other five are determined by important general events, such as the establishment of the Ptolemaic dynasty, the reigns of Constantine and Heraclius in the fourth and seventh centuries respectively, the reestablishment of the Roman Empire by Charlemagne in 800 C. E. and other events. In this sketch, he notes of course all important events in universal history, but he includes also a large part of the political history of the Jews during the Second Commonwealth, such as the story of the rise of the house of Joseph ben Tobiah, the deeds of the Hasmonean kings and those of Herod and similar events. He even gives, following Josephus, a description of the Sadducees and the Essenes, their opinions, and of the latter also their conduct of life.

On the whole, Zacuto displays a fair knowledge of universal history. He chronicles not only the deeds of the kings but also mentions the names of the popes and the order of their succession. He is well acquainted with the history of the Byzantine Empire and the affairs of the Mohammedan world. He is quite detailed about the latter and records extensively the deeds of the Tartar empire and especially of the Ottoman Turks. There is little system in the arrangement of the material of that section, inasmuch as the affairs of the various nations are mixed together. The use of three different eras, namely, that of creation for the Jews, the Christian for the Western and the Hegira for the Mohammedan nations adds to the confusion.

Zacuto must have used different sources for his books. Besides the *Book of Tradition* of Ibn Daud, he also employed the historical chapter in the *Yesod Olam* by Isaac Israeli and other unknown Jewish Chronicles. He frequently quotes the history of Josephus which he read in Latin, and he calls it either the long history of Joseph ben Gorion, or the history written by him for the gentiles. Like all Mediaeval scholars, he thought that the *Jossippon* (Vol. I, Sect. 188) had been written by Josephus himself in Hebrew as a kind of abbreviation of his longer history in Greek, and though he knew him to be the son of Matthias, he still calls him ben Gorion, for like others he thought that this was his surname. For the latter period, he undoubtedly employed many Latin chronicles and most likely several Eastern ones which dwelt especially upon Mohammedan history.

Zacuto displays much knowledge in his book but little critical acumen. He is very conservative in his views and hesitates to accept any statement which may differ slightly from a view expressed in the Talmud. Like earlier chroniclers, he fixes the birth of Jesus to have taken place in the time of Alexander Januaus to correspond with a Talmudic statement which makes him a disciple of Joshua ben Perahya, though he is quite aware of the common view. Again, in spite of the fact that he himself incorporated Isaac of Acco's letter about the *Zohar* he speaks of its miraculous revelation as a certain fact, though he concedes that it was not composed by Simon ben Yohai himself but by his disciples about sixty years after his death.

The *Yuhasin* was first printed in 1566 by Samuel Shulam who edited it and added many valuable documents, among them, the text of the letter of Sherira Gaon (Vol. I, Sect. 190), a treatise on the order of the academies in Babylonia, a translation of Josephus' *Contra Apionem,* and many notes by the editor. It was later reprinted many times but with omissions of the treatise of Josephus and the letter of Isaac of Acco. On the other hand, the later editions contain additional notes by Moses Isserlis (Sect. 60) and Jacob Emden. The best edition is that of Filipowsky issued in 1857 from an Oxford manuscript.

The *Book of Genealogies* is a valuable contribution to Jewish historical literature and serves as an important source for our knowledge of the past, especially of the Talmudic period.

130. HISTORIES OF PERSECUTIONS

Suffering forms the very stuff of which Mediaeval Jewish history is made. It is not to be wondered at then that some of the historians directed special attention to this important phase of the past life of their people and undertook to chronicle all the principal persecutions during the ages and describe their origin and results. Of such histories, we have two, the *Shebet Yehudah* (The Scourge of Judah) and the *Emeḳ ha-Baḳah* (The Vale of Tears). They, of course, contain common material but only to an extent, inasmuch as each of these comprises records of a number of persecutions not found in the other.

The *Shebet Yehudah* is a composite work participated in by three authors of three generations. The nucleus of the book was provided by the notes of Judah Ibn Verga of Seville, Spain, who lived around 1480. He was a mathematician and astronomer and the representative of the Jews at court. The notes were found at the end of one of his books. Solomon Ibn Verga of the same family and a relative of Judah who was an eye witness of the expulsion from Spain and later settled in Turkey, copied these notes, added his own material and named the book *Shebet Yehudah* in honor of the first compiler. Solomon's son, Joseph Ibn Verga, added some more material to the work and brought it down to his own times. Joseph lived in Adrianople and was the author of a book on the methodology of the Talmud named *Shearith Yoseph* (The Remnant of Joseph), which was published in 1554. It seems that the *Shebet Yehudah* was also printed in the same year. The real author of the book, however, is undoubtedly Solomon Ibn Verga. It is he who composed the greater part of the work.

The *Shebet Yehudah* can be called a history only by courtesy for the form of the book hardly entitles it to that name. There is no definite plan in the arrangement of the material, nor do the authors follow any systematic division into periods or epochs in the narration of events. On the whole, it is a confused list of persecutions that took place at various times, for no chronological sequence is observed and events which had taken place in earlier times are preceded by those which occurred later. The only thread which supplies some kind of unity to the book is the numeration of the various persecutions, namely that each event is given a number.

The author pays special attention to the persecutions that took place in Spain and Portugal describing them in great detail, while the persecutions of the Jews in other countries are referred to very briefly, and some of the most important ones, such as those of the Crusades, are entirely omitted. In the record of the persecutions earlier than the twelfth century there is complete confusion, and some of the anachronisms arouse our curiosity. Thus, as the first persecution, the author records an attack by Augustus against the Jews in Palestine after his victory over Anthony, as a result of which tens of thousands of the people were killed and the city of Jerusalem destroyed. He tells us that he copied the story from a work entitled the History of the Aragonian Kings, but that he confused the name of Augustus with that of Pompey or Titus is quite evident.

Again, he names as the second persecution one that took place in the time of Joshua ben Sira, and tells us that about thirty thousand Jews forsook the faith of their fathers. He gives no date for this event and frankly confesses that he does not know its cause, though he knows that Ben Sira is the author of Ecclesiasticus. We are entirely unable to trace the origin of this strange record, and the only thing that we may venture to assert is that he refers to the persecutions of Antiochus Epiphanes which occurred about thirty-five years after the death of Ben Sira. But why the author should have omitted to mention the name of the Maccabees and the great struggle for liberation, especially since Joseph, the last author, was well versed in Latin and read Josephus' history, we are at a loss to understand. There is considerable carefulness exercised in the recording of events from the twelfth century on, though many anachronisms occur even in that part.

Yet the book has great value, for inasmuch as the persecutions that befell the Jews in Spain and Portugal are told in detail, many historical data are thus supplied. A special feature of the book is the inclusion of numerous debates between Jews and Christians that took place in the presence of kings or popes. A good number of these debates are of an imaginary character, for in some of them the interlocutors are kings and Christian scholars who defend the Jews against their calumniators. They are, of course, of an apologetic character and are intended to bring out the good qualities of the people, but they also contain reproaches against the mode of life of the upper classes of Spanish Jewry. These debates or dialogues are written in a brilliant style and contain many witty remarks and anecdotes. It is to be noted that one of these dialogues contains an early version of Lessing's story of the three rings, told in his famous drama, Nathan the Wise. The story is put in the mouth of the Jewish savant Isaac Shangu who was asked by Don Pedro the III, King of Aragon (1275-1285) to state which religion is the better of the two, Judaism or Christianity. In his reply, Isaac relates the following story: A neighbor of his who had departed for distant lands, gave him two precious stones to keep in trust for his children. When they came to him and asked to be told the difference between the stones as well as their respective values, his answer was that their father is the only one who could give the required information as he is the owner and the expert jeweler. Likewise, concluded the savant, Jacob and Esau were brothers, and their Father, God, gave them each a jewel, a religion. Who but He can tell the difference between the two and appraise their distinctive values? Whether Lessing used the *Shebet Yehudah* as the source of his parable is not known.

The work records also several debates that actually took place, the most important of which is the one at Tortosa, where a number of Jewish scholars, among whom was Joseph Albo, disputed with the apostate Geronimo de Santa Fē or Joshua Lorki. The report of this debate forms a valuable historical document as it is full and detailed.

The editor omitted to tell much about the expulsion from Spain and refers the reader to Isaac Abrabanel's introduction to his commentary on the Book of Kings, where a description of the events is given. He does, however, describe the events following the expulsion. Very characteristic and worthy of record are the reasons given by Solomon Ibn Verga for the great suffering undergone by the Spanish Jews. The first, is the one stated by Amos, that because God chose the Jewish people for their moral excellence, he chastises them severely for any infraction of law in their conduct. (Amos III, 2.) He then gives other reasons, namely the separation of the Jews from the Christians in matters of food and drink, the hatred of the latter for the former because of the alleged crucifixion of Jesus, and finally the actual transgressions committed by the Jews of that period, such as the intercourse of the younger Jews with Christian women, the habit of taking false oaths, and above all the sin of pride by which the Jews were distinguished. These offences show us the moral laxity of the Jews in Spain before the expulsion.

The book contains also a number of extraneous matters, such as a description of the Temple of Jerusalem said to have been sent by a certain Christian scholar to Alphonso X, king of Castile. The description is ascribed to Titus himself but was most likely modelled after Josephus' description of the building and other sources. There are also included in the book the text of Josephus' speeches to the Jews in Jerusalem at the time of the siege and other matters, even a dialogue between a king and a Christian scholar concerning certain problems in physics.

The *Shebet Yehudah* is written in excellent Hebrew style and is replete with dramatic moments and emotional outbursts. Taking in consideration these qualities together with the large number of true historical data and documents it supplies, we can safely say that its virtues overbalance the faults, and on the whole, the *Shebet Yehudah* is a valuable contribution to Jewish literature.

The *Emek ha-Baka* (The Vale of Tears) was written by Joseph ha-Cohen (1496-1580). He was born at Avignon, South of France, but at the age of five, his family removed to Genoa, Italy, where he spent the rest of his life. Joseph was greatly interested in history and in the year 1554, he published his first book, a history of the Kings of France and the House of Ottoman. When he later came across the book, *Consolations for the Sorrows of Israel,* written in Portuguese by the poet Samuel Usque, where the various persecutions are forcibly described, he determined to write a similar one in Hebrew and the *Emek ha-Baka* is the result.

The work judged as a historical record of Israel's suffering is on a much higher plane than the *Shebet Yehudah.* It is sober, earnest and systematic. The author begins with the destruction of the Temple and the revolt of Bar Kokhba and records in comparatively fair sequence all persecutions down to the year 1575.

His record of events up to the middle of the eleventh century is brief and contains a number of errors. He places the revolt of Bar Kokhba in the reign of Domitian though he is aware that Bethar fell in the time of Hadrian, but he makes the leader of the second revolt Romulus, the son of Kusiba. It is evident that Joseph confuses the events here, but we can not ascertain the source whence he derived his information. He is also quite hazy about the date of certain early German and Italian scholars and poets and antedates them considerably. From the middle of the eleventh century on his reports are fairly accurate. He gives full and detailed descriptions of the persecutions of the first and second Crusades which he derived from the Chronicles of Eliezer ben Nathan (Vol. I, Sect. 192) and which he supplemented by information taken from the history of the German kings. His record of the subsequent events up to the year 1505, though brief, is complete as it embraces all important persecutions in France, Germany and Austria as well as those in Spain. From the year 1505, he devotes his main attention to Italy. Here he is extensive and detailed, and his narrative is very valuable for the history of the Jews of Italy in that century. The book was originally brought down to the year 1564, but he later added some more data bringing it up to 1575. In this added narrative, we find also the story of the rise of Joseph Nasi in Turkey and of his attempt to rebuild the city of Tiberias in Palestine. The *Emek ha-Baka* is found in two versions, the one of 1564, and the other of 1575. The first version was later edited by a subsequent anonymous Italian scholar and supplied by him with additional notes carrying the history to the year 1605. The style of Joseph is Biblical and is distinguished by its lucidity and brevity. From time to time, though, his sympathy for his people's suffering expresses itself in passages of deep pathos which add a poetic touch to the otherwise prosaic narrative.

131. GENERAL HISTORIES

There are two books written in the sixteenth century which deal primarily not with Jewish but with general history and only touch indirectly upon events in Jewish life. The first of these is the *Seder Eliyahu* (The Order of Elijah) written by Elijah Kapsali of the Island of Crete in the year 1523. We know little about the life of Elijah except that in his youth he studied at Padua under the famous rabbis, Judah Mintz and Meir Katzenelenbogen (Sect. 68), and that later he became rabbi in the city of Candia in Crete. The history was written by him, during the time when the pestilence raged on the island, for the purpose of diverting his mind from dwelling upon morbid thoughts arising from the constant fear of death.

The *Seder Eliyahu* is a history of the rise and development of the empire of the Ottoman Turks, and it is quite extensive as it is divided into four books comprising one hundred and sixty-six chapters. It contains also, as said, numerous reports about events in the history of the Jews of Spain, Turkey and the Island of Rhodes. The data on episodes of Jewish history are valuable as some of them are not found in any other source. Of special importance are the narratives concerning the history of Spanish Jewry and particularly those regarding the period of the expulsion. Kapsali gathered his material from exiles passing through Crete who were eye witnesses to the events and it possesses the quality of a first hand source.

The book is still in manuscript and only a small portion of it was printed in 1869 by Dr. Moses Lattes under the title Selections (Likuttim) from the *Seder Eliyahu*. The style of the book is florid and the author often breaks forth in rhymed prose.

The second book is the above-mentioned History of the Kings of France and of the Ottoman Turks (Dibrē ha-Yamim le-Malkē beth Ottoman ha-Tuger) by Joseph ha-Cohen. It is a work of great importance and testifies to the skill of its author and to his wide knowledge of the historical literature of his time. In spite of its name which limits it to the history of France and Turkey the book is really an epitome of universal history for a period of over a thousand years, namely from the foundation of the Frankish kingdom by Clovis at the end of the fifth century to 1550. France and Turkey are used by Joseph as synonyms for the Christian and Mohammedan worlds, and he really chronicles all the important events which transpired in both these worlds during that period.

The book is divided into two parts, the first of which carries the story down to 1520, and the second is devoted to the history of thirty years from 1520 to 1550 and primarily to the wars in Italy between Francis the First of France and the Emperor Charles the Fifth. In the narration of events of this period, Joseph is exceptionally detailed and hence the large space devoted to a comparatively short time. However, he is not sketchy even in the first part of the work, but on the contrary records almost every event of importance that took place during the long period. He pays, of course, special attention to the two nations he singled out, but the others are not neglected. Very detailed and painstaking is the narrative of the first three Crusades and the resulting occupation of Palestine by the Christians. The struggles between the Crusaders and the Mohammedans for the retention of that country, lasting close to a century, are described by our author almost minutely without omitting even a single battle. He undoubtedly used for this epoch first hand sources written by those who participated in the events.

Joseph does not fail to mention in his general history the important incidents in the life of his own people. Of these, his reports of the deeds of David Reubeni (Sect. 138) and Solomon Molcho in the first half of the sixteenth century is of great value. Joseph did not place great faith in the story of David that he was an ambassador sent by his brother, ruler of a Jewish kingdom in Arabia, and calls him an adventurer. He was more impressed though by Solomon and incorporates in the history a long letter of his to the Jewish leaders and scholars. This letter contains some biographical data and reveals to us the psychosis of the strange but enchanting personality of the young Marrano who turned mystic and apostle of the Messiah. He tells there of his strange visions and of their interpretation by the voice of an angel, in good apocalyptic style. There is also evidence in that letter that while Molcho never announced publicly that he is the Messiah, he entertained the idea secretly. He tells in that letter of his living for thirty days among the poor and sick of Rome. This according to the Talmud[1] is supposed to be an act performed by the Messiah himself.

The style of the history is like that of the *Emek ha-Baka,* Biblical but not ornate and is well suited to that of an historical narrative. His chronology is on the whole correct and contains few errors.

132. THE HISTORIES OF IBN YAHYA AND GANZ

Towards the end of the sixteenth century there appeared two books on Jewish and to a certain extent on general history, one the *Shalsheleth ha-Kabbala* (The Chain of Tradition) by Gedalya Ibn Yahya (1522-1588) and the other the *Zemah David* (The Sprout of David) by David Ganz (1541-1613).

Gedalya was a descendant of the famous Yahya family of Portugal. His grandfather David left Lisbon during the exile in 1497 and settled at Ravenna, Northern Italy. His father Joseph was a scholar of note and wrote several works, among them a commentary on the Hagiographa. He gave his son a good Jewish and secular education which enabled him to amass extensive knowledge in many fields. Gedalya was a rich man and possessed a good library. On account of certain circumstances, he was compelled to wander about a great part of his life. In 1575, he left Italy and went to Turkey and later settled in Alexandria, Egypt, where he spent the rest of his life. Yet, his wanderings did not prevent him from writing many works. According to his own testimony, he composed twenty books, but the *Shalsheleth ha-Kabbala* is the most popular. He wrote this book for his eldest son and completed it on the day when the latter became thirteen years old.

In the preface, Gedalya points out to his son the many benefits which may be derived from a study of Jewish history. Among them are the increase of the desire for knowledge, the strengthening of the love of God, and the belief in His special providence over the destinies of the Jewish people. A study of the list of sages, scholars and martyrs, as well as of the many vicissitudes of fortune that befell Israel during the long exile, he asserts, would stimulate the student to endeavor to emulate the great men of his people, both in acquisition of knowledge and in the love of God and inculcate in him a sense of trust in the future of his nation.

[1] B. Sanhedrin, 98a.

The author further informs his son that he had drawn upon many sources in the writing of this book, both Jewish and non-Jewish, and also tells him of the relation of the Christian and Mohammedan eras to those of creation and the destruction of the Temple. He continues to inform him of the method he employs in dividing history according to generations and fixing the length of each generation at fifty years, and finally of the nature of the book and its divisions.

The book is divided into three parts. The first deals with the history of tradition from early days to his own day, the second contains a number of discourses on a variety of subjects, namely on the spheres and their movements, on embryology, on the soul, on coins and measures, on hell and paradise, on the division of humanity into seventy nations, on forms of idolatry, on the development of arts and crafts and on the origin of language and its ramifications. The third part comprises a collection of historical essays on important events during the Second Commonwealth, on the Roman emperors, on events in general Mediaeval history, and finally a list of persecutions of the Jews during the ages.

The book as we can see from its contents is an encyclopaedia in miniature, as it intends to impart information on many subjects. To do so, the author had to have a vast knowledge in many branches of learning, and in fact, Gadalya was a very learned man. He mastered besides Hebrew, Latin and Italian and was well read in historical and geographical literature and had access to many sources. He read Eusebius and St. Augustine and many other Christian Chronicles and quotes frequently from their works. Yet, with all his knowledge, Gedalya was a very poor historian, as he absolutely lacked the faculty of discerning between fact and fable. His book is, therefore, a hopeless confusion of historical data and a multitude of legends, stories and a recital of miracles and wonderful events.

The first part of the work where the chain of the bearers of tradition is recorded is the most important of the entire work. This part contains hardly any record of events but is devoted entirely to the lives of the leading scholars who succeeded one another. There is one great advantage in this work, for up to the twelfth century the author lays stress upon the great personalities in each generation and it therefore assumes the character of a biographical history. However, because of lack of critical ability and on account of his love for the great men of his people, Gedalya marshalls all popular legends and tales about the lives of the sages of history. Distance and time seem to form no obstacles to him. Thus, according to our author, Abraham Ibn Ezra was the son-in-law of Judah ha-Levi, and he tells the story of the alliance, which has a romantic touch. Judah ha-Levi, says Ibn Yahya, was a very rich man and had only one daughter. His wife frequently entreated him to search for a suitable candidate for the hand of the daughter. These entreaties angered the poet, and one day he swore to give his child in marriage to the first Jew he meets in the morning. It so happened that Ibn Ezra in his wanderings, dressed as a poor man, came to the house in the early hours of the morning. The poet was not at home, and his wife remembering her husband's oath was frightened at the sight of her future son-in-law and hastened to acquaint her husband with the matter. Judah began to investigate the capabilities of the stranger, but Ibn Ezra dissimulated as an illiterate. Ha-Levi then bowed to the inevitable and accepted the unknown man as the candidate and began to instruct him in various studies. One night Judah found great difficulty in the construction of a certain poem as he could not find the proper line which should begin with the letter *Resh,* and he sat late in his study. When he finally left the poem unfinished, the stranger asked Judah's wife to show him the manuscript. She reluctantly consented and the stranger made some correction in the poem and inserted the missing line. When Judah saw the corrections and insertions, he immediately divined the identity of the stranger and the anxiety of the aged couple turned to joy.

Again, Gedalya makes Rashi wander for seven years and meet Maimonides in Egypt. He is greatly confused with the fact that there were two Isaac Iraelis, the earlier, the physician and philosopher, and the latter the astronomer and mathematician, the disciple of Asher ben Yehiel (Sect. 99), and he makes the first the grandfather of the second, bringing him down from the tenth to the thirteenth century. These are only a few of the errors he commits. What is interesting to note is that even when his sources contain the right data he, for spurious reasons, confuses them. He saw the record of the *Yuhasin* that Rashi died in 1105, yet he decides that he lived a generation later in the time of Maimonides. Likewise he read somewhere else that Rashi lived only sixty-four years which is only one year short of the correct number, yet he follows the error of the *Yuhasin* and asserts that he lived seventy-five years.

On account of these anachronisms and the many legends and fables incorporated in the work, the *Shalsheleth* was severely condemned by later historians, and Joseph Solomon del-Medigo named it *Shalsheleth ha-Shekorim* (The Chain of Falsehoods), a name which was frequently repeated by modern scholars. Still the epithet is not justified, for not only does Gedalya's work contain many true historical data but the very legends and at times even the anachronisms have peculiar charm. The legends about the great men bring out the personalities in full relief and show the impression they made upon the mind of the people. The people at large seemed to have appreciated the work of Gedalya more than the historians, for of all the chronicles and histories, the *Shalsheleth* was the one most read for several centuries. They were attracted to it by these very legends and stories and also by the mass of information it gives on various subjects.

Gedalya likes to introduce variety in his historical narrative and incorporates many extraneous matters in his record. Thus, when he speaks of Shealtiel, the father of Zerubabel, he tells the mode of election of the princes of the exile in Babylonia, and when talking of Solomon he gives a graphic description of the Temple. He also incorporates certain documents in the narrative, such as the letter of Aristeas (Vol. I, Sect. 65) concerning the translation of the Bible into Greek, and other records. Being a Kabbalist of the school of Luria and believing in the theory of the impregnation (Ibbur) of souls (Sect. 110) he notes the souls of the earlier sages and scholars which joined those of the savants of the later generations.

These traits in the work caught the fancy of the students of the Talmud and made the book a book of the people. It is to the merit of Gedalya Ibn Yahya that he popularized the knowledge of Jewish history among the Jews, even though the information he offered was mixed to a certain degree with errors in dates and other details.

ii. David Ganz, the author of the *Zemah David,* the second history, was, as we have seen above (Sect. 100), a scientist of note, and his scientific training is greatly reflected in his history. The *Zemah David* belongs to the best Jewish books on the history of the Middle Ages. It is divided into two parts, the first dealing with Jewish and the second with general history. The author is quite conscious that there were many Jewish histories written before him, for he even saw Ibn Yahya's *Shalsheleth* and he finds it therefore necessary to apologize for his writing a new history. He believes though that most of them are defective in one thing or another, as they do not observe the correct chronology nor do they arrange the data on the lives of men and events in the right sequence. Some, he says, treat the periods of the Judges and of the Second Commonwealth in an incomplete manner overlooking the importance of political life, and others possess various shortcomings. He, therefore, proposes to remedy all these defects. David, being interested not only in tradition but in Jewish life as a whole, treats both of men and events alike. However, since he wrote his history, as he says, not for scholars but for laymen, he is very brief and limits himself to a statement of facts. The book assumes, of course, a dry character but this is overbalanced by the fine order of the narrative and the comparative correctness of the data.

He divides the history from creation to his own time according to the millenia and discusses the men and the events in the proper order in each cycle. He is very careful to note the dates of every fact. Chronology is his fortē and he is very much troubled in adjusting the difficulties of Biblical chronology, especially that of the period of the Judges and of the kings of Israel and Judah. He is also aware of de Rossi's (Sect. 144) objections to the calculations according to the era of creation. Being of a conservative trend of mind, he endeavors to meet these objections and maintain the correctness of the traditional view. He does, however, display some critical spirit and deviates in some matters from the views propounded in the Talmud, such as that Saul reigned only two years and similar things.

David, having been a resident of Prague and a student of Moses Isserlis at Krakow, was well acquainted with the Polish and German Jewish history and the great men of these Jewries. He, therefore, gives correct and important data concerning events and scholars in these countries during the latter centuries of the Middle Ages and the work thus acquires special value.

The second part dealing with general history is arranged in the same fair order and correct sequence. It is a little longer than the first for the material is more exhaustive. David gives a fair sketch of the entire history of all nations, ancient as well as Mediaeval, and is careful to note the date of the appearance of certain nations on the arena of history, such as the Goths, Vandals, Huns and others. He also notes the important events in the Church and like all Mediaeval chronists, the exceptional natural phenomena which occurred during the ages.

Both parts are provided with excellent chronological tables, where the dates of the births and deaths of great men and the occurrence of leading events are given in as exact a manner as possible. This was a great improvement in Jewish historiography and a thing of merit for David Gans.

In the preface to the second part, David gives a list of his sources upon which he drew for this information. They are quite extensive and display a wide knowledge of the historical literature of his time.

133. CONFORTE'S KORE HA-DOROTH

The seventeenth century was not as prolific in the production of historical literature as the preceding one. Only one work of this nature of considerable value was produced during the period and that is the *Korē ha-Doroth* by David Conforte (1617-1676). Little is known of Conforte's life except that he was born in Salonika where he resided until 1644. He then visited Palestine and after staying in Jerusalem a few years, returned to his native city. In 1652 he came for a second time to Jerusalem and settled there permanently; however, but a few years before his death he went to Egypt and evidently died there. Conforte was a great Talmudic scholar and wrote also a book of Responsa which was never published and ultimately lost. We have, though, some of his Responsa which were included in the works of other scholars. Of secular sciences he knew little.

His main purpose in his book was to give a complete literary history from the close of the Talmud to his own days. He, therefore, devoted himself primarily to the intellectual and literary side of Jewish history and mentions but few events.

The book is divided into three sections, one dealing with the Saburaim (Vol. I, p. 428), the second with the period of the Gaonim and the third with the succeeding scholars. The first two sections are brief accounts of the periods taken mainly from Sherira's letter and Ibn Daud's *Book of Tradition,* while the third forms the body of the book. It is this section which imparts importance to the work.

He divides the entire Rabbinic period from 1038 to 1675 into eleven generations, and proceeds to record the scholars and their works in succession. He does this work thoroughly and completely. He is the first historian who gives a complete list of all the scholars whose names are mentioned in the *Tosofoth,* or the Tosafists. He is especially extensive and detailed when recording the history of learning during the last two centuries preceding his time. However that applies only to the scholars of Turkey, Egypt and Palestine. He seemed to have known but little of those who lived in Germany and Poland.

Conforte was painstaking in his work as he had gone through many volumes of Responsa and noted down the names of all correspondents and all other data so as to have a full record of all scholars. The book is more of a technical source book for historians of Rabbinic literature than a history, but in this field it is of great value.

It is rather surprising that Conforte who lived during the great Messianic movement of Sabbatai Zevi and who was on friendly terms with many of its leaders, should pass it over in total silence. Whether this was due to the fact that he entertained some sympathy towards it and probably grieved over its miserable failure, as a recent scholar surmised,[2] or for some other reason, we cannot tell.

The book was left in manuscript for seventy years. It was first published in 1764 anonymously by the editor, Eliezer Ashkenazi, and only subsequent editions restored the name of the author. David Cassel published in 1846 a scientific edition of the work.

134. HALPERIN'S SEDER HA-DOROTH

The last of the more important histories is the *Seder ha-Doroth* (The Order of Generations) written by Rabbi Yehiel Halperin (1660-1749) of the city of Minsk, Poland. Rabbi Yehiel was a great Talmudic scholar, one of the leading rabbis of his generation, and like all the scholars of his day wrote Responsa and Talmudic *Novellae*. But unlike them, he became interested in history early in life and devoted much time to its study. The result of his researches is the *Seder ha-Doroth* which was greatly admired by his own contemporaries and the scholars of the succeeding generations.

In the introduction, the author points out at length the many uses which a knowledge of history can be put to. He dwells especially upon the use which can be made of this knowledge in the decision of legal and Halakic matters, and quotes a number of errors found in the books of great Rabbinic scholars which can be traced primarily to a lack of historical knowledge. From this we can see that his main interest, like that of Zacuto's, lay in the Talmudic period and in the literary phase of past Jewish life. And it is in these fields that his real contribution consists.

The book is divided into three parts, the first dealing with general Jewish history from creation to his day, the second devoted entirely to the generations of the Tanaaim and Amoraim, while the third

[2] See Z. Rubastrow's article in Ha-Goren, Vol. X, pp. 122-131.—The Author of the Kore ha-Doroth and the Events of his Generation.

called *Maarekheth ha-Sephorim* (The Order of Books) forms one of the early treatises on bibliography. In the first part, he follows the order and arrangements of the *Zemah David* dividing history into millenia and taking up events and biographies in proper succession. On the whole, he added little new but followed his sources, the *Yuhasin,* the *Shalsheleth* and the *Zemah David.* He displays, however, a more critical view than Gedalyah Ibn Yahya whom he condemns for his many errors some of which he corrects. Yet he repeats all the fables and legends of the former, even when they contradict his own data. Thus he gives the correct dates of Rashi's birth and death, and also the date of the birth of Maimonides, which is twenty-nine years after the death of the former, and yet he reiterates the story of Gedalyah that the two met in Egypt, without noting the incongruity. This indicates that he did not endeavor to ascertain the truth of the statements of his sources but incorporated them as he found them being uncertain which is the correct one. Halperin includes also important events in general history and tells also, as chroniclers before him, of exceptional natural phenomena which occurred at certain times.

The second part is the most important one of the book. It is an exhaustive study of all the generations of the Tanaaim and Amoraim. Halperin follows the *Yuhasin* in arranging the biographical articles in alphabetical order and utilizes Zacuto's material to a great extent, but improves considerably upon him. The author displays exceptional Talmudic erudition in this part for hardly a single statement of a scholar of that age escapes him. The articles are very detailed; all data concerning the biography of the sages are collected and lists of their Halakic and Agadic statements in the entire Talmudic literature are given. If we note that in the article on Judah ben Ilai, the disciple of Rabbi Akiba, close to three thousand statements of his are listed, we are able to appreciate the amount of labor the author put into the work. This part of the *Seder ha-Doroth* is of inestimable value and was used extensively as a source by all subsequent writers on the history of the Talmud.

The third part is likewise of great value as a work of bibliography, especially in the field of Rabbinic literature. Halperin, like Gedalyah Ibn Yahya and David Ganz, helped to spread the knowledge of Jewish history among the Rabbinic students, for though he had written other works, he is primarily known as the author of the *Seder ha-Doroth.*

135. MINOR WORKS

There are a number of small historical treatises which record the story of special events that occurred in the life of the Jews of a certain country or even in that of a single Jewish community. Thus, we have two scrolls (Megilloth) written by Egyptian scholars to commemorate the miraculous escape of the Jews of Alexandria and Cairo from pending persecutions. The first event took place in 972 immediately after the death of Shemariah ben Elhanan, one of the four captives (Vol. I, p. 257) who was ransomed by the Jews of Egypt and who later settled there. The scroll was composed by Samuel ben Hosanah. The second event occurred in 1524. Ahmed Pasha, the governor of Egypt, rebelled against the Sultan Suleiman and celebrater his victory over the Sultan's forces by an attack against the Jews in Cairo. He was, however, soon defeated and the Jews escaped further prosecution. They celebrated this event and Samuel ben Nahman wrote a scroll to commemorate it.

The most important of such treatises, however, are those narrating the terrible persecutions and massacres suffered by the Jews of Poland during the years 1648-49 which are known as Gezeroth, ת"ח, ת"ט i. e. the years 5408-5409 of the era of creation. In these massacres perpetrated by the rebellious Cossacks under the leadership of Bogdan Chelminicki close to two hundred thousand Jews perished and hundreds of Jewish communities were destroyed. The Jews of Poland commemorated these tragic events by observing the 20th of the month of Sivan as a fast day, on which special prayers of penitence (Shelihoth) and elegies (Kinoth) were recited. The *Yeven Metzulah* (The Deep Mire, after Ps. LXIX) by Nathan Hanover and the *Megilath Eifa* (Scholl of Darkness) by Sabbatai Cohen (Sect. 65), eye witnesses of the persecutions, contain stories of the massacres. Hanover was a resident of Zaslov in Volhynia which was attacked by the Cossacks, but he managed to escape and later settled in Livorno, Italy. From there he went to Wallachia, and for a time held rabbinical positions in Yassi and Fakshan, and finally became rabbi in Ungresh Brod, in Moravia, where in the year 1683 he was killed by a stray bullet during the siege of the city.

The chronicle of Hanover is quite a detailed one and tells in an orderly manner the history of the rebellion of Chelminicki, the progress of the war between the Cossacks and the Poles, and gives full accounts of the massacres perpetrated in the important Jewish communities, especially those of Nemirow, Tultshin and Polnoh, in each of which cities the number of Jews slain ran into the thousands. The book contains also a short description of the educational, charitable and social institutions of the Polish Jewish communities which is a valuable historical document.

The scroll of Sabbatai Cohen is a brief account of these events written in rhymed prose. It was originally appended to his elegic and penitential poems which he composed for public recitation on the 20th of Sivan, but later printed separately.

B. Geography and Travel

136. GEOGRAPHICAL BOOKS

The geographical literature of this period, as stated, consists largely of books of travel and itineraries, and these are mainly descriptions of Palestine and journeys thither. Very few of these itineraries deal with other countries and still fewer books deal with geography proper. Besides the few works discussed above, (Sect. 100), which deal with astronomy but include also some geographical data, there are two books devoted to geography only. The first is the *Orhoth Olam* (The Ways of the World) by Abraham Farissol (1451-1526).

Farissol was born in Avignon, Provence, and in the year 1468 he migrated to Italy and settled in Ferrara. He was by profession a cantor and writer of scrolls, but also a student of the sciences. He became acquainted with the Duke Hercules d'Este who was a patron of learning, and at his invitation often held theological debates with Catholic priests, and at their request, wrote his apologetic work named *Magen Abraham* (The Shield of Abraham). Farissol also wrote other works, among them commentaries on some books of the Bible and several treatises on philosophical subjects, but the *Orhoth Olam* is the one best known.

In the introduction, the author states the purpose of his book to be, first to provide useful reading for those who in their leisure time peruse light stories and fabulous histories; second to instruct people in the wonders of God manifested in the natural changes occurring in different parts of the earth. In order to prove the importance of geographical knowledge, he points to the carefulness with which the Torah described the boundaries of Palestine and the genealogy of nations and the countries where they dwelt.

The book is divided into two parts; the first containing twelve chapters, is devoted to the general description of the earth, its division into climatic zones and continents and the individual countries. The second, consisting of fifteen chapters, deals with the new discoveries made by the Portuguese and the Spaniards. Ferissol displays in his work considerable knowledge of geography in accordance with the standard of his time. Ptolemy, is, of course, still his authority both for astronomy and geography, and the geographical treatises of the Arabs in Latin translations supplemented by later works are his sources. He at first describes the division of the inhabited part of the globe into three continents, Asia, Africa and Europe, and delineates the boundaries of each. He next deals with the seven climatic zones and states the sections which each one embraces. This is followed by descriptions of the extent of the inhabited part in each continent and detailed narratives of the countries known to him, with special attention to those around the Mediterranean.

The second part is a detailed story of the discoveries made by Vasco de Gama during his cruises around the Cape of Good Hope on the way to India. He begins with a description of the lands lying on the Western coast of Africa up to the Cape and ends by depicting parts of India. He gives also some data about the peoples inhabiting these strange countries. His description contains, of course, much exaggeration and many fables and unfounded stories. He insists on calling the entire region of Central and Western Africa Lower Cush, i. e. Ethiopia. In this rather unknown region, he places Ophir of the Bible, though in another chapter, he places it somewhere in India. He also believes that Paradise was somewhere in this region. But before he substantiates this theory, he attempts first to solve a difficult problem in connection with it. The Bible states that four rivers issue from the Garden, namely Pishon, Gihon, Hidekel (the Tigris) and Perath (the Euphrates), (Gen. II, 10-14). He is aware that Pishon, according to the description of the Bible, is the Nile, and Gihon is another river in Africa, but the Tigris and Euphrates are in Asia thousands of miles distant from the other rivers. How then can all the four rivers issue from one source? A difficult problem indeed, but Farissol solves it easily. He assumes that the Tigris and the Euphrates do issue from the same source, but that they flow a long distance under ground until they come to the surface in the mountains of Armenia. He congratulates himself on his ingenious solution. However, this represents an attempt to reconcile some Biblical statements with scientific and geographic data.

Farissol, as said, derived his information from Latin sources, but was not careful in the transcription of the names into Hebrew, and as a consequence a modern reader finds difficulty in recognizing the places they denote. His carelessness caused him to commit a number of errors, some very curious, and one deserves to be quoted. In describing the countries of the far East, he mentions several times the Kingdom of the Great Dog (Malkuth ha-Keleb ha-Godol). By this peculiar name, he designates the kingdom of the Tartar Khans, the error having arisen by confusing the word *Khan* or its genitive *ḳhanis* with *canis,* a dog, and hence the great Khan became the great Dog.

Farissol has also a chapter on the discovery of America where he describes both the land and the people living there, according to the current stories, and also a chapter on David Reubeni. He does not doubt the existence of independent Jewish tribes in Arabia, but is rather skeptical of Reubeni's story about his mission as an ambassador of the Jewish king to the Christian nations.

The second geographical book is the *Kitzur Limudē ha-Geographia,* a manual of the Science of Geography by Menahem Emanuel Porto of Trieste which was printed at Padua in the year 1604. It contains mainly excerpts from books on geography in Italian.

We have also several maps where the places are designated in Hebrew letters. They were drawn in the year 1695 by Jacob Tzadik and Abraham ben Jacob, a proselyte, and were included as an addition to a Passover Haggadah printed at Amsterdam in 1712.

137. PALESTINE ITINERARIES

Palestine, as is known, always exerted a great influence upon the Jews of the diaspora. Scattered as they were to the four corners of the world, they always considered the land of their fathers as a center to which they were drawn and a visit to that country was considered not only a holy pilgrimage but a goal which the chosen spirits of Israel strove to reach. It is not to be wondered at, therefore, that we possess so many itineraries of Palestine during this post-Classical period, for almost in every century there were a few scholars who visited the country, and even settled there, and considered it their duty to impart information to their brethren in exile concerning Eretz Israel, either in the form of letters or small treatises. As a result, the greater part of the travel literature consists of Palestine itineraries with the exception of one book which deals with other countries, and that is the *Book of Travel* by David ha-Reubeni.

Since visiting or settling in Palestine was usually accomplished from a religious motive, it is but natural that the descriptions of the land should contain to a great extent matters of religious interest, such as the locations of the holy places and the graves of the sages as well as some legends and tales about the lives of the holy men and their wondrous deeds. Accordingly, many of these itineraries are but lists of holy places and graves. Some of them, however, contain valuable descriptions of the life of the Jews in Palestine as well as in various other countries and also many important geographical data. Even those of the first class contain here and there some interesting information about the land and the life of the people. Consequently, all of these works have both historical and geographical value and add to our knowledge of Palestine during the ages. We will now proceed to survey the works according to the centuries in which they were produced.

i. The Thirteenth Century.

The thirteenth century saw, as we know from Jewish history, an exodus of many German and French scholars from their native countries to Palestine. Parts of that country were then occupied by the Christians, and the immigrants settled in these parts for, after all, they could adapt themselves more easily to the life of their former neighbors than to that of the Mohammedans. Two of these scholars have left us short itineraries. The first is Samuel ben Samson who wrote the *Mas'a de-Plishtina* (A Journey to Palestine) and the second is one by the name of Jacob who was sent by the Tosafist Rabbi Yehiel of Paris to collect money for the support of his academy in that city[3] and whose treatise *Ele ha-Masa'oth* (These Are the Journeys) is preserved.

The *Mas'a* of Samuel is a small pamphlet of two chapters which relates very briefly of a hurried trip from Jerusalem to Hebron and from there to Galilee and into Syria and even into Mosul, the place of the ancient city of Nineveh. The author describes mainly the loca-

[3] It is a curious fact worth while noting that at the beginning of the thirteenth century the Jews of France thought it advisable to seek support for their institutions of learning from the Jews of Palestine, a reverse process from the one that went on during later centuries, namely, that Palestine is continually supported by the Jews of the diaspora. This fact testifies both to the poverty of French Jewry and to the well-being of the Jews who settled in the Holy Land at the period.

tion of certain holy places, such as ancient synagogues and the graves of sages, and narrates also several brief stories about the sanctity of these places. It is curious that among the sacred graves, are counted also those of Adarmelek and Asharazar, the children of Sennacherib (Kings XIX, 37), who according to the legend,[4] became proselytes and of whose descendants there came forth the pair of sages, Shemaya and Abtalyon.

According to Samuel, the Assyrian princes are buried in Giscala near the above-named scholars. This Samuel went to Palestine in the company of Rabbi Jonathan of Lunel (Sect. 43), but he returned to France while the former remained in the Holy Land.

The itinerary of Jacob the emissary is a more elaborate affair. It is intended for the same purpose, for in fact it is designated as a guide book to the holy places and graves of the saints, but it is more systematic and contains other data. It is divided into eight chapters, each devoted to the mapping out of the places of religious interest in the environs of a principal city. The first six are devoted to the Palestinian cities, Acco, Nablus, (Shechem) Jerusalem, Bethlehem, Hebron, Meron in Galilee and Tiberias. The chapter on Jerusalem contains also a brief description of the city and the Temple Mount. Among the graves, he marks also peculiarly enough those of Seth the son of Adam, of Shem the son of Noah and that of Queen Esther, though there is no reference anywhere that her body was transported to Palestine for burial, and Benjamin of Tudela. (Vol. I, Sect. 195) distinctly speaks of her grave in Susa (Sushan), Persia.

The last two chapters deal with the descriptions of the environs of Damascus, Palmyra (Tadmor) and Bagdad. It is interesting to note the large number of synagogues, the founding of which was ascribed to the prophet Elijah. There are at least eight of them, and some were situated in Syrian cities. But strangest of all is the description by the author of a synagogue at Aleppo said to have been founded by Moses, the Law-giver, though according to the Bible, he never even entered Palestine, let alone Syria. Such is the power of credulity.

ii. Fourteenth Century

The fourteenth century was quite productive of a number of itineraries and descriptions of Palestine. The earliest geographical study of the Holy Land during the period is contained in an impor-

[4] *B. Sanhedrin,* 96b.

tant Halakic work written by Estori ha-Parhi (1282-1357) under the name of *Kafter we-Ferah* (A Knop and a Flower, after Ex. XXV, 33). Estori descended from a noble family which originally lived in Florencia, in the province of Andelusia, Spain, and hence it acquired the name *Parhi* (Perah, meaning flower) after the name of the city. Later, members of the family settled in Provence. Little is known of the life of the author, for we do not even know his Hebrew name nor does he reveal it to us, for in his preface he calls himself *Ish Toriyi,* i. e. a man obedient to the Law, a play upon the name Estori. We only know that he was forced to leave his native country in 1306 during the exile of the Jews from France. He then went to Barcelona and finally in 1312 set sail for Palestine whither he arrived after a short stay in Egypt in the year 1314. Estori's love for the Holy Land was unbounded, and he wanted to learn all that there was to know about the land, and for that purpose he explored it for seven years, two of which he spent in Galilee and five in the other parts of the country. During his wanderings, he endeavored to ascertain the true boundaries of the land as a whole, the area each tribe had occupied during the Biblical times, and took great pains to identify the location of many cities mentioned in the Bible and the Talmud. After completing his wanderings, he settled at Scytopolis (Beth Shean) and there he composed his book, naming it so as to include his family name in the title.

The *Kaftor we-Ferah* is really an encyclopaedia on all things related to Palestine with special reference to the laws dependent upon the land such as the giving of tithes *(M'aaser)* to the Levites and the offerings to the priests (Terumah), the question of the Sabbatical cycles *(Shemitah)* and the jubilee year, and many more legal phases connected with that country. But while the greater part of the book is devoted to legal matters, the geographical and topographical phases of the country receive, as said, great attention. He devotes a chapter to a detailed description of the Temple area, and displays great erudition in delineating the plan of the various parts of that famous edifice. Another long chapter deals with the topography of Palestine. Here the boundaries are traced, the areas occupied by each tribe defined and historical places identified. A third deals with special cities such as Ascalon, Gaza, Tiberias and also with the Jordan. These chapters are very valuable for the student of Palestine from the historical and topographical points of view.

The book contains also discourses on the Biblical and Talmudic coins and measures and their Palestinian and French equivalents, on the calculation of the Jubilee years and Sabbatical cycles and on the beginning of the Selucid era. Here and there are scattered data on the flora and minerals of Palestine as well as other useful information. All these qualities make the geographical parts of the book an important contribution to Palestine literature.

An interesting itinerary of Palestine is the *Shebilē di-Yerushalayim* (The Paths of Jerusalem) written in the year 1333 by Isaac Hilo of Larisa, Spain, who later settled in Palestine. It was written in the form of a letter addressed to his father and relatives. The name is misleading, for it deals with the entire country and only the introduction is devoted to a description of Jerusalem. Hilo is brief but does not omit any important detail. In his description of Jerusalem, he gives us several data on the life and occupation of the Jews there. He tells us that there are among them many artisans and business men but that a number of Jews devote themselves to the pursuit of the sciences, such as medicine, astronomy and mathematics.

The body of the book is divided into seven chapters or paths as each describes a route from Jerusalem to a certain city in Palestine. The termini of the routes are 'Arad in the South, Jaffa, Shechem (Nablus), Acco, Tiberias, Safed and Banaias in the North. Hilo, while he like the preceding writers pays special attention to places of religious interest, does not neglect to tell us of the Jewish communities in the various cities situated on the routes and of the occupation of the Jews. We learn that there was at that time a large Jewish settlement in Ramlah and that the inhabitants came from Spain, that the Jews of Jaffa were wealthy and possessed a fine library but that there were few scholars to make use of it. Again, we are informed about the communities of Haifa and Acco, that the first contained many great scholars who came from France and Germany and the members of the second carried on an extensive business and possessed great riches. We thus get a first hand glimpse of Jewish life in Palestine during the first half of the fourteenth century. The book contains, of course, a few legends and stories and some erroneous facts such as that Beter is near Samaria and that the Samaritan alphabet does not contain the letters *Alef, Heth* and *'Ain,* but such things are to be expected, and on the whole the itinerary makes interesting reading.

iii. Fifteenth Century

We have several fragmentary reports of visits to Palestine written during the first half of the fifteenth century, one by Isaac Ibn Alfasi of Malaga, Spain, composed in 1411, and a second by Elijah of Ferrara, dated 1435. Both, though, are of little significance. The second half of the century, however, compensates us for the meagerness of the first, inasmuch as two itineraries written towards its close are excellent specimens of travel literature. Both were composed by Italian Jews, the first in 1481 by Meshulam ben Menahem of Voltelia and the second by the famous commentator of the Mishnah, Obadiah di Bertinoro in the year 1488.

Meshulam was a wealthy merchant who seemed to have made several trips to the Orient, for we find him again in 1486 on a trip together with Obadiah from Messina to Alexandria. The trip, described in the book, however, must have been the first one for he tells of the cities he passed through with the enthusiasm of one who sees things for the first time. Part of the first chapter is missing so that we do not know where his route started, but from the island of Rhodes it followed to Alexandria, Cairo, and from there by caravan to Gaza, thence to Hebron, terminating at Jerusalem. He then returned to Italy by way of Jaffa, Beirut, Rhodes, Corfu and Ragusa. He also visited Damascus.

As we can see, Meshulam visited only a part of Palestine and consequently his itinerary is devoted largely to the other countries. He was well equipped for his task, for he had a knowledge of the affairs of the world and an observant eye. His narrative is therefore full and detailed. He takes note of the general as well as of Jewish life in the countries he visited and little escapes him. He devotes considerable space to the description of Egypt and its principal cities, Alexandria and Cairo, and tells at length of the customs of the inhabitants, of the mode of dressing of both men and women, of the manner of riding and eating. As a Westerner, he was repelled by the way of living of the Arabs and the Jews as they ate and slept on the ground. He describes the wonders he saw there, such as the Pyramids and the crocodiles and similar things. In his, as well as in Obadiah's time, the main Jewish settlement in Egypt was Cairo, for he tells us that the number of Jewish families in that city was eight hundred and fifty, and only sixty in Alexandria. There were also several hundred Karaite and fifty Samaritan families in the former city but none of the sectarians resided in the latter.

After a lengthy description of the travails of travel by caravan from Cairo to Gaza, Meshulam gives a graphic account of the disorderly conditions which reigned in Palestine at that time, of the conduct of the Bedouin bands of robbers and of their life in general. His description of Jerusalem is limited primarily to the city proper and dwells little upon the life of the Jews there. He is exceedingly brief in his narrative of his travels to Beirut, but is enraptured with Damascus and its famous bazaars which he depicts in detail. He tells us that there were at the time four hundred and fifty Jewish families in the latter city and that they were wealthy. He concludes his itinerary by a long description of his trip by sea from Beirut, but it is filled with personal incidents, though he gives a fair account of the many islands he passed and their principal cities. Meshulam lacks literary grace and his narrative is marred by an excessive use of Italian words.

Bertinoro's itinerary is of a much higher quality and of great interest. As a Jewish scholar, he paid more attention to Jewish life and customs and his data shed much light upon the life of the Jews in several countries. It was written in the form of three letters to his father, brother and to an anonymous person. The first letter, however, forms the body of the book.

Obadiah set out in the fall of 1486 from Naples for Palermo, Sicily, in order to sail from there to Palestine. The people of Palermo, however, did not allow him to depart for some time and he had to stay there perforce and act as rabbi and preacher for nine months. He finally left in October 1487, immediately after the Feast of Tabernacles (Succoth) for Alexandria by way of Rhodes; thence he followed the same route as Meshulam to Gaza, Hebron and Jerusalem where he settled.

Like the itinerary of Meshulam, that of Bertinoro is to a great extent devoted to the description of other countries. He begins with a description of the Jews in Sicily in which he informs us that there were at that time nine hundred and fifty Jewish families in Palermo, and four hundred in Messina, besides those in other cities. He tells of their occupations as artisans and workers in the field, and that they do not command the respect of their neighbors on account of their dress and conduct. Bertinoro likewise has little respect for them, for he informs us that they were lax in their morals and that the habit of informing was quite prevalent among them. On the other hand, we learn that the Jews of Sicily conducted their public affairs in an organized manner and that their leaders had full jurisdiction over the people even to the extent of arresting offenders of the law and inflicting upon them corporal punishment. He faithfully records their peculiar religious and social customs, such as funeral rites and wedding ceremonies. This is followed by the story of his visit to Rhodes in which he tells us of the pitiable state of the small Jewish community there and does not fail to note any peculiarity in their customs and praises them for their conduct and bearing.

He devotes much space to Egypt but principally to the life of the Jews there, though he does not omit to mention the crocodiles and the beautiful buildings. He tells in detail of the customs of the Jews in Alexandria especially of their conduct on the Sabbath day. He also narrates of the Karaites in Cairo, of their mode of living and even of their rare books. We are informed that Nathan ha-Cohen was at the time the head of the Jews (Nagid) in Egypt and that there were already fifty families of former Spanish Marranos in Cairo.

Following the same route of Meshulam, he came to Jerusalem. His description of the Holy City is entirely devoted to the Jewish phase. It is interesting to compare his data about the Jews there with those of Hilo. The latter, writing about one hundred and fifty years before, speaks of a large community whose members were wealthy and important, and some of whom were engaged in scientific pursuits. Bertinoro tells us that there were in his time only seventy Jewish families in Jerusalem, all poor and ignorant, and that not a single one among them knew anything of philosophy or the other sciences. In general, he has a very low opinion of the Palestinian Jews of his time. The itinerary ends with descriptions of the Temple Mount, the Mount of Olives and the environs of the city.

The other two letters are brief and supplement the book by stories about the Jews in Abyssinia and other data. The style of Bertinoro is flowing, clear and light, and the itinerary on the whole, makes pleasant reading.

To this century belongs also an anonymous itinerary written by a Venetian scholar in the year 1496. He made his journey through Rhodes, Corfu, Cypress to Beirut and thence via Damascus and Safed to Jerusalem. He does not describe his return trip nor his travels in Palestine proper, but his narrative ends with the visit to Jerusalem. There is little new in his description except a few data which shed light upon Jewish life in Palestine cities. We learn that Safed had at the time about three hundred Jewish families, which shows that the tide of emigration of Spanish exiles which a few decades later made the city a great intellectual center, had not as yet reached it. On the other hand, we learn that the number of Jews in Jerusalem had more than doubled within seven years, for Bertinoro in 1488 speaks of seventy families in that city, while our author gives the number as two hundred. He also speaks of them as God-fearing and generous, and in general with great respect, in quite a different tone than Obadiah. This change in the character of the Jews of Jerusalem was in a great measure due to the influence of Obadiah himself. In fact, our author pays great tribute to his renowned countryman and is justly proud of him.

iv. Sixteenth Century

The sixteenth century can only boast of one itinerary written in 1523 and this an anonymous one. We do not even know the country where the author lived, but from his work it is evident that he was a scholar and an important man in his community. In all probabilities, he was an Italian as he started on his trip from Venice. His tour lay through Corfu, Tripoli, Beirut, Safed, Nablus (Shechem) and Jerusalem. He returned by way of Tiberias, Meron, Damascus and Beirut and thence by sea to Venice. He describes all the places he visited, but adds little to the geographical and topographical knowledge of the country except some data of historical value. He speaks of Safed as a large Jewish community and tells us that the Jews there carry on an extensive trade with Damascus, but is surprisingly silent about its intellectual prominence at the time, for even in those years, Safed was already a great seat of learning, the place of residence of such men as Jacob Berab and Levi ben Hahib (Sect. 69). The author is more eloquent, though, about Jerusalem. We are informed that the Jewish community consisted of six hundred families, an increase of four hundred since 1496 and he names a number of scholars, both Spanish and German, among them David Ibn Shoshan Rofē, and Rabbi Israel, heads of the Sephardic and Ashkenazic academies respectively. It is evident that Levi ben Habib had not as yet settled in Jerusalem, for our author, describing in detail the spiritual life of the Jews there, would not have passed him over in silence.

His description of Damascus is also a detailed one. He tells of the various kinds of business carried on in the city, of the rates of interest and of the conditions of credit. He seems to have been specially interested in these matters. He further tells us that the Sicilian Jews had a special synagogue in that city, which shows that there was an extensive immigration from Sicily to the Oriental cities and especially to Damascus. It is, however, possible that under the name Sicilian are included all Italian Jews. Our author gives also a list of the holy places and graves of the saints he visited, and narrates a few current legends, among them the story that Rabbi Simon ben Yohai built twenty-four synagogues in Palestine.

v. Seventeenth Century

There are a number of itineraries and descriptions of travel dating from the seventeenth century. The earliest is one written by the well known Talmudic scholar and Kabbalist Isaiah Hurwitz (Sect. 119) in the year 1622. It is in the form of a letter to his children in Prague describing his trip. Isaiah left Prague in August 1621 and went through Vienna and the Balkan countries to Turkey where he boarded a ship to Tripoli and thence through Aleppo and other Syrian cities to Damascus, Safed and Jerusalem. He stopped for a month with the Jews of Aleppo who accorded him great honor. He praises them highly and tells us that Hebrew is spoken among them and that he also held discourses there in that language. He informs us further that on coming to Safed, the leaders of the community entreated him to settle in the city as their rabbi, but as he had already received a similar offer from Jerusalem, he chose the latter city as his residence. The reason for the rivalry between these two cities to retain Rabbi Isaiah is, that each hoped to attract more settlers and also money for the support of its institutions from the lands of the diaspora through the fame of that scholar, which shows us that the zenith of the Palestine cities as intellectual centers had already passed at that time. We also learn from the letter that the tide of settlers from the exile had, in the first quarter of the seventeenth century, definitely turned toward Jerusalem, for the author says that Ashkenazic settlers are arriving in great numbers daily to the Holy City.

A very popular book of travel which is frequently quoted by historians and chronists is the *Geliloth Eretz Israel* (The Environs of Palestine) by Gershon ben Eliezer of Prague written in 1624. It is a peculiar booklet written by a peculiar man. Gershon was smitten by the *wanderlust* and spent a great part of his life travelling through Oriental countries. According to his own story, he went via the Balkan countries to Constantinople and from there to the Crimea and thence by land to Armenia and Nisibis. From there, through Mesopotamia and Syria, he came to Palestine. He later tells of a second journey he made by caravan to Arabia, the land of the ten tribes, parts of India, and again to Persia and Media, and thence by sea to North Africa and finally to Rome. The report of the second journey is so vague, and as we will see, full of such inaccuracies and exaggerations, that it is doubtful whether he really made it.

The *Geliloth,* though written late in the period, is a typical Mediaeval legendary book of travel, for the credulity of the author and his capacity for recording legends and seeing wonderful natural phenomena seems boundless. He was especially interested in marking the location of the graves of the great men. He gives quite an extensive list of those in Babylonia, Syria and Palestine. He expatiates upon the legends clustering around the graves of Ezekiel, Ezra, and Daniel, which were told by Benjamin and Petahia (Vol. I, Sect. 195) and adds many of his own. He saw many wonderful natural freaks, men whose Adam's apple extended to the middle of the body, animals with three eyes, flies as large as pigeons and frogs the size of geese and also the particular pillar of salt into which the wife of Lot was turned at the time of the destruction of Sodom; and he even tells us that the pillar is nigh consumed by goats daily but resumes its original size during the night. There was no definite route to his travels, as he continually crossed from one point to another, made a circuit and returned to the place he started from. There is no doubt that his descriptions contain some important data but the truth is hopelessly mixed with fiction, so that it is difficult to extricate it.

The story of his journey to Arabia and the land of the ten tribes is still more vague and miraculous. He says that while in Alexandria, he heard of the arrival in Salonika of a caravan from a distant country, the members of which told stories about independent Jewish tribes, and about the river Sambatyon and its curious ways. Gershon immediately hastened to Salonika and joined the caravan on its return trip. He tells us that he came to Mecca where he found many free Jewish tribes living in the desert, and further informs us that Jews live on islands in the Indian Ocean. He seems to confuse India and Abyssinia, for he says that he traveled by land to India that is to the environs of Calcutta which is on the coast of Malabar, and that the Sambatyon is somewheres there, and then again he places it in the neighborhood of the kingdom of Prester John[5] which is Abyssinia. Then he proceeds to describe in detail the river Sambatyon and the Jews who live on the other side. He even tells us of a headless man with mouth and eyes in his chest who was sent as a present by Prester John to Eliezer, King of the ten tribes living across the Sambatyon. Surprisingly enough he refrains from informing us why he himself did not cross the river though so close to it, while we are told by him that in the year 1528, Jews from Europe crossed the Sambatyon. From the vicinity of the Sambatyon, Gershon passed again to Arabia and thence by way of the Red Sea to Crete and continued his journeys.

Endeavoring to explain the character of Gershon according to the stories of his book of travel, we face a real mystery. We are uncertain whether we have before us a Jewish Münchausen or a man with a highly inflamed imagination who concocted his stories from tales and fiction of other travelers or a combination of both.

The booklet, as said, enjoyed great popularity on account of these stories and was translated into Judaeo-German and printed many times. The part relating to the ten tribes and Sambatyon was also translated into German by Eismenger and incorporated by him in his work *Das Endecktes Judentum.*

To this century, there belong also two itineraries written by Karaite Pilgrims. The first was composed by Samuel ben David of the Crimea in 1642 and the second by Moses ben Elijah Yerushalmi in 1655. Samuel was a leader and a man of learning. His knowledge is reflected in the work for it is extensive, detailed and skilfully written.

He left Koslow (Eupatoria in the Crimea) in the year 1641, and went by sea to Constantinople, and from there through Rhodes to Alexandria and thence through Cairo to Gaza and Jerusalem. He returned by way of Hebron, Nablus, Safed, Damascus, Aleppo, Antioch and other Syrian cities and part of Asia Minor to the coast of the Sea of Marmora whence he returned to Constantinople and the Crimea.

Samuel had an eye for architectural beauty and is careful to describe all imposing structures he saw on his travels. He tells also about the nature of the countries he visited, prices of food and similar

[5] Prester John is the name by which the King of the Ethiopians or the Abyssinians was known in Europe during the later period of the Mediaeval Ages. He was supposed to be both high priest and ruler, and hence his title of *Prester* or Presbyter as he was at times called. As Abyssinia was the only Christian country in a continent dominated by Moslems, a halo of legend surrounded its ruler, and many strange stories were told both of the powerful king and the wonderful country over which he held sway.

matters. The special interest of the book lies in the author's description of the life in the Karaite communities of the East.

He speaks with pride of his brethren in Cairo, their well being and piety. He tells us that they do not buy any meat, bread nor wine from the Rabbanites for all these articles of food are provided by members of their own sect. He concludes therefore that they, i. e. the Karaites, are the true Jews and Israelites. In his description of Jerusalem and other cities in Palestine he differs litlte from those of the earlier travelers except to pay more attention to the graves of Biblical personages. He devotes considerable space to Damascus giving details about the city proper, about the Jews in general and the Karaites in particular. He tells us of their synagogue and the old crolls of the Law he saw there. According to him, one scroll was written in 567 C. E. His descriptions of the other Syrian cities are rather brief, but he does not fail to tell us something of the Jews who live there though they are Rabbanites. His style is lucid and flowing, and the work as a whole makes good reading.

The second itinerary is much briefer and deals more with the description of the countries proper. Moses Yerushalmi followed the same route as Samuel both on going to and returning from Palestine. He adds therefore little that is new except that his narrative is more concise and varies here and there by adding certain data.

vi. Eighteenth Century

There are only two itineraries extant from this century, both composed towards the end, one by a Karaite, Benjamin Yerushalmi of Crimea who visited Palestine in the year 1786, and the other by Simha ben Joshua of the city of Zalasitz, Poland, who made his trip in 1774.

The first is a brief description of the cities of Jerusalem and Hebron and of the holy places located there. It contains no new material except for a few stories about some personal incidents which happened to the author during his travels. As he landed at Jaffa and did not visit Egypt, he has little to tell about the Karaite life, for the Karaite community in Jerusalem, the only one in Palestine, was small and poor. Benjamin writes in a good Hebrew style, free from any admixture of foreign words, a fact which indicates his mastery of the language and to a certain extent his high scholarly training.

The itinerary of Simha known as the *Sipurē Eretz ha-Galil* (Stories of the Land of Galilleo) is more extensive and contains a number of interesting descriptions. The story of the author's visit to Palestine is quite pathetic and is indicative of the great love the pious Polish Jews bore for Palestine. Simha must have belonged to the Hassidic sect and was seized with the great desire prevalent then among certain circles of that faction to settle in Palestine, though he knew all the difficulties attached to such an act. His wife, who accompanied him against her will insisted upon returning home in the midst of the journey. He then divorced her and was about to continue his way alone, but she changed her mind and begged him to remarry her and take her with him. His way lay along the Balkan Peninsula to Galatz, Roumania, from there by sea to Constantinople, and thence via Rhodes and Jaffa to Acco. On arriving there he went to Safed where he stayed for seven months, but was ultimately forced, much against his will, by economic necessity, to return home.

Simha was a good observer and he noted every detail of interest in the lands he passed. He gives a good description of Constantinople and especially of the life of the Jewish community. He tells us of a fine custom instituted by the Sephardic Jews of that city, namely that in the month of Elul (August) of each year a ship was chartered by the community in order to carry all who desired to make a pilgrimage to Palestine over the high holy days. The traveling expenses were paid out of the community chest. As Simha did not visit Judea nor even Jerusalem, his descriptions are limited to the cities of Galilee, especially Safed, Tiberias, and Meron, the burial place of Simon ben Yohai. His narrative regarding Safed is full and detailed and we obtain a graphic picture of Jewish life in that city in the last decade of the eighteenth century. His book contains, of course, a description of the graves of the sages in the environs of Safed and Tiberias and a few stories about the holy places. It is concluded with a short narrative about his return trip which led through Italy, and from there by sea to Danzig. In Livorno he found a patron, a very rich man who supported him during his stay in that city and also endowed him liberally with traveling expenses. As a mark of gratitude, Simha wrote for his patron, whom he does not name, the record of his journey.

138. THE TRAVELS OF DAVID HA-REUBENI

We had occasion to mention several times the name of David Reubeni (1490-1537) who appeared suddenly and declared himself an ambassador from the Jewish king in Arabia on a political mission to some of the Christian kings in Europe. His appearance aroused hope in the hearts of the Jews and wonder and astonishment on the part of the Christians. His deeds and exploits during the eight years that passed since his appearance (1524) until his arrest by Charles the Fifth in 1532 certainly testify to his remarkable personality. But history has not succeeded as yet in solving the riddle which this peculiar personality presents. We can not know whether Reubeni was a shrewd adventurer who relied upon the credulity of the people at the time, or a dreamer and visionary who deluded himself and involuntarily misled others. His itinerary, therefore, which is quite an extensive work and describes not only his travels but many of his deeds and visits in royal courts, is of great interest, for, though it does not solve the riddle, it sheds much light upon his character and supplies many data in the Reubeni episode.

The travel narrative begins with a short statement of his genealogy and the purpose of his trip. He calls himself David, son of King Solomon and the brother of King Joseph who rules over 30,000 men belonging to the tribes of Gad, Reuben and half of the tribe of Menasseh, who live in the desert of Habur, Aarbia. He informs us that the king and the council of seventy elders sent him on a mission to the pope in Rome but does not acquaint us with its nature. He then begins to describe his route and the adventures he met with. From the desert of Habur, he traveled for ten days until he came to Jedda on the coast of the Red Sea. Thence he crossed into Africa and arrived at Suakin in Nubia. There he tarried for about ten months, and finally by crossing the desert succeeded in reaching Cairo, Egypt. Thence he went by land to Gaza, Hebron and Jerusalem.

During the time he sojourned in Mohammedan countries, he posed as a follower of the prophet and even claimed to be one of his descendants. In order that he should not be detected, he wore the dress peculiar to the members of the prophet's family. This guise enabled him not only to pass safely through all the places inhabited by fanatical tribes, but also to receive great honor from various chiefs and princes. He kept up the dissimulation even during his visit in Palestine and on his second visit to Egypt, and therefore had to communicate with the Jews in those cities in secret. He told those of his brethren he met that the end of the exile is near and that redemption is close at hand. Returning to Alexandria, he made arrangements to sail for Italy. In Alexandria, he finally threw off the disguise and associated with the Jews openly, telling them of his mission, and of course was greatly honored by them and even given monetary support. Thus ends the first part of his journey leading up to his appearance in Italy. In the narrative he describes briefly the nature of the countries in Africa and also gives some information on the Temple Mount and the cave of the graves of the patriarchs in Hebron. On account of his guise as a Mohammedan, he had a better opportunity than other Jewish travelers to visit these places.

The second part of the work deals with Reubeni's travels and sojourn in Italy where he tarried for about a year and a half from the late fall of the year 1523 to the spring of 1525. It is a detailed account of his trips to Rome and thence to various cities, interspersed with data of his daily conduct and personal incidents. The gist of it is that he arrived first in Venice where he disclosed to several Jewish leaders his identity and his mission. When they asked for details he refused to tell them, saying that it is a great secret. They were a bit skeptical about his words, yet they honored him and paid his expenses to Rome and even sent some men to accompany him thither. In Rome, he had an audience with the pope, and apparently he had some authentic documents with him, for the pope took his propositions earnestly and promised to help him in his endeavors and write to the king of Portugal to comply with his requests. The nature of his request he does not entirely disclose but from numerous places in this book it is evident that he asked the Christian kings to supply his brother Joseph and his men with arms and assist them otherwise, so as to enable them to drive the Turks out of Palestine. The pope was, of course, interested in the weakening of the Mohammedan power, and David most likely promised special rights for the Christians in Palestine, but he never mentions any details of his conversation.

The reception by the pope and the honor paid him by the cardinals raised his esteem in the eyes of the Jews, for they honored him, contributed towards his expenses and gave him presents. While he was staying at Rome waiting for the pope to write to the kings of Portugal and Abyssinia (Prester John), his fame spread to other cities of Italy and many Jews came to see him, among them great scholars and famous men, such as Obadiah Sporno (Sect. 19) and others. One of these, Daniel of Pisa, a very rich man and a friend of the cardinals even undertook to act as his guide and interpreter, for David spoke only Hebrew. However, there were also some Jews who believed his activities dangerous and who tried to impede his work. He speaks of informers and enemies quite frequently.

Finally he received the letter of recommendation from the pope, but a new difficulty presented itself. The ambassador of the King of Portugal, a certain Dom Michael, was slow in issuing the necessary safe conduct papers for the journey to Portugal. He promised to send the documents to Pisa whither David went for a short stay, but did not keep his promise. Only after Dom Michael was recalled by his king and a new man, Dom Marten took his place did David finally get the necessary documents and he began to make preparations for his journey. The Jews of Italy were greatly interested in his visit to the king of Portugal and the leaders of that Jewry assisted him in his endeavors. In Pisa, David was entertained by its most distinguished Jewish citizen, Yehiel, whose generosity towards the exiles from Spain is recorded in history. The wife of Don Samuel Abrabanel sent him a beautifully embroidered silk flag and other presents. He was also supplied liberally with money so that he might make his appearance before the royal court as befits an ambassador of a Jewish king. After many delays, David finally set sail for Portugal.

In the third part of the book Reubeni describes his stay in Lisbon, his dealings with the king and his return from there to Italy. It is very detailed and contains the record of many small personal incidents of daily occurrence which exhibit more strongly the character of the writer. We learn that at first the king of Portugal received David with exceptional honor treating him like a prince of a foreign country and was favorably inclined to accept his proposition. He even drew up a covenant in which the king obligated himself to supply Joseph, the ruler of the Jewish tribes, with eight warships and four thousand pieces of arms as well as some cannon. But all the promises came to naught. Dom Michael, the former Portuguese ambassador to Rome, who was now a royal counsellor, threw many obstacles in the way and ultimately succeeded in frustrating the entire plan. Another factor in the undoing of David was his carelessness in fraternizing with the Marranos. These were greatly encouraged by the honor with which the Jewish ambassador was received by the king and began to turn openly to Judaism. Such action aroused great objection on the part of many nobles and protests were made to the king which resulted in his dismissing Reubeni from his presence and disregarding his former promises. On the return trip, the boat in which David sailed touched the port of Almera in Spain and there he was arrested by the authorities. After many tribulations, however, he was ordered to be freed by the emperor Charles the Fifth. With this episode, the itinerary breaks off and the rest of the story of Reubeni's adventures as told by himself, is unfortunately missing.

The last part of the book is the most valuable for in it is reflected the remarkable character of this adventurer. We see in it that he took himself very seriously. His bearing in the royal court was like that of a real prince. He never quaked before his enemies who were the highest nobles of Portugal and treated their haughtiness with open contempt. Even in his relations with the king himself, he displayed the utmost dignity. He tells us that once when he thought himself insulted by the king's refusal to see him at a certain hour, he in turn refused to come before him later in the day when he was sent for, in spite of the entreaties of the royal messengers, and came to court only on the following day. He continually tells the king that he came to Europe from his distant land not only for the sake of the Jews but for the benefit of the Portuguese dominion as well.

Where lay the source of that pride, the princely bearing, the complete confidence in himself which was not shaken even after the disappointment in the promises of the king? Again, what was the nature of the documents which he presented to pope and king which made them receive him as a real ambassador of a reigning house? To these questions, history will probably never give an answer, and the personality of Reubeni will forever remain a mystery.

139. MINOR WORKS

We have two more itineraries written during this period which describe travels to other countries besides Palestine. Both of them, however, are of minor importance, one on account of the short distance of the trip it describes, and the other because of the insufficiency of its description. The first is called *Miktab Mas'a* (A Letter of Travel) by Elijah of Pesaro, Italy, written in 1564. Elijah who, as can be seen from his letter was a scholar and a rich merchant, intended to go to Palestine with his family for the purpose of settling there. He sailed from Venice on the 4th of August, 1563, to reach his destination. His route lay via the Adriatic Sea, the islands of Corfu and Crete to Cyprus. At the last island, the boat stopped for some time and Elijah visited the city of Pamgusta where he heard that the pest was raging in the East. He therefore decided to discontinue his journey and settled at Pamgusta for some time. It is from there that he wrote the letter.

Our author tells the story of his rather short trip in great detail. He begins with a description of the boat itself, its structure, its equipment and its management. He does not neglect to tell us about the prices of tickets and the amount of special taxes that Jews had to pay and other things connected with a sea voyage. His vessel called at many ports, among them also at some Albanian cities, and Elijah tells about the life of the Jews in those places. Most of the Jews who resided in Albania and the islands of Corfu and Cyprus were engaged primarily in money lending, and on the whole were ignorant and not very pious. The last part of the book is devoted to Pamgusta in particular and Cyprus in general. We get an adequate description of the city, the climate of the island, the life of the people, and customs of their religion. There were at that time twenty-five Jews in the whole island who resided at that city and were engaged in money lending. There Elijah met Rabbi Eliezer Ashkenazi of Cairo, Egypt, who later became rabbi at Krakow, Poland, and it is he who undertook to deliver Elijah's letter while on a visit to Venice.

The second book of travel is a record of a journey through most of the European countries in the years 1753-58 by the famous bibliographer Hayyim David Azulai (Sect. 145) called *Maagal Tob* (The Good Path). Azulai left Jerusalem in 1753 on a trip to Europe as an emissary of the Sephardic educational (Yeshiboth) and charitable institutions in the Holy City to collect funds for their support. He went by land to Cairo and thence to Alexandria, where he set sail for Italy. He visited Italy, Germany, Holland, England and France. From there, he returned to Italy by way of Provence.

The book is primarily a record of personal events, but it does contain many data on Jewish life in all those countries. He visited almost every important Jewish community in Europe, but met with little success for his mission in Germany, for the Jews there sent their money to Palestine solely for the support of Ashkenazic (German) institutions, and he records in great detail his tribulations in the various cities. He fared better in the Sephardic communities. Of great interest is his meeting in Paris with Jacob (Giacobbo) Rodriguez Pereire, the pioneer in deaf mute education and the inventor of the sign language. Pereire's method was investigated by a commission of the French academy and approved. He later, according to Azulai, attracted the notice of the king, and the latter granted him an annual pension of 800 francs. This Pereire, we learn from Azulai, was a pious and observant Jew who took great interest in community affairs. He befriended our author and provided him with lodgings during his stay at Paris. Azulai took advantage of his trip to search through the libraries for Jewish books and manuscripts and he does not fail to record his finds in this field in the itinerary. He also describes here and there some exceptional sights or public building which attracted his attention. Thus he tells in detail about what he saw in the Tower of London and a few other places of interest. From a historical point of view, the itinerary of Azulai, though marred by innumerable reports of collections of funds, is valuable.

C. Biography and Autobiography

140. INTRODUCTORY

The art of biography by means of which the life of a famous man is described to us on the basis of certain data and the record of his deeds and actions, was entirely unknown in the Middle Ages. Needless to say that no attempt was made to analyze the character of the one described and to penetrate into the inner recesses of his soul. The best that we can expect in the line of biography are collections of tales and legends touching upon the life of the hero or heroes who caught the imagination of the people. These collections contain at times a few true data about the life and activities of the hero. Still even in the field of legendary biography there is no prolific productivity. With the exception of numerous tales and legends concerning the life of Jewish great men scattered in the various histories and chronicles of the period, we have only two special legendary biographies, one of which is a semi-autobiography.

On the other hand, we have extant a number of autobiographical works and personal memoirs written by distinguished men and women at various times which are a distinct contribution to Jewish literature. They are authentic and full of interest, for the writers were not only learned and good observers of life, but also leading men and women in their generation, as well as active in public work. Their works are therefore not only testimonies of the life of distinguished personalities, but historical documents as well, for they throw light upon the events and vicissitudes in the history of generations.

141. BIOGRAPHIES

The first of these so-called biographies is the *Shivhē ha-Ari* (The Praises of the Ari, i. e. Isaac Luria). Isaac Luria, the famous Kabbalist (Sect. 118) became, as his theories of mysticism spread to all parts of Jewry, a popular hero, a man of wondrous deeds and miraculous life. It is but natural that some kind of legendary biography of his should be written shortly after his death, and accordingly it was composed by the Kabbalist Solomon Shlumel, a devoted follower of Luria who settled in Safed. The biography was written in the form of three letters sent by Shlumel in the year 1609 to the mystic Issachar Ber at Krementz, Poland. A part of the first letter contains authentic data about the youth of Luria, his sojourn at Egypt, his ascetic and saintly conduct and his settlement at Safed. The rest is devoted to the description of his wondrous deeds. Many tales are told about the high degree of his sanctity, his all-embracing mystic knowledge, and his frequent ascensions to heaven for the purpose of learning the deep secrets of the Kabbala. Among other things, we are told that Luria was the Messiah of the house of Joseph (Meshiah bene Yoseph), who is supposed to precede the Davidic Messiah, and that on several occasions he was about to initiate the *Geulah,* i. e. the redemption, but that the disciples in their ignorance, prevented it.

The secon dletter is devoted chiefly to a description of Luria's life in Safed, and contains also a few data about the extreme piety of the *Ari.* The third letter is again devoted to Luria, the miracles he performed, his ability to see things hidden and at a distance, and especially his relation to his disciple, Rabbi Hayyim Vital. The author repeats the story often told by Vital himself that Luria came to this world only for the purpose of revealing the secrets of the Kabbala to Hayyim, the great apostle of the new teaching.

The letters of Shlumel were printed first in the *T'alumoth Hoḳmah* (Secrets of Wisdom) by Solomon Joseph del-Medigo in the year 1649, but were later reprinted a number of times under the above title with many additions from other sources.

The second biography is the *Sepher ha-Hesyonoth* (Book of Visions) by Hayyim Vital. As said, it is really an autobiography, for it is written by the author himself, but only partly so, for the greater portion is devoted to the description of visions experienced by the writer which he interprets in good apocalyptic style. As indicated above, Vital was a great aspirant for honor and fame and had an extremely exaggerated opinion of himself. This passion for self glorification is nowhere as strongly reflected as in the autobiographical part of his book.

He tells us with exceptional modesty that two years before his birth, his father, while still in Italy, was advised by a famous man to go to Palestine where a son would be born to him who will be the greatest sage in his generation. He again tells us nonchalantly that Rabbi Joseph Karo, the author of the *Shulhan Aruk*, said that half of the world subsists because of the merit of Hayyim's father, especially on account of the phylacteries (Tephilin) which he writes, and the other half through the merit of Hayyim himself. In another chapter, he tells of his revelation as a saint, quoting the statement of another Kabbalist about him, namely that he, Hayyim, was destined to become the Messiah of the house of Joseph, provided, of course, the generation deserved redemption. He further tells of his greatness as a Kabbalist, that he received all of Luria's secrets and the purpose of the latter's life was only to transmit the secrets to him.

The visions also are mainly intended for self-glorification. In one of them he relates of his visit in Paradise and describes quite minutely his own place there which is one of the highest order. The other visions follow in similar style and for like purpose. It is interesting to note that in spite of the too evident tendency of the autobiography and of the visions, the stories were readily accepted by the people. Strong indeed was the faith placed by the people in those whom they considered great.

142. AUTOBIOGRAPHY

i. The first authentic autobiography written in an orderly way, where the author tells of his accomplishments as well as of his failures and defects, is the *Hayē Yehudah*, by Judah Aryē de Modena (1571-1648). The work is of great interest for it gives us a glimpse into the inner life of a man of a most peculiar personality. In fact, his character was many-sided. He was, at one and the same time, a believer not only in tradition, but also in superstition and a skeptic, a man of a serious bent of mind, and yet with a great deal of frivolity in him, a dignified rabbi and teacher, and a director of and participant in the production of comic plays on the stage. And just as his character exhibits many-sidedness and variety, so does his life. He constantly varied his occupation and tried his hand at many a trade with the hope of succeeding in one of them, but as is the case with many such people, he spent his life in poverty and in bitter struggle for existence. In his despair he frequently grasped at a chance at the card table, but his luck deserted him even there, and as a rule he was the loser. He records in his autobiography twenty-six occupations with which he busied himself during his life, among them teaching both Jews and gentiles, preaching, Rabbinic work, writing poems, composing comedies, giving instruction in dramatic art, writing amulets, translating books, acting as business agent and match-maker (shadkhan) and similar things.

Equally varied were Modena's writings. He composed a book of sermons called *Midbar Yehudah* (The Speech of Judah), a divan of poems, a pastoral by the name of *Jacob and Rachel,* a Biblical dictionary in Hebrew and Italian, a dialogue both in defense and in derogation of the oral law, another dialogue in praise and disparagement of card playing, additions to the Agadic collection *En Yaḳob* by Jacob Habib, an exposition or a code of Jewish laws in Italian called the Ritus, and several more works. He also wrote dedicatory poems for authors and prefaces to their works, besides editing and indexing the books.

All these vicissitudes, changes and variations are faithfully recorded in his autobiography. He tells us of his youth, his education, his teachers and of his display of precocious ability. He informs us that he read the prophetic portion (Haftorah) in the synagogue at the age of two and one-half years[6] and performed several other scholastic feats in early youth. He narrates of his study at Ferrara under Hezekiah Finzi and later at Padua with Samuel Arkevolti (Sect. 9), famous grammarian and poet. We learn that he was also instructed in Latin, in music, both vocal and instrumental and in dancing. These subjects of education in which Judah was trained show us the great difference in the view of life held by the Italian Jews, on the one hand, and their brethren in Germany and Poland, on the other hand. No youth of a pious family in either of these latter countries would have been instructed in such unholy secular subjects as instrumental music and dancing.

He continues to tell of his early ventures both in business and in poetry, and that he failed in the former and succeeded in the latter. After failing in commerce, he drifted into teaching, a profession in which he was engaged most of his life, in spite of his detestation of it. He describes the tragic death of his fiancee, Esther, with quite some pathos and his marriage to her sister, Rachel, which took place in 1590, and later the checkered record of his life. Modena lived at

[6] It was customary in Italy to have very young children read the Haphtorah in the synagogue.

first in Montegana, but in 1592 he settled in Venice where he lived, except for several intervals of short residence in Ferrara, for the rest of his life.

In the other chapters, he tells in some detail all the incidents of his own life and those of his family, the birth of his children, their education, their accomplishments and short-comings. He also narrates with great emotion the death of his oldest son, Mordecai, and that of his son-in-law, Jacob Levi. He records his various ventures in business, in the publishing of books and other occupations, and also his frequent losses at the card table which amounted to large sums. In the six months from December 1595 to May 1596, he lost more than three hundred ducats. He struggled bitterly with his passion for gambling but was unable to overcome it. He resolved many times to cease playing but broke his resolution as often as opportunity presented itself. The narrative is interspersed with reports and visions for, as said, he was a believer in things supernatural as well as a skeptic.

He concludes his book with his testament, giving instructions regarding his coffin, the book that is to be placed on it, the psalms to be recited and the content of the funeral oration. He would prefer not to have any such oration, but knowing that he will not be obeyed, asks the orators not to exaggerate his virtues but to say that he was no hypocrite, God-fearing and fearless in telling the truth to others and even to himself. In fact, he began to compose his own funeral oration on condition that it be delivered by his son-in-law, Jacob Levi, but since the latter preceded him in death, he abandoned the writing. In the last admission, there is revealed a bit of the theatrical in the nature of Modena.

This autobiography is supplemented by a collection of letters left by Modena and published by Dr. L. Blau. The letters over two hundred in number, throw further light upon the life of Modena, his character and his relations with friends and acquaintances, and also illuminate some points in Italian Jewish life. They are written in a flowing but ornate Hebrew style (Melitzah). Through them, as well as through his autobiography, there runs the tragic note of the bitter struggle of a man possessing a deep, feeling soul and striving towards noble things against a cruel destiny.

143. GLUCKEL VON HAMMELN'S MEMOIRS

A work of exceptional value and interest is the autobiography of a remarkable Jewish woman, Glückel Von Hammeln (1647-1724), known under the name of *Memoirs.* The book is written in the Judaeo-German of the time, but its content is of such importance and uniqueness that it deserves a more lengthy discussion than a mere passing notice in a short survey of the literature of that dialect.

The author of the *Memoirs,* Glückel, was the daughter of Löb Pinkerle, the president of the Jewish community of Hamburg. When she was two years old, her parents, due to the temporary expulsion of the Jews from that city, took up their residence in the neighboring city of Altona. There, Glückel attended the elementary Hebrew school (Heder) where she obtained her Jewish education which is so excellently manifested in her work. Her father was later instrumental in obtaining permission for the Jews to return to Hamburg and her family was the first to go back to its old home. Nothing remarkable occurred during her girlhood; her life was spent quietly in the house of her father where the atmosphere was saturated with piety, love of learning and unbounded sympathy for the unfortunate sufferers. In this atmosphere her character was moulded and her personality perfected to be able to fulfill her functions as a faithful and devoted wife and mother of a large and distinguished famliy. The roles seem ordinary enough, but with Glückel they became somewhat more than that, worthy to attract our attention.

At twelve she was engaged to Hayyim of Hammeln, a small town in the northwest of Germany, and at fourteen she was married to him. Though, in accordance with the custom of the time, matches were then made by the parents and Glückel had not set eyes upon her fiance before marriage, the match was nevertheless a most happy one. The love of the couple for each other was an exalted one as she speaks of her husband in the most endearing terms. At first, the couple lived at Hammeln, but soon moved to Hamburg where Hayyim engaged in the jewelry business on a large scale. For thirty-two years Glückel's life flowed happily, marred here and there by the usual troubles arising from the vicissitudes of commerce, and the raising of a large family of twelve. In 1689, the first serious painful episode came into her life which was the death of her Hayyim, "the apple of her eye," as she constantly calls him. She was only forty-five years when that occurred and she was left alone in the world with a large troop of children to provide for, educate and give into marriage. She assumed her burdens dutifully, carried on her husband's business, brought up her children in the best Jewish style and married them into the leading Jewish families of Germany. During the eleven years of her widowhood, she attained wealth and even fame. But in spite of her being busily engaged in commercial and family affairs, she was very lonely without Hayyim, and it was in order to assuage her loneliness and pacify the melancholy thoughts that took hold of her during the winter nights, that Glückel began to write her *Memoirs* in the year 1691.

She planned to settle in Palestine in her old age, but her children objected to that, and at the importunities of some of them, she entertained a second marriage proposal. In 1700, she married the rich Cerf (Hertz) Levy of Metz, Alsace. Levy was the leader of the Jewish community there and the head of a great banking house. But she was not destined to enjoy her second wedded life. Only two years after the marriage, Levy went bankrupt causing great loss even to his wife who had invested her own money and the dowry of her youngest daughter with him, and Glückel experienced for the first time in her life the pangs of poverty. Matters grew worse when Levy died in 1712, and she remained a widow for the second time, and poor in addition. For a time she refused the hospitality of her rich daughter, Esther, the wife of Moses Krumbach of Metz, as she preferred to live alone in a garret, but due to illness she ultimately yielded to the requests of her children and spent the rest of her life with them. She bore her adversity with equanimity and speaks in her *Memoirs* of her days of misery with the same implicit faith and trust in the justice of God as manifested in the records of her days of affluence.

The life of this woman who verily represents the ideal Jewish wife and mother which we sketched here briefly, is described in the *Memoirs* in all its ramifications very vividly. In fact, it is so vividly pictured that we obtain an indelible impression not only of Glückel's own character and personality but also of all those that came in contact with her. Her education was limited for, as she tells us, the years of her attendance at *Heder* were few, and though she could read Hebrew, she did not master that language and knew no other language. Yet so saturated was the atmosphere of her environment with piety, learning and morality that she imbibed unconsciously a great amount of Jewish lore and displays in her writings a wide knowledge of the Jewish religion, the Bible and Jewish ethical literature. She undoubtedly derived all this knowledge from the extensive Judaeo-German religious and ethical literature, and most likely read the Bible also in translations. Still she succeeded in acquiring sufficient mastery of a large number of Hebrew phrases and expressions to be able to use them appropriately and correctly. Her book is replete with such phrases and quotations. In addition she also drew upon her wide reading and illustrates her narrative by many moral stories, fables and tales which enhance the value of the *Memoirs* and give it the status of a literary creation.

Of the seven books into which the Memoirs are divided, the first serves as an introduction to the entire work, and is devoted to the statement of both of her view of life and the purpose of the book. It is in fact a small ethical treatise. Her view of life is simple but noble. God's providence in the world extends to everybody, and is permeated with mercy, intended for the good of man though we can not always scrutinize its ways. Man must therefore be thankful for the good happenings, accept the bad events with patience and resignation, and his main concern must be to live in such wise as to please God. In business relations, he must be careful to deal honestly, not to bring any dishonor upon the name of God and Israel (Hilul-ha-Shem) and to be free from debt. Honest business dealing is the first point upon which man is judged in the hereafter. This was a sacred principle to Glückel in her life which she observed at the greatest sacrifice. It is for the purpose of inculcating in the hearts of her children these principles of conduct by examples from her own life and that of her dead husband Hayyim that she wrote these memoirs in order that they should know who their ancestors were and model their own life after theirs. She is however modest enough to say that she does not deserve a special biography and therefore adds that her loneliness after her husband's death was another reason for the writing of the *Memoirs*. The first book also contains several lengthy stories of a moral nature.

The second book embraces her life story from early youth to about a year after her marriage when the young couple decided to move from Hammeln to Hamburg. Here we get a description of her father's home, a fine picture of an ideal Jewish home. Among other things she tells us that when the refugees from the massacres in Poland in the years 1648-49 came to Hamburg, they were lodged at her father's house and though afflicted with a contagious disease they were cared for by her family. Her grandmother attended to them personally and as a result she took sick and died. Glückel herself and her sister also fell sick, and yet the *Parnas* (head of the community), Pinkerle, her father, did not complain and continued to care for the refugees. We are further told of her wedding ceremony and her life at Hammeln which was rather dreary as the place was small, but she informs us, that she was compensated for the monotony of life by her admiration for her father-in-law, Joseph, who was a model of good conduct and piety.

The third and fourth books describe the events that transpired during the happiest period of her life, that is from the time the family settled in Hamburg to the death of her husband. In these books numerous events are recorded which unroll before us the vicissitudes of the Hammeln family in all their ramifications together with many things that throw light upon Jewish life in Germany. We are informed of the commercial relations of Hayyim Hammel, of his various visits to the fairs of Leipzig and the jewelry mart of Amsterdam, the people he did business with and their code of conduct. We thus obtain an inner glimpse into the business methods of some of the leading Jews of Germany at the time. From the narratives about the marriages of her children, we learn how the Jews combined business with match-making, for several matches of Glückel's children were concluded at the fairs. Thus, she tells us, that the match between her eldest daughter Zippora and Koshman, son of Gompertz of Emmerich, a wealthy man and the agent of the Kurfürst of Brandenburg, was concluded at the meeting of merchants at Amsterdam. She further relates that the news aroused great interest at the exchange there, for many people did not credit it as Gompertz was one of the wealthiest Jews of the country, while Hammel was as yet unknown, and bets were placed on the probability of the consummation of the matter. We have a description of the wedding which was a grand affair. It was attended by the Prince of Brandenburg and Prince Maurice of Nassau with whom Gompertz had business relations.

The first alliance with one of the leading families of German Jewry brought about the affiancing of several other of the Hammel children to scions of noble families, the transpiring of which are told in detail. Among other things Glückel narrates also of the impression the reports of the doings of Sabbatai Zevi, the false Messiah, made upon German Jews. Hamburg was a center of Sabbatism, for the Sephardic community there contained a large number of followers of the Messiah, but even among the Ashkenazic Jews there were some staunch believers that redemption was near. Glückel's father-in-law, Joseph Hammel, sold his property and made all preparations to depart for Palestine. He even packed two barrels full of smoked meats and dried fruits and sent them to Hamburg to be ready for the day of sailing to the Holy Land. The old man, however, was doomed to disappointment, and the food, Glückel tells us, had to be consumed by her family.

The fifth book contains the story of her widowhood, her struggle to raise her family of eight children who were yet young, to educate them and marry them off. Glückel performed her duties in a most masterly manner. She carried on the business and amplified her fortune, made seven marriage alliances for her younger sons and daughters, all of the highest degree, and endowed each one with a respectable dowry. In the narration of these events, her character as a mother, as a business woman and as the head of a large family is drawn in strong relief. She followed her own maxims pronounced in the first book, namely strict honesty in business, and paid several times large sums to the creditors of her children so that the name Hammel remain unsullied. In selecting matches for her children, nobility of family and learning were her first concern, though the matter of dowry was not discarded. Her children were scattered after their marriages through the leading cities of Germany, Austria and Alsace, such as Metz, Berlin, Vienna and other cities, but she was still the head of the family. The narratives of the affairs of the Hammel family are full of human interest.

The sixth and the seventh books are devoted to Glückel's life in Metz, her second marriage and widowhood. She describes fully her first two years of happy life with Cerf Levy, his bankruptcy and poverty. In the description of the sudden adversity that came upon the rich banker and her fall from great wealth into the abyss of misery, the fine qualities of her personality are shown at their best. No complaint escapes her pen, but she accepts the vicissitudes of fortune with stoic resignation. On the other hand, she is very proud of the fact that her husband gave to his creditors even the last tin spoon in order to save the integrity of his name.

The same stoic equanimity is manifested in her description of her misery after Levy's death when she lost her home and was forced to live in a small garret room without stove or fire-place.

The Memoirs of Glückel are of great interest to the student of human life and that of Jewish history.

To the autobiographic literature of the period belong also the Memoirs of Dob of Bolihow (1723-1805) which were only recently published. Dob received, in addition to the usual Hebrew education, also instruction in Polish and Latin, and was on the whole a well read man. Though he was engaged like his father in the wine business, he devoted his leisure to study and reading, and even tried his hand at literary composition. He composed a kind of history of Jewish sects by the name *Dibrē Binah* and began to translate the German rendering of Humphrey Pridaw's treatise *On the Old and New Testaments,* into Hebrew. In his leisure moments he wrote down his memoirs.

Unfortunately, the last work has not come down to us either completely or in an orderly and systematic arrangement. The Memoirs do not constitute a coherent story of his life but consist of isolated chapters, each containing more or less connected narratives of events in his life with no specific order of arrangement, as some of the later happenings precede the earlier ones.

The greater part of the book consists of records of his commercial transactions and his various business trips and dealings. Here and there, however, we find notices about Jewish communal life in various cities in Galicia, as well as a number of facts concerning the relations of the Polish government to the Jews during the period. Dob also records some important changes that took place at the time in the Polish commonwealth. The book though not distinguished as a literary prdouction, is yet valuable on account of the historical material it contains.

D. Critical and Literary History

144. *AZARYA DE ROSSI'S MEOR ENAYIM*

As we have seen in our survey of the historical literature of the period, most of the books written in this field merely convey information regarding the past life of the people and no attempt is made by their authors to test critically the material they are dealing with. Yet criticism was not entirely neglected, as there is at least one valuable contribution to this important branch of literature, and that is Azarya de Rossi's collection of historical essays called *Meor Enayim* (The Light of the Eyes).

Azarya ben Moses de Rossi (1513-1678) was a descendant of one of the noblest Jewish families in Italy. The family called itself *ha-Adumim* (The Red People, hence de Rossi) and cherished a tradition that its ancestors were brought to Rome from Jerusalem by Titus. Moses, Azarya's father, lived in Mantua and it is there where the gifted son spent his youth and received his education. Azarya was trained both in Jewish and secular learning, and he attained an exceptional mastery of almost all branches of science of his time. He knew besides Hebrew also Latin, Italian and Greek, though he did not master the latter sufficiently. He studied medicine and most likely practiced it, but his real interest lay in historical and theological studies to which he devoted himself with great energy. Azarya's erudition was remarkable and the extent of his reading all-embracing. He was at home in the entire Jewish literature in all its branches, and equally at home in the writings of Philo, Josephus, Plato, the Church Fathers, the works of Cicero, Quintilian, Thomas Aquinas and a host of others; in short in the entire philosophical, theological and historical literature of his time.

He seemed to have made his home at Ferrara, though from time to time he sojourned temporarily in several of the papal cities. In 1571, an earthquake took place in Ferrara and Azarya's home was destroyed along with others, though none of his family was injured, and he was forced to move to a place across the River Po. There he began to devote himself to literary composition. He first wrote a short treatise on the earthquake called *Kol Elohim* (The Voice of God). Next he translated from the Latin into Hebrew the Apocryphal book known as the *Letter of Aristeas* (Vol. I, Sect. 65); where the story of the Septuagint translation is told, calling his work *Hadrath Zeḳenim* (The Glory of the Elders) and finally he composed his various essays. He included them all in one work, *Meor Enayim* which was printed in 1574 at Ferrara. The book aroused great discussion and many scholars took issue with him for his assertions. The author, therefore, prepared a second edition where he replied to his critics, and added another treatise called *Mazref la-Keseph* in which the main problem of his work, that of the authenticity of the era of creation, is further elucidated and the entire question of the calendar is gone into in a thorough manner.

The *Meor Enayim* is divided into three parts, the first two are the above mentioned, the treatise on earthquakes and the translation of the *Letter of Aristeas,* and the third called *Imrē Binah* containing sixty chapters consists of various essays and constitutes the body of the book. Of the first two parts, there is little to be said, except that the *Kol Elohim* is a description of the events of the earthquake together with a short discussion of the causes of the quakes, and that the translation of the letter of Aristeas is rendered in an accurate manner and in good Hebrew style.

The third part is divided into four sections (Maamarim), each subdivided into chapters. The aim of the work as a whole is to examine critically many of the views contained in Talmudic literature on certain events in Jewish history, or literary matters, or the nature of institutions, and to ascertain whether the cherished views are really true, especially as compared with those held by oher writers both Jewish and gentile. Azarya was not exactly the first Jewish scholar who utilized in his studies the works written by gentiles, but he was the first who studied them thoroughly and brought to bear the results of these studies upon his investigations. He cites more than ninety works written in Greek, Latin or Italian and displays a thorough knowledge of the works of Philo, Josephus, Eusibius, Jerome, St. Augustine and the later divines and historians. He collates the statements on Jewish history and antiquities contained in the writings of these men with those contained in Talmudic literature and by critical methods endeavors to elicit the truth.

The opening two chapters of the first section are devoted to apologies both for the variety of the content of his book and for the extensive use he makes of the writings of gentiles. As to the former, the author felt that he is introducing something new in Jewish literature, namely the short essay, and he attempts to prove the advantage of a book which discusses many subjects rather than only one exhaustively. Regarding the latter, he holds forth a long apology telling us that even the authors of the Talmud followed, in matters of science, the opinions of non-Jews, and that scholars throughout the ages had studied the works of gentiles, and finally assures us that he will not quote anything derogatory to the Torah but, on the contrary, things which will corroborate its truth and add to its glory. He then introduces to the readers Philo and his works, and in connection with this, he discusses the Jewish sects during the Second Commonwealth as described both by Philo and Josephus. Here Azarya suggests that since we have no characterization either in Talmudic literature or in the works of these historians of the character of the Bethusians, that this sect was identical with the Essenes.

A few more chapters are devoted to Philo, where the author quotes on the one hand, a number of excerpts from his writings which agree with the accepted Jewish views, and on the other hand, many passages which do not agree with them. He observes correctly that Philo did not read the Bible in the original but used the Septuagint, and hence many of his mistaken notions. He even devotes a special chapter to an apology on behalf of the philosopher. The discussion of Philo brings Azarya to a discussion of the Septuagint, namely the statements about this translation in the Talmud, its deviaions from the Masoretic text and the question how these differences arose. In all these matters de Rossi displays great critical skill in the examination of the documents. He makes an interesting suggestion regarding the text underlying the Septuagint which is, that during the early part of the Second Commonwealth there were two texts of the Bible, one in Hebrew which was carefully guarded and the other a popular edition in Aramaic, written in the ancient Hebrew script. It is this second text which was translated into Greek, and since it was not guarded, there were a number of changes which crept into it, and the same variations were incorporated into the Septuagint. It is worth while noting that this supposition was revived in our own days by some Biblical scholars.

The last four chapters of the section deal with such subjects as the comparison of the stories about Alexander the Great found in the Talmud and in Plutarch, the massacre of the Jews at Alexandria under Trajan, the large number of Jews at the time of the destruction of the Second Temple and a vindication of the Rabbis for some of their erroneous views on matters of science. In the apology for the Rabbis, he proves first of all that they did not possess a thorough knowledge about astronomy and kindred sciences, and consequently they erred at times. He lays down his principle that their authority is to be accepted only in matters of law and tradition, for in subjects which concern other departments of knowledge they were limited by the conditions of their time, but their glory is not diminished, even if we assume that they erred occasionally.

The second section paves the way for his main thesis given in the third section, namely that we must revise our reckoning according to the era of creation, for there are some errors in the Biblical chronology, as well as in the Talmudic tradition, namely that the period of the First Temple lasted for 410 years and that of the second 420. The second section therefore deals with subjects pertaining to the main thesis which affect the chronological calculations mentioned. In the opening chapters, Azarya quotes the earlier commentators of the Bible, such as Kimhi, Gersonides and Abrabanel who differed in their interpretation of certain verses from the one adopted in the Talmud and in the *Seder Olam* (Vol. I, Sect. 74). Thus, Kimhi computes the length of the existence of the First Temple to be 429 years, Gersonides 419, Abraham Ibn Daud 430, but all disregard the figure 410 fixed in the *Seder Olam* and adopted by the Talmud.

He then discusses various questions such as the time of Simon the Just, the number of the Persian kings from Cyrus to Alexander, the beginning of the Seleucid era,[7] the time when the Jews began to reckon according to creation and several kindred subjects. He also discusses in several chapters the method of the Rabbis in interpreting the Bible for purposes of instruction in ethics and religion, and enunciates principles of great value for the understanding of the Agada. First, that these Agadic interpretations are not to be taken literally but metaphorically or symbollically, and that their main purpose was to draw from the verse the lesson the Rabbis had in mind and not to explain the verse in accordance with its plain meaning. Moreover, the Rabbis themselves were conscious of the fact that the *peshat* and the homiletic interpretation were two different things and that the verse must always be understood plainly. Second, that the Rabbis imposed their authority only in such matters, mostly legal, which they believed either to have been handed down from Sinai or deduced from the Pentateuch by the fixed rules of interpretation, or that were established by them as a fence around the law. In all other matters, such as astronomy, chronology and related studies, they merely expressed an opinion and one is permitted to differ with them. For the establishment of these principles, he cites a number of quotations from Talmudic literature and opinions of various authorities.

The third section which contains the main thesis of the book is devoted primarily to chronology and is denominated *Yemoth Olam* (The Days of the World). As the question of he length of the years of existence of the Second Temple is the crux of the problem, he concentrates on that point. The acceptance of the number of 420 years for the duration of that period is based primarily on the number of years the Persian rule extended before the conquest of Alexander. The *Seder Olam* followed by the Talmud fixed that number as thirty-four. Such a short period, of course, can not account for all the events that took place from the building of the Temple to the con-

[7] This era began in 312 B. C. E. with the victory won by the combined forces of Seleucus Nicator and Ptolemy Soter at Gaza over those of Antigones. This year marks the beginning of the reign of the Seleucid dynasty over Syria, and hence also that of the era. The Jews who lived in the land under the sway of the Seleucids also adopted it at the time. In Palestine, though, it was discarded immediately after the victory of the Hasmoneans, but the Jews of Babylonia continued to use that era for over a thousand years after the Syrian kingdom ceased to exist.

quest of Alexander, and the Rabbis were forced to assume that the four names of the Persion kings mentioned in the Bible in reality refer only to two kings and so make Cyrus bear three names. Likewise the Talmudists placed Zerubabel, Ezra and Nehemiah in one generation, and Simon the Just, the last of the Great Assembly in the following generation. The days of the Great Assembly were thus shortened to a few years. All these errors resulted from the assumption that the length of that period was only 420 years. And it is primarily against this erroneous historical conception that Azarya directs his criticism.

As usual, he begins the section with an apology for his attempting to disprove the opinions of the Rabbis. Next he marshals in four chapters the testimonies of four historians, the Greek Xenophones, the Persian Metastenes, Philo and Josephus all of whom speak of a considerable number of Persian kings between Cyrus and the last Darius. He then concentrates his attack on the entire Biblical chronology, pointing out errors in the traditionally assumed period of duration of the residence of the Jews in Egypt and in the extent of the periods of the First and Second Temples. He proves from the long chain of high priests that held office between the time of the Restoration and Simon the Just, from the eight descendants of Zerubabel mentioned in I Chronicles, Ch. II, and from the lists of the Persian kings, that the assumption of thirty-four years to be the span of time from the Restoration to Alexander is preposterous.

He therefore comes to the conclusion that we must add to the era of creation at least a hundred years. Azarya does not fix the number of years for the duration of the Second Temple, but surmises it to have been at least 490. We know it now to have been 586.

The fourth section contains a number of essays on such subjects as the translations of Onkelos and Aquila, on the form of the priestly vestments, on the ancient Hebrew script, on the origin of the vowels and accents and on the forms of poetry in the Bible. Every essay is very elucidating, and our knowledge of the subjects is greatly enriched by numerous quotations from the entire Jewish literature as well as from other sources. It is interesting to note that in regard to the origin of the vowels and accents, Azarya is very conservative. He differs with Elijah Levita (Sect. 8) who ascribes the invention of the vowels and accents to the period after the close of the Talmud, and believes that the vowels at least were already known to Moses, but that the accents might have been invented later. His essay on forms of poetry in the Bible displays a keen understanding of the poetic portions of Scriptures, and constitutes a contribution to Biblical knowledge.

The work of Azarya, *Meor Enayim,* is one of the few books that really deserve their name, for it shed light on many knotted problems in Jewish history and blazed the path for a real scientific study of Jewish history and literature. The founders of Jewish science in the nineteenth century saw justly in de Rossi the pioneer who made possible the continuation of their own work.

However, the contemporaries of the author were not as favorably inclined toward the book as were the later generations, and on the contrary, considered it pernicious and heretical. The appearance of the *Meor Enayim* raised a storm of protests, especially in Safed, the center of Talmudic and mystic scholarship at the time, and according to reports, the great scholar Joseph Karo was about to issue a ban against all readers of the work. But before he carried out his intention he took sick and died. When these reports reached Italy, the rabbis there took counsel and finally issued a decree that no pious Jew should read the *Meor Enayim* until he reached the age of twenty-five and then only by special permission by the scholars of his city. This decree was signed by the Rabbinical courts of Venice, Ferrara, Padua, Pesaro and other leading communities. Later, however, the decree was revoked and was soon forgotten altogether. Such were the struggles of the first attempt at critical history.

145. LITERARY HISTORY

Just as Mediaeval literature is meager in histories written from a critical point of view, it is likewise poor in works dealing with the history of literature. This is partly explained by the fact that most Jewish histories include to a great extent the record of literary progress and give the names of the works of the men whose life they tell. Some of these histories, as the *Seder ha-Doroth,* (Sect. 134) even have a section dealing with bibliography. Yet there were a few writers who paid special attention to this branch of literature and left us several works dealing with books and authors. These books are primarily bibliographical works, but they embrace more than a mere catalogue of titles, inasmuch as they contain also some biographical data and short notes on the contents of the books they mention, and they thus furnish good material for a literary history.

i. The earliest of these works is the literary letter of Joseph Solomon del Medigo (1591-1657) to Zerah of Troki, the Karaite, (Sect. 126) which for want of a specific name is called *Miktob Ohuz* after the opening words of the epistle. The letter written in rhymed prose and with excessive euphuism gives a short sketch of the most important productions of Mediæval Jewish literature with the exception of Rabbinics. It begins with a tirade against the Kabbalists and their works, in which not only the important books on mysticism are mentioned but also its principal theories. He next turns to praise the scientists and scholars of former ages who devoted their time to worthy studies, such as astronomy and mathematics, gives a list of their principal works in these fields, and outlines for his correspondent a reading course in Jewish literature. He begins with the science of language, recommends the works of the best grammarians and turns to poetry and prose citing the Classical works in these fields. From these, he proceeds to philosophy and enumerates the important productions in the field. Bible exegesis and miscellaneous books, such as histories, works on ethics and tales of travel are next listed and discussed. He concludes the letter by a list of his own works.

The letter is of literary interest for it is not a catalogue but contains pointed remarks about the character of the books, either of a complimentary or derogatory nature. Some of del Medigo's remarks became standard quotations in literary history and were frequently cited without mention of the author. Thus, the name he gave to Ibn Yahya's history, calling it *Shalsheleth ha-Shekarim* instead of *Shalsheleth ha-Kabbala* clung to the work through the ages. Equally famous is his statement about the four principal commentators of the *Guide* of Maimonides, namely Moses Narboni, Shem Tob ben Joseph, Asher Crescas and Ephodi, or Profit Duran. These four, says del-Medigo, are like the four sons mentioned in the Passover Haggadah. Narboni is the *Rosha,* the wicked, for he is the radical, Shem Tob is the *Hakam,* the wise, for his commentary explains the words of Maimonides well and also analyzes them; Grescas is the *Tam,* the simple one, for his explanation is insufficient, and Ephodi is the *She-Ainē Yodea Lishol,* as he comments briefly and clearly but raises no difficulties against Maimonides.

The letter is also a human document, for it reveals the double personality of del-Medigo. The same man who wrote a number of Kabbalistic works himself (Sect. 119) and speaks there of the Kabbala and of Luria in the most exalted terms, mocks in this letter at its teachings in a most atrocious and undignified manner. He also makes light of the Talmudic studies which he lauds in his other works.

ii. The second work on literary history which is in the nature of a bibliography is the *Sifthē-Yeshenim* (The Lips of the Sleeping), a euphuistic name for the works of dead authors by Sabbatai Bass (1641-1718). Sabbatai was a cantor by profession, hence his name *Bass,* i. e. possessor of a bass voice. He first served the Jewsih community in Prague, then in other cities. Finally, after many years of travel he settled in Dyhenfurth, a town near Breslau, and established there a Hebrew press. On his travels and especially during his stay at Amsterdam, he gathered material for his work.

The book is divided into two sections or parts, each of which he calls *Deleth* (Door). The first part is devoted to the Bible and all books dealing with it. The second part embraces the literature centering around the Oral Law or the Talmud, including of course all works on other subjects, besides those of Rabbinics, though the latter are given special attention. Bass listed over twenty-four hundred books and arranged them in alphabetical order in twenty divisions according to subject matter. At the end of the book there is an index of the authors, and lists of the Tannaim, Amoraim, and Gaomim. Bass' *Sifthē,* though far from complete, is a very useful work and is well organized. It was frequently utilized by the succeeding bibliographers.

iii. Another valuable book of bibliography is the *Shem ha-Gedolim* (Glory of the Great) by Joseph Hayyim Azulai (Sect. 139). Azulai, as we saw above, traveled extensively throughout Europe, and during these journeys visited many public and private libraries gathering material for his work. As is evident from his writings, he himself possessed a number of manuscripts. He wrote many works but is primarily known for this particular one.

There are two divisions to the *Shem ha-Gedolim,* the *Maareketh ha-Gedolim* and the *Maareketh ha-Sepharim,* (The Order of Great Men and The Order of Books). In the first, over three thousand short biographies are given, and in the second an equal number of books are listed. Both divisions are arranged alphabetically. Azulai intersperses the first part with quotations from the works of the men he describes, and also notes, in accordance with his Kabbalistic teaching, the kind of soul the scholar possessed and at times even enters into polemical discussions refuting the view of his predecessors on certain matters. In a similar manner, he comments upon the books he lists in the second part.

Azulai was subjective in his selection of the works. As a Kabbalist and primarily a Talmudic scholar, his main interest lay in Rabbinics, works on Kabbala and other books of purely religious nature. Of the other branches of literature, he thought lightly. He therefore either omitted such productions or gave them brief mention, mostly including them in the biography of the author. Thus, he makes no mention of Gersonides' *Milhamoth,* nor of his commentaries on the Bible, though he allots a few lines to his biography. The *Kuzari,* the *Emunoth we-Deot* and the *Guide of Maimonides* are not dealt with in separate articles but included in the biographies of their authors. All that he has to say of Hasdai Crescas' *'Or Adonai* is that it advises to study the Talmud and observe the precepts, passing over in silence its higher value as a philosophical book. But with all its shortcomings, the *Shem ha-Gedolim* is a valuable contribution to Jewish literary history.

Chapter X

POLEMICS AND APOLOGETICS

146. GENERAL OBSERVATIONS

The adherents of every monotheistic religion which claims to possess the whole truth must, in the course of time, on coming in contact with the followers of other religions which advance a similar claim, produce an extensive polemic literature. They must necessarily defend the teachings of their own religion from the attacks of the representatives of other faiths, and very often they are forced to take the offensive and attack the principles of these faiths themselves. This necessity was greatly intensified in the course of history, in the case of the Jews, on account of both their own peculiar position and that of Judaism.

It has been the tragic destiny of Judaism from its very inception to stand alone and face a hostile or at best an unfriendly world. In the ancient world, it formed an anomaly in the history of humanity for it advocated unity in life and nature, while all other nations favored multiplicity. In the Mediaeval world it had to take issue with its own daughter religions which claimed to have superseded it in the possession of truth, and even attacked their progenitor with weapons drawn from its own Scriptures.

Not less tragic has been the fate of the Jewish people. Scattered through the greater part of their history to the four corners of the world, the Jews formed a minority in most of the countries in which they resided, and as such, were subjected not only to the political but also to the cultural power of the majority. They were forced therefore to constantly justify their separateness as a cultural and religious entity, and whenever they dared, also to prove the superiority of their religion over that of the majority. For these reasons, Jewish literature contains an exceedingly large number of books which are either entirely devoted to polemics and apologetics, or at least exhibit a tendency to defend Judaism and vindicate its superiority over other religions.

The place each of the two elements occupied in literature, namely the polemic and the apologetic, varied according to the position of the Jews and their relations to the surrounding world. Thus, in the Biblical and in the early post-Biblical periods, when Israel still lived on his land, the polemic element predominated. The prophetic books abound with diatribes and passages full of mockery against idolatry and idol worshippers, as for example Isaiah Chap. XL, 18-27; XLIV, 19-21; Jeremiah Chap. X, 1-17; Habakuk Chap. II, 18-20; Psalms Chap. CXV and many more places. The Apocryphal and Apocalyptic books are likewise full of stinging denunciations and biting satires against paganism and its adherents, such as the *Letter of Jeremy,* Chaps. VIII-XV in the *Wisdom of Solomon,* and the fourth book of the *Sybilline Oracles* (Vol. I, pp. 19, 24, 43) in addition to many scattered passages in other books.

In the later period, when the Jew went into exile and even during the Second Commonwealth outside of Palestine in the lands of the diaspora, the apologetic element on the whole predominated in literature, though from time to time, a bold Jewish spirit ventured to carry the war into the camp of the enemy and deliver a vigorous attack in the form of a trenchant polemic work. These characteristics were vividly reflected in the Hellenistic literature of the Jews of the diaspora discussed in Volume I (Ch. IV, A and B).

In the Talmudic period, as long as Jewish life was organized on a well established autonomous basis in the two great Jewish centers, Palestine and Babylon, the pressure of the outside life and culture was not strongly felt in Judaism. Hence there was no urgent need for a special literary activity of a polemic or apologetic nature. But whenever such tendency found expression, it was more of a polemic character rather than an apologetic one. In the entire wide Talmudic and Midrashic literature, we do not find a single treatise or book devoted either to a discussion of the qualities of Judaism or to a criticism of the principles of other religions. We do find, though, hundreds of passages scattered throughout these literatures where paganism, Christianity, and in the younger Midrashim also Islam are mentioned, and their teachings severely criticized and often bitterly satirized. That these literatures contain an equal number of passages extolling the superiority of the teachings of Judaism goes without saying. But in all these expressions, there is little of the apologetic except on one point and that is the explanation of the low state of the Jews. The dispersion of Israel and their sufferings was, as we will see, a strong weapon wielded by the representatives of the other religions, and especially of Christianity and Islam, in their polemics against the adherents of Judaism. It was considered by them proof of their claims that the Jewish religion was superseded by the later revelations to Jesus or Mohammed. Consequently, the Rabbis were forced to combat this argument and find some justification for the exile and the resultant suffering of the Jews.

It is therefore with the rise of Christianity and Islam, the two daughter religions, to complete power, each in its own sphere, that an extensive polemic and apologetic literature began to develop. Both of these religions were aggressive and propagandistic and saw in Judaism a living protest against their claims to the possession of truth. Consequently, their representatives made repeated attacks against it, and attempted to prove their superiority over Judaism. Moreover, the frequent persecutions which resulted in the increase of Jewish converts, the forced religious disputations prevalent in Christiandom, the emoluments held out to apostates and libelers of Judaism, all these produced a large anti-Jewish literature, and the Jewish scholars were forced to defend their faith and sometimes meet these attacks with counter charges. Thus this kind of literature gradually increased through all the centuries of suffering of the Middle Ages, and especially from the twelfth century on.

We must, therefore, note a great difference between the polemic and apologetic works produced in Christian countries and those in Mohammedan. The difference is both quantitative and qualitative. The fact that the teachings of Islam are closer to Judaism than those of Christianity, inasmuch as they emphasize the purity of the conception of God and His unity and command the performance of many religious ceremonies resembling those of Judaism, as well as the better position of the Jews, their participation in the general culture, and the comparative ignorance of the Mohammedans of Jewish literature, prevented the development of polemics in the countries under the sway of Islam. In addition we must also take into consideration that the Mohammedans abstained from forced religious disputations and often endeavored to hide their sacred scriptures from the Jews. Only on rare occasions, especially during the infrequent persecutions, do we find Mohammedan scholars writing polemic works against Judaism, for most of these, written in Arabic were composed by Syrian Christians. Finally, the polemic works of the Islam sages deal primarily with the limitation of the rights of the adherents of other religions, and dwell but little on the refutation of their principles.

As a result of all these factors, the Jewish polemic and apologetic works dealing with Islam are limited in number and comparatively milder in tone. The great mass of works belonging to this particular literature was produced in Christian countries and deals mainly with the teachings of Christianity and the attacks and charges of its representatives.

The nature and character of this literature accumulated through the centuries are many-sided. While this literature is largely defensive and apologetic, aiming to refute the many charges and libels against Judaism as well as the claims of Christianity to the possession of truth, it is yet of a decided polemic tone and color. Not only do the special polemic works display a belligerent quality but even in the apologetic works, the line between the defensive and the offensive attitudes is not drawn fast. For we really can not defend ourselves against the charges of an opponent without implying that the views on which the charges are based are erroneous and worthless. And just as the arguments of the representatives of Christianity against Judaism, as well as their claims to the veracity of their teachings were various and drawn from several fields of literature, such as exegesis, philosophy, theology, history and kindred subjects, so were the polemic and apologetic works of the Jewish authors varied in nature.

First of all comes the question of Biblical exegesis. Almost all Christian sages, from the Church Fathers down, based the claims of their religion to be the ultimate revelation, on a large number of passages in the Old Testament which they interpreted as prophesying the advent of Jesus and the establishment of the Church as a substitute for the synagogue. Then there are the philosophical-theological questions, such as the reconciling of the unity of God and His relation to the world with the conceptions of the divinity of Jesus and his role in the conduct of the affairs of men, as well as the problem of original sin, the Messiah and similar questions. There is also an historical phase bearing upon the origin of Christianity.

As a result, almost all branches of Jewish literature had to deal to a greater or lesser extent with some phase of these complicated problems. The greatest burden fell to the exegetes, philosophers and theologians. The leading exegetes and interpreters of the Bible such as

Rashi, Ibn Ezra, Nahmanides, Gersonides, Kimhi, Abrabanel and others devoted more or less attention to polemics or apologetics in their commentaries and some of them dealt with the questions quite extensively. Again the philosophers and theologians in their enunciation of the principles of Judaism and dogmas had to meet the objections of the representatives of the other faiths and elucidate their conceptions.

Some of these longer excursuses of the exegetes and philosophers were at times collected into separate works and thus constitute a part of this special literature, but much of the material remained as an integral part of the original works. We have then two different types of polemics and apologetics, one which is dealt with in special works devoted to that purpose, and the other which forms parts and sections of other works.

This literature has in addition to the many phases indicated also a humorous phase, for besides the intellectuality displayed in the various productions, there is also expressed here and there a biting and sharp wit. As in all polemics and clash of opinions, wit forms the spice of the argument, so is it in this branch of Jewish literature. Of course, due to the position of the Jews and the fear of the zealous guardians of the honor of the ruling religion, the inquisitors and the censors, these particular flashes of wit are often veiled. However, to the one who can read between the lines, the keen irony and biting satire are fully revealed.

We have hitherto discussed the polemic literature which has for its object of discussion the tenets and principles of other faiths. But there is also a species of polemics which attacks the opinions of a sect or a faction of the same faith or defends the views of the ancient faith against dissenters and this type is not to be neglected. Many schisms had arisen in Judaism, the most important of which was that of Karaism. These schisms and differences of opinion likewise called forth an extensive literature. However, the polemic works of Karaism were already discussed in the proper chapters on the literature of the sect (Vol. I, Ch. XIII and Vol. II, Ch. VII) and the works of the Rabbanites, their opponents, were also described in the respective places. There were, though, minor differences of opinion which also created small eddies in the current of literature, such as the movement in opposition to philosophy, to the Kabbala and the individual opposition to the oral law expressed in works of certain scholars and thinkers. These also will have to be considered in the present chapter.

Finally, as in all other surveys of extensive departments of literature, the present one will be limited to the salient works in the field.

A. Polemics Against Other Religions

147. EARLY POLEMIC LITERATURE

During the Classical period no special works devoted to apologetics or polemics were produced until its very end (see below, Sect. 148), but many chapters dealing with the subjects were incorporated in other works. The earliest author who dealt with these matters in connection with other works was the philosopher David Al-Mukamis (Vol. I, p. 325) who lived towards the end of the ninth century. In his philosophic work, *The Book of Twenty Tractates,* in which he discussed primarily the proofs for the existence and the unity of God, he devoted two tractates (IX, X) to arguments against the theories of Christianity showing that its conceptions undermine pure monotheism. The book was written in Arabic and was lost, but it must have been translated into Hebrew, as fragments of such a version exist. Moses Ibn Ezra who quotes the work of Al-Mukamis tells us that it contained also a polemic section against Islam, especially against the view stated by Mohammed that the wonderful style of the Koran is sufficient proof for its Divine origin as it can not be imitated. The same author wrote also another treatise which he incorporated in his commentary on Genesis, entitled, *Against the Abrogation of the Torah,* where he endeavored to show the immutability of the latter. This was directed both against Christianity and Islam which advance the same claim, that their revelations superseded that of the Old Testament.

The vindication of the superiority of the monotheistic conception of Judaism over that of Christianity, and the refutation of the claim of the Abrogation of the Law made by both daughter religions was taken up by Saadia in a number of chapters in his *Emunoth we-Deoth* (Vol. I, Sect. 166). The former is dealt with in three chapters in the second book of the work (Chaps. VI-IX) where he describes the four theories current among Christians regarding Jesus, his nature and the incarnation. He seems to have been well versed in the views of the Eastern churches concerning the doctrine of incarnation, for he quotes the views of the Nestorians and the Monophysites besides the one of the orthodox Christians. He also quotes the opinion of a rationalist sect which sees in Jesus only a prophet. He refutes all the views, as well as evidences from the Old Testament adduced by their propounders, for the pre-existence of Jesus. The question of the Abrogation of the Law is discussed by Saadia in three chapters (VII-X) in the third book. He explains that miracles do not constitute proof of the veracity of any religion. It is to be judged primarily on its own merit of nobility. By this he wishes to say that the miracles claimed by the followers of Christianity and Islam to have been performed by their founders do not prove the revelation of the religions even if the facts were as stated. He advances an argument for the immutability of the Torah from the eternity of the Jewish people as promised by God through the prophets. This eternity, says Saadia, can not be accomplished unless the Torah is eternal, for it is the Law which makes the Jews a nation. He then refutes several exegetical interpretations of verses which make them refer to future revelations by Jesus and Mohammed. He further polemizes against the Christians in the eighth book dealing with the coming of the Messiah.

The question of the Abrogation of the Law was also discussed by the last Gaon of Sura, Samuel ben Hofni (Vol. I, Sect. 152) in an apologetic and polemic work written in Arabic entitled *Nasih al-Sharia* (The Abrogation of the Law). The book itself is lost but we possess a number of quotations by Moses Ibn Ezra in two of his works. From these we can infer that not only did Samuel ben Hofni defend the immutability of the Torah, but also refuted the claim of Islam to the divine origin of the Koran on account of its wonderful style.

Judah ha-Levi's *Kuzari* (Vol. I, Sect. 170) considered as one of the Classical works in Jewish philosophical literature was originally composed with an apologetic tendency in view. In fact, its Arabic name clearly indicates this purpose, for it is entitled *A Book of Proofs and Arguments* in *Defense of the Humiliated Religion*. The book aims, as evidenced from its prologue, where it is told how the Khazar king interviewed first representatives of Christianity and Islam before taking up the discussion with the Jewish scholar, to vindicate not only the veracity of Judaism, but also its superiority, and contains therefore much of polemic material. Thus, in answer to the arguments of the Mohammedan representative that the Koran is of divine origin on account of its style, the author makes the king say that this is no proof to a non-Arabic speaking man, for he can not appreciate the qualities of the style. Again, speaking on prophecy (Sect. I, 87) and the condition necessary for its attainment, ha-Levi deliberately enumerates continence as one of the conditions, referring thus to Mahammed's well known passion for women which accordingly disqualifies his claim to prophecy. He refutes the argument advanced both by Christian and Mohammedans that the low state of the Jews proves that God had forsaken them, from the fact that both religions speak of the poor and the humble as being closer to God than the rich and powerful, and that consequently this proof is valueless.

In another place, (Sect. IV, 2), he charges both religions with retaining many pagan customs in their ceremonies, and with bestowing special honor on places which were formerly seats of idolatry, namely Rome and Mecca. Similar polemic passages or refutations of arguments advanced by the professors of the daughter religions are numerous in the book, which together with its general tendency of vindicating the superiority of Judaism, thus impart to the work a pronounced polemic and apologetic character. This tendency, however, by no means detracts from the value of the *Kuzari* as being an excellent exposition of the principles of Judaism.

Much apologetic and polemic material is also contained in the famous letter of Maimonides to the Jews of Yemen in South Arabia known as *Iggereth Tēman* (Tēman is the Hebrew equivalent for Yemen). The Jews of that country were forced in the year 1171 by the decree of the Sultan to embrace Islam publicly in order to escape death or exile. This apparent conversion soon wrought havoc in the South Arabian Jewry. On the one hand, there arose an apostate who endeavored to convince his former brethren of the veracity of Islam by pointing to certain passages in the Bible which are supposed to presage the coming of Mohammed, and the substitution of the Torah by his religion. On the other hand, there appeared a false Messiah who told the Jews that these sufferings are signs of the nearness of redemption. The Jewish leaders of Yemen were greatly distracted at seeing these dangerous movements in their midst. At the advice of a pupil of Maimonides, Solomon ha-Cohen, who was visiting the country at the time, Jacob Al-Fayumi, a leading Tēmanite scholar turned to the sage of Egypt for counsel and comfort.

In his letter of response, Maimonides first reminds his unfortunate brethren of the steadfastness of their ancestors to the Jewish religion and admonishes them to act likewise under all circumstances. With words of comfort and encouragement, he tells them that the sufferings of the Jews are entailed through no fault of their own but as a result of the hatred of the nations for the Torah and the Jewish religion. The nations thus oppose the will of God, and the Jews must therefore not be discouraged, for His will will ultimately triumph.

He then turns to the claims of the apostate and refutes his interpretations of the Biblical passages. He says further that even the Mohammedans themselves do not believe in the evidence as adduced by the renegade, for they accuse the Jews of falsifying the Bible and deleting every reference to Mohammed. This charge again is not true for the Bible was translated into Aramaic, Greek and Latin long before Mohammed, and all of these translations agreed with the Hebrew text current at the time of the appearance of the prophet of Islam or subsequent to it.

He devotes the last part of his letter to the false Messiah denouncing his utterings and admonishing his brethren not to be misled by him. He encourages them to wait patiently for the coming of the real Messiah though they must suffer for the time being. He concludes his letter with words of comfort and assures his coreligionists once more of the eternity of the Jewish people by saying that just as it is impossible to doubt in the eternal existence of God, so is it impossible to waver in the belief of the continued existence of Israel, His people.

148. POLEMIC WORKS OF THE TWELFTH AND THIRTEENTH CENTURIES

As was indicated above, the Jewish scholars of the Classical period though greatly interested in the defense of their religion and the vindication of its truths, with few exceptions, did not devote special works to these subjects but incorporated this kind of material in parts of other works. We have to look therefore primarily to the post-Classical period for distinct polemic and apologetic books. It is with the end of the twelfth century that a prolific activity in this field began. At that time, there was also a change in the place of production of this literature as well as in its language and direction. Hitherto, as we have seen, most of the works of this kind were produced in the East or in Mohammedan Spain, the language was Arabic and Islam the center of attention. Henceforth, the place of production was the West, the language mostly Hebrew, and the direction of the works, with several exceptions, against Christianity.

i. The earliest of these polemic works is the *Sepher ha-Berith* (The Book of the Covenant) by the grammarian and Bible commentator, Joseph Kimhi (Vol. I, Sect. 104). The book is written in the form of a dialogue between a believer, (Maamin), i. e. a Jew and a heretic (Min, i. e. a Christian. *Min* is the usual term for Christian in Rabbinic and in Talmudic and Midrashic literature). The subjects dealt with in the work are the interpretations of prophecies and Biblical passages which the Christians say refer to Jesus, the questions of original sin and Jesus' redemption of humanity, and finally the charges against the Jews.

The first matter occupies a large part of the book. Kimhi refutes all the Christian interpretations and explains the verses in a logical and rational way. Typical of these is his refutation of the well known claim that the words in Isaiah VII, 14 "Behold an *Almah* shall conceive and bear a son and thou shalt call his name Immanuel" refer to the birth of Jesus for they translate *"Almah,"* virgin. Kimhi besides agreeing with many other Jewish commentators in explaining *Almah* to mean merely a young woman, irrespective whether married or unmarried, refutes the reference on other grounds. The birth of the son, he says, was given by the prophet as a sign to Ahaz king of Judah, to convince him of God's promise that he has nothing to fear from the alliance of the kings of Ephraim and Syria who were attacking Jerusalem at the time. If, he concludes, the event refers to the birth of Jesus which took place seven hundred years later, how could it convince Ahaz of the truth of Isaiah's prophecy? In connection with the interpretation of the Bible in which the Christians use to a great extent the allegorical method, the author lays down the rule that with the exception of anthropomorphic expressions found in the Bible which contradict the pure conception of God, we have no right to say that Moses or the prophets spoke in allegory or metaphor. He proves his view in a logical manner.

Regarding the contention of the Christians that the original sin of Adam pursued his descendants and that all of them were, as a punishment, sentenced to hell until Jesus through his suffering redeemed the righteous from further damnation, Kimhi has the following to say. First, the very conception of original sin contradicts the Bible, where it is explicitly stated "Neither shall the children be put to death for the fathers; every one shall be put to death for his own sin." (Deut. XXIV, 2.) Second, if Jesus came to redeem the sin of Adam, why did he not remove also the other curses pronounced against his descendants, namely the pain of child birth for women and the malediction "In the sweat of thy brow shalt thou eat thy bread"? Third, if the suffering of Jesus were intended to expiate that sin, why then do people still suffer death and agonies long after his coming? Was not the sin of Adam which brought death into the world wiped out by his passion? He adduces several other arguments against these theories, including quotations from the gospels which contradict these views.

He then takes up the question of Jesus as the incarnation of divinity saying that the view is untenable because of the fact that he himself prayed to God for help at the time of the crucifixion, for, were he God or the spirit of God incarnated, to whom did he pray, why did he not help himself? This argument is frequently repeated in all polemic works.

Kimhi exonerates the Jews from the charges made against them such as the killing of the Messiah, their low state and the taking of usury and similar accusations. As for the first, he says, did not Jesus himself pray for them and ask for their forgiveness? If he forgave them, says the author, why bring the charge again? As for the low state of the Jews, he argues that they have no government, they lead a fine communal moral and virtuous life, while the Christians fall much below the standard of the Jews. Again, the taking of usury by the Jews is limited to gentiles in accordance with the injunction of the Old Testament (Deut. XXIII, 21); but says the author, there are many Christians who in spite of the prohibition of the Church, lend money on usury both to Jews and their own brethren. The author thus vindicates Jews and Judaism from all charges and attacks at times severely the very fundamentals of the Christian faith.

ii. The son of Joseph, David Kimhi also left us a small polemic work entitled *Vikkuah* (Disputation), containing the gist of the arguments presented in a debate he held with a Christian scholar. It does not, however, add much that is new, for he reproduces in the main the polemic material of his father's book. Only occasionally do we find some new refutation of certain claims presented by Christianity. Thus, he devotes some space to the question whether Jesus is the promised Messiah or not. He proves by a series of quotations from the Old Testament that he did not fulfill the conditions of the Messiah as promulgated by the prophets. He did not redeem Israel from exile, he did not rule over all the kings of the world, and finally, he did not bring peace to the world. The prophecies of Isaiah and others have not been fulfilled as yet, and hence, the Messiah is still to arrive.

Besides this *Vikkuah,* David Kimhi incorporated many long polemic passages in his commentary on the Bible. They are especially numerous and lengthy in his commentary on the Psalms and these were collected after his death and printed in a separate book under the title *Teshuboth le-Notzrim* (Arguments against the Christians). In this book, as well as in many polemic passages in the other commentaries, our author argues with the Christian exegetes about the interpretation of numerous verses in the prophetic books. It is regrettable that many of these passages were deleted in the later editions of the commentaries by the censor and are only contained in the very old editions. Both Kimhis show a fair acquaintance with the New Testament, and David even gives several quotations in Latin.

iii. Another small book likewise entitled *Vikkuah* was left to us by one of the Tosafists, Rabbi Yehiel of Paris. It contains the apology on behalf of the Talmud which he advanced in the disputation with the apostate, Nicholas Dunin, held in the year 1240 in the presence of the king and queen of France and dignitaries of the Church. There were associated wtih him other rabbis, among them Moses of Coucy, the codifier (Sect. 51), but it seems that Rabbi Yehiel was the spokesman at this disputation, and the Talmud formed the target of the charges, as Dunin wanted to obtain a verdict for its destruction.

The charges were divided into two classes, first that the Talmud contains many abusive anti-Christian passages, and second that it contains numerous irrational statements on religion and morality. Rabbi Yehiel parried with his antagonist with great skill and refuted all his arguments. In answer to Dunin's accusation regarding the abusive references to Jesus, he stated that there were two persons by the name of Jesus, one, the founder of Christianity, and another, who lived about one hundred and fifty years earlier, and that all the statements quoted refer to the latter. As for the irrational statements, he asserted that they are found in the Agadic part which is not obligatory upon the Jews to believe. The Agada represents individual opinions, and if one wants to accept these views, he may do so, and if not, he is at liberty to take any difficult statement as an exaggeration or as incorrect. He added that he himself believes that all the words of the Rabbis are true and that the strange statements must be interpreted to contain a hidden meaning, but he does not want to force his views upon any one else. Yehiel was also asked about some Talmudic laws which express animosity to gentiles, and he explained each law and statement in a rational manner. Among other things, he was asked about the *Kol Nidrē* formula recited on the eve of the Day of Atonement which annuls all vows a Jew may make during the year. The charge was made that it is intended to annul all oaths and promises made by Jews to gentiles. His answer was that the annulment is intended for vows, oaths and promises made by a Jew irrespective whether to a fellow Jew or to a gentile, only if transgressed unconsciously. The purpose of this annulment in advance is to save the offender from punishment, but no wilfull transgression of an oath or promise given to anybody is tolerated in Judaism. The *Vikkuah,* as it seems, was not written by Yehiel himself, but was compiled from his notes by a contemporary scholar, Joseph ben Nathan, the official (officiali).

iv. A very important apologetic and polemic work is the *Vikkuah* composed by Moses ben Nahman which contains his discussion held with the apostate Pablo Christiano at Barcelona in the year 1263. The disputation was held at the invitation of the king Jayme I in the presence of many bishops and cardinals, and the questions laid down for the debate were three: (1) whether the Messiah had already arrived? (2) whether the Messiah is God incarnate or a human being? (3) whether Judaism is a true and just religion? The third question, however, was not discussed, for the disputation was terminated before the expiration of the allotted time at the request of Nahmanides and with the consent of the king.

To prove his first two assertions, Pablo cited Biblical and Talmudic passages which according to his interpretation prove both that Jesus is the Messiah and that the Messiah is Divine. The Biblical passages are Genesis XLIX, 10—a well known verse in polemic literature—, Isaiah LII, 13-15, Ch. LIII, and Daniel IX, 25-27, and the Talmudic passages are found in the Agada and various Midrashim. Nahmanides interpreted the Biblical passages in a logical manner and showed that they contain no references to Jesus. He admitted that the Rabbis in the Talmud interpret the chapter LIII in Isaiah speaking of the servant of the Lord (Ebed Adonai) to refer to the Messiah, but this is merely a homiletic interpretation and does not express the real meaning of the chapter. He argued that the term "Servant of the

Lord" the subject of that chapter refers to the entire Jewish people, and that the verses picture its suffering.

As for the Talmudic passages, though Nahmanides refuted Pablo's interpretation of each passage, he laid down a general rule about the authority of the Agada, a rule similar to the one pronounced by Yehiel. He said, we have three kinds of books, the Bible which all Jews consider the prime authority, the Talmud, the accepted commentary of the Bible and its laws and precepts, and the Midrashim which are like the sermons preached by the representatives of the Church. A Jew may and may not accept their views. On this ground, he said openly that he does not believe in the story told in the Midrash on Lamentations (Ch. I, 51) that the Messiah was born on the day the Temple was destroyed. Moreover, he added that the story, even if taken literally, does by no means refer to Jesus, for he was born seventy years before that date. He was not satisfied though with mere answers to Pablo's questions but also made several attacks on certain principles of Christianity, among them that of original sin and Jesus' redemption of humanity from that taint, but his arguments have little new material. They are similar to those produced by Joseph Kimhi.

v. To the thirteenth century belongs most likely the preposterous concoction of legends and folk stories about the character and activities of Jesus known under the name *Maasē Yeshu or Toldoth Yeshu* (The Story or Biography of Jesus). The work is an anonymous one and probably is an outgrowth of several collections of such stories. According to some scholars[1] it was originally compiled in the fifth century in Aramaic, of which version there are some fragments, and it was later translated into Hebrew. The first Hebrew version seemed to have been composed around 1240. Subsequently, other versions appeared. However, Jewish polemic authors never referred to it, and it only attracted the attention of apostates and enemies of Judaism who accused the Jews of hatred of Christianity on the basis of the booklet. It was first published by Wagenseil in 1681 in his collection of Jewish polemic works under the title *Tēla Ignea Satanae* (The Arrows of Satanic Fire).

The booklet begins with the story of the illegitimate birth of Jesus and is followed by tales of his exploits. We are told that he was both a very bright and arrogant student and that both qualities are to be

[1] Dr. Samuel Kraus: Das Leben Jesu.

attributed to the fact of his illegitimate birth, for such children, according to a popular adage, quoted also in the Talmud,[2] possess these qualities.

His performance of miracles is assumed, but it is explained that he possessed the Ineffable Name (Shem ha-Meforosh) and by its use he accomplished the wonders. It is only when Judas Iscariot, who is here represented not as a disciple but as a Pharisee scholar, managed by devious means to defile the Holy Name, that Jesus lost his power, and the Jews were able to capture him and bring him to trial. According to the story, he was not executed immediately but was first rescued by his followers, escaped to Antioch where he learned witchcraft and then returned to Palestine. It was after his return that one of his disciples Papa ben Ritzitza identified him, and he was then captured and sentenced a second time.

There are many more absurd stories told about his death and burial. But what is interesting is that the separation of the Christians from the Jews, that is their abandoning the observance of the laws and the establishment of their institutions, is here attributed to two Pharisaic scholars who carried this out at the behest of the Jewish leaders. This was done with the purpose that the followers of Jesus should not intermingle with the Jews. These scholars, absurd as it may seem, were no other than Elijah* (Paul) and Simon (Peter). They themselves, according to the account of this booklet, remained pious Jews, and all their activities among the Christians was for the purpose mentioned above. The story about Peter is quite prevalent in Jewish literature, for we have even two versions of a legendary Midrash about his assumed apostleship, called *Agadata di Shimon Kaifa* (The Story of Simon the Rock, i. e. Petra). But of the pseudo-apostleship of Paul, we learn only here. The booklet knows also of the later schisms of the Church, especially of the Nestorian, which it records in a distorted manner.

vi. Some apologetic works were also written during the century by several anonymous German and French scholars, primarily intended to refute the Christian interpretation of certain Biblical passages. They are all called by the name *Nitzahon* (Victory). Two of them are extant and were first printed by Wagenseil in his above-mentioned collection of Jewish polemic works, one called *Nitzahon*

[2] Jerusalem Talmud, Kiddushin, Ch. IV, II.

* It is curious that the Toldoth Yeshu gives Paul's Hebrew name as Elijah and not Saul.

Yashan (The Old Nitzahon) written by a German Jew toward the end of the thirteenth century, and the other *Nitzahon Yashan Noshan* (the oldest), written by a French scholar about the middle of that century. Both books use the same method, namely arranging the disputed passages according to the order of the Bible from Genesis to Proverbs. The method is typified in Yom Tob Lippman's *Nitzahon,* the best example of such works, which will be discussed in the proper place.

149. FOURTEENTH AND FIFTEENTH CENTURIES

These two centuries were prolific in the production of polemic literature, for during this period a large number of religious disputations were held and great efforts were made by the Christians to convert the Jews. Moreover, due to the persecutions that took place in Spain at the end of the fourteenth century, many Jews became Christians and the number of apostates who desired to find favor in the eyes of their masters by libelling their former religion, increased. These wrote books and pamphlets for the purpose of proving to the Jews their error in not accepting Christianity, and attempted to indicate the veracity of the new religion they embraced and the abrogation of the old they had forsaken. This insidious activity on the part of the apostates called forth a counter activity on the part of the rabbis, and they in turn wrote books where they attacked the dogmas of Christianity and showed their untenability. As a result, we have a considerable number of polemic works written by great scholars of a high philosophic training.

i. The first polemic book written during the fourteenth century is one by the great Talmudic scholar Solomon ben Adret (Sect. 42). The book consists of three parts, the first of which is entitled *'Al-Yishmoel* (A Tractate against Ishmael, i. e. Islam). In it ben Adret, in the form of a dialogue with a Mohammedan, defends the Bible from the charges of the abrogation of the Law and the Jews from that of falsifying its text. After vindicating the veracity and the eternity of the Torah, he turns against the dogmas of Islam, especially that of the Divine origin of the Koran. The other two parts are devoted to Christianity and contain the gist of the dispute he held with the Christian scholar, Raymond Martin. The main arguments turn on the questions of allegorical interpretations of the Bible and the eternity of the Law. Ben Adret defends the plain meaning of the precepts and the immutability of the Law. He refutes some proofs of Martin based on quotations from the Talmud—Martin was well versed in Rabbinic literature—and gives the right interpretation of the passages.

ii. Around the middle of the century, Moses of Narbonne, the commentator of the *Guide* of Maimonides (Sect. 75) translated a polemic work of the famous Arabic philosopher Al-Gazali into Hebrew. The work is entitled *Yihud Elohuth* (The Unity of the Godhead). The book, which attacks the doctrine of the Trinity, seems to be a compilation of discourses contained in several of his works.

iii. Very important are the two polemic works of Isaac Profiat Duran, the grammarian and commentator of the *Guide,* known as *Ephodi* (Sect. 75). The first of these is the famous satiric letter called after its initial words *Al Tehi ḳa-Aboteḳha* (Be Not Like Your Ancestors), and the second is the *Klimath ha-Goyim* (The Shame of the Gentiles), a treatise on the untenability of the dogmas of Christianity. Profiat Duran was himself forcibly converted during the great persecution in Spain in 1391 but soon regretted his step, and together with his friend, another Marrano, Bonnet Goren, he decided to leave for Palestine. Duran went first to an appointed place on the coast, and there he awaited the arrival of Goren. The latter, however, did not come but instead informed him by letter that after meeting at Avignon the apostate Solomon ha-Levi or Paul de Burgos who convinced him of the veracity of Christianity, he decided to cling to his new faith and asks Duran to do likewise. It is then that Duran sent his former friend the epistle.

The letter is a masterpiece of ironic writing, for each of its sections begins with the formula, "Be not like thy ancestors," which imparts to it the tone of ambiguity. In fact, the Christians were for a time misled by the formula and considered the missive as an admonition to Goren not to return to Judaism. Duran in the several sections satirizes the dogmas of incarnation, original sin, transubstantiation (eucharist) and the abrogation of the Law. He urges his friend not to be like his ancestors who believed in the pure unity and spirituality of God, but accept His corporeal incarnation; not to explain philosophically the sin of Adam and his punishment but take it literally, and believe that this sin clung to all his descendants. He advises him not to follow the ancestors who accepted the principles of logic and mathematics, but to throw these to the winds and believe that the large body of the Messiah can enter into a small wafer, or to assume that Jesus can be simultaneously present in the wafer and in heaven. He further advises him not to observe the precepts of Judaism like his fathers but reminds him that the leading apostles did observe them. He ends with a request to Goren that henceforth in his letter to him, he shall not sign the name of his father, saying that "were he alive he would rather have chosen the loss of a son like thee, than his existence." However, Duran assures Goren that if he will repent, he will accept him again as friend and comrade.

The epistle was written in 1392, and five years later in 1497, Duran wrote, at the request of Don Hasdai Crescas, his larger treatise intended as a systematic criticism of the basic principles of Christianity. Profiat Duran, as we can see from his work, was well versed not only in the New Testament but in the entire Christian theological literature of his time and was well qualified for his undertaking. The book is divided into twelve chapters, nine of which deal with the principles of the Christian religion and the other three with the errors found in the Gospels and in the translation of Jerome (The Vulgate), both in quotations from the Old Testament and in the rendition.

The doctrine of the divinity of Jesus is dealt with first. His method is the literary-historical one, namely he traces the doctrine to its sources, John, Ch. X, 30 and Ch. XIV, 9, where we read, "I and my Father are one," and "He that hath seen me had seen the Father." Against these two short statements which identify Jesus directly with God and several other passages which indicate this assertion indirectly, Duran amasses a number of quotations from all the Gospels, proving that neither Jesus himself nor all the apostles ever thought of such identification. In connection with the discussion he also refutes some interpretations of Scriptural verses, and points out the wilfull changes made in the verses by the interpreters in order to suit the text to their purpose. He even quotes the well known Christian commentator Nicholas de Lyra, as one who had already noted such doubtful interpretation.

The question of the Trinity is taken up next, and this doctrine is traced to the First Epistle of John V, 7, where it is said, "There are three that bear record in heaven, the Father, the Word and the Holy Ghost, and these three are one." Duran argues that the words, "And these three are one" mean not absolutely one, but that they agree in testimony, for when it is said in the following verse "And there are three that bear witness in earth, the spirit, the water and the blood, and these three are one," it certainly means agreement and not identification. He states that commentaors had already noted the difficulty and that in some later copies of the New Testament verse eight was changed. He further cites many quotations from the Gospels which contradict the doctrine of the Trinity. Incarnation and redemption are severely criticized in the third chapter while the question of the abrogation of the Law is discussed in the fourth. With remarkable erudition in the Gospels and other writings he proves that most of the apostles insisted on the observance of the Law, as a whole, though deviating here and there in smaller matters. Even Paul who proclaimed the abrogation of the Law did so insofar as the gentiles were concerned, for he himself stated that it was never abrogated for those who were once born Jews. This was a mighty challenge to the Church, based on its own authoritative writings, to prove its right to force conversion upon the Jews.

From the fifth to the ninth chapter, Duran discusses the Biblical references to the doctrine of abrogation, the question of the bread and wine sacraments (Transubstantiation), baptism and the institution of the papacy. He shows from the New Testament that there is no real authority for all these doctrines and institutions. Regarding the passages in the Gospel, where Jesus refers to the sacred bread and wine as his body and blood, the author argues that they are mere figures of speech, as he always used parables and metaphors.

Of great interest are the last chapters where the author gives a number of misquotations from the Old Testament found in the writings of the Church Fathers. These errors concern both text and facts. Not even the learned Jerome escapes criticism, for Duran proves, from the quotations from the Old Testament found both in the Gospels and in Jerome, that the latter deliberately changed them in his translation, as the Gospel text agrees with the Masoretic. The purpose of all this severe criticism was to show that Christianity, as practised by Catholicism, is only of later growth and has no firm roots in its own sacred writings. On the whole, the *Klimath ha-Goyim* of Profiat Duran is one of the strongest polemic works ever written by a Jew. It was utilized by many writers on the subject during the generations though it was not printed until 1913.

iv. The book of Profiat Duran was undoubtedly made use of to a great extent by Hasdai Crescas in his polemic treatise written originally in Spanish but later translated into Hebrew under the title *Maamer be-Bitul Ikrē ha-Notzrim* (A Treatise on the Refutation of the Dogmas of Christianity). We have good reason to assume that the material in Crescas' treatise, which closely resembles that of Duran,

A page from the Nitzahon, 15th Century Ms., in the Jewish Theological Seminary, New York.

was directly taken from the latter's book. In the dedicatory epistle of Duran to Crescas, prefacing the *Klimath ha-Goyim* he says, "I have written little on the subject, for I know that you with your wide knowledge will be able to amplify it." In fact, Crescas did not enlarge upon the arguments advanced by Duran, but deepened them and gave to some of them a philosophic aspect.

The treatise is divided into ten chapters and deals with the dogmas of the Trinity, Sonship of God, incarnation, original sin, abrogation of the Law, Jesus' descent from the House of David, his Messiahship, baptism, miraculous birth and several others. In most of his arguments about the dogmas, Crescas, as said, repeats those of Duran in more or less altered form. But in the refutation of the doctrine of the Trinity, the Sonship of God and incarnation, he follows his own way. Great philosopher that he was, he treats these principles philosophically and shows that considering these doctrines as mental conceptions, they contradict every logical principle in the Aristotelian canon. He buttresses, of course, his logical arguments by literary proofs from the Gospels and the writings of the Apostles as Duran had done, but in these there is little that is new.

On the whole, the treatise of Crescas is a powerful polemic work written in a very learned and dignified manner. It aroused great comment in Church circles at that time and provoked Christian theologians to compose several apologetic treatises in defense of their faith.

150. THE NITZAHON OF YOM TOB LIPPMAN MULHAUSEN

One of the best polemic works written at the beginning of the fifteenth century which made a great impression not only in the Jewish but in the Christian world as well was the *Sepher ha-Nitzahon* (The Book of Triumph) by Yom Tob Lippman Mülhausen. (d. 1459.)

As his surname indicates, his family must have lived in earlier times in the city of Mülhausen, Alsace, but whether Rabbi Lippman himself was born there can not be determined, for neither the date nor the place of his birth is known. We do, however, know that he lived for a great part of his life in Prague where he filled the positions of Dayan and head of an academy. Rabbi Lippman was held in great esteem by the contemporary scholars, for we find many references in the Responsa of the time to his legal decisions and Rabbinic ordinances.

Mülhausen's activity, however, was not limited to the field of Jewish law, but extended to other branches of Jewish knowledge. He was greatly interested in the studies of Biblical exegesis, religious philosophy and mysticism. He wrote many books, among them the *Eshkol,* an exposition of his system in Kabbala, the Sepher *Aleph Beth* (The Book of the Alphabet), a mystical treatise on the form of the letters of the alphabet and the importance of their various combinations, commentaries on the *Sepher Yetzira* and the *Hymn of Unity* (Shir ha-Yihud). His fame, though, rests on the *Nitzahon* which was an outgrowth of his frequent disputations with the representatives of the Church and also with Jewish converts. Lippman was thoroughly equipped for the writing of such a book, for besides his great erudition in Jewish subjects, he also mastered the Latin language and was well versed in the New Testament and other authoritative Christian writings. This book can rightly be considered his Magnum Opus, for he displays in it his extensive knowledge in all fields of Jewish learning, and also his view of Judaism, which is a fine combination of moderate rationalism and deep piety.

The *Nitzahon* is not merely a polemic book against Christianity but a complete apology and defense of the teachings of Judaism and its laws both written and oral. It intends to remove all difficulties raised by all opponents and skeptics against the Bible, the dogmas of the Jewish religion and certain Talmudic statements. As a secondary purpose, it aims to enunciate the dogmas of Judaism which according to the author number sixteen. Of these, nine dogmas are borrowed from Maimonides' Thirteen Articles and seven are added by Lippman. These seven, though, are not his own innovations but mere expansions and conceptual subdivisions of several of those of Maimonides relating to the unity and purity of the conception of God. There is only one dogma which is not included in the Thirteen Articles and that is the belief in the creation of the world *de novo.*

These aims are briefly stated by the author in his preface. He says, many have arisen against us, namely Jewish heretics, Sadducees or Karaites and Christians. These three classes who attack the teachings of traditional Judaism together with those Jews who are pious but lack the true conception of the dogmas of the Jewish religion, constitute four categories of people who misunderstand the teachings of the Bible and the Talmud in various ways. He designates them by the names of the traditional four sons of the Passover Haggadah, the wise (Hakam), the wicked (Rosha), the simple one (The Tam), and the one who does not know how to ask a question (she-Eno-Yodea Lishol). The first represents those who are learned but do not apply their learning towards the understanding of Judaism; the second represents both heretics and Karaites who mock either at the written or oral law; the third symbolizes the simple Jews who observe the Law but do not understand the meaning of the precepts and take Talmudic statements literally; and the fourth characterizes the Christians whose queries are without true knowledge. To refute the arguments of the second and fourth classes and to guide the first and third towards the rational and right understanding of Judaism, the *Nitzahon* was written. And in order to make it as complete an exposition as possible of the nobility of the Jewish religion, Rabbi Lippman added also sections dealing with the reasons for the precepts. (Ta'ame ha-Mitzvoth.)

The arrangement of the material in the book is a logical one though not very systematic. The author adopted the method of the earlier polemic books by the name *Nitzahon,* namely of following the sections of the Bible. Accordingly, the book of Lippman is arranged in the order of the books and the weekly portions of the Bible, from Genesis to II Chronicles. In addition, the book is divided into small sections each dealing with a separate subject. The number of these sections is 354, corresponding to the days of the lunar year, which is the Jewish calendar year. The number is symbolic of the duty of the Jews to think about their religion every day in the year. There is also a third division of the work which is not contained in the book proper but in an especially prepared index. "I have divided," says the author, "the *Nitzahon* into seven parts corresponding to the seven days of the week." These divisions contain sixty-six sections dealing with refutations of the arguments and views of the Christians; thirty-nine explaining some apparently dubious actions of the righteous men of the Bible; forty-one offering comments of difficult verses in the Scriptures; thirty-four stating reasons for the precepts; fifty-five aiming to refute the arguments of the skeptics against the Bible and Talmud; and forty-seven intended against heretics and Karaites. Finally, the last division consisting of forty-eight sections and reserved for reading on the Sabbtah deals with the sixteen dogmas and their elucidation. These groups of sections are not consecutive but scattered throughout the book, and the individual sections are related to each other only by their content. Lippman by supplying this remarkable index aimed to make his work a practical text for all those interested in the understanding of Judaism.

The *Nitzahon* is not a commentary on the Bible but a systematic collection of notes, comments and discussion on selected passages from the Scriptures, which either present difficulty or afford a basis for interpretation to the Christians or Karaites, or contain any basic teaching of Judaism which is to be unfolded. Lippman makes passages of the last kind the vehicle for his views on many important beliefs. In general, he appears to us in the book as a rationalist, as a follower of Maimonides and the other Jewish philosophers who endeavored to show that there is little in Judaism which does not agree with reason.

This tendency runs throughout the book in all its divisions. Thus, he insists again and again that it is not enough for a righteous Jew to merely know the Law and observe it, but that it is his prime duty to understand God philosophically. He even says explicitly that one who thinks of God in corporeal terms commits the sin of heresy (Sect. 124). In his long excursus on reward and punishment contained in sections 76-78, he discusses the question in detail, and is inclined to accept the view of Maimonides that the reward and punishment is of a spiritual nature and not of a physical one. He attempts, though, to reconcile this veiw with the belief in paradise and hell. The first he considers as a symbol for the spiritual pleasure that the soul will enjoy, and the second, disagreeing with Nahmanides who places the *Gehinom* in the bowels of the earth, he locates somewhere in the lower part of the zone of the element of fire which is above the earth. He says that when the soul of the wicked attempts to ascend to heaven, it is weighed down by its sins and is caught up by the element of fire and is thus brought to hell. He admits, however, that the fire of hell is not purely corporeal, for even the soul of a sinner retains its primary spiritual quality.

In a similar rationalistic way, he expounds his view of creation. He places a number of media between God and the earth. These are the separate intelligences and the spheres, and through these the lower world was evolved. He also attempts to remove all difficulties connected with creation otherwise.

In his explanations of the reasons of the precepts, the same rationalistic strain is evident. Most of his explanations are borrowed from the *Guide* of Maimonides but there are many of his own.

In his polemics against the Christians, he is more thorough and complete than many of his predecessors. He hardly omits a single passage in the Bible which any one of the Christian theologians utilized in one way or another, without interpreting it in the proper manner. At times, he is not satisfied with a mere refutation of the Christological interpretation of the verse, but analyzes at length the fundamental dogmas of Christianity and attempts to show their baselessness. Thus, in section eight, commenting upon the words in Genesis II, 17, "For in the day thou eatest thereof thou shalt surely die," from which the Christian theologians derive the doctrine of original sin and Jesus' redemption of humanity, Lippman launches upon a complete refutation of these doctrines together with those of incarnation, miraculous birth, the eucharist and others. This section is in fact his principal polemic attack against the dogmas of Christianity. Here he presents all arguments that were offered on the subject by his predecessors, and adds some of his own. Like those before him, Lippman points out that the New Testament distinctly calls Joseph the husband of Mary and the father of Jesus and asks the question why do the Gospels say that Jesus is a descendant of David, if according to them, Joseph who is of the Davidic line was not his father? In other places, he asks why did Jesus whom the Christians call God incarnate say the words, "My God, my God, why hast Thou forsaken me (Matthew, XXVII, 46)?" How then, concludes Lippman, according to these statements, can the Christians apply to Jesus the term God?

In his many refutations of the interpretation of Biblical verses advanced by Christians, Lippman makes a general charge against them, that they misunderstood the passages where such verses are found. On the whole, they emphasized only a few words in the verse and did not pay attention to the context. He utilizes in his refutations all exegetic means and very often proves that the gentile interpreters disregarded grammatical rules, meanings of words, and above all, the general meaning of the context. Lippman displays in his exegetical remarks a fine sense of understanding of the Bible. His comments are based on a deep knowledge of grammar and exegesis. He drew, of course, upon the commentaries of Saadia, Rashi, Ibn Ezra, Kimhi, Shemaria of Negroponti and others whom as a rule he quotes by name.

Lippman's tone in his arguments with the Christians is extremely polemical. He uses very acrid language in his refutations and calls his opponents by opprobrious names. He often employs sharp barbs of humor and wit and not always of a dignified character. He is especially bitter against the apostates of his own faith and spares no epithets for their characterization. So zealous is he in his polemics that at times he even adopts an argument of his opponents and uses it against them without detecting its dangerous tendency. Thus, in his efforts to refute the Christian argument that Jewesses who can not be circumcised should not be considered members of the faith he says, "They do not know that faith does not depend on circumcision but on the conviction of the heart." But this is the very Pauline argument against the obligation of circumcision in general. Lippman overlooked this because he was eager to make a sally against the Christians who force Jews to become converts and are satisfied with their baptism without paying attention to the fact that they remain unbelievers in their hearts.

Our author is equally thorough in his apologetics for the dubious actions of the righteous men in the Bible as well as for those of the people of Israel at large. He even attempts to defend the making of the golden calf by the Jews in the desert, insisting that the Jews themselves were not idol worshippers but merely wanted a visible image of the glory of God, and that the image of the calf was substituted by the Egyptian proselytes for the less corporeal image desired by the Jews.[3] He likewise defends Moses and Aaron for their act of disobedience told in Numbers XX, 7-13, when they struck the rock instead of talking to it as commanded by God. He attempts to show that they did not mean to disobey God, but on the contrary, to glorify His name, only that they erred. In this manner, he explains all matters pertaining to the subject.

Taking into consideration the several aspects of the *Nitzahon* and the thoroughness and completeness with which the purposes set by the author are carried out, we must accord it a place among the best apologetic works on behalf of Judaism. Lippman was not very original but he used his derived knowledge to great effect and made his work practical and useful.

It is, therefore, not to be wondered at that a polemic and apologetic work of this kind spread among the Jews very quickly and was frequently used by their scholars, who were called upon to dispute with the representatives of the Church, as an armory whence they drew

[3] In this view, he was, however, preceded by Judah ha-Levi, of Kuzari, B. I. 97.

their weapons in their verbal warfare. Consequently, many manuscripts of the book circulated in Jewish hands. However, some of them found their way into the Christian world, and immediately, an anti-Lippman literature, the purpose of which was to refute the attacks of Mülhausen began to arise. As early as the year 1459, the Bishop of Brandenburg, Stephanus Bodeker, wrote his book *Contra Judaeos* (Against the Jews), in which he refers to Lippman and his book in the most opprobrious terms. He accuses him of possessing only a slight knowledge of Latin and of being a frequent visitor in churches, where he heard the sermons of the priests. These, he says, he did not understand thoroughly and consequently he misquoted their arguments.

The real campaign against Lippman and the *Nitzahon* began when Theodore Hackspan, a professor of theology at Altdorf published the book in 1644. Hackspan obtained a manuscript of the work from a rabbi in the town of Schnattach by actually seizing it from his hands by force. Hackspan himself added an introduction in Latin where among other things, he attempts to refute Lippman in a dignified manner. Others, though, were not so generous. As soon as the book appeared, Latin translations of it were made and works combating it in a vituperous manner appeared. In 1659, Christian Schotan published a work called Anti-Lippaniana devoted entirely to the *Nitzahon*. The bitterest opponent of the work though was the well known Christian Hebraist, John Christoff Wagenseil. In 1681, he published his *Tēla Ignea Satanae* (The Fiery Satanic Arrows), where, as mentioned, he collected a number of Jewish polemic works and translated them into Latin. Among them is a polemic poem *Zikron ha-Nitzahon* (The Memorandum of the Nitzahon) which Wagenseil ascribed to Lippman but which in reality is not his.

In this poem, the author renders the most potent polemic arguments of Mülhausen in verse. Wagenseil devoted to it a refutation of five hundred pages, where he denounces Lippman in vitriolic terms. The storm around the *Nitzahon* continued to rage through the first half of the eighteenth century, but from that time on it waned and subsided. Thus, one Jewish book created almost an entire library of Christian theological literature.

The second important polemic work produced during the fifteenth century is the *Kesheth U-Mogen* (Bow and Shield) by Simon ben Zemah Duran (Sect. 80). This work really formed a part of his larger treatise *Mogen Aboth* nominally a commentary on the ethical tractate *Aboth* of the Mishnah, but in reality a philosophical-theological treatise, as pointed out above.

The Kesheth U-Mogen is directed both against Islam and Christianity. The first is treated in detail and at great length in five sections, each containing a number of chapters which are devoted to the discussion of the Koran and its teachings. In these sections, Duran endeavors to show that the valuable laws and precepts contained in the Koran as well as its dogmas were borrowed from Judaism. He further refutes the arguments produced by the Mohammedans for the divinity of the Koran by pointing to its contradictions, its lack of clearness and its excessive rhetoric. Duran also devotes several chapters to the refutation of the well known charge made by the Mohammedans against the Jews that they falsified the text of the Bible.

In dealing with Christianity, the author devotes his attention to four important points, namely the argument that the Old Testament was superseded by the New, the doctrine of the Trinity, the coming of the Messiah, and the interpretation of the Scriptural passages. He utilizes to a great extent the arguments on these subjects quoted in Profiat Duran's treatise, but at times, he adds some new ones.

He proves by numerous citations from the Gospels, that neither Jesus nor His disciples ever intended to aver that the Mosaic law was abrogated for the Jews, and that the abrogation of the Law by Paul was intended only for the gentiles in order to attract them to the new faith. He points to the passage in the Acts of the Apostles, XV, 1-20 where it is told that at the advice of James, the Apostles, including Paul, wrote to the Christians at Antioch that they must abstain from idolatry, adultery, from strangled things and from blood. These prohibitions, Duran argues, tally almost with the seven laws of the Noachides which, according to Judaism, a proselyte of the gate (Ger Toshab) must observe, and therefore, the Apostles wanted to make the gentiles second degree proselytes. He further proves from the Gospels that Jesus considered himself a man not a God, and points to the fact that in Matthew III, 16, we are told that when Jesus was baptized by John, the spirit descended upon him like a dove, and therefore, says the author, only then was he imbued with the Holy Spirit and not before. How then can the Christians say that Mary conceived from the Holy Spirit?

Considerable attention is devoted by him to point out the contradictions in the Gospels, and moreover, the ignorance of their writers of the Hebrew Scriptures. He cites many passages where verses from the Old Testament are misquoted. There is little new in his refutation of the Christian interpretation of certain verses, but at times, he adds an important point. In general, he accuses many of the interpreters and especially Jerome of changing the text to suit their purpose. He cites several instances where Jerome changed the tenses and punctuation, and finally quotes fifteen proofs that the Messiah had not as yet come, but most of them are taken from Saadia's *Emunoth we-Deoth.*

Simon Duran shows a thorough acquaintance with the New Testament and the Bible translation of Jerome, and he undoubtedly mastered the Latin language to a considerable degree. His work, though it can not compare in systematic treatment and thoroughness with that of Profiat Duran, is nevertheless a valuable contribution to Jewish polemic literature.

Solomon, the son of Simon Duran also left us a short polemic treatise called *Milhamath Mitzvah* (The Battle of Duty) in defense of the Talmud. It was intended as a reply to the attack on the Talmud made by the apostate Geronimo de Santa Fē, known formerly as Joshua ha-Lorqi. In his introduction, Solomon lays down a few rules about the nature and character of the Talmud and Jewish Law. He proves especially the necessity of the Oral Law and shows that even in the New Testament the Oral Law is considered binding and obligatory. He repeats the distinction already made by Nahmanides between Halakah and Agada, namely, that the first is authoritative while the second is not, and then proceeds to the detailed refutation of Santa Fē's attack, taking up the charges against the Halakic statements which seem either unjust or illogical and endeavors to justify them. From Halakah, he passes to Agada and explains a considerable number of curious Agadic passages in a logical and rational manner. The treatise was written in the year 1438 in he lifetime of his faher, Simon Duran.

151. MINOR POLEMICS OF THE FIFTEENTH CENTURY

There are several minor polemic treatises produced in the fifteenth century, the most important of which are the following: The first is a letter written before his conversion by Joshua ha-Lorqi to his former teacher, the apostate Solomon ha-Levi. In this letter, the disciple asks Solomon for the reasons which prompted him to forsake the faith of his fathers. In veiled irony, he suggests that the reason could not have been the love of pleasure or gain nor even the miserable state of the Jews, and he therefore concludes that it must have been the conviction that Christianity is really the better religion. He then advances his doubts in the doctrine of the Messiahship of Jesus. His arguments are not original for we meet with them in other books, but are logically arranged and expressed in forceful style. To these arguments, Solomon made a feeble reply of which only a small fragment is extant.

Unfortunately the zeal displayed by Joshua on behalf of Judaism was not of long duration. It did not take long and he himself "saw the light." In his new state as Geronimo de Santa Fē, he was a most zealous apostate and at his instigation, the Jewish leaders were invited in the year 1418 by Pope Benedict XIII for a disputation at Tortosa, Aaragon, in which the greatest Jewish scholars of Spain headed by Don Vidal Beneveniste and Joseph Albo participated. The record of this disputation constitutes the second treatise.

The debate turned on the question whether the Talmud asserts that the Messiah had already come or not? Santa Fē undertook to show from several passages of the Talmud that the Messiah had arrived. His principal argument was based on a statement in the Babylonian Talmud, tractate *Abodah Zarah,* 9a which says, "We have learned in the Book of Elijah that of the six thousand years which the world is to exist, two thousand were moral chaos, i. e. without law and order, two thousand were under the reign of Law (Torah) and two thousand will constitute the period of the Messiah." Santa Fē wanted to prove that the author of the statement was Elijah the Prophet and that he admitted that the Messiah came at the end of four thousand years after creation. The rabbis in their reply pointed to the statement following the above quoted passage which says, "Because of our sins, many years of the two thousand period passed and Messiah did not come as yet." Santa Fe argued that this is an addition by later scholars but not the words of Elijah. The Jewish leaders then replied that the meaning of the statement, "That the last two thousand years are the Messianic period," is that during this period Messiah *may* come at any time God wills, but not that he had come, and proved their interpretation by many citations from the Talmud. Santa Fē then quoted several other passages but his interpretations were skillfully refuted.

The third treatise is by Joseph Albo and was originally a chapter in his book *The Ikkarim.* It is the gist of a discussion with a Christian scholar who argued that the Torah is deficient in several respects, namely that it does not contain the doctrine of the Trinity; it promises only material reward but not spiritual salvation; and finally that its laws are gross and unjust, as it commands sacrifices and it allows the taking of usury from a gentile and similar things.

To these objections, Albo replies that the doctrine of the Trinity is opposed to reason and that the Torah teaches pure monotheism. Further, it speaks of material reward, for the majority of the people will believe rather in such compensation than in a pure spiritual one. But there are many references in the Bible also to that spiritual salvation. As for the grossness of the laws, the sacrifices were, as Maimonides pointed out, a concession to the usage of the people and a means to purify their hearts and bring them ultimately to the conception of pure monotheism. Again, usury is permitted only with regard to idol worshippers who do not acknowledge any stable law. On the contrary, says Albo, the Torah is replete with humane laws which prove its perfection. He then shows many inconsistencies in Christian teachings. Some of Albo's arguments were utilized by Simon Duran in his treatise. The chapter was deleted from the *Ikkarim* by the censors and was later printed separately.

The fourth treatise is called *Ahitub we-Zalmon,* written by a scholar named Mattatias. It describes a dispute held in the presence of a king between Ahitub, a Jew of Turkey, Zalmon, a Mohammedan and Akar ha-Karhi, a Christian priest. The Jew, of course, issues victorious and the Moslem praises the Jews, pointing to the facts that on the other side of the river Sambatyon powerful Jewish kingdoms exist, that flourishing Jewish communities thrive in Spain, and that even in Germany and France where the Jews are oppressed, they evoke respect by their readiness to undergo martyrdom rather than forsake their faith. He therefore, renounces Islam and allows himself to be converted to Judaism by Ahitub.

152. *SIXTEENTH CENTURY*

The sixteenth century was, like the preceding one, productive of a large number of polemic and apologetic works. However, most of these can not compare in quality and thoroughness to the earlier books. On the whole, the authors repeat the arguments of their predecessors. The earliest of the apologists is Don Isaac Abrabanel (Sect. 20) who, though he had not written a special treatise on the subject, had incorporated in his commentaries on the Biblical books and also in his several books on the Messianic hope, numerous pas-

length with the fundamental Christian doctrine of the divinity of sages dealing with the refutations of the Christian interpretation of Biblical verses, as well as with the proofs that the Messiah is still to come. Of these excursuses, the most important is the one contained in the eighth section of his *M'aenē ha-Yeshuah* (The Fountains of Salvation), a commentary on Daniel. In this excursus, he deals at Jesus. The polemic passages were translated into Latin by A. Hulsius under the title *Capitulatio Libri Fontes Salutes,* who added a lengthy refutation of their arguments.

Another Jewish apologist of the century hails from Italy. He is the above mentioned geographer Abraham Farissol (Sect. 136), who in his treatise *Magen Abraham* (The Shield of Abraham), wrote down the gist of the disputations he held at the request of Hercules d'Este, Duke of Ferrara, with Dominican friars. The book is divided into three parts; the first contains a polemic against the dogmas of Christianity as well as a refutation of certain accusations against the Jews; the second deals with Islam; and the third is devoted to a critical analysis of the Gospels. The tone of the work is dignified, for Farissol treats the beliefs of his opponents with respect. His arguments are weak and are not distinguished by deep reasoning, though at times he displays a practical turn of mind. To the accusation that the Jews occupy themselves with money lending, he replies that society can not be conducted on pure humanitarian principles, and he sees no difference between renting the use of a house and the use of money, inasmuch as the interest paid for loans is merely rent for its use. The part against Islam is borrowed verbatim from Simon Duran's *Kesheth U-Magen.*

The two Nasi brothers, David and Joseph, the latter famous as the Duke of Naxos, wrote polemic treatises in the second half of the century. David's work is called *Hodoath Baal Din* (The Testimony of the Plaintiff). It is divided into two parts, in the first of which the author quotes a number of passages from the Gospels that corroborate the Thirteen Articles of faith of Judaism, while in the second he attempts to refute the nine fundamental Christian doctrines.

It is interesting to note that in his preface he tells us that he wrote the book for the Cardinal Francesco di Bentivelo of Crete whose secretary and business agent he was. He taught the Cardinal Hebrew and read with him the Old Testament in the original. Being certain of his friendship and his liberal views, he composed this treatise to convince him of the unsoundness of Christian doctrine. He asserts that this prelate not only did not rebuke him for his boldness but rewarded him munificently.

Don Joseph's small treatise is the *Ben Poroth Yoseph* (Joseph is a Fruitful Vine, after Genesis XLIX, 22), written in the year 1577, originally in Portuguese and later translated into Hebrew. It contains the arguments advanced by Joseph in his dispute with a Christian and is not distinguished by any depth of thought. The main interest of the book lies in the fact that its author, occupied as he was with affairs of state of great importance, still found time to engage in literary pursuit. Another Turkish Jewish scholar, Abraham Ibn Megas, the physician of the Sultan Suleiman (d. 1585), wrote a more thorough polemic work named *Kabod Elohim* (The Glory of God). Its eighteen chapters deal critically and in a systematic way with all important doctrines of Christianity. Among the dogmas and beliefs attacked are the Trinity, the divinity of Jesus, the eucharist, sacraments, baptism, original sin, the view that Jesus came to redeem the suffering souls and even the rights of the Roman pontificate, i. e. the papacy. Besides he proves that the Jews were driven out of Palestine for other sins and not because as the Christians say they killed Jesus, that the Messiah is still to come and that the Law was not abrogated. In the last two chapters, the author refutes the Christological interpretations of Biblical verses. In general, we can see in his system and division of the subject matter the influence of Profiat Duran's and Crescas' treatises. Ibn Megas shows wide acquaintance with the Gospels and other writings and even knows of Luther and the Protestant Reformation.

153. THE SEVENTEENTH CENTURY

The seventeenth century can be rightly denominated as one of controversy. The representatives of both factions in Christianity, those of Protestantism and Catholicism, displayed remarkable zeal for the conversion of the Jews. Their efforts often bore fruit, for they succeeded in snaring some weak members of the race who had converted themselves and then turned against their brethren. These apostates published vituperous pamphlets and books against the Jews, and of course, Jewish scholars were forced to defend their faith and race in polemic works. Such works are quite numerous and we will mention the outstanding among them.

i. The earliest is a book written by Zalmon Zevi Openhausen, a resident of the German city by that name called *Der Judischer The-*

riac (The Jewish Medicine). It was directed against the venemous attack by the apostate Frederick Von Ittingen, named *Der Judischer Schlangenbalg* (Jewsih Serpent Hissing).

In this libelous writing, the apostate piled up all accusations that were ever made against the Jews and charged them with making frequent derogatory references in their daily speech to Jesus and to Christianity, with fostering animosity to the Christians and referring to their writings as well as to the priests and dignitaries of the Church by insulting epithets, and that they even speak of Latin as an unclean language. He also accused the Talmud of being full of blasphemies against Jesus and Christianity, and that it allows the Jews to cheat the Christians in their commercial dealings with them. He further repeated the oft made accusations that the *Kol Nidrē* formula, recited on the eve of the Day of Atonement, is intended to annul all vows and oaths made by Jews to gentiles, and accused them of practicing witchcraft and using incantations in the name of the devil. These charges form only a part of his diatribe, and the book really deserved its name, for it is a veritable "hissing of a serpent."

To refute all these monstrous charges was the task undertaken by Openhausen. His work contains seven chapters, each dealing with a group of accusations. The author is very cautious and takes care not to offend the feelings of the Christians, although he is not sparing in opprobious epithets for the apostate. He proves by numerous citations from the Talmud that the Jews are commanded to show mercy and friendliness to the gentiles, and that even the few laws of an unfriendly character are directed against the pagans and not the Christians. He corroborates his contention by facts from life that the Jews do not follow these laws in their dealings with their neighbors. As for the statements in the Talmud concerning Jesus, he revives the thesis which was stated by earlier Jewish apologists that they refer to an earlier Jesus, and proves his contention by the discrepancies in the facts given about his life and family in the Talmud and those in the Gospels.

With great contempt, he rejects the accusation of witchcraft, stating that it proves both the ignorance and the maliciousness of the apostate, for the Bible and Talmud are full of injunctions against such practices. As for certain incantations used by the Kabbalists, he points to the testimony of many Christian scholars and especially Reuchlin and Pico-de-Mirandola, who extolled the Kabbala. Again the *Kol Nidrē* is only intended for vows made unconsciously and does not annul any conscious oaths. In this manner, Openhausen refutes every charge made by the apostate. The book written in a good German style made a favorable impression on the Christian world, and was reprinted several times and also translated into Latin by Johann Wilber. The author also issued a Judaeo-German version of his work, so that every Jew might be able to use the arguments contained therein in defense of the Jewish name.

ii. Another treatise in this field was written about the same time by an Italian Jew, Jacob of Venice, as a reply to an apostate, Peter Paul, who attacked the Talmud on account of its strange Agadic statements. Jacob, in his answer, states that many of these Agadic passages and stories are allegorical and contain noble thoughts and ideas, while numerous Christian writings are full of superstitious legends and miraculous stories of the saints and their deeds. Finally, he reproaches the apostate for his evil deeds against his own brethren and warns him of the dire punishment which is bound to overtake any enemy of Israel, citing many examples from the past history of the Jews.

iii. In the year 1617, a dispute was held at Ferrara between Don Alfonso Caracciolo, a Christian divine and a Jewish scholar. The contents of this dispute is contained in a book called *Vikkuah Al-Nitzhiuth ha-Torah* (A Debate about the Immutability of the Torah). As can be seen from the name of the book, it deals chiefly with the question of the abrogation of the Law. The main argument of the Jewish scholar in defending the immutability of Judaism was that the truth and Divine origin of a religion is proved by four things: (a) from the character of the religion itself; (b) from the nature of the giver; (c) from the character of those who received it; and (d) the manner of its inception. He then proceeds to unfold the exaltedness of the Mosaic Law; points to the fact that God Himself gave the Law; that Moses the mediator, was the greatest prophet; that the Jews who received the Torah are called in the Bible the chosen people; and that the Torah was given in such a manner that there is no doubt of its truth. He, therefore, concludes that no one can appeal to the Jews to change their religion, for none of them can doubt the veracity of the faith received from their fathers. The argument is really borrowed from Albo's *Ikkarim,* but the anonymous author developed it in his own way.

iv. Judah Leon de Modena (Sect. 141), the prolific writer of that century and well known composer of several apologetic treatises on behalf of the Oral Law and a polemic against the Kabbala also left us a work against Christianity named *Magen we-Hereb* (Shield and Sword). It was one of his last writings, composed in the year 1644 and unfortunately was not preserved in its entirety.

What is left of it is divided into five sections subdivided into chapters, each section dealing with a fundamental Christian doctrine. The first section discusses the dogma of original sin, and in ten chapters the author shows the impossibility of assuming such a doctrine. Most of his arguments repeat what was said before by Jewish controversialists, but some are new, among them one where he states that the sin of Adam was not so great that all future generations should be punished with eternal suffering. The transgression of making the golden calf was greater, he says, and yet the punishment was not so severe. The second section deals with the Trinity, where he points out that this conception contradicts the unity of God, for notwithstanding all efforts of the theologians to justify it, the fact remains that it posits multiplicity in the nature of God. He also refutes the interpretation of Biblical verses by which the Christian savants usually substantiate that doctrine.

In the third section, the question of incarnation is taken up and besides analyzing the view and proving its untenability, Modena devotes a long excursus to the development of the conception as a whole. He asserts that Jesus never claimed divinity, that he used the title "Son of God" merely as a means to convince the people that he is above all prophets, and that he consistently denied imputing to him the possession of Divine power. The fourth section is devoted to the dogmas of the immaculate conception and to the birth of Jesus. Modena quotes many objections to this theory, among them the following: If Mary did not in any way help towards the birth of Jesus as everything was accomplished without her participation, wherefore was the whole purpose of the birth through her? Here he also deals with a number of suspicious passages quoted in the book of Peter Galatinus in the name of the Midrash. These passages are not found in the copies of the Midrash and Modena suspects that Galatinus invented them himself and imputed them to the Rabbis to show that there are favorable references to Jesus in the Agada. In the last section, he proves that the Messiah had not yet come and that he will be a man of pure human nature.

v. The last apologetic work produced during the century was the *Kur-Metzaref ha-Emunoth* (Purifying Crucible of Belief) by Isaac

Lupis. It contains the gist of a dispute held at Marseilles, France, between him and two representatives of the Church, Fra Francesco, the provincial and an apostate, Pedro.

The crux of the debate centered about the question as to whether the Messiah had already come and whether we can find testimony in the Talmud to that effect. The Christian side is championed by the apostate but the monk opens the dispute with a general attack upon the Talmud, claiming that it is full of superstition and erroneous views concerning heaven and God and produces a few distorted and misquoted statements in support of his assertion. Lupis, after settling him right in his quotations, lays down six rules in the interpretation of the Agada and shows that the Rabbis used allegory, metaphor, exaggeration and cryptic expressions in their statements.

The apostate then steps in and endeavors to prove from a considerable number of Talmudic and Midrashic passages that the Messiah had already arrived. Lupis refutes each passage. The interesting thing about these quotations is that many of them are not found in our Midrashim. It is not exactly known whether the apostate had a different text before him or whether he drew upon a Christian source where these Agadic statements were doctored, for they possess a Christological color. We have, however, fair proof that the apostate borrowed his rather colored Agadic statements from Peter Galatinus' work, for Modena in his *Shield and Sword*, attacks Galatinus for spurious Agadic statements, and among the few examples he quotes, there is one statement also cited by Pedro. This statement Modena proves to be distorted. According to Modena, Galatinus quotes frequently from *Bereshith Rabbatai* of Moses ha-Darshan, a doubtful source, and Pedro likewise cites Moses ha-Darshan several times. All these prove that the Agadic statements of the apostate Pedro were borrowed from the work of Galatinus and do not constitute genuine Midrashic passages.

With the end of the seventeenth century, the interest in controversial literature, at least on the part of the Jews, began to wane. As a result, little of importance was produced in this field during the eighteenth century with the exception of Moses Mendelssohn's famous letter to Lavater. But this belongs to the modern period of Jewish literature.

B. Polemics Against Jewish Factions

154. THE STRUGGLE AGAINST PHILOSOPHY

We have hitherto described the extensive polemic and apologetic literature which was aimed against other faiths. We will now turn to works of a similar nature aimed either at attacking certain new tendencies in Judaism proper or defending its teachings from the encroachments of new intellectual currents which made their way into Jewry.

The first great intellectual clash of opinions which gave rise to a number of polemical works of this character was the strife that took place early in the thirteenth century between the followers of philosophy and their opponents. With the passing of the Classical period a change entered in the spiritual and cultural status of the Spanish Jewry. The interest of its leaders in secular studies began to wane and more emphasis began to be placed upon the study of the Talmud and Jewish law, and gradually these became, at least in some centers, the all-absorbing subjects of education while all other studies were looked upon with distrust and suspicion. Under these circumstances, it is not to be wondered at that certain Spanish leaders looked with disfavor upon the spread of the views of Maimonides, which since the translation of the *Guide of the Perplexed* into Hebrew, gained access to wide circles. A similar attitude was adopted in the Provence towards the philosophy of Maimonides. This country, as indicated above (Sect. 73), became the heir to the rich harmonious Jewish culture of the Golden Age of Spain and consequently became also the place of strife against it. Being in close proximity to northern France, a large number of its leaders were adherents of the Franco-German type of Judaism which looked upon all secular and philosophic studies with suspicion. These took alarm at the spread of philosophy among the Jews of Provence, especially since it bore the sanction of the great Talmudic authority, Moses ben Maimon.

The signal for the war against philosophy, however, was given by a Spanish Jewish scholar, Meir ben Todros ha-Levi Abulafia, Rabbi of Toledo. Meir Abulafia was a great Talmudist and was not averse to other studies as he knew Arabic and mastered the Hebrew language and its grammar thoroughly, but he was ultra-conservative in his religious views. He, therefore, could not agree with the views expressed by Maimonides in the first book of his Code where he deals with the fundamental principles of the Jewish religion. He especially took umbrage at Maimonides' conception of the state of existence of the righteous in the world to come (Olam-ha-Ba). According to Maimonides, the existence of the righteous in the new world after the Messianic days and after resurrection, will be merely a spiritual and not a bodily one. He relies upon a statement in the Talmud which says, "In the world to come there will be no eating nor drinking, but the righteous will all sit crowned and enjoy the glory of the Divine presence."[4] Abulafia saw in this conception a deviation from the Talmudic views of resurrection and *Olam ha-Ba.* According to him, the resurrection will be a bodily one and the righteous will continue to exist in body forever, though they may not necessarily partake of food and drink.

These strictures on Maimonides, he expounded in a polemical letter to Rabbi Jonathan of Lunel who was a great admirer of the former. He added also some refutations of a number of legal matters contained in the Code with the intention of minimizing the authority of Maimonides. In fact, he expressed his dissatisfaction with the acceptance of his Code as the authoritative one.

This attack on the Code of Maimonides and some of the views expressed therein provoked a number of replies from his admirers. The aged scholar and poet, Shesheth Beneveniste of Barcelona, wrote a long letter to the community of Lunel in defense of Maimonides and also indited several epigrams against Meir Abulafia. Other poets did likewise and as a result, we have a considerable number of polemic poetic compositions which were described above (Sect. 23). The most stinging rebuke, however, was administered to Abulafia by Aaron ben Meshulam of Lunel in a long letter written in defense of the master and his Code. Aaron, who was a famous scholar in his day and at one time the teacher of Meir, speaks with great authority and chastises the latter severely. He accuses him of undue pride in daring to attack a man who was the teacher of all Israel and whose mind embraced all branches of wisdom and knowledge. He then proceeds to refute the attacks of Abulafia, first proving that Maimonides by no means denied the bodily resurrection but that the spiritual existence of the righteous he speaks of refers to their existence in the new world which will come into being later. He corroborates his view by quotations from the Talmud. Aaron then turns his atten-

[4] T. B. Berakot, 17a.

tion to Abulafia's strictures on certain legal decisions in the Code, refutes them and justifies the master's opinions.

Upon receipt of Aaron's letter, Abulafia immediately sent him a long rejoinder where he defends his own views both in the matter of eschatology and that of law. He speaks of Aaron with great respect, acknowledges him as his former teacher, but still persists in pointing out the errors in his reasoning and in his legal opinions and does not neglect even to indicate several mistakes in grammar and in the usage of words. These three letters are written in a fine flowing Hebrew full of euphuisms, and in accordance with the custom of the day, in rhymed prose. Abulafia collected his polemic letters together with the apology of Aaron in a book which he called by an Arabic name *Kitab Al-Rasaid* (A Treatise of Letters).

This early polemic against the writings and views of Maimonides which probably took place in his lifetime, namely, at the beginning of the thirteenth century (c. 1203) was rather a mild outburst as compared with the storm that broke out against he study of philosophy thirty years later. During the three decades, the books of Maimonides, especially the *Guide* in the Hebrew translation, found their way into constantly increasing circles of Jews both in Spain and the Provence. The number of the adherents of the philosophical view grew by leaps and bounds and rationalism spread among the Jewish intellectual classes. This phenomenon was, of course, viewed with great alarm by the rabbis of northern France and by many of their likeminded colleagues in the Provence. Finally, about the year 1232, one of them, Rabbi Solomon of Montpelier, raised the cry of heresy against the spread of rationalism.

Solomon was a man of deep piety and a great Talmudic scholar, but of ultra-narrow theological views as he was even accused by his opponents of believing in a kind of corporeality of God. On the other hand, he must have been a man of great energy for he carried on the war against philosophy with zeal and bitterness. In conjunction with his two disciples, Rabbi Jonah Gerundi (Sect. 87) and Rabbi David ben Saul, he proclaimed a ban (1232) against all those who would study the *Guide* or the first book of the Code of Maimonides (Sepher ha-Mad'a) or any philosophical works in other languages. In the epistle which they attached to the ban, they openly averred that the theological views of Maimonides undermine the teachings of true Judaism and even spoke derogatively of Maimonides himself.

This action aroused a great storm among the followers of the philosopher. They rushed to the defense of the master and, led by the aged exegete and grammarian David Kimhi, immediately issued a counter ban against Solomon and his associates and sent letters to all communities in the Provence and Spain, calling upon the faithful to rally to the support of reason and knowledge and their exponent, Moses ben Maimon.

Most of the communities responded favorably to the appeal of the Maimonists and condemned severely the actions of the opponents of philosophy. But Solomon and his associates had also some sympathizers, the most noted of whom were Meir Abulafia and the venerable scholar and physician, Judah ben Joseph Al-Fakhar, both of Toledo. The first openly espoused the cause of Solomon while the second was more cautious, but when David Kimhi turned to him in a letter soliciting his aid on behalf of the Maimonists, Al-Fakhar rebuked him severely. It did not take long and the strife between the parties took on an exceedingly acrimonious aspect.

Nahmanides, the great authority of the day, at first endeavored to make peace between the parties, but when he failed, he ranged himslf on the side of Maimonides, though somewhat hesitatingly. Public opinion turned then against Solomon, and even a number of rabbis of northern France, who at first had joined him deserted his ranks. In despair, he committed a grave offence, for he sought help from the Franciscan monks by informing them of the heresy contained in the writings of Maimonides. These seized the opportunity of confiscating the books and burned them publicly in Paris early in the year 1234. This action horrified the Jews and many of Solomon's followers forsook him but he remained undismayed and with exceeding stubborness carried on the strife. Some of his associates stooped to still lower means and informed against the leading Maimonists, who were seized and put into prison, but soon the falsity of the accusation was discovered, and the informers were barbarically punished by having their tongues cut out. The tragic episode put an end to the strife, proving to all how dangerous inner dissension is to a scattered people.

This strife produced, of course, a considerable polemic literature, both in poetry and prose. The most important of the latter writings is the collection of polemic and apologetic letters, published together with the letters of Maimonides (Iggroth ha-Rambam), in Constantinople around the year 1530. There are fifteen letters in the collection written by different men but unsystematically arranged, and it is difficult to determine their chronological sequence, for with the exception of one, all are undated. The historian Graetz, however, succeeded in unravelling the mystery and establishing a kind of sequence. According to him, the earliest letter is the shorter missive of Nahmanides which was written early in the year 1232 to the communities of Aragon. The writer pleads that these communities should not join the ranks of the Maimonists against Solomon of Montpelier,—for though the name "Maimonists" is not mentioned, yet it is evident that this was his intention. It is conciliatory in tone and condemns mildly the French rabbis who endeavored "to cover the midday sun," referring by this title to Maimonides, but urges that the entire matter be judged with deliberation and that both parties be forced to come before a court of justice.

To this letter there is extant but one response, that of Meir Abulafia, the old controversialist. He openly avows his sympathy for Solomon and assures Nahmanides that he will use his influence to prevent Spanish communities from agreeing to the excommunication of the Rabbi of Montpelier. He speaks, however, with great respect of Maimonides, but claims that the *Guide,* though it strengthens the roots of the Jewish religion, yet destroys some of its branches, and it is, therefore, best to restrict its study. There is no mention, though, of issuing a ban against its reading.

However, neither the appeal of Nahmanides nor the efforts of Abulafia succeeded in keeping the communities of norhern Spain from joining the ranks of the Maimonists. Only a few months later in August 1232 (Ab 4992 A. M.), the community of Saragossa sent a letter to the other communities condemning in severe terms the attack on Maimonides. This letter is followed by four other epistles sent by the communities of Huesca, Monzon, Calatyud and Lorida, which confirmed the judgment contained in the epistle of the Saragossa community. Simultaneously with all these missives, another letter by the leading scholar of Aragon, Bahya ben Moses, was sent out as a call to arms to all those to whom the name of Moses ben Maimon, the Light of Israel, is dear, to rally and excommunicate the vituperators of his books. These six letters, contained in the collection are distinguished by unbounded love and admiration for Maimonides.

The epistle of the Aragon communities aroused Nahmanides to a second effort for peace which he advocated in a long letter addressed to the rabbis of France. This time, the writer expresses himself more definitely on behalf of Maimonides, extols his piety and extensive erudition, praises the *Guide of the Perplexed,* and rebukes the rabbis for their issuing a ban against the study of Moses ben Maimon's works. He is especially bitter against their prohibition to read the first book of the Code and refutes all the objections raised to some of its teachings. For the sake of peace, Nahmanides says, he would consent to the limitation of the study of the *Guide* only to selected men. He demands that the rabbis of France rescind their ban and use their offices for peace. The letter, though distinctly pro-Maimonides, is yet conciliatory in tone and speaks with great respect of Solomon of Montpelier even if it decries his narrow theological views.

Very interesting are the seven letters which comprise the correspondence between David Kimhi and Judah Al-Fakhar of Toledo. Kimhi, believing the latter a sympathizer of Maimonides, went to Spain to solicit his aid on behalf of the cause, but on the way, he became sick and sent Al-Fakhar a short letter expressing his request. Al-Fakhar in his reply administers Kimhi a stinging rebuke as he calls him "Satan," i. e. one who brings about quarrels, as well as other undignified epithets and delivers an attack on the teachings of the *Guide,* saying that we can not reconcile the views of Aristotle and Judaism. He openly justifies the stand of Solomon of Montpelier. This letter did not reach Kimhi who meanwhile sent Al-Fakhar a second epistle written with great humility, telling him of the change of mind of some of the French rabbis who left the ranks of Solomon and asking him to interfere in the strife. Al-Fakhar's answer to the second letter is more respectful but he declines to grant his request. In the third letter, Kimhi reproaches Al-Fakhar for the insulting tone of his first epistle, for though he did not see it he had heard of its wording. He further informs him of the alliance of Solomon with the Christian monks against the works of Maimonides. In his final reply, Al-Fakhar makes a rather stiff apology for his undignified style of writing but remains adamant to Kimhi's pleas. To this correspondence, we must add the letter sent by Abraham Ibn Hasdai of Barcelona, the poet and scholar (Sect. 24) to Al-Fakhar in which he rebukes him for his treatment of Kimhi. All the letters are written in rhymed prose and in superb Hebrew style.

Besides this collection of polemic writings, a number of similar works exist. Among them are two long epistles by Samuel Sasportas against the opponents of philosophy and a treatise named *Milhamoth Adonai* (The Wars of the Lord) by Rabbi Abraham, son of

Maimonides, which contains a number of letters in defense of the master and also excerpts from the polemics against his views.

The third stage in the struggle against philosophy began about sixty-five years later, also in the Provence and by a remarkable coincidence in the same city of Montpelier. The strife, on the whole, was of a much milder character and was conducted in a quite dignified way. During those sixty odd years, the study of philosophy and the sciences struck roots in Provence Jewry, and as a consequence, even the ultra-pious were not entirely averse to it and could not entertain any idea of prohibiting it entirely but hoped to put some restrictions and limitations upon its cultivation.

The cause for the anti-philosophic movement was the writings and sermons of the allegorists who, as we have seen above (Sect. 94) had gone quite far in their allegorical interpretation of the historical portions of Genesis and also of some of the precepts of the Law. One of the Provence scholars, a very energetic man Abba Mari Lunel of Montpelier took alarm at he spread of such methods of interpretation of the Bible and called the attention of the leading Rabbinic scholar of the day, Solomon ben Adret, to the danger. In a letter addressed to him in the year 1304, Abba Mari asks the scholar to find ways and means to restrain the allegorists. Ben Adret at first hesitated to issue a general prohibition against secular studies, but was not entirely averse to the attempt. He wrote to several leaders of the Provence communities, especially to he brothers, Bonafoux and Crescas Vidal, soliciting their opinion on the matter. These being of the same mind as Abba Mari, urged him to begin the struggle against the philosophers.

Their answer encouraged Abba Mari to offer to ben Adret a definite proposal, namely to prohibit by a ban the study of all sciences except medicine to any one under the age of thirty. Ben Adret, still cautious, prepared a letter on the subject addressed to the community of Montpelier calling upon them to join in the restraining of the activities of the allegorists. The letter was signed by himself and a number of other scholars. When Abba Mari read the communication to the council of the community, it met with great opposition and a party was formed to oppose the proposed prohibition on the study of the sciences. At the head of this party was Jacob ben Makir, famous mathematician and translator. It was soon discovered that the followers of the sciences had great strength and numerous friends in all Provence and Aragon communities. Jacob ben Makir also wrote to ben Adret in defense of the pursuit of the sciences, and other men joined in the protest against the proposed ban.

This unexpected opposition somewhat deterred ben Adret and he wrote Abba Mari that he must first obtain the consent of twenty communities to the issuance of such prohibition and then he would be ready to proclaim it. He also asked him and Kaloynmos ben Todros, the Nasi of Narbonne who joined the ranks of the opponents of philosophy, to compose the version of the ban. Abba Mari, though his party was strengthened by new adherents, was still reluctant on account of the strong opposition, to be severe in the form of the ban and composed a lenient version. He recommended that the study of physics and metaphysics from books written by non-Jews be prohibited to any one below the age of twenty-five. It is to be noted that only physics and metaphysics were excluded but not medicine and mathematics, and that books on the subjects written in Hebrew by Jews were also not included in the prohibition. This was done, of course, in order not to cast any slur on the works of Maimonides or any other Jewish philosopher.

This version, however, was found to be too lenient by ben Adret. He, therefore, encouraged by the support of Asher ben Yehiel (Sect. 43) who had meanwhile settled in Toledo, issued on the 31st of July, 1305 (ninth of Ab), a more severe prohibition. This read that no one is allowed to study the books of the Greeks on physics and metaphysics whether written in that language or translated before he reaches the age of twenty-five, but medicine, though based on physics, is expressly permitted. The new feature was that such books even when translated into Hebrew were included in the prohibition. However, it seems that even this new version did not include the works of Maimonides or any other Jewish philosopher.[5]

The ban, however, was not accepted by the Provence communities and the lovers of philosophy proclaimed a counter ban against those who will prevent their children from the study of the sciences, or who will speak evil of Maimonides, or who will accuse any Jewish rationalist for his books before proving the charges made against him. The counter ban caused a good deal of anxiety to Abba Mari and his associates, and they endeavored to prove that it is not valid. Meanwhile,

[5] Graetz' assertion to the contrary is not borne out by the text which distinctly reads *Siphre ha-Yevanim* (The Books of the Greeks), i. e., those of Aristotle. This is also evident from the letters of the signers of the ban, who expressly state that Maimonides' works were never intended to be excluded. See Minhath Kanaoth letters, 84-85.

Yedayah Bedersi wrote a long letter to ben Adret in defense of the study of philosophy and science. The letter made a great impression upon ben Adret and the other signers of the ban who wrote to Abba Mari asking him to desist from the strife and avowing that not the slightest slur was intended against the works of Maimonides in the prohibition proclaimed. In the communication, they do not rescind the ban but hint that if a community will not accept it, they will overlook such action. Thus ended the third stage in the struggle against philosophy and science.

The literary results of this struggle are expressed in several polemic and apologetic works. The first is the *Minhath Kanaoth* (Offering of Zeal) a collection of a hundred and one letters arranged by Abba Mari which tell the tale of the last strife. Most of the letters deal with the events of the strife and form excellent material for its story. A few, however, deal with legal matters containing inquiries by Abba Mari and Responsa by ben Adret and Asher ben Yehiel. The bulk of the letters comprise the correspondence between the editor and ben Adret, but there are many written by other men, among them several from opponents, such as Jacob ben Makir and others.

In his introduction, Abba Mari states that the reason for his initiating the movement to limit the study of philosophy was the activity of the allegorists which brought about the spread of irreligious ideas. He says that he loves knowledge but that the sciences of physics and metaphysics should be restricted to men of mature age who had been first instructed in Bible and Talmud. He quotes Maimonides as an example and praises the first book of the Code and the *Guide* exceedingly.

The second work is a treatise called *Hoshen Mishpat* by Simon ben Joseph of Provence, surnamed En Duran, intended as a reply to a pamphlet by the famous scholar and Talmud commentator Menahem ha-Meiri of Perpeignan (Sect. 43). Meiri or Don Vidal Solomon, who was a great lover of sciences and who did not sympathize with Abba Mari in his zeal for prohibiting their studies, sent the latter a pamphlet where he raised a number of objections to the proposed ban. Abba Mari asked his disciple En Duran to reply to Meiri's writing. The original of Menahem's brochure is lost, but En Duran preserves for us a considerable number of fragments, and these constitute one of the points of interest of his work.

From these excerpts, we learn that Meiri objected to Abba Mari's activity on the grounds that it degrades the value of science in general, that ben Adret is not the proper judge in these matters since he is a Kabbalist, and that the prohibition will bring bitter strife among the communities as was the case during the earlier struggle. He further objects to the tone of Abba Mari's writings which implies that philosophers are not pious and cites many scientists who were known to be God-fearing. He also argues that books are not to be condemned because some opinions found in them are erroneous, and in general, we are not responsible for the actions of the individuals. It is our duty to reproach them, but if they do not obey we should leave their punishment to God. Finally, he objects to the terms of the prohibition, namely of excluding the study of physics and the limit of twenty-five years. Such exclusion, Meiri argues, would deprive one from the study of parts of the *Guide* or logic which are based on the principles of physics. As to the age limit, he says, if one is not allowed to study these sciences before twenty-five, he will not study them later, for then men are married and have little leisure for study. Knowledge and science, he concludes, would thus automatically be excluded from the House of Israel, a condition greatly to be regretted.

To all these objections, En Duran attempts to find answers and in a respectful tone endeavors to allay Meiri's doubts. The second point of interest in En Duran's treatise is his extensive exposition of the ways of the allegorists, how they applied their method to sublimate all historical facts of the Bible.[6] His difficult style, however, minimizes to a certain extent the value of the treatise, for it is a conglomeration of parts of verses and Talmudic expressions.

The third work is the long letter of apology on behalf of the sciences addressed by Yedayah Bedersi to ben Adret. It is a brilliant brief for the necessity and urgency of the study of the sciences, and as we know made a great impression. It is written in a fine flowing Hebrew but the style is exceedingly ornate.

155. LEON DE MODENA'S DEFENSE OF ORAL TRADITION

Among the numerous works of Leon de Modena, there are two which aim to defend the Oral Law against attacks by Jewish unbelievers. The first is a somewhat longer work called *Behinat ha-Kabbala* (The Test of Tradition) and the second called *Magen we-Tzinah* (Shield and Buckler), is a shorter treatise on the same subject.

[6] For their method and examples thereof, see sect. 94.

The *Behinat ha-Kabbala*, however, is a peculiar kind of apology and the well known adage "Guard me from my friends, and I will guard myself against my enemies," can be fittingly applied to it, for in reality, it is more of a polemic against the Oral Law than a defense. The work is divided into two unequal parts, one called *Kol Soḳol* (The Voice of the Fool) contains the arguments of the supposed opponent and comprises the greater part of the book, and the other named *Shaagath Aryē* (The Roar of the Lion, with reference to the author's name) is devoted to the defense of the Law. It consists of a few chapters and is left in an incomplete state for it deals only with the refutation of a few arguments of the polemic. Whether the balance of the apology was lost or was never written by the author can not be definitely determined.

In his short preface, the author says that by accident he chanced upon a book written by a certain Amitai ben Yedayah Ibn Roz in the year 1500 at Al-Kalah in Spain which contains a severe polemic against the Talmud and Rabbinic Judaism. He decided to refute his arguments and publish both the book of the polemist and his answer. He does not give us the original title of the *Kol Soḳol*. Whether there even existed an author by that name, or whether the story is mere fiction invented by Modena to cover his own authorship of the first part, will become evident after we survey the contents of the arguments.

The *Kol Soḳol* contains three sections. The first enunciates the dogmas of the Jewish religion which the supposed mysterious author had come to believe in, not merely by tradition but by his own reasoning. These are: the existence of God, creation, man being the purpose of creation, Providence, reward and punishment, Divine origin of the Torah, immortality of the soul, and reward and punishment in the hereafter. The author finds little difficulty with all these dogmas except with the doctrine of the immortality of the soul, for in the entire Pentateuch there is not a single explicit statement referring to the survival of the soul, as all promises speak of material good or evil. Yet in spite of that, says the author, reason compels us to accept the doctrine and he also believes that Moses hinted at it in a veiled way in a number of places.

This section, though containing little which contradicts tradition, yet reveals before us the author's attitude towards it. He would, on the whole, not accept anything which could not be proved directly and simply from the Torah. His general views regarding Rabbinic tradition of the Law is expressed in the second section. He opens up with the question whether the interpretation of the Torah pursued by Rabbinism is the right one or whether it represents a deviation from the original intention of Moses? He claims that it is a deviation.

There are, he says, two wrong methods of interpretation of the Law, the literal one adopted by the Karaites, and the allegoric used by the Christians. The Rabbis, though, used both methods in any manner they saw fit. He then delivers his main attack against the Rabbinic claim of the existence of an oral tradition from Moses to the men of the Great Assembly. He admits that the laws of the Torah need explanation and interpretation and that Moses undoubtedly gave such to Joshua but argues that this tradition was not transmitted from Joshua on. The Jews, he says, during the entire period of the First Commonwealth, did not observe even the written law let alone the oral. Even the Pentateuch was preserved by the few. It was Ezra who made the Torah the heritage of the people, and though our author believes that Ezra gave the right text and the proper necessary explanation, yet he insists that he did not institute the Oral Law, nor did he introduce all the ordinances (Takonoth) which the Talmud ascribes to him.

It is from Ezra on that the deviation began; the Sopherim (scribes) introduced new rules of interpretation and deduced new laws which have no basis in the Torah nor in true tradition. As a proof that there was no continuous oral tradition, he cites the rise of the Sadducean party. How, argues the author, could such a party arise in face of an uninterrupted personal tradition which enjoins the performance of the Law in the Rabbinic manner? How could they differ when the people conducted themselves in the way of the Pharisees for ages? He, therefore, comes to the conclusion that much of Rabbinic law is a pure innovation. He does not, however, deny the need for interpretation, but claims that it must be based on a right understanding of the Torah.

From this general statement, the author passes on to a detailed criticism of Rabbinic law and arranges it in the order of the four parts of the Code of Jacob ben Asher, the *Tur* (Sect. 57). It must be said that his detailed criticism is much milder than his general opposition to Rabbinic law would indicate. He merely wants to reform the Code and no more; for he almost accepts all the laws in principle with the exception of a few, but he desires to have them modified and made light so that the Jews could perform them under the severe conditions of the exile. He begins with a series of attacks on the first part of the Code, *Orah Hayyim,* containing the synagogue ritual, and the Sabbath and festival laws. His first charge is directed against the Phylacteries (Tephilim) and the complicated system of prayers (Tephilah). He would abolish the wearing of phylacteries altogether for such injunction is not stated in the Bible. The verse in Deuteronomy VI, 8 which reads, "And thou shalt bind them for a sign upon thine hands, and they shall be as frontlets between thine eyes," he says, should not be taken literally. Again, while a Jew must pray three times a day, the prayers should be very brief and individual; public worship should be held only on the Sabbaths and festivals and this must also be very brief; the entire services together with the reading of the Law must not last more than an hour. He even composed a short text of prayers which in his opinion should suffice.

In regard to the Sabbath, he protests against the rigorousness of the day imposed by the Rabbis, especially against the prohibitions of carrying things of slight weight and of going beyond a fixed boundary. In general, he demands only slight modification of the Sabbath Law. He is also dissatisfied with the rigor of the Passover laws which require scrupulous abolition of all vestiges of leaven (Hametz) and many more things. As for the Holy Days, he advocates the abolition of the second day. In his strictures upon the second part of the Code *Yore Dea,* he finds fault with the laws regarding the mixture of milk and meat claiming that the words of the Bible, "Thou shalt not seethe a kid in its mother's milk" are to be taken literally, and also with the laws of *Terephah* in slaughtered animals, arguing that there is no Biblical injunction for all the various kinds of *Terephah,* i. e. signs of disease, which the Rabbis have prohibited.

He similarly finds flaws in the parts of the Code devoted to the civil and family laws, namely *Hoshen Mishpat* and *Eben ha-Ezer,* but these are of comparative minor importance. His most serious objections are to the retention of the laws concerning the Aaronides (Kohanim), for he asserts that all these laws are no more valid and should be openly declared so. The author likewise demands the abolition of the numerous rules connected with the writing of a bill of divorce (Get) and advocates a simple formula consisting of one or two sentences.

The second part which is called by the grandiloquent name *Shaagath Aryē* (The Roar of the Lion) consists only of two brief chapters devoted to the refutation of the general theses in the second section of *Kol Sokol.* Modena points out that the Pentateuch must have interpretation and that Moses himself refers several times to the explanation of the laws. As to the opponent's argument that tradition ceased with Joshua and was not continued to be transmitted on account of the people's relapse from the Torah, he avers that the case was not so, for in every generation there were a few outstanding men who guarded the Torah and its interpretation. They were either priests or prophets. Thus, when Joshua died, his colleague Phineas who together with him received the tradition from Moses survived, and he transmitted the tradition to the judges and they to the priest Eli, and he in turn to the prophet Samuel and after him there followed a continuous uninterrupted chain of bearers of tradition, for from Samuel on, prophecy in Israel did not cease until Malachi. The back-sliding of the people could not, therefore, have affected the transmission of tradition.

With this refutation, the *Roar of the Lion* ceases to rumble. It is on the whole a very feeble roar to terrify such a formidable opponent as the author of the *Kol Sokol.* As said above, the balance of the refutation is missing and we do not know whether the rest of Modena's apologetic was lost or not completed. The solution of this question, though, is dependent on the other question whether the *Kol Sokol* was really composed by the man whose name it bears or is the handiwork of Modena himself?

There is overwhelming proof that the author of the polemic against oral tradition is none other than Modena. His story of finding the manuscript sounds very suspicious. First, the name of the supposed Amitai ben Yedayah Ibn Roz is not known in the entire Jewish literature; second, the name itself which means the True Man, the son of one who possesses Divine knowledge of the family of secrecy, sounds like an invented one and indicates that truth and knowledge and secrecy are contained in the arguments. Third, Modena does not give the name of the original manuscript which is rather strange as an author always designates his work by some name. Fourth, there are numerous parallels both of the style and the views expressed in the *Kol Sokol* in other works of Modena which compel us to assume that this work was also written by him. As we have seen above, Modena was a man of contradictory characteristics, both pious and free thinking at the same time. We should, therefore, not be surprised to learn that both the vehement attack on the Oral Law and the feeble defense of it were written by one and the same hand. Almost all Jewish scholars who have dealt with the matter have come to this conclusion.

We can now approach the solution of the second question, namely did Modena write a complete refutation of the *Kol Sokol* or was he merely satisfied with the two chapters extant to show that he attempted the refutation of all arguments but was prevented from completing it? Isaac Samuel Reggio, the editor of Modena's book, who published it for the first time in 1852, thinks that the second alternative was the case. According to him, Modena was more interested in the polemic against the Oral Law than in its defense, and the two chapters of apologetics were merely used by him as a ruse to lead people to believe that the first part was not written by him, and that he, like all other pious people, was wroth against such utterances.

This harsh judgment, though not an entirely improbable one, is not borne out by facts. We find that our author did in fact give a more complete though brief refutation of a considerable number of the arguments contained in the *Kol Sokol,* in his second apologetic work *Magen we-Tzinah.* We may, therefore, assume that he either completed the *Shaagath Aryē* but that a large part of it was lost, or that he abandoned its completion when he conceived the composing of the second work where the apology is given in a more popular form.

The other book referred to, namely the *Magen we-Tzinah,* was written in the year 1617 as a reply to the arguments of a Jewish rationalist against the Oral Law. According to the inscription at the beginning of the book, the propounder of the arguments who is characterized as "A fool who is wise in his own eyes" lived in Hamburg, and when his arguments were published they were sent by the leaders of the Portuguese community of that city to Modena with a request to refute them. He readily consented to the request and the treatise was the result.

The theses of the opponent are twelve in number. One (No. 7) attacks the validity of the Oral Law in general, and the others object to particular laws and institutions. The general attack states four reasons for the rejection of Rabbinic Judaism: (a) There is no explicit statement in the Pentateuch that there is another Torah or that it needs interpretation; (b) that Moses warns numerous times against adding to or detracting from the law; (c) that in the time of Moses, laws were decided according to the written Torah and not by tradition, for the Jews asked Moses to explain difficult cases, and likewise in later generations, the priest or judge decided according to the Pentateuch and not according to tradition; (d) Solomon in asking aid from God in the decision of the laws, requested that He grant him an understanding heart, which proves that he relied on reason in this matter and not on Oral Law.

Eight theses deal with the phylacteries, with the custom of sucking out the blood (Mezizah) and making further incision after circumcision (Periaḥ), with the annulling of vows, with the "fences of the Law," i. e. Rabbinic prohibitions, and with the benediction pronounced on the performance of Rabbinic precepts. The author argues that these observances are opposed to the plain meaning of the Bible and he strenuously opposes the pronouncing of the benediction over Rabbinic precepts as they were not commanded by God. The other three theses deal with civil law. He would apply the *lex talionis* literally, and, likewise, he demands the actual killing of the owner of a goring ox if it killed a man and the meting out of the prescribed punishment of burning at the stake for certain capital offences, and not as the Rabbis say that the owner of the ox should merely pay a ransom and that molten lead should be poured down the throat of the culprit. Only few of these theses are found in the *Kol Soḳol* of Modena, and even those are given in a different form.

In his defense, Leon Modena begins with the refutation of the general attack upon the Oral Law and advances three reasons why that law was necessary. First, says he, we are not even certain whether the vowels and accents date from the time of Moses or from that of Ezra. But this is certain that the Pentateuch of Moses did not contain vowels or accents, for our own scrolls do not contain them. If that is the case, we must assume that the manner of reading of the Torah was handed over by tradition from Moses, and this is an important part of the Oral Law, for how can we know any part of the written law if we do not know how to read the commandments? Second, the brevity of the laws as stated in the Torah, compels us to accept the Oral Law as a complement to the written, for otherwise the precepts can not be carried out. Third, we may assume that God purposely left many things obscure so that the explanation be given by authority and be not left to the understanding of each individual Jew as the case would have been were the laws stated clearly. Every one would have placed his own interpretation on the laws, for even clear statements need explanation, and confusion would have resulted. Modena then refutes the four reasons of the opponent against tradition and goes on to refute the other theses. All his refutations are executed with skill and knowledge.

In connection with the *Magen we-Tzinah,* the question likewise arose whether "The fool who is wise in his own eyes" is not a fiction and that in reality the questions were written by Modena himself? In fact, all Jewish scholars beginning with A. Geiger and including Modena's latest biographer[7] assert with definiteness that he wrote both the theses and refutations. However, this assertion is proved utterly false by the publication of Uriel da Costa's *Propostas Contra a Tradicao* (Propositions against Tradition) by Carl Gebhardt[8] which are the very same contained in the *Magen we-Tzinah.* The fact that da Costa published these theses in Hamburg in 1616 the year given by Modena, establishes the authenticity of the opponent beyond any doubt. Leon Modena is thus vindicated, at least as far as this particular charge is concerned.

The other two polemic works of Modena are directed against the Kabbala. The first is a small treatise called *Ben David* which was written at the request of his pupil, the physician Joseph Hamitz. It deals with the belief in the transmigration of souls (Gilgul). Modena begins by stating that were the inquirer some one else, he might have dissimulated in his answer and probably agreed to this belief but to his beloved pupil he tells the truth, namely that there is no support for such doctrine in the Bible or the Talmud, and it is only the mystics who teach it. He speaks ironically of them for seeking support for this teaching in the views of Pythagoras, and says, if they have a tradition from the prophets, why seek succor from the pagan philosopher? As for Pythagoras, Modena assumes that he taught the doctrine of transmigration as a means to make people love their fellowmen believing that strangers may possess the souls of their deceased relatives.

Of the prominent Jewish scholars, only Isaac Abrabanel believed in transmigration and Modena sets forth to refute all his arguments on its behalf. He concludes by quoting the opinions of Saadia, Albo and others against the doctrine of transmigration.

Of more importance is Modena's second work against the Kabbala called *Ari Nohem* (The Roaring Lion). Here he really raises a mighty voice against the presumption of the mystics who claimed the sole

[7] N. Leibowitz, Leon Modena, New York, 1901, pp. 43-46.
[8] C. Gebhardt, Da Costa, Opera, Amsterdam, 1922, pp. 1-10.

possession of truth. He was one of the few Jewish scholars who dared to attack the Kabbala in an age when it was considered all supreme.

His main point in this work is that the teaching which goes by the name *Hokmat ha-Kabbala* (The Science of the Tradition) is neither science nor tradition. Science it can not be, for science is based on reason and logic, while Kabbala has very little of either. Again, it can not be tradition, for the older Jewish literature, i. e. Talmud and Midrash know nothing about it, and the great authorities of Judaism fought against its teachings. Again, a traditional doctrine must be uniform and its adherents usually follow the same principles. It is not so with the Kabbala where there is much divergence among its adherents.

The author then goes on to refute the assertion of the Kabbalists that one must possess a special aptitude to penetrate into the depths of the teachings. He asks how it is that men of mighty intellect who are otherwise the lights of Judaism did not possess that aptitude while mediocre men did? As for the piety of the followers of the Kabbala, that is no proof for the veracity of the teachings, for in all religions the ignorant are the most pious. He finally attacks the literature of the Kabbala and declares the *Sepher Yetzira* and the *Zohar* as pseudepigraphic works and quotes proofs that the *Zohar* was not written by Simon ben Yohai but much later. The author is especially bitter against the wonted boastfulness of the Kabbalist teachers, as for example, it is said of Luria that he once asserted that he could not impart in a period of eighty years the instruction his soul received in one hour on ascending to heaven. Such stories, says Modena, display not only a lack of modesty but an intention to overawe the people. Finally, he points to Maimonides whom he esteemed above all as a proof that the Kabbala is of very late origin, for how could he be ignorant of any Jewish teaching of importance? He thus continues to undermine the foundations of mysticism. The *Ari Nohem,* though not printed for a long time—for it was not published until 1840—yet made a great impression upon his contemporaries and a number of works were written against it, among them a work by the poet and Kabbalist, Moses Hayyim Luzzato. In concluding our survey of Modena's works, we may say that although he appears as one wayward in his opinion, still, when he was fired by a zeal for what seemed to him as truth, he expressed it with remarkable courage.

156. MISCELLANEOUS WORKS

There are numerous treatises of a polemic character, which either attack one or another kind of aberration in Judaism or, on the contrary, defend some of its aspects. But since we can not enumerate all of them, we will only select the most important. To these belong Jacob Emden's polemic books, *Mitpahat Sepharim* (The Cover of Books) andd the *Torath ha-Kanaoth* (The Law of Religious Zeal). Jacob Emden inherited his belligerent attitude against deluded mystics and aspirants to Messianic leadership from his father Rabbi Zevi Ashkenazi (Sect. 70) who was a redoubtable fighter against Sabbatai Zevi and his successors. He spent a large part of his life in stamping out the roots of evil which were planted in Jewish life by the movement of false Messianism, and many of his years passed in quarrel and strife. The most notable among his strifes is the battle he waged against the famous Talmudic scholar of his time, Jonathan Eybenshütz, whom he accused of being a follower of Sabbatai Zevi.

Emden was a pious man and even narrow in his theology, but with a keen critical sense and a fearless courage. When he saw that the Kabbala, in the teachings of which he believed, lay claim to ancient origin, which in his eyes was not justified, he wrote the *Mitpahat* to disprove such claim. In this book, which was already discussed above (Sect. 113), he quotes two hundred and eighty proofs to show that the *Zohar* could not have been written by Simon ben Yohai. His criticism is thorough and incisive. He analyzes every part of the *Zohar* and assigns each one to a proper date. Emden's work is a veritable contribution to the literary criticism of the *Zohar,* and was drawn upon by all subsequent Jewish scholars.

The second work is primarily a collection of documents bearing upon the struggle of one hundred years against the movement of Sabbataism and its followers. It contains bans, court decisions and letters by various Rabbinical courts against Sabbatai himself, his followers and subsequent impostors. Among other things, it contains also material for the strife and struggle against the poet and Kabbalist Moses Hayyim Luzzato and polemic letters against his contemporary opponent, Jonathan Eybenshütz. The book, as a whole, possesses great historical value.

A very fine apology which undertakes to straighten out the difficulties raised against the doctrines of Judaism and certain passages in the Bible is Abraham Hayyim Viterbo's *Emunath Hakomim* (The

Faith of the Wise). The book is divided into six sections treating of various subjects but not in a very systematic way. In his preface, the author informs us that the purpose of his work is to defend especially the Talmud and Midrash from the attacks of the people who, misled by secular studies, take the words of the Rabbis lightly. He also apologizes for differing with the views of Maimonides in a number of points, for he says when there is a question of truth, no deference is paid even to a teacher.

Viterbo was a very pious man but was also a rationalist and at times goes further than Maimonides in his rationalization. His first topic is the question of the sin of Adam and his punishment, a question which had already taxed the ingenuity of commentators and philosophers. Viterbo after rejecting the solution of Moses ben Maimon in his *Guide* offers a novel explanation of the matter. According to him, God never intended that Adam should live forever for that is against the constitution of the body. Death would have been the fate of man even if Adam would not have eaten of the Tree of Knowledge. Nor was Adam punished for his acquiring knowledge. The Tree of Knowledge was prohibited only because it aroused passion, and Adam was punished for transgressing the command of God. The Garden of Eden was merely a fruitful stretch of land embracing all the countries extending from Ethiopia to Mesopotamia. The extending of the Garden to include all these countries solves another difficulty, a geographic one, for according to Genesis II, 10-14, the Nile in Egypt and the Euphrates and the Tigris in Mesopotamia are supposed to issue from one source, namely the Garden of Eden. When Adam was punished, God caused the fruitfulness of this stretch of land to diminish and man henceforth had to work for his sustenance. Viterbo's explanation is a bold attempt to rationalize a very difficult passage.

In the other sections, the author endeavors to remove other difficulties in the Bible. Thus he explains that the builders of the Tower of Babel were not heretics who wanted to war with God, but that they merely contradicted the will of God that men should settle in all parts of the world while they congregated in one place. Their punishment was dispersion. He mitigates the act of the sons of Jacob in putting all the inhabitants of Shechem to the sword by saying that the judges of the city should have punished Shechem for his ravishing of Dinah, and when they failed to do so they were accomplices to the crime. He also explains, citing proof for his view, that the stern command of Moses to kill all inhabitants of Palestine referred only to those that would show resistance but not to those who would submit to the Israelites. He justifies the lending of money on interest, for there is no difference between lending money or selling goods, yet when the borrower is a Jew, we are enjoined to act more equitably and lend him money without interest. Still, he says, interest must be proportionate, and if a Jew exacts an exorbitant rate from a gentile, he should be punished.

Viterbo differs in the dogmas with Maimonides and fixes only six instead of thirteen. These are: the existence of God, His unity and incorporeality, revelation at Sinai, the veracity of the prophecy of Moses, the Divine origin of the Torah and reward and punishment. He holds a long polemic with Maimonides on dogmas and objects especially to the dogma of the Messiah. On the whole, Viterbo's work deserves its name *Emunath Hakomim* for much wisdom and logical reasoning is displayed in it. It can be counted among the best attempts made to reconcile the beliefs of Judaism with the principles of reason.

Chapter XI

PROSE LITERATURE

TALES, FABLES, SATIRE AND HUMOR

157. INTRODUCTORY

The works composed during the post-Classical period which aim not only to instruct but also to entertain, differ, on the whole, little in quality from the works of the former period. They retain, at least those books composed during the early part of the period, the characteristics of the productions of the twelfth century described in Vol. I (Sect. 203). The Oriental nature, the grotesque and fanciful still predominate; and the tale, the fable, and the proverb abound as illustrations of the moral teachings the author intends to convey and often constitute the body of the books. The influence of the Arabic models of this type of literature is in great evidence, and in fact, some of the works are either direct translations from that language or imitations of popular Arabic books.

Yet this literature possesses an individuality of its own, for even the translations and imitations are endowed with a peculiar spirit not found in the original. Not only are the names of the characters of the tales and fables changed to Biblical ones, but the entire content is infused with the Jewish spirit. That the original works possess this individuality in a marked degree goes without saying, though even these do not escape the influence of this type of general Mediaeval literature. This influence is especially evident in the numerous proverbs and fables employed by the writers of these books. As is well known, of all species of literary expressions, that of fable and proverb is the most migratory, and there is hardly a nation that can claim originality for this type of expression as it can always be traced to one foreign source or another. Fables, tales and proverbs were in a way the common property of the Mediaeval world and the Jews of the period availed themselves of the opportunity and appropriated their share of the common treasure and added to it a modicum of their genius by dressing it in a Jewish garb.

This literature can roughly be divided into three classes, namely (a) didactic works, (b) collections of tales and fables and (c) satire and humor. To the first class belong all books which aim primarily to delineate in a popular and attractive way the right conduct in life. They can not, though, for this reason be called strictly ethical works for their aim is not only to teach, but also to entertain. The second class includes all such works in which the entertaining and pleasing characteristics predominate over the instructive or ethical ones, though even here the goal the author set for himself may rightly be the inculcation of moral teachings in the hearts of the readers. The third class contains all such works where the author aims either to satirize and ridicule certain phases of the life of the generation, or peculiar weaknesses of human nature, or merely to amuse and entertain by a display of sparkling wit and keen flashes of humor.

The last class of works is especially marked by originality, for the humor displayed there is a typical one, adapted entirely to the ghetto life of the Jew. That life was undoubtedly a gloomy one, yet it had its moments of mirth, namely the holidays which enlivened the hard life of oppression and religious sternness. Of these, the feast of Purim was the most hilarious one, and this single day practically created a literature of its own, sparkling with wit and humor. However, the humor of this peculiar Purim literaure is expressed more in form than in content. And this can really be said about a large number of the humorous works in general, for the form most prevalent in them is that of parody.

Parody is usually defined as "A composition in which the form or expression of grave and dignified writings are closely imitated, but are made ridiculous by the subject or method of treatment."[1] The writers of a nation that produced the Bible, the Talmud, the Midrashim and other grave and dignified works could not help, when the spirit of mirth descended upon them, but to avail themselves of this ready arsenal and forge weapons for their darts of wit by parodying these writings. Hence we have numerous "tractates" dealing not with weighty legal questions but with drinking and merry-making, which are formed in the fashion of Talmud treatises, and are provided with commentaries and additions (Tosofoth) and other

[1] Century Dictionary, S. V. On the entire subject of parody in Jewish literature, see Prof. Israel Davidson's most complete and interesting work, Parody in Jewish Literature, N. Y., 1907.

paraphernalia. Other works dealing with similar subjects, imitate certain Biblical books.

Purim, however, was not the only subject dealt with in these works. Other subjects were also drawn upon for targets of the arrows of wit and humor. Of these, the most prominent were women, cantors, teachers, and other public officials. Thus, the literature grew and increased, and taking into consideration that the average Jew of the Middle Ages was sufficiently learned to understand the quips and puns and the parodies of the humorous works, we can safely conclude that this type of literature was exceedingly popular and widespread.

During the early part of the post-Classical period, the prose literature was primarily produced in Spain and was almost entirely subjected to the influence of the Arabic and Oriental world. But with the middle of the fourteenth century, the center of the literary activity, at least of the secular phase, as we know, shifted to the Provence and then to Italy. It is, therefore, in these two countries that the greater part of this type of literature was produced and where it was, of course, influenced by the spirit of these two centers.

158. DIDACTIC WORKS

The earliest didactic treatise of this period, written with the purpose not only of instructing but also of amusing and pleasing the reader, is a small book entitled *Milhamoth ha-Hokmah Im ha-'Osher* (The Strife between Wisdom and Riches) by Judah ben Isaac Ibn Shabbatai ha-Levi of Toledo, Spain. The author is well known by his two longer satirical works which will be discussed later. The work, though written in a humorous vein and in a style bristling with puns and parodies, can not be considered a satire as it aims to point out to man the right way of life and conduct. Its tendency is, therefore, primarily a didactic one.

The strife between wisdom and riches is carried on in the form of a dialogue between two twin brothers Peleg and Yaktan. Peleg is devoted to the pursuit of riches while Yaktan is an ardent follower of wisdom. Their father at his death, divided his property between them in proportionate shares, but left a very precious crown which possessed the magical quality of assuaging the pain of its bearer, without giving instruction as to who of the two sons should own it. The brothers then contend for the possession of the crown. Peleg argues that riches is the strongest factor in life and that wisdom and even religion are subservient to it, and he is therefore entitled to the crown. Yaktan, on the other hand, shows that wisdom rules the world and he is accordingly the rightful claimant to the heirloom. Each of the contestants draws upon the Bible, Talmud and Jewish history for proofs of his contention and it is in the clever use made of Biblical verses and Talmudic passages that the humor of the work is expressed. The brothers finally decide to try their case before the leader of Spanish Jewry, Todros Abulafia of Toledo. At the trial, Peleg produces a document signed by Jereboam ben Nabat and Elishah ben Abuya, notorious apostates who turned from a career of learning to the pursuit of pleasure,[2] to the effect that learning is of little value in the world, while Yaktan produces a similar document extolling wisdom and signed by Joseph, the son of Jacob and Solomon, son of David. Each tries to invalidate the testimony of the other, but to no avail. The decision is then given in the form of a regular court statement (Pesak Din) that both wisdom and wealth are the necessary means for a happy life, and that one can not reach this aim without the help of the other. The moral of the dialogue is that man must pursue in life both wisdom and wealth and must not follow one to the exclusion of the other. True, the instruction derived from the dialogue is not very deep nor lofty but the main interest of this treatise does not lie in its content but in its form. To one who is conversant with Hebrew, the brilliant puns, the clever twists of parody and the witty arguments of the contestants afford great delight and pleasure.

A larger and more important didactic book and a more serious one, though it possesses all the characteristics of such works, is the *ha-Mebaḳesh* (The Inquirer) written in the year 1264 by the philosopher Shem Tob Ibn Falaquera (Sect. 77). In the introduction, the author tells us that his purpose is to compose a treatise or an epistle (Iggereth), as he calls it, to instruct people in the right way of conduct. But in order that it be read by all and its words remembered, the teachings are epitomized at the end of each section in short poems and pointed proverbs which are easily retained in memory. The book is divided into two epistles, the first of a lighter nature dealing with the various occupations in life is written in a semi-poetic man-

[2] Jeroboam led after the death of Solomon, the secession of the ten tribes from the rule of the house of David and established the Israelitish kingdom in the North. Elishah ben Abuya, called also Ahar, was one of the Tannaim in the generation of Akiba who became an apostate and led an evil way of life.

ner. The second epistle devoted to an exposition of religious beliefs and the sciences possesses a graver and more serious tone, and as such, it contains no poems. Both epistles or parts are written in the form of a series of dialogues between an Inquirer, a young man in search of wisdom and knowledge, and various representatives of pursuits and occupations in life and of the sciences. The first part opens with a discussion between the Inquirer and a rich man. The young man attempts to dissuade him from accumulating wealth and asks him to devote his attention to the study of the Law, but the latter defends his pursuit, and a lively repartee develops interspersed with epigrammatic poems and pointed aphorisms. They part, and the Inquirer being convinced that happiness does not lie in the acquisition of riches, turns to investigate the quality of strength and holds a series of arguments with a man of might in a similar manner as the preceding one. The Inquirer praises wisdom as real nobility and extols its virtues, but the man of might is equally valiant in defense of prowess.

From the man of strength, the young man turns to the craftsman and engages him in a dialogue on the merits of the crafts. In this as well as in the remaining dialogues of the first part, the Inquirer enters deeper into the subjects of investigation for not being satisfied with a mere recital of their merits, he wants to learn their nature and essence. He, therefore, propounds numerous questions to the representatives of the various arts to which they give answers, but invariably there is one question to the answer of which ignorance is confessed. Thus, six questions are propounded by the Inquirer to the craftsman which touch on the difference between art and nature, the most necessary things for the artificer and the principal arts under which all others can be subsumed. Five are answered dexterously, but as for the sixth, the interlocutor simply answers I do not know. The same process is repeated with the physician, ethicist, grammarian, and poet who are the interlocutors of the last four dialogues.

These last dialogues are executed with great skill, for the author really united in himself all these arts, and we, therefore, get a fair survey of the art of medicine, its purpose and methods. We are told that nature is really the great healer of sickness and that the art of the physician and his medicines are only means to help nature in its work. We are also informed of the history of medicine and are given a list of the great physicians of the ages and their works beginning with Hippocrates and ending with Maimonides. Likewise, we are treated to an interesting summary of the current ethical theories and to an epitome of the arts of grammar and poetry.

The second part begins with a dialogue between the Inquirer and a pious but simple believer in the Jewish religion. The former raises a number of difficulties both in the Bible and in the Oral Law, but the latter merely asserts that such is the tradition and we are not allowed to question it. The Inquirer is not satisfied with this assertion and turns to a Jewish sage who avers that happiness is to be found in the Torah, but that the study of the sciences and philosophy is a prerequisite to the understanding of the Torah. The Searcher then interviews an arithmetician, geometrician, astronomer, logician, physicist and philosopher. By means of these interviews and dialogues, he obtains a survey of all knowledge and comes to the conclusion that philosophy is the acme of all sciences and the man of intellect must make it his aim. We thus discover the purpose the author had in mind which is that a real understanding of religion can be attained only through a mastery of science and philosophy, and in that lies happiness.

The book, as a whole, in its encyclopaedic character is instructive but through its poems and proverbs also pleasant and delightful. The poetic part, however, has its own value and samples of its charm were quoted above (Sect. 24).

A very noble treatise on the aim and purpose of human life written in a most exquisite style of pure Hebrew is the *Behinath Olam* (The Examination of the World) by Yedayah Bedersi or ha-Penini, composed in the first half of the fourteenth century.

In this work, the author discusses the vicissitudes of human life, the hazards of fortune, the various pursuits of men and points out the right path which the wise should follow.

The *Behinath Olam* can be divided, according to its contents, into three parts, though it is not actually done so by the author, each dealing with a certain general subject. The first part containing four chapters is devoted to the delineation of the character of man in general and that of the wise man in particular, his dignity, his all-embracing flight of thought and his ultimate destiny. The author begins with the wise man and speaks of his capabilities and his achievements. Man, he says, has scanned the heavens and has penetrated the depths of the earth and his knowledge is wider than the sea. He goes into raptures on contemplating the capabilities of the human intellect and exclaims, "Can the wide earth encompass the thought of man, the seat of which is only a chamber as small as the palm of a human hand?" Against this elevated position of man, he contrasts his ultimate destiny, death, which places him on an equal with all other animals. He concludes this part by offering us one comfort in this sad situation, namely that man possesses immortality, and this should be his striving during life. All other aims in life are vain and their futility is depicted by Bedersi in a striking sentence saying, "The love of the pleasures of life (Time in text) is like the shadows at eventide which vanish quickly and the disappointment experienced in their pursuit can be compared to that of the youth who gathers the rays of the sun in his closed hand but on opening it finds it empty."

In the second part, the author devotes himself entirely to a masterful description of the vicissitudes of life and the vanity of the pursuit of temporal pleasures or possessions. In a short chapter (VIII), he draws a beautiful poetic picture of the world and life (the translation of which was given above, p. 57) where the first is compared to a roaring sea and the second to a narrow bridge thrown across it. In other chapters, he bewails the blindness of the man who does not reflect upon the shortness of his sojourn on earth and is dazzled by the ephemeral glamor of wealth and passion. These chapters can not be translated, but their gist is as follows: "Oh, that passions should only lead to darkness, pearls become thistles, and roses thorns; pride is only a glimmering flame that vanishes and *guldens* (a kind of coins) have wings like flies." In another chapter, he depicts the precarious position of man in this grea tworld, his littleness as compared with the forces of nature and his subjection to the influences of the heavenly bodies. In still another, he denounces the world for its whims and caprices and exclaims, "Oh world, I have seen thee select the husks and reject the kernels, befriend the low-minded and estrange the noble souls, reach for the empty vessel but remove the full one."

The third part deals with the soul and the cultivation of the right kind of life. In a beautifully written chapter, he describes the nature of the soul, its heavenly origin and its tribulations and its struggles during its earthly sojourn when joined with the body. He finally points out the right conduct in life. "Happiness", he says, "can be found in the observance of the Law. The Torah is a flame issuing from the heavenly spark, man in his two parts is the torch which this flame enkindles, the body is the wick and the soul the pure oil." Yet Yedayah would not have man devote himself entirely to study. On the contrary, he must attend to all necessary pursuits and enjoyments in life, but must use moderation. He decries laziness and blind belief in predestination and urges man to diligence and industry. The book closes with a semi-poetic version of the Thirteen Articles of Maimonides.

There is, of course, an ascetic note in Bedersi's *Behinath Olam* only of the kind which does not lower and degrade life but dignifies and ennobles it. On the whole, this little didactic work, both on account of its content and its stately style, is a gem in Jewish ethical prose literature.

159. TALES AND FABLES

The books subsumed under the title, Tales and Fables, are likewise didactic in nature, for all Mediaeval stories and collections of fables have a moral point and their purpose was to instruct people in the way of life. But the line of demarkation between them and the class of books which we have called purely didactic consists in their narrative character. The number of stories, parables and fables they contain as a rule exceeds any other matter. It is primarily the appeal to the imagination and the emotions of the readers which made the books so exceedingly popular that they became the staple folk literature during the Middle Ages.

The earliest of such books in Jewish literature during this period is the *Ben ha-Melek̲ we-ha-Nazir* (Prince and Hermit). It was not written originally in Hebrew but translated by the poet Abraham Ibn Hasdai from an Arabic version which is no more extant . However, it is not a mere translation, but as will be evident, practically a new version, and the poetic part of it testifies to the great skill of the translator as poet, just as the delightful style of rhymed prose proclaims him a veritable master of Hebrew.

The Prince and Hermit is one of the celebrated books of Mediaeval literature and is found under different names in almost all Oriental and European languages. The Arabic literature possesses several versions of the work under the title *Kitab Balahuar wa-Budasaph.* In the Greek and the Latin versions as well as in those of other European languages it usually bears the title Barlaam and Josaphat. For a long time, it was thought that the work was an original Greek production, for in that language it has a Christian color, and Barlaam and Josaphat, the names of the Hermit and the Prince respectively, were even entered by both the Greek and the Roman Catholic churches in their lists of saints. But patient scholarly research in modern times and the discovery of Oriental versions have established beyond doubt that the story is Indian in origin and that the Prince Josaphat is no other than the Hindu founder of Buddhism, Gautama. It was transmitted to Europe through a Pahlavi translation and thence through a Syriac version was rendered, around the end of the sixth century, into Greek, and from the Greek, it began to make its rounds in all the other European languages.

In its long wandering through all these lands and languages, the story underwent many metamorphoses of content and in fact, the older versions hardly agree with each other. In general, in all European versions, beginning with the Greek, the story was thoroughly Christianized. In the Moslem versions, however, less zeal was shown to convert the Prince and the Hermit into Moslems, but a strong element of Biblical and Koranic character was added to the content of the parables and stories with which the book is replete.

The Hebrew version likewise retains the general human character of the story and no attempt is made to convert the Prince to Judaism, but the Biblical element is quite in evidence. On the whole, *Ben ha-Melek̠ we-ha-Nazir* is a unique work and differs greatly from all the other versions. It contains ten parables which are not found anywhere else and also deviates in content from these versions, toward the end of the story, for the last eleven chapters of the Hebrew book follow an original way. These chapters tell of teachings, moral and psychological, which were current in the philosophical schools of the twelfth century. Especially is this true of the theories about the separate intelligences, the nature of the soul, its destiny, and reward and punishment after death.

As the Arabic original of the Hebrew version is lost, it can not be determined whether the added material was contained there or the additions constitute Abraham Ibn Hasdai's contribution to the book. At any rate, these additions enhance the value of the work and make it not only a collection of fine parables and tales but a real book of instruction.

The central theme of the book in the Oriental versions including the Hebrew, is the vanity of the world and its allurements and the praise of an ascetic life. It is conveyed in the following story. There lived once in India a king, mighty and powerful,[3] who was of a mean character and addicted to the pleasures of the world. One day, he

[3] In the Hebrew version, the king is unnamed. In Arabic, he is called Jandisar, in Greek, Abenner. In giving the gist of the story, I follow primarily the Hebrew version.

discovered that one of his chief counsellors had become a follower of the faith of the hermits and that he leads an ascetic life. He is greatly incensed at the news and summoning the noble, he reproaches him for his conduct. The counsellor defends his way of life and in a series of monologues tells of the vanity of the world, the instability of fortune and the inconstancy of friends and counsellors. He proves to the king that an ascetic and secluded life is preferable to that of a kingly court. The king, however, is not convinced and in his rage, expels the nobleman from his country.

Some time later, a son is born to the king who greatly rejoices at the new arrival as he was hitherto childless. But when his horoscope is cast by the court astrologers, the father is told that the Prince will, when he grows up, become an ascetic. The prophecy greatly disturbs the king and to forestall the possible event, he orders a palace to be built on an island far from the haunts of men and places the child there so that he would never learn the common lot of man or his ultimate destiny, death. He continues to persecute the ascetics and upon hearing that even the vizier was inclined towards their teachings, he drives them out of the country, confiscates their property, and issues an edict that no hermit shall appear within the boundaries of the kingdom.

Meanwhile the Prince grows up and becomes dissatisfied with his life of seclusion. He asks his teachers for the reason of his confinement, and after much entreaty, one of them reveals the secret to him. He then pleads with his father, on one of his visits to the palace, to release him, and the latter yields to his request and grants him permission to return to court. On his way, though, he meets a blind man, a leper, an old man and a corpse and thus learns the evils which befall man during life and his ultimate end—death. He is told that only hermits may allay the fear of death, but that they were driven out of the country.

At that time, a hermit came to court in the guise of a merchant under the pretext that he had some precious stones to show to the young Prince. On being introduced to him, he produces his books and says, "These are my wares." When asked by the Prince what they contain, the hermit relates a number of parables extolling the value of wisdom thereby proving that the real dignity of man consists in his intellectual attainments. A series of dialogues then develop between the two in which the hermit discusses the vanity of the world, the fleetness of its pleasures and contrasts with these the calm of the contemplative life and the permanence of the other world. The Prince asks the hermit his age to which he replies, "twelve years." The explanation for this curious statement is given that only the years the hermit lived an ascetic life are considered real living, for the years spent in pleasures are as naught. Many other teachings are imparted in the dialogues and illustrated by parables. Finally, the Prince expresses his desire to follow the hermit, but the latter dissuades him.

At this point, the resemblance between the Hebrew and the other versions ceases altogether. Both the Arabic and the Greek versions continue the story by telling of many attempts on the part of the king to lead his son away from the new path of life. Among them are attempts to entice the Prince to enjoy the world by the charms of a very beautiful woman, and the arranging of a disputation upon the faith he intends to embrace—in the Arabic version it is the Buddhistic religion and in the Greek it is the Christian. All attempts fail, and the Prince flies into the desert. In the Hebrew version, all these features are missing. The nature of the narrative remains of general human interest with no attempt at a particular religious inclination. In the last ten chapters, the dialogues as indicated above, assume more and more a philosophical character. The conclusion is that the Hermit goes on his way and the Prince remains at home, a sadder but a better and nobler man.

It is my personal opinion that the part of the *Ben ha-Meleḳ we-ha-Nazir* which deviates entirely from all other versions was not contained in the Arabic original, but is the work of Abraham Ibn Hasdai himself. He took only the kernel of the story from the current versions and reworked it in an original way. I believe also that the many poems of the book which epitomize the teachings of the parables and dialogues are his work, though the models for such poems inserted in didactic works were not lacking in the Arabic literature. Of the many parables with which the book is replete and on account of which it was so popular we will cite several. The first two are found in the Hebrew version only while the last one is found also in the other versions.

Here is one which illustrates the value of wise management of one's own affairs. Once there was a man whom King Solomon, in recognition of his great devotion to him, taught to understand the language of the birds and animals on condition that he shall not betray the secret lest he die. One night, he overheard the ass advise the ox to feign illness so as to escape work, and he laughed aloud. His wife pressed him to tell her the cause of his laughter, but he refused to do so. On the following day, when the ox pretended illness, he put the ass to work in his place, and at night when the ass returned from the field fatigued from a day's hard labor, he told the ox that he would be slaughtered on the morrow if he should not feel better. The ox immediately applied himself diligently to the food placed before him devouring it entirely. The man seeing this laughed again. This time, his wife would not be put off and insisted that her husband tell her the reason for his laughing twice. The man told her that he could not reveal the secret for it would mean his death. "Either your death or mine," said the woman and vowed that she would not eat until she knew the secret. The man then promised to disclose the secret on the following day, and accordingly prepared to die. Sadness reigned in the household and even the dog would not touch food, but the cock and his wives continued to eat without any concern. The dog observing their conduct reproached them saying, "Do you not know that our master is going to die today?" "Mere fool," said the cock, "I can rule ten wives while he can not rule one." "What can he do?" asked the dog. "Take a stick to her and I will guarantee that she will desist from her demand to know his secret," was the answer. The man who heard this followed the cock's advice and thus saved his life.

The following parable teaches the fleetness of life and its pleasures. A king invited a shepherd to lunch with him in the heat of the day. Said the shepherd, "I can not eat with thee for I have already promised another greater than thee." "Who is he?" asked the king. "God who has invited me to fast," came the answer. "But the day is too hot to fast," protested the king. "I fast for a day still hotter than this" (i. e. to be saved from the torments of hell), said the shepherd. "Then," said the king, "eat to-day, fast to-morrow." "Yes, if you will guarantee that I shall see to-morrow," was the reply.

In the comparison quoted below, wisdom is exalted. "Wisdom," says the hermit, "is like the sun which shines exerywhere and upon all, yet its effects vary in respect to the recipients of the light. Some have weak eyesight and can not bear its brilliance, others are blind and can not see at all. Only a few there are whose eyes are strong and whose sight is clear and can enjoy the full glare of the radiance of the sun." This parable must have been current at the time, for it is used also as an illustration by Bahya in his Duties of the Heart.[4]

The credulity of man and his greed is artfully depicted in the story of the man and the bird. A man caught a bird in his garden which proffered him three pieces of valuable advice if he would set it free. He agreed, whereupon the bird said, "Do not sigh for what is past; do not attempt the impossible; believe not the improbable." The man then freed the bird. The bird, desiring to tease him cried while perched on the topmost branch of a tree: "Fool, you know little what treasure you have lost. I have within my body a pearl as large as an eagle's egg." The man greatly vexed began to tear his hair and attempted to entice the bird again within his power. The bird replied, "Oh fool, now I can see how you observe the advice I gave you. I told you not to regret the past and yet you are sorry for freeing me. I advised you not to try the impossible, and yet you are endeavoring to get me in your power again. I warned you never to believe the improbable, and yet you believed when I told you that I have within me a pearl larger than my whole body."

We will also cite at random a few of the numerous proverbs of the book bristling with keen wit and instruction. The following deal with the vicissitudes of life. "The life of man is full of disappointments; if it is long he grieves at the loss of relatives and friends who died during its span; if short he grieves at his own speedy end." "Time," said a wise man, "thou settest free the fly, but placest the eagle in a cage." On characterization of the divisions of time, "The past is a good and instructive teacher; the present is a trusty friend, but often disappointing; beware therefore, of its delusions; the future is a stranger and should be met with caution." On the evil of falsehood, "Lying and death are equal, for the distinguishing quality of man is his speech, and if his speech can not be trusted, then his *human* life is gone." Again, "A liar is worse than a thief, for the latter steals your money while the former steals your reason or confidence." On friendship with the great, "The friendship of the great is like a garment; if it is short it uncovers the nakedness, if long one stumbles over it." The meaning of it is that if the friendship of the great is slight the contrast between the two will be evident, if it is great, the humble man will sooner or later stumble over it. On God, "A philosopher was asked, 'Where is God?' 'In the heart of every seeker

[4] Duties of the Heart, end of Portal I.

after Him,' was the reply. 'And when did He come into being?' 'And when was He non-existent?' answered the philosopher." On counsellors, "The best horse needs a whip, the strongest man a sword, and the wisest man a counsellor." On men who display great submissiveness, "Said the wise man, my children, do not be deceived by submissiveness for the more the bow bends, the more dangerous is the arrow it shoots."

The second book of this kind written originally in Hebrew in the year 1281 is the *M'shal ha-Kadmoni* (The Fable of the Ancients) by Isaac Ibn Sahulah (b. 1244) of Guadalxara, Spain. We know little about the life of the author, not even the year of his death except that he wandered about for a great part of his life. He cultivated both the muses and the sciences, as we find a considerable number of short poems in his book, and the work contains evidence of a complete mastery of the knowledge of his day. From the many passages in the book bearing on the nature of diseases and the various medical cures, we can surmise that Ibn Sahulah, like many Jewish scholars, was a physician by profession.

In the introduction, the author tells us that he was moved to compose his book out of zeal for the Hebrew language, the cultivation of which was neglected by his generation, on account of their assiduous reading of Arabic stories, fables and parables which gave them pleasure and enjoyment. He was, therefore, determined to provide them with the same literary amusements in the sacred tongue which is as elastic and adaptable for fine and ornate writing as any other language, and is even more suitable to convey moral and religious instruction through fables and parables. He tells us further that while he uses the animal fable as a means of instruction, a method common in the current Arabic literature, yet he is not a mere imitator of Islam writers, for in fact, the Bible contains numerous fables and parables and it is these that served him as models. He finally informs us that his book contains many original stories which are merely the external garments for the precious teachings of the Torah, philosophy and religion.

The book is divided into five portals each devoted to the inculcation of a certain virtue. The first extols the value of wisdom, the second of repentance, the third of good counsel, the fourth of humility, and the fifth of piety in general. The form is that of a dialogue between the author and an opponent. The opponent attempts to prove that the cultivation of virtue is useless, while the author defends the urgency and necessity of each of the virtues stated and demonstrates their efficiency in directing man to the right conduct which leads to happiness. Both sides employ tales and animal fables as a means for expressing their ideas, but they possess a peculiar flavor. They are unnatural, for not only do the animals talk and discuss, but actually hold long discourses on matters scientific and philosophic and are made the mouth-piece of the author's views on all branches of knowledge. Thus, in one of the portals the deer delivers a discourse on the classification of the sciences, and the dog lectures on the principles of psychology. In another portal, the cock holds forth a learned talk on the four humours and the principles of medicine, and the ram expounds the theory of positive and negative judgments. In the last portal, the gazelle develops before us the complete system of astronomy. These animals are, of course, also well versed in the Bible and the Talmud and apply dexterously Biblical verses and Talmudic passages to the subjects under discussion. As a result, the work assumes rather the character of a concise encyclopaedia of the knowledge of the time than a book of fables. Yet the fables do impart to the work a peculiar glamor and naivete which make the contents more palatable to the reader and afford him amusement as well as instruction.

The style of the book enhances its value. It is written in rhymed prose and is replete with quips, puns and bits of parody on Biblical and Agadic expressions.

A real book of fables which well deserves its name and which practically can be considered the first of its kind in Hebrew literature is the *Mishlē Shualim* (Fox Fables) by Berakya ha-Nakdan (the punctator (c. 1260). Berkaya ha-Nakdan also called Crespia is not a total stranger in Jewish literature. He is the author of a paraphrase of Saadia's *Emunoth we-Deoth,* and the translator of Adelard of Bath's *Questiones Naturales,* a collection of questions and answers on natural phenomena under the title, *Dodi we-Nekdi* (Uncle and Nephew). He also translated another work of an ethical character under the name of *Mezarof* (The Purifier).

Yet with all his literary activity, we know little of his life and we can not even determine definitely whether he lived in the South or North of France. Even his age is not accurately established. It is surmised that the book was in circulation by 1280, for on a manuscript copy of the fables dated 1286, we find a deed of its sale. From the title *Nakdan,* we can infer that he was by profession one who busied himself with punctuating the Bible and copying the Masoretic rules. It seems though that he also mastered the Talmud and was greatly interested in the sciences as evidenced from his works.

The *Mishlē Shualim* contains one hundred and seven short fables with animals as actors and speakers. The fox plays, as in other collections, an important role, yet he does not occupy the stage completely for there are numerous fables where he is left out altogether. The name of the book, *Fox Fables,* should be construed to mean animal fables, and Berakya merely adopted it from the Talmud where *Mishlē Shualim* is used as a generic name for fables.

Berakya himself tells us that he got his fables from other sources, but claims that he added some of his own. He also indicates the moral to be drawn from each fable by a few lines of prose appended at the end and also epitomizes it in the manner of Ibn Hasdai and Ibn Sahulah in a short metric poem.

Most of the fables collected by Berakya are of the well known popular type that usually go under the name of Aesop's Fables. But as there were numerous versions of these fables current in Mediaeval Ages, each differing from the other and bearing different names, it is impossible to determine the exact source of Berakya's book. A collection of fables in French by a woman called Marie de France, and supposed to have been written about 1220, bears a striking resemblance to that of Berakya, inasmuch as a number of fables belonging to the cycle of Aesop are given in the same form by both Berakya and Marie retaining the same variations from other versions. Yet it can not be said that Berakya utilized Marie's collection as his chief source. First, the number of fables common to both is only fifty-three, one half of the number contained in the *Mishlē Shualim*. Second, Marie herself avers that her book is a translation of a collection of fables compiled by Alfred the Englishman, and we may then suppose that both used a common source. Further on analyzing Marie's or Alfred's collection, we come to the conclusion that it differs greatly from the ordinary Latin version of Aesop's Fables. According to Joseph Jacobs[5] these variations could come only from one source and that is the Arabic Aesop, and since Berakya most likely was conversant with Arabic as can be surmised from his paraphrase of the *Emunoth* which differs greatly from the translation of Ibn Tibbon, it is safe

[5] Joseph Jacobs; Aesop's Fables, Vol. I, pp. 97-99.

to assume that his chief source was the Arabic Aesop which likewise was the source of Alfred's collection and subsequently that of Marie's.

Besides the fables drawn from the versions of the Aesop Cycles, Berakya incorporated several from the Talmud which he expanded and beautified. In addition, there are eighteen fables for which no parallels can be found in any of the collections and we may, therefore, surmise that they are his own. In fact, they differ greatly from the usual type of fables, inasmuch as they lack in naturalness and bear the stamp of artificiality and are often merely the expansion of a well known proverb.

The contribution of Berakya consists primarily not in the content of the fables but in the form and style in which they are written. In fables especially, the form plays a great role, for it is thus that those of one nation are distinguished from those of another, as the content is on the whole universal. Berakya's fables, therefore, bear a Jewish stamp. In them the animals and birds not only converse in Biblical language and here and there even quote a Talmudic proverb, but they also display typically Jewish characteristics. His style is flowing, light, and full of Biblical and Agadic parodies thus making the book delightful reading. The puns and twists of verses lend to the fables a humorous flavor which is not found in similar versions in other languages. On account of that quality, they can really not be translated, for they lose much of their peculiar charm in the process. Yet we will cite one in the masterly translation of Dr. Jacobs who in order to retain the flavor of the original imitated the author's rhymed prose style. It belongs to the Aesop cycle and bears the title *The Wolf and the Animals,* and reads as follows:

The Wolf, the Lion's prince and peer, as the foe of all flesh did appear; greedy and grinding, he consumed all he was finding. Birds and beasts, wild and tame, by their families urged to the same, brought against him before the Lion an accusation, as a monster worthy of detestation. Said his Majesty, "If he uses his teeth as you say, and causes scandal in this terrible way, I'll punish him in such a way as to save his neck, if I may, and yet prevent you becoming his prey." Said Lion to Wolf, "Attend me to-morrow, see that you come, or you'll come to much sorrow." He came sure enough, and the Lion spoke to him harsh and rough, "what by doing this do you mean?" Never more raven the living or live by ravening. What you shall eat shall be only dead meat. The living you shall neither trap nor hunt. And that you may my words obey swear me that you'll eat no flesh for two years from to-day, to atone for your sins, testified and seen: 'tis my judgment, you had better fulfill it, I ween." Thereat the Wolf swore right away no flesh to eat for two years from that day. Off went Sir Wolf on his way, King Lion stopped at court on his throne so gay. Nothing that's fleshy for some time did our Wolf eat, for like a gentleman he knew how his word to keep. But then came a day when he was hungry and he looked hither and thither for meat, and lo, a fat goat, fair to look on and goodly to eat. (Gen. III, 6.) Then to himself he said, "Who can keep every law?" and his thoughts were bewildered with what he saw. He said to himself, "It overcomes me the longing to eat, for two years day by day must I fast from meat. This is the oath to the king that I swore but I've thought how to fulfill it as never before. Three sixty-five are the days in a year. Night is when you close your eyes, open them, then the day is near." His eyes he closed and opened straightway. It was evening and it was morning one day. (Gen. I, 5.) Thus he winked till he had numbered two years and his greed returned and his sin disappears. His eyes fix the goat they had seen and he said, "See beforehand I have atoned for my sin," and he seized the neck of the goat, broke it to pieces, and filled up his throat as he was wont to do before, and as of yore his hand was stretched out to the beasts, his peers, as it had been in former days and years.

A tale of great interest and much information on the nature of man and beast which also contains a deep moral lesson is the *Iggereth Baalē Hayyim* (The Book of Animals and Man) by Kalonymos ben Kalonymos. The book is not an original composition but a translation from the Arabic. It forms a part of the famous encyclopaedia of the Society of Pure Brethren which flourished in the city of Basra in the second half of the tenth century. This was a peculiar society professing an eclectic philosophy and heterodox religious views tinged with mysticism. Their philosophy was a mixture of Neo-Pythagorianism and Neo-Platonism together with some elements of Oriental thought. They laid great emphasis both on intelligence and on the striving to assimilate the soul to God in a degree possible to man.

The encyclopaedia aimed to give a popular presentation of all branches of knowledge. It consisted of fifty-one volumes dealing with mathematics, logic, physics, philosophy and religion. In the treatise of the *Book of Animals and Man,* the authors aimed to present a general criticism of human society and even of religious doctrines and views. They endeavored to show that men do not excel the beasts in industry nor in practical conduct both as individuals and as groups. Their excellence lies mainly in the possession of reason and in the attained perfection of the soul. This criticism and the derived moral is given in the form of a debate between the animals and man.

The book contains five portals each of which is subdivided into a number of chapters. Its gist is as follows: It happened in olden times that a group of men representing all nations and creeds embarked on a sea voyage. A storm arose and wrecked the boat, but the passengers saved themselves by swimming ashore on an island nearby. The island belonged to demons or jins whose king Borsif ruled his domain justly. The men finding their new place of habitation fruitful and peopled with all kinds of animals, settled there, built houses and palaces, and began to enslave the animals who had hitherto roamed free over hill and dale. The animals revolted against the men and fled back to their former pastures, but the latter, pursued them and employed all means to bring them back to servitude. The beasts then decided to bring their case before king Borsif.

The king summoned the contestants to court, and after acquainting himself with the nature of the arrival of the men in his domain, asked them by what right do they enslave the animals. An Islam scholar arose and quoted verses from Scripture where it is stated that God granted men the right to rule over beasts, birds and fishes. The mule representing the animals replied that the right was conferred by God only for the purpose that men may derive some use from the beasts, but not to destroy and torture them, and related at length all the suffering which the creatures undergo at the hands of their cruel masters. Borsif challenged the men to prove their right of complete mastery over the animals. The representative of the former pointed to the beautiful form of man, his erect body, the proportion of his limbs and fine senses, all of which he said demonstrate the superiority of the human genus and consequently confer upon him the right of mastery. The mule was not dismayed though and proceeded to refute the arguments of the opponents. Erection of stature he averred, is no advantage and pointed to the trees as an example, and likewise the proportion of the limbs is no distinct sign of superiority, for the disproportion of the limbs of various animals is for a definite use and purpose. He was about to discuss the relative value of the senses of man and animals when he was interrupted by the other beasts who were desirous to relate their plight to the king. The ass, lamb, elephant and others told tales of woe and suffering of which man was the cause. Borsif was impressed with their words and adjourned court until the following day in order to confer with his counsellors.

A large council of the wisest of the realm of the jins was called and the king asked their opinion in the matter. Various views were offered, some saying the animals should be freed by force, other advising purchase by the king, and still others that the *status quo* continue until a change in the cycle of time when the beasts will be freed by Divine decree like the Israelites from Egypt. Since opinions were divided, the case was continued. Meanwhile the animals sent delegates to the kings of six families of beasts, birds, reptiles and insects asking them to appoint representatives of all the divisions to come and argue the case. The jackal, the nightingale, the parrot, the bee, the frog and the cricket came as representatives of all classes of beasts, birds, insects and reptiles and presented themselves at court.

The trial opens with a talk by one of the wise jins who praises God and the king and introduces the representatives of the creatures by expounding the Platonic doctrine that these creatures in their various shapes are merely copies of the eternal generic forms existing in the spiritual world. The king then calls upon the representatives of the men to speak. There rise then in succession, the Babylonian, the Hindu, the Jew, the Byzantine, the Moslem and the Persian and tell of the qualities and excellences of their nations and the contributions each had made to civilization. The wise jin, however, acts as a kind of procureur and reminds every spokesman of the faults and misdeeds of the people he represents. The representatives of the other creatures then rise and tell likewise of the qualities and virtues of the class they represent. We thus get a good deal of information on the subject of natural history and instruction in zoology. In these descriptions, the first day of the trial passes.

The real debate begins on the morrow. One after another, the men come forward and narrate of human achievements. The Roman tells of human industries, the Arab of the skill in cooking and preparation of foods, the Jew of his Torah and worship, the Babylonian of the fine garments, the Greek and other spokesman of the sciences of medicine, astrology and astronomy. All these accomplishments however, are subjected to a withering criticism by the spokesmen of the creatures. The bee tells at length of her own great industry as well as of that of the other insects, the spider and the the ant, and extols the mathematical precision of their work, their craftiness and ability. The jackal minimizes the value of clothes, saying that the animals and birds are by nature endowed with beautiful pelts and colorful feathers. Besides, man manufactures his clothing by robbing the materials from animals, birds and insects. Thus wool is taken from the lamb, skins from wild animals, feathers from the birds and silk from the silkworm. The art of medicine is decried by the parrot who says that the life of pleasure brings on sickness, and likewise the worry and the hustle and bustle of man engenders many diseases. Even the boast of possessing equitable laws and established forms of worship is minimized. These, said the representatives of the animals, were given to men as a remedy for their numerous sins and as a means for restraining their passions, but the other creatures which have no sins and whose passions are not so fierce are in no need of remedies.

Finally a philosopher rises and begins to extol the advantages of reason and speaks of the ultimate aim of man which is to draw as near to God as possible and describes the excellence of the life of the ascetics and the virtues of the prophets and the holy men. His words silence the opponents, and they admit that man truly excels in these qualities and is, therefore, superior to all other creatures. The king then issues the decision that the animals which are of help to man in his various pursuits in life are to return to his service, but that he must use them kindly and equitably.

We are thus taught by the authors a lesson in human conduct and given a criticism of the ordinary ways of human life by way of a fine parable. In addition, we are furnished with information on many subjects of science.

The translation of Kalonymos is a clear and lucid one, the style is of the narrative type, flowing and light with no attempt at turning Biblical verse or Agadic sayings to particular use. It is not to be wondered at that the *Iggereth Baale Hayyim* was popular among the Jews in Mediaeval Ages.

160. SATIRE AND HUMOR

While the books enumerated above contain a fair portion of wit and humor expressed in various ways, in puns, and quips and parodies, yet their main purpose was to instruct and teach. The humor contained in them is only a by-product. The case is not so with the works of the type described below. There the author intends mainly to amuse the reader, and endeavors to pass before him some aspects of life in an exaggerated and grotesque form which, *volens nolens,* call forth a smile on his lips and often provoke a hearty laugh. True, every satire contains a criticism of life and is thus instructive, but in the case of satirical and humoristic works, instruction is not usually the objective unless especially intended.

The earliest satire of the post-Classical period, the *Minhath Yehudah* (The Gift of Judah) was composed by the writer already referred to, Judah Ibn Shabbatai in 1208. It has also a second title, *Sonē ha-Nashim* (The Women Hater) which gives us an intimation of its contents. Women, as we know, formed a favorite subject for the humorists of all literatures and thus a number of books discussing them pro and con is considerable. Shabbatai ranges himself apparently on the side of those who are against women and marriage and was so considered by his contemporaries and successors. But Davidson had already shown,[6] and everyone who reads the satire carefully must agree with him, that the author is not a misogynist, but really wants to show us both sides of the question and tells us that if there is evil in marriage no one can escape it. The best way to follow, therefore, is moderation in dealing with women and carefulness in choosing a life companion.

The gist of the book is as follows: Tahkemoni, a very wise man who was disappointed in married life calls his son Zerah before his death and asks him for a promise never to marry. He draws before him a picture of the wiles of women and of the suffering men undergo at their hands when wedded to them. Zerah promises to obey his father's commands faithfully, and choosing three friends who are like-minded, he preaches with their assistance a crusade against women and marriage. The women are terrified at his success and lay plans how to defeat Zerah. One of them Kozbi with the aid of her husband Sheker (both names signifying falsehood) concocts a plan to bring about Zerah's downfall. She induces a very beautiful woman to ensnare him into the meshes of matrimony. The maiden meets Zerah and practices her charms upon him, to which he succumbs so that he asks her hand in marriage. All arrangements are made to celebrate the nuptials, but under the canopy an ugly garrulous woman is substituted for the beautiful maiden wooed by Zerah. In the morning when he discovers his mistake and is greatly mortified, the situation can not be helped, and to aggravate his misery, his bride pours forth a torrent of abuse and sends him forth to provide for her

[6] Parody in Jewish Literature, pp. 8-10.

food, drink and costly articles of apparel. His three friends, in the manner of those of Job, come to console him in his misery, and after delivering pointed epigrams bewailing his fall, counsel him to divorce her. Zerah proceeds to act upon their advice, but the women interfere, and the case is brought before the king. The spokesmen on behalf of the women arraign Zerah for his perfidy to the gentle sex and picture the disastrous consequences which would ensue if he be permitted to divorce his wife, as many a husband would follow his example. The king is about to pass severe sentence upon Zerah when the author approaches and confesses that the whole episode is a fiction.

The satire is written in delightful style and brims with parodies. The Bible, the liturgy and the marriage contract (the Ketubah) are all drawn upon and are made to do service in the interests of humor. The Ketubah is parodied completely and the marriage contract drawn up for Zerah is given in very grotesque and ridiculous terms. Ibn Shabbatai was also a poet, and his satire contains numerous short poems, expressing various sentiments.

As a kind of rejoinder to this satire, Yedayah ha-Penini, the famous didactic writer wrote in his eighteenth year (1298) a defense of women called *Oheb Nashim* (The Lover of Women). In it, the author tells of a decree issued by a wicked king who suffered at the hands of an ill-tempered wife that all husbands who are displeased with their spouses may divorce them. The ignorant rejoice at this decree but the wise men together with the women consider this a calamity. Both parties plead their cases before the king, and even Reason herself speaks on behalf of the women and quotes history and Bible and Talmud to vindicate their cause. Pharaoh who decreed that all male children of the Israelites be thrown into the river but spared the daughters is acknowledged a wise man. The arguments, however, do not prevail and the king refuses to rescind the decree. The champions of the women, however, are not dismayed, their leader Seraya gathers an army and prepares to defend the cause of the fair sex by force. In the war that breaks out the king is killed, and when Seraya ascends the throne the cause of women triumphs of course. The author concludes by telling that even Shabbatai in Paradise heard of the news and comes down to this world and arraigns the writer for his defense. They bring their case before the noble brothers, Meir and Judah, sons of Solomon, scholars and men of judgment. They decide against Ibn Shabbatai and reprimand him for his attitude. He acquiesces in their judgment and peace is established.

The *Oheb Nashim* written by Yeadayah in his youth is far from an accomplished work. It is much inferior to the satire of Ibn Shabbatai both in style and humor. His style, though displaying a mastery of language, is heavy and cumbersome and lacks the flashing wit, the darting pun and the twists of parody of the former. It is on the whole, more of a euphuistic composition than a humorous piece of literature.

Real satire and keen humor are found in the several Purim treatises written during the fourteenth century of which the most outstanding are the *Maseketh Purim* by Kalonymos ben Kalonymos (Sect. 159) and the *Megillath Setorim* (Scroll of Secrecy) by the famous exegete and philosopher, Levi ben Gerson. The basis of both these works is parody, for they are written in the form of Talmudic treatises with Mishnah and Gemarah and employ the style, the methods of interpretation and discussion of the Talmud.

The humor, though, is expressed in the spirit of levity with which the works are permeated. There, the customs of drinking wine and eating good food and making merry on Purim day are raised to the dignity of the most important precepts, and the obligation to fulfill them in all their minutae are deduced from the Bible in the most orthodox Midrashic manner. The levity is carried even to names of the Tannaim and Amoraim who carry on the discussion. Their names are such as Rabbi Samhan, i. e. the merry-maker, Rabbi Kàmzan, the miser, Rabbi Shakran, the drunkard and Rabbi Bibē, a name actually found in the Talmud, but in the *Megillath Setorim* it is derived from the Latin *Bibere,* to drink.

The *Maseketh Purim* is a close imitation of a Talmudic treatise and is divided into four chapters or *Perakim.* The first chapter describes the preparations to be made before Purim and fixes the time when they are to begin, namely at least two weeks in advance. It tells of the duties of women to prepare the feast and gives a list of twenty-four dishes that are eaten on that day. The second discusses the details of the feast such as the quantity of food and drink to be consumed. It fixes the quantity of meat to be placed on each plate as not less than three pounds and gives a grotesque reason for that quantity. A glutton once dived into a bowl of soup to discover the portion of meat at the bottom and he was in great danger of drowning. Three pounds of meat then is, in the opinion of the scholar, sufficient to avert the repetition of such an act for it will be seen even by a near sighted glutton. The other two chapters tell of other Jewish Mediaeval customs of merry making practiced on that day. We are told that the Jews used to ride on horses through the streets and carry long staffs in their hands performing various feats. They also made a puppet representing Haman and the people gathered around it singing, dancing, blowing trumpets and shouting *Ira, Ira,* Italian for vengeance.

The forte of the treatise is primarily its style, for in it lies the humor, and that of course, can not be translated. But to those who are conversant with the Talmud and its language, the book offers much delight and provokes laughter and merriment.

The *Megillath Setorim* resembles in its style the Midrash more than the Talmud, though like the latter, it states the Mishnah first and then the Gemarah as a commentary. It is divided into three chapters which deal, like those of the *Maseketh Purim,* with the subjects of drinking, feasting and merry making. The first statement imitates the first Mishnah in Aboth, where the chain of the bearers of tradition is given. Likewise, the chain of tradition of drinking is stated here in the following manner:

"Habakbuk (bottle) received the law (of drink) from Karmi (Kerem, meaning vineyard), and handed it down to Noah and Noah to Lot, and Lot to the brothers of Joseph, and they handed it down to Nabol the Carmelite, and he to Ben-Hadad, and Ben-Hadad to Belshatzar, and Belshatzar to Ahasuerus, and Ahasuerus to Rabbi Bibē (Rabbi Drunkard)."

On the whole, there is much keener wit and greater spirit of levity in the *Scroll of Secrecy* of Levi ben Gerson than in the treatise of Kalonymos. There is also a stronger personal note in it, for many sayings and Midrashic statements are quoted in the name of Rabbi Levi, and he does not hesitate to laugh even at himself. The levity is manifested in numerous passages where the duties of merry making, eating and drinking are continually emphasized. In one long Midrashic passage it is conclusively proved from the Bible that one who does not share in the pleasures of the world will also be denied a portion of the world to come. What a dissonant note such a statement struck, even if only uttered in jest, in a literature saturated with a spirit of distrust to the pleasures of this world. No wonder then the graver men in Jewry looked askance at such works.

In the *Megillath Setorim,* we learn of a custom which was prevalent among the Jews of Provence in the fourteenth century, to appoint a master of ceremonies for the joyful day, called the *Purim King.*

His functions are not exactly defined, but we can surmise from the frequent references in the *Scroll of Secrecy* that he supervised the merry making. The custom later spread to other countries, for we possess several poems written in Italy, during the sixteenth century, in honor of such kings.

From the fourteenth century, there is also extant an anonymous Purim parody called Habakbuk ha-Nabi (The Prophet of the Bottle) which is a parody of the prophetic book of Habakuk. Besides the prophet Habakbuk, two other leaders of the people are mentioned, Karmi (Vineyard) and Beeri (Well), each of whom endeavors to persuade the people to follow his way. The prophet, however, ranges himself on the side of Karmi. This parody must have been written early in the century, for Levi ben Gerson in his Scrolls had, as we have already seen, utilized it as a partial text.

A satire which represents a more elevated species of wit and humor is another book of Kalonymos ben Kalonymos named the *Eben Bohan* (The Touch Stone). But though it is classed as a satire, it is not strictly so, for there is a large didactic element in it, and in fact, instruction seems to have been its main purpose. Yet the satire upon the life of his generation forms not only an important part of the book but imparts to it its real value, as the instruction it affords adds but little new to what has been stated in numerous other books of this kind. The frame of the work is a dialogue between the author and his soul, or as he calls it, his heart. He opens up with a complaint against himself for having spent his time in the pursuit of the pleasures of the world. He tells in fine language, replete with puns and short parodistic passagse, how he was addicted to good food and sparkling wine, how he was charmed by the beauty of women and spurred on by the glamor of the world. He reproaches his heart for wanting all these things and calls upon it to reflect upon its destiny and prepare for the ultimate journey.

Here he suddenly turns from his adopted grave mood to a lighter one. Speaking of the duties which face every Jew in life, he expresses his regret that he was not born a woman and draws a contrast between the comparatively easy life of the Jewish girl and the duty-laden existence of the Jewish boy. The picture makes delightful reading, and closes with a very beautiful passage expressing resignation to the sad lot which nature imposed upon him. It is written in the style of the old prayers and is a parody. We reproduce it here in the excellent translation of Professor Davidson.

"O Thou, in heaven, our Sire,
Thou hast saved our fathers from flood and from fire;
The heat of Ur-Kasdim, Thou hast cooled
The sperm *Be-Dinah,* Thou hast ruled;[7]
Hast turned staff into snake,
And clean hands didst leprous make;
Hast changed the Red Sea into land,
And the bed of the Jordan into dry sand;
At thy bidding water gushed from rocky mass;
O, that Thou wouldst refashion me a lass.
Were I blessed with fortune rare,
I would be a lady free from care.
But, alas, it is of no avail
My bitter fortune to bewail.
Since my lot in heaven was willed,
To change it no one is so skilled.
Thus, my burden I'll bear with grace,
Until I have run my race.
And conforming with our belief
To thank the Lord in joy or grief,
I offer thanks in speech faint and worn:
'Praised be Thou, O Lord, that I no woman was born.' "[8]

He then begins to satirize the life of his generation. The object of his satire must have been the Jews of Provence, the country where he resided before he left for Naples and Italy. Th book was written in 1323 and he left for Italy immediately after that. There are even references to the first expulsion from France which took place in 1306 seventeen years earlier and to the massacres caused by the shepherds and the lepers in the year 1320-1321. All these facts prove that the *Touch Stone* was written when the author was still in Provence and the picture of Jewish life he draws there is of the life of the Jews in that country, though he occasionally refers to Jews of other countries.

The picture he paints of the social and moral life of the Provence Jews is a rather gloomy one and is no doubt exaggerated. He describes the observances of the holy days, beginning with the New

[7] The line alludes to the story told in B. Berakot, 60a. Leah, the wife of Jacob, was destined to give birth to seven male children, but not wishing to shame her sister Rachel who at the time had only one son, she prayed to God that the embryo be changed to a female. Her prayer was granted and she gave birth to Dinah.

[8] Parody in Jewish Literature, p. 28.

Year and ending with Shabuoth as being mainly perfunctory with no real religious spirit prevailing among them. The Jews are, he says, very scrupulous in preparing the various foods and drinks for each holiday and are also careful in observing the merry games and festivities on Hanukah and Purim, but little attention is paid to the import of all these holidays. Kalonymos describes minutely the kinds of food and delicacies the Jews made for each festival and the description is of quite some value to the student of folk lore.

He then passes before us the various classes of aristocracy in the communities. Some, he says, boast of their wealth and some of their descent, some of their wisdom and some of their honesty. Others again parade their little Talmudic knowledge or their smattering of philosophy and the sciences, while still others display their mastery of medicine and astronomy. Others again endeavor to impress the world with their erudition in grammar or with their ability to compose poems and epigrams, and some brag about their physical beauty or power of oratory. The description contains keen wit and genuine humor. Especially ludicrous is the picture drawn by him of the *medicii* (physicians) of his day. The portraying of their pedantism, their exaction of fees, the concoction of their medicines and the preparation of the various devices they employ in their practice really provoke laughter.

After this satire, Kalonymos becomes serious again, turns to the analysis of human life, examines the various pursuits of men, and shows the vanity of a worldly life. There are several lofty passages in this part of the book, some of them bearing a striking resemblance to those of Yedayah ha-Penini in his *Examination of the World*. There are also several parables of the moral type, one of which we will quote here. It is found in several versions of Barlaam and Josaphat but is missing in the Hebrew version of the *Prince and the Hermit*. It is called the *Man in the Well*.

A man once fell into a pit, but while falling, caught hold of a branch which saved him from crashing to the bottom. Looking around, he saw two mice, one black and one white, gnawing at the root of the branch he was clinging to, while at the bottom of the well, he saw serpents crawling around. Raising his eyes, he noticed some honey on a projecting ledge, and forgetting his precarious position, the serpents and the mice, he devoted himself wholly to the lapping up of the honey.

The moral is clear. The well represents the world, the branch the span of life, the mice night and day which eat away at the branch of life, the serpents the dissolving elements of the human body, and the honey the pleasures of life. The book ends with a fervent prayer to God on the author's behalf and in behalf of the suffering children of Israel.

The first part containing the introduction and the satire is written in rhymed prose and is full of puns and parodies of Biblical phrases and Talmudic adages. The second part is written in a plain style flowing and pure and tinged with a euphuistic flavor.

In the fifteenth and sixteenth centuries many humorous works were composed most of which center around Purim. A number of them parody the Purim treatises of Levi ben Gerson and Kalonymos; others parody parts of the Passover Haggadah and well known liturgical poems. One, a polemic poem against Christianity written by Elijah Hayyim ben Benjamin parodies the dogmatic poem of *Yigdal.* It ridicules the Christian beliefs and is rather harsh and virulent.

A satirical work which deals with an entirely different subject than those hitherto mentioned is the *Sur-Me-Ra* (Turn from Evil) written by Leon de Modena in 1859, the eighteenth year of his life. It is a dialogue on card playing. Eldad and Medad, two friends are discussing the pros and cons of gambling. Eldad denounces and Medad defends the practice. During the greatest part of the booklet the author remains impartial as his arguments on behalf of card playing are as strong and as pointed as those against it. Medad, the advocate of gambling claims that it is a species of business and that its hazards are no greater than in any other business. In the fifth chapter, each of the contestants recites a poem epitomizing his view. The poem against gambling is a quotation from Ibn Ezra, the one in its favor is a parody on it. The dialogue ends with an admission on the part of Medad that gambling after all is a great evil and that he intends to turn from its ways.

The satiric works produced during the seventeenth and eighteenth centuries center, as in the previous centuries, around Purim, and some excel even those of the fourteenth century. Of these, there are several versions of Purim treatises, a number of imitations of prayers, of epitaphs, and of other kinds of standard writings. Only two works deal with other subjects and both imitate the Passover Haggadah. The first is *Haggadah Shel Jonah Rapa* written by a man of that name in the year 1680 and the second *Seder Pesah ḳe-Hilḳoto* (The

Order of Passover according to the Laws). The former is a polemic against Christian ceremonies and the holidays of the Church. Rapa seems to have been well versed in the Christian ceremonies and his criticism is keen and sharp. The latter is a satirical description of a miser and a woman-hater who fell in love with an ill-tempered woman and the miserable life he led afterwards. It resembles the *Sonē Nashim* of Ibn Sabbatai, but falls much below it in style and humor. Its novelty consists primarily in the imitation of the Haggadah.

Chapter XII

JUDAEO-GERMAN LITERATURE

161. RISE OF JUDAEO-GERMAN LITERATURE

Of the many vernaculars employed by the Jews, in the course of their long exile and sojourn in various lands, none was so deeply influenced by Jewish life and in turn exerted its own influence upon that life as the German. True, the works produced by the Jews in that tongue can not compare either in originality or in literary value to those produced by them in other vernaculars such as the Aramaic or the Arabic. But instead, the Jews allied themselves so closely with that language that they reformed and reshaped it into a distinct dialect of their own, which in the course of time also acquired a special name, that of *Yiddish*.

In this new form the vernacular absorbed much of the energy of the folk spirit and was stamped with the characteristics of the Jewish mind, thought and expression. Judaeo-German or *Yiddish,* therefore, reflects to a great extent, the soul of a great part of Jewry during a long period of history. Consequently, the literature created in that dialect be its character what it may, has a distinct value of its own, and no history of Jewish literature can be complete without taking account of it.

Scholars differ as to the time when the German vernacular spoken by the Jews of Germany began to change and assume the form of a distinct dialect. Those of the last generation such as Zunz[1] and others maintain that up to the sixteenth century, there was comparatively little difference between the German spoken by the Jews of the Germanic countries and that spoken by their neighbors. The changes introduced were slight and unimportant. It is only from that time on, that the differentiation between the Jewish medium of expression and the general German language became more and more distinct. This is attributed by them to two causes. The first is the

[1] L. Zunz Gottesdienstlichen Vorträge, pp. 438.

influence exerted upon the speech of the Jews of Germany, by the Jews of the Slavonic countries, who had emigrated thither from Germany, in the twelfth century, and clung to the language they brought with them from the fatherland. The speech of the latter, on account of their residence in non-Germanic countries was by necessity deviated from the current and living German, which deviation was communicated to the speech of their German brethren on their coming in contact with them and it thus assumed its different form. The second cause is the changes that the German language itself underwent during the centuries, namely the difference between middle and new German. The Jews, assert the scholars, on account of their isolation in the ghettoes, and their constant expulsions from old places of settlement, did not keep pace with the changing language and clung to old forms and expressions, and hence the marked differentiation in their speech.

The younger scholars of the present generation who made the origin of *Yiddish* their subject of study, argue on the other hand, that the differentiation between the speech of the Jews of Germany and that of their neighbors began much earlier, probably in the thirteenth century. They support their assertion by literary documents which, however, may date from the second half of the fourteenth century, yet point to a distinct earlier differentiation in the form of the language in which they are written.

Not going into detail regarding the controversy, it seems to us that the opinion of the younger scholars is nearer the truth. Undoubtedly the speech of the Jews of Germany, during the three centuries, namely from the thirteenth to the sixteenth, was much nearer to the German, and the differences between the two were not as greatly marked as in the later period. But on the other hand it is certain that the deviations from the standard German in the language spoken by the Jews began as early as the thirteenth century. These deviations were bound to follow from a number of causes. First, we must not forget that the Jews wrote the German they spoke in Hebrew letters. Such a change in the writing of the language necessarily involved a change in the pronunciation of the words, for the German and the Hebrew belong to two different groups of tongues and the sounds of the one can not be represented by the letters and vowels of the other without changes in their expression. Second, there was the isolation of the Jews in the Ghetto, and their peculiar life brought about variations of expression and usage. Thirdly, we must take account of the wide spread of Hebrew among the Jews. True, it was not a spoken language but almost every Jew was acquainted with it and even the women were not totally ignorant of it. It was, therefore, quite reasonable that even the masses should employ a large number of Hebrew words in their daily conversation or join parts of Hebrew words to German verbs or suffixes. Fourth, in view of the fact that the Jews were very mobile and constantly moved about, voluntarily or involuntarily, from place to place, they had thus acquired in their speech a mixture of various dialects of the same language which due to their isolation they retained even after these dialectic peculiarities passed out of usage. Besides, in their movement from place to place and often from country to country a large number of foreign words found their way in the speech of the Jews and amalgamated with the other elements of the language. Lastly, there was the influence exerted by the Polish Jews upon the speech of their German brethren spoken of above which caused a further deviation in the speech of the latter from the general language.

All these causes undoubtedly brought about a distinct change in the Jewish-German vernacular even as early as the second half of the thirteenth century, and we may safely trace the rise of Yiddish as a dialect to that date.

And simultaneously with the differentiation of the vernacular into a dialect, there arose also a need for a literature. It is quite true that the Jews of Germany and the neighboring countries had attained a comparatively high degree of culture and education, and as a result, Hebrew was understood by a large number of the members of the communities and the literature produced in that language sufficed for all those instructed in Jewish lore. But on the other hand, there were the women and also many men whose education was deficient, who though they were undoubtedly able to read Hebrew, as they recited their prayers in it, yet were not able to understand it. The feminine part of the Jewish population and the uneducated men evinced, therefore, a desire to have a literature in the language they understood best. They also wanted to be instructed in the Holy Torah, to be inspired by the beautiful legends and stories of the Talmud and Midrash, and to be aroused to good deeds by the teachings of pious men and masters of ethics. And what is more, these women and the men of the masses were not always moved by a holy desire but were also stirred by secular or pure human motives. The atmosphere in the ghetto was indeed a religious one and saturated with piety but it was not entirely a gloomy one. The dwellers behind the walls were not unmindful of a desire for joy and amusement. This desire was especially manifest on the part of the women as well as the men who did not belong to the intellectual class. From the outside world, there penetrated into the ghetto the echoes of the songs of the Minnesänger, and the voices of the wandering troups of actors who travelled through the length and breadth of Germany and recited the glories of the valorous knights and of the heroes of old. These wandering actors, singers and reciters created, during the twelfth and thirteenth centuries, an entire literature of romances, stories and epics, which is often called by a technical name, the literature of the "Spielman" (actor in middle German).

All these activities and means of amusement did not pass unnoticed by the Jews. They also wanted to be amused, aroused and stirred by the glories and feats of valor of heroes whether of their own or of their neighbors. This double desire for both instruction and amusement had to be satisfied. And soon there arose men who ministered to the needs of the masses and created a literature for them. We will see how in the course of the centuries a quite extensive literature grew up, dealing with all forms of religious and ethical life, and beside it there rose also a secular literature consisting of romances, stories, legends and even drama.

That the first type of literature exceeded in quantity that of the second is needless to say. But on the other hand, it seems quite probable that the secular literature preceded the religious in time. It may be safely asserted that the German *"Spielman"* soon found its counterpart in a Jewish "Spielman." There undoubtedly arose troops of wandering Jewish singers, reciters and declaimers who, like their Christian colleagues, amused Jewish audiences by heroic songs and stories and romances. For their material, they utilized to a great extent the German popular romances and songs. References to the well known Mediaeval German romances "Herzog Erenst," "Hildebrand Lied" and "Dietrich Von Bern" are numerous in Mediaeval Judaeo-German literature, and these acclaim their popularity. Although there exist no early manuscripts of these romances, but only late printed editions, yet the references to their popularity which hail from the first half of the sixteenth century show clearly that they were long current among the masses. These versions of the romances were, of course, like their prototypes, first recited orally, but were greatly modified to suit the Jewish audience. Later, they were put into writing. However, the Jewish actor or wandering singer (Spielman) was not entirely satisfied with borrowed material but soon began to elaborate the literary resources of his people. The Biblical historical books furnished him the themes for his versions.

The Books of Samuel, the stories of which center around the heroic figure of David were before long recast into an epic poem, which was most likely first sung (see below) or recited and then put into writing. This was followed by other books of the Bible. Soon Biblical dramas began to appear and finally original poems and songs. Thus as the centuries passed, a literature ramifying into several branches and reflecting the life of the Jewish masses in Germany and the Slavonic countries was gradually created until at the beginning of the eighteenth century, it assumed respectful proportions.

We stated above that the Judaeo-German literature probably arose simultaneously with the differentiation of the vernacular into a dialect, that is about the end of the thirteenth century. This probability, however, refers more to the oral literature than to the written. The rise of the latter can not be placed before the middle of the fourteenth century. In fact, the earliest Judaeo-German manuscript we possess dates as late as the year 1490. It is a translation of the Psalms in that dialect. But this does not prevent us from assuming the existence of other books written about a century earlier, for the very language and technique of the translation point to a literary tradition of at least a century old. The lack of fourteenth century manuscripts can be easily explained by the fact that due to the frequent expulsions and persecutions which took place during the fourteenth and fifteenth centuries, they were lost, for the Jews did not attach to manuscripts in the vernacular the sanctity bestowed upon those written in Hebrew, and consequently took less care of them.

The loss of the earlier records of this literature makes it difficult for the historian to follow its development and fix with certainty the various epochs and divisions. In general, though, we can divide the Mediaeval Judaeo-German literature into two epochs, the first lasting from the middle of the fourteenth to the end of the sixteenth century, and the second from the end of the sixteenth to the middle of the eighteenth century. During the first epoch, both religious and secular works were produced, but the second is characterized by an extremely pious ethical spirit, and the greater part of the works written during its span were of an ethical nature.

162. CHARACTER AND NATURE OF THAT LITERATURE

As can be seen from the above survey of the rise of the Judaeo-German literature, it is by the conditions of its development, primarily one of translation. Little that is original was created in that vernacular during the four hundred years of its growth, with the exception of a number of poetic pieces penned by ghetto singers on certain occasions. To the class of original works, we may also count some recastings of Biblical episodes in dramatic form, and the composing of special prayers intended mainly for women usually called *Tehinoth.* The majority of the works of this literature were translated either from the Hebrew or the German or, in a few cases, also from the Italian.

It could not be otherwise, for the demand for literature in that dialect came from the women and the uneducated men, and that need expressed itself in a desire for knowledge of religious things and instruction in piety and conduct on the one hand, and the desire for amusing and easy reading on the other hand. Those that undertook to satisfy these desires were not men of great literary talent, for the intellectuals among the Jews of Germany looked down upon the Judao-German dialect, though they used it in their daily conversation, and considered it beneath their dignity to compose works in it. They were, with few exceptions, men who merely possessed skill in writing and for their purposes they found ample material for translation in the rich Hebrew literature, on the one hand, and in the European languages with which they were conversant on the other hand. Thus before long, the Pentateuch, other books of the Bible, the prayer book and some of the Apocryphal books were rendered into the dialect, and likewise, the outstanding romances of several languages and similar books were made accessible to the Judaeo-German reading public. And these translations fully satisfied the need and craving of that public for instruction and amusement. Only in some cases, such as those mentioned above was there an incentive for original creation.

The second fundamental characteristic of this literature is that it was primarily written for women and that it arose under their patronage. Only in later times do the writers and publishers of Judaeo-German books mention in their introduction also the uneducated men. But even then the pious women and girls, who are denominated by the Hebrew word *Bahuroth,* constituted the main reading public, whom the writers addressed in their prefaces. In earlier times, it was only the women who in their need called forth such works. The writers knew their patronesses and catered to their wants, spoke to them in the proper terms, in their long rhymed prefaces and expected their reward from them, and quite often received it from their hands in a generous manner.

A few illustrations will demonstrate to us the extent of influence the women exerted upon this dialect literature. In most of the Judaeo-German manuscripts (and in a good number of the books printed during the sixteenth and seventeenth centuries), the author calls himself "Der Schreiber Fun Alle Frume Weiber" or "Diener Fun Alle Frume Weiber." (The writer for or the servant of all pious women.) This title implies, as one historian of Yiddish literature aptly remarks,[2] that these writers were professionals who earned their living by composing books for women and girls. In fact, we find a number of manuscripts where this fact is clearly stated. Thus, in a manuscript of a translation of the Books of Psalms and Proverbs written by Eliezer ben Israel of Prague in 1532 the writer says, "I wrote this book with great energy and diligence for my patroness Pesslin, the daughter of Rabbi Jacob." The Hamburg manuscript of the *Schemuel Buch* dating undoubtedly from the beginning of the sixteenth century bears the dedication by a writer, a certain Liva (Leib) of Regensburg, to his good patroness Freidlin. Another copyist or maybe the author of a translation of the Sayings of the Fathers (Pirke Aboth), written in Italy in 1579, indites a long poem in honor of the woman at whose request he copied or composed this work. In the poem, the writer enumerates the virtues of the woman, Perlen by name, and gives a list of her immediate relatives, ending with praises and blessings. In these dedications of the writers or copyists there is often mention of the reward they received from their patronesses, from which we can see that the compensation was not always in cash but frequently in kind; these literary-minded women at times paid the writers by presents of various foods which they sent to the homes of the latter.

Likewise, the authors and publishers of printed Judaeo-German books address themselves primarily to the women and request them to buy the works. Thus, Elijah Bahur begins the rhymed preface to his translation of the Psalms printed by Cornelius Adelkind in 1545, at Venice, with the following words:

[2] M. Eric, Die Geschichte fun der Judischer Literatur, p. 31.

"Ihr Frume Frauen die andechtigen
Die begeren zu loben dem Almechtigen
Do hebt auf eure augen un secht
Dos heilig Tillim das gut un gerecht."
(Ye pious and virtuous women who desire to praise the Almighty,
Raise your eyes and see the holy book of Psalms
Which is good and righteous.)

In a similar manner writes Isaac ben Aaron of Prostiz in his introduction to the edition of the translation of the Books of Kings printed by him at Cracow 1582, saying, "Das Melochim Buch wohl verteitscht in Teutscher Sprach gor hübsch und besheidlich. Un'gor kurzweilig derinen zu leinen fur weiber and meiddlach." (The Book of Kings well rendered in Teitch, i. e. Yiddish language, in the fine and proper manner. It will be amusing for women and girls to read therein.) Such examples could be multiplied but the foregoing will suffice to prove the all-important role played by the Jewish women in the development of the Judaeo-German literature.

This fundamental tone of the Mediaeval Yiddish literature had imparted to it a number of peculiar traits and had stamped it with its impression in all its ramifications. Its influence affected first the content of the work translated. The prime motive of Mediaeval Jewish life was the religious one, and consequently the women of Israel were greatly interested in religious instruction and inspiration, in all its forms. The greater part of the books were, therefore, of a religious, pietistic character. But the character of the religious works was determined by the public to whose needs it ministered, the women. The translations consisted primarily of the narrative and lighter part of the extensive Hebrew literature. It is the numerous Bible translations which first made their appearance in the ghetto and even these were at first limited to the historical books and the narrative portions of the Pentateuch which became popular. Of the post-Biblical literature, it is the Apocryphal fiction books, portions of the Agada, and works of fables, stories and legends which were rendered into *Yiddish* and gained extensive circulation. Again, of the many ethical books in Hebrew translated into that dialect, only those were selected which are of a popular nature. The more difficult and scientific treatises were left out, and very often even in the books chosen for translation, the more complicated passages or sections were omitted.

On the whole, very few legal or Halakic books were translated into the Judaeo-German. But the few that were rendered bear a different character. These are either primarily compilations of the special laws regarding the conduct of women, or of such laws the execution of which belongs to them, as the salting of meat, preparation of food and others. Of the extensive philosophic and scientific literature in Hebrew, almost nothing was made accessible in Yiddish with the exception of Bahya's Duties of the Heart, which is more of an ethical than a philosophic treatise. However, the first portal of this book which deals with philosophy was not translated.

The fact that the reading public for whom the Judaeo-German books were intended consisted mainly of women influenced also the very tone of these books. Not only were difficult passages originally contained in the Hebrew texts omitted, but the entire character of the texts was frequently altered in order to suit the taste of the readers. In the ethical books, sections which exalt and enjoin the meticulous observance of the special duties and tasks of women were added. The type of rewards promised to law-abiding persons was changed to one appealing mostly to women as the readers are frequently told that if they will be God-fearing and law-observing, they will have and raise pious and virtuous children. Again, the models of piety and virtue are not the patriarchs, scholars and saints so frequently mentioned in the Hebrew texts but the matriarchs and the prophetesses and other pious women mentioned in the Agada and Bible.

This change of motive and tone is especially evident in the prayers, both those translated from the Hebrew and those originally composed in that dialect. They lack the dignity and the grandeur of the Hebrew prayers, and the tone of the appeal to God is entirely feminine. The people of Israel and the vicissitudes of its fortunes which occupy such an important place in our prayer book are relegated in the *Yiddish* prayers to the second place. Instead, there are projected the needs of the praying individual. These Yiddish prayers rightly deserve the name given to them, *Tehinoth,* i. e. supplications. In them, the supplicant pours out her woes and suffering before God in an intimate and detailed manner and demands immediate redress. God is seldom spoken of in these prayers as the just but stern judge who scans the deeds of men, but is addressed as the merciful and forgiving father and his love and mercy are mainly appealed to. Finally, it is not the merit of the fathers which is invoked but the deeds of the mothers and pious women.

Equally great was the influence of women on the form of that literature. It is intimate, permeated with deep feeling and pathos; intended more to arouse the emotions than the thoughts, and appeals to the heart rather than to the mind. The writers of the Judaeo-German books not only employed simple language but endeavored painstakingly to make the works intelligible even to the most uneducated readers. They utilized all kinds of devices, quotations, stories, parables and long explanations of the subject.

The style is, of course, verbose, but possesses at the same time a certain charm and sweetness which is primarily expressed by the intimacy between the writer and the reader. Very often, as stated, long prefaces are given by the authors, in which they turn to their feminine readers, extolling their virtues and appealing to them to buy the books, enumerating their qualities and uses. Sometimes, they stop in the middle of a discourse on a matter of ethics, piety and instruction and enter upon a long excursus of a personal character, speaking directly to the readers addressing them by endearing terms. Even in books dealing with law where the details of observance and performance of precepts are given, the injunctions are not stated in an impersonal manner as is the case in the Hebrew codes. In the Judaeo-German legal manuals, the writer often begins the statements with a phrase like this, "Hearken ye, kind people, (Liebe Leute) the precepts are to be performed in this manner." Again, at the end of the chapter, a paragraph is added where promises of reward for the performance of the precepts are given and the kinds of rewards described. In these and many other ways, did the peculiar character of the soul of the feminine reading public exert its influence upon the style of the works constituting the greater part of the Mediaeval Judaeo-German literature.

All these characteristics combined make the entire literature real folk literature. It is saturated with the spirit of the home and reflects the life of the ghetto in all its phases. It echoes its joys and its sorrows, and portrays its various moods. It is the only part of the extensive mass of literary productions of the Jewish people which was not only greatly influenced by the Jewish woman but was also partly created by her. In the long list of writers and composers of Judaeo-German works, there are found many names of women authors who contributed their share to the development of the dialect literature.

As a folk production, arising in response to the desire of the Jewish women and the uneducated masses for religious instruction and amusement, this literature exerted great influence upon life. In it, the Jewish woman found the source of her spiritual strength. From the numerous Bible translations, embellished with Agadic stories, fables and legends, she drew her inspiration, her comfort and amusement, and the books of piety and ethics strengthened her faith and elevated her soul. If the Jewish woman during the ages was the main stay of the home, the backbone of the family, and her character and deep faith was the source of inspiration and encouragement to her children, we have to thank partly for these fine traits the Judaeo-German literature which helped to inculcate them in her easily impressionable soul.

163. RELIGIOUS LITERATURE

As was noted in the introduction, the rise of the Judaeo-German literature had its origin in the desire on the part of women and the uneducated men to participate in the religious knowledge of their people, in the center of which stood the Bible. Bible translation formed, therefore, the backbone of the early literary activity in that dialect. But before such activity could have been undertaken, some preliminary work had to be done, a certain method of rendering Hebrew words and phrases had to be developed and a vocabulary had to be created. This preliminary work was done by the writers of glosses on the margin of Bibles and the compilers of Biblical glossaries.

These glosses and glossaries were written by men who either occupied themselves with Biblical exegesis or by teachers who noted the translation of difficult words in the texts which they employed in class. There are numerous Bible manuscripts which contain such glosses, and also a considerable number of separate Bible glossaries. We will mention the most important of such works.

The earliest extensive Judaeo-German glosses extant date from the end of the thirteenth century. They are contained in a commentary on the Prophetical Books—from Joshua to Malachi—by a disciple of Moses ben Eliezer ha-Darshan (the exegete or homiletist). As the said Moses is known to have lived around 1270 the glosses by the disciple must have been written at the end of the century. The glosses consist primarily of numerous renderings of Hebrew words into their German equivalents. But here and there, whole phrases are also translated.

Many Judaeo-German glosses are also contained in another manuscript of the Prophetical Books. The manuscript itself probably dates from the thirteenth century but the glosses are of later origin, most likely from the fourteenth century. They are very numerous and are written all around the text, above and below the lines. The glosses are not limited to mere translations of words or even phrases but very often contain comments and Agadic embellishments of verses. In these glosses, we can see the nuclei of the translations of Biblical books, for they mark the first attempt at lengthy renderings into the Judaeo-German vernaculars.

From the glosses written on the margin of the text, more ambitious writers passed over to composing separate glossaries either to individual books or even to the entire Bible. Several such incomplete glossaries exist in manuscript. The most noted of them is a glossary to almost the entire Bible, for only Genesis, the larger part of Exodus and the Book of the Twelve Prophets are missing. It was undoubtedly originally complete but these parts were lost in the copying. The glossary, judging from the character of its language dates from the first half of the fourteenth century. The glosses render single words, phrases and frequently even entire verses into German. The glosses to most of the books are limited to selected passages, but those to the Book of Psalms are so numerous that they form almost a continuous translation. The other glossaries are not as complete and several of them are only to the Hagiographa. They date from the second half of the fourteenth century. From the fifteenth century, there is extant in manuscript a glossary to the Pentateuch. It was written by a certain Isaac Cohen of Alessandria in the year 1513, but it is evident that the material was compiled from earlier works. The glossary is arranged according to the weekly portions read in the synagogue, and was undoubtedly intended as a manual to be used in the instruction of children.

The writers of the glosses and glossaries laid the foundation for a further literary activity which branched off into two directions, one that of Bible translations and the other that of composing more perfected and improved lexicons and dictionaries. As the first kind of literary expression is the more important of the two, it will take precedence in our survey of the Judaeo-German literature.

ii. Bible Translations

As noted above, we possess comparatively few Judaeo-German manuscripts antedating the sixteenth century. We can not, therefore, gauge with precision to what extent the activity in the field of Bible translation was carried on during the earlier centuries. The period of bloom for this branch of the dialect literature begins with the sixteenth century, for it is with the spread of printing that Judaeo-German translations of Biblical books begin to increase in a prolific manner. Yet, we do possess several manuscripts of translations of a number of Biblical books, which supposedly date from the fifteenth century and some may possibly go back to the fourteenth, though the copying of the manuscripts is of a much later date. The difficulty in determining the time of the composition of a translation consists in the fact that we can not be certain whether the writer of a manuscript was actually the translator or merely the copyist. The actual date of composition must then be determined by the language used in the translation as well as by other criteria which are not always decisive.

Of these manuscripts, we will describe briefly several of the important ones. (a) The earliest of them seems to be a manuscript containing the translations of the Books of Psalms, Proverbs and Job. It is not dated and is anonymous, but by the antique form of its language, it is evident that it was originally composed not later than the first half of the fifteenth and possibly even at the end of the fourteenth century. There are in the manuscript a number of corrections from a later hand which substituted different words and expressions for the more obsolete ones. The translation clings closely to the original and attempts no embellishments or additions. (b) A translation of the Psalms written in 1490 is the oldest dated manuscript, but the author undoubtedly utilized still older material. This translation is likewise a literal one but its style is more free and flowing than the one which preceded it.

(c) A more improved translation of the Psalms and Proverbs intended primarily for women is contained in a manuscript written in the year 1532 by Eliezer ben Israel of Prague. He wrote it, as indicated above, for his patroness Peslin, the daughter of Rabbi Jacob. In the preface to the rendition of the Book of Proverbs, the writer addresses his readers and assures them that if they will read the book, they will become as wise as Bath Sheba, the mother of Solomon, and will rear their children in the spirit of the fear of the Lord as she had done. This indicates clearly the class of readers for whom the work was intended. The Psalms are divided into seven groups, each to be recited during a special day of the week, and instructions for such recitations are given. The translation evinces the characteristics of a later age, for while the verses are, on the whole, rendered literally, yet there are frequent additions and Agadic embellishments. Such additions are more numerous in the Book of Proverbs, but they are also found in the rendition of the Psalms. They were, of course, added in order to make the translations more suitable to the taste of the readers. Though the name of the writer of the manuscript is distinctly given, yet it is possible that he was rather the editor of the translation than the author, as most likely a large part of the work dates from earlier times.

(d) To the fifteenth century belongs also a manuscript translation of the Pentateuch found in München. No date, nor place of composition, nor name of the author is given, but by a number of criteria, especially that of style and language, the great Jewish bibliographer Steinschneider had termed it one of the older Pentateuch translations produced in Judaeo-German. (e) Another manuscript of a translation of the Pentateuch to which is also added the rendition of the weekly prophetic portions (Haftaroth) and of the two Scrolls, Esther and Canticles, is extant in the Parma library. It was originally in the possession of the famous bibliographer de Rossi and he assigned its composition to the fifteenth century without any proofs. The language, however, seems to be old and to an extent corroborates de Rossi's assertion. This manuscript, like the translation of the Psalms by Eliezer ben Israel described above, proves definitely that the books were written for women. At the end of the *Haftarah* for the ninth of Ab, the author suddenly digresses and says, "Kind sister, bear me no grudge for the poor writing of this *Haftarah,* for my hand was injured while I wrote it." The statement shows both the spirit of friendliness which existed between the writer and his readers and his confidence that only women will read the work.

These then were the early steps made in the Judaeo-German Bible translations which later developed into an extensive branch of literature. It is to be noted that as far as the manuscripts are concerned, the translations of the Books of Psalms and Proverbs outnumber those of the Pentateuch, which indicate that these two books were very popular in early times, the first on account of its lyrical character and the second because of its epigrammatic form. In later times, when books began to be printed, the process was reversed and the Pentateuch came into its own, for during six decades, from 1544 to 1610, more than a dozen translations of the Pentateuch were issued. However, even then the Psalms took precedence over other books of the Bible, for its translations are numerous.

The first printed translation of the Pentateuch together with the *Haphtaroth* and the Five Scrolls was issued at Constance in the year 1544. This translation was formally ascribed to Elijah Bahur, but it is now definitely established that it was done by the Jewish convert Michael Adam. He undoubtedly had the assistance of the Christian Hebraist Paul Fagius who a year previously (1543) published a rendition of the first four chapters of Genesis, and most likely several others collaborated in the work. Adam, however, was chiefly responsible for the version. At that time, there were a number of Christian Hebraists and theologians who were interested in promoting the development of the Judaeo-German literature. Whether their interest arose from missionary zeal, from their hoping to gain in this way the confidence of the Jewish masses or merely from literary curiosity, can not be definitely determined. But if Adam and his collaborators had any intention of spreading Christian propaganda, it is not revealed in the translation, as it is executed in the best manner of Jewish tradition.

In the preface, the translator says that his motive in making the Pentateuch accessible in the vernacular was to increase the knowledge of the Scriptures among the Jews. On account of persecutions, he asserts many Jews settled in villages and they could not engage teachers for their children and these consequently grew up without any instruction. By using this translation, he continues, the fathers themselves will be able to teach the children. Besides, even poorly equipped teachers will be able to utilize it.

The translation is a very literal one and follows the text scrupulously. Even Hebrew prepositions and particles are rendered into the vernacular. The style is, therefore, strained and follows the Hebrew construction. On the margin, however, freer renderings based on the exegetic commentaries of Rashi and Kimhi are given.

Shortly after the appearance of Adam's translation, there was issued in the same year, 1544, at Augusburg another one, and curiously enough by another Jewish convert, Paulus Aemilius. Aemilius in a letter preceding the translation which was intended to serve as a preface, says that he undertook this work in order to prove to the Christians that not all Jews converse in Hebrew, but that many of them employ a German dialect as the medium of their speech. It is, however, doubtful whether this was exactly his motive in issuing this translation, and most likely he also had intended to use the translation as a means for future propagandistic activity.

The translation itself is as traditional as Adam's. In fact, it is not a new translation but as stated explicitly on the title page, it is based on an older Pentateuch translation. Aemilius had only improved the language, modernizing its forms and substituting words current in the sixteenth century for the obsolete ones.

The steps taken by renegade Jews to supply the Jewish women and the uneducated masses with the means to acquire a knowledge of the Bible gave a great impetus to the development of Judaeo-German literature. The field was soon entered by faithful Jews who had the welfare of the people at heart. Sixteen years later, in 1560, a new Pentateuch, *Haftaroth* and Scroll translation, appeared at Cremona. The editor of this work was a Polish Jew Judah Leib ben Naphtali Bresh who settled in Italy. Bresh's translation is primarily a reprint of Adam's version, but greatly improved. Its main value consists in the fact that an abbreviated translation of Rashi's commentary was appended to the text, thus making the reading of the Pentateuch more attractive and interesting. Bresh had written a rhymed preface to his translation which shows us definitely the reading public for whom the work was intended. In it, the editor calls himself "the writer of all pious women" (der schreiber fun alle frume weiber) and asks the women and girls to read the book which is "as tasty as milk and cake." He advises them to sell even their dresses or to hire themselves out for housework in order to obtain the money for the price of the book. As a whole, the rhymed preface or the poem is typically characteristic of the age and of the attitude of the writer and printer to his readers. Bresh's translation evidently filled some need, though his passionate call to the women to buy his book was not answered to the extent he expected. Twenty-three years later in 1583, a second edition of the work appeared at Basel by the publisher, Israel Zitroni, and twenty years after that in 1603, a third. In both later editions little change in the original was made.

The Pentateuch translation of Bresh which was reprinted several times, broke a new path in Bible translations. The tendency became prevalent to deviate more and more from the literal form of translation and adopt the form of embellishing the text with Midrashic comments, stories, and exegetic remarks. The first translation of this kind was issued at Prague in the year 1608 by a well known Talmudic scholar, Rabbi Isaac ben Samson, the son-in-law of the famous Rabbi Bezalel Levy (Maharal) of Prague who was said to have created a homunculus (Golem). In this translation, the Midrashic passages and the digest of the Rashi are still kept separated from the text proper. But the later translations incorporated the Agadic passages and comments in the text, so that the versions became extensive and assumed more the character of a paraphrase. It seems that Rabbi Isaac's translation was the first to receive the well known appellation "Teutsch Humesch." Under this name there were published, during the seventeenth and eighteenth centuries, many embellished Pentateuch translations with slight variations in the form of exposition and incorporated Midrashic matter. The "Teutsch Humesch" was the most popular book in the ghetto, the source of inspiration and Biblical knowledge for generations of Jewish mothers.

Simultaneously with the frequent appearances of the various Pentateuch translations, there began to be issued also translations of the other books of the Bible. The translations of these books assumed, however, several literary forms. The first is the ordinary prose translation in which the text is rendered into Judaeo-German in a more or less literal manner without embellishment. The second is the rhymed translation where the content of the text is necessarily altered in order to suit the rhymed form. The third is the rhymed paraphrase where the content of the book is not only embellished with legends and stories but is entirely reworked in a dramatic manner in order to present the subject in the most attractive form. The last kind of literary productivity in reality transcends the bounds of a translation and becomes an original literary creation based on Biblical episodes.

Of the first type of translation, the earliest is the rendering of the Psalms in the Judaeo-German by Elijah Bahur (Levita), published at Venice in the year 1545 by the famous printer, Cornelius Adelkind. In the rhymed preface, the translator, as stated, turns to the virtuous pious women and tells them that the book was rendered for the purpose that they may praise God by reciting the Psalms of David, the great singer in Israel, and they are, therefore, urged to buy the book. He also tells that the rendering was done according to all rules of grammar and can be used by the teachers in their classes. Adelkind adds a few lines in prose telling how he came to publish the translation. He informs us that in his younger days he had published many important books, but ultimately felt that he had done little for the uneducated laymen and the pious young women (Baḥuroth) who spend their Sabbaths and holidays reading romances. He, therefore, asked the great scholar, Elijah Bahur, to render the Psalms into the vernacular, so that it might be read by those who do not understand Hebrew. The translation clings closely to the text and contains no embellishments, except Jewish exegetic interpretations. It seems, though, that Elijah was not the real translator of the book, but more of an editor of an older translation, for as we have seen above, there were several translations of the Psalms hailing from the fifteenth century. Elijah undoubtedly utilized one of them improving its style and bringing it up to date. This translation was in the course of the ages reprinted many times.

Besides the translation of the Psalms we have also a translation of the Book of Proverbs. It was rendered by Mordecai Teplitz and printed in Krakow in the year 1582.

Of the Prophetic Books, we have only a single translation of the Book of Isaiah printed in Krakow in the year 1586. The work, an anonymous one, was intended by the author for pedagogic purposes. It contains besides the translation of the text also an abridgement of David Kimhi's commentary and a summary of the contents placed at the end of each chapter.

The second type of translations is represented first by the anonymous rhymed rendering of the Book of Judges printed in Mantua in 1564. The author mentions in his preface that he was prompted to undertake the translation by the example of the "Schmuel Buch" which appeared earlier (see below) and that he hopes to render in a short time also the Book of Joshua. This hope, however, seems never to have been realized. He further tells us that his translation is not only to be read but to be sung, for it is done in real poetic manner. He uses the *Ottava Rima,* namely, strophes of eight lines, which was at the time a popular poetic form. The rendering is not strictly literal for the author incorporated a good deal of Agadic material.

It did not take long and the popular book, the Psalms, was also rendered in rhyme. The translator was Moses Stendel, the publisher, a patroness of literature, Roesel, the daughter of Rabbi Joseph ha-Levi or Roesel Fishel's, the printer, Isaac Prostitz of Krakow, and the year of publication 1586. The publisher tells us in her short preface, of her great desire to make the Psalms accessible to every man and woman and how she found the author in the city of Hanover and saw his rendering which pleased her greatly. She then copied the manuscript with her own hands and published it. She further informs us that the translation is done in the "Schmuel Buch" strophe, i. e. in the eight line strophe, and that it will certainly please the readers, men and women and pious girls. The same printer, Isaac Prostitz, published two years later in 1588 a rhymed version of the Book of Daniel and six years afterwards a similar version of the Book of Kings.

The rhymed versions of Biblical books evidently became popular for their production continued for generations and assumed various forms. The most interesting variation of such rhymed translations is a rhymed Biblical anthology under the name *Mismor Le Toda* (Songs of Praise) by David Cohen, published in 1644 at Amsterdam. It consists of selections of the narrative parts both of the Pentateuch and the Scrolls. The author relates in his preface that he composed his book at the request of some pious women who, desiring to raise their daughters to be God-fearing and virtuous, were anxious to provide for them spiritual nourishment which should be both religious and amusing. The girls, he tells us, preferred to play games or sing songs rather than to read the "Teutsch Humesh," and even the popular Agadic commentary on the Pentateuch, the Zeena U-Reena, (see below) the delight of women, used to put them to sleep. He, therefore, hopes that his poetic narratives will afford that type of religious literature which will be interesting even to the young women, as they will be able to recite and sing some of the poems.

The desire to provide religious literature in an interesting and amusing form was the primary motive in the production of the third type of translation, namely the poetic paraphrases of Biblical books. This kind of literature began, as noted above, to develop very early and was probably first recited orally in the manner of the German heroic poems. The narrative of the Bible heroes was elaborated into a kind of Jewish heroic epic. The most important of such works is the oft-mentioned "Schmuel Buch." The book appeared in Augsburg in 1544. The name of the author is not given, but in several manuscripts of the work, we find different names of "writers" such as the above mentioned Liva of Regensburgh, one by the name of Zanvil and others. There is, however, no doubt that "writer," "*schreiber,*" in German, means only copyist. The author, therefore, remains unknown. There is also no doubt that the book hails from an earlier time than the sixteenth century, at least a hundred years earlier. The book is probably the most original production of the Mediaeval Judaeo-German literature, for though it follows the text of the two Books of Samuel, it is an epic poem. Its central figure is king David, to whose life and exploits it is primarily devoted, and Franz Delitsch had justly called it a Daviada. The author reworked the entire Biblical material and incorporated many Agadic elements and produced a work which projects the life and deeds of his hero vividly and graphically. Some episodes which occupy a few lines in the Bible are told by the author in great detail and with poetic flavor, while others are shortened. Thus the story of Hannah and the birth of Samuel which in the Bible occupies only two chapters is lengthened in our book to forty-nine strophes. Likewise is the Biblical order of events not followed strictly. Some events or songs which in the Bible come at the end are placed by the author earlier in order to produce a stronger effect. The writer endeavors to draw the portrait of his hero- David, in the brightest colors and of course utilizes the Agada in his defense. He tells us that Bath Sheba was divorced from her husband when David took her to his palace, an explanation which is found in the Talmud. Finally, in order to complete the life of David, the author transcends the bounds of the Books of Samuel and draws upon the first Book of Kings for the last acts of the life of his hero and his death.

The book is written in real vigorous poetic style in the eight line strophe and was undoubtedly intended to be sung. For that purpose, it had a special melody as later authors often tell us that their books were composed "Benigun Schmuel Buch," that is both in the strophe and melody of this work. It was, as we have already noted, very popular and served as a model of imitation for many authors.

A year earlier, 1543, there appeared in Augsburg a rhymed paraphrase of the Books of Kings called "Melochim Buch." It bears a great likeness to that of the "Schmuel Buch" but is not as poetic and masterly as the former. It is also an older production and was originally written as a separate book and not as a sequel to the "Schmuel Buch." The author wanted to make it a complete story of the life of the nation on their own land. It begins with a hymn of praise to God in three strophes, after which there follow nine strophes which recite the history of Israel from the Exodus to the last days of David. Then follow the contents of the Books of Kings and as a sequel, it relates the history of the Jews from the destruction of the First Temple to the end of the Second Commonwealth in thirty strophes. The entire book contains twenty-two hundred and sixty-one strophes. The

"Melochim Buch" possesses the same characteristics as the "Schmuel Buch." The book bears at the end a colophon saying that it was published by Paulus Aemilius, but it is very doubtful whether he was really the publisher, and it is more probable that Hayyim Shahor and his son-in-law Isaac ben Yakar who were associated with Aemilius in printing enterprises were the publishers of both works. Aemilius himself later adopted the text of the "Schmuel Buch" as the basis for his high German version of the Books of Samuel printed in 1562 at Ingolstadt.

The "Melochim" and "Schmuel" books were later reprinted several times and, as stated, served as models for new translations. Of the more important later rhymed paraphrases of the Biblical books is the *Kehillath Yacob* (The Assembly of Jacob) by Jacob ben Isaac Segal, printed at Fürth in 1692. It paraphrases the content of the Pentateuch and the Books of Joshua and Judges. It falls much below the earlier models in poetic strength, but is more verbose than they. Its main value consists in the fact that the author embellished the content of the text with matter drawn from all sources, from the Talmud, the Midrashim, commentaries and the quasi-historical books, the *Sepher ha-Yashar* and the *Jossipon*. In addition, he added parables and fables to make the work more attractive and amusing. Like the authors who preceded him, Jacob hoped that the appearance of his book would cause people to break away from games of cards and dice and turn to perusing the beautiful stories and narratives contained therein.

Paraphrasing, however, was not limited to the rhymed form. There appeared also many prose paraphrases of the Pentateuch or other Biblical books. The general characteristic of these books is that they deviate more and more from the text and emphasize the embellishments and stories to such a degree that the extraneous matter becomes the dominating element. Thus, we have a paraphrase of Canticles composed by Isaac Sulkus and printed in Krakow in 1579, where the author collected all stories and allegoric interpretations of Canticles, found in Jewish literature, and as a result, the entire content of the book assumed a different form. The author complains in his preface very bitterly against the scholars and intellectuals who look down upon the literary productions in the vernacular. He believes that it is a pious deed to write such books in Yiddish so that the people should spend their time in the study of the words of God rather than in the reading of such romances as Dietrich von Bern and others. A similar work is a paraphrase of the Book of Esther published in 1589 at Krakow by Isaac Prostitz but written by an unknown author. It is at times called the *Long Megillah* (Die Lange Megilla) for it is an extensive compilation of all legends and stories contained in the Targumim and Midrashim.

The most typical example, however, of all such deviating paraphrases is the classic book known as the *Zeena U-Reena* composed at the end of the sixteenth century by Rabbi Jacob ben Isaac Ashkenazi of Janow, Poland, but printed in Krakow in 1620. It is, however, quite probable that it was printed in Lublin in 1600. The title is borrowed from Canticles Ch. III, 11 where it is said, "*Zeena U-Reena Bnoth Zion ba-Melek Shlomeh*" (Go out, ye daughters of Zion and look at king Solomon), and in its popular form, *Zenna Renna* it was a household word in every Jewish family for many generations.

The book can not even be said to be a paraphrase of the Pentateuch, for the actual content of the text constitutes but a small part of the book. The greater part consists of Agadic passages, Midrashic homilies and exegetic comments of all kinds including mystic and Kabbalistic elements. Its proper name would therefore, be a Judaeo-German Midrash to the Pentateuch. Jacob Janow drew upon the entire Jewish literature for the material, the Talmud, Midrashim, books of legends and stories and almost upon all leading Jewish commentaries especially those of Rashi and Bahya ben Asher. These are his favorites, the first for its Agadic matter and the second on account of its mystic strain. At times, he even cites oral comments or bon mots from contemporary scholars who are otherwise unknown to us. Rabbi Jacob displays great literary skill in his weaving together of the thousands of remarks, comments and homiletic statements into one harmonious work. His method varies. At times, he gives the plain translation of the verse first and then begins to expound it by the numerous quotations, and at other times, he marshalls his moral teachings first and concludes with the verse. Thus, the section of *Noah* begins, with a short discussion on three types of *Tzadikim* (Righteous Men) and this is concluded by pointing out the three epithets applied in the verse to Noah. The section *Lek Lekah* begins with a short homily on the influence of a man's environment upon his character and the necessity of departing from bad company, and the conclusion is the explanation of Abraham's departure from his fatherland. There is quite a large number of verse translations, but they are interwoven in the general narrative.

To the qualities of the book must be added its style which is simple, flowing and tinged with a poetic glow. The influence exerted by this book upon successive generations of Jewish women can hardly be described. It was their encyclopaedia of Jewish knowledge. From it, they drew their love and reverence for the past of their people, and the portrayals of the Jewish saints and righteous men and women contained in the book became the models of conduct in their daily lives. It inculcated in their hearts a desire for virtue and an impassioned love for the Torah, and implanted in their souls a living hope for the redemption of Israel and deliverance from its sufferings. The popularity of the *Zenna Renna* equalled its influence, for in a period of one hundred and twenty years it went through more than thirty known editions.

The same Jacob Janow wrote a companion volume to the *Zeena U-Reena,* a paraphrase of the Prophetic and Hagiographic books of the Bible entitled *ha-Magid.* It differs, though, from the first book as it is a kind of commentary on the text which is given in the original Hebrew. It is less voluminous, but otherwise possesses the same characteristics. It was also popular and underwent many editions, but never attained the degree of popularity of the *Zeena U-Reena.*

The hitherto surveyed Bible translation activity was limited to the Pentateuch and single Biblical books. A need, therefore, arose for a translation of the entire Bible. This need was satisfied by two translations which appeared almost simultaneously at Amsterdam in the years 1676-1679. These translations are by Jekuthiel Blitz and Joslen Witzenhausen. The printer Uri Phoebus engaged Blitz in the year 1676 to undertake the translation for him. Blitz executed the work and even obtained endorsements from famous rabbis together with bans against other translators warning them not to encroach upon his rights. But as soon as the printing began, another printer by the name of Hayyim Etiash engaged Witzenhausen to undertake a similar translation. Etiash also obtained endorsement of rabbis for his undertaking. Meanwhile, Blitz's translation was prevented from appearing on account of the anti-Christian passages it contained. Only after it was corrected and the passages expunged was it allowed to appear in the year 1579, while that of Witzenhausen was issued a year earlier in 1678. The latter translation was corrected by the famous bibliographer, Sabbatai Bass (Sect. 145).

The purposes of both translations were similar. They both intended to give a complete and systematic rendering of the Bible which should follow the *Peshat* method without intermixture of Agadic interpretation. These translations were attempts to supplant the Agadic and embellished translations which prevented the readers from understanding the right meaning of the Scriptures. Both state their motives in the prefaces. Blitz says it is to be regretted that the Jewish scholars had not provided up to his time an adequate translation of the Bible which should give a correct understanding of its teachings. He complains bitterly that the translations of the gentiles are better than those of the current Jewish ones, which being full of exotic Agadic comments only confuse the reader. And what is more regrettable, he continues, is that these perverted interpretations are taught to the children in the schools by their teachers, and none of them know the proper meaning of the words or verses. It is for the purpose of correcting these errors, Blitz informs us, that he undertook this work. In a similar strain speaks the publisher Etiash in his preface to Witzenhausen's translation. He adds one more complaint against the teachers who came from Poland and settled in Amsterdam that they teach but little of the Bible and concentrate mainly on the instruction of the Talmud.

Blitz's translation though better than the various "Teutsch Humoshim" and the translations of the different books of the Bible falls short of the mark. It seems that he did not possess the necessary equipment for such a work. He was neither a master of Hebrew nor German, and his translation contains many errors. In addition, his style is poor and his language is not better than that of the older translations. Witzenhausen's rendition is decidedly preferable to that of Blitz. He displays greater skill and more knowledge of both languages, the Hebrew and the German, and in fact, he informs us that he utilized all the best commentaries and consulted scholars on numerous occasions. His style and language are of a higher quality. His translation was included in the *Biblia Pentapla,* that is the five-language Bible published in 1711, but there the style was much Germanized. Both translations are primarily literal, but at times, in order to give a better understanding of the verses, freer renderings are given which are enclosed in brackets.

As stated above, the activity of the earlier writers of glosses and explanations to the Bible branched out into two lines of literary productivity, that of Bible translations and that of lexicography and the composition of books which were of great value in the study of the Bible. We have hitherto studied the first branch of this productivity, and it is time now to turn to the second. This branch of Judaeo-German literature is not as extensive as that of Bible translations. Yet, it contains some important works which helped to spread the knowledge of both the Hebrew language and the Bible among the Jews who used Yiddish as their medium of speech.

The purpose of these books was primarily a pedagogical one, and they were intended not for the women and the uneducated masses but for teachers and students of all ages.

The first printed lexicographical work and practically the first printed Judaeo-German book is the *Merkebet ha-Mishnah* or as it is usually called *Sepher Shel Rabbi Anshel* which appeared at Krakow in 1534. The author whose name was Anshel can not be definitely identified, though various suggestions have been offered by different scholars. The book is both a concordance and a dictionary of the Bible. The words are arranged in accordance with the principle laid down by David Kimhi in his Book of Roots, namely the root of a word is given first and then all words connected with that root are subsumed under it. Each word is translated into Judaeo-German, and its place in the Bible is indicated by giving the chapter and verse where it is found. In the preface, the author states the great value of the book which is that it can serve as a means for studying the Bible without the help of a teacher. He points out that especially the Jews who live in villages and have no instructors for their children can with the help of the book teach them the Bible. The author, however, seemed to have had another purpose in mind besides the pedagogic and that is a polemic one. It is the same purpose which the author of the first Hebrew concordance, Isaac Nathan (Sect. 7), had in mind, namely, to help the Jews in their disputations with the Christians, as for such discussions a thorough knowledge of the Bible is necessary.

The year 1534, when the *Merkebet ha-Mishnah* appeared is the same year when Luther's translation of the Bible was issued. It is possible that the publishers of the book, the brothers Halitz, were anxious to emulate the example of the Christians to a certain extent and present their brethren with a book which would enable them to study the Bible thoroughly and efficiently. The book itself, however, seems to antedate the sixteenth century, for the German words the author uses are of earlier currency. They were in vogue in the fourteenth and fifteenth centuries. The Book of Rabbi Anshel was evidently used by many generations of teachers, for many of his Judaeo-

German equivalents of Hebrew words, though long obsolete, were used by teachers in Hebrew schools among the Jews of Eastern Europe as late as the end of the last century, and probably are employed even to-day.

Eight years after the appearance of Rabbi Anshel's book, there was published in 1542 at Isny, by the Christian Hebraist, Paulus Fagius, Elijah Bahur's dictionary, *Shemoth Debarim* (The Names of Things). It is a practical dictionary, translating the words from the Judaeo-German into Hebrew, and is primarily limited to the nouns, adjectives and phrases commonly employed in speech. It does, however, contain a number of verbs. It is arranged in four columns; the first contains the Judaeo-German words in Hebrew script arranged according to the Hebrew alphabet; the second and third give the Hebrew and Latin equivalents, and the fourth, the Judaeo-German words in German script. The purpose of this work was to enable both Jews and Christian Hebraists to translate from German into Hebrew and to compose Hebrew letters with the help of a vocabulary. The work also contains thirty phrases commonly used in greetings and well wishings. Bahur's dictionary went through a number of editions among them one issued in 1652, where the Judaeo-German column is omitted altogether.

A very popular Biblical dictionary was the *Beēr Moshe* (The Well of Moses) by Moses Sertles, first published at Prague in 1604. The work, however, can be called a dictionary only by courtesy, for in reality, it is a kind of interlinear translation. It is arranged according to the chapters and verses of the Pentateuch and each word is translated into the vernacular. Often more than one equivalent is given, and here and there, an exegetic comment is included. The same author also wrote a similar book under the name *Leḳah Tob* (Good Instruction), covering the Prophets and Hagiographa. The *Beēr Moshe,* though, was the more popular of the two. It underwent many editions, and was used as a manual for the teaching of the Pentateuch by many generations of teachers. In the community of Krakow an ordinance was passed by the school authorities prohibiting the teachers to use any other manual for the teaching of *Humesh* (Pentateuch) except the *Beēr Moshe.*

Of the many other glossaries and dictionaries which were current among the Yiddish speaking Jews, there are to be noted the *Sapha Berurah* (Correct Language) by Nathan Hanover (Sect. 135), the Judaeo-German version of Benjamin Musfia's *Seḳer Rab* (Sect. 9), the *'Ayala Sheluha* by Naphtali Altschuler, and the *Dabar Tob* by an anonymous author. The first book is a dictionary in four languages where the Hebrew words are translated into Judaeo-German, Latin and Italian. The work is arranged not according to the alphabetical order, but according to the subjects. It contains twenty chapters, each embracing a group of words relating to a certain subject. The dictionary was originally undoubtedly bi-lingual, namely Hebrew and Judaeo-German, for it is questionable whether Nathan Hanover knew any other languages besides these two. The Latin and Italian translations were, therefore, supplied by other scholars. It was later reprinted several times, but these editions contain only the Hebrew and the Yiddish. The second is a recast version of Musfia's short Hebrew and Latin dictionary written in the form of a connected series of hymns of praise to God. The number of such hymns is seven corresponding to the seven days of the week, and they contain all the root words of the Hebrew language. Yerahmiel Falk substituted the Judaeo-German equivalents instead of the Latin. The third work is a dictionary limited to the prophetic and Hagiographic books, and arranged according to the chapters. It appeared at Krakow in 1590. The fourth, published likewise, in the same place and at the same time is arranged in regular dictionary order, namely according to the alphabet. The words are translated both into Judaeo-German and into Italian. These frequent inclusions of Italian in Hebrew-Yiddish dictionaries points to a continual migration of Polish and German Jews into Italy.

iii. Prayer Book Translations and Supplication Prayers (Tehinoth)

The desire for religious instruction on the part of the Jewish women in the ghetto was matched and even exceeded by a desire for religious expression. The mothers and daughters of Israel felt an inner urge to pour out their heart before God in a language which they understood. It follows, therefore, that simultaneous with the activity in the field of Bible translations, a similar activity went on which aimed to make the treasures of the Jewish liturgy accessible to all those who were not conversant with the Hebrew.

There are extant in manuscript several translations of the prayer book which go back to the fifteenth century, and one manuscript from the same century contains also a complete translation of the sacred poems (Piutim) for New Year and the Day of Atonement. The first printed translation of the prayer book is the one rendered by Joseph Yakar and published by him in 1544 at Ichenhausen. The translation embraces the standard collection of prayers with no omissions, including also the treatise of *Aboth,* the chapters of which are recited on the Sabbaths during the summer and also the Passover Haggadah. It does not contain the Hebrew text which may indicate that the translator intended that the women should say their prayers exclusively in Judaeo-German.

In his preface, Joseph expresses his view on the subject quite explicitly. He admits that the sacred tongue is the best of all languages, but claims that the uneducated do not understand the prayers, and consequently their praying lacks the proper devotion. It is better, therefore, that they should pray in the vernacular and thus express their inner feelings. He then turns to the pious women and urges them to buy his book. At the end of the book, there is a rhymed epilogue where the writer in a humorous tone turns again to his public and tells them the value of the book. He informs them that the price he fixed, one crown, is only a tenth of what the book is really worth and praises his work in a loud and vulgar manner which is typically expressed in the following remark: "The difference between my book and the other translations," he says, "is like the one between an old dame and a young charming girl." Evidently, both the writer and his readers considered such a comparison proper enough to insert it on the last page of a prayer book.

This translation was followed by many others, the most important of which are the Mantua version which appeared in 1562, containing also the text in Hebrew, the Venice edition in 1599 and the translation known as the *Derek Yesharah* (The Straight Path) by Michael Epstein, published in 1697 at Frankfurt on the Main. The last edition contains besides the translation of all prayers also a digest in the vernacular of all laws and customs bearing upon the liturgy and worship in the synagogue. Another translation of the prayer book deserves to be singled out, not because it contains any special features but on account of its publisher and the manner of its printing. This is the Judaeo-German version of the *Siddur* published by the proselyte Moses ben Abraham at Halle, in the year 1720. This Moses ben Abraham was a Christian who embraced Judaism early in life, married the daughter of Rabbi Israel Katz and established a Hebrew printing press at Amsterdam which he later moved to Halle. This prayer book version was set up in type by the twelve year old daughter of Moses who informs us of the fact in her prefatory note to the work. The note is permeated with a deep spirit of piety and closes with an expression of longing for the coming of the Messiah.

The activity in this field was not limited to the prayer book but extended to all phases of the liturgy. We have numerous translations of the *Selihoth,* penitential prayers, *Piutim,* the Passover Haggadah and all kinds of prayers recited on special occasions. In this literary pursuit, there participated, for the first time, also women as translators and editors. A number of special collections of prayers were rendered into Judaeo-German by scholarly women. The most prolific among these women translators was Elis the daughter of Mordecai of Slutzk who lived in the second half of the seventeenth century. She rendered into the vernacular several collections of prayers including the popular *Maabar Yabbok,* a collection of prayers recited in the house of the sick and dying.

The demand for religious expression, however, was not satisfied entirely by translated prayers, but called forth also a supply of prayers originally composed in the vernacular. These are known as prayers of supplication or *Tehinoth.* In this particular form of literary activity both men and women participated, the latter predominating.

The *Tehinoth* were the special medium of devotion of the women of Israel and were adapted, as noted above, both in form and content to their needs. Generation after generation of pious souls had poured forth their hearts before their Maker and pleaded for the health and welfare of their near and dear ones in the semi-lyrical language of these supplication prayers. The *Tehinoth* are of a heterogenous character, as they were made to suit every phase of life. There are prayers for health, for sustenance (Parnassah), for the giving birth to children, for raising them as pious Jews, for brides, for pregnant women, for lighting the Sabbath candles and for numerous other occasions. The tone is usually a very intimate one. The supplicant speaks of herself as the servant of God and usually addresses Him directly. The requests are detailed and specific, and the style verbose and euphuistic. The whole breathes the spirit of a private conversation with the merciful and all-forgiving God.

The first printed collection of *Tehinoth* dates from the year 1590. It was composed by Abraham Apoteker and printed at Prague. Since that year, the collections multiplied in an exceptionally prolific manner. The women authors who soon appeared in the field almost replaced the male authors though some of the latter clung to this kind of literary expression. A very interesting collection of *Tehinoth* is the one composed by Aaron ben Samuel which bears a curious title. It is called *"A Libliche Tephilah, oder a Greftige Arzenai fur Guf und Neshomah"* (A Lovely Collection of Prayers, or a Strong Medicine for the Body and the Soul). The author aimed that the prayers in the vernacular included in his collection should gradually take the place of the Hebrew prayers for at least the women and uneducated men to whom these were unintelligible. He stated his intention quite frankly in his preface to the book. It, of course, kindled the wrath of the rabbis and the book was laid under ban and consequently was not sold.

The most prolific of the women writers was one by the name of Sarah, the daughter of Mordecai, known under the pen name of *Sarah Bath Tobim* (Sarah the Daughter of the Pious). She wrote prayers for all occasions in life in a typical feminine style and form. Her popularity in this field was so great that later, during the nineteenth century, many *Tehinoth* were composed by men under the pseudonym *Sarah Bath Tobim.*

The prayer book translations contained, as we have seen, also digests of laws and customs relating to the liturgy and the synagogue. But such digests were considered insufficient for a complete knowledge of religious conduct and a demand arose for separate manuals of laws affecting the daily life of the masses and especially that of the women. This need was soon filled. Many such books were written in the Judaeo-German vernacular. The earliest is a booklet dealing with the precepts which are to be observed by women only, published at Venice in the year 1552 under the name *Mitzvoth ha-Nashim* (The Laws for Women). The names of the authors are not given. The title page simply bears the words, "Composed by a pious rabbi and a virtuous rabbi's wife." The booklet is a rhymed manual of the details of the special laws and the modes of their observance. It must have been very popular, for it was reprinted several times. The Basel edition of 1602 replaced the Hebrew title by a Judaeo-German one, calling the booklet *Frauen Büchlein.* Other manuals dealing with other sets of laws soon appeared, such as one on the laws of salting meat by the famous scholar, Yom Tob Lippman Heller (Sect. 48), entitled *Brith Melah* (The Covenant of Salt). To this class belongs also the *Leḳet David* by David Leib Orshitz, published in 1731 and *Siah ha-Sade* by Judah Leib of Fürth which deal with various laws practiced in daily life. The last one is devoted especially to the mode of observance of the dietary laws while on a journey.

A very important manual of religious law is the *Sepher ha-Hayyim* (The Book of Life) by Simon Frankfurter which appeared in 1703 at Frankfurt on the Main. The book deals, as its name indicates, with the laws and religious practices relating to the various events in human life, such as birth, circumcision, marriage, sickness, death and burial. It describes in great detail the practices on such occasions and the way of their performance. It attained great popularity and was reprinted numerous times.

Besides these and other original manuals and digests of laws, there appeared also many translations and compendia of Hebrew codes, especially of the shorter ones and of the books of *Minhagim*. (Sec. 53).

As noted above, the manuals of law, though treating of laws and precepts are not written in the severe and precise legal style, for the writers had their reading public in mind. Like all Judaeo-German books, they are addressed to women and are written in the mild tone of exhortation rather than in the form of a command and injunction.

164. ETHICAL OR MUSAR LITERATURE

We have hitherto surveyed the branches of Judaeo-German literature which aimed both at religious instruction and religious expression in their various forms. But there is still another literary branch and quite an extensive one which though permeated with the same spirit of piety and Divine devotion is yet wider in its scope and embraces also other forms of life besides the pure religious one. This is the ethical literature, which, in its aim to teach man the conduct of life as a whole, must necessarily embrace also the social and the secular phases of it.

The Yiddish ethical literature, though it is, like the other branches of literary productivity, dependent to a great extent on its Hebrew prototypes, displays on the whole a certain individuality of character. Not only were there many books of an ethical nature written originally in that language, but even the translated Hebrew books present an entirely different aspect. The folk character of the Judaeo-German literature is especially expressed in the ethical works. First, they are not as abstract as the Hebrew and are thoroughly saturated with a practical spirit. They discuss the phases of actual life and go more into detail in depicting the conditions and circumstances of conduct, and consequently, we feel in them the actual pulsations of life as it was lived by the Jewish masses in the ghetto a few centuries ago. Second, they aim not only to instruct the reader but also to amuse him, that is to inculcate the moral teachings not by injunctions but by means of stories, parables and illustrations. The ethical works contain, therefore, a large narrative element, which in some books even outweighs the purely moral. It follows that because of these characteristics this type of literature was very popular and in great demand. It reached the height of its development in the seventeenth century, but its beginnings appeared simultaneous with the other forms of the Judaeo-German literary activity, namely they took place in the fifteenth and sixteenth centuries.

The first printed ethical book in Judaeo-German is the *Sepher Midoth* (The Book of Good Qualities) which appeared at Isny in the year 1542. The book which is the largest Yiddish ethical work, was printed anonymously and neither the name of the author nor that of the publisher is given. However, it is now assumed that the publisher was Paulus Fagius, the Christian Hebraist who caused the book to be printed. He was the only one who established a Hebrew printing press at Isny in that year where he printed several of Elijah Bahur's works. It is different with the author of the book, his identity still remains unknown. Nor is it definitely determined whether the book is an original composition or a translation from the Hebrew ethical work entitled *Orhoth Tzadikim* which was described above (Sect. 87). The identity of the two versions is undeniable, but in view of the fact that the *Orhoth Tzadikim* was only published in 1581, it was maintained by several Jewish scholars that the Judaeo-German version is the original one and that the Hebrew is only a translation. But on the other hand, in view of the discovery of two Hebrew manuscripts of the *Orhoth Tzadikim,* one in Leningrad and one in Hamburg, the first dating from the fifteenth century and the second from 1503, which contain some differences from the Yiddish version but agree with the printed Hebrew text, it is impossible to maintain the originality of the Judaeo-German version. It is, therefore, now held by most scholars that the *Orhoth Tzadikim* was composed in Hebrew at the beginning of the fifteenth century and circulated for a long time in manuscript form, and that the Yiddish translation was made from one of these manuscripts. The content of this excellent manual of conduct was described above in connection with the Hebrew version. It remains for us to say a few words regarding the translation. It is on the whole more of a free translation than a literal one. The translator adapted his version to the character of his readers. He abbreviated the more difficult Talmudic quotations of the Hebrew text and at times omitted them altogether. On the other hand, he enlarged upon the narrative part of the original, often giving *in extenso* the stories and parables which were merely referred to in the Hebrew text. Here and there, the translator also added parables and snatches of poems of his own. Besides there are also some other changes. All this was done in order to give the book a popular and folk character.

The Judaeo-German version is dedicated to a woman by the name of Murada, living at the city of Günzburg, who is called doctor of the liberal art of medicine. That a Jewish woman should at that time hold a degree of doctor of medicine is certainly a curious phenomenon but her identity can not be established. At the end of the book there are appended some rules for Yiddish orthography which show that both the translator and the publisher were anxious to train the Jewish masses, for whom the work was intended, in the reading of a literature which was just making its appearance in print.

The translation of the *Orhoth Tzadiḳim* was followed soon by other translations of Hebrew ethical works. Four years later in 1546, there appeared at Zurich an anonymous translation of Rabbi Jonah Gerundi's *Sepher ha-Yirah* (The Book of Reverence). It is a free translation of this well known ethical work which reflects the deep spirit of piety and righteous conduct of life typical of the thirteenth century. A modern historian of early Yiddish literature[3] maintains that it was the convert Michael Adam, the editor of the 1544 Constance edition of the Pentateuch who rendered the book in Judaeo-German, but his thesis is not definitely established. Another Yiddish recension of Gerundi's work appeared at Freiburg in 1583 under the title *Hayē Olam* (Eternal Life) by a man named Israel. This is not a translation but a recast of the contents of the book in rhymes. It is much abridged and contains about half of the pages of the Zurich version. Its semi-poetic form, though, made it more popular and it ultimately replaced the first translation.

It did not take long and the writers in the Judaeo-German began to compose original works. The first of such books is *Der Brant Spiegel,* bearing also a Hebrew title *Marēh ha-Sorefeth* (A burning or Gross Mirror) written by Moses Henoch's, i. e. the son of Henoch, of Prague. It first appeared at Basel in 1602. In his rhymed preface,

[3] N. Stiff, in Philologische Schriften, Vol. II, pp. 135-167.

the author after praising his work and inviting the people to buy it, explains the title. He gave his work that name because it reflects to the readers their spiritual uncleanliness and moves them to purify their souls. He continues to say that his mirror is not of the poor quality which reflects images in a diminutive form, but is a *Brant Spiegel* which shows the spots and defects in a gross way. The readers will therefore see the transgressions they often commit in a projected outline and will take care not to repeat them.

Although the book was primarily intended for women, the author in his preface urges also men to buy it. As a result most of the material in the book deals with such phases of conduct as are peculiar to women. The book is divided into seventy-four chapters, each dealing with a certain subject. Thus, one chapter is entitled "On the Use Derived by Man from the Faculty of Speech" which describes the value of restraining oneself from evil speech. Another one is named "How a Wife Should Encourage Her Husband To Do Good." Still another advises housewives how to treat their servants. There are chapters on the training of young children, on rejoicing at a wedding, on comforting the mourner, on marital relations and on many more subjects embracing the details of daily life. The work also reflects the social conditions of the time. The author chastises the young married women for their expensive dressing and unseemly manners. He claims that these matrons dress in silks and velvets and ornament themselves with jewels in order to attract the attention of men, and that they dance with men and deprive the girls of that privilege. He bewails the lack of modesty in women, their arrogance and their interference in the conversation of men. There is undoubtedly some exaggeration in the complaint of the pious author but also some truth, and his words reflect the beginnings of the change in the life of the Jews in the ghetto which appeared as early as the seventeenth century. The *Brant Spiegel* is illustrated with numerous fables, stories and parables culled from the entire Jewish literature so that the narrative element forms a considerable part of the book.

Another important ethical book produced early in the seventeenth century is the *Leb Tob* (A Good Heart) by Isaac ben Elyakim of Posen and published in 1620, at Prague. This work, intended for a larger reading public including both men and women, is distinguished by a spirit of rigorous piety. It is divided into twenty chapters dealing with various subjects, especially with the sanctity of the Sabbath and the festivals, the scrupulous observance of which is urged. For this purpose, the author copied from the *Shulhan Aruk* many of the laws relating to the day of rest and the holidays. He also chastises the uneducated for their light-minded attitude towards study, points out many other deficiencies in the conduct of the masses and discusses at length the principles of general conduct which he calls by the Talmudic name *Derek Eretz* (The Way of the World), i. e. manners and etiquette. He treats the subject under four heads, (a) manners of scholars, (b) of old men, (c) of laymen and young people, and (d) of women and girls. Isaac drew much upon the later Hebrew books of ethics such as the *Reshit Hokmah* by Vidas (Sect. 89) and others. Like his models, he depicts graphically the tortures of hell intended for sinners and in general reminds the reader very frequently of death and its terrors. The book was evidently suited to the taste and spirit of the times, for it was reprinted many times during the century and became the leading ethical book of the masses.

To the other books written before the eighteenth century belong the *Rosen Garten* (The Garden of Roses) by Moses Eliezer which appeared in 1579 at Krakow and the *Meneketh Rivkah* (The Nurse of Rebecca) by Rebecca Tiktiner published in 1609. The last book represents the entrance of the Jewish woman as authoress, not only in the field of *Tehinoth* but also in that of ethics. Its literary value is not great, for it is primarily a compilation of statements culled from the Agada and Hebrew ethical books. Many ethical works and brochures were also composed during the eighteenth century but few are of special importance. To the last belongs the *Simhath ha-Nephesh* (The Joy of the Soul) by Elhanan Hendel Kirchan. The book appeared in two parts, the first in 1707 and the second twenty years later in 1727. It is a unique ethical work, for as its name indicates, its purpose is to teach ethics as well as to inculcate a feeling of joy in life. The spirit pervading it is that of extreme optimism opposed to the usual spirit of rigorism and asceticism prevailing in most of the ethical compositions. The author states in his preface that he intends to cure people from the habit of worry which is injurious both to the body and the soul, and will endeavor to prove that man must not be beset by sorrow in all circumstances of life.

The first part of the book contains chapters teaching the ways of conduct, the cultivation of the proper manners (Derek Eretz) together with abstracts of laws and customs. But its most distinguishing characteristic is the wealth of stories, legends, and parables, drawn both from Jewish and even non-Jewish sources, found there. The narrative and folkloristic part entirely overshadows the ethical one. The stories and other folkloristic matter illustrate the main thesis of the author, namely that one is to derive joy from life.

The second part consists entirely of poems and songs with an ethical tendency. There are poems for the Sabbath, for the festivals, for weddings and circumcision feasts and for other occasions in life. The poems are mostly of his own composition, but some are recasts of current folk songs. The songs are accompanied by notes of the melodies to which they are to be sung.

The *Simhath ha-Nephesh* serves also as a source for numerous data upon the social and the cultural life of the Jews in Germany at the beginning of the eighteenth century. In long poems devoted to the description of Jewish life in the villages, the author cites a number of accusations against these village dwellers from which it is to be seen that there prevailed among them much ignorance, laxity in manners and lack of proper moral conduct. Elhanan is especially severe against the women who in his opinion had lost the quality of Jewish feminine modesty.

Another work which appeared only one year earlier in 1706 is the well known *Kab ha-Yashar* written by the father-in-law of the author of the *Simhath ha-Nephesh,* the Talmudic scholar Zevi Hirsh Kaidonower. The book which was described above (Sect. 90) appeared both in Hebrew and Yiddish, and represents the opposite of the spirit prevailing in Elhanan Kirchan's work. It is one of rigorism, ascetism and mysticism, and yet it was widely read.

The smaller ethical books are too numerous to recount and are, on the whole, of little value as they consist mostly of compilations. Besides the ethical works originally written in Judaeo-German, there were numerous translations of the standard ethical books in Hebrew, such as Bahya's Duties of the Heart, Isaac Aboab's *Menorath ha-Maor* (Sect. 88) and the *Shebet Musar.*

Close in spirit to the ethical books are the collections of aphorisms, proverbs and bon mots. Several of such didactic and semi-humorous productions are found in this literature. Such a collection by Judah Regensburg appeared in 1566 under the title *Mishlē Haḳomim* (The Proverbs of the Wise). It is primarily a translation of fifty passages taken from Harisi's *Tahḳemoni* (Vol. I, Sect. 204) but there are twenty more passages added by the translator which he collected from other sources.

A more important work is Seligman Ulma's book called *Der Zuchts*

Spiegel or *Marēh Musar* (The Mirror of Virtue) which appeared in 1610. It is a valuable collection of many proverbs and elegant sentences culled from the Talmud and post-Talmudic works with a fair admixture of apothegms of his own. They are cast in rhyme and contain wholesome wit and humor. Some of his chosen sentences were quoted above (Sect. 90) and need not be repeated.

It may be added, though, that Ulma made woman the special target of his wit, as the epigrams which display their defects and shortcomings are quite numerous. One deserves to be quoted: "Nobles and pretty women," says Ulma, "one should serve faithfully, but trust little, for their heart is like a bath-house, one enters and the other makes his exit."

165. ROMANCES, NOVELS, TALES AND FABLES

The various forms of literary expression in the Judaeo-German vernacular hitherto surveyed can be subsumed under the general name of religious literature. The domniating motive in each of these branches is the desire to elevate the reading public to a higher degree of devotion, piety and good conduct. We will now turn to a different phase of this literature of the masses, which can be rightly termed the secular one. It is true that here and there the religious motive crops up even in that type of literature, but it is merely a subordinate one. The main purpose of the works termed secular is to amuse and entertain the readers, and in many cases even the content is thoroughly worldly and borrowed from other literatures. The number of such books is considerably large and exceeds that of similar productions in Mediaeval Hebrew literature.

The mass of Judaeo-German belletristic literature can be rightly divided into three classes, romances with a heroic motive, novels which are shorter than the romances and whose motives run closer to ordinary life, and tales and fables. The tale or the short story usually known by the name *Maase* (Tale of an Event) was very popular in the ghetto and numerous collections of *Maases* are extant as will be seen.

The romances belong to the earlier period of Yiddish literature, to the fifteenth and sixteenth centuries, and are as a rule, translations and recasts of such works in other literatures. The period of bloom of the novels and tales is the last two centuries of the Jewish Middle Ages, the seventeenth and eighteenth. The novel is still dependent in its content to a great extent upon borrowed non-Jewish material though it is mostly an original composition, but the tale or the *Maase* is almost wholly Jewish as it is usually taken either from the extensive Agadic works or from the multitudinous legends current in the ghetto.

As was pointed out in the introduction to this chapter, the romances had their origin in the oral recitations of the Jewish actor who, like the German "Spielman," his model, entertained the audiences with declamations and the singing of poems. The contents of these recitations were likewise borrowed, together with the form from the current German sagas and the heroic epic cycles. The most popular romances were those already referred to, *Herzog Erenst, Dietrich von Bern* and the *Hildebrand Lied*. They were all very popular as we have seen from the protests of the writers of religious books against their reading. They had special melodies to which they were sung or recited, for we find many other poetical works written later where the authors indicate that they are to be sung "Benigun" (melody) *Herzog Erenst,* or *Dietrich von Bern*. Undoubtedly there were many written copies of these romances circulating in the ghetto in the fifteenth century but few of these reached us. Only as late as the eighteenth century, there appeared a printed text of *Herzog Erenst*. The romance of *Dietrich von Bern* in Yiddish translation appeared much earlier, in 1597, while the *Hildebrand Lied* was never printed but is found in manuscript. The contents of all these romances are similar in nature, the leading motive being the story of the valiant knight who meets with many adventures, overcomes all obstacles and issues victorious. *Herzog Erenst* is based on the conflict that took place between the Emperor, Conrad the Second and his stepson, the Herzog Erenst. The romance sings of the struggles of the young knight with the emperor, of his defeat and flight to the Orient where he meets with many adventures. It concludes with the tales of his marriage to a princess in India whom he saved from the attentions of a beak-faced bridegroom and of his reconciliation with his stepfather.

The hero of *Dietrich von Bern* (Verona) is no other than Theodoric, the king of the Ostrogoths, who later became king of Italy (493-526), but whose historical role was entirely changed by the legends of the romance. Here he is represented as a valiant knight who protects the weak and is the friend of the poor. Driven out of his land by the enemy, Dietrich in company with his friend Hildebrand, wanders about in foreign lands and meets with many adventures. He fights many battles among them also several with a giant Zigenot, but issues forth victorious and returns to his throne.

The *Hildebrand Lied* is a sequel to the *Dietrich von Bern* cycle. It is similar to the Persian poem, Rustram and Sohrab but with a different ending. Hildebrand returning to his dukedom after the absence of thirty years meets at the boundary a young knight who bars his way. He is Hildebrand's son but unknown to him. They fight and unlike Rustram and Sohrab, father and son recognize each other and both return happily to the wife and mother. The Judaeo-German translations follow closely the German texts but are careful to omit the references to Christ and the saints which are found in the original.

Another very popular belletristic work was the King Arthur romance. It was a Judaeo-German recast of one of the many German versions of the Arthurian cycle of romances, which were current in all European languages. This particular romance tells of the adventures of one of the knights of the Round Table, Gabain by name, who was overpowered by an adversary and carried captive to the latter's land. There, Gabain is set free by his captor who is the king of the foreign country, and in addition gives him his daughter in marriage. Gabain stays for some time in that land, but finally leaves his wife pregnant with child and returns to Arthur's court. Gabain's wife gives birth to a son, names him Weeduwilt and when he grows up sends him to Arthur's court to meet his father. There follow a series of adventures met with by both Gabain and his son. The romance was printed several times, the first edition appearing at Prague in 1652. All printed editions give the story in two line verses, but the Prague text is arranged in the eight line strophe. There are also three manuscripts of this romance likewise in two line verses. It seems, therefore, that there were several versions of this story current in the ghetto representing two or more different translations and recasts of the same romance. The manuscript copies date at least a century earlier than the first printed edition, which shows that these romances were composed in the first half of the fifteenth century and were probably known still earlier.

Of the romances translated during the sixteenth century, the most important are the *Bova Buch,* and "Paris and Vienna" rendered into Judaeo-German from the Italian by Elijah Bahur. The first was so popular that its name became ultimately a synonym for any fantastic tale. It is preserved in the well known Yiddish expression "A Bobe

Maase" which, however, is erroneously understood to mean a story told by the grandmother deriving it from the word *Bobe,* grandmother. In reality it comes from *Bova* the name of this romance. This name, however, is in itself an error, for it should really read Beauvais, the French name of the hero of the story. Bahur, though, translated it from the Italian version of the romance. The translation was completed in the year 1507, but it was not printed until the end of the sixteenth century. The first edition, however, was not preserved, and we posses this book only in the second edition of 1660. There are also two manuscript copies of the book.

The contents of the story which captivated the hearts of generations of readers of Judaeo-German, is of the usual romantic fantastic type and runs as follows: The Herzog Guidon marries late in life a beautiful princess named Brandonia. Of this union a boy named Beauvais is born. Brandonia, however, hates both her aged husband and her child and she invites her former lover, Herzog Dodon, to come and free her from her husband. He responds to the invitation, comes and kills Guidon, becomes ruler in his place and marries the treacherous wife. Brandonia plans next to get rid of Beauvais. She makes several attempts on his life, but he succeeds in escaping from her power and disguising himself becomes a stable boy at the court of the king of Flanders. There the beautiful daughter of the king, Drusina falls in love with him. The match, however, is opposed by the father and hence there begins a series of adventures both for Beauvais and Drusina. In the end, of course, after many wanderings, battles and overcoming of obstacles, Beauvais and Drusina are happily united and the guilty ones, Dodon and Brandonia, are deservedly punished, the first killed and the second sent to a cloister to spend there the rest of her life.

Bahur's rendition is not a mere translation but a recast as he altered the original in many ways. Besides, he added Jewish features to the work, as it opens with a hymn to God, and ends with a poem expressing the pious wish for the coming of the Messiah and the redemption of Israel from exile. There are other passages interwoven in the romance which appeal distinctly to the Jewish reader, and many remarks of a personal character. In these, Elijah reveals bits of his own life and experience.

The second romance, Paris and Vienna, is another translation and a recast by Bahur of a popular Italian work. It was printed in Verona in 1594, but composed in the twenties of the century. From a literary point of view, it is of higher quality and shows more skill on the part of the author. Its theme is again a story of two lovers whose union is opposed but whose devotion and fidelity to each other finally triumph. Paris and Vienna are not names of cities but of the lover and the beloved. The first is a poor knight who attends the court of king Dolfin and the second is the daughter of the king. They fall in love with each other, but the king would not entertain a proposition to marry off his daughter to a poor knight, and finally decides upon the prince of Burgenland as his future son-in-law. Paris leaves the court but Vienna remains faithful to him and refuses to see her suitor. The romance continues to tell about the various devices employed by her in escaping an enforced marriage, as well as the schemes of the lover to return to court and meet his beloved. The conclusion is that Vienna becomes sick from longing after Paris, and her father announces that he who will cure her will take her for wife and succeed to the throne. Paris presents himself in the disguise of a physician, cures Vienna from the fateful malady and as a matter of course, the lovers are united.

In the translation of the romance, the skilful hand of Bahur is displayed even more than in the *Bova Buch.* The content is borrowed but the form and the style is typically Jewish. Bahur imparted, in the recast of the narrative, Jewish characteristics to the heroes, for though they hail from an entirely different world, they yet act in a Jewish manner in their expressions and in their demeanor. In many cases, the translator also incorporated Biblical phrases and idioms so that the work as a whole assumed a certain originality.

Both of Bahur's romances are written in rhyme and in the eight line strophe. These romances were followed by a host of translations of similar stories and other belletristic books from several European languages and also from the Hebrew. Among these the following are worthy of mention: *Kaiser Octafianus,* a recast of a popular German story which is in itself a translation of a French romance; *Sigmunt und Magdalina; Tristan und Isolde; Wieland der Schmid* and others. Very popular was the book *Die Sieben Weisen Meister,* a story which originated in India and later made its rounds in all European languages and was also translated into Hebrew under the name of *Mishlē Sandabar.* Its motive is the treacherousness and infidelity of women. From the Hebrew there were translated the famous book "The Prince and the Hermit" (Ben ha-Melek we-ha-

Nazir) and the *Gehinom und Gan-Eden Buchel,* a rendition of Immanuel di Romi's twenty-sixth Maqama in his *Mahboroth* (Sect. 30) and similar works.

With the beginning of the seventeenth century, there becomes manifest a great demand on the part of the Jewish masses for a literature of amusement and entertainment and this demand called forth a supply of all kinds of novels and especially of tales (Maases) written in prose. Some are translated but most of them are original compositions. To the translations belong also Boccaccio's Decameron stories which appeared in 1710 in Amsterdam. The original works are based mainly on Jewish stories either drawn from the treasures of the Agada or from the current legends. These works are too numerous to discuss in detail and we will only select several specimens which typify the two classes of belletristic composition, the novel and the tale.

The most important Yiddish novel of the time is one called *Maase Briah we-Zimra.* The content is very similar to that of Paris and Vienna but with an entirely different ending. Zimra is a brilliant young counsellor of a Jewish king but it seems of low origin. He falls in love with Breah, the daughter of the high priest who returns his affection. The father opposes the match on account of Zimra's social status and even the intercession of the king does not alter matters. The high priest concocts a scheme to get rid of the persistent lover and he manipulates to send him as a delegate to the pope to ask for the repeal of decrees against the Jews. Briah's father being confident that Zimra will be killed by the pope readily promises him his daughter in marriage if he will be successful. The high priest does not keep his promise, though Zimrah succeeds in his mission, and from disappointment, Briah takes sick and dies. In some miraculous way, Zimrah visits the other world and meets his beloved. She warns him not to kiss her for if he does so he will die within three days. He does not heed the warning and accordingly dies after his return to the lower world within the appointed time. His body is carried to Paradise by angels and there he is united with his beloved.

The motive is a general human one but the development and ending is typically Jewish. The author was not very careful of his facts for he groups together a Jewish king, a high priest and a pope who decrees laws against the Jews as if all lived at the same time. The readers, however, did not seem to pay much attention to historical anachronisms. The novel was first printed in 1597 at Venice and since then it was reprinted several times.

The numerous short stories, novels and tales which appeared in Judaeo-German during the two centuries, the seventeenth and the eighteenth, could not have been produced without the existence of sources upon which the authors drew for the materials of the content of their works. These sources were, besides the extensive Agadic literature, two collections of legends, stories and folk tales which were published at the end of the sixteenth century, namely the *Maasē Nissim* (Miraculous Stories) by Yuspe Shamesh (The Beadle) and the anonymous *Maase Buch*.

The first, as said, was composed by Yuspe (a diminutive of Joseph), the beadle of the community of Worms around 1670, originally in Hebrew. It was later translated by his son, Eliezer Liberman, into Judaeo-German and printed in 1696. It consists of twenty-five legends and stories which were current in and around Worms from ancient times. The legends contained in the cycle are of the following classes: (a) those that center around the origin of the Jewish community in Worms as well as several concerning the city itself; (b) those that tell of the lives and character of the great men; (c) tales of miraculous escapes of the Jews from persecutions; (d) those of a general fantastic and folk nature. The great men who are the heroes of the stories are the well known scholars Eleazar of Worms known as the *Roḳeah* (Vol. I, Sect. 156), Rashi, Judah ha-Hassid and Meir of Rothenburg.

We will reproduce here one of the stories of the collection as an illustration of their character and nature. It was very popular in the ghetto during the ages and is even related by people to-day. It runs as follows: Once there lived in Worms at the *House of the Crown* a very pious man who was constantly followed by bad luck (Schlim Masal). He was very poor and led a hard life. He determined to leave the community and settle in a village where he thought he would find an easier livelihood. However, he was very loath to do so as in his new habitation he would lack the religious environment of the community. The Jew went to the rabbi for advice. The latter confirmed him in his decision, and he consequently made preparations for departure. When the household goods were packed and loaded on the wagon and the family likewise took their seats there, a loud knocking at the locked door was heard from the inside of the house. The man was astonished, for he knew that none of his family was left there. When he asked who was knocking, the answer came, "It is I, the Schlim Masal. I wish to accompany you to your new home." The Jew was frightened and immediately decided to remain in Worms. He sold his house, built another one, and henceforth his lot improved.

The second collection, the *Maase Buch* is a much larger one and is more varied in content. It was collected and edited around 1580, but appeared in print only in 1602 at Basel, the publisher being a Jewish book-seller by the name of Jacob of Meseritsch. The work contains two hundred and fifty-seven tales which can be divided into several cycles. The first cycle consists of one hundred and fifty-seven stories taken from the Talmud and Midrashim, but presented in a much embellished form often containing extraneous elements. The second cycle numbers twenty-five tales based on legends that were current in the community of Regensburg, and center around Samuel and his son, Judah Hassid. The third is a collection of seventy-five stories drawn from various sources, Jewish and non-Jewish. These are recasts of folk tales which were recited in the ghetto for centuries. To many of them we find parallels in the folk lore collections of other nations. Their form is, of course, typically Jewish.

We will select also from this large collection a story for reproduction which will give us an inkling of the literary and folk lore value of the material.

Once, runs the tale, there lived a pious Jew who had three sons. Before his death, he distributed his wealth among them in equal shares, but in addition left a large chest full of gold with the instruction that it be opened by the heirs only when in extreme need. The leaders of the community signed as witnesses to his testament and the chest was placed in charge of one of the sons while the key was given to another, each of the brothers taking turns in the custody of the treasure and key. Of the three sons, the two older ones were thrifty but the youngest was improvident. Before long, he lost his share of the inheritance and came to the brothers demanding that the chest be opened as he was in need. The oldest brother being loathe to do so, offered to lend him five thousand gulden for the present, which offer was accepted, but within a year, he lost also this money. Again, he demanded the opening of the chest and this time a loan was given him by his second brother. The third year, the chest came into his custody and being once more in need, he duplicated a key, opened the chest and took out the gold and replaced it with stones.

A short time later, the oldest brother was impoverished and the youngest likewise lost his newly acquired money. A demand was then made by both to open the chest which was acceeded to. When it was opened in the presence of the elders of the community and no gold found, the brothers began to accuse each other of stealing the treasure. They finally decided to go to the rabbi of a nearby community and ask him to determine who the culprit was.

The brothers went on their journey and on the way met a man who asked them whether they saw his runaway horse. One of the brothers asked, whether the horse was white? "Yes," eagerly answered the owner. The second inquired whether it was blind in one eye? This was also confirmed. The third then asked whether it did not carry on its back two barrels, one of wine and one of oil? "Quite so," replied the owner, "and now," he added, "since you know all about the animal, return it to me." The brothers denied having seen the horse and were, of course, invited to the rabbi for judgment.

When the four appeared before the rabbi, the case of the lost horse was taken up first. The first brother explained that he knew the horse was white because he saw some white hair clinging to the bridle held by the owner. The second brother said that he guessed at its blindness in one eye because the grass was nipped only on one side of the road; and the third asserted that he knew the nature of the load because he noticed that the drops on one side of the road were dried up while those on the other side were not. The case was dismissed and their own taken up. The rabbi then turned to them and said, "I see that all of you are very wise, I therefore, ask you to help me render a decision in another case which was communicated to me by a rabbi and then I will attend to the matter at hand."

The correspondent, continued the rabbi, tells the following story: Once there were two pious Jews who were great friends and each one had an only child, a son and a daughter respectively. They decided that the two should marry and left such instruction in their wills. When the children grew up, the young man turned out to be a reckless spendthrift who lost his father's fortune, while the young woman, on the other hand, was thrifty and consequently rich, in addition to being very beautiful. On reaching marriageable age, the girl asked her fiance to carry out their parent's will and take her to wife. The young man, however, refused to comply with the request saying that he does not want to bring misfortune upon her by his conduct. The girl repeated her request numerous times but was persistently rebuffed. She finally chose a suitable young man as a candidate for her hand, but told him that she will appeal three times more to her fiance. If he still refuse, she will marry the man of her choice. She accordingly made these appeals, each time dressed in costlier and finer clothes, hoping thereby to fascinate him by her beauty and charm. The young man, though, remained adamant to her pleas, insisting that he does not wish to make her unhappy by his conduct which he is unable to change. The girl then married her chosen one. After the wedding the bridal party was attacked by a band of robbers and the groom and bride carried away. The chief of the robbers, captivated by the beauty of the bride wished to force his attentions upon her. She pleaded with him, and he finally heeded her appeal and returned both bride and groom to safety, together with the money he had taken from them. Now, the rabbi concluded, the question arises who of the three, the first suitor, the bride or the robber chieftain performed the noblest deed? He waited for the answers of the brothers. "The first suitor," replied the oldest brother, "is to be praised above all for he refused to cause the bride the loss of her money." "The bride," said the second, "for she was faithful to her father's will." "The robber," responded the third, "first because he restrained his passion and secondly, because he returned the money." "You are the one who stole the gold from the chest," thundered the rabbi. "If you evinced a desire for money which you have never seen, how much greater was that desire to take the gold which was in your possession." He confessed and was punished accordingly.

As we can see, there are three distinct stories in this tale, and we find a parallel in the Midrash on Lamentations to the tale of the meeting of the brothers with the owner of the horse. But the separate motives are skilfully combined into a unified whole, which shows that the unknown author of the tales had some literary taste.

166. DRAMA AND POETRY

As pointed out in the introduction to the chapter, much of the later Judaeo-German literature had its origin in oral recitations by wandering actors and declaimers. Life in the Mediaeval German ghetto was not always gloomy. There were moments of mirth and joy. These were weddings, circumcision feasts, engagement parties, and above all, the annual Purim feast. On these happy occasions, special persons appeared whose business was to amuse the people. They were called by different names; in earlier times, their name was "fools" (Narren), the German technical name for the clowns of the plays; later they were given a Hebrew name *Badhan* (one who amuses). Besides these, there were professional men and amateurs who dabbled in poetry and dramatic composition. As writing took the place of recitation, the production of poetry increased and ramified. Originally, the poetic and dramatic arts were interwoven and were not distinctly separated. In the course of time, though, the poetic element proper in all its phases predominated, while dramatic productions with few exceptions were limited to Purim plays.

The Judaeo-German drama, like the Mediaeval drama in general, originated in the Biblical stories which possess a certain dramatic motive. The first dramatic or rather the quasi-dramatic work in that vernacular is a poem entitled *Akedath Yitzhak* (The Sacrifice of Isaac). It was written in the fifteenth century, though the oldest manuscript dates from the year 1574. It is a dramatic presentation of the story and the contents are told with great passion. It served as a model for later plays which dealt with the same subject.

The Purim plays proper are, as a rule, limited to Biblical subjects and especially to the story of the day. But there were also some exceptions. In a collection of poems written about 1630, we find reference to a comedy which used to be presented on Purim in the city of Worms, named, *Toeb Yeklein und sein Weib Kendlein und seine Zwei Sindelach fein* (The Deaf Yeklein and his wife Kendlein and his two fine sons). The comedy itself did not reach us but the contents are more or less known to have been of a gross burlesque type. More popular were the dramas based on the story of Esther. The earliest of these is a *Purim Spiel* written during the sixteenth century by an unknown author.

The number of plays increased during the eighteenth century. In 1708, there appeared in Frankfurt on the Main a play called *Achaschverocsh Spiel*. It is a gross and vulgar dramatization of the story, full of erotic jests and caricatures, and was primarily intended to make the audience laugh. It was very popular, for though it was condemned to be burned by the elders of the Frankfurt community, yet it continued to be played in Jewish communities for a long time. Of a much better quality is a play entitled *Akta Esther et Achaschverosh* which appeared at Prague in 1720. The play was presented by the students of the academy (Yeshivah) of Rabbi David Oppenheim. The printed version is, on the whole, free from vulgar remarks but it is evident that they were omitted. Mordecai plays here the role of the comical "fool," besides the historical role.

Of the other Biblical plays presented on Purim there is first, *David und Goliath,* which was staged in Frankfurt on the Main in 1711 with great success. The police stopped its presentation on account of the large crowds who came to see it. Another one is the *Mechirath Yoseph* (The Sale of Joseph, i. e. Joseph and His Brethren). In both these plays, the authors are not true to the text but add popular embellishments of a comical nature. Both contain also a special comical character who bears a peculiar name. In the second play his name is *Pickleherring,* one which was usually employed in Holland for the clown.

Towards the end of the century, several plays portraying contemporary life appeared. These did not, however, become popular and the Purim plays continued as the theatrical fodder with which the children of the ghetto regaled themselves until late in the nineteenth century.

Turning to the other forms of poetry we find such a large number of poems and songs written and sung on different occasions that it is a difficult task to enumerate even a part of them. Most of the poetic compositions are anonymous, as they are real folk productions. In general this mass of poetic outpourings can be divided into several classes, (a) humorous and satiric songs; (b) didactic, i. e. historical and ethical poems; (c) holiday and festival songs; and (d) love poems.

Humor and satire played a great role in the life of the Jews of the ghetto. The "Fool," the official jester had its place in it. Even in a manuscript of a Yiddish legal manual dating from the fifteenth century, we find a drawing of a "Fool" dressed in his comic costume and it is indicated that his function was to amuse the people on Purim. It is these jesters who were the anonymous composers of many humorous songs which we find scattered in various books. In an early collection of Judaeo-German poems gathered by Isaac Walich, an elder of the Worms community around 1681, we find several songs ascribed to jesters. But while the purpose of these songs was primarily to amuse, there were many poems which intended to satirize and even ridicule certain persons. Of such poems, we have many, some directed against the leaders of communities and some against private individuals. The content of these humorous and satiric poems is not of an elevating character. They are replete with erotic remarks and the satiric poems often assume the form of pasquils.

However, widespread as this type of poetry was in earlier times, it was not preserved in its entirety, for we have very few collections of such poems, and with the sixteenth century the rise of the more serious and exalted poems begins. The religious and pious tenor of life found expression in poetry as well as in prose. Even the professional merrymaker who is no mere jester but *Badhan,* whose business it was to amuse the people at weddings and other festal occasions, injects a serious tone in his songs and couplets. In fact, it is these *Badhanim* who were to a great extent also the poets of the ghetto.

As a consequence, the number of religious, didactic and ethical poems constantly increased. There is a group of poems known by the name of *Getlich Lied* or *Stroff Lied* in which the authors sing of the praise of God or call upon man to improve his conduct or remind him of death, the destined end. There is even a poem called *Teiten Lied* in which the departure of man from the world is described in detail. This poem was written by Jacob Teplitz around 1600 and served as a model for imitation. Among the writers of such poems we may mention Shlome Singer and Isaac of Wilna. The first was, as his name indicates, a professional reciter and singer of poems at weddings. He lived at the beginning of the seventeenth century at Prague and was very popular among the Jews of Germany. Several later poets advise the readers that their poems are to be sung to the tune of Shlome Singer's melodies. A number of his own compositions of the type of the *Gettliche Lied* is extant. There is also a humorous poem of his where the rooster is depicted as a prophet whose prophecy always comes true, for day always follows his crowing.

Another group of this class comprises songs on the cure of the soul and poems in praise of the Torah known as the *Toire Lied.* One of such poems under that name was composed by the same Jacob Teplitz mentioned above. Allied to these are epic poems where the deeds of Biblical heroes are recited and their righteousness portrayed, or on the contrary their sins noted. Such are the *Odom we-Have Lied* and the *Yoseph ha-Tzadiḳ Lied* where the sins of the first and the righteous conduct of the other are respectively portrayed. Another called by the general name *Getlich Lied* recites the deeds of Jacob and his sons. In a similar strain many other poets sing.

Numerous poems belong to the third class and are devoted to the Sabbath and the holidays. Thus we have Hanukah songs, Purim and

Simhath Torah songs. One of these a *Simhath Torah Lied* was written by a woman, Rebecca Tiktiner.

Love poems are well represented in this poetic productivity. Many of them were sung by the young girls of the ghetto and were preserved orally and many were written down. A love poem is even found in a manuscript of Rashi's commentary on the Pentateuch.

To the miscellaneous class belong various groups of poems, such as those recited by the *Badhanim* at weddings and known as the *Kallah Lied,* poems against gambling, historical poems and others. The *Kallah Lied* has a number of variations. At times, the singer describes the beauty of the bride, her life as a girl and her separation from her friends; at other times, he pictures married life with its joys and duties; and at still others, he reminds the young couple of the righteous conduct they are to follow.

Gambling was widespread in the ghetto and many poems are devoted to the description of its evils. Likewise, there are poems portraying certain events that took place in the life of Jewish communities. Of such the best known are Elijah Bahur's *Serepha Lied* (Song of the Conflagration) and the historical poem *Megillath Winz* composed in 1616 by Elhanan Heln. It describes the expulsion of the Jews from Frankfurt in that year through the instigation of Fettmilch Winz. There are also many other poems of the same type, among them several which tell about the Messianic movement of Sabbatai Zevi.

From all that was said, it can be seen that the poetic expression was widely prevalent in the Mediaeval ghetto. The rhythm and the rhyme appealed greatly to the Jewish masses and every event, great or small, was deemed worthy of recording in a *Lied.* Many were the authors who tried their hand at composing poetry, professional *Badhanim,* pious writers, students and in general people of various callings and occupations who had an inclination for writing.

Several women also participated in this productivity. Besides Rebecca Tiktiner mentioned above, there were also Roesel Fishel's (1588) Toybi Pan (c. 1700) and Hanna Katz. The first wrote a poem as a preface to Moses Stendel's translation of the Psalms; the second composed a long poem where she portrays the state of the Jews in her time; and the third is the author of a rhymed sermon (Drasha) for women and a Sabbath prayer (Tephila le-Shabath).

That the real poetic quality of the mass of these productions is not high goes without saying, yet these poems and songs express real feelings of living and throbbing hearts, mirroring the joys and sorrows of generations of Jews and hence their value.

167. HISTORY, GEOGRAPHY AND POPULAR SCIENCE

The popular desire both for knowledge and for entertainment found satisfaction in books on history, travel, as well as those that deal with some aspect of science in a light and easy manner. We have, therefore, a considerable number of such books. The more important historical books however, are mainly translations from the Hebrew or from other languages. The books on history originally written in Judaeo-German describe, with few exceptions, single episodes or special events in the life of the Jews of certain communities.

The first books of historical character that attracted the attention of the translators were those included in the Apocrypha. As early as the year 1548, there appeared at Venice, a translation of the books of the Maccabees or rather a digest of these books. Later translations of several other Apocryphal books which can be called historical fiction, such as the stories of Tobit, Judith and Susana, appeared. The last two books were especially popular and they are found in several Yiddish versions, both in prose and rhyme. The most complete collection of such versions is the *Sepher ha-Maasim* (Book of Stories) by Hayyim ben Nathan printed at Basel in 1625. This collection contains nine Apocryphal books, namely the first and second Maccabees, the stories of Judith, Tobit, Susana, Bell and the Dragon, the letter of Jeremy and the Prayer of Menasseh. Of the books of wisdom contained in the Apocrypha, only the sayings of Ben Sira was rendered into Judaeo-German several times.

Of the Hebrew historical books, the first that was rendered in that vernacular was the Jossipon (Vol. I, Sect. 188). The translation was made by the convert Michael Adam, the very same who edited the Constance version of the Pentateuch. It was printed by him at Zurich in 1546. It is an excellent rendition of the Hebrew text with no omissions and contains also some additional notes of an explanatory character. The work is decorated with a large number of wood cuts illustrating important events in history. The *Jossipon* was followed by translations of the *Shebet Yehudah* and the *Zemah David* (Sect. 132). The former appeared first in a somewhat abridged form in 1591 at Krakow, and later in several improved editions, and the latter was published in 1698 at Frankfurt on the Main.

The only historical works on a larger scale originally written in Judaeo-German are, the *Shearith Israel* (The Remnant of Israel) by Menahem Man Amelander and the *Beth Israel* by Alexander Ethausen. The first was printed in 1743 and was intended to be a continuation of the *Jossipon*. It begins, therefore, with the destruction of the Second Temple and covers the events up to 1740. It consists primarily of excerpts from Jewish and non-Jewish works systematically arranged. The only original matter contained in that work is that concerning the history of the Jews in the Netherlands. The book is embellished with many narratives and stories which made it popular and attractive to the masses. The second work is a history of the Jews from the beginning of the nation to the destruction of the Second Temple. It also contains an appendix called *Beth ha Behirah* (The Chosen House) where a description of Jerusalem is given. The large number of historical works can be divided into two classes, those written in prose which are to a great extent translations from the Hebrew and only partly original compositions, and those written in rhyme originally composed in the vernacular. To the first class belong such works as the *Yeven Mitzulah* (Sect. 135) by Nathan Hanover, and the *Megillath Ephah* (Sect. 135) by Sabbatai Cohen, both of which tell of the persecutions in Poland under Chmelnicki, the leader of the Cossaks.

Of the second type, there are numerous poems or *Lieder* which commemorate a single event, either an expulsion, persecution, or a deliverance from an impending evil. Thus we have one called *Klog Lied Al Srefath Prog* (A Chant on the Conflagration at Prague), another called *Ein Nai Klog Lied Al Hurban Wirmischa,* a third one bears the name *A Shein Lied für Wein* and similar ones. There are several dirges on the Cossak persecutions, elegies on the death of martyrs and similar subjects. A number of these poems commemorate the occurrence of epidemics in various cities, some tell of wars and others of other extraordinary occurrences. The most important of such poems is the *Megillath Winz* described above. To the class of historical works belong also the Memoirs of certain individuals who tell the story of their lives, of their families and of their times. The Memoirs of Gluckel von Hammeln was described in detail above (Sect. 143). The second important Memoir is the *Megillath Evah* (The Scroll of Animosity) by the famous scholar, Yom Tob Lippman Heller, in which he tells of the suffering he endured at the hands of his enemies who informed against him to the government.

This was also described above. The Scroll is found in several manuscripts, both in Hebrew and Yiddish, and it is not definitely known whether the latter is a translation from the former, or that the Memoirs were originally composed in both languages.

Judaeo-German also possesses translations of the important books of travel written in Hebrew. Thus, there are versions of the itineraries of Benjamin of Tudela, of Petahia of Regensburg (Vol. I, Sect. 195-6) and even of some later Palestine travel stories, such as the *Geliloth Eretz Israel* (Sect. 137) and others.

The books that deal with scientific knowledge are limited primarily to three sciences, the elements of which every intelligent man or woman is desirous to know. These are arithmetic, geography and medicine. There are several books which deal with the elements of arithmetic, such as the *Yediath ha-Heshbon* (The Knowledge of Reckoning), a translation from the Hebrew by Aryeh Hasar and the *Meleketh Mahshebeth* (The Art of Arithmetic) by Zerah Eidlitz. In addition, there is also a translation of Elijah Misrahi's Arithmetic and several other elementary works.

As far as geography is concerned, the works extant contain besides the translations of the Hebrew itineraries, a few books which deal with geography proper, the most important of which is the *Horē Olam* (The Mountains of the Earth). The book is devoted to the description of the mountain ranges of the world as well as of the countries wherein these are situated.

The Judaeo-German medical literature consists primarily of books devoted to hygiene, dietetics, and the general conduct of life, and only very few deal with medicine proper. The works of the last class are either translations or compilations from the German or compilations of excerpts from such books. Those that deserve to be mentioned are, *Spiegel der Arzenei* (Mirror of Medicine), a rendition of the work of Laurenius Fries by Moses ben Jacob which was completed around 1583, the *Yerushath Moyshe* (Inheritance of Moses) by the physician Moses of Meserich printed in 1677 and the *Refuoth Buch* by an anonymous author.

Bibliography

List of Abbreviations

J. J. L. G.—Jahrbuch der Jüdisch Literarischen Gesellschaft.
J. Q. R. O. S.—Jewish Quarterly Review Old Series.
J. Q. R. N. S.—Jewish Quarterly Review New Series.
M. G. W. J.—Monatsschrift für die Geschichte und Wissenschaft des Judentums.
R. E. J.—Revue des Etudes Juive.
Z. D. M. G.—Zeitschrift der Deutschen Morgenländischen Gesellschaft.
Z. F. H. B.—Zeitschrift für Hebräische Bibliographie.
Z. G. J. D.—Zeitschrift für Geschichte der Juden in Deutschland.

CHAPTER I

Grammar and Lexicography

BACHER, W. *Aus den Wörterbuche Tanchum Jeruschalmis,* Budapest, 1903.
—— Die Hebräische Sprachwissenschaft Vom. 10ten bis zum 16ten jahrhundert, in *Winter und Wünsche II,* Trier, 1894.
—— "Elija Levitas Wissenschaftliche Leistungen," *Z. D. M. G.* Vol. XLIII, pp. 206-272.
BAUCH, G. "Die Einführung des Hebräischen in Wittenberg," *M. G. W. J.* Vol. XLVIII, 1904.
FRIEDLANDER & KOHN. Introduction to Edition of *Efodi's Maasē Efod,* Wien, 1865.
FÜRST, J. Geschichte der Hebräischen Lexicographie, in Introduction to his *Dictionary,* Leipzig, 1876.
GEIGER, L. *Das Studium der Hebräischen Sprache in Deutschland,* Breslau, 1876, pp. 55-89.
GOLDZIHER, I. *Studien über Tanchum Jeruschalmi,* Leipzig, 1870.
HIRSCHFELD, H. *A Literary History of Hebrew Grammarians and Lexicographers,* London, 1926.
KLUGE, OTTO. "Die Hebräische Sprachwissenschaft in Deutschland in Zeitalter des Humanismus," *Z. G. J. D.* III-IV, 1931-32.
KOHN, S. "Mordechai ben Hillel," *M. G. W. J.* Vol. XXVI, especially pp. 167-171, 272-275.
KRONER, TH. *De Abraham Bedersi, Vita et Operibus,* Breslau, 1868.
LEVY, J. *Elia Levita und seine Leistungen als Grammatiker,* Breslau, 1888.

NEUBAUER, A. "Berachiah Naqden," *J. Q. R. O. S.* Vol. I, pp. 516-20.
PERLES, J. *Beiträge zur Geschichte der Hebräischen und Arämaischen Studien,* Munich, 1884, pp. 31ff and 131-144.
POLAK, G. J. Introduction to his Edition of Bedersi's *Hotam Toknith,* Amsterdam, 1865.
RENAN-NEUBAUER. *Les Rabbins Francais,* pp. 484-487.
STEINSCHNEIDER, M. *Jewish Literature,* Chas. XVI, XXVII.
—— *Bibliographisches Handbuch über die Theoretische und Praktische Literatur für Hebräische Sprachkunde,* Leipzig, 1859.
—— *Zusatze und Berichtungen,* Leipzig, 1896.
ZUNZ, L. *Zur Geschichte und Literatur,* 2nd Edition, Berlin, 1919, pp. 107-122.

CHAPTER II

BIBLE EXEGESIS

BACHER, W. Die Bibelexegese, in *Winter und Wünsche,* Trier, 1894,
—— "Joseph Ibn Caspi als Bibelerklärer" *Festschrift Judaica,* Cohen, Berlin, 1912.
—— "Aus den Bibelerklärung Joseph Ibn Caspis," *M. G. W. J.* 56-7.
BERNSTEIN, B. *Die Schrifterklärung des Bachja ben Asher,* Berlin, 1891.
GEIGER, A. *Schemarja Negroponti, Kebuzath Maamorim, ed. Poznanski,* pp. 285-286.
GÜDEMANN, M. *Geschichte des Erziehungswesen und der Kultur der Juden in Italien,* pp. 116ff, 181ff.
JOEL, M. *Die Bibelcommentarien des Gersonides, Beiträge zur Geschichte der Philosophie,* Vol. I, pp. 87-105.
LAST, I. Introduction to his Edition of Kaspi's, *Mishnē Keseph, Commentary on the Pentateuch,* Krakow, 1905.
LOW, L. *Hamafteah,* Vol. I, Gross-Kanischa, 1855.
MEISELS, "Isaac Abrabanel" *J. Q. R. O. S.* Vol. II, pp. 37-52
NEUBAUER, A. "Joseph Ibn Aknin," *M. G. W. J.* Vol. XIX, pp. 394-401 and 445-448.
"Jewish Controversy and De Pugio Fidei"—*The Expositor* 3rd Series, VII, 1886, 81-105, 179-95.
PERLES, J. "Nachmanis Pentateuch Commentar," *M. G. W. J.* Vol. VII, pp. 81-97, 117-136.
POZNANSKI, S. "Tanchum Jeruschalmis Psalmen Commentar," *Z. F. H. B.* Vol. V, pp. 122-126, 184-189.
—— Introduction to his Ed. of Eliezer of Beaugency's *Commentary on Ezekiel and Minor Prophets,* Warsaw, 1913.
RENAN-NEUBAUER, *Les Rabbins Francais,* pp. 435-443.
SCHWAAB, M. *Abrabanel et son Epoque,* Paris, 1865.
STEINSCHNEIDER, M. *Jewish Literature,* Chas. XVII, XXVII.
—— Joseph Caspi, *Gesammelte Schriften,* Vol. I, pp. 89-135.

—— Joseph Ibn Aknin, *ibid.* pp. 35-89, 575-590.
—— Levi ben Gerson, *ibid.* 233ff.
WEISS, I. H. *Dor, Dor We-Dorshow,* Vol. V, Ch. I.
WIESNER, "Abrabanels Thoracommentar," *Ben Chanania,* Vol. X.
ZUNZ, L. *Zur Geschichte und Literatur,* pp. 60-107.

CHAPTER III

POETRY

BERNFELD, S. *Neim Zemiroth Yisroel,* Biography of I. Najara, ha-Asif, Warsaw, 1887, pp. 18-25.
BERNSTEIN, S. Introduction to his Ed. of Modena's *Diwan,* Philadelphia, 1932.
BERNSTEIN, S. Introduction to his Ed. of *Emanuel Frances Diwan,* Tel-Aviv, 1932.
BERLINER, A. Introduction to *Luhoth Abanim,* Frankfurt am Main, 1861.
—— Ed. of M. Zacuto's *Yesod Olam* with intro. and notes, Berlin, 1874.
BRODY, H. Introduction to his Ed. of Emanuel Frances' *Metek Sphataim.*
—— *Shushan Eduth,* a collection of poems by Todros ben Abulafia, Ziunim, Berlin, 1929.
DAVIDSON, I. *Shirē Abraham ben Halphon,* Ziunim, Berlin, 1929.
DELITZSCH, F. *Zur Geschichte der Jüdischen Poesie,* Leipzig, 1836.
FRIEDLANDER, M. H. Ed. of Najara's *Pizmonim* with introduction and notes, Wien, 1858.
FRIEDMAN, Introduction to his Ed. of Zacuto's *Tofte Aruk,* Berlin, 1923.
GEIGER, A. *Tzitzim U-Prahim,* a collection of poems by various Mediaeval poets with notes and introduction, Leipzig, 1856.
GOLDENTHAL, JACOB. Ed. of Rieti's *Mikdash Meat,* with introduction and notes, Wien, 1851.
KARPELES, G. *Geschichte der Jüdischen Literatur,* Berlin, 1886, pp. 791-809.
MILLER, D. H. *ha-Shahar,* Vol. III, pp. 479-487.
NEPPI GHIRONDI. *Toldoth Gedolē Israel,* Triest, 1853.
RENAN-NEUBAUER. *Lés Rabbins Francais,* pp. 702-726.
RHINE, A. B. *The Secular Poetry of Italy,* J. Q. R. N. S. Vls. I, II.
STEINSCHNEIDER, M. *Jewish Literature,* Chas. XIX, XX.
—— *Die Poeten und Polemiker in Nord Spanien, ha-Maskir.* Vols. XIV-XVII.
—— *"Manna."*
—— *Ges. Schriften I.* 271-326.
—— Ed. of Ezobi's *Kaarath Keseph* with intro. and notes, Berlin, 1860.
SULZBACH, A. Die Poetische Literatur, in *Winter und Wünsche,* Vol. III.
TSCHERNICHOWSKI, S. *Emanuel ha-Romi,* Berlin, 1925.
YELLIN, D. *Gan Hamscholim we-ha-Hidoth L'Todros Abulafia,* Jerusalem, 1932.
ZUNZ, L. *Die Synagogale Poesie des Mittelalters,* 2nd Ed. Berlin, 1919.

—— *Zur Geschichte und Literatur,* pp. 459-484.
—— *Die Literaturgeschichte der Synagogalen Poesie,* Berlin, 1865.

CHAPTER IV

Rabbinic Literature

Atlas, E. "*ha-Ribash U-Bne Doro,*" *ha Kerem,* pp. 1-26, Warsaw, 1888.
Bäck, S. Die Halachistische Literatur vom 15ten bis 18ten Jahrhundert, in *Winter und Wünsche,* Vol. II, Trier, 1897.
Brüll, N. *Jakob Pollak, Jahrbücher,* Vol. VII, pp. 31-37.
Buchholtz, L. Die codification des Halachastoffes, *M. G. W. J.* Vol. XIII.
Chones, S. *Toldoth ha-Poskim,* Warsaw, 1922.
Dembitzer, V. N. *Klilath Yofi; Geschichte der Rabbiner der Stadt* Lemberg, Krakow, 1888.
Epstein, I. *The Responsa of Solomon ben Adret,* London, 1925.
—— *The Responsa of Simon ben Zemah Duran,* London, 1930.
Frankel, Z. *Entwurf einer Geschichte der Nachtalmudischen Responsa,* Breslau, 1865.
Freiman, Alfred. *Kuntres, ha-Mefarash Hasholem,* Berlin, 1914.
——"Ascher ben Jechiel" *J. J. L. G.,* 1919, (XII), pp. 237-317.
—— Die Ascheriden, *ibid.,* (XIII), 1920, pp. 142-254.
Fünn, S. J. *Kiryah Neemanah,* Wilna, 1860.
Ginsburg, L. Art. "Codification of Law," *Jewish Encyclopaedia,* Vol. III.
Graetz, H. *Geschichte der Juden,* Vols. VII, VIII, IX; Heb. Trans. Vols. V-VIII, Eng. Trans. Vol. III, Ch. XV-XVIII, Vol. IV and Vol. V, Chs. I-VII.
Gross, H. "Isaac ben Moses Or Sarua," *M. G. W. J.* Vol. XX, pp. 248-264.
Güdemann, M. *Geschichte des Erziehungswesens und der Kultur der Abendländischen Juden,* Vol. II.
—— "Der Pilpul," *M. G. W. J.* Vol. XIII.
Harkavy, A. *Hadashim Gam Yeshanim,* II, No. 3 Addenda to *Graetz's Geschichte,* Heb. Trans. Vol. VII.
Hoffman, D. *Der Schulchan Aruch,* Berlin, 1894.
Horodetzky, S. A. *Le-Koroth ha-Rabonuth,* Warsaw, 1910.
Horowitz, M. *Frankfurter Rabbiner,* Vols. II, III.
Jaulus, H. "Simeon ben Zemach Duran," *M. G. W. J.* Vols. XXIII, XXIV.
Jellinek, A. *Kuntres ha-Rambam, Bibliographie der Schriften über Maimonides Gesetzbuch,* Wien, 1878, 1893.
—— *Kuntres ha-Kellalim, Bibliographie zur Methodologie des Talmuds,* Wien, 1878.
Kaminka, A. Die Rabbinische Literatur, in *Winter und Wünsche,* Vol. II.
—— Die Halacha in Italien, Frankreich und Deutschland, *ibid.*
Kaufman, J. *Rabbi Yom Tob Lippman Mühlhausen,* New York, 1927, pp. 1-12.
Kohn, S. *Mordechai ben Hillel,* Breslau, 1878.

PERLES, J. "Moses ben Nachman," *M. G. W. J.* Vol. VII and Vol. IX, pp. 175-195.
—— *Salomo ben Aderet,* Breslau, 1863.
ROSEN, S. *Ein Compendium der Jüdischen Gesetzeskunde (Hahinuk),* Breslau, 1871.
STEINSCHNEIDER, M. *Jewish Literature,* Ch. IX.
TSCHERNOWITZ, CH. *Le-Toldoth ha-Shulhan Aruk V'hispashthutho, ha-Shiloah,* Vols. II-VI.
—— *Die Entstehung des Schulchan Aruch,* Berlin, 1915.
WEISS, I. H. *Dor Dor We-Dorshow,* Vol. V.
—— *Mebooth ha-Talmud We-Toldotham, Beth Talmud,* Vol. V.
—— Intro. to Ed. of Isaac Campanton's *Darké ha-Gemarah,* Wien, 1891.
WELLEZ, J. "Isaac ben Mose Or Sarua," *M. G. W. J.* 48, 1904.
——Über R. Isaak ben Mose "Or Sarua," *J. J. L. G.* 1906.
—— "Meir ben Baruch de Rothenburg," *R. E. J.* 58-61.
ZUNZ, J. H. *Ir ha-Tzedek, Geschichte der Kraukauer Rabbinat,* Lemberg, 1874.
ZUNZ, L. *Die Ritus der Juden,* 2nd Ed. Berlin, 1919, pp. 36ff.
—— *Zur Geschichte und Literatur,* pp. 29-60.

CHAPTER V

PHILOSOPHY, THEOLOGY, AND ETHICS

ABRAHAMS, I. *Hebrew Ethical Wills,* Ed. with introductions and notes, 2 vols., Philadelphia, 1926.
ADLERBLUM, N. *A Study of Gersonides,* New York, 1926.
BÄCK, S. *Die Philosophie des Joseph Albo.*
BERNFELD, S. *Daath Elohim,* 2 Vols., Warsaw.
BLOCH, PH. Die Jüdische Religionsphilosophie, in *Winter und Wünsche,* III.
BRÜLL, N. Zur Geschichte der Judisch-ethischen Literatur, *Jahrbücher,* Vol. V. pp. 79-93.
EFROS, I. *The Problem of Space in Jewish Philosophy,* N. Y., 1919.
—— "Menorath ha-Maor," *J. Q. R. N.* S. Vol. X, pp. 337-357.
ENELOW, G. H. Introduction to his Ed. of al-Nakawa's, *Menorath ha-Maor,* New York, Vol. I, 1927, and Vol. III, 1932.
GEBHARD, C. *Leone Hebreo,* Heidelberg, 1920.
GUTTMAN, JAKOB, *Die Scholastik des Dreizehnten Jahrhunderts in ihren Beziehungen zum Judentum und Jüdische Literatur,* Breslau, 1902.
—— "Die Stellung des Simeon ben Zemach Duran in der Geschichte der Jüdischen Philosophie," *M. G. W. J.* Vol. LII.
—— *Die Religionsphilosophischen Lehren des Isaak Abrabanel.*
—— "Die Familie Shem Tob in Ihren Beziehungen zur Philosophie," *M. G. W. J.* Vol. LVII.
HUSIK, I. *A History of Jewish Philosophy,* New York, 1918.

Joel, M. *Beiträge zur Geschichte der Philosophie*, 2 Vols., Breslau, 1876.
Munk, S. *Mélanges de Philosophie Juive et Arabe*, Paris, 1927, 2nd Edition.
Renan-Neubauer. *Les Rabbins Francais*, pp. 571-646.
Neumark, D. *Geschichte der Jüdischen Philosophie*, Vols. I, II, Heb. Trans. Vols. I, II.
—— *Toldoth ha-Ikkarim Be-Yisrael*, Vol. II.
Neumark, D. *Crescas and Spinoza.*
Steinschneider, M. *Jewish Literature*, Ch. XII.
—— "Abraham Bibagos Schriften," *M. G. W. J.* Vol. XXXII.
—— Die Metaphysic des Aristotles in Jüdishcen Bearbeitungen, *Zunzs Jubelschrift*, Berlin, 1884.
Waxman, M. *The Philosophy of Don Hasdai Crescas*, New York, 1920.
—— "Baruch Spinoza's Relation to Jewish Philosophic Thought and to Judaism," *J. Q. R. N. S.* Vol. XXIX.
Wolfson, H. A. "Crescas on the Problem of Divine Attributes," *J. Q. R. N. S.* Vol. VII, pp. 1-44, 175-221.
—— *Crescas' Critique of Aristotle*, Cambridge, 1928.
Zimmel, B. *Leone Hebreo*, Breslau, 1886.
—— *Leone Hebreo, Neue Studien*, Wien, 1892.
Zunz, L. *Die Ritus*, Beilage IV, pp. 204-211.
—— *Zur Geschichte und Literatur*, pp. 122-157.

CHAPTER VI

Science

Carlsbach, *Levi b. Gerson als Mathematiker*, Berlin, 1910.
Carmoly, E. *Històire de la Medicine Juive*, 1884.
Cassel, D. Introduction to his Ed. of Israeli's *Yesod Olam*, Berlin, 1849.
Gross, H. *Geschichte der Juden in Arles.*
Haskins, C. H. *Studies in the History of Mediaeval Science*, Cambridge, 1924.
Jacobs, Joseph. *Jewish Contribution to Civilization*, Philadelphia, 1919, Ch. IV.
Levinson, A. *Tubia Ha-Rofé*, Berlin, 1923.
—— "A Medical Cyclopedist of the Seventeenth Century," a biography and estimate of Amatus Lusitanus, *Bulletin of the Society of Medical History of Chicago*, 1917.
Loeb, I. *Magazin für die Wissenschaft des Judentums*, Vol. III, pp. 101-110.
Renan-Neubauer. *Lés Rabbins Francais*, pp. 571-646.
Singer, Ch. "The Jewish Factor in Mediaeval Thought," in *Legacy of Israel*, pp. 173-283.
Steinschneider, M. *Jewish Literature*, Chas. XXI, XXX.
—— *Hebräische Uebersetzungen des Mittelalters*, 1893.

CHAPTER VII

Kabbala

Abelson, J. *Jewish Mysticism*, London, 1913.
Bloch, Ph. Die Jüdische Mystik und Kabbala, in *Winter und Wünsche.*
—— Die Kabbala auf ihren Hohepunkt und ihre Meister, *M. G. W. J.* Vol. XLIX, pp. 129-166.
Epstein, A. *Le-Koroth ha-Kabbala ha-Ashkenazit, ha-Hoker,* Vol. II, pp. 28-48.
Ehrenpreis, M. *Die Entwicklung der Emanationslehre,* Frankfurt, 1895.
Frank, A. *Die Kabbala,* German Trans. 3rd Ed. Berlin, 1922.
—— *The Kabbala,* Eng. Trans. New York, 1926.
Ginsburg, Ch. D. *The Kabbalah,* London, 1865.
Ginzberg, L. Art. "Cabala," *Jewish Encyclopaedia,* Vol. III.
Graetz, H. "Ursprung der Kabbala," Note 3 in *Geschichte der Juden,* Vol. VII.
Gross, H. Die Kabbalistische Traditionsketten des R. Eleasar aus Worms, *J. G. W. J.* Vol. XLIX, pp. 692-700.
Horodetzki, S. *The Teachings of Moses Cordevero* (Heb.), Berlin, 1824.
Jellinek, A. *Auswahl Kabbalistischer Mystik,* Leipzig, 1855.
—— *Beiträge zur Geschichte der Kabbala,* Leipzig, 1857.
—— *Philosophie und Kabbala,* Leipzig, 1854.
Joel, D. H. *Midrash ha-Zohar,* Leipzig, 1849.
Joel, M. *Ibn Gabirol's Bedeutung für die Geschichte der Philosophie, Beiträge,* 1876.
Landauer, M. H. *Studien, Orient,* Vol. VI, pp. 212ff.
Kahana, D. *Toldoth ha-Mekubalim, ha-Shabtaim We-ha-Hasidim,* 2 Vols. Tel-Aviv, 1926-27.
Meyer, I. *The Qabbalah,* Philadelphia, 1888.
Munk, S. *Melanges,* 2nd Ed. Paris, 1927, Ch. V.
Neumark, D. *Geschichte der Jüdischen Philosophie,* Vol. I, Berlin, 1907, pp. 179-236 Heb. Trans. pp. 166-354.
Sholem, G. *Zur Frage der Entstenhung der Kabbala,* Berlin, 1928.
—— *Im Hibber Moshe de Leon Eth ha-Zohar?* publications the Institute for Jewish Studies at the Hebrew University, Vol. I, Jerusalem, 1926, pp. 16-28.
—— *Perakim L'Toldoth ha-Kabbala,* Jerusalem, 1931.
—— "Reste Neuplatonischer Spekulation in der Mystik der Deutschen Chassidim," *M. G. W. J.* Vol. LXXV, pp. 172-91.
—— "Le-Heker Kabbalath Yitzhak ben Shem Tob Gaon," *Tarbitz* Vol. II-IV.
—— Art. "Kabbala," *Encyclopaedia Judaica,* Vol. IX.
Steinschneider, M. *Jewish Literature,* Chas. XIII, XXVI.
Waite, A. E. *The Holy Kabbala,* London, 1927.
Yabetz (Jacob Emden) *Mitpahat Sepharim,* Altona, 1768.
Zunz, L. *Die Gottesdienstlichen Vorträge,* pp. 320ff.

CHAPTER VIII

Karaite Literature

Delitzsch, F. Introduction to his Ed. of *Etz Hayyim,* Leipzig, 1841.
Fürst, J. *Geschichte des Karäertums,* Parts II and III, Leipzig, 1865.
Gottlober, A. B. *Bikoreth Le-Toldoth ha-Karaim,* Wilna, 1865.
Hamburger, J. Die Karäer und ihr Schriftthum, in *Winter und Wünsche* Vol. II.
—— *Real Encyclopaedie,* respective articles.
Harkavy, A. Art. "Karaites," *Jewish Encyclopaedia,* Vol. VII.
Husik, I. *History of Jewish Philosophy,* New York, 1918, pp. 362-388.
Jost, M. *Geschichte des Judentums und seiner Sekten,* Vol. II, Ch. XVI-XIX, Leipzig, 1858.
Kahana, D. *Moses Darai, Ha-Shiloah.*
Lutzki, S. I. *Orboth Tzadikim,* Pt. III.
Markon "Karäer," *Encyclopaedia Judaica,* Vol. IX.
Neubauer, A. *Aus der Petersburger Bibliothek,* Leipzig, 1866.
Pinsker, S. *Likkutè Kadmonioth,* Wien, 1860.
Poznanski, *The Literary Opponents of Saadia,* London, 1908.
—— Art. "Qaraites" in *Hasting's Encyclopaedia of Religion and Ethics,* Vol. VII.
—— Articles, Yisroel and Samuel ha-Maarabi, *Simha Isaak Lutzki, Ozar Yisroel,* Vols. V, X.
—— *ha-Karai Abraham ben Yoshiahu Yerushalmi, ha-Goren,* Vol. VIII, pp. 58-75.
—— Introduction to Ed. of Sultanski's *Zeker Tzadikim,* Warsaw, 1920.
Steinschneider, M. *Jewish Literature,* Ch. XIV.
—— *Hebräische Uebersetzungen,* 1893.
—— *Arabische Literatur der Juden,* 1902.

CHAPTER IX

History, Geography, Travel, and Biography

Adler, E. N. *Jewish Travellers,* New York, 1930.
Baer, F. *Untersuchungen über die Quellen und Composition des Shebet Jehudah,* Berlin, 1923.
Baron, S. *Azariah de Rossi's Attitude to Life,* Israel Abrahams' Memorial Vol. 1927, pp. 12-52.
—— *La Methode Historique d'Azaria de Rossi,* R. E. J., Vol. 86-7, 1928-9.
Blau, L. *Iggroth Yehudah,* a collection of the Letters of Leon Modena with introduction and notes. 1905.
Carmoly, E. *Itineraires Terre Sainte.*
Cassel, D. Ed. of Conforte's *Kore ha-Doroth,* Berlin, 1846.

EISENSTEIN, D. *Ozar Masaoth,* introduction, New York, 1927.
FÜNN, S. J. *Kiryah Neamanah,* pp. 74-80.
GRAETZ, H. *Geschichte der Juden,* Vol. IX, note 4.
GEIGER, A. *Melo Chofnaim,* collection of historical and literary essays, Berlin, 1840.
HYDE Ed. *Orhoth Olam* with Latin Trans. and notes, Oxford, 1691.
KAHANA, A. *Safruth ha-Historiyah ha-Yisraelith,* Vol. II, Warsaw, 1923.
—— Introduction to his Ed. of Zacuto's *Yuhasin.*
—— Introduction to his Ed. of *Modena's autobiography,* Kiew, 1912.
KAUFMAN, D. *Gesammelte Schriften,* Vol. III, pp. 83-95.
—— Introduction to his Ed. of *Glückel Von Hammelns Memoiren,* Frankfurt am Main, 1896.
LIBOWITZ, N. *Yehudah Aryé de Modena,* New York.
LEWIN, A. Geschichte Geographie und Reise Literatur, in *Winter und Wünsche,* Vol. III.
LOEB, IS. *Joseph ha-Kohen, et les Chroniqueurs Juifs,* R. E. J. Vol. XVI, XVII.
NEUBAUER, A. *Mediaeval Jewish Chronicles,* Vols. I, II, Oxford.
RUBASHOW, Z. *Conforte as Historian,* Ha-Goren, Vol. X.
SCHECHTER, S. *Studies in Judaism,* Vol. II, pp. 126-148, Philadelphia, 1908.
STEINSCHNEIDER, M. *Geschichtsliteratur der Juden,* Frankfurt, 1905.
—— *Jewish Literature,* Chas. X, XXIX.
VOGELSTEIN UND RIEGER *Geschichte der Juden in Rom,* Vol. II, pp. 41-58.
WIENER, M. Introduction to German Translation of *Shebet Yehudah,* Leipzig, 1858.
ZUNZ, L. *Geographische Literatur der Juden,* Ges. Schriften, Vol. I.
—— "Toldoth Rabbi Azariah min ha-Adumim," in ben Yakab's Ed. of *Meor Enayim,* Wilna, 1863.

CHAPTER X

POLEMICS AND APOLOGETICS

BÄCK, S. Die Apologeten, in *Winter und Wünsche,* Vol. III.
BAER, F. *Le-Bikkoreth ha-Vikkuchim shel Yechiel mi-Paris, we-R. Moshe b. Nahman, Tarbitz,* II, 172-187.
EISENSTEIN, J. D. *Ozar Vikkuhim,* introduction, N. Y., 1928.
GEBHARD, CARL. Introduction to his Ed. of Uriel Da Costa's opera, Amst. 1927.
GEIGER, A. *Melo Chofnaim,* Berlin, 1840.
—— Proben Jüdischer Vertheidigung, *Liberman's Jahrbücher,* Vol. III.
GRAETZ, H. *Geschichte der Juden,* Vol. VII, note 1. Hebrew Trans. Vol. V, note 1.
KAUFMAN, D. Simeon ben Joseph's Sendschreiben, *Zunz's Jubelschrift,* 1884.

KAUFMAN, J. *Rabbi Yom Tob Lippman Mülhausen,* Phil. 1928.
KRAUS, S. *Das Leben Jesu nach Jüdischen Quellen,* Berlin, 1902.
LIBOWITZ, N. *Yehudah Aryé de Modena,* New York.
LOEB, I. "La Controverse de 1240 sur Le Talmud," *R. E. J.* Vol. I-III.
—— "La Controverse de 1263 a Barcelona," *R. E. J.* Vol. XV.
—— "La Controverse religieuse entre les Chretiens et les Juifs en Moyen age," Paris, 1888.
—— "Polemistes Chretiens et Juifs en France et Espagne," *R. E. J.* Vol. XVIII.
NEUBAUER, A. *The 53rd Chapter of Isaiah according to the Jewish Interpreters,* Oxford, 1896.
—— "Jewish Controversy and the Pugio Fidei," *Expositor,* 3rd Series, Vol. VII.
POZNANSKI, Ad. *Shiloh,* Leipzig, 1904.
RENAN-NEUBAUER. *Lés Rabbins Francais,* pp. 647-700.
ROSSI DE, J. B. *Bibliotheca Judaica Anti-Christiana,* Parma, 1800.
STEINSCHNEIDER, M. *Jewish Literature,* Chas. XV, XXIV.
—— *Polemische und Apologetische Literatur in Arabische Sprache,* Leipzig, 1877.
WAGENSEIL, J. *Tela Ignea Satanae,* 1681.
ZIEGLER, I. *Die Religiosen Disputationen der Juden.*
ZUNZ, L. *Zur Geschichte und Literatur,* pp. 261-268.

CHAPTER XI

PROSE LITERATURE

DAVIDSON, I. *Parody in Jewish Literature,* New York, 1907.
JACOB, JOSEPH. *Barlaam and Josephat,* London, 1896.
—— *The Fables of Aesop,* Vol. I, London 1889.
LANDSBERGER. German Translation of Kalonymos' *Iggereth Baale Hayyim* with introduction and notes, Darmstadt, 1892.
MEISEL. German Translation of Kalonymos' *Eben Bohan,* with introduction by Kayserling, Budapest, 1878.
STERN, M. E. German translation of *Behinat Olam* with introduction by Weiss, Wien, 1847.
STEINSCHNEIDER, M. *Jewish Literature,* Ch. XX.
—— *"Manna"*
—— *Hebräische Übersetzungen.*
—— *Ha-Maskir,* Vol. XIII.
—— Purim und Parodie, *M. G. W. J.* XLVI.
SULZBACH, A. Die Weltliche Poesie, in *Winter und Wünsche,* Vol. III.

CHAPTER XII

Judaeo-German Literature

Berliner, A. *Aus dem Inneren Leben der Deutschen Juden im Mittelalter*, Berlin, 1900.

Erik, M. *Geschichte fun der Yiddischer Literatur*, Warsaw, 1928.

—— *Wegen Altyudischen Roman und Novelle*, Warsaw, 1926.

Geiger, L. *Das Studium der Hebräischen Sprache in Deutschland*, Breslau, 1870.

Grünbaum, M. *Jüdischdeutsche Chrestomatie*, Leipzig, 1882.

—— Die Jüdischdeutsche Literatur, in *Winter und Wünsche*, Vol. III.

Guedemann, M. *Geschichte des Erziehungswesens und Kultur der Abendländischen Juden*, Wien, 1880-88, Vol. I, pp. 273-280; Vol. III, pp. 69, 79, 280, 299.

Karpeles, G. *Geschichte der Jüdischen Literatur*, pp. 1000-1029.

Korman, E. *Jüdische Dichterinens*, Chicago, 1928.

Niger, S. *Studien zu der Geschichte fun der Yiddischer Literatur*, Pinkas, Wilna, 1912, pp. 75-138.

Perles, J. *Beiträge zur Geschichte der Hebräischen und Aramäischen Studien*, München, 1884.

Pines, M. *Geschichte fun der Yiddischer Literatur*, Warsaw, 1912.

Schulman, E. *Sephath Yehudith Ashkenazith We-Saphrutah*, Riga, 1913.

Staerk und Leitzmann. *Dis Jüdisch Deutschen Bibel Übersetzungen*, Frankfurt am Main, 1923.

Steinschneider, M. *Jüdischdeutsche Literatur, Serapeum*, 1848, 1849, 1864, 1869.

—— *Cat. Bod.* 1852-60.

—— *Geschichtsliteratur der Juden*, Frankfurt am Main, 1905.

Weinreich, M. *Staplen*, Warsaw, 1923.

—— *Bilder fun der Yiddischer Literaturgeschichte*, Wilna, 1928.

Zinberg, I. *Der Kampf fur Yiddish in der Alt Yiddischer Literatur, Schriften fun Yiddisch Wissenschaftlichen Institut, Philologische Schriften*, Vol. II, Wilna, 1929, pp. 69-100.

—— *Aus der Altjudischer Literatur, ibid.* Vol. III, 1928. pp. 173-184.

Zunz, L. *Gottesdienstlichen Vorträge*, pp. 438-449.

—— *Zur Geschichte und Literatur*, pp. 268, 304.

INDEX

A

B

C

F

G

H

I

J

K

L

M

Q

R

T

Z